Operations Management for MBAs

Operations Management for MBAs

Third Edition

Jack R. Meredith

Scott M. Shafer

Wake Forest University

John Wiley & Sons, Inc.

Publisher: Susan Elbe
Executive Editor: Beth Lang Golub
Senior Production Editor: Trisha McFadden
Marketing Manager: Jillian Rice
Senior Designer: Kevin Murphy
Senior Photo Editor: Lisa Gee
Editorial Assistant: Jennifer Snyder
Senior Media Editor: Allison Morris
Cover Design: David Levy

This book was set in 10/12 Times Roman by Wiley/Australia
and printed and bound by Hamilton Printing. The cover was printed by Phoenix Color.

This book is printed on acid free paper. ∞

To order books or for customer service please, call 1-800-CALL WILEY (225-5945).

ISBN 13   978- 0-471-35142-9
ISBN 10   0-471-35142-3

Printed in the United States of America

10 9 8 7 6 5 4 3 2 1

This book is dedicated to the Newest Generation:

Avery and Mitchell

J. R. M.

Brianna, Sammy, and Kacy

S. M. S.

Preface

The continuing enthusiastic reception of this MBA-oriented book has been gratifying!

The Need

It was originally written because of the express need we felt in our MBA-only program at Wake Forest University for an operations management textbook directed specifically to MBA students, and especially to those who had some real-world experience. We tried all of the current texts but found them either tomes that left no time for the cases and other materials we wanted to include or shorter but simplistic quantitative books. Moreover, all the books were so expensive they did not allow us to order all the cases, readings, and other supplements and class activities (such as Harvard's "Beer Game," see Chapter 7 Supplement) that we wanted to include in our course.

What we were looking for was a short, inexpensive book that would cover just the introductory, basic, and primarily conceptual material. This would allow us, as the professors, to tailor the course through supplementary cases and other materials for the unique class we would be teaching: executive, evening, full-time, short course, and so on. Although we wanted a brief, supplementary-type book so that we could add other material, we have colleagues who need a short book because they only have a half-semester module for the topic. Or they may have to include another course (e.g., management science or statistics) in the rest of the quarter or semester. In addition, we didn't need the depth of most texts that have two extensive chapters on materials management, two long chapters on scheduling, two chapters on quality, and so on; one chapter on each topic would be sufficient for our needs.

Changes in this Third Edition

We also wanted a contemporary book that included topics our MBAs currently or would soon be facing in industry. In this edition, we have dramatically reorganized the book to stress these recent topics: outsourcing and offshoring, six sigma improvement projects, enterprise resource planning, lean management, process and value planning, and of course, supply chain management. Moreover, we wanted a book that kept the marketing or finance major in mind—what did these students need to know about operations to help them in their careers? Certainly not shop floor control and many of the other details we traditionally taught in our undergraduate classes! So we tossed these topics, and in this edition we also dropped the more technical and engineering aspects of product design. And we tossed much of the heavier quantitative material, keeping only discussions and examples that illustrate a particular concept since finance and marketing majors would not be solving operations problems. Moreover, even operations managers probably wouldn't themselves be solving those problems; more likely, they would be assigned to an analyst.

We also wanted a book with a more strategic point of view since our MBAs were working at the managerial rather than entry level, and in this edition we have attempted to further stress the strategic role of these operations topics. In addition, we have added substantial additional material to Chapter 2: Strategy, Operations, and Global Competitiveness. And we added even more service examples throughout the text, and converted some manufacturing examples to service examples, since the great majority (over 80 percent these days!) of our students would be or are already employed in a service organization. And since these students will be working and competing in a highly global economy, we added a great many international examples and changed many problems and cases to an international setting.

To illustrate the topics and their organization in each chapter, we include an organization chart of the topics at the beginning of each chapter so the instructor and students can quickly and easily see what is coming and how it is organized. We intentionally changed the textual flow of material in the chapters away from the current undergraduate trend. Instead of fracturing the material flow by adding sidebars, examples, applications, solved problems, and so forth, in an attempt to keep the students' interest and attention, given the maturity of MBA students we instead worked these directly into the discussions to attain a smoother, clearer flow. We also altered the end-of-chapter materials by cutting down the questions to just a few that would intrigue and engage more experienced and mature students. We similarly limited the bibliography to what would be of interest to current or soon-to-be midlevel managers. We also considered the caselettes to be of interest for this level of student. For those chapters in which exercises are included, they are intended only to help illustrate the concept we are trying to convey rather than make experts of the students. As noted below, the Instructor's Manual includes suggestions for readings, cases, videos, and other course supplements that we have found to be particularly helpful for MBA classes since this book is intended to be only a small part of the MBA class.

Supplements

Our approach to supplementary MBA-level material here is to reference and annotate in the Instructor's Manual good cases, books, video clips, and readings for each of the 11 textbook chapters. The annotation is intended to help the instructors select the most appropriate materials for their unique course. Although there are brief caselettes at the end of each chapter in the text that we have personally class-tested and found can form the basis of an interesting class discussion, we primarily rely on our favorite Harvard, Darden, Western Ontario, and European cases, plus *Harvard Business Review* readings to fully communicate the nature of the chapter topic we are covering. Although we didn't think that test bank questions, videos or PowerPoint slides would be used by most MBA instructors, these materials are available from the publisher also. For that matter, the publisher can also custom bind with selected content from this text, our larger undergraduate (or any other) Web text, along with cases and articles, should this approach be of interest to the professor. Please contact your local Wiley sales representative for more details.

Your Inputs Appreciated

We would once again like to encourage users of this book to send us their comments and suggestions. Tell us if there is something we missed that you would like to see in the next edition (or the Instructor's Manual or web site) or if there is perhaps material that is unneeded for this audience. Also, please tell us about any errors you uncover, or if there are other elements of the book you like or don't like. We hope to continue keeping this a living, dynamic project that evolves to meet the needs of the MBA audience, an audience whose needs are also evolving as our economy and society twist and change.

We want to thank the many reviewers of this book and its previous editions: Satya Chakravorty, Kennesaw State University; James A. Fitzsimmons, University of Texas; Lawrence D. Fredendall, Clemson University; Robert Handfield, North Carolina State University; Janelle Heineke, Boston University; David Hollingworth, Rensselaer Polytechnic Institute; Mehdi Kaighobadi, Florida Atlantic University; William C. Giauque, Brigham Young University; Damodar Golhar, Western Michigan University; Suresh Kumar Goyal, Concordia University, Canada; Hector Guerrero, The College of William & Mary; Manoj Malhotra, University of South Carolina; Gus Manoochehri, California State University, Fullerton; Robert F. Marsh, Sacred Heart; Ivor P. Morgan, Babson College; Seungwook Park, California State University—Fullerton; Sue Perrott Siferd, Arizona State University; Jaime S. Ribera, IESE-Universidad de Navarra, Spain; Gary D. Scudder, Vanderbilt University; Asoo J. Vakharia, University of Florida; Jerry C. Wei, University of Notre Dame.

For this edition we thank Mike Godfrey, University of Wisconsin, Oshkosh; Mark Gerard Haug, University of Kansas; James L. Hoyt, Troy State University; Archie Lockamy III, Samford University; Ron McLachlin, University of Manitoba; Donald E. Simmons, Ithaca College; and William J. Tallon, Northern Illinois University.

Jack Meredith
Babcock Graduate School of
  Management
Wake Forest University, P.O. Box 7659
Winston-Salem, NC 27109
jack.meredith@mba.wfu.edu
www.mba.wfu.edu/faculty/meredith
336.758.4467

Scott Shafer
Babcock Graduate School of
  Management
Wake Forest University, P.O. Box 7659
Winston-Salem, NC 27109
scott.shafer@mba.wfu.edu
www.mba.wfu.edu/faculty/shafer
336.758.3687

Contents

The Nature of Operations

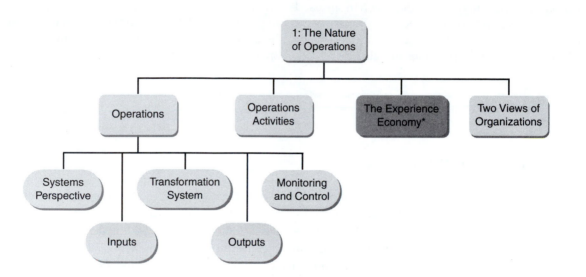

CHAPTER IN PERSPECTIVE

This first chapter serves as an introduction to the field of operations management. At the beginning of the chapter, *operations* is defined as the activities associated with transforming inputs into useful outputs in order to create a result of value. It is also shown that the actual production system is defined in terms of environment, inputs, transformation system, outputs, and the mechanism used for monitoring and control. The four primary ways that value can be added to an entity and the major subject areas within operations are also discussed.

The chapter overviews two alternative ways for organizing work activities. In the traditional functional approach, companies organize activities on the basis of the type of work performed. With this approach, operations, marketing, and finance are defined as the three core functional areas in companies. Recently, however, many companies have found that they can significantly improve organizational efficiency and effectiveness by organizing activities on the basis of specific value-creating processes.

INTRODUCTION

- Facing increased competition and customers who are smarter, more demanding, and less brand-loyal, McDonald's reevaluated the way it made some of the items on its menu. For example, it considered switching to a hamburger bun that does not require toasting. In trial tests, customers seemed to prefer the new bun's taste and texture. Furthermore, not toasting buns would translate into substantial cost savings due to reduced preparation time and the elimination of commercial toasting equipment. At first, such savings may seem trivial; however, consider that McDonald's processes several billion buns for its hamburgers, chicken, and fish sandwiches (Gibson 1995).

- Getting the Olympic flame to Atlanta for the summer Olympics of 1996 was a major undertaking. Ten thousand runners carried the flame 15,000 miles, passing through 42 states in 84 days. More than two years of planning went into this operation. For example, plans had to be coordinated with 2970 local police jurisdictions. Additionally, plans had to be made to deal with rush-hour traffic, no-show runners, or runners who were not able to complete their leg of the relay. In all, it was estimated that the Olympic flame relay cost in the neighborhood of $20 million, not including transportation, computers, and communication equipment used to support the project (Ruffenach 1996).

- It is not well known that the Kmart and Wal-Mart chains both date back to 1962. By 1987 Kmart was clearly dominating the discount chain race, with almost twice as many stores and sales of $25.63 billion to Wal-Mart's $15.96 billion. However, for the retail year that ended in January 1991, Wal-Mart had overtaken Kmart, with sales of $32.6 billion to Kmart's sales of $29.7 billion. Interestingly, although Wal-Mart had taken the lead in sales in 1991, it still had fewer stores—1721 to Kmart's 2330. By the 2000 retail year, Wal-Mart had clearly established itself as the dominant discount chain, with sales of $188.1 billion to Kmart's $36.4 billion. Perhaps equally telling is the shift in market share experienced by these two companies. For the period from 1987 to 1995, Kmart's market share declined from 34.5 percent to 22.7 percent, while Wal-Mart's increased from 20.1 percent to 41.6 percent.

What accounts for this reversal in fortunes? Kmart's response to the competition from Wal-Mart was to build on its marketing and merchandising strengths and invest heavily in national television campaigns using high-profile spokespeople such as Jaclyn Smith (a former Charlie's Angel) and Martha Stewart. Wal-Mart took an entirely different approach and invested heavily in operations in an effort to lower costs. For example, Wal-Mart developed a companywide computer system to link cash registers to headquarters, thereby greatly facilitating inventory control at the stores. Also, Wal-Mart developed a sophisticated distribution system. The integration of the computer system and the distribution system meant that customers would rarely encounter out-of-stock items. Further, the use of scanners at the checkout stations eliminated the need for price checks. By Kmart's own admission, its employees were seriously lacking the skills needed to plan and control inventory effectively (Duff and Ortega 1995).

Fast forward to 2004 and analysts are still commenting on Kmart's problems with getting merchandise on its shelves. Given its apparent inability to address its operational problems, Kmart appears to have adopted a new strategy to compete with Wal-Mart, namely, merging with Sears, Roebuck & Co. Analysts have speculated that a key benefit of such a merger is potential synergies between Kmart's convenient locations and Sears' strong brands. However, it remains to be seen to what extent the merger between Kmart and Sears helps close the significant performance gap between these chains and Wal-Mart. For example, in 2003, Wal-Mart was ringing up sales of $433 per square foot compared with $184 per square foot at Kmart and $286 at Sears. When multiplied across Wal-Mart's 3,033 stores and Kmart and Sears' combined 2,374 stores, this translates into sales of $256 billion at Wal-Mart versus combined sales of $63 billion at Sears and Kmart (Duff and Ortega 1995, Merrick and Zimmerman 2004).

These brief examples highlight the diversity and importance of operations. Take the description of McDonald's. This example provides a glimpse of two themes that are central to operations: *customer satisfaction* and *competitiveness*. This example also illustrates a more subtle point—that improvements made in operations can simultaneously increase customer satisfaction and lower costs. The Wal-Mart example demonstrates how a company obtained a substantial competitive advantage by improving basic operational activities such as controlling its inventory. Finally, all three examples illustrate that the field of operations is as applicable to service organizations as it is to manufacturing.

Today, in our international marketplace, consumers purchase their products from the provider that offers them the most value for their money. To illustrate, you may be doing your course assignments on a Japanese notebook computer, driving in a German automobile, or watching a sitcom on a television made in Taiwan while cooking your food in a Korean microwave. However, most of your services—banking, insurance, personal care—are probably domestic, although some of these may also be owned by, or outsourced to, foreign corporations.

There is a reason why most services are produced by domestic firms while products may be produced in part, or wholly, by foreign firms, and it concerns an area of business known as operations.

A great many societal changes that are occurring today intimately involve activities associated with operations. For example, there is great pressure among competing nations to increase national productivity. Similarly, businesses are conducting national crusades to improve the quality of their offerings, build effective supply chains, and improve their processes through "six-sigma," "lean management," and other operations-based programs.

Another characteristic of our modern society is the explosion of new technology. Technologies such as cell phones, e-mail, notebook computers, personal digital assistants, and the Web, to name a few, are profoundly affecting business and are fundamentally changing the nature of work. For example, many banks are shifting their focus from building new branch locations to using the Web as a way to establish and develop new customer relationships. Banks rely on technology to carry out more routine activities as well, such as transferring funds instantly across cities, states, and oceans. Our industries also rely increasingly on technology: robots carry and weld parts together, and workerless, dark "factories of the future" turn out a continuing stream of products. And soft operations technologies, such as "supply chain management" and "lean production" (Feld 2000; Womack, Jones, and Roos 1991) have transformed world markets and the global economy.

This exciting, competitive world of operations is at the heart of every organization and, more than anything else, determines whether the organization survives in the international marketplace or disappears into bankruptcy or a takeover. It is this world that we will be covering in the following chapters.

$\mathscr{O}$PERATIONS

Why do we argue that operations be considered the heart of every organization? Fundamentally, organizations exist to create value, and operations involves tasks that create value. Michael Hammer (2004) maintains that operational innovation can provide organizations with long-term strategic advantages over their competitors. Regardless of whether the organization is for-profit or not-for-profit, primarily service or manufacturer, public or private, it exists to create value. Thus, even nonprofit organizations like the Red Cross strive to create value for the recipients of their services in excess of their costs. Moreover, this has always been true, from the earliest days of bartering to the modern-day corporations.

Consider McDonald's as an example. This firm uses a number of inputs, including ingredients, labor, equipment, and facilities; transforms them in a way that adds value to them (e.g., by frying); and obtains an output, such as a chicken sandwich, that can be sold at a profit. This conversion process, termed a *production system*, is illustrated in Figure 1.1. The elements of the figure represent what is known as a **system**[1]: *a purposeful collection of people, objects, and procedures for operating within an environment*.

---

[1]Note the word *system* is being used here in a broad sense and should not be confused with more narrow usages such as information systems, planning and control systems, or performance evaluation systems.

Note the word *purposeful;* systems are not merely arbitrary groupings but goal-directed or purposeful collections. Managing and running a production system efficiently and effectively is at the heart of the operations activities that will be discussed in this text. Since we will be using this term throughout the text, let us formally define it. **Operations** is concerned with transforming inputs into useful outputs and thereby adding value to some entity; this constitutes the primary activity of virtually every organization.

Not only is operations central to organizations, it is also central to people's personal and professional activities, regardless of their position. People, too, must operate productively, adding value to inputs and producing quality outputs, whether those outputs are information, reports, services, products, or even personal accomplishments. Thus, operations should be of major interest to every reader, not just professionally but also personally.

Systems Perspective

As Figure 1.1 illustrates, a production system is defined in terms of environment, inputs, transformation system, outputs, and the mechanism used for monitoring and control. The environment includes those things that are outside the actual production system but that influence it in some way. Because of its influence, we need to consider the environment, even though it is beyond the control of decision makers within the system.

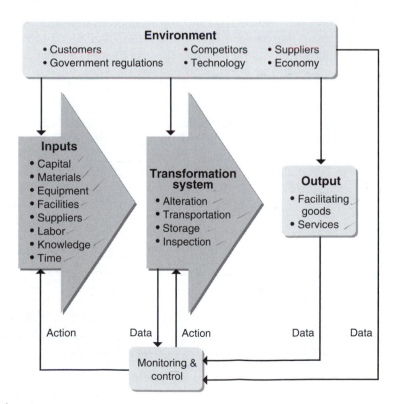

Figure 1.1   The production system.

For example, a large portion of the inputs to a production system are acquired from the environment. Also, government regulations related to pollution control and workplace safety affect the transformation system. Think about how changes in customers' needs, a competitor's new product, or a new advance in technology can influence the level of satisfaction with a production system's current outputs. As these examples show, the environment exerts a great deal of influence on the production system.

Because the world around us is constantly changing, it is necessary to monitor the production system and take action when the system is not meeting its goals. Of course, it may be that the current goals are no longer appropriate, indicating a need to revise the goals. On the other hand, it may be determined that the goals are fine but that the inputs or transformation system or both should be acted upon in some way. In either case, it is important to continuously collect data from the environment, the transformation system, and the outputs. Then, on the basis of an analysis of these data, appropriate actions can be devised to enhance the system's overall performance.

Thinking in terms of systems provides decision makers with numerous advantages. To begin, the systems perspective focuses on how the individual components that make up a system interact. Thus, the systems perspective provides decision makers with a broad and complete picture of an entire situation. Furthermore, the systems perspective emphasizes the relationships between the various system components. Without considering these relationships, decision makers are prone to a problem called *suboptimization*. Suboptimization occurs when one part of the system is improved to the detriment of other parts of the system, and perhaps the organization as a whole. An example of suboptimization from the medical field is "the operation was a success but the patient died!" As another example of suboptimization, suppose that a retailer decides to broaden its product line in an effort to increase sales. Such a decision could actually end up hurting the retailer as a whole if it does not have sufficient shelf space available to accommodate the broader product line, sales, and service personnel that are knowledgeable about the new products, or if the broader product line increases inventory-related costs more than profits from the increased sales. The point of this example is that decisions need to be evaluated in terms of their effect on the entire system, not simply in terms of how they will affect one component of the system.

It is interesting to note that the components of systems are often themselves systems, called *subsystems*. For example, a factory that assembles personal computers is a system. Within this system there are many subsystems, such as the system that reports financial information, the system for assembling the computers, the system for ordering the raw materials, the system for designing new products, and the system for recruiting and hiring workers. And many of these subsystems could be further divided into sub-subsystems. To illustrate, the system that reports financial information may be composed of a system that reports information to sources outside the organization and another system that provides financial information to employees within the organization.

It also stands to reason that since systems can be divided into component subsystems, it should also be possible to combine them into larger systems. This is indeed the case. Consider the example of a personal computer assembly plant. This plant may be just one of a number of plants making up a particular division of the company. Thus, combining these plants would form a system corresponding to the division of this company. Furthermore, combining the divisions of the company would create a system for the whole company. This logic could be extended to creating systems for the entire industry, and all the way up to creating a system for the entire economy.

This discussion highlights the importance of defining a system's boundary appropriately. Specifically, defining a boundary determines what a decision maker will and will not consider, since things outside the system boundary are considered to be part of the environment and beyond the decision maker's control. Defining a system boundary is important, because if it is defined too narrowly, important relationships among system components may be omitted. On the other hand, extending the boundary increases the complexity and costs associated with developing and using the model. Unfortunately, determining the system boundary is more of an art than a science and is based on the experience, skill, and judgment of the analyst.

Regardless of where the system boundary is defined, all production systems receive inputs from their environments, transform these inputs, and create value in the form of outputs. In the remainder of this section we elaborate on inputs, the transformation system, and outputs.

Inputs

The set of inputs used in a production system is more complex than might be supposed and typically involves many other areas such as marketing, finance, engineering, and human resource management. Obvious inputs include facilities, labor, capital, equipment, raw materials, and supplies. Supplies are distinguished from raw materials by the fact that they are not usually a part of the final output. Oil, paper clips, pens, tape, and other such items are commonly classified as supplies because they only aid in producing the output.

Another very important but perhaps less obvious input is knowledge of how to transform the inputs into outputs. The employees of the organization hold this knowledge. Finally, having sufficient time to accomplish the operations is always critical. Indeed, the operations function quite frequently fails in its task because it cannot complete the **transformation activities** within the required time limit.

Transformation System

The transformation system is the part of the system that adds value to the inputs. Value can be added to an entity in a number of ways. Four major ways are described here.

1. *Alter:* Something can be changed structurally. That would be a *physical* change, and this approach is basic to our manufacturing industries where goods are cut, stamped, formed, assembled, and so on. We then go out and buy the shirt, or computer, or whatever the good is. But it need not be a separate object or entity; for example, what is altered may be *us*. We might get our hair cut, or we might have our appendix removed.

Other, more subtle, alterations may also have value. *Sensual* alterations, such as heat when we are cold, or music, or beauty may be highly valued on certain occasions. Beyond this, even *psychological* alterations can have value, such as the feeling of worth from obtaining a college degree or the feeling of friendship from a long-distance phone call.

2. *Transport:* An entity, again including ourselves, may have more value if it is located somewhere other than where it currently is. We may appreciate having things brought to us, such as flowers, or removed from us, such as garbage.

3. *Store:* The value of an entity may be enhanced for us if it is kept in a protected environment for some period of time. Some examples are stock certificates kept in a safe-deposit box, our pet boarded at a kennel while we go on vacation, or ourselves staying in a motel.

4. *Inspect:* Last, an entity may be more valued because we better understand its properties. This may apply to something we own, plan to use, or are considering purchasing, or, again, even to ourselves. Medical exams, elevator certifications, and jewelry appraisals fall into this category.

Thus, we see that value may be added to an entity in a number of different ways. The entity may be changed directly, in space, in time, or even just in our mind. Additionally, value may be added using a combination of these methods. To illustrate, an appliance store may create value by both storing merchandise and transporting (delivering) it. There are other, less frequent, ways of adding value as well, such as by "guaranteeing" something. These many varieties of transformations, and how they are managed, constitute some of the major issues to be discussed in this text.

Outputs

Two types of outputs commonly result from a production system: services and products. Generally, products are physical goods, such as a personal computer, and services are abstract or nonphysical. More specifically, we can consider the characteristics in Table 1.1 to help us distinguish between the two.

*T*ABLE   1.1 • Characteristics of Products and Services

Products	Services
Tangible	Intangible
Minimal contact with customer	Extensive contact with customer
Minimal participation by customer in the delivery	Extensive participation by customer in the delivery
Delayed consumption	Immediate consumption
Equipment-intense production	Labor-intense production
Quality easily measured	Quality difficult to measure

However, this classification may be more confusing than helpful. For example, consider a pizza delivery chain. Does this organization produce a product or provide a service? If you answered "a service," suppose that instead of delivering its pizzas to the actual consumer, it made the pizzas in a factory and sold them in the frozen-food section of grocery stores. Clearly the actual process of making pizzas for immediate consumption or to be frozen involves basically the same tasks, although one may be done on a larger scale and use more automated equipment. The point is, however, that both organizations produce a pizza, and defining one organization as a service and the other as a manufacturer seems to be a little arbitrary. In addition, both products and services can be produced as commodities or individually customized.

We avoid this ambiguity by adopting the point of view that *any physical entity accompanying a transformation that adds value is a **facilitating good*** (e.g., the pizza). In many cases, of course, there may be no facilitating good; we refer to these cases as *pure services*.

The advantage of this interpretation is that every transformation that adds value is simply a service, either with or without facilitating goods! If you buy a piece of lumber, you have not purchased a product. Rather, you have purchased a bundle of services, many of them embodied in a facilitating good: a tree-cutting service, a saw mill service, a transportation service, a storage service, and perhaps even an advertising service that told you where lumber was on sale. We refer to these services as a bundle of "benefits," of which some are tangible (the sawed length of lumber, the type of tree) and others are intangible (courteous salesclerks, a convenient location, payment by charge card). Some services may, of course, even be negative, such as an audit of your tax return. In summary, ***services* are bundles of benefits, some of which may be tangible and others intangible, and they may be accompanied by a facilitating good or goods.**

Firms often run into major difficulties when they ignore this aspect of their operations. They may think of, and even market themselves as, a "lumberyard" and not as providing a bundle of services. They may recognize that they have to include certain tangible services (such as cutting lumber to the length desired by the customer) but ignore the intangible services (charge sales, having a sufficient number of clerks).

While the broader perspective of the facilitating good concept helps clarify the ambiguity associated with whether an organization produces a product or service, it also blurs the distinction between operations and marketing. To illustrate, earlier we defined operations as including the tasks that add value. However, when outputs are viewed broadly as a bundle of benefits, it becomes clear that marketing, as well as other areas of an organization, contribute to the value outputs provide.

Another reason for not making a distinction between manufacturing and services is that making such a distinction can be harmful. Specifically, when a company thinks of itself as a manufacturer, it tends to focus on measures of internal performance such as efficiency and utilization; and when companies classify themselves as services they tend to focus externally and ask questions such as "How can we serve our customers better?" This is not to imply that improving internal performance measures is not desirable. Rather, it suggests that improved customer service should be the primary impetus for all improvement efforts. It is generally not advisable to seek internal improvements if these improvements do not ultimately lead to corresponding improvements in customer service and customer satisfaction.

In this text we will adopt the point of view that all value-adding transformations (i.e., operations) are services, and there may or may not be a set of accompanying facilitating goods. Figure 1.2 illustrates how the tangible product (or facilitating good) portion and the intangible service portion for a variety of outputs contribute to the total value provided by each output. The outputs shown range from virtually pure services to what would be known as products. For example, the Plush restaurant appears to be about 75 percent service and 25 percent product. Although we work with "products" as extensively as with services throughout the chapters in this book, bear in mind that in these cases we are working with only a *portion* of the total service, the facilitating good. In general, we will use the non-specific term *outputs* to mean either products or services.

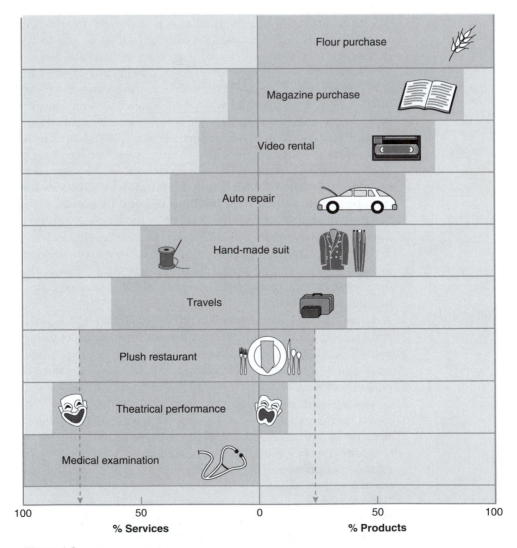

Figure 1.2   The range from services to products.

With the current revolution in information technology, particularly the Internet, it is also instructive to consider the extent to which outputs are physical or information entities. As is illustrated in Table 1.2, the economics associated with physical and information outputs differ substantially and therefore have important implications for managers. One key difference concerns ownership of the output once it is sold. More specifically, sellers of physical outputs no longer own the output once it is sold while sellers of information outputs still possess the output once it is sold. To illustrate, when a music CD is purchased from a retailer, the retailer ceases to own it and the CD becomes the property of the purchaser. On the other hand, when music is purchased over the Internet from sites such as MP3.com, the retailer simply provides the purchaser with digital copies of music files and does not give up its ownership of its music files. This example also illustrates another important difference, namely, that replicating physical outputs typically requires some type of manufacturing operation while replicating information outputs can be done with virtually zero cost and without limit.

in terms of self manufacturing the O/P

$\mathcal{T}$ABLE 1.2 • Economics of Physical and Information Outputs

Physical Outputs	Information Outputs
Seller no longer owns when sold	Seller continues to possess after sale and can sell again
Replication requires manufacturing	Replication at negligible cost and without limit
Output exists in single location	Output can exist in multiple locations simultaneously
Subject to diminishing returns	Subject to perfectly increasing returns
Wears out	Does not wear out

The types of returns associated with physical and information outputs also differ. Physical outputs are typically subject to the law of diminishing returns. In other words, as the scale of the operation used to produce physical outputs is increased, the marginal cost of producing incrementally more units tends to increase beyond the point where the physical facilities can be operated at optimal efficiency. Information outputs tend to have perfectly increasing returns since they consist primarily of one-time fixed costs and can be replicated with little variable cost or other physical resources. To illustrate, consider a software program that is distributed over the Internet. If only one person were to buy this program, then this person would have to absorb the entire cost of developing the program. However, if two people purchase this program, then the development cost can be evenly divided across these two people. Given the nature of this product with its negligible variable cost, this logic continues, resulting in proportionally lower per unit cost as more people purchase the software program.

Imp →

A final distinction worth noting between physical and information outputs is that physical outputs eventually wear out while information outputs do not. Of course, information can certainly become outdated and even obsolete, often faster than physical outputs!

Monitoring and Control

Suppose that in our production system we make a mistake. We must be able to observe this through, for example, accounting records (monitor), and we must change our system to correct for it (control). The activities of monitoring and control, as illustrated in Figure 1.1, are used extensively in systems, including management systems, and will be encountered throughout this text. In essence, the monitoring process must tell the manager when significant changes are occurring in any part of the production system. If the changes are not significantly affecting the outputs, then no control actions are needed. But if they are, management must intercede and *apply* corrective control to alter the inputs or the transformation system and, thereby, the outputs.

Table 1.3 lists some components of the five elements of the production system for a variety of common organizations.

*T*ABLE   1.3 • Examples of Production System Components

Organization	Inputs	Transformation System	Outputs	Monitor/Control	Environment
Post office	Labor Equipment Trucks	Transportation Printing	Mail deliveries Stamps	Weather Mail volumes Sorting/loss errors	Transportation network Weather Civil service
Bank	Checks Deposits Vault ATMs	Safekeeping Investment Statement preparations	Interest Electronic transfer Loans Statements	Interest rates Wage rates Loan default rates	Federal Reserve Economy
Cinema	Films Food People Theater	Film projection Food preparation	Entertainment Snacks	Film popularity Disposable incomes	Economy Entertainment industry
Manufacturer	Materials Equipment Labor Technology	Cutting Forming Joining Mixing	Machines Chemicals Consumer goods Scrap	Material flows Production volumes	Economy Commodity prices Consumer market
School	Books Teachers Facility Students	Learning Counselling Motivating	Educated students Skills Research	Demographics Grievances	State and county boards Tax system

*O*PERATIONS ACTIVITIES

Operations include not only those activities associated specifically with the production system but also a variety of other activities. For example, purchasing or procurement activities are concerned with obtaining many of the inputs needed in the production system. Similarly, shipping and distribution are sometimes considered marketing activities and sometimes considered operations activities. Because of the important interdependencies of these activities, many organizations are attempting to manage these activities as one process commonly referred to as *supply chain management*.

As organizations begin to adopt new organizational structures based on business processes and abandon the traditional functional organization, it is becoming less important to classify activities as operations or nonoperations. However, to understand the tasks more easily, we divide the field of operations into a series of subject areas as shown in Table 1.4. These areas are quite interdependent, but to make their workings more understandable we discuss them as though they were easily separable from each other. In some areas, a full-fledged department may be responsible for the activities, such as quality control or scheduling, but in other areas the activities (such as facility location) may be infrequent and simply assigned

*T*ABLE   1.4 • Major Subject Areas in Operations

Chapter	Subject Area
2	*Strategy:* Determining the critical operations tasks to support the organization's overall mission.
2	*Output planning:* Selecting and designing the services and products the organization will offer to customers, patrons, or recipients.
3	*Transformation process design:* Determining the physical transformation aspects of the production activities.
3	*Facility layout:* Devising an appropriate material flow and equipment layout within the facility to efficiently and effectively accommodate the transformation activities.
4	*Quality control:* Determining how quality standards are to be developed and maintained.
4	*Reliability and maintenance:* Determining how the proper performance of both the output and the transformation system itself is to be maintained.
4	*Process improvement:* Applying process design techniques to improve the flow and efficiency of production systems.
5	*Capacity planning:* Determining when to have facilities, equipment, and labor available and in what amounts.
5	*Facility location:* Deciding where to locate production, storage, and other major facilities.
6	*Schedule planning:* Anticipating the yearly needs for labor, materials, and facilities by month, week, or day within the year.
7	*Supply chain management:* Organizing the activities from the customer's order through final delivery for speed, efficiency, and quality.
8	*Inventory management:* Deciding what amounts of raw materials, work-in-process, and finished goods to hold.
9	*Enterprise and material requirements planning:* Using information management systems to coordinate enterprise-wide activities, especially for ordering or producing materials to meet a master delivery schedule.
10	*Lean management:* Using techniques from the Toyota Production System and JIT to eliminate waste and nonvalue-added activities.
11	*Project management:* Learning how to plan and control project activities to meet specifications for performance, schedule, and cost.

to a particular group or project team. Moreover, some of the subareas such as supply chain management or maintenance are critically important because they are a part of a larger business process or because other areas depend on them. Finally, since we consider all operations to be services, these subject areas are equally applicable to organizations that have traditionally been classified as manufacturers and services.

$\mathcal{T}$HE EXPERIENCE ECONOMY[2]

Commodities are outputs that have become standardized to the extent that there are typically no perceived differences across the offerings of different suppliers. In these cases the price of the output becomes the primary distinguishing feature of alternative offerings. Of course, many organizations attempt to differentiate their outputs so that they are not perceived to be commodities. However, in their thought-provoking book, *The Experience Economy*, B. Joseph Pine II and James H. Gilmore argue that in many cases the Web has done much to undermine efforts aimed at differentiating outputs and has in fact resulted in the *commoditization* of numerous product and service outputs. To illustrate, consider how the Web has impacted the purchase of personal computers. Specifications such as memory, amount of RAM, CPU type, and hard disk storage space have largely become standardized, and consumers frequently compare the price of these offerings via the Web. In a similar fashion, consider how the Web is impacting traditional services such as term life insurance and home mortgages.

To help better understand this phenomonon, Pine and Gilmore offer a classification of economic offerings. As shown in Figure 1.3, the classification suggests that economic offerings have evolved over time and in fact are continuing to evolve. Thus, according to this framework, commodities were the first economic offering. Organizations that further processed commodities into goods next evolved. In the following phase, the tangible characteristics of goods were combined with intangible benefits to create services. Finally, in the present phase, services are evolving into experiences.

Pine and Gilmore use the example of coffee to illustrate this framework. Specifically, the growing and harvesting of coffee beans represents the commodity stage. Organizations that grind, package, and brand coffee beans provide a "good" or physical output (e.g., Folgers, Maxwell House). Organizations that brew and then sell cups of coffee provide a service (e.g., McDonalds). Finally, organizations that engage customers and provide memorable events such as five-star restaurants stage experiences.

It is worth pointing out that there can be significant economic benefits associated with progressing to more evolved positions in this framework. Again using the coffee example, Pine and Gilmore note that the amount of money a Peruvian grower and harvester of coffee beans receives is but a few cents for each cup of coffee sold. The amount of money the manufacturer receives per cup of coffee after grinding and packing the coffee beans increases to between five and twenty-five cents.

---

[2]Shaded headings indicate especially timely topics.

Continuing this example, the amount a fast-food restaurant or convenience store receives for brewing a cup of coffee is typically in the neighborhood of a dollar. Finally, five-star restaurants and specialized cafes are often able to charge upwards of $2 to $5 for a similar cup of coffee. The point is that customers pay to enjoy memorable events or experiences. Table 1.5 summarizes key differences across these economic offerings.

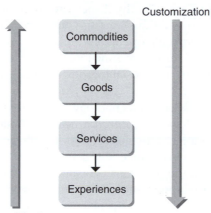

Customization

Commoditization

Figure 1.3   Classification and evolution of economic offerings.

$\mathcal{T}$ABLE   1.5   •   Comparison of Alternative Economic Offerings

	Commodities	*Goods*	*Services*	*Experiences*
Value added by:	Extracting	Producing	Delivering	Staging
Form of output:	Fungible	Tangible	Intangible	Memorable
Key characteristic:	Natural	Standardized	Customized	Personalized
Buyer:	Market	User	Client	Guest

Adapted from B. J. Pine II and J. H. Gilmore, *The Experience Economy*, HBS Press, 1999, p. 6.

Also, as shown in Figure 1.3, there are two counteracting forces that impact economic offerings. On the one hand, commoditization occurs when outputs become less differentiated based on their features. Commoditization implicitly moves economic offerings to less evolved levels. For example, commoditization would lead to services being perceived as goods (e.g., term life insurance and home mortgages) and goods being perceived as commodities (e.g., personal computers). One way to counteract commoditization is by increasing the amount of customization. For example, by maintaining and repairing its medical equipment, GE has been able to profitably expand its position from offering a good to delivering a service.

TWO VIEWS OF ORGANIZATIONS

Traditionally, companies have been organized on the basis of the type of work performed. Thus, organizations were divided into marketing, finance, accounting, engineering, operations, and other departments. This type of organization is referred to as a *functional organization* because work is organized on the basis of the function performed.

In the functional view, all organizations must perform three core functions: operations, finance, and marketing. Clearly, if they are to continue to exist, all organizations must create value (operations), get the output to the customer (marketing), and raise capital to support their operations (finance). Additionally, organizations perform a number of other important functional activities such as reporting financial information (accounting) and designing new products (engineering)—to name just two.

As a result of recent advances in technology and increased international competition, many organizations have recognized a need for better methods of grouping and integrating organizational activities. Figure 1.4 illustrates how organizational structures are currently evolving to meet this need. Figure 1.4*a* depicts the traditional functional organization. In the functional organization, employees at any level are coordinated by having a common supervisor, who controls the information that is shared across the groups and resolves problems that arise between groups.

In the 1980s Michael Porter, a professor at the Harvard Business School, developed the concept of a *value chain* as a way to improve the coordination among various functional groups. The value-chain approach (Figure 1.4*b*) emphasized the organization as a system of interdependent activities that create value for the customer. Superimposing the value chain over the functional hierarchy provides a coordinating mechanism for linking sequentially related organizational activities. In effect, this is accomplished by organizational groups viewing subsequent organizational groups along the value chain as their "internal" customers. Thus, Porter's value chain presented a new view of management, depicting the organization as a system of value-creating vertical processes rather than a collection of independent activities.

As business became increasingly globalized and competition grew fiercer, organizations were forced to become even more efficient and effective. The current phase of the evolution is shown in Figure 1.4*c*: Organizations are now adopting organizational structures based on specific value-creating processes rather than simply using the value chain to coordinate separated functional groups. Thus, the traditional vertical structure based on functional specialists is being abandoned in favor of a horizontal structure based on process generalists. Furthermore, in comparing Figures 1.4*b* and *c*, we observe that the traditional management positions are also changing. For example, vice president (VP) and general management (GM) positions that were responsible for specific functional activities such as operations, marketing, and finance are evolving into process management positions. Managers of processes, often referred to as process owners (PO), have responsibility for entire value-creating processes, such as supplying a product from the receipt of raw materials to the distribution of the final product.

The evolution to process organizational structures makes the topics in this course all the more relevant. Specifically, in the old functional organizational structure, only people in the operations area thought in terms of value-creating processes. However, in the new process-centered organization, all employees are organized on the basis of specific value-creating processes. Thus, all employees must now think in terms of how their efforts fit into and support a particular value-creating process.

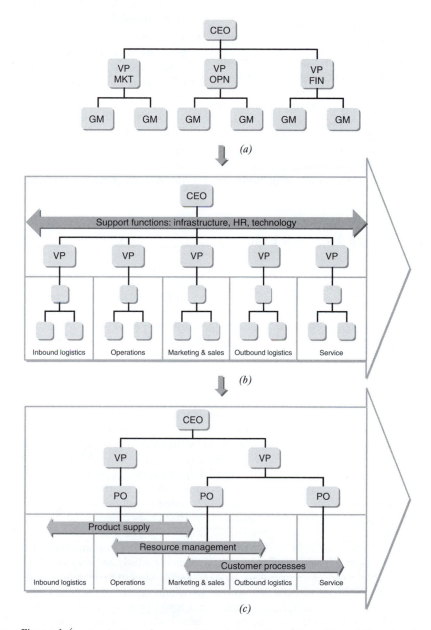

Figure 1.4   Evolution of organizational structures: (*a*) traditional functional organization; (*b*) value-chain approach; (*c*) process-centered structure. *Source:* Adapted from Shafer, S. M., and S. L. Oswald. "Product Focused Manufacturing for Strategic Advantage." *Business Horizons* (November–December 1996): 24–29.

EXPAND YOUR UNDERSTANDING

1. Since value is always in the mind of the beholder, how does altering a product differ from advertising or guarantees in terms of added value?

2. Why is it so hard to increase productivity in the service sector?

3. Identify other major differences between services and products in addition to those listed in Table 1.1.

4. Some countries have strict laws regarding pollution, antitrust activities, and bribery by their domestic firms. Yet many other countries have no such laws. Indeed, firms and individuals in those countries may well expect to receive a kickback (return of cash) for orders placed or delivered. How ethical is it for a firm based in the former to meet the latter's kickback expectations? How ethical is it for the former to restrict the activities of domestic firms but not those of foreign firms operating in their country?

5. Many foreign firms have been successful in the following areas: steel, autos, cameras, radios, and televisions. Are services more protected from foreign competition? How?

6. It is commonly said that Japanese firms employ 10 times as many engineers per operations worker as U.S. firms and 10 times fewer accountants. What effect would you expect this to have on their competitiveness? Why?

7. While the value of economic offerings tends to increase, moving from commodities to experiences, do profits exhibit a similar pattern?

8. How might the concept of a "facilitating good" alter the way we perceive a product? A service?

APPLY YOUR UNDERSTANDING
Taracare, Inc.

Taracare, Inc. operates a single factory in Ensenada, Mexico, where it fabricates and assembles a wide range of outdoor furniture for the USA market, including chairs, tables, and matching accessories. Taracare's primary production activities include extruding the aluminum furniture parts, bending and shaping the extruded parts, finishing and painting the parts, and then assembling the parts into completed furniture. Upholstery, glass tabletops, and all hardware are purchased from outside suppliers.

Jorge Gonzalez purchased Taracare in 2001. Before that, Jorge had distinguished himself as a top sales rep of outdoor furniture for the western region of one of the leading national manufacturers. However, after spending 10 years on the road, Jorge wanted to settle down and spend more time with his family back in Mexico. After searching for a couple of months, he came across what he believed to be an ideal opportunity. Not only was it in an industry that he had a great deal of knowledge about, but he would be his own boss. Unfortunately, the asking price was well beyond Jorge's means. However, after a month of negotiation, Jorge convinced Jesus Garza, Taracare's founder, to maintain a 25 percent stake in the business. Although Jesus had originally intended to sell out completely, he was impressed with Jorge's knowledge of the business, his extensive contacts, and his enthusiasm. He therefore agreed to sell Jorge 75 percent of Taracare and retain 25 percent as an investment.

Jorge's ambition for Taracare was to expand it from a small regional manufacturer to one that sold to major national retailers. To accomplish this objective, Jorge's first initiative was to triple Taracare's sales force in 2002. As sales began to increase, Jorge increased the support staff by hiring an accountant, a comptroller, two new designers, and a purchasing agent.

By mid-2005, Taracare's line was carried by several national retailers on a trial basis. However, Taracare was having difficulty both in meeting the deliveries its sales reps were promising and in satisfying the national retailers' standards for quality. To respond to this problem, Jorge hired Alfredo Diaz as the new manufacturing manager. Before accepting Jorge's offer, Alfredo was the plant manager of a factory that manufactured replacement windows sold by large regional and national retailers.

After several months on the job—and after making little progress toward improving on-time delivery and quality—Alfredo scheduled a meeting with Jorge to discuss his major concerns. Alfredo began:

> I requested this meeting with you, Jorge, because I am not satisfied with the progress we are making toward improving our delivery performance and quality. The bottom line is that I feel I'm getting very little cooperation from the other department heads. For example, last month purchasing switched to a new supplier for paint; and although it is true that the new paint costs less per gallon, we have to apply a thicker coat to give the furniture the same protection. I haven't actually run the numbers, but I know it is actually costing us more, in both materials and labor.

> Another problem is that we typically run a special promotion to coincide with launching new product lines. I understand that the sales guys want to get the product into the stores as quickly as possible, but they are making promises about delivery that we can't meet. It takes time to work out the bugs and get things running smoothly. Then there is the problem with the designers. They are constantly adding features to the product that make it almost impossible for us to produce. At the very least, they make it much more expensive for us to produce. For example, on the new "Destiny" line, they designed table legs that required a new die at a cost of 250,000 pesos. Why couldn't they have left the legs alone so that we could have used one of our existing dies? On top of this, we have the accounting department telling us that our equipment utilization is too low. Then, when we increase our equipment utilization and make more products, the finance guys tell us we have too much capital tied up in inventory. To be honest, I really don't feel that I'm getting very much support.

Rising from his chair, Jorge commented:

> You have raised some important issues, Alfredo. Unfortunately, I have to run to another meeting right now. Why don't you send me a memo outlining these issues and your recommendations? Then perhaps I will call a meeting and we can discuss these issues with the other department heads. At least our production problems are really no worse than that of our competitors, and we don't expect you to solve all of our problems overnight. Keep up the good work and send me that memo at your earliest convenience.

Questions

1. Does Alfredo's previous experience running a plant that made replacement windows qualify him to run a plant that makes outdoor furniture?
2. What recommendations would you make if you were Alfredo?
3. Given Jorge's background and apparent priorities, how is he likely to respond to Alfredo's recommendations? On the basis of this likely response, is it possible to rephrase Alfredo's recommendations so they are more appealing to Jorge?

BIBLIOGRAPHY

Bowen, D. E., R. E. Chase, and T. G. Cummings & Associates. *Service Management Effectiveness.* San Francisco: Jossey-Bass, 1990.

Duff, C., and B. Ortega. "How Wal-Mart Outdid a Once-Touted K-Mart in Discount-Store Race." *Wall Street Journal* (March 24, 1995): A1, A4.

Evans, P., and T. S. Wurster. *Blown to Bits.* Boston: HBS Press, 2000.

Feld, W. M. *Lean Manufacturing: Tools, Techniques, and How to Use Them.* Boca Raton, FL: CRC Press, 2000.

Fitzsimmons, J. A., and M. J. Fitzsimmons. *Service Management: Operations, Strategy, and Information Technology.* New York: Irwin/McGraw-Hill, 2001.

Gibson, R. "At McDonald's, New Recipes for Buns, Eggs." *Wall Street Journal* (June 13, 1995): B1, B6.

Hammer, M. "Deep Change: How Operational Innovation Can Transform Your Company." *Harvard Business Review*, April 2004: 85-93.

Merrick, A. and Zimmerman, A., "Can Sears and Kmart Take On a Goliath Named Wal-Mart?" *Wall Street Journal* (November 19, 2004): B1, B2.

Pande, P. S., R. P. Neuman, and R. R. Cavanagh. *The Six Sigma Way.* New York: McGraw-Hill, 2000.

Pine, J., and J. Gilmore. *The Experience Economy,* Boston: HBS Press, 1999.

Porter, M. E. *Competitive Advantage.* New York: Free Press, 1985.

Ruffenach, G. "Getting the Olympic Flame to Atlanta Won't Be a Simple Cross-Country Run." *Wall Street Journal* (February 29, 1996): B1.

Womack, J. P., D. T. Jones, and D. Roos. *The Machine That Changed the World.* New York: Harper Perennial, 1991.

CHAPTER 2

Strategy, Operations, and Global Competitiveness

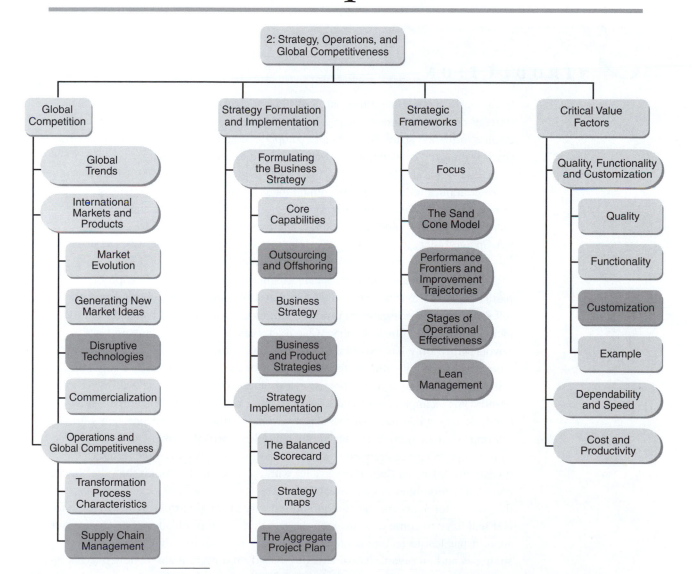

Shaded headings indicate especially timely topics.

CHAPTER IN PERSPECTIVE

This chapter describes the critical role of operations to the global competitiveness of the organization. We start the discussion with a review of global trends in the economy, the evolution of international markets and products, and the impact of operations on competitiveness and the global supply chain. Next we describe the process of formulating and implementing the business strategy, including the role of outsourcing and offshoring. Following this, we describe five strategic frameworks available to businesses as underpinnings for their strategy, and then close the chapter with a description of those operations factors that are critical to offering value to the customer.

INTRODUCTION

- In the early 2000s, GM's Chairman and CEO, Richard Wagoner Jr., relied on the strategy of using rebates to help generate cash and reverse GM's long, downward decline in market share. In the highly competitive auto industry, maintaining market share is critical. For example, analysts estimate the impact of each percentage point of market share at GM is $1 billion in profits. Unfortunately for GM, as its market share continues to erode, it is becoming increasingly clear that the rebate strategy it pursued over the last several years is not working. A recent indication of this was that in the first two months of 2005, GM's market share declined by over two percentage points to just under 25 percent. Based on this decline, GM projected a loss for the first quarter of 2005 of over $800 million.

  A closer examination of GM's situation suggests more fundamental problems. In particular, some analysts have suggested that GM's reliance on rebates is simply a reflection of weaknesses in its product offerings. Currently, GM has eight brands including Cadillac, Buick, Pontiac, Chevrolet, Saturn, and Saab compared with Toyota which only has two brands (Toyota and Lexus). Aside from the issue of whether a company with less than 25 percent of the market needs so many brands, one result of having so many brands is a proliferation of similar vehicles across the brands. For example, six of GM's divisions offer similar front-wheel-drive midsize family sedans while four offer similar minivans. Furthermore, the problem with offering so many models creates another problem for GM, namely, that it is unable to redesign its cars as frequently as its competitors do. For example, it took GM 9 years to replace its Chevrolet Cavalier with the Cobalt. Honda, on the other hand, completely redesigns its Civic every five years. On average, GM's cars have been on the market for 3.7 years compared to an industry average of three years. In the end, GM will have to come to terms with the fact that it will not likely regain the market share it has lost to its international competitors and will then have to develop strategies and an organizational structure based on a more realistic view of what its sustainable market share actually is. (Welch 2005)

- Having rung up combined profits of $8 billion in 2004, manufacturers of flat-panel TVs appear to be especially optimistic about the profit potential for the TV market in the years ahead. Indeed, a battle of epic proportions appears to be brewing in the consumer electronics industry. On one side there is a group of Asian manufacturers that have spent $35 billion adding flat-panel capacity in 2004 and 2005. Among the Asian players are a joint venture between LG Electronics and Royal Philips Electronics that invested $5.1 billion to build the world's largest liquid-crystal display factory, a $2 billion joint venture between Sony and Samsung to produce LCDs, and Matsushita Electronics' new $1.3 billion plant for producing chips for thin TVs. On the other side, North America's Dell is attempting to leverage its streamlined supply chain and direct-sales model and thereby shift the basis of competition from features to price. For example, in the fall of 2004 Dell introduced a high-definition 42-inch plasma TV for under $3,000 while the similar offerings of its Asian competitors were still priced above $4,000. As a result, Dell was able to capture 10 percent of the market in a span of only a couple of months. In the years ahead it will be interesting to observe whether the Asian strategy based on product innovation and appealing designs will win out over Dell's strategy that seeks to commoditize the market and thereby shift the basis of competition to price. In addition, Dell faces another challenge that the other manufacturers do not face. Namely, Dell must determine the extent to which it is willing to allow its TV offerings functionality that overlaps with its computers. Such a strategy could cannibalize sales of its lucrative PCs but may be necessary to compete with other TV manufacturers that do not have to worry about cannibalizing this part of their business. (Einhorn 2005)

- While most other steelmakers struggled during an industry-wide downturn throughout the early 2000s, Nucor distinguished itself as the only domestic steelmaker to remain profitable. In fact, Nucor actually capitalized on the opportunity created by the downturn and invested $1.1 billion to acquire 10 steel plants, increasing its annual production capacity by 5 million tons. Even better for Nucor, it was able to acquire this capacity for an average of 17 cents on the dollar. From its entry in the steel industry, Nucor has pursued unique strategies relative to the other major players in the industry. For example, Nucor's first minimills utilized electric arc furnaces, an experimental technology at the time, to melt scrap metal into finished steel. A key advantage of this approach is that scrap metal is significantly cheaper than the iron ore traditionally used to make finished steel. Currently, Nucor is once again attempting to utilize technology to leap ahead of the competition and gain yet another significant cost advantage. In particular, Nucor is implementing strip casting, a radically new production process that extrudes steel through nozzles into thin strips of metal. Because of the thinness of the strips, the strips will require little additional processing. This therefore should translate into a significant cost advantage over traditional approaches where thick metal strips are produced which then require substantial amounts of additional processing to get the steel strips into sheets. (Foust 2005)

Making and keeping an organization competitive is top management's job, and this is accomplished partly through the business strategy that top management adopts. This strategy gives the firm its direction and vision for the future and guides its decisions in both the short term and the long term. In the case of GM, its previous strategy of relying on rebates to stem its downward spiral in market share proved ineffective and therefore suggests the need for a new strategy, perhaps one based on further contracting its capacity and placing greater emphasis on the frequency with which it updates its product offerings. In the case of the consumer electronics industry, recent strategic decisions addressed issues related to the development of strategic partnerships and joint ventures as well as how to position product offerings in the marketplaces (e.g., to compete on the basis of innovative products versus product costs). In Nucor's case, strategic decisions revolved around the use of technology as a way to gain significant cost advantages over the competition.

Furthermore, the examples illustrate the extent to which the marketplace has become globalized. In GM's case, virtually all of its loss in domestic market share can be attributed to gains made by international competitors. The consumer electronics industry demonstrates how dynamic the marketplace has become. For example, we see two organizations that compete with one another in a range of markets and headquartered in different countries (i.e., Sony, a Japanese company, and Samsung, a Korean company) forming a joint venture to produce LCDs.

A common strategy in the recent past, particularly for small firms, was to be a local supplier who could react quickly to the immediate needs of its customer. But global producers are now competing in virtually all markets, whether local, domestic, or foreign. Thus, even if a firm sees itself as only a small, local business, it must be globally competitive to survive. For example, small regional foundries have been driven out of business by the thousands and replaced by international competitors. Thus, it is incumbent on every firm's top management to consider international competition in its business strategy.

Our description of the production system in Chapter 1 assumed that the organization had some specific, well-defined goal—such a goal might be making gourmet cookies for an upscale market, for example. This goal implies awareness of marketing: What services and facilitating goods do customers want? But any independent financial goal (to make the company rich) or marketing goal (to increase sales 10 percent) is only wishful thinking unless the operations of the organization can deliver what is needed with the available resources. What transformation activities are needed? What level of quality is required? Is transportation necessary?

The organization's business strategy provides the information needed to design business processes for the firm to achieve its goals. The business strategy also provides the information for all activities carried out in the organization to support the production system in its task. In the functional organization, this specification of how each function is going to support the overall business strategy was known as a functional strategy. Thus, there was a marketing strategy, a finance strategy, an operations strategy, and so on.

GLOBAL COMPETITION _____

long-term

short term →

Competitiveness can be defined in a number of ways. We may think of it as the long-term viability of a firm or organization; or we may define it in a short-term context such as the current success of a firm in the marketplace as measured by its market share or its profitability. We can also talk about the competitiveness of a nation, in the sense of its aggregate competitive success in all markets. The U.S. President's Council on Industrial Competitiveness gave this definition in 1985:

> Competitiveness for a nation is the degree to which it can, under free and fair market conditions, produce goods and services that meet the test of international markets while simultaneously maintaining and expanding the real incomes of its citizens.

Global Trends

The United States provides a graphic example of global trade trends. The trend in merchandise trade for the United States is illustrated in Figure 2.1. Although some might think that foreign competition has been taking markets away from U.S. producers only in the past decade, this figure indicates that U.S. merchandise imports have grown considerably in the last 30 years. Although *exports* have increased over this period as well, they have not increased as fast as imports; the result is an exploding trade deficit with foreign countries as shown by the cumulative net exports curve in Figure 2.1. Partly as a result of this deficit, the United States is now the biggest debtor nation in the world, with a cumulative deficit of about half a trillion dollars, nearly half of the U.S. annual gross domestic product (GDP), and an annual deficit running about 6 percent of GDP.

Although the trade deficit has received major attention only since it burgeoned in the early 1980s, Figure 2.1 indicates that it is actually part of a long-term trend. One danger of such a growing deficit, however, is the historical currency "run rate" of about 5 percent of GDP. For most countries, when their annual trade deficit hits about 5 percent of the GDP, there is a run on their currencies as other countries and currency traders dump the currency so as to not be left with a loss when the currency is forced into devaluation. The United States has so far been able to avoid this fate primarily because of its strong economy, the fact that most major commodities (oil, gold) are priced in U.S. dollars, and the fear by other countries holding vast U.S. dollar reserves that if they try to unload their reserves now, they will create the run that will reduce the value of those reserves. This results in a highly unstable and dangerous situation.

Newspapers and network news programs often report on the bilateral trade deficit of the United States with various foreign countries. These stories frequently focus on the bilateral trade gap between the United States and Japan, or China. There are a number of problems, however, with bilateral trade statistics. For instance, when Japan shifts some of its production to other countries such as China or Thailand, it appears that the trade gap between the United States and Japan has decreased. Similarly, Japanese-owned companies operating in the United States are partly responsible for the increase in exports to Japan. Both of these occurrences tend to distort the true nature of the balance of trade between the United States and Japan or China.

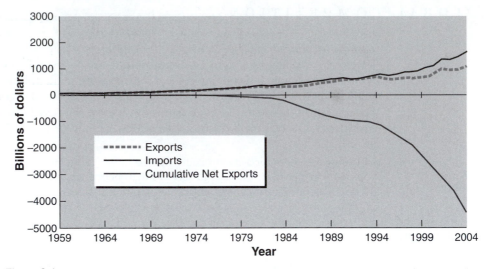

Figure 2.1   The United States's merchandise trade. *Source:* Economic Report of the President.

When the United States buys more imports from overseas with dollars, and foreigners buy fewer American exports, a surplus of U. S. dollars accumulates abroad that tends to reduce the desirability of holding dollars, so the value of the dollar falls. This is illustrated in the price-adjusted (for inflation) broad dollar index plotted in Figure 2.2. This index is the weighted-average price of the U.S. dollar to the foreign currencies of 26 countries, such as the Euro (€), Japanese yen (¥), British pound (£), South African rand (R), Swiss franc (F), Indian rupee (Rs), and so on. A large value of the index indicates a strong dollar, making it easier for Americans to afford imports but also making it more difficult for people in other countries to afford U.S. exports. Although other factors, such as intervention by a central bank and changes in national interest rates, can alter the exchange rate in the short term, the basic economic factors of competitiveness tend to show through over the long term.

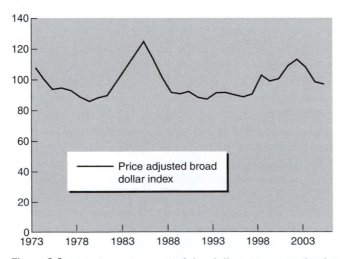

Figure 2.2   Purchasing power of the dollar. *Source:* Federal Reserve Board, *www.federalreserve.gov/releases/h10/Summary/indexbc= m.txt*, March, 10, 2001.

Although the value of the dollar often fluctuates widely relative to the value of a particular country's currency, Figure 2.2 indicates that the price-adjusted broad dollar index has been relatively stable since the late 1980s, averaging about 96.1. However, as seen in the figure, the strength of the dollar increased substantially relative to the currencies of the United States' key trading partners in the mid-1980s. By the late 1980s and through the mid 1990s this situation had reversed with a dollar weaker than its long-term average. Finally, as the 1990s came to an end, the dollar once again began to strengthen and remained above its long-term average through 2002, though it is beginning to drop again, primarily due to the large trade deficits.

Let's consider in more detail what it means to Americans and to the average foreign consumer when the dollar declines in value relative to a foreign currency. A weaker dollar means that Americans will have to pay more for products imported from the foreign country in question. Meanwhile, however, the prices for products produced in the United States and exported to the foreign country will decline. Thus, a decline in the value of the dollar is a double-edged sword. Such a decline makes imported goods more expensive for Americans to purchase but at the same time makes exports less expensive for foreign consumers, increasing the demand for domestic products.

According to economic theory, a weaker dollar should make American products more desirable (or competitive) in foreign markets, and imports less desirable in American markets. However, some market actions that governments and businesses often take to keep from losing customers can alter this perfect economic relationship. For instance, when the price of Japanese products in the United States started increasing in terms of dollars, Japanese firms initiated huge cost-cutting drives to reduce the cost (and thereby the dollar price) of their products, to keep from losing American customers. This strategy has been largely successful. Similarly, China limits the exchange rate of its currency, the renminbi, at about 8.3 to the dollar so it always sells its goods at a competitive price.

Also, instead of American products becoming significantly cheaper in Japan, some claim that many of these products have been politically blocked from access to Japanese markets by the Japanese government, which tries to protect domestic firms from foreign competition. When a government does this to protect a developing domestic industry while it is struggling to become competitive in world markets, the short-run strategy may seem wise. But in Europe, a result of protectionism has been that consumers buy only half as many electronic products (TV sets, VCRs, and such) as Americans and yet pay two to three times as much for them.

International Markets and Products

In the last decade, particularly with the economic rise of China and India, global markets, manufacturers, and service producers have evolved in a dramatic fashion. In this subsection we describe the dynamic changes occurring in the global marketplace and the roles of research and development, technology, and commercialization in bringing new products and services to market.

Market Evolution

The way current trends are developing, there now seem to be three major trading regions in the world: Europe, North America, and Asia, as illustrated in Figure 2.3.

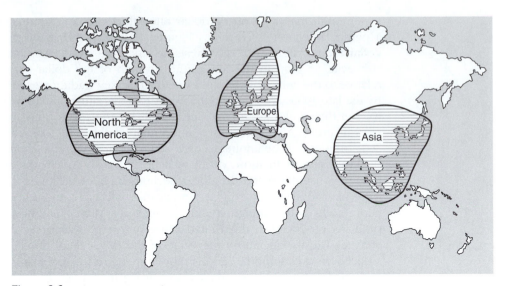

Figure 2.3   Three major trading regions.

Note that Africa, middle and northern Asia, and Latin America are not included. (Australia and New Zealand are moving into the Asian regions with major exports and imports from countries in that region.) In the last two decades, under the sponsorship of the European Union (EU), one of the largest unified markets in the world has emerged. This region is even larger than the North American region, which consists (mainly through the influence of NAFTA, the North American Free Trade Agreement) of the United States, Mexico, and Canada, and continues to grow with the addition of eastern European countries, including the Balkans and now even Turkey! However, there are still several issues in the process of being resolved, such as currency (Euros) and sovereignty, before the goal of a unified European market is realized. The Asian region is composed of Japan, Korea, Indonesia, Malaysia, Taiwan, Hong Kong, Singapore, and now the giants India and China, the latter growing at over 9 percent a year! These countries are primarily exporters of goods rather than importers.

With the changes occurring in the World Trade Organization (WTO), international competition has grown very complex in the last decade. Previously, firms were domestic, exporters, or international. A domestic firm produced and sold in the same country. An exporter sold goods, often someone else's, abroad. An international firm sold domestically produced as well as foreign-produced goods both domestically and in foreign countries. However, domestic sales were usually produced domestically, and foreign sales were made either in the home country or in a plant in the foreign country, typically altered to suit national regulations, needs, and tastes.

Now, however, there are global firms, joint ventures, partial ownerships, foreign subsidiaries, and other types of international producers. For example, Canon is a global producer that sells a standard "world-class" camera with options and add-ons available through the local dealer. And American automobile producers—Ford and General Motors—both own stock in foreign automobile companies. Mazak, a fast-growing machine tool company, is the U.S. subsidiary of Yamazaki Machinery Company of Japan. Part of the reason for cross-ownerships and cross-endeavors is the spiraling cost of bringing out new products. New drugs and memory chips run in the hundreds of millions to billions of dollars to bring to market. By using joint ventures and other such approaches to share costs (and thereby lower risks), firms can remain competitive.

Whether to build offshore, assemble offshore, use foreign parts, employ a joint venture, and so on is a complex decision for any firm and depends on a multitude of factors. For example, the Japanese are expanding many of their automobile manufacturing plants in the United States. The reasons are many and include: to circumvent U.S. governmental regulation of importers, to avoid the high yen cost of Japanese-produced products, to avoid import fees and quotas, and to placate U.S. consumers. Of course, other considerations are involved in producing in foreign countries: culture (e.g., if women are part of the labor force), political stability, laws, taxes, regulations, and image.

Other complex arrangements of suppliers can result in hidden international competition. For example, many products that bear an American nameplate have been totally produced and assembled in a foreign country and are simply imported under the U.S. manufacturer's or retailer's nameplate, such as Nike shoes. Even more confusing, many products contain a significant proportion of foreign parts, or may be composed entirely of foreign parts and only assembled in the United States (e.g., toasters, mixers, hand tools). This recent strategic approach of finding the best mix of producers and assemblers to deliver a product or service to a customer has come to be known as "supply chain management," a topic we discuss a bit later but cover in detail in Chapter 7.

Generating New Market Ideas

The field of Research and Development (known as R&D) is primarily responsible for developing new product ideas. R&D activities focus on creating and developing (but not producing) the organizational outputs. On occasion, R&D also creates new production methods by which outputs, either new or old, may be produced. *Research* itself is typically divided into two types: pure and applied. Pure research is simply working with basic technology to develop new knowledge. Applied research is attempting to develop new knowledge along particular lines. For example, pure research might focus on developing a material that conducts electricity with zero resistance, whereas applied research could focus on further developing this material to be used in cable products. *Development* is the attempt to utilize the findings of research and expand the possible applications, typically along the sponsor's line of interest (e.g., the development of cable to connect computers together in a local-area network).

The development end of R&D is more on the applications side and often consists of modifications or extensions to existing outputs. Figure 2.4 illustrates the range of applicability of development as the output becomes more clearly defined. In the early years of a new output, development is oriented toward removing "bugs," increasing performance, improving quality, and so on. In the middle years, options and variants of the output are developed. In the later years, development is oriented toward extensions of the output that will prolong its life.

Currently—as compared to a few decades ago—the development effort in R&D is much, much larger than the research effort. Some scholars of R&D attribute the shift away from research and toward the simple extension of existing outputs to the extensive influence of marketing on organizations. These scholars postulate that the marketing approach, "giving the customers what they want," is basically wrong because neither the customer nor the marketer has the vision to see what new technology can offer. By draining off funds from research and spending them on ever greater development of existing outputs, and on advertising those outputs, the organization leaves itself vulnerable to those competitors who are willing to invest in research and "disruptive technologies" (discussed in the next subsection) to develop entire new generations of products and services.

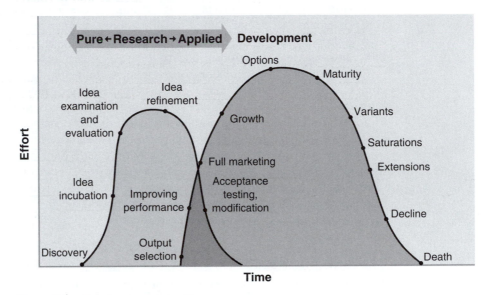

Figure 2.4   The development effort.

Unfortunately, the returns from R&D are frequently meager, whereas the costs are great. Figure 2.5 illustrates the ***mortality curve*** (fallout rate) associated with the concurrent design, evaluation, and selection for a hypothetical group of 50 potential chemical products, assuming that the 50 candidate products are available for consideration in year 3. (The first three years, on the average, are required for the necessary research preceding each candidate product.) Initial evaluation and screening reduce the 50 to about 22, and economic analysis further reduces the number to about 9. Development reduces this number even more, to about 5, and design and testing reduce it to perhaps 3. By the time construction (for production), market development, and a year's commercialization are completed, there is only one successful product left. (Sometimes there are none!) A recent study found that, beyond this, only 64 percent of the new products brought to market were successful, or about two out of three.

Two alternatives to research frequently used by organizations are *imitation* of a proven new idea (i.e., employing a second-to-market strategy) or outright *purchase* of someone else's invention. The outright purchase strategy is becoming extremely popular in those industries where bringing a new product to market can cost huge sums, such as pharmaceuticals and high technology. It is also employed in those industries where technology advances so rapidly that there isn't enough time to employ a second-to-market strategy. Although imitation does not put the organization first in the market with the new product or service, it does give an opportunity to study any possible defects in the original product or service and rapidly develop a better design, frequently at a better price. The second approach—purchasing an invention or the inventing company itself—eliminates the risks inherent in research, but it still requires the company to develop and market the product or service before knowing whether it will be successful. Either route spares the organization the risk and tremendous cost of conducting the actual research leading up to a new invention or improvement.

In addition to *product research* (as it is generally known), there is also *process research*, which involves the generation of new knowledge concerning *how to produce* outputs. Currently, the production of many familiar products out of plastic (toys, pipe, furniture, etc.) is an outstanding example of successful process research. Motorola, to take another example, extensively uses project teams that conduct process development at the same time as product development.

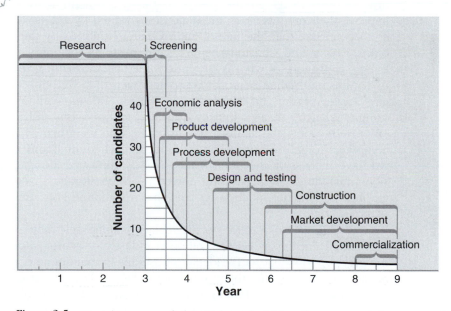

Figure 2.5 Mortality curve of chemical product ideas from research to commercialization. *Source*: Adapted from *This is Dupont 30*. Wilmington, DE by permission of DuPont de Nemours and Co.

Disruptive Technologies

Certainly the importance of identifying and meeting customer requirements in developing new outputs cannot be overstated. However, is it possible for organizations to actually stay too close to their customers? The answer according to Harvard Business School Professors Joseph Bower and Clayton Christensen (1995) is that many organizations do indeed fall into a trap of staying too close to their existing customers, particularly when **disruptive technologies** are involved.

When disruptive technologies are introduced, they typically offer a set of performance characteristics that are not valued by current mainstream customers and actually perform worse along the performance characteristics of interest to them. Therefore, outputs based on disruptive technologies tend to initially appeal to niche markets. The apparently small market for outputs based on the disruptive technology compared with the size of the established market makes it difficult for traditional organizations to justify shifting resources to meet the needs of this niche market.

However, these disruptive technologies are often able to improve their performance along the dimensions valued by the mainstream customers at a faster rate than outputs based on traditional technologies. In other cases, there may be a shift in the performance characteristics valued by mainstream customers toward the characteristics provided by the disruptive technology. In either case, the organizations that introduced the new outputs based on the disruptive technology are often able to successfully invade the mainstream market with the familiar result that industry leadership changes. During this period of time, the traditional companies tend to focus on the needs of the mainstream market and continue to improve their outputs along the dimensions valued by mainstream customers—but at a slower rate than the rate of improvement exhibited by the disruptive technologies. Bower and Christensen refer to innovations that provide mainstream customers with more of what is currently valued as *sustaining technologies*.

To illustrate, when personal computers were first introduced, the performance gap between them and mainframe computers and minicomputers was quite substantial. As a result, PCs initially appealed to hobbyists and technically oriented employees, not to the mainstream customers who were using mainframe and minicomputers for payroll processing, production scheduling, and so on. However, as we have witnessed, the performance of PCs improved along a variety of dimensions, including raw processing power, memory, storage space, ease of use, and graphics capabilities much faster than their mainframe and minicomputer counterparts.

And while PCs may never totally replace mainframes, they have certainly had a very significant impact on the computer industry. It is also interesting to note that the organizations that had leadership positions in mainframe computers were slow to offer minicomputers, thereby providing Digital Equipment Corporation with an enormous opportunity. Furthermore, both mainframe and minicomputer manufacturers were slow to offer PCs, providing significant opportunities to Apple Computer, Compaq, Dell, Gateway, and so on. Of course many mainframe and minicomputer manufacturers offered PCs, but none led the PC market like they had in their traditional market, and many of them are now gone.

As an example of a disruptive technology that is currently playing out, consider the impact that the Web is having on graduate business education. On the one hand, many professors and administrators find it difficult to imagine that network technology will ever progress to the point that it can provide the same classroom experience online as they currently provide in the physical classroom. This seems particularly true of professors who lean more toward a discussion-oriented format versus a lecture format. Of course, many institutions of higher education do successfully offer distance learning programs online and through a variety of other technologies. But given the current state-of-the-art including streaming video, hypertext links, chatting, and email, it is probably fair to say that pure distance education programs still cannot provide the same rich experience as the physical classroom.

However, it is also important to point out that while they may not provide the same experience as their physical classroom counterparts, they do excel along other performance dimensions such as providing students with the convenience of not having to travel to a physical classroom and the flexibility of being able to review course content at times when it is most convenient for the student. These benefits appear to be especially attractive to working professionals who travel frequently, who do not live in close proximity to a physical university, or who otherwise value flexibility more than close interactions with other students and their professors.

[handwritten margin note: Online classrooms provide flexibility of being able to review course content at times when it is most convenient for the student]

[handwritten margin note: suitable for grad or higher forms of education]

Will the Web turn out to be a disruptive technology relative to graduate business education? As is illustrated in Figure 2.6, it certainly may! Already, many consumers have broadband access in their homes, and some even have video cameras and microphones hooked up to their computers. Furthermore, given the rate of improvement or the performance trajectory of network technologies on dimensions such as bandwidth, streaming video, monitor resolution, collaborative software applications, and network conferencing, we foresee a day in the not too distant future where professors will be able to offer as rich a classroom experience, if not richer, online as they currently do in their physical classrooms.

From a managerial perspective, there are several important implications associated with disruptive technologies. First, since industry leadership often changes after the introduction of a disruptive technology, it is important that organizations develop the ability to identify potential disruptive technologies. Second, Bower and Christensen (1995) argue that disruptive technologies must initially be protected, perhaps by being placed in separate and independent business units. For example, the prospect of cannibalizing sales of their expensive and highly profitable mainframe computers with much less expensive and less profitable PCs probably did not excite many managers at IBM. Indeed, their reluctance to cannibalize the mainframe computer may be a primary reason contributing to why IBM is selling their PC division. Thus the lesson is, if you are not willing to obsolete your own products and services, you can be certain that one of your competitors is more than willing to do so!

[handwritten margin note: Imp =>]

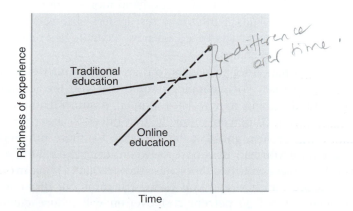

Figure 2.6 Performance trajectories of traditional and online distance education programs.

Commercialization

In the previous subsections, we discussed the importance of designing new products and services that meet customers' requirements and can be produced by the firm. The final ingredient in determining whether a new product or service will succeed is the organization's ability to commercialize its new offerings. *Commercialization* refers to the process of moving an idea for a new product or service from concept to market. It is frequently noted by top managers and academics alike that although quality and manufacturing excellence were the key to competitive success in the 1980s and 1990s, commercialization of technology may be the key to competitive success in future decades. Couple significantly shorter product life cycles with a marketplace that is becoming increasingly competitive as a result of globalization, and you begin to get an idea of how important it is for organizations to be able to rapidly move ideas for new products and services from concept to market.

In the late 1980s, McKinsey & Company conducted a study of the differences between leading and lagging companies with respect to commercialization (Nevens, Summe, and Uttal 1990). The results of the study indicated that leading companies had the following four characteristics in common:

1. The leading companies commercialized two to three times as many new products and processes as their competitors (given equal sizes of firms).
2. The leading companies incorporated two to three times as many technologies in their products.
3. The leading companies were able to get their products to market in less than half the time of their competitors.
4. The leading companies generally competed in twice as many product and geographic markets.

This study provided a number of other interesting insights related to commercialization. First, it was observed that the leading companies tended to view commercialization as a highly disciplined process. Also, not surprisingly, a strong relationship was observed between an organization's competitiveness and its commercialization capabilities. Further, the researchers observed that those companies first to market with products based on new technologies realized higher margins and increased market shares.

It is not uncommon for managers to dramatically underestimate the benefits of being first to market. For example, assume that you are leading a design team charged with designing a new laser printer. Assume that the market for laser printers is growing 20 percent annually, that prices for laser printers are declining by 12 percent per year, and that the life cycle for these printers is five years. As project leader, if you had to choose between incurring a 30 percent cost overrun to finish the project on schedule or miss the deadline by six months but meet the original budget, which would you choose? It turns out that under these circumstances, incurring the 30 percent cost overrun will reduce cumulative profits by only 2.3 percent, whereas launching the printer six months late will reduce cumulative profits by approximately 33 percent!

*[handwritten margin notes: duty
& responsibility]*

[handwritten left margin: What types of commercialization capabilities should be considered? production? financial? marketing? geographic?]

The first step an organization should take to improve its commercialization capabilities is to begin to measure this capability. The McKinsey study suggested a number of measures of commercialization capability, including the following:

- ***Time to market.*** It is crucial to get products to the market as quickly as possible.
- ***Range of markets.*** Since the cost of developing new outputs is increasing, it is important for organizations to spread this development cost across multiple product and geographic markets. Note that this is consistent with the competency/capability view that suggests organizations leverage these strengths to offer a variety of outputs and serve multiple markets.
- ***Number of markets.*** The McKinsey study found that the leading companies tend to serve more market segments than the laggards.
- ***Breadth of technologies.*** This refers to the number of different technologies a company integrates into its new products and services.

Once appropriate measures for assessing commercialization capability have been established, organizations can begin working toward improving them. The McKinsey researchers recommend the following actions:

- Make commercialization a top priority in the organization.
- Set goals and benchmarks to motivate progress.
- Build cross-functional teams to speed up the handoffs and reduce roadblocks.
- Promote hands-on management to speed actions and decisions.

[handwritten left margin: store sale per sq. ft. => $ sale per sq. ft.]

Operations and Global Competitiveness

Operations commonly plays a critical role in international competitiveness. Its activities are concerned with such factors as the efficiency and effectiveness of domestic production compared with outsourcing, the appropriate locations for international facilities, the output capacities needed for various plants, and the labor-machinery trade-offs in each facility. For example, in some countries there may be an excess of low-cost labor and a high cost of capital to buy equipment, so the transformation system should be designed to be labor intensive.

Transformation Process Characteristics

In general, six primary characteristics of the transformation system are critical. Each of these can also be an area of organizational "focus," as noted later in the chapter.

*[handwritten left margin: transformation system.
1. Efficiency doing the thing right
2. Effectiveness doing the right thing.
3. Capacity]*

1. ***Efficiency.*** This is usually measured as output per unit of input. The problem in trying to compare different transformation systems, of course, is choosing good measures for outputs and inputs. In a store, it might be dollars of sales per square foot. In a maternity suite, it might be deliveries per day. High efficiency usually results in low cost per unit of output, clearly a major competitive factor.

2. **Effectiveness.** Whereas efficiency is known as "doing the thing right," effectiveness is known as "doing the right thing." That is, is the right set of outputs being produced? Are we focused on the right task? Do our outputs have the *functionality* desired by the market?

3. **Capacity.** Capacity, too, is different from efficiency in that it specifies the *maximum* rate of production that is attainable. Equipment and tools tend to significantly increase capacity, though if their cost is too high they may reduce overall efficiency.

4. **Quality.** The output may not work well or last long, in which case we say it is of poor quality. Another important aspect of quality is reliability—the continued proper functioning of the product when it is used. High quality is a primary requirement of most products and services in our current highly competitive global economy.

5. **Response time.** How quickly can the output be produced? If a custom output or a totally new output is desired, response time refers to the time needed to produce the first unit of this different output.

6. **Flexibility.** Can the transformation system be used to produce other, different outputs? How easily? How fast? What variety or level of customization can be achieved? Are major changes in volumes achievable without altering the efficiency of the transformation process?

Supply Chain Management

As one of the major functions of operations, supply chain management (SCM) has taken on a major role in the global marketplace and in the business strategy of competing businesses. Originally driven by the desire to reduce costs, SCM has now taken on a much more strategic role (Handfield and Nichols 1999).

As the costs of first labor, and then overhead, continued to shrink as a percentage of the cost of products delivered to customers, the costs of logistics and other elements of the supply chain became a significant portion of the remaining cost. This cost includes not only transportation and warehousing but also inventories, defects, scheduling, backordering, and all the other costs of production. The idea of SCM was to thus consider the total value chain of global production—all the suppliers back to basic materials plus all the contractors to customer delivery as well as all third-party resources—and coordinate this long supply chain to eliminate inefficiencies in both time and cost throughout the chain.

This coordination consists of many elements. One is providing accurate information between the links in the value chain to minimize costs of errors as well as costs of storage and inventories. Another is finding the most efficient producers for each link of the chain. A third is identifying the best transportation options between and within the links. And so on. Clearly, this model will dictate working extremely closely with only a limited number of suppliers—often, in a sole-source mode.

Coordination also takes advantage of the many new technologies available today, such as *enterprise resource planning* (ERP) and other internal intranets, *electronic data interchange* (EDI), bar coding, and of course, the Internet. Probably the most flexible of these new technologies is the Internet, allowing the construction of virtual value chains such as those of Dell Computer and Cisco Systems, joint sites among manufacturers of common products, joint supplier sites,

Web sites for reverse auctions and other bidding mechanisms, business-to-business (B2B) and business-to-consumer (B2C) sites, and a range of other new endeavors. The flexibility of the Internet allows its creative use for purposes as innovative as the next entrepreneur can envision.

These technologies facilitate not only planning and execution for seamless flow, but also the selection of the most appropriate global group of players for the production project at hand. Thus, the selection of the appropriate supplier for each link in the chain (as well as third parties) might change from project to project, each supplier being sole-source for only that particular project. The strategic aim is to deliver the right products to the right location at the right time so everyone in the supply chain makes the "highest possible profit." It is worth noting that the goal is not necessarily the fastest possible delivery, but rather delivery at the *right* time. In the process of minimizing cost, fast production will probably be required but the initiation of production may be delayed in order to deliver at precisely the time that the customer desires; otherwise, expensive storage may be needed to hold the product until the proper time.

apply lean manufacturing concepts to achieve this goal.

As now envisioned, SCM involves many more strategic factors than just cost and efficiency. The proper management of the supply chain must include consideration of all six transformation process characteristics in order to deliver the proper output to the correct location at the right time.

$\mathcal{S}$TRATEGY FORMULATION AND IMPLEMENTATION

The organization's business strategy is a set of objectives, plans, and policies for the organization to compete successfully in its markets. In effect, the business strategy specifies what an organization's competitive advantage will be and how this advantage will be achieved and sustained. As we will see, a key aspect of the business strategy is defining the organization's core competencies and focus. The actual strategic plan that details the business strategy is typically formulated at the executive committee level (CEO, president, vice presidents). It is usually long range, in the neighborhood of three to five years.

In fact, however, the decisions that are made over time *are* the long-range strategy. In too many firms, these decisions show no pattern at all, reflecting the truth that they have no active business strategy, even if they have gone through a process of strategic planning. In other cases these decisions bear little or no relationship to the organization's stated or official business strategy. The point is that an organization's actions often tell more about its true business strategy than its public statements.

Formulating the Business Strategy

The general process of formulating a business strategy is illustrated in Figure 2.7. Relevant inputs to the strategic planning process include the organization's vision/mission statement, a variety of factors external to the organization, and a range of factors internal to the organization. One school of thought—the **Resource Based View**—considers the set of resources (an internal factor in Figure 2.7) available to the organization as the primary driver of the business

(handwritten margin note: how much resource do we have to create a product?)

strategy. For further discussion of this topic and its impact on the development of corporate strategy, consult Barney (1998, 2001) or Collis and Montgomery (1997).

After collectively considering these inputs, strategic planning is often initiated by developing a vision statement, a mission statement, or both. ***Vision statements*** are used to express the organization's values and aspirations. ***Mission statements*** express the organization's purpose or reason for existence. In some cases, organizations may choose to combine the vision and mission statements into a single statement. Regardless of whether separate statements or combined statements are developed, the intent is to communicate the organization's values, aspirations, and purpose so that employees can make decisions that are consistent with and support these objectives.

(handwritten margin notes: vision - values & aspirations; mission - reason for existence)

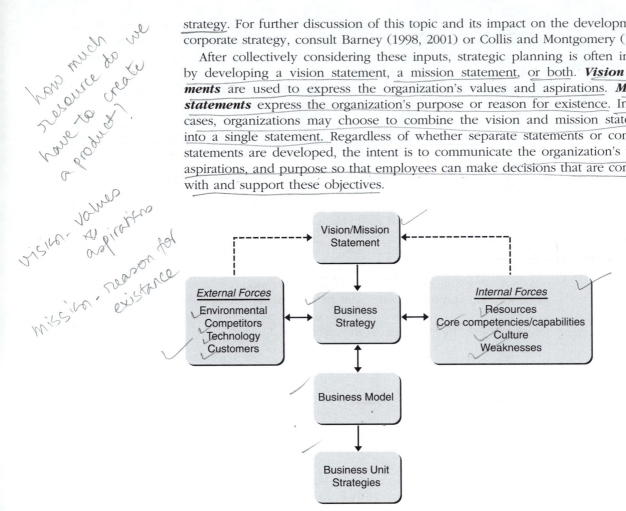

Figure 2.7   Strategy formulation.

(handwritten margin note: edict?)

Effective vision and mission statements tend to be written using language that inspires employees to high levels of performance. Further, to foster employees' commitment, it is advisable to include a wide variety of employees in the development of the vision or mission statement, rather than enforcing top management's view by edict. Once the vision and mission statements are developed for the organization as a whole, divisions, departments, process teams, project teams, work groups, and so on can develop individual vision-mission statements that support the organization's overall statement. For example, after a university develops its overall vision-mission statement, each college could develop its own unique statements specifying the role that it will play in supporting the overall mission of the university. Likewise, once each school develops its own vision-mission statement, the departments within the school can develop unique statements. Having each organizational unit develop its own unique statements promotes wider participation in the process, helps employees think in terms of how their work supports the overall mission, and results in statements that are more meaningful to a select group of employees. Some examples of actual vision-mission statements are provided in Figure 2.8.

COCA-COLA COMPANY'S MISSION STATEMENT

Our Mission

We exist to create value for our share owners on a long-term basis by building a business that enhances the Coca-Cola Company's trademarks. This also is our ultimate commitment.

As the world's largest beverage company, we refresh the world. We do this by developing superior soft drinks, both carbonated and noncarbonated, and profitable nonalcoholic beverage systems that create value for our Company, our bottling partners and our customers.

In creating value, we succeed or fail based on our ability to perform as steward of several key assets:

1. Coca-Cola, the world's most powerful trademark, and other highly valuable trademarks.
2. The world's most effective and pervasive distribution system.
3. Satisfied customers, who make a good profit selling our products.
4. Our people, who are ultimately responsible for building this enterprise.
5. Our abundant resources, which must be intelligently allocated.
6. Our strong global leadership in the beverage industry in particular and in the business world in general.

THE CENTRAL INTELLIGENCE AGENCY

Our Vision

To be the keystone of a U.S. Intelligence Community that is pre-eminent in the world, known for both the high quality of our work and the excellence of our people.

Our Mission

We support the President, the National Security Council, and all who make and execute U.S. national security policy by:

- Providing accurate, evidence-based, comprehensive, and timely foreign intelligence related to national security; and
- Conducting counterintelligence activities, special activities, and other functions related to foreign intelligence and national security as directed by the President.

APICS — THE EDUCATIONAL SOCIETY FOR RESOURCE MANAGEMENT

Vision

To inspire individuals and organizations toward lifelong learning and to enhance individual and organizational success.

Mission

To be the premier provider and global leader in individual and organizational education, standards of excellence, and information in integrated resource management.

Sources: www.cocacola.com/co/mission.html, www.odci.gov.cia/information/mission.html, www.industry.net/c/orgunpro/apics/plan (February 12, 1997).

Figure 2.8 Examples of vision and mission statements.

APICS – Resource Mgmt.

In addition to the vision/mission statement, other important inputs in the formulation of the business strategy are categorized as forces external to the organization and forces internal to the organization in Figure 2.7. Although both sets of forces are considered to some extent in formulating the vision/mission statement (as shown by the dotted lines in the figure), they are considered at a more detailed level and more directly when developing the business strategy. Important external forces include the environment (e.g., the economy, government regulations, climate), competitors (e.g., new product introductions, industry consolidation, new entrants from outside the industry), the technology available, and customer requirements. Relevant internal forces include organizational resources, the organization's core competencies/capabilities, its culture, and its weaknesses. As shown in Figure 2.7, there is a bi-directional relationship between the organization's business strategy and both the internal and external forces. For example, an action by a key competitor may impact the organization's strategy just as its business strategy may force a reaction by a key competitor.

One important result of developing a business strategy is identifying the organization's core competencies and capabilities that provide those product/service dimensions important to customers and hence the source of customer value. ***Core competencies*** (Prahalad and Hamel 1990) are the collective knowledge and skills an organization has that distinguish it from the competition. In effect, these core competencies become the building blocks for organizational practices and business processes, referred to as ***core capabilities*** (Stalk et al. 1992). (Hereafter we will refer to both of these simply as "core capabilities.") The importance of these core capabilities derives from their strong relationship to an organization's ability to integrate a variety of technologies and skills in the development of new products and services. Clearly, then, one of top management's most important activities is the identification and development of the core capabilities the organization will need to successfully execute the business strategy. Given this importance, we discuss core capabilities in more detail in the next section.

Core Capabilities

Core capabilities are the collective knowledge, skills, organizational practices, and business processes that distinguish an organization from its competition. In effect, core capabilities provide the basis for developing new products and services and are a primary factor in determining an organization's long-term competitiveness. Hammer (2004) points out the importance of "operational innovation" in the organization as one basis for sustained competitive advantage, the clear result of a core capability. Therefore, two important parts of strategic planning are identifying and predicting the core capabilities that will be critical to sustaining and enhancing the organization's competitive position. On this basis, an organization can also assess its suppliers' and competitors' capabilities. If the organization finds that it is not the leader, it must determine the cost and risks of catching up with the best versus the cost and risks of losing that core capability.

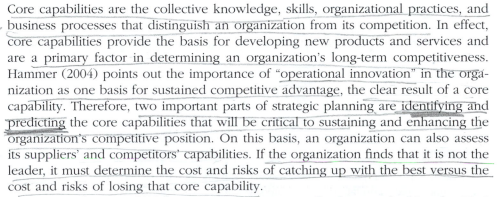

Hayes and Pisano (1994) stress the importance of a firm not looking for "the" solution to a current competitive problem but rather the "paths" to building one or two core capabilities to provide the source of customer value for the indefinite future. Moreover, the firm should not think in terms of "tradeoffs" between core capabilities (e.g., moving from flexibility as a strength to low cost), but rather "building" one capability on top of others, and which *set* will provide the most customer value.

Often, it is more useful to think of an organization in terms of its portfolio of core capabilities, rather than its portfolio of businesses or products. For instance, Sony is known for its expertise in miniaturization; 3M for its knowledge of substrates, coatings, and adhesives; Black and Decker for small electrical motors and industrial design; Boeing for its ability to integrate large-scale complex systems; and Honda for engines and power trains. Had Sony initially viewed itself as primarily a manufacturer of Walkmans, rather than as a company with expertise in miniaturization, it might have overlooked several profitable opportunities, such as entering the camcorder business. As another example, Boeing has successfully leveraged its core capability related to integrating large-scale systems in its production of commercial jetliners, space stations, fighter-bombers, and missiles.

As these examples illustrate, core capabilities are often used to gain access to a wide variety of markets. Cannon used its core capabilities in optics, imaging, and electronic controls to enter the markets for copiers, laser printers, cameras, and image scanners. In a similar fashion, Honda's core capabilities in engines and power trains comprise the basis for its entry into other businesses: automobiles, motorcycles, lawn mowers, and generators.

In addition to providing access to a variety of markets, a core capability should be strongly related to the benefits provided by the product or service that customers value. In Sony's case, its expertise in miniaturization translates directly into important product features such as portability and aesthetic designs. Alternatively, suppose Sony developed a core competence in writing understandable user manuals. Since people who purchase a Walkman or camcorder rarely base their decision on the quality of the user manual (when was the last time you read a user manual?), this core capability would provide little if any competitive advantage.

Another characteristic of core capabilities is that they should be difficult to imitate. Clearly, no sustainable competitive advantage is provided by a core capability that is easily imitated. For example, Sony's expertise in miniaturization would mean little if other electronics manufacturers could match it simply by purchasing and taking apart Sony's products (this is called *reverse engineering*). Bartmess and Cerny (1996) identify three elements of a core capability that hinders imitation:

- It is complex and requires organizational learning over a long period of time
- It is based on multiple functional areas, both internal and external to the organization
- It is a result of *how the functions interact* rather than the skills/knowledge within the functions themselves.

Outsourcing and Offshoring

The topic of core capabilities is also strongly related to the recent surge in outsourcing and offshoring. **Outsourcing**—an approach increasingly common—involves subcontracting out certain activities or services. For example, a manufacturer might outsource the production of certain components, the management and maintenance of its computer resources, employee recruitment, or the processing of its payroll.

When we consider the concept of core capability, it is important to recognize that not all parts, services, or activities are equal. Rather, these activities and parts can be thought of as falling on a continuum ranging from strategically important to unimportant. Parts and activities are considered strategically important when:

- They are strongly related to what customers perceive to be the key characteristics of the product or service.
- They require highly specialized knowledge and skill, a core capability.
- They require highly specialized physical assets, and few other suppliers possess these assets.
- The organization has a technological lead or is likely to obtain one.

Activities that are not strategic or core are candidates for outsourcing. These parts or activities are not strongly linked to key product characteristics, do not require highly specialized knowledge, do not need special physical assets, and the organization does not have the technological lead in this area. Thus, if it is beneficial to outsource these parts or activities—perhaps because of lower cost or higher quality—no loss in competitiveness should result. On the other hand, when a firm's strategic parts and activities have been outsourced, particularly to a foreign supplier, called **offshoring**, the firm has become *hollow* (Jonas 1986). As we have stated, the wise firm will outsource only nonstrategic, simple, relatively standard parts such as nuts and bolts that are not worth the time for the firm to produce itself; the complex, proprietary parts that give their products an edge in the marketplace are produced internally. If the firm outsources these parts as well, it soon finds that the engineering design talent follows the production of the part outside the firm, too, and its core capabilities have been lost. Then, the firm has been **hollowed out**, becoming merely a distributor of its supplier's products.

Given the huge potential effects of outsourcing, both positive and negative, a firm should consider such a move *very* carefully. They need to think about the long-term and short-term effects. And they also need to consider the impact of this decision on their core capabilities, and everything else they do within the company. Such a major decision as outsourcing will affect other decisions as well, such as sourcing materials, hiring/releasing labor and management, marketing, finance, and a wide range of other areas.

So what is the problem? If a supplier can deliver the parts at lower cost and better quality when they are needed, why not use them? The problem is that the supplier gains the expertise (and core capabilities) to produce the critical parts you need, and as Hayes and Pisano (1994), among others note, organizations quickly forget how they produced those critical parts. After a while, when the supplier has improved on the process and you have forgotten how to make the parts, it is likely to start competing with you, producing the products you have been selling and dropping you as a customer. This is even more dangerous if, as already noted, the product and transformation system has also been hollowed out, following the production activities to the supplier. This happened extensively in the television industry, where the Japanese learned first how to produce, and then how to engineer black-and-white and, later, color television sets. They then started tentatively introducing their own brands, to see if U.S. customers would buy them. Their products were inexpensive, of high quality, and caught on quickly in the free-enterprise American markets. The Japanese now virtually control this industry.

An example of a company involved in this issue is Sara Lee Corporation (Miller 1997, Rose and Quintanilla 1997). In September 1997, Sara Lee announced a "fundamental reshaping" of its business away from in-house production of its brand-name products which include L'eggs hosiery, frozen desserts, Wonderbras, Coach leather goods, and Kiwi shoe polish. Referring to the plan as to "de-verticalize," Sara Lee's chairman and CEO, John Bryan, stated, "The business of Sara Lee Corporation has been and will continue to be the building of branded leadership positions," not manufacturing. Mr. Bryan mentioned Nike and Coca-Cola as model companies that have chosen to avoid manufacturing. Indeed, company officials estimated the program would reduce costs up to $125 million annually.

Sara Lee exemplifies a growing trend among U.S. manufacturers. The Big Three automakers are well-known examples of manufacturers that extensively outsource. As other examples, Deere & Co. puts its name on midrange utility tractors produced by a Japanese company, and Agco Corp. outsources the production of almost all of the transmissions and engines used in its farm equipment. Of course, not all manufacturers are jumping on the outsourcing bandwagon. New Balance Athletic Shoes, for example, invested $25 million in its manufacturing facilities as part of an overall strategy to do more assembly in-house.

Kodak's Business Imaging Systems Division (BIS) is one firm that looked into offshoring and decided against it (Bartmess and Cerny 1996). Initially they took the "traditional" perspective and discovered that overseas wage rates were 75 percent cheaper than domestic rates. [*Note*: Recent research reveals that wages in China are now commonly 96 percent cheaper than domestic U.S. wages!] The traditional perspective is one dominated by: considering only current conditions with no thought about the future, a short-term response to a competitive threat, a heavy emphasis on cost (primarily labor), and a singular focus on one function, typically operations, to the exclusion of other functions such as engineering, marketing, and design.

But then BIS considered a capabilities perspective and discovered that:

- Offshore productivity was also low, negating the benefit of low wage rates.
- Large overhead costs were primarily fixed and would not shrink with overseas labor.
- Engineering would also have to accompany manufacturing overseas, but offshore engineering wages were almost equal to domestic wages. Moreover, BIS did not want to lose their domestic engineering competence.
- Over time, foreign wages would be increasing: "... once trained and experienced, labor does not stay cheap very long."
- Cost advantages almost equal to the benefit of low offshore wages were available through product redesigns.

BIS hence decided not to move their operation overseas, though they did decide to start an offshore plant for a low-end product for the foreign market, mainly to educate themselves in the advantages and disadvantages of offshore production as well as to learn ways to improve their internal low-cost manufacturing capabilities. (For another view on offshoring, see Markides and Berg 1988.)

Regarding the purpose for outsourcing, it is also important to be aware of another danger of outsourcing activities or parts primarily on the basis of "cost." To illustrate, assume a manufacturer produces four product lines each with an annual volume of 100,000 units. Further assume that the company's overhead is £1.2 million (British pounds). Allocating this overhead evenly across the four product lines would result in each unit being allocated £3 in overhead charges. Now suppose that in the interest of lowering its cost and increasing its competitiveness, the manufacturer investigates outsourcing products that can be produced at lower unit costs by external suppliers. In fact, suppose that a supplier is found for one of its product lines. What is the impact of outsourcing this product line? Clearly on one hand, the company obtains the product at a lower unit cost. But what is the impact on the remaining product lines and the organization's overhead?

More than likely, outsourcing one product line will not have a dramatic impact on total overhead; however, the amount of overhead each unit must now absorb increases from £3/unit to £4/unit. In effect, each unit now appears to be more expensive to produce internally. Thus, outsourcing other product lines now appears to be warranted and likely will be investigated. As you can see, this logic results in a vicious cycle commonly referred to as the **creeping breakeven phenomenon.** As outputs are outsourced, the remaining outputs appear to be more expensive to produce in-house. This creates an incentive to outsource even more outputs. The logical conclusion of this process is that the organization ends up producing no outputs and going bankrupt.

Business Strategy

Perhaps the most difficult aspect associated with discussing strategy is that a single widely accepted definition of strategy does not exist. The problem is further compounded, as strategist Henry Mintzberg (1994) points out, due to the tendency on the part of managers to define strategy generally speaking in one way and then to describe their organization's specific strategy in a way that conflicts with their original general definition. However, while a single generally accepted definition of strategy may not yet exist, Mintzberg identifies five major strategy schools of thought: (1) strategy as a plan, (2) strategy as a pattern, (3) strategy as a position, (4) strategy as a perspective, and (5) strategy as a ploy. Based on this categorization, one way to reconcile these different schools of thought is to recognize that each view is fundamentally concerned with making a set of *choices*. For example, in the "strategy as a plan" view, the required choices relate to the paths or courses of action while the "strategy as a pattern" view focuses on the consistency of the choices made over time. Likewise, the "strategy as a position" view, which Michael Porter of the Harvard Business School promotes, focuses on choices about products and markets, the "strategy as a perspective" view is concerned about choices related to the way activities are accomplished, and the "strategy as a ploy" relates to choices made to outmaneuver the competition.

While the preceding discussion highlights strategy's orientation toward making choices, the business model (see Figure 2.7) is simply a reflection (model) of the choices made. To better understand this, it is helpful to parse the term business model. To begin, business can be broadly viewed as creating value and then capturing returns from the value created. Models are simplified representations of reality. Combining these definitions, a business model can be viewed as a representation of an organization's core logic and strategic choices for creating value and capturing returns from the value created (Shafer, Smith, and Linder 2005). In effect, the choices made in the strategic planning process define the business model. Thus, strategy is primarily concerned with making sets of choices and the resulting business models that reflect the choices made are tools to help further analyze the strategy and communicate the strategy. In particular, analysis of the business model can help an organization verify that the elements of the strategy are consistent with one another, that they are logical, and that they are mutually reinforcing. Business plans in turn provide a much more detailed view of the business model typically including expanded verbal discussions of key elements of the strategy and the business model as well as quantitative projections for important operational, marketing, and financial aspects of the business.

To help further understand the distinction between strategy and a business model, consider the construction of a custom home. Initially, the architect consults with the future homeowners to understand how they envision the home and their life within it. The architect then creates a design to fulfill this vision. This corresponds to strategy. Next, the architect prepares a detailed floor plan and elevation based on the choices made during the design process. These correspond to the business model. Just as a business model can be used to help analyze and communicate strategic choices, the floor plan can be used to help understand, analyze, and communicate the design choices that were made.

Once the business strategy has been developed and the resulting business model analyzed, the final step in strategy formulation is the development of business unit strategies. At this stage, each business unit develops its own strategy to guide its activities so that they are consistent and support the organization's overall business strategy. Although formulating the business strategy is displayed as rather straightforward in Figure 2.7, in reality it is very iterative.

Business and Product Strategies

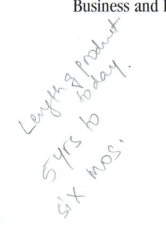

A wide variety of common business strategies are described in this subsection and the following subsection. A number of them are tied to the stages in the standard **life cycle** of products and services, shown in Figure 2.9. Studies of the introduction of new products indicate that the life cycle (or *stretched-S growth curve*, as it is also known) provides a good pattern for the growth of demand for a new output. The curve can be divided into three major segments: (1) introduction and early adoption, (2) acceptance and growth of the market, and (3) maturity with market saturation. After market saturation, demand may remain high or decline; or the output may be improved and possibly start on a new growth curve.

The length of product and service life cycles has been shrinking significantly in the last decade or so. In the past, a life cycle might have been five years, but it is now six months. This places a tremendous burden on the firm to constantly monitor its strategy and quickly change a strategy that becomes inappropriate to the market.

The life cycle begins with an **innovation**—a new output or process for the market. The innovation may be a patented product or process, a new combination of existing elements that has created a unique product or process, or some service that was previously unavailable. Initial versions of the product or service may change relatively frequently; production volumes are small, since the output has not caught on yet; and margins are high. As volume increases, the design of the output stabilizes and more competitors enter the market, frequently with more capital-intensive equipment. In the mature phase, the now high-volume output is a virtual commodity, and the firm that can produce an acceptable version at the lowest cost usually controls the market.

Clearly, a firm's business strategy should match the life-cycle stages of its products and services. If a firm such as Hewlett-Packard is good at innovation, it may choose to focus only on the introduction and acceptance phases of the product's life cycle and then sell or license production to others as the product moves beyond the introduction stage. If its strength is in high-volume, low-cost production, the company should stick with proven products that are in the maturity stage. Most common, perhaps, are firms that attempt to stick with products throughout their life cycle, changing their strategy with each stage.

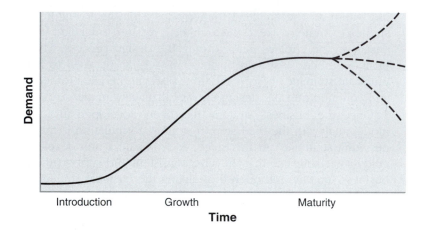

Figure 2.9   The life-cycle curve.

One approach to categorizing an organization's business strategy is based on its timing of introductions of new outputs. Two researchers, Maidique and Patch (1979), suggest the following four product development strategies:

1. ***First-to-market.*** Organizations that use this strategy attempt to have their products available before the competition. To achieve this, strong applied research is needed. If a company is first to market, it has to decide if it wants to price its products high and thus skim the market to achieve large short-term profits or set a lower initial price to obtain a higher market share and perhaps larger long-term profits.

2. ***Second-to-market.*** Organizations that use this strategy try to quickly imitate successful outputs offered by first-to-market organizations. This strategy requires less emphasis on applied research and more emphasis on fast development. Often, firms that use the second-to-market strategy attempt to learn from the mistakes of the first-to-market firm and offer improved or enhanced versions of the original products.

3. ***Cost minimization*** or ***late-to-market.*** Organizations that use this strategy wait until a product becomes fairly standardized and is demanded in large volumes. They then attempt to compete on the basis of costs as opposed to features of the product. These organizations focus most of their research and development on improving the production system, as opposed to focusing on product development.

4. ***Market segmentation.*** This strategy focuses on serving niche markets with specific needs. Applied engineering skills and flexible manufacturing systems are often needed for the market-segmentation strategy.

Be aware that a number of implicit tradeoffs are involved in developing a strategy. Let us use the first-to-market strategy to demonstrate. A first-to-market strategy requires large investments in product development in an effort to stay ahead of the competition. Typically, organizations that pursue this strategy expect to achieve relatively higher profit margins, larger market shares, or both as a result of initially having the market to themselves. The strategy is somewhat risky because a competitor may end up beating them to the market. Also, even if a company succeeds in getting to the market first, it may end up simply creating an opportunity for the competition to learn from its mistakes and overtake it in the market. To illustrate, although Sony introduced its Betamax format for VCRs in 1975, JVC's VHS format—introduced the following year—is the standard that ultimately gained widespread market acceptance.

Such tradeoffs are basic to the concept of selecting a business strategy. Although specific tasks must be done well to execute the selected strategy, not everything needs to be particularly outstanding—only a few things. And of course, strategies based on anything else—acquisitions, mergers, tax loss carry-forwards, even streams of high-technology products—will not be successful if the customer is ignored in the process.

Strategy Implementation

Once the strategy has been formulated, the next step is to implement it. However, in spite of business's enthusiastic acceptance of strategic planning, the implementation of these strategic weapons has commonly been near an outright disaster. Two techniques for implementing business strategies have recently met with more success. The earliest one to experience some level of success was the balanced scorecard. More recently, the aggregate project plan has also had substantial success.

The Balanced Scorecard

The ***balanced scorecard*** approach (Kaplan and Norton 1996) is becoming increasingly recognized for helping organizations translate their mission and strategy into appropriate performance measures. In the past, it was not uncommon for managers to rely primarily on financial performance measures. However, when the inadequacies of these measures were discovered, managers often responded by either trying to improve them or by abandoning them in favor of operational performance measures such as cycle time and defect rates. Many organizations now realize that no single type of measure can provide insight into all the critical areas of the business. Thus, the purpose of the balanced scorecard is to develop a set of measures that provides a comprehensive view of the organization.

Organizations that have developed a balanced scorecard report numerous benefits, including:

- An effective way to clarify and gain consensus of the strategy.
- A mechanism for communicating the strategy throughout the entire organization.
- A mechanism for aligning departmental and personal goals to the strategy.
- A way to ensure that strategic objectives are linked to annual budgets.
- Timely feedback related to improving the strategy.

One problem with traditional performance measurement systems based primarily on financial measures is that they often encourage short-sighted decisions such as reducing investments in product development, employee training, and information technology. The balanced scorecard approach corrects this problem by measuring performance in four major areas: (1) financial performance, (2) customer performance, (3) internal business process performance, and (4) organizational learning and growth.

The financial performance measures included in the balanced scorecard are typically related to profitability, such as return on equity, return on capital, and economic value added. Customer performance measures focus on customer satisfaction, customer retention, customer profitability, market share, and customer acquisition. The internal business process dimension addresses the issue of what the organization must excel at to achieve its financial and customer objectives. Examples of performance measures for internal business processes include quality, response time, cost, new-product launch time, and the ratio of processing time to total throughput time. Finally, the learning and growth dimension focuses on the infrastructure the organization must build to sustain its competitive advantage. Learning and growth performance measures include employee satisfaction, employee retention, worker productivity, and the availability of timely and accurate information.

The process of developing a balanced scorecard begins with top management translating the mission and strategy into specific customer and financial objectives. Based on the customer and financial objectives, related measures for the internal business processes are identified. Finally, investments in employee training and information technology are linked to the customer, financial, and internal business process objectives. Note that a properly constructed balanced scorecard contains an appropriate mix of outcome measures related to the actual results achieved and measures that drive future performance.

The balanced scorecard is based on the premise that a strategy is a set of hypotheses about cause-and-effect relationships that can be stated as if–then statements. For example, management of a department store might hypothesize that increasing the training that sales associates receive will lead to improved selling skills. These managers might further hypothesize that better selling skills will translate into higher commissions for the sales associates and will therefore result in less turnover.

Happier and more experienced sales associates would likely lead to increased sales per store, which ultimately translates into an increase in return on investment. Since a properly developed balanced scorecard tells a story about the cause-and-effect relationships underlying the strategy, all measures included in the scorecard should be an element in the chain of cause-and-effect relationships.

Strategy Maps

In extending their earlier work on the Balanced Scorecard, Kaplan and Norton (2000) proposed the development of Strategy Maps as a way to show the cause-and-effect relationships identified through the development of a Balanced Scorecard. In particular, Strategy Maps provide organizations with a tool that helps them communicate important details about the business strategy, thereby enhancing their employees' understanding of the strategy which in turn facilitates implementing the business strategy.

Like the Balanced Scorecard, Strategy Maps address four perspectives: the financial perspective, the customer perspective, the internal business process perspective, and the learning and growing perspective. An example Strategy Map for a department store that desires to improve its performance is shown in Figure 2.10.

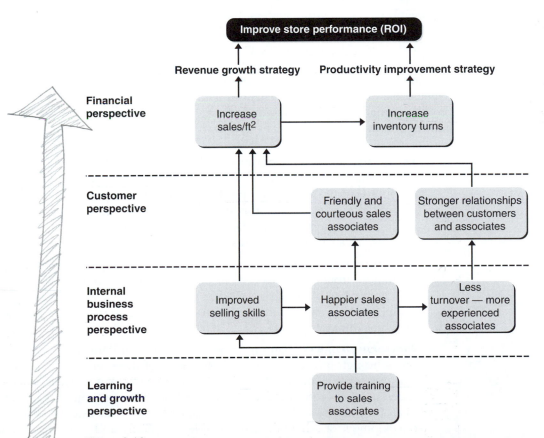

Figure 2.10   Example strategy map for a department store.

At the top of the Strategy Map the goal is specified, which in our example is to improve the store's ROI. Management has determined that the goal of improving the store's ROI can be accomplished by increasing revenue and/or improving the store's productivity. The remainder of the Strategy Map explicitly shows the chain of cause-and-effect relationships management has hypothesized about how the store's ROI can be improved. For example, it is hypothesized that providing the sales associates with additional training will lead to improved selling skills, which should then result in increased sales per square foot of retail space and happier associates. Happier associates in turn should result in both friendly and courteous sales associates and less turnover among the sales associates. Ultimately, the Strategy Map hypothesizes that increased sales per square foot will help the store increase its revenue and also increase its inventory turns.

The Aggregate Project Plan

In an attempt to better tie the firm's product development projects to their strategic objectives, Professors Wheelwright and Clark (1992) of the Harvard Business School developed a framework for categorizing projects that they call the Aggregate Project Plan. The purpose of the framework is to illustrate the *distribution* of all the organization's product/service design projects across a variety of measures such as resource demands, innovativeness, product lines, time, and project type. It is important to point out, however, that it is typically not a single project that determines the organization's long-run success, but rather the set of research projects pursued by the organization, or its **project portfolio**. Therefore, in making project selection decisions, it is vital to consider the interactions among various projects and to manage the projects as a set in order to achieve the organization's strategic objectives.

Using this framework, output development projects are categorized along two dimensions: (1) the extent of changes made to the output and (2) the degree of process change. Based on these two dimensions, projects can then be categorized into the following four categories as shown in Figure 2.11:

1. **Derivative projects.** Derivative projects seek to make incremental improvements in the output and/or process. Projects that seek to reduce the output's cost or make minor product line extensions exemplify these types of projects. Developing a stripped down version of an existing modem or adding a new menu item at a fast-food restaurant would qualify as derivative projects. This category accounts for a large majority of all innovations.

2. **Breakthrough projects.** These projects are at the opposite end of the continuum from derivative projects and typically seek the development of a new generation of outputs. A modem that would work with fiber-optic cable as opposed to copper wire or an entirely online grocery store is an example of a breakthrough project.

3. **Platform projects.** Platform projects fall between derivative and breakthrough projects. In general, the result of these projects is an output that can serve as the *platform* for an entire line of new outputs. A key difference between platform projects and breakthrough projects is that platform projects stick with existing technology. As an example, the development of a new modem capable of sending and receiving data at 256 kb would qualify as a platform project. If this modem succeeds, it could

serve as the basis for a number of derivative projects focusing on cost improvement and the development of other modems with different features.

4. **R&D projects.** R&D projects entail working with basic technology to develop new knowledge. Depending on its focus, an R&D project might lead to breakthrough, platform, or derivative innovations.

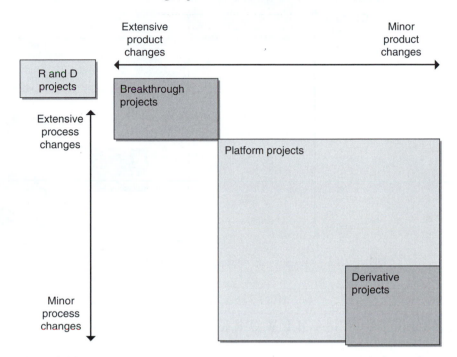

Figure 2.11 The aggregate project plan.

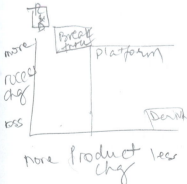

Use of the aggregate project plan requires that all projects be identified and plotted. The size of the points plotted for each project should be proportional to the amount of resources the project will require. In Figure 2.12, we have used different shapes to indicate different types of projects. Internal projects are plotted using circles while projects pursued as part of a strategic alliance with other firms are plotted using squares.

There are a number of ways the aggregate project plan can be used. The identification of gaps in the types of projects being undertaken is probably most important. For example, are the types of projects undertaken too heavily skewed toward derivative type projects? This might indicate an inadequate consideration of the firm's long-run competitive position. Also, the aggregate project plan facilitates evaluation of the resource commitments of the ongoing as well as proposed projects. Finally, this framework can serve as a model for employee development. New employees can be initially assigned to a team working on a derivative project. After gaining experience, employees can be assigned to a platform project, then assigned to *manage* a derivative project. As managerial skill accumulates, the employee will qualify for larger and more valuable projects. Of course, we must remember that the fundamental purpose of this entire process is to ensure that the set of projects accurately reflects the organization's strategic goals and objectives.

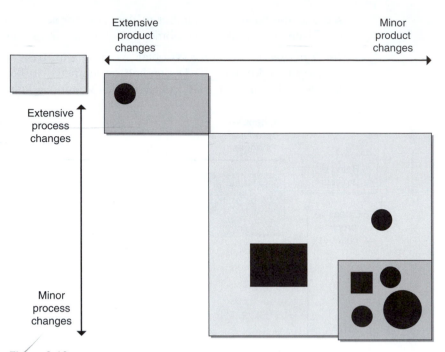

Figure 2.12   An example aggregate project plan.

STRATEGIC FRAMEWORKS

In the previous section, we discussed the general aspects of formulating and implementing the organization's business strategy. In this section we build on the foundation established in the previous sections and overview five well-known strategic frameworks. As you will see, these frameworks are not only useful for helping define and describe an organization's current operational strategy; they can also be used to help develop future strategies.

Focus

The goal of the business strategy is to utilize an organization's core capabilities to establish and maintain a unique strength(s), or *focus* (Skinner 1974), for the firm that leads to a sustainable competitive advantage. McKinsey & Company, a top management consulting firm, studied 27 outstanding successful firms to find their common attributes. Two of the major attributes reported in *Business Week* are directly related to focus:

1. ***Stressing one key business value.*** At Hewlett-Packard, the key value is developing new products; at Dana Corporation, it is improving productivity.

2. ***Sticking to what they know best.*** All the outstanding firms define their core capabilities (or strengths) and then build on them. They resist the temptation to move into new areas or diversify.

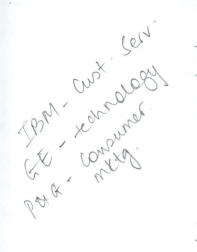

When an organization chooses to stress one or two key areas of strength, it is referred to as a *focused organization.* For example, IBM is known for its customer service, General Electric for its technology, and Procter & Gamble for its consumer marketing. In general, most but not all areas of focus relate to operations. Some firms, such as those in the insurance industry, focus on financial strength and others focus on marketing strengths. Kenner Toys, for example, considers its strength to be a legal one: the ability to win contracts for exclusive production of popular children's toys. Harley-Davidson considers its strength to be in building relationships with its dealers and motorcycle owners. As a final example, many health care organizations are achieving significant operational efficiencies by focusing on a narrow range of ailments. For example, by treating only long-term acute cases, Intensiva HealthCare has been able to reduce its costs to 50 percent of those of a traditional intensive-care ward.

Table 2.1 identifies several areas of focus that organizations commonly choose when forming their competitive strategy; all are various forms of differentiation. Recent competitive behavior among firms seems to be dividing most of the factors in Table 2.1 into two sets that Terry Hill (2000), an operations strategist and researcher in England, calls *order qualifiers* and *order winners*. An **order qualifier** is a characteristic of the product or service that is required if the product is even to be considered or in the running. In other words, it is a prerequisite for entering the market. An **order winner** is a characteristic that will win the bid or the purchase. These qualifiers and winners vary with the market, of course, but some general commonalties exist across markets. For example, response time, performance, customization, innovation, quality, and price seem to be frequent order winners, and the other factors (e.g., reliability and flexibility) tend to be order qualifiers. Working with marketing and sales to properly identify which factors are which is clearly of major strategic importance.

$\mathcal{T}$ABLE 2.1 • Common Areas of Organizational Focus

- *Innovation:* Bringing a range of new products and services to market quickly
- *Customization:* Being able to quickly redesign and produce a product or service to meet customers' unique needs
- *Flexibility of products and services:* Switching between different models or variants quickly to satisfy a customer or market
- *Flexibility of volume:* Changing quickly and economically from low-volume production to high volumes and vice versa
- *Performance:* Offering products and services with unique, valuable features
- *Quality:* Having better craftsmanship or consistency
- *Reliability of the product or service:* Always working acceptably, enabling customers to count on the performance
- *Reliability of delivery:* Always fulfilling promises with a product or service that is never late
- *Response:* Offering very short lead times to obtain products and services
- *After-sale service:* Making available extensive, continuing help
- *Price:* Having the lowest price

In addition to the advantages of being focused, there are also some dangers. A narrowly focused firm can easily become uncompetitive in the market if the customers' requirements change. In addition to being focused, a firm must also be flexible enough to alter its focus when the need changes and to spot the change in time. Frequently, a focus in one area can be used to an advantage in another way, if there is enough time to adapt—for example, to move into a new product line or alter the application of the focus.

An organization can also easily lose its focus. For example, in the traditional functional organization, purchasing may buy the cheapest materials it can. This requires buying large quantities with advance notice. Scheduling, however, is trying to reduce inventories so it orders materials on short notice and in small quantities. Quality control is trying to improve the output, so it carefully inspects every item, creating delays and extensive rework. In this example, each functional department is pursuing its own objectives but is not focusing on how it can support the organization's overall business strategy.

There may even be a loss of focus at the top management level. For example, one firm decided to consolidate its production of made-to-order products in a remodeled central plant. Previously, the products were made in three separate plants that were obsolete and inefficient. One plant produced high volumes of cheap fasteners (screws, nails) on demand for the construction industry. It used large, dirty equipment to stamp out the fasteners in short lead times with minimal quality control. The second plant produced expensive, high-quality microwave ovens. Engineering design was the critical function, with long lead times, extensive testing, and purchases in small lots. The third plant produced custom integrated circuits in clean rooms with expensive computerized equipment. The consolidation proved to be a disaster.

How do organizations lose their focus and get into trouble? There are a number of ways this can happen, such as the following:

- **New outputs:** Managers, in an attempt to reap what they feel will be economies of scale, add products or services to the organization's offerings that require expertise in a wide variety of areas. Unable to control the variety of expertise required of each line, the organization becomes unfocused.

- **New attributes:** This loss of focus occurs when management adds, or the market demands, a new twist to the output that conflicts with the existing focus, a new twist that the firm cannot meet.

- **New tasks:** Management may add new goals that compromise the firm's existing focus, such as reducing costs, raising quality, or improving product safety.

- **Life-cycle changes:** As products go through their life cycle, the task of operations often changes, as shown in Figure 2.13, from being flexible enough to accept changes in design, to meeting the growing demand in the marketplace, to cutting costs. Throughout this life cycle, the focus of the organization has to change, if it stays with the same output. Many firms, however, choose to compete at only one stage of the life cycle and abandon other stages, so that they can keep the strength of their original focus.

- ***Departmental professionalism:*** Sometimes an organization loses its focus when particular specialties follow their own interests rather than the needs of the organization. For example, finance may pressure production to reduce inventory levels in an effort to lower inventory-related costs, while marketing may simultaneously pressure production to increase inventory levels so that delivery dates can be shortened and sales increased.

However, the most common reason a firm loses its focus is simply that the focus was never clearly identified in the first place. Never having been well defined, it could not be communicated to the employees, could therefore not gain their support, and thus was lost. Sometimes a focus is identified but not communicated throughout the organization, because management thinks that lower-level employees don't need to know the strategic focus of the firm in order to do their jobs.

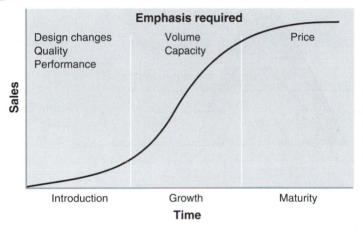

Figure 2.13 Product life cycle: stages and emphasis.

The Sand Cone Model

Earlier in this chapter we discussed the concept of core capabilities. Related to this is the competitive dimension(s) an organization chooses to compete on, such as quality, dependability, speed, or cost. Clearly, the capabilities an organization possesses can significantly affect its ability to compete on various competitive dimensions.

For many organizations, the traditional view was that competing on one competitive dimension required trading off performance on one or more other dimensions (e.g., higher quality results in higher costs). More recently, however, research suggests that, at least in some cases, building strengths along alternative competitive dimensions may in fact be cumulative and that building a strength on one dimension may facilitate building strengths on other dimensions (Ferdows and De Meyer 1990).

Furthermore, according to this research there is a preferred order in developing strengths on various competitive dimensions. According to the Sand Cone Model (as it is called) shown in Figure 2.14, organizations should first develop the capability to produce quality outputs. Once an organization has developed this proficiency, it is next appropriate to address the issue of delivery dependability.

Next, according to the model, the competitive dimensions of speed and cost should be addressed, respectively.

In addition to providing guidance to organizations regarding the order in which to focus their attention and initiatives, the model has intuitive appeal. For example, it makes little sense to focus on improving delivery dependability before an organization can provide a consistent level of quality. In today's competitive marketplace, providing defective outputs in a timely fashion is not a recipe for long-term success. Likewise, organizations should achieve consistent quality levels and delivery dependability before attempting to reduce lead times. Of course, the model is not set in stone (remember it is called the Sand Cone Model) and organizations facing different circumstances may choose to address the competitive dimensions in a different order. We will return to these critical competitive factors in the final section of this chapter.

choose your own Sand Cone Model.

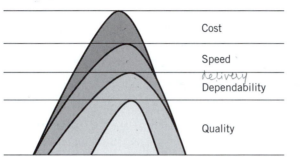

Cost

Speed

delivery
Dependability

Quality

Figure 2.14 The Sand Cone Model. (Adapted from Ferdows and De Meyer 1990, p. 175.)

Performance Frontiers and Improvement Trajectories

According to the Sand Cone model, building multiple capabilities to simultaneously address a variety of competitive dimensions can be complementary. However, at other times, performing better on one dimension may only be attainable by sacrificing performance on another dimension. For example, as shown in Figure 2.15, in some industries increasing output variety results in higher unit costs.

More specifically, curve 1 in Figure 2.15 is called a *performance frontier* (Clark 1996). In effect, this curve represents the level of performance that organizations in an industry can achieve across two dimensions given the technology available. According to the figure, company A is apparently pursuing more of a variety strategy than the two other competitors shown, offering a wider variety of outputs but incurring greater cost. We might think of J.C. Penney as perhaps fitting point A. Company C, perhaps K Mart, seems to be pursuing a standardization strategy, offering a smaller range of outputs but incurring lower unit costs.

Performance frontier curve.

(@ what cost?)

An interesting use of this framework is to investigate and evaluate the impact of a change in technology or operational innovation (Hammer 2004). For example, in Figure 2.16, assume a new innovation such as "cross-docking" has been developed by company B, perhaps represented by Wal-Mart, shifting its performance frontier to curve 2. In this case, company B could hold its unit price constant and offer higher output variety than company A and at lower unit cost (position B1). Alternatively, company B could maintain its current level of output variety and lower its unit cost to levels below company C's (position B2), or perhaps choose a position somewhere between points B1 and B2.

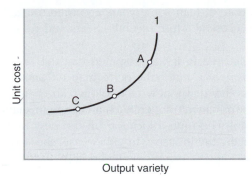

Figure 2.15 Example performance frontier.

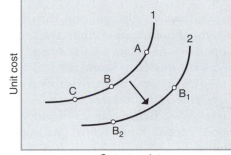

Figure 2.16 Development of new technology results in shift in the performance frontier.

Suppose you were employed at company A and company B chose to operate at point B1. In effect, company B can now offer a wider variety of outputs and at lower unit costs. What are your options? As it turns out, there are two generic options or **improvement trajectories** company A could try to follow. One improvement trajectory would be for company A to streamline its operations and make cost-variety tradeoffs, moving down curve 1 toward company C. Upon streamlining its operations, company A could then attempt to adopt the new technology and choose a position on the new frontier. A second improvement trajectory would be for company A to attempt to directly adopt the new technology and move to the new frontier without streamlining its current operations.

There are advantages and disadvantages associated with both trajectories. An advantage of streamlining operations first is that this may provide a better understanding of current processes. In turn, this better understanding may increase company A's options in choosing a location on the new frontier and may even better position it to adopt the new technology. One drawback of streamlining its current operations first is that the knowledge gained may be irrelevant when the new technology is eventually adopted, and delaying the adoption of the new technology may mean reduced market share and profits. Another important factor is the amount of time required to execute the improvement trajectory and get to the new position on the new performance frontier. However, although it might appear that streamlining the current operation first before adopting the new technology should take more time than immediately adopting the technology, when ease of implementation is considered, the former approach may in fact be more expedient.

On a more practical note, K-Mart some years ago tried to challenge Wal-Mart on low prices but was unsuccessful. More recently, Sears and K-Mart have announced plans to merge instead.

One final point. In Figure 2.16 it was assumed that the result of the new technology/innovation was simply a shift in the performance frontier. It is also important to be aware of the possibility that a new technology can change the shape as well as the location of the performance frontier. Such a change in shape can have important implications regarding choosing a location on the new frontier as well as the nature of the tradeoff facing the industry. In either case, the way to beat your competition is through developing or using new technology to move to a new frontier.

Stages of Operational Effectiveness

The next framework, articulated by Wheelwright and Hayes (1985), suggests that organizations can progress through four stages of effectiveness in terms of the role their operations play in supporting and achieving the overall strategic objectives of a business. As a diagnostic tool, this framework helps determine the extent to which an organization is utilizing its operations to support and possibly attain a sustainable competitive advantage. As a prescriptive tool, the framework helps focus an organization on appropriate future courses of action because it is argued that stages cannot be skipped. Important managerial challenges are also identified for each stage of effectiveness.

Organizations in stage 1 of the model are labeled ***internally neutral***. These organizations tend to view operations as having little impact on the organization's competitive success. In fact, these organizations often consider the operations area as primarily a source of problems (e.g., quality problems, late shipments, too much capital tied up in inventory). Thus, believing that operations have little strategic importance, the emphasis in these organizations is on minimizing the negative impact of operations.

Stage 2 is labeled ***externally neutral***. As the name suggests, organizations at this stage attempt to match the operational practices of the industry. Thus, organizations in this stage still tend to view operations as having little strategic importance, but they at least attempt to follow standard industry practices. Because these organizations follow industry practice, they tend to be more reactive than proactive in the operations area. Furthermore, operational investments and improvements tend to be tied to reducing costs.

Stage 3 is called ***internally supportive***. In this stage of development the organization expects its operations to support the overall business strategy and competitive position. In many cases this is stated as a formal operations strategy. Thus, operational decisions are evaluated based on their consistency with and the extent to which they support the organization's overall mission. Internally supportive organizations tend to be more proactive in terms of identifying opportunities to support the organization's overall competitiveness. It is important to point out, however, that while stage 3 organizations expect operations to support the overall business strategy, operations is typically not involved in actually formulating it.

Stage 4 organizations depend on their operations to achieve a competitive advantage and are referred to as ***externally supportive***. In effect, these organizations use core capabilities residing in the operations area to obtain a sustainable competitive advantage. Because different parts of an organization may evolve at different rates, determining an organization's stage of effectiveness may require making a judgment about where the balance of the organization is positioned. Thus, it is possible that some departments or areas of a stage 2 organization exhibit characteristics of a stage 3 organization. However, if the majority of the organization is most appropriately characterized as being in stage 2, then the organization should be categorized as being in stage 2. Thus, evaluating an organization's evolution is based not on its most evolved area, but rather on the balance of organizational practices.

Lean Management

[handwritten margin note: Based on minimal use of resources & eliminating all forms of waste, including time.]

Lean management is a framework that has grown out of the Toyota Production System and is based on the minimal use of resources and elimination of all forms of waste, including time. Many production techniques, such as just-in-time, Six Sigma, and even supply chain management, tend to overlap with this framework, each often including elements of the others. The subject is broad; therefore, Chapter 10 is devoted entirely to its description.

CRITICAL VALUE FACTORS

Operations must provide, through the transformation system, products and services that embody those factors critical to success in the marketplace. In general, customers seek to maximize the value of their transactions; basically, they desire the most *benefit* for the lowest possible *cost.* As we saw in the Sand Cone model, some of the most critical value factors for customers involve those that provide benefit—quality, functionality, customization, delivery dependability, and speed. In this section we discuss these benefit and cost elements in more detail. In the first subsection we include other elements of effectiveness that tend to accompany quality: reliability, functionality (what the product or service offers the consumer), and degree of customization. The second subsection then covers dependability and speed, and the final subsection discusses cost and its primary driver: productivity.

Quality, Functionality, and Customization

Quality

One of the most important factors affecting a business unit's competitive ability is the quality of its products and services, relative to those of competitors, a topic we address in detail in Chapter 4. Quality also usually implies **reliability**, that is, being able to depend on a product or service to continue providing the benefits intended. In the days of craftspeople and guilds, the quality of an individual's output was his or her *advertising*, a declaration of *skill*, and a source of *personal pride*. With the coming of the Industrial Revolution and its infinite degree of specialization and interchangeability of parts (and workers), pride in one's work became secondary to effective functioning of the individual as simply one cog in an enormous organizational system. Quite naturally, quality deteriorated and therefore had to be specifically identified and controlled as a functional aspect of the output, particularly as production systems and organizations have evolved into the complex arrangements we see today.

Many benefits are associated with providing products and services that have high quality. Obviously, customers are more pleased with a high-quality product or service. They are more apt to encourage their friends to patronize the firm, as well as giving the firm their own repeat business. Top quality also establishes a reputation for the firm that is very difficult to obtain in any other manner, and it allows the firm to charge a premium price. This was verified in the Profit Impact of Market Strategy (PIMS) study conducted by the Strategic Planning Institute. It was found that high-quality products and services were not only the most profitable but also garnered the largest market shares.

High quality also tends to protect the firm from competition, which may have to offer competing outputs at an especially low price (with correspondingly low margins) in order to stay in business. It also enhances the attractiveness of follow-up products or services so that their chances of success are much improved. And, of course, high quality minimizes risks to safety and health and reduces liability for the firm.

High quality has implications for production as well. If quality is built into the production system, it improves workers' morale, reduces scrap and waste, smooths work flows, improves control, and reduces a variety of costs. As a result, Philip Crosby, a well-known quality consultant, and others state that "quality is free." Crosby estimates that firms can lose up to 25 percent of the amount of their sales because of poor quality. A study conducted by Ken Matson of Litton's Industrial Automation Systems Division found that the annual cost of nonconformance in quality, by itself, was about 14 cents for every dollar of equipment assets.

Functionality

Many people confuse quality with **functionality**, which involves the functions the product or service is intended to perform, thereby providing the benefits to the customer. However, many products, especially electronics, as well as services, are advertised to provide purchasers with a new, unique benefit and they may do so, but it may not work well, or correctly, or for long. The former involves functionality, the middle concerns quality, and the latter has to do with reliability. Clearly, these are all different attributes of the output, and one can be well addressed while other attributes disappoint.

Customization

Customization, as noted in the discussion of the experience economy in Chapter 1, refers to offering a product or service exactly suited to a customer's desires or needs. However, there is a range of accommodation to the customer's needs, as illustrated in Figure 2.17. At the left, there is the completely standard, world-class (excellence suitable for all markets) product or service. Moving to the right is the standard with options, continuing on to variants and alternative models, and ending at the right with made-to-order customization. In general, the more customization the better, if it can be provided quickly, with acceptable quality and economy.

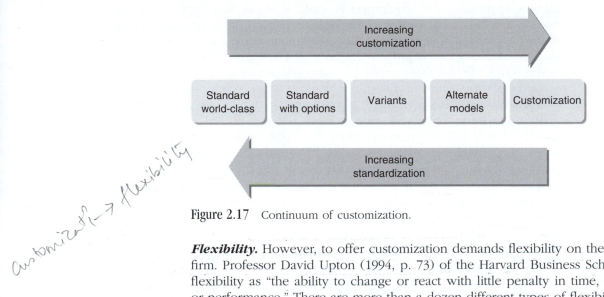

Figure 2.17   Continuum of customization.

Handwritten note (left margin): Customization → flexibility

Flexibility. However, to offer customization demands flexibility on the part of the firm. Professor David Upton (1994, p. 73) of the Harvard Business School defines flexibility as "the ability to change or react with little penalty in time, effort, cost, or performance." There are more than a dozen different types of flexibility that we will not pursue here—design, volume, routing through the production system, product mix, and many others. But having the right types of flexibility can offer the following major competitive advantages:

- Faster matches to customers' needs because changeover time from one product or service to another is quicker.
- Closer matches to customers' needs.
- Ability to supply the needed items in the volumes required for the markets as they develop.
- Faster design-to-market time to meet new customer needs.
- Lower cost of changing production to meet needs.
- Ability to offer a full line of products or services without the attendant cost of stocking large inventories.
- Ability to meet market demands even if delays develop in the production or distribution process.

Mass Customization. Until recently, it was widely believed that producing low-cost standard products (at the far left in Figure 2.17) required one type of transformation system and producing higher-cost customized products (far right) required another type of system. However, in addition to vast improvements in operating efficiency, an unexpected byproduct of the continuous improvement programs of the 1980s was substantial improvement in flexibility. Indeed, prior to this, efficiency and flexibility were thought to be tradeoffs. Increasing efficiency meant that flexibility had to be sacrificed, and vice versa.

Thus, with the emphasis on continuous improvement came the realization that increasing operating efficiency could also enhance flexibility. For example, many manufacturers initiated efforts to reduce the amount of time required to set up (or change over) equipment from the production of one product to another. Obviously,

Handwritten note (left margin): Mass Customization! emphasis on continuous improvement

Handwritten note (bottom): Technology can greatly advance this

all time spent setting up equipment is wasteful, since the equipment is not being used during this time to produce outputs that ultimately create revenues for the organization. Consequently, improving the amount of time a resource is used productively directly translates into improved efficiency. Interestingly, these same reductions in equipment setup times also resulted in improved flexibility. Specifically, with shorter equipment setup times, manufacturers could produce economically in smaller-size batches, making it easier to switch from the production of one product to another.

In response to the discovery that efficiency and flexibility can be improved simultaneously and may not have to be traded off, the strategy of mass customization emerged (see Pine 1993, Pine et al. 1993, and Gilmore and Pine 1997). Organizations pursuing **mass customization** seek to produce low-cost, high-quality outputs in high variety. Of course, as was mentioned earlier, not all products and services lend themselves to being customized. This is particularly true of commodities such as sugar, gas, electricity, and flour. On the other hand, mass customization is often quite applicable to products characterized by short life cycles, rapidly advancing technology, or changing customer requirements. However, recent research suggests that successfully employing mass customization requires an organization to first develop a transformation system that can consistently deliver high-quality outputs at a low cost. With this foundation in place, the organization can then seek ways to increase the variety of its offerings while at the same time ensuring that quality and cost are not compromised.

In an article published in *Harvard Business Review*, James Gilmore and Joseph Pine II identified four mass customization strategies:

1. ***Collaborative customizers.*** These organizations establish a dialogue to help customers articulate their needs and then develop customized outputs to meet these needs. For example, one Japanese eyewear retailer developed a computerized system to help customers select eyewear. The system combines a digital image of the customer's face and then various styles of eyeware are displayed on the digital image. Once the customer is satisfied, the customized glasses are produced at the retail store within an hour.

2. ***Adaptive customizers.*** These organizations offer a standard product that customers can modify themselves, such as closet organizers. Each closet-organizer package is the same, but includes instructions and tools to cut the shelving and clothes rods so that the unit can fit a wide variety of closet sizes.

3. ***Cosmetic customizers.*** These organizations produce a standard product but present it differently to different customers. For example, Planters packages its peanuts and mixed nuts in a variety of containers on the basis of specific needs of its retailing customers such as Wal-Mart, 7-Eleven, and Safeway.

4. ***Transparent customizers.*** These organizations provide custom products without the customers knowing that a product has been customized for them. For example, Amazon.com provides book recommendations based on information about past purchases.

Example: Hewlett-Packard.

Faced with increasing pressure from its customers for quicker order fulfillment and for more highly customized products, Hewlett-Packard (HP) wondered whether it was really possible to deliver mass-customized products rapidly, while at the same time continuing to reduce costs (Feitzinger and Lee 1997). HP's approach to mass customization can be summarized as effectively delaying tasks that customize a product as long as possible in the product supply process. It is based on the following three principles:

- Products should be designed around a number of independent modules that can be easily combined in a variety of ways.
- Manufacturing tasks should also be designed and performed as independent modules that can be relocated or rearranged to support new production requirements.
- The product supply process must perform two functions. First, it must cost-effectively supply the basic product to the locations that complete the customization activities. Second, it must have the requisite flexibility to process individual customers' orders.

HP has discovered that modular design provides three primary benefits. First, components that differentiate the product can be added during the later stages of production. This method of mass customization is generally called ***postponement***, and is one form of the assemble-to-order production process, discussed in more detail in Chapter 3. For example, the company designed its DeskJet printers so that country-specific power supplies are combined with the printers at local distribution centers and actually plugged in by the customer when the printer is set up. Second, production time can be significantly reduced by simultaneously producing the required modules. Third, producing in modules facilitates the identification of production and quality problems.

Dependability and Speed

The competitive advantages of faster, dependable response to new markets or to the individual customer's needs have occasionally been noted in the business media (Vessey 1991). For example, in a study of the U.S. and Japanese robotics industry, the National Science Foundation found that the Japanese tend to be about 25 percent faster than Americans, and to spend 10 percent less, in developing and marketing new robots. The major difference is that the Americans spend more time and money on marketing, whereas the Japanese spend five times more than the Americans on developing more efficient production methods.

Table 2.2 identifies a number of prerequisites for and advantages of fast, dependable response. These include higher quality, faster revenue generation, and lower costs through elimination of overhead, reduction of inventories, greater efficiency, and fewer errors and scrap. One of the most important but least recognized advantages for managers is that by responding faster, they can allow a customer to delay an order until the exact need is known. Thus, the customer does not have to change the order—a perennial headache for most operations managers.

Faster response to a customer also can, up to a point, reduce the unit costs of the product or service, sometimes significantly. On the basis of empirical studies reported by Meredith et al. (1994) and illustrated in Figure 2.18, it seems that there is about a 2:1 relationship between response time and unit cost. That is, starting from typical values, a 50 percent reduction in response time results in a corresponding 25 percent reduction in unit cost. The actual empirical data indicated a range between about 5:3 and 5:1, so for a 50 percent reduction in response time there could be a cost reduction from a high of 30 percent to a low of 10 percent.

$\mathcal{T}$ABLE   2.2 • Prerequisites for and Advantages of Rapid Response

1. *Sharper focus on the customer*. Faster response for both standard and custom-designed items places the customer at the center of attention.

2. *Better management*. Attention shifts to management's real job, improving the firm's infrastructure and systems.

3. *Efficient processing*. Efficient processing reduces inventories, eliminates non-value-added processing steps, smoothes flows, and eliminates bottlenecks.

4. *Higher quality*. Since there is no time for rework, the production system must be sufficiently improved to make parts accurately, reliably, consistently, and correctly.

5. *Elimination of overhead*. More efficient, faster flows through fewer steps eliminate the overhead needed to support the remaining steps, processes, and systems.

6. *Improved focus*. A customer-based focus is provided for strategy, investment, and general attention (instead of an internal focus on surrogate measures such as utilization).

7. *Reduced changes*. With less time to delivery, there is less time for changes in product mix, engineering changes, and especially changes to the order by the customer who just wanted to get in the queue in the first place.

8. *Faster revenue generation*. With faster deliveries, orders can be billed faster, thereby improving cash flows and reducing the need for working capital.

9. *Better communication*. More direct communication lines result in fewer mistakes, oversights, and lost orders.

10. *Improved morale*. The reduced processing steps and overhead allow workers to see the results of their efforts, giving a feeling of working for a smaller firm, with its greater visibility and responsibility.

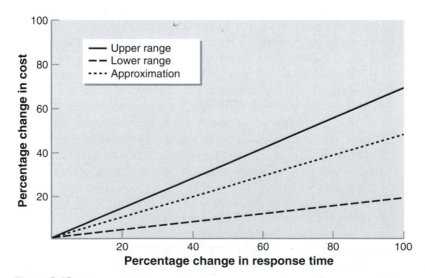

Figure 2.18   Cost reductions with decreases in response time.

This is an overwhelming benefit because if corresponding price reductions are made, it improves the value delivered to the customer through both higher responsiveness and lower price. The result for the producer is a much higher market share. If the producer chooses not to reduce the price, then the result is both higher margins and higher sales, for significantly increased profitability.

Cost and Productivity

Operational activities play a major role in determining the cost of a product or service, particularly during the up-front design for the output. This is certainly true for acquisition cost, but even truer for the **life-cycle cost** of an output, a cost consideration that more and more firms and individuals are now taking into consideration. It is commonly said that approximately 70 percent of the cost is built in at the design-engineering stage. That is, anything happening after this point, even high productivity, can affect the cost by only about 30 percent. Thus, in the traditional functional organization, it is important for all interested parties—research and development, marketing, engineering, and especially operations—to be represented on the design team. Such integration is the foundation upon which activities are grouped together in process-centered organizations.

It is worth noting that cost to the producer and price to the customer are two very different factors. You might expect that the price would always be set greater than the cost, but in many situations it is not. For example, in a recession or an oversupply situation, a producer may "dump" its product on the market to salvage any revenue it can. Or a firm may try to break into a market by offering a product at a low price as a "come-on" to encourage consumers to become familiar with its brand. Or a producer may even try to capture an entire market by driving out competitors with its low prices, planning to raise prices after the competition has left the market.

Yet it is not always clear when a firm is dumping, because costs are never a clear-cut issue. First, on many occasions American firms have claimed that foreign firms were dumping when, in fact, the foreign firms were simply more efficient and were able to offer the same goods at much lower prices while still making a profit. Second, if a firm is producing one product successfully but has excess capacity on some of its resources (e.g., machines), it may be able to produce another product for simply the additional cost of the raw materials. It can then make a nice profit at a much lower price to the consumer. That is, the "marginal contribution" becomes the full profit, since the normally fixed expenses were available free.

Nevertheless, it is always to the producers' advantage to keep their absolute costs as low as possible. This allows them the flexibility of reducing price and still making a profit if competition moves into the market, or of making an excellent profit on a reasonable price if competition is minimal. The primary method of keeping production costs low is through high *productivity*.

Productivity (Skinner 1986) is a special measure of efficiency and is normally defined as output per worker-hour. Note that there are two major ways to increase a firm's productivity: increase the numerator (output) or decrease the denominator (worker-hours). Also, of course, productivity would increase slightly if both increased but output increased faster than worker-hours, or if both decreased but worker-hours decreased faster than output.

This definition of productivity is actually what is known as a *partial factor* measure of productivity, in the sense that it considers only worker-hours as the productive factor. Clearly, productivity could easily be increased by substituting machinery for labor, but that doesn't mean that this is a wise, or even cost-saving, decision. A *multifactor* productivity measure uses more than a single factor, such as both labor and capital. Obviously, the different factors must be measured in the same units, such as dollars. An even broader gauge of productivity, called *total factor* productivity, is measured by including *all* the factors of production—labor, capital, materials, and energy—in the denominator. This measure is to be preferred in making any comparisons of productivity.

Improving productivity is important because for a society to increase its standard of living, it must first increase its productivity. How can a country improve its productivity growth? It has been estimated that technology has been responsible for at least half of the growth in productivity in the United States between 1948 and 1966. It would appear, then, that this approach holds the solid promise for continuing increases in productivity. Technology in the past resulted in the substitution of mechanical power for human physical labor (**mechanization**). This trend is continuing even faster today, where electronic equipment is replacing human sensing skills (**automation**) and information technology (IT) is allowing firms to be both more efficient and effective. We read in magazines and newspapers about these new "factories and offices of the future" that are improving productivity and frequently replacing factory workers.

We must be careful, however, not to focus solely on productivity as the problem, but rather, to consider overall competitive ability. Any solution must include quality, lead time, innovation, and a host of other such factors aimed at improving customers' satisfaction. Furthermore, since 50 to 60 percent of a typical manufacturer's cost is for materials, improved supply-chain management (covered in Chapter 7) is also critical to long-term competitiveness.

EXPAND YOUR UNDERSTANDING

1. Why is supply chain management so important in the new global economy?

2. What technologies do you see today that may be "disruptive?" Consider medicine, science, computers, transportation, technology, communications, financial transactions, the media.

3. Is it wise for a firm to stick to what it knows best, or should it expand its market by moving into adjoining products or services? How can it avoid losing its focus?

4. What do you think the result will be of the continuing escalation of the U.S. trade deficit? Will a gradual devaluation of the dollar solve the "problem?" If it does, how far do you think it needs to devalue and what will be the resulting conditions in the United States?

5. Can you think of any other areas of possible focus for a firm besides those identified in Table 2.1?

6. How might the addition of equipment to a production system *lower* efficiency? What does this say about replacing labor with equipment to increase productivity?

7. What core capabilities do you think China possesses? India? Japan? The United States?

8. According to K. Blanchard and N. V. Peale (*The Power of Ethical Management,* New York: Morrow, 1988), the following three ethical tests may be useful: (1) Is it legal or within company policy? (2) Is it balanced and fair in the short and long term? (3) Would you be proud if the public or your family knew about it? Apply these tests to the following situations:

   a. A foreign firm subsidizes its sales in another country.

   b. A foreign firm dumps its products (sells them for less than cost) in another country.

c. A country imports products that, had they been made domestically, would have violated domestic laws (e.g., laws against pollution).

9. Why do Americans invest more in marketing new products while the Japanese invest more in engineering? What advantages accrue to each investment?

10. In responding faster to customers' needs, where might the cost savings come from?

11. Can you think of companies that have moved the performance frontier of their industries?

12. How does an Aggregate Project Plan help a firm implement its strategy?

13. What is your reaction to Sara Lee's "de-verticalize" strategy? What is Sara Lee implying about its core competency?

14. How might Kaplan and Norton's strategy map help a firm implement its strategy?

15. With the increasing trend of offshoring in the United States, although companies may get richer, what will happen to the workers? What will the future hold?

16. What are the order winners and order qualifiers for Wal-Mart? Toyota? BMW? Sony?

17. Given the recent trends in products and services, does the focus strategy or sand cone strategy seem most applicable these days?

18. Why don't we see more mass customization in products and services?

19. Where would you place the following firms among the four stages of operational effectiveness? Honda; Dell; Ford; Hewlett-Packard; Citibank; American Airlines; McDonalds; J.C. Penney.

20. Using new technologies, it is not uncommon for firms to cut their response times by a factor of ten. What effect would you expect this to have on their unit costs?

APPLY YOUR UNDERSTANDING
Izmir National University

Izmir National University (INU) was chartered in 2000 to facilitate Turkey's expected eventual entry into the economy of Europe, via the EU. To foster growth and development in the European economy, engineering, science, and business were deemed to be the institution's primary areas of intellectual endeavor. The university grew rapidly during its first three years. By 2005, the enrollment reached just over 9300 students. However, with this rapid growth came a number of problems. For example, because the faculty had to be hired so quickly, there was little real organization, and curriculum seemed to be decided on the basis of which adviser a student happened to consult. The administrative offices were often reshuffled, with vague responsibilities and short tenures.

The faculty of the new Business School was typical of the confusion that gripped the entire university. The 26 faculty members were mostly recent graduates of doctoral programs at major European and Turkish universities. There were 21 Assistant Docents and Lecturers, 3 Docents, and 2 full Professors, spread fairly evenly over the four Departments, each overseen by a Kürsü professor (department head). In addition, funds were available to hire 3 additional faculty members, either assistant or regular Docents. The background of the newly recruited Dekan (administrative head, dean) of the Business School included five years of teaching at a primarily Muslim university in Turkey and two years of departmental administration at a large southern European university.

Upon arriving at the Business School, the Dekan asked the faculty to e-mail their concerns to her so that she could begin to get a handle on the major issues confronting the school. Her office assistant selected the following comments as representative of the sentiments expressed.

- "Our student-teacher ratio is much higher than what it was at my former university. We need to fill those open slots as quickly as possible and ask the university to fund at least two more faculty positions."

- "If we don't get the quality of enrollments up in the MBA program, the Graduate School will never approve our application for a doctoral program. We need the doctoral program to attract the best faculty, and we need the doctoral students to help cover our courses."

- "Given that research is our primary mission, we need to fund more graduate research assistants."

- "The travel budget isn't sufficient to allow me to attend the meetings I'm interested in. How can we improve and maintain our visibility if we get funding for only one meeting per year?"

- "We need better staff support. Faculty members are required to submit their exams for copying five days before they are needed. However, doing this makes it difficult to test the students on the material covered in class right before the exam, since it's difficult to know ahead of time exactly how much material we will cover."

- "I think far too much emphasis is placed on research. We are here to teach."

- "Being limited in our consulting is far too restrictive. In Europe we were allowed one day a week. How are we supposed to stay current without consulting?"

- "We need a voice mail system. I never get my important messages."

Questions

1. What do the comments by the faculty tell you about INU's strategy?
2. What would you recommend the Dekan do regarding the Business School's strategic planning process? What role would you recommend the Dekan play in this process?
3. Productivity is defined as the ratio of output (including both goods and services) to the input used to produce it. How could the productivity of the Business School be measured? What would the effect be on productivity if the faculty all received a 10 percent raise but continued to teach the same number of classes and students?

BIBLIOGRAPHY

Barney, J. *A Resource Based View of the Firm.* Cincinnati, OH: Thompson Learning, 1998.

Barney, J. B. *Gaining and Sustaining Competitive Advantage*, 2nd ed Upper Saddle River, NJ: Prentice-Hall, 2001.

Bartlett, C. A. and S. Ghoshal. "Going Global: Lessons from Late Movers." *Harvard Business Review* (March–April 2000): 132–142.

Bartmess, A. and K. Cerny. "Building Competitive Advantage through a Global Network of Capabilities." Chapter 7 in R. A. Hayes, G. P. Pisano, and D. M. Upton: *Strategic Operations: Competing through Capabilities.* New York: The Free Press, 1996.

Bernstein, A. "Backlash: Behind the Anxiety of Globalization." *Business Week*, April 24, 2000: 38–44.

Bower, J. L., and C. M. Christensen. "Disruptive Technologies: Catching the Wave." *Harvard Business Review* (January–February 1995): 43–53.

Clark, K. "Competing Through Manufacturing and the New Manufacturing Paradigm: Is Manufacturing Strategy Passé?" *Production and Operations Management*, 5 (1996): 42–58.

Collis, D. J., and C. A. Montgomery. *Corporate Strategy: A Resource Based Approach.* McGraw-Hill/Irwin, 1997.

Einhorn, B. "Your Next TV." *Business Week* (April 4, 2005): 33—36.

Eisenhardt, K., and S. Brown. "Time-Pacing: Competing in Markets that Won't Stand Still." *Harvard Business Review* (March–April 1998): 59–69.

Feitzinger, E., and H. L. Lee. "Mass Customization at Hewlett-Packard: The Power of Postponement." *Harvard Business Review* (January–February 1997): 116–121.

Ferdows, K., ed. *Managing International Manufacturing.* New York: North-Holland, 1989.

Ferdows, K., and A. DeMeyer. "Lasting Improvements in Manufacturing Performance: In Search of a New Theory." *Journal of Operations Management*, 9 (1990): 168–184.

Fitzsimmons, J. A., and M. J. Fitzsimmons. *Service Management for Competitive Advantage.* New York: McGraw-Hill, 2001.

Gilmore, J. H., and B. J. Pine II. "The Four Faces of Mass Customization." *Harvard Business Review* (January–February 1997): 91–101.

Goldstein, S. M., R. Johnson, J. Duffy, and J. Rao. "The Service Concept: The Missing Link in Service Design Research?" *Journal of Operations Management*, Vol. 20 (2002): 121-134.

Hammer, M. "Deep Change: How Operational Innovation Can Transform Your Company." *Harvard Business Review*, April 2004: 85-93.

Hammer, M. and S. Stanton. "How Process Enterprises Really Work." *Harvard Business Review*, November-December 1999: 108–120.

Handfield, R. B., and E. L. Nichols, Jr. *Introduction to Supply Chain Management.* Upper Saddle River, NJ: Prentice-Hall, 1999.

Hayes, R. H., and G. P. Pisano. "Beyond World-Class: The New Manufacturing Strategy." *Harvard Business Review* (January–February 1994): 77–86.

Hayes, R. H., G. P. Pisano, D. M. Upton, and S. C. Wheelwright. *Operations, Strategy, and Technology: Pursuing the Competitive Edge.* New York: John Wiley, 2004.

Heskett, J. L., W. E. Sasser, Jr., and L. A. Schlesinger. *The Service Profit Chain.* New York: Free Press, 1997.

Hill, T. *Manufacturing Strategy: Text and Cases*, 3rd ed., Homewood, IL: Irwin, 2000.

Jonas, N. "The Hollow Corporation." *Business Week* (March 3, 1986): 57–85.

Kaplan, R. S., and D. P. Norton. *The Balanced Scorecard.* Boston: Harvard Business School Press, 1996.

Kaplan, R. S., and D. P. Norton. *The Strategy Focused Organization.* Boston: Harvard Business School Press, 2001.

Kaplan, R. S., and D. P. Norton. "Having Trouble with Your Strategy? Then Map It." *Harvard Business Review* (September-October 2000), pp. 167–176.

Maidique, M. A., and P. Patch. Corporate Strategy and Technological Policy. *Harvard Business School Case 9-679-033*, Boston, 1979.

Markides, C. C. and N. Berg. "Manufacturing Offshore is Bad Business." *Harvard Business Review* (September–October 1988): 113–120.

McCutcheon, D. M., A. S. Raturi, and J. R. Meredith. "The Customization-Responsiveness Squeeze." *Sloan Management Review,* 35 (Winter 1994), no. 2: 89–100.

Meredith, J. R., D. M. McCutcheon, and J. Hartley. "Enhancing Competitiveness Through the New Market Value Equation." *International Journal of Operations and Production Management,* 14 (November 11, 1994): 7–21.

Mintzberg, H., *The Rise and Fall of Strategic Planning*, (New York: The Free Press, 1994).

Miller, J. P., "Sara Lee Plans 'Fundamental Reshaping,' " *The Wall Street Journal* (September 16, 1997): A3, A10.

Nevens, T. M., G. L. Summe, and B. Uttal. "Commercializing Technology: What the Best Companies Do." *Harvard Business Review* (May–June 1990): 60–69.

Pine, B. J., II. *Mass Customization: The New Frontier in Business Competition.* Boston: Harvard Business School Press, 1993.

Porter, M. "What is Strategy?" *Harvard Business Review* (November–December 1996): 61–78.

Prahalad, C. K., and G. Hamel. "The Core Competence of the Corporation." *Harvard Business Review* (May–June 1990): 79–91.

Rose, R. L., and C. Quintanilla. "Sara Lee's Plan to Contract Out Work Underscores Trend among U.S. Firms." *The Wall Street Journal* (September 17, 1997): A3.

Skinner, W. "The Productivity Paradox." *Harvard Business Review* (July–August 1986): 55–59.

Skinner, W. "The Focused Factory." *Harvard Business Review* (May–June 1974): 113–122.

Shafer, S. M., H. J. Smith, and J. C. Linder, "The Power of Business Models." *Business Horizons*, 48 (May–June 2005): 199–207.

Slack, N., and M. Lewis. *Operations Strategy.* New York: Financial Times Prentice-Hall, 2001.

Stalk, G. "Time—The Next Source of Competitive Advantage." *Harvard Business Review* (July–August 1988): 41–51.

Stalk, G., P. Evans, and L. E. Shulman. "Competing on Capabilities: The New Rules of Corporate Strategy." *Harvard Business Review* (March–April 1992): 57–69.

Upton, D. M. "The Management of Manufacturing Flexibility." *California Management Review* (Winter 1994): 72–89.

Vessey, J. T. "The New Competitors: They Think in Terms of 'Speed-to-Market.'" *Academy of Management Review,* 5 (April 1991): 23–33.

Welch, D., "Running Out of Gas." *Business Week* (March 28, 2005): 29–31.

Wessel, D. "With Labor Scarce, Service Firms Strive to Raise Productivity." *The Wall Street Journal* (June 1, 1989): A1, A16.

Wheelwright, S. C., and K. B. Clark. "Creating Project Plans to Focus Product Development." *Harvard Business Review* (March–April 1992): 70–82.

Wheelwright, S. C., and R. H. Hayes. "Competing Through Manufacturing." *Harvard Business Review* (January–February 1985): 99–109.

Zachary, G. P. "Service Productivity Is Rising Fast—and So Is the Fear of Lost Jobs." *The Wall Street Journal* (July 8, 1995): A1, A10.

Zeithhaml, V. A., A. Parasuraman, and L. L. Berry. *Delivering Quality Service and Balancing Customer Expectations.* New York: The Free Press, 1990.

CHAPTER 3

Process Planning and Design

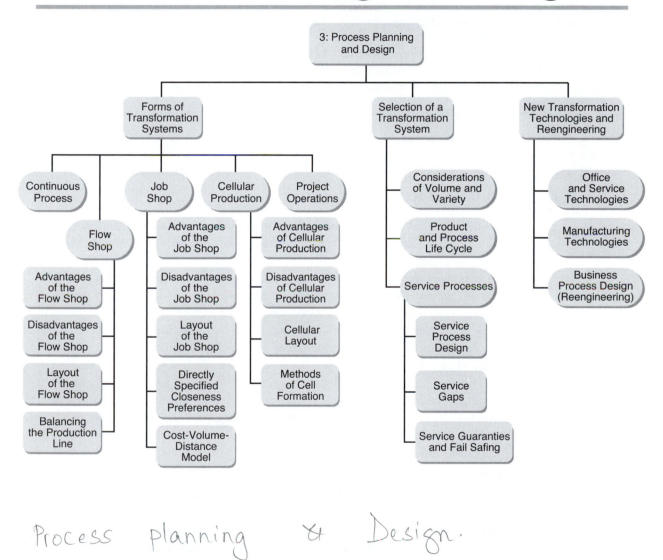

Process planning & Design.

CHAPTER IN PERSPECTIVE

Chapter 2 identified the critical factors in providing value to the customer. This chapter discusses the selection and design of the transformation process that can deliver those factors—low cost, high quality, enhanced functionality, speed, and so on—in an efficient and effective manner. If an organization is using the wrong transformation process, either because the organization has changed or the market has changed, the organization will not be competitive on these critical value factors. The chapter begins with an overview of the five types of transformation processes, their layouts, and their respective advantages and disadvantages. Next, issues related to the selection of an appropriate transformation process such as considerations of volume, variety, and product life cycles are discussed. Next, explicit attention is given to the unique requirements of designing service operations. Last, we describe some new technologies to help in redesigning the transformation process for both services and manufacturing in order to improved their efficiency and effectiveness in providing value to the customer.

INTRODUCTION

- Fender's Custom Shop has produced guitars for many famous and gifted guitarists, including Eric Clapton, John Deacon (Queen), David Gilmour (Pink Floyd), Yngwie Malmsteen, and Stevie Ray Vaughan, to name a few. The Custom Shop uses relatively new equipment and in some cases, prototypical equipment. To produce guitars, computer-controlled routers and lathes are first used to shape the bodies and necks to precise tolerances. Also, Fender has a state-of-the-art machine called a neck duplicator, which can produce a copy of the neck of any existing guitar. After the necks and bodies are fabricated, they are hand- and machine-sanded. Next, detailed inlay work is done with a Hegner precision scroll saw. Following this, paint and finishing operations are done in a special room where air is recirculated 10 times per minute to keep dust and impurities out of the finishes. After paint and finishing, the guitar parts are buffed and then hung up to be seasoned for two weeks. Next, they are moved to the final assembly area, where necks are attached to bodies, and the electronics and hardware are installed. Final assembly of the guitars is done by actual musicians (Bradley 1988).

- The assembly line at IBM's plant in Charlotte, North Carolina, is unlike any other in the world. What makes it unique is that it was designed to produce 27 significantly different products. Indeed, the variety of products produced by the team of 40 workers who operate this line is astounding; these products include hand-held bar-code scanners, portable medical computers, fiber-optic connectors, and satellite communications devices. The assembly line operates by delivering to each worker a "kit" of parts based on the production schedule. Since each product requires different assembly procedures, each worker has a computer screen at his or her station that displays updated assembly instructions for the current product (Bylinsky 1994).

72

- Rickard Associates, an editorial production company that produces magazines and marketing materials, was a pioneer in the mid-1990s of a new type of organization structure, the virtual organization. If we traveled back to that time, we would have found only two of its employees actually working at its headquarters in New Jersey: the art director worked in Arizona; the editors were located in Florida, Georgia, Michigan, and the District of Columbia; and the freelancers were even more scattered. To coordinate work, the Internet and America Online were used. For example, art directors were able to submit electronic files of finished pages to headquarters in a matter of minutes using these computer networks (Verity 1994).

- Martin Marietta's aerospace electronics manufacturing facility in Denver, Colorado, was initially set up as a job shop with numerous functional departments. As is typical of most job shops, the Marietta plant had high levels of work-in-process and long lead times, and parts had to travel long distances throughout the plant to complete their processing. Also, as is typical of functional organizations, departmental divisions created barriers to communication and often resulted in conflicting goals. To address these problems, Martin Marietta organized its plant into three focused factories. Each focused factory was completely responsible and accountable for building electronic assemblies for a particular application (e.g., flight, space, or ground use). The intent was to make each focused factory a separate business enterprise.

  A factory manager was assigned to each focused factory. The factory managers then engaged in a sort of "NFL draft" to select employees for their teams. Workers not drafted had to find other positions either inside or outside the company. Within the focused factories, product families were identified; these were based on the technology and processing requirements of the products. Next, standardized routings and sequences were identified for each product family. The plant realized a number of improvements as a result of these and other changes, including seven consecutive months of production with no scrap, a 50 percent reduction in work-in-process inventory, a 21 percent average reduction in lead times, and a 90 percent reduction in overtime (Ferras 1994).

- In the early 1990s, Nynex released Robert Thrasher from his duties as chief operating officer and assigned him to lead an effort aiming to reinvent the company. From the very beginning, Thrasher chose not to examine the company in the traditional way in terms of its divisions, departments, and functions. Rather, he opted to analyze the company in terms of four core processes that cut across the entire organization. Thrasher defined these processes as customer operations, customer support, customer contact, and customer provisioning. With the processes defined, Thrasher decided to obtain the services of the Boston Consulting Group (BCG) to help reengineer the process. Teams were then formed from 80 Nynex employees and 20 BCG consultants with the charge of reducing operating expenses by 35 to 40 percent.

  To stimulate their thinking and to learn from the best, team members visited 152 "best practice" companies, thereby identifying a number of major inefficiencies at Nynex. For example, the teams learned that Nynex purchased 83 different brands of personal computers, that $500 per truck was being spent painting newly purchased trucks a different shade of white, and that $4.5 million was spent to identify and pursue $900,000 in unpaid bills. After identifying these problems, the teams developed a list of 85 "quick wins." For instance, Nynex will save $7 million a year in postage costs by printing on both sides of customers' bills and will save $25 million by standardizing on two personal computer models. Companywide, the teams' suggestions reduced Nynex's $6 billion operating expenses by $1.5 to $1.7 billion in 1997. Doing this was expected to provide Nynex with an internal rate of return of 1025 percent and pay back its investment in two years (*Business Week* 1994).

These examples illustrate several transformation systems. The Fender Custom Shop is a job shop that has specialized departments for routing, lathe operations, inlaying, paint and finishing, and final assembly. Likewise, because work is organized by the task performed, Rickard Associates is also a job shop—even though the work is not performed in one location. Actually, and as mentioned in the example, companies like Rickard that rely on information technology to bring separated workers together are referred to as *virtual organizations*. Martin Marietta converted into *focused factories*. And assembly lines like the one IBM uses are referred to as flow shops.

As we noted in Chapter 2, the Sand Cone Model of additive and complementary competitive strengths emphasizes operations that can deliver quality, delivery dependability, speed, and low cost. The most important ingredient in achieving these strengths is selecting the most appropriate transformation process design and layout for the organization's operations. There are various basic forms of transformation process designs, each with their own layout, as well as myriad combinations and hybrids of them. This chapter describes these transformation systems, how the operations are laid out for each of them, and how to select the most appropriate one for maximum competitiveness.

The five basic forms of transformation systems are (1) continuous process, (2) flow shop, (3) job shop, (4) cellular, and (5) project. The continuous process industries are in many ways the most advanced, moving fluid material continuously through vats and pipes until a final product is obtained. Flow shops produce discrete, usually standardized outputs on a continuous basis by means of assembly lines or mass production, often using automated equipment. Cellular shops produce "families" of outputs within a variety of flow cells, but numerous cells within the plant can offer a range of families of outputs. Job shops offer a wide range of possible outputs, usually in batches, by individualized processing into and out of a number of functionally specialized departments. These departments typically consist of a set of largely identical equipment, as well as highly skilled workers. (Potentially, job shops could also produce unique—that is, one-of-a-kind—customized outputs, but job shops that do this are commonly called *model shops* or, in Europe, *jobbers*.) Finally, projects are temporary endeavors to achieve a unique outcome. The most commonly known projects are those performed on a massive scale when the labor and equipment are brought to each site rather than to a fixed production facility, such as dams, buildings, roadways, space launches, and so on.

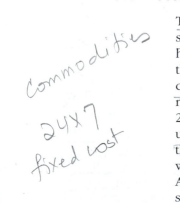

Considerations in selection

efficiency
effectiveness
capacity
lead time
flexibility

layout of operations.

waiting line theory used to design a service delivery system.

The general procedure for selecting a transformation system is to consider all alternative forms and combinations to devise the best strategy for obtaining the desired outputs. The major considerations in designing the transformation system—*efficiency, effectiveness, capacity, lead time, flexibility,* and so on—are so interdependent that changing the system to alter one will change the others as well. And the layout of the operations is another aspect that must be considered in the selection of the transformation system. The main purpose of *layout analysis* is to maximize the efficiency (cost-orientation) or effectiveness (e.g., quality, lead time, flexibility) of operations. Other purposes also exist, such as reducing safety or health hazards, minimizing interference or noise between different operational areas (e.g., separating painting from sanding), facilitating crucial staff interactions, or maximizing customers' exposure to products or services.

In laying out service operations, the emphasis may instead be on accommodating the customer rather than on operations per se. Moreover, capacity and layout analyses are frequently conducted simultaneously by analyzing service operations and the wait that the customer must endure. Thus, *waiting line* (or *queuing) theory,* a topic discussed in Chapter 5, is often used in the design of a service delivery system. The layouts of parking lots, entry zones, reception rooms, waiting areas, service facilities, and other points of customer contact are of top priority in service-oriented organizations such as clinics, stores, nightclubs, restaurants, and banks.

In a constantly changing environment, the transformation system and its layout will have to be constantly maintained and even redesigned to cope with new demands, new products and services, new government regulations, and new technology. Robots, computers, increasing global competition, and shortages of materials and energy are only a few examples of changes in the past decade that have forced organizations to recognize the necessity of adapting their operations.

FORMS OF TRANSFORMATION SYSTEMS _____

Continuous Process

Commodities

Commodities

24 × 7
fixed cost

The **continuous transformation process** is commonly used to produce highly standardized outputs in extremely large volumes. In some cases these outputs have become so standardized that there are virtually no real differences between the outputs of different firms. Examples of such *commodities* include water, gases, chemicals, electricity, ores, rubber, flour, spirits, cements, petroleum, and milk. The name *continuous process* reflects the typical practice of running these operations 24 hours a day, seven days a week. One reason for running these systems continuously is to spread their enormous fixed cost over as large a volume as possible, thereby reducing unit costs. This is particularly important in commodity markets, where price can be the single most important factor in competing successfully. Another reason for operating these processes continuously is that stopping and starting them can be prohibitively expensive.

The continuous process industries constitute about half of the manufacturing industry in the United States. Although not all of this industry produces commodities, those are what is typically envisioned. The operations in these commodity industries are highly automated, with very specialized equipment and controls, often electronic and computerized. Such automation and the expense it entails are necessary because of strict processing requirements. Because of the highly specialized and automated nature of the equipment, changing the rate of output can be quite difficult. The facility is typically a maze of pipes, conveyors, tanks, valves, vats, and bins. The layout follows the processing stages of the product, and the output rate is controlled through equipment capacity and flow and mixture rates. Labor requirements are low and are devoted primarily to monitoring and maintaining the equipment.

Recent research (Dennis and Meredith 2000), however, has shown that there is a much wider range of continuous process industries than just commodity manufacturers. In fact, these industries range all the way from intermittent forms akin to *job shops* to rigidly continuous *flow shops* (both described next). In fact, there appear to be at least seven clearly differentiable forms of continuous processes. Some run for a short time making one product and then switch over to make another product, largely on demand and by the specification of individual customers, which is almost the opposite of commodity production. In addition to these two extremes, there are also blending types of continuous processes as well as unusual hybrids of both job and flow shops.

The major characteristic of processing industries, especially commodities, is that there is often one primary, "fluid"-type input material (gas, wood, wheat, milk, etc.). This input is then often converted to multiple outputs, although sometimes there may be only one output (e.g., clean, chlorinated water). In contrast, in discrete production many types of materials are made or purchased and combined to form the output.

Although human variation in continuous processing firms does not usually create the problems it creates in discrete manufacturing, the demands of processing are usually more critical. For example, chemical reactions must be accurately timed. The result is that the initial setup of equipment and procedures is even more complex and critical than it is for flow shops. Fixed costs are extremely high; the major variable cost is materials. Variable labor (excluding distribution) is usually insignificant.

Flow Shop

Industrial

The ***flow shop*** is a transformation system similar to the continuous process, the major difference being that in the flow shop there is a discrete product or service, whereas in continuous processes the end product is not naturally divisible. Thus, in continuous processes an additional step, such as bottling or canning, might be needed to get the product into discrete units. Like the continuous process, the flow shop treats all the outputs as basically the same, and the flow of work is thus relatively continuous. Organizations that use this form are heavily automated, with large, special-purpose equipment. The characteristics of the flow shop are a fixed set of inputs, constant throughput times, and a fixed set of outputs. Examples of the flow form for discrete products are pencil manufacturing, steelmaking, and automobile assembly, whereas for services, some examples include the car wash, processing insurance claims, and the perennial fast food restaurant.

An organization that produces, or plans to produce, a high volume of a small variety of outputs will thus probably organize its operations as a flow shop. In doing so, the organization will take advantage of the simplicity and the savings in variable costs that such an approach offers. Because outputs and operations are standardized, specialized equipment can be used to perform the necessary operations at low per-unit costs, and the relatively large fixed costs of the equipment are distributed over a large volume of outputs.

Continuous types of materials-handling equipment, such as conveyors—again operating at low per-unit costs—can be used because the operations are standardized and, typically, all outputs follow the same path from one operation to the next. This standardization of treatment provides for a known, fixed throughput time, giving managers easier control of the system and more reliable delivery dates. The flow shop is easier to manage for other reasons as well: routing, scheduling, and control are all facilitated because each output does not have to be individually monitored and controlled. Standardization of operations means that fewer skilled workers can be used and each manager's span of control can increase.

The general form of the flow shop is illustrated in Figure 3.1, which shows a *production line*. (If only assembly operations were being performed, as in many automotive plants, the line would be called an *assembly line*.) This production line could represent new military inductees taking their physical exams, small appliances being assembled, or double-decker hamburgers being prepared.

Note that both services and products can be organized as flow shops and can capitalize on the many advantages of this form of processing.

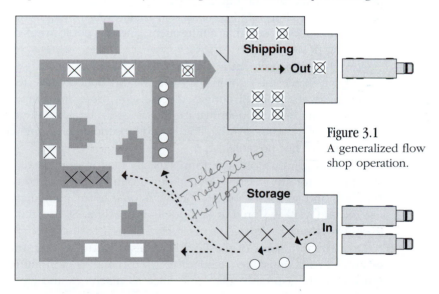

Figure 3.1
A generalized flow shop operation.

Advantages of the Flow Shop

The primary advantage of a flow shop is the low per-unit cost that is attainable owing to specialized high-volume equipment, bulk purchasing, lower labor rates, efficient utilization of the facility, low in-process inventories, and simplified managerial control. In addition, with everyone working on all the required tasks simultaneously, referred to as **overlapping**, product or service outputs are produced very quickly and fast response to changing markets is possible.

Because of the high rate of output, materials can often be bought in large quantities at a significant savings. Also, because operations are standardized, processing times tend to remain constant so that large in-process inventories are not required to queue up for processing. This minimizes investment in in-process inventory and queue (*buffer*) space. Furthermore, because a standardized product is produced, inventory control and purchasing decisions are routine.

Because the machines are specialized, less-skilled operators are needed, and therefore, lower wages can be paid. In addition, fewer supervisors are needed, further reducing costs. Since the flow shop is generally continuous, with materials handling often built into the system itself, the operations can be designed to perform compactly and efficiently with narrow aisles, thereby making maximum use of space.

The simplification in managerial control of a well-designed flow shop should not be overlooked. Constant operations problems requiring unending managerial attention penalize the organization by distracting managers from their normal duties of planning and decision making.

Disadvantages of the Flow Shop

Despite the important cost advantage of the flow shop, it can have some serious drawbacks. Not only is a variety of output difficult to obtain, even changes in the rate of output are hard to make. Changing the *rate* of output may require using overtime, laying off workers, adding additional shifts, or temporarily closing the plant. Also, because the equipment is so specialized, minor changes in the design of the product often require substantial changes in the equipment. Thus, important changes in product design are infrequent, and this could weaken the organization's marketing position.

A well-known problem in flow shops is boredom and absenteeism among the labor force. Since the equipment performs the skilled tasks, there is no challenge for the workers. And, of course, the constant, unending, repetitive nature of the manufacturing line can dehumanize the workers. Because the rate of work flow is generally set (*paced*) by the line speed, incentive pay and other output-based incentives are not possible.

The flow production line form has another important drawback. If the line should stop for any reason—a breakdown of a machine or conveyor, a shortage of supplies, and so forth—production may come to an immediate halt unless work-in-process (WIP) is stored at key points in the line. Such occurrences are prohibitively expensive.

Other requirements of the flow shop also add to its cost and its problems. For example, parts must be standardized so that they will fit together easily and quickly on the assembly line. And, since all machines and labor must work at the same repetitive pace in order to coordinate operations, the work loads along the entire line are generally *balanced* to the pace of the slowest element. To keep the line running smoothly, a large support staff is required, as well as large stocks of raw materials, all of which also add to the expense.

Last, in the flow shop, simplicity in *ongoing operation* is achieved at the cost of complexity in the initial *setup*. The planning, design, and installation of the typically complicated, special-purpose, high-volume equipment are mammoth tasks. The equipment is costly not only to set up originally but also to maintain and service.

Furthermore, such special-purpose equipment is very susceptible to obsolescence and is difficult to dispose of or to modify for other purposes.

Layout of the Flow Shop

The crux of the problem of realizing the advantages of a flow shop is whether the work flow can be subdivided sufficiently so that labor and equipment are utilized smoothly throughout the processing operations. If, for example, one operation takes longer than all the others, this single operation (perhaps a machine) will become a bottleneck, delaying all the operations following it and restricting the output rate of the entire process.

Obtaining smooth utilization of workers and equipment across all operations involves assigning to groups tasks that take about the same amount of time to complete. This balancing applies to production lines where parts or outputs are produced, as well as to assembly lines where parts are assembled into final products.

Final assembly operations usually have more labor input and fewer fixed-equipment cycles and can therefore be subdivided more easily for smooth flow. Either of two types of lines can then be used. A *paced line* uses some sort of conveyor and moves the output along at a continuous rate, and operators do their work as the output passes by them. For longer operations the worker may walk or ride alongside the conveyor and then have to walk back to the starting workstation. The many disadvantages of this arrangement, such as boredom and monotony, are, of course, well known. An automobile assembly line is a common example of a paced line. Workers install doors, engines, hoods, and the like as the conveyor moves past them.

In unpaced lines, the workers build up queues between workstations and can then vary their pace to meet the needs of the job or their personal desires; however, average daily output must remain the same. The advantage of an unpaced line is that a worker can spend longer on the more difficult outputs and balance this with the easier outputs. Similarly, workers can vary their pace to add variety to a boring task. For example, a worker may work fast to get ahead of the pace for a few seconds before returning to the task.

There are some disadvantages to unpaced lines, however. For one thing, they cannot be used with large, bulky products because too much in-process storage space is required. More important, minimum output rates are difficult to maintain because short durations in one operation usually do not dovetail with long durations in the next operation. When long durations coincide, operators downstream from these operations may run out of in-process inventory to work on and may thus be forced to sit idle.

For operations that can be smoothed to obtain the benefits of a production line, there are two main elements in designing the most efficient line. The first is formulating the situation by determining the necessary output rate, the available work time per day, the times for operational tasks, and the order of precedence of the operations. The second element is actually to solve the balancing problem by subdividing and grouping the operations into balanced jobs. To more clearly communicate the concept of a balanced production line, we will give an example that addresses both of these main elements. In reality, of course, one of a variety of computer packages would be employed.

Balancing the Production Line

We illustrate the formulation of the ***line balancing*** situation with an example. Longform Credit receives 1200 credit applications a day, on the average. Longform competes on the basis of its ability to process applications within hours. Daily application processing tasks, average times, and required preceding tasks (tasks that must be completed before the next task) are listed in Table 3.1.

The *precedence graph* for these tasks is shown in Figure 3.2; it is constructed directly from Table 3.1. This graph is simply a picture of the operations (boxed) with arrows indicating which tasks must precede others. The number or letter of the operation is shown above the box, with its time inside.

𝒯ABLE   3.1 • Tasks in Credit Application Processing

Task	Average Time (minutes)	Immediately Preceding Tasks
a Open and stack applications	0.20	none
b Process enclosed letter; make note of and handle any special requirements	0.37	a
c Check off form 1 for page 1 of application	0.21	a
d Check off form 2 for page 2 of application; file original copy of application	0.18	a
e Calculate credit limit from standardized tables according to forms 1 and 2	0.19	c, d
f Supervisor checks quotation in light of special processing of letter, notes type of form letter, address, and credit limit to return to applicant	0.39	b, e
g Secretary types in details on form letter and mails	0.36	f
Total	**1.90**	

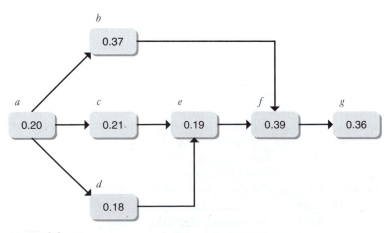

Figure 3.2   Precedence graph for credit applications.

In balancing a line, the intent is to find a *cycle time* in which each workstation can complete its tasks. A workstation is usually a single person, but it may include any number of people responsible for completing all the tasks associated with the job for that station. Conceptually, at the end of this time every workstation passes its part on to the next station. Task elements are thus grouped for each workstation so as to utilize as much of this cycle time as possible but not to exceed it. Each workstation will have a slightly different *idle time* within the cycle time.

$$\text{Cycle time} = \text{available work time/demand}$$

$$= \frac{8 \text{ hr} \times 60 \text{ min/hr}}{1200 \text{ applications}} = (0.4 \text{ min/application})$$

The cycle time is determined from the required output rate. In this case, the average daily output rate must equal the average daily input rate, 1200. If it is less than this figure, a backlog of applications will accumulate. If it is more than this, unnecessary idle time will result. Assuming an eight-hour day, 1200 applications per eight hours means completing 150 every hour or one every 0.4 minute—this, then, is the cycle time.

Adding up the task times in Table 3.1, we can see that the total is 1.9 minutes. Since every workstation will do no more than 0.4 minute's work during each cycle, it is clear that a minimum of 1.9/0.4 = 4.75 workstations are needed—or, always rounding *up*, five workstations.

$$\text{Number of theoretical workstations, } N_T = \sum \text{task times/cycle time}$$

$$= \frac{1.9}{0.4} = 4.75 \text{ (i.e., 5)}$$

It may be, however, that the work cannot be divided and balanced in five stations—that six, or even seven, may be needed. For example, precedence relationships may interfere with assigning two tasks to the same workstation. This is why we referred to N_T as the *theoretical* number of workstations needed. If more workstations are actually needed than the theoretical number, the production line will be less efficient. The *efficiency* of the line with N_A actual stations may be computed from

$$\text{Efficiency} = \frac{\text{output}}{\text{input}} = \frac{\text{total task time}}{(N_A \text{ stations}) \times \text{cycle time}}$$

$$\frac{1.9}{5 \times 0.4} = 95 \text{ percent if the line can be balanced with 5 stations}$$

$$\frac{1.9}{6 \times 0.4} = 79 \text{ percent if 6 stations are required}$$

In the formula for efficiency, input is represented by the amount of work required to produce one unit, and output is represented by the amount of work that actually goes into producing one unit.

Now that the problem has been formulated, we can attempt to balance the line by assigning tasks to stations. We begin by assuming that all workers can do any of the tasks and check back on this later. There are many heuristic rules for which task to assign to a station next. We will use the LOT rule; select the task with the *longest operation time* next. The general procedure for line balancing is:

- Construct a list of the tasks whose predecessor tasks have already been completed.
- Consider each of these tasks, one at a time, in LOT order and place them within the station.
- As a task is tentatively placed in a station, new follower tasks can now be added to the list.
- Consider adding to the station any tasks in this list whose time fits within the remaining time for that station.
- Continue in this manner until as little idle time as possible remains for the station.

We will now demonstrate this procedure with reference to Longform, using the information in Table 3.1 and Figure 3.2. The first tasks to consider are those with no preceding tasks. Thus, task *a*, taking 0.2 of the 0.4 minute available, is assigned to station 1. This, then, makes tasks *b* (0.37 minute), *c* (0.21 minute), and *d* (0.18 minute) eligible for assignment. Trying the longest first, *b*, then *c*, and last *d*, we find that only *d* can be assigned to station 1 without exceeding the 0.4-minute cycle time; thus, station 1 will include tasks *a* and *d*. Since only 0.02 minute remains unassigned in station 1 and no task is that short, we then consider assignments to station 2.

Only *b* and *c* are eligible for assignment (since *e* requires that *c* be completed first), and *b* (0.37 minute) will clearly require a station by itself; *b* is, therefore, assigned to station 2. Only *c* is now eligible for assignment, since *f* requires that both *e* and *b* be completed and *e* is not yet completed. But when we assign *c* (0.21 minute) to station 3, task *e* (0.19 minute) becomes available and can also be just accommodated in station 3. Task *f* (0.39 minute), the next eligible task, requires its own station; this leaves *g* (0.36 minute) to station 5. These assignments are illustrated in Figure 3.3 and Table 3.2.

We now check the feasibility of these assignments. In many cases, several aspects must be considered in this check (as discussed later), but here our only concern is that the clerk or the secretary does not do task *f* and that the supervisor does not do task *g* (or, we hope, much of *a* through *e*). As it happens, task *f* is a station by itself, so there is no problem.

As we saw, short tasks are often combined to reach the cycle time. However, long tasks may have to be split up to meet the cycle time requirements. If a task cannot be split, we can "clone" the station as many times as needed to effectively reduce its cycle time, with each station alternating in its output to match, in essence, the required cycle time.

Job Shop

The **job shop** gets its name because unique jobs must be produced. In this form of transformation system each output, or each small batch of outputs, is processed differently. Therefore, the flow of work through the facility tends to be intermittent. The general characteristics of a job shop are *grouping* of staff and equipment according to function; a large *variety* of inputs; a considerable amount of *transport* of staff, materials, or recipients; and large *variations* in system flow times (the time it takes for a complete "job"). In general, each output takes a different route through the organization, requires different operations, uses different inputs, and takes a different amount of time.

This transformation system is common when the outputs differ significantly in form, structure, materials, or processing required. For example, an organization that has a wide variety of outputs or does custom work (e.g., custom guitars) would probably be a job shop. Specific examples of product and service organizations of this form are tailor shops, general offices, machine shops, public parks, hospitals, universities, automobile repair shops, criminal justice systems, and department stores. By and large, the job shop is especially appropriate for service organizations because services are often customized, and hence, each service requires different operations.

$\mathcal{T}$ABLE   3.2 • Station Task Assignments

Station	Time Available	Eligible Tasks	Task Assigned	Idle Time
1	.40	a	a	
	.20	b, c, d	d	
	.02	b, c	none will fit	.02
2	.40	b, c	b	
	.03	c	c will not fit	.03
3	.40	c	c	
	.19	e	e	.00
4	.40	f	f	
	.01	g	g will not fit	.01
5	.40	g	g	.04

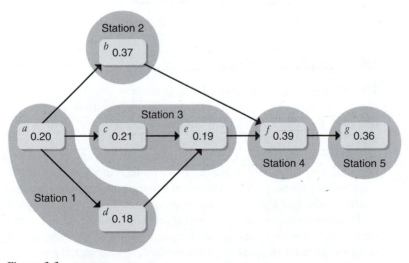

Figure 3.3   Station assignments.

Clearly, the efficient management of a job shop is a difficult task, since every output must be treated differently. In addition, the resources available for processing are limited. Furthermore, not only is it management's task to ensure the performance of the proper functions of each output, where considerations of quality and deadlines may vary, but management must also be sure that the available resources (staff, equipment, materials, supplies, capital) are being efficiently utilized. Often there is a difficult tradeoff between efficiency and flexibility of operations. Job-based processes tend to emphasize flexibility over efficiency.

Figure 3.4 represents the flow through a job shop. This facility might be a library, an auto repair shop, or an office. Each particular "job" travels from one area to another, and so on, according to its unique routing, until it is fully processed. Temporary in-process storage may occur between various operations while jobs are waiting for subsequent processing (standing in line for the coffee machine).

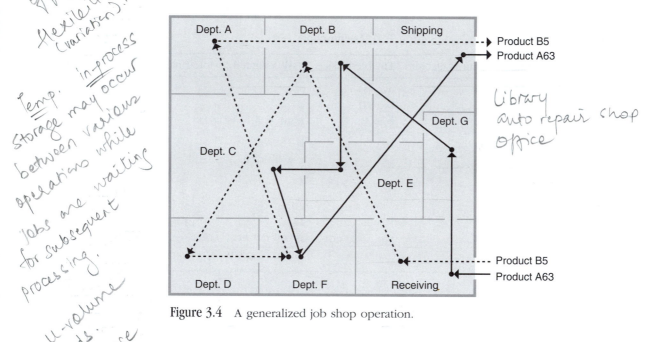

Figure 3.4   A generalized job shop operation.

Advantages of the Job Shop

The widespread use of the job shop form is due to its many advantages. The job shop is usually selected to provide the organization with the flexibility needed to respond to individual, small-volume demands (or even custom demands). The ability to produce a wide variety of outputs at reasonable cost is thus the primary advantage of this form. General-purpose equipment is used, and this is in greater demand and is usually available from more suppliers at a lower price than special-purpose equipment. In addition, used equipment is more likely to be available, further reducing the necessary investment. There is a larger base of experience with general-purpose equipment; therefore, problems with installation and maintenance are more predictable, and replacement parts are more widely available. Last, because general-purpose equipment is easier to modify or use elsewhere and disposal is much easier, the expense of obsolescence is minimized.

Because of the functional arrangement of the equipment, there are also other advantages. Resources for a function requiring special staff, materials, or facilities (e.g., painting or audiovisual equipment) may be centralized at the location of that function, and the organization can thus save expense through high utilization rates. Distracting or dangerous equipment, supplies, or activities may also be segregated from other operations in facilities that are soundproof, airtight, explosion-proof, and so forth.

One advantage to the staff is that with more highly skilled work involving constantly varying jobs, responsibility and pride in one's work are increased, and boredom is reduced. Other advantages to the staff are that concentrations of experience and expertise are available and morale increases when people with similar skills work together in centralized locations (all market researchers together). Because all workers who perform similar activities are grouped together, each worker has the opportunity to learn from others, and the workers can easily collaborate to solve difficult problems. Furthermore, because the pace of the work is not dictated by a moving "line," incentive arrangements may be set up. Last, because no line exists that must forever keep moving, the entire set of organizational operations does not halt whenever any one part of the operation stops working; other functional areas can continue operating, at least until in-process inventory is depleted. Also, other general-purpose resources can usually substitute for the nonfunctioning resource: one machine for another, one staff member for another, one material for another.

Disadvantages of the Job Shop

The general-purpose equipment of job shops is usually slower than special-purpose equipment, resulting in higher variable (per-unit) costs. In addition, the cost of direct labor for the experienced staff necessary to operate general-purpose equipment further increases unit costs of production above what semiskilled or unskilled workers would require. The result, in terms of costs of the outputs, is that the variable costs of production are higher for the general-purpose than for the special-purpose equipment, facilities, and staff, but the initial cost of the equipment and facilities is significantly less. For small-output volumes the job shop results in a lower total cost. As volume of output increases, however, the high variable costs begin to outweigh the savings in initial investment. The result is that, for high-production volumes, the job shop is not the most economic approach (although its use may still be dictated by other considerations, as when particular equipment threatens workers' health or safety).

Inventories are also frequently a disadvantage in the job shop, especially in product organizations. Not only do many types of raw materials, parts, and supplies have to be kept for the wide variety of outputs anticipated, but *in-process inventories*, that is, jobs waiting for processing, typically become very large and thereby represent a sizable capital investment for the organization. It is not unusual for batches of parts in these environments to spend 90–95 percent of the time they are in the shop either waiting to be moved or waiting to be processed. Furthermore, because there are so many inventory items that must travel between operating departments in order to be processed, the cost of handling materials is also typically high. Because job routings between operations are not identical, inexpensive fixed materials-handling mechanisms like conveyor belts cannot be used.

Instead, larger and more costly equipment is used; therefore, corridors and aisles must be large enough to accommodate it. This necessitates allocating even more space, beyond the extra space needed to store additional inventories.

Finally, managerial control of the job shop is extremely difficult, as mentioned earlier. Because the output varies in terms of function, processing, quality, and timing, the managerial tasks of routing, scheduling, cost accounting, and such become nearly impossible when demand for the output is high. Expediters must track down lost jobs and reorder priorities. In addition to watching the progress of individual jobs, management must continually strive to achieve the proper balance of materials, staff, and equipment; otherwise, highly expensive resources will sit idle while bottlenecks occur elsewhere.

Layout of the Job Shop

Because of its relative permanence, the layout of the operations is probably one of the most crucial elements affecting the efficiency of a job shop. In general, the problem of laying out operations in a job shop is quite complex. The difficulty stems from the variety of outputs and the constant changes in outputs that are characteristic of organizations with an intermittent transformation system. The optimal layout for the existing set of outputs may be relatively inefficient for the outputs to be produced six months from now. This is particularly true of job shops where there is no proprietary product and only for-contract work is performed. One week such a shop might produce 1000 wheels, and the next week it might produce an 8000-gallon vat. Therefore, a job-shop layout is based on the historically stable output pattern of the organization and expected changes in that pattern, rather than on current operations or outputs.

A variety of factors can be important in the interrelations among the operations of a job shop. If all the qualitative and quantitative factors can be analyzed and combined, the relative importance of locating each department close to or far from each of the other departments may be used to determine a layout. This approach is particularly useful for service operations where movements of materials are not particularly significant. To illustrate how this concept might be achieved in practice, we next present a simplified example. Following this, we illustrate how a purely cost-based layout could be achieved.

Directly Specified Closeness Preferences

As a simplified example, consider Table 3.3, where six departments have been analyzed for the desirability of closeness to each other. Assume we are given the organization's *closeness preferences,* indicated by the letters A, E, I, O, U, and X, with the meanings given in the table. In general, the desirability of closeness decreases along the alphabet until U, which is "unimportant," and then jumps to "undesirable" with X; there is no range of undesirability in this case, although there could be, of course.

One way of starting the layout process is simply to draw boxes representing the departments in the order given in the table and show closeness preferences on the arcs (line segments) joining them. Figure 3.5a illustrates this for Table 3.3. The next step is to shift the departments with A on their arcs nearer each other and those with X away from each other. When these have been shifted as much as possible, the E arcs, then the I arcs, and finally the O arcs will be considered for relocation, resulting in an improved layout, such as in Figure 3.5b.

$\mathcal{T}$ABLE 3.3 • Directly Specified Closeness Preferences*

Department	Department					
	1	2	3	4	5	6
1		E	A	U	U	U
2			U	I	I	U
3				U	U	A
4					I	U
5						I
6						

*Note:

A = Absolutely necessary   O = Ordinary closeness OK

E = Especially important   U = Unimportant

I = Important   X = Undesirable

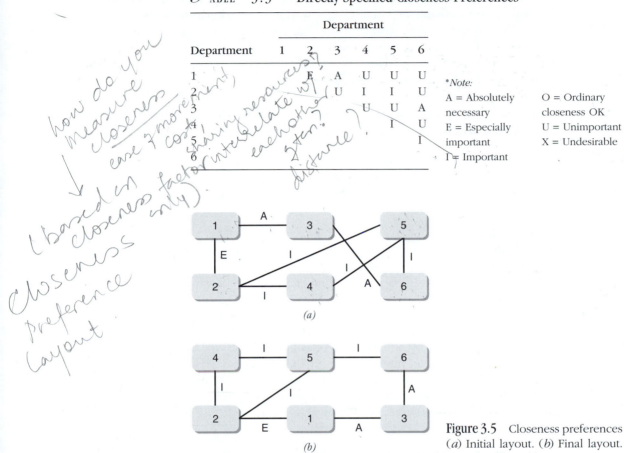

Figure 3.5   Closeness preferences layout: (a) Initial layout. (b) Final layout.

Cost–Volume–Distance Model

In the cost–volume–distance (CVD) approach, the desirability of closeness is based on the total cost of moving materials or people between departments. Clearly, a layout can never be completely reduced to just one such objective, but where the cost of movement is significant, this approach produces reasonable first approximations. The objective is to minimize the costs of interrelations among operations by locating those operations that interrelate extensively close to one another. If we label one of the departments i and another department j, then the cost of moving materials between departments i and j depends on the distance between i and j, D_{ij}.

In addition, the cost will usually depend on the amount or volume moving from i to j, such as trips, cases, volume, weight, or some other such measure, which we will denote by V_{ij}. Then, if the cost of the flow from i to j per-unit amount per-unit distance is C_{ij}, the total cost of i relating with j is $C_{ij}V_{ij}D_{ij}$. Note that C, V, and D may have different values for different types of flows and that they need not have the same values from *j* to *i* as from *i* to *j*, since the flow in opposite directions may be of an entirely different nature. For example, information may be flowing from *i* to *j*, following a certain paperwork path; but sheet steel may flow from *j* to *i*, following a lift truck or conveyor belt path.

Adding the flows from *i* to every one of *N* possible departments, we find that the total cost of department *i* interrelating with all other departments is

$$\sum_{j=1}^{n} C_{ij} V_{ij} D_{ij}$$

(It is normally assumed that $C_{ii}V_{ii}D_{ii} = 0$, because the distance from *i* to itself is zero.) Adding together the costs for all the departments results in the total cost.

$$TC = \sum_{i=1}^{N} \sum_{j=1}^{N} C_{ij} V_{ij} D_{ij}$$

Our goal is to find the layout that minimizes this total cost. This may be done by evaluating the cost of promising layouts or, as in the following simplified example, by evaluating *all possible* layouts.

The section of a business school containing the administrative offices of the operations management department is illustrated in Figure 3.6. Each office is approximately 10 feet by 10 feet, so the walking distance (*D*) between adjacent offices (i.e., offices 1 and 2, and offices 2 and 3) is 10 feet, whereas the distance between diagonal offices (offices 1 and 3) is approximately 15 feet.

The average number of interpersonal trips made each day is given in a travel or load matrix (Table 3.4). According to Table 3.4, each day the assistant makes five trips to the chairperson's office and 17 trips to the secretary's office. Thus, the assistant would travel 305 feet (10 feet × 5 trips + 15 feet × 17 trips) each day.

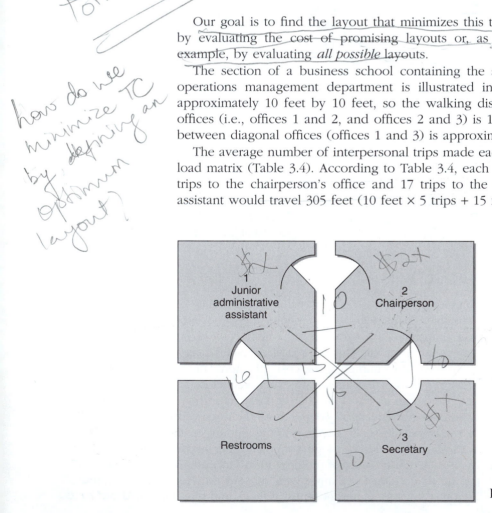

Figure 3.6 Office layout.

Assuming that the chairperson is paid approximately twice as much as the secretary and the junior administrative assistant, determine if the current arrangement is best (i.e., least costly) in terms of transit time and, if not, what arrangement would be better.

For convenience, the offices are numbered in Figure 3.6. Before calculating total costs of all possible arrangements, some preliminary analysis is worthwhile. First, because of special utility connections, restrooms are usually not considered relocatable. In addition, the relocation of the restrooms in this example would not achieve any result that could not be achieved by moving the other offices instead.

Second, many arrangements are mirror images of other arrangements and thus need not be evaluated, since their cost will be the same. For example, interchanging offices 1 and 3 will result in the same costs as the current layout. The essence of the problem, then, is to *determine which office should be located diagonally across from the restrooms.* There are three alternatives: chairperson, assistant, or secretary.

(handwritten margin notes: "Analysis of problem", "restrooms cannot be relocated / not necessary", "interchanging 1 & 3 will result in same issue", "determine which office should be located diagonally across from restrooms", "3 possibilities: assistant, chair, secretary", "TC =")

TABLE 3.4 • Load Matrix, V_{ij} (trips)

	To		
From	1 Assistant	2 Chair	3 Secretary
1 Assistant	—	5×10	17×15 = 305
2 Chair	10×10	—	5×10 = 150
3 Secretary	13×15	25×10	— = 445

(handwritten: "assumption")

Now, let us evaluate each of the three possibilities as the "diagonal office"—first the chairperson, then the assistant, and last the secretary. The costs will simply be denoted as 1 for the assistant and the secretary or 2 for the chairperson (who earns twice as much as the others). As noted, the V_{ij} "volumes" will be the number of trips from i to j taken from the load matrix, and the distances will depend on who has the diagonal office across from the restrooms. The calculations for each arrangement are shown here.

1. Chairperson: $TC = 1(5)10 + 1(17)15 + 2(10)10 + 2(5)10 + 1(13)15 + 1(25)10$
   $= 1050$

2. Assistant: $TC = 1(5)10 + 1(17)10 + 2(10)10 + 2(5)15 + 1(13)10 + 1(25)15$
   $= 1075$

3. Secretary: $TC = 1(5)15 + 1(17)10 + 2(10)15 + 2(5)10 + 1(13)10 + 1(25)10$
   $= 1025$ (lowest)

To better understand these calculations, consider the current arrangement in which the chair has the office diagonal to the restrooms. In this case, the assistant must travel 305 feet each day, as was explained earlier. Each day the chairperson would have to travel 150 feet: (10 feet × 10 trips to the assistant) + (10 feet × 5 trips to the secretary). Finally, the secretary would have to travel 445 feet each day: (15 feet × 13 trips to the assistant) + (10 feet × 25 trips to the chair).

Because the chairperson is paid twice as much as the secretary and assistant, we weight the chairperson's travel distance as twice that of the other two workers. Using this weighting scheme provides a total cost of the current office arrangement of 1050: that is, 305 + (2 × 150) + 445. The best arrangement is to put the secretary in the office diagonal to the restrooms for a relative cost of 1025. Again, if faced with an actual layout task, a computer package could be used.

good analysis

DILBERT: ©Scott Adams/Dist. by United Feature Syndicate, Inc.

Cellular Production

customized

Cellular production is a relatively new type of transformation system that many firms have recently been adopting. It combines the advantages of the job shop and flow shop to obtain the high variety possible with the job form and the reduced costs and short response times available with the flow form. Figure 3.7 contrasts the job shop with cellular production for a manufacturing firm. The job shop in Figure 3.7a has separate departments for welding, turning, heat treat, milling, and forming. This type of layout provides flexibility to produce a wide range of products simply by varying the sequence in which the products visit the five processing departments. Also, flexibility is enhanced, as machines are easily substituted for one another should a specified machine be busy or nonoperational.

Reduced cost
Short response times
Variety of products.
enhanced flexibility

Figure 3.7b shows a reorganization of the plant for cellular production. The cellular form is based on ***group technology***, which seeks to achieve efficiency by exploiting similarities inherent in parts. In production, this is accomplished by identifying groups of parts that have similar processing requirements. Parts with similar processing requirements are called *part families*. Figure 3.8 provides an example of how a variety of parts can be organized into part families.

Based on group technology

After the parts are divided into families, a *cell* is created that includes the human skills and all the equipment required to produce a family. Since the outputs are all similar, the equipment can be set up in one pattern to produce the entire family and does not need to be set up again for another type of output (as is necessary in a job shop). Some cells consist of just one machine producing a complete product or service. Other cells may have as many as 50 people working with dozens of machines.

identify part families

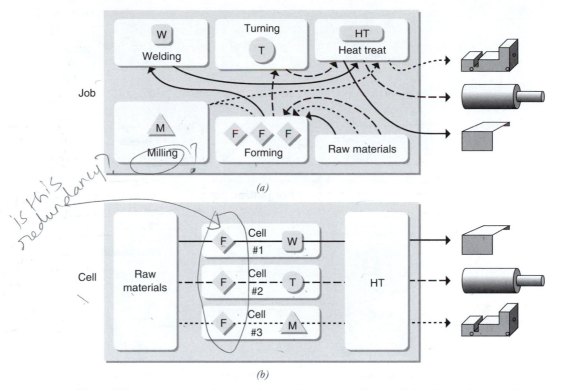

Figure 3.7 Conversion of (*a*) a job shop layout into (*b*) a cellular layout for part families.

A facility using cells is generally organized on the basis of *teams*. That is, a team is completely responsible for conducting the work within its cell. The team members usually schedule and inspect the work themselves, once they know when it is due. Occasionally, work must be taken outside a cell for a special treatment or process that is unavailable within the cell, but these operations are minimized whenever possible.

The families are derived from one of a number of different approaches. Sometimes the basis is the machines that are needed to produce the output, or the families may be based on the size of the equipment, the quality required, the skills needed, or any other overriding consideration. This is called the *classification* stage. Items are classified into families—sometimes by simple inspection and other times by complex analysis of their routing requirements, production requirements, part geometry, and the like. It is generally not feasible to classify all the outputs into one of a limited number of families, so at some point all the miscellaneous outputs are placed in a "remainder" cell, which is operated as a minijob shop.

Advantages of Cellular Production

Organizations adopt the cellular form to achieve many of the efficiencies associated with products and services that are mass-produced using flow transformation systems in less repetitive job shop environments. However, not all the advantages of a full flow shop or a full job shop can be obtained, because not enough high-volume equipment can be purchased to obtain the economies of scale that flow shops enjoy.

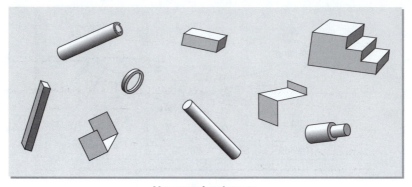

Unorganized parts

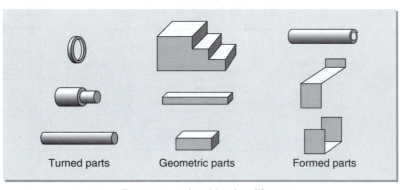

Turned parts   Geometric parts   Formed parts

Parts organized by families

Figure 3.8   Organization of miscellaneous parts into families.

And because the equipment is dedicated to part families, some of the variety afforded by job shops is lost.

One of the most important advantages of the cellular form is reduced machine setup times. In the job shop, when a worker completes the processing of one batch, the machine is set up for the next batch. Because a wide variety of parts typically flow through each department in a job shop, the next batch of parts processed by the worker will likely be different from the one just completed. This means that the worker may have to spend several hours or more simply setting up and preparing the machine for the next batch of parts. In cellular production, machine setup times are minimized because each cell processes only parts that have similar (or identical) setup and processing requirements. It is extremely desirable to minimize machine setup times, because setup time takes away from the amount of time machines can be used to produce the outputs.

Decreasing machine setup times provides several benefits. First, as we have just noted, when setup times decrease, the amount of time equipment is available to process parts increases. Second, increased capacity means that the company can produce at a given level with fewer machines. Reducing the number of machines used not only reduces the costs of equipment and maintenance, but also reduces the amount of floor space needed. Third, shorter setup times make it more economical to produce smaller batches. For instance, if the setup time is four hours, it would not be efficient to produce a small number of parts using a particular machine, only to spend another four hours to set it up for the next batch. However, if the machine required only a few minutes of setup time, it might be practical to produce a few parts on the machine.

There are numerous benefits associated with producing parts in small batches. To begin, producing small batches enhances an organization's flexibility in responding to changes in product mix. Also, reducing the size of batches leads to reductions in work-in-process inventory. Less inventory means that less space is needed to store it and less capital is tied up in it. Also, product lead times are shorter, and throughput times are faster due to overlapping the tasks. Shorter lead times and faster throughput facilitate more accurate forecasting, faster response to market changes, faster revenue generation, and perhaps the most important advantage of all—less time for engineers to change the output or customers to change (or cancel) the order!

Another major advantage of the cellular form is that parts are produced in one cell. Processing the parts in one cell simplifies control of the shop floor. To illustrate this, compare the amount of effort required to coordinate the production activities in the job shop and the cellular layout shown in Figure 3.7. Producing parts in a single cell also reduces the amount of labor and equipment needed to move materials because travel distances between successive operations are shorter. Additionally, producing the parts in one cell provides an opportunity to increase the workers' accountability, responsibility, and autonomy. Finally, reducing material handling and increasing the workers' accountability typically translate into reduced defects. In a job shop, it is difficult to hold the workers accountable for quality because the product is processed in several different departments and the workers in one department can always blame problems on another department.

A unique advantage of the cell form is that it maximizes the inherent benefits of the team approach. In a flow shop, there is little teamwork because the equipment does most of the work; the labor primarily involves oversight and maintenance. Job shops are organized by department, and this allows for some teamwork—but not in terms of specific jobs, because everyone is working on a different job. In a cell, all the workers are totally responsible for completing every job. Thus, the effect is to enrich the work, provide challenges, encourage communication and teamwork, meet due dates, and maintain quality.

An additional advantage for manufacturers is the minimal cost required to move to cellular production. Although some cells may be highly automated, with expensive special-purpose equipment, it is not necessary to invest any additional capital in order to adopt the cellular form. It requires only the movement of equipment and labor into cells. Or, with even less trouble—though with some loss of efficiency—the firm can simply designate certain pieces of equipment as dedicated to a single part family, but not relocate them. The term used in this case is **virtual cell** or *logical cell* (also known as *nominal*), because the equipment is not physically adjoining but is still reserved for production of only one part family.

Another form of cellular production is called a miniplant. Here, the cell not only does the manufacturing but also has its own industrial engineer, quality manager, accountant, marketing representative, and salesperson, and almost all the other support services that a regular plant has. Only far-removed services, such as R&D and human resources, are not dedicated to the miniplant. The entire facility of the firm is thus broken down into a number of miniplants, each with its own general manager, production workers, and support services so that it can operate as an independent profit center.

Disadvantages of Cellular Production

Some disadvantages of the cellular form are those of the flow shop and the job shop, but they are not as serious. As in a flow shop, if a piece of equipment should break down, it can stop production in the cell; but in a cell form—unlike a flow shop, where that might be the only piece of equipment in the facility—work might, if permissible, temporarily be shifted to other cells to get a job out.

However, obtaining balance among the cells when demands for a product or service family keep changing is a problem that is less in both flow and job shops. Flow shops are relatively fixed in capacity and they produce a standard output, so there is no question of balance. Job shops simply draw from a pool of skilled labor for whatever job comes in. With cells, by contrast, if demand for a family dries up, it may be necessary to break up that cell and redistribute the equipment, or reform the families. In the short run, though, labor can generally be assigned to whatever cell needs it, including the remainder cell.

Of course, volumes are too small in cellular production to allow the purchase of the high-volume, efficient equipment that flow shops use. The cellular form also does not allow for the extent of customization usually found in job shops, since the labor pool has largely been disbursed to independent cells (although the remainder cell may be able to do the work). Moreover, the fostering of specialized knowledge associated with various operational activities is reduced because the workers who perform these activities are spread out and therefore have limited opportunities to collaborate.

Cellular Layout

Cellular production creates teams of workers and equipment to produce families of outputs. The workers are cross-trained so that they can operate any of the equipment in their cell, and they take full responsibility for the proper performance or result of the outputs. Whenever feasible, these outputs are final products or services. At other times, particularly in manufacturing, the outputs are parts that go into a final product. If the latter is the case, it is common to group the cells closely around the main production or assembly line so that they feed their output directly into the line as it is needed.

In some cases, a *virtual cell* is formed by identifying certain equipment and dedicating it to the production of families of outputs, but without moving the equipment into an actual, physical cell. In that case, no "layout" analysis is required at all; the organization simply keeps the layout it had. The essence of the problem, then, is the identification of the output families and the equipment to dedicate to each of them.

It is more common for an organization to actually form physical cells. When physical cells are created, the layout of the cell may resemble a sort of miniflow shop, a job shop, or a mix of these, depending on the situation. Thus, we will direct our attention here to the formation of the part or product families and their associated equipment, leaving the issues of physical layout to be addressed in the discussions of the flow shop and job shop.

In practice, organizations often use the term cell to include a wide range of very different situations: a functional department consisting of identical machines, a single machine that automatically performs a variety of operations, or even a dedicated assembly line. Earlier, we also referred to the portion of a shop that is not associated with a specific part family as a cell: a *remainder cell*. Nevertheless, we do not consider all these groups as part of what we are calling cellular production.

Organizations that formally plan their shop layouts typically choose to group their equipment on the basis of either the function it performs (i.e., job shops) or the processing requirements of a product or group of products (i.e., flow shops). As we discussed, the purpose of grouping equipment on the basis of its function is to maximize flexibility, whereas the purpose of grouping it on the basis of processing requirements is to maximize efficiency.

Companies that adopt cellular manufacturing typically create a *pilot cell* initially to experiment with the cellular approach, and therefore most of the equipment in the shop remains in functional departments at this stage. As these firms gain experience with the cell and become convinced that it is beneficial, they begin a phase of implementing additional cells. This can be referred to as the *hybrid stage* because as the shop is incrementally converted to cells, a significant portion of the facilities are still arranged in functional departments. At some point, the formation of additional cells is terminated and the firm may or may not have the majority of its equipment arranged in cells. Often companies stop creating new cells when the volume of the remaining parts is insufficient to justify forming additional cells. To clarify the concept of a cellular layout based on product families and machine cells, we present a detailed example based on one of the more common approaches to cell formation in the next subsection.

Methods of Cell Formation

There are a variety of ways to determine what outputs should constitute a family and be produced in the same cell. Sometimes a family is dictated by the size or weight of the output; for example, huge pieces of steel may require an overhead crane to lift them onto the machines for processing. Sometimes electronic parts have special requirements for quality, such as being produced in a "clean room" or being welded in an inert gas environment. Sometimes it is obvious what family a part belongs in simply by looking at it and seeing how it was made (i.e., by what machines).

Most commonly, some form of manual determination based on human judgment is used. One relatively simple approach involves taking photographs of a sample of the parts and then manually sorting these photographs into families based on the geometry, size, or other visual characteristics of the parts. Another approach is to sort the parts based on the drawing name.

A more sophisticated manual procedure is called **production flow analysis** (PFA). In this approach, families are determined by evaluating the resource requirements for producing the outputs. Outputs that have the same complete set of resource needs are grouped into a single family. It should then be possible to cluster a set of the necessary resources together in a cell to produce that family. However, this is not always the case because there may not be enough of all resources to place each one in each of the cells that needs it or low levels of usage may not justify placing each resource in each cell. In these cases the resources can be shared between cells or additional resources acquired. For example, maternity wings at many hospitals are set up as cells having their own

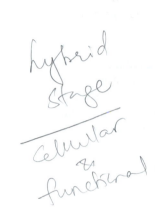

handwritten margin notes:

hybrid stage

cellular & functional

size weight

Production flow analysis ↓ based on resource requirements

[handwritten margin note: consider usage of each & every resource based on current & near-term market forecasting]

dedicated doctors, nurses, and even operating rooms. However, typically the amount of time the anesthesiologists are needed in the maternity wing does not justify dedicating anesthesiologists to the unit. Thus, the anesthesiologists split their time supporting several hospital units. At other times, even if there are sufficient quantities of the resources to assign each to the appropriate cells, two or three such resources may be needed in one cell to handle its capacity requirements while half a resource or less is needed in another cell. These difficulties are handled case by case.

The essence of PFA is to determine the *resource-output matrix* and then identify the outputs (parts or services) with common resource requirements. In manufacturing operations, the matrix is based on information contained in the part routings and is formed by listing all the outputs (parts, patients, services) across the top and all the resources (workers, machines, nurses) down the side. Then 1's are written in the matrix wherever, say, a part uses a machine. For example, Table 3.5 shows a matrix with seven parts that together require six machines. The objective is to reorder the parts and machines so that "blocks" of 1's that identify the cells are formed along the diagonal, as shown in Table 3.6. Similar resource-output matrices could be developed for service organizations. For example, a hospital might identify type of treatment as the output (e.g., maternity, cardiac, oncology) and the resources as the equipment required (X-ray, respirator, defibrillator, heart monitor). Once the treatment-equipment matrix was developed, it could be reordered to identify the resources needed to set up dedicated treatment cells.

TABLE 3.5 • Original Machine-Part Matrix

	Parts						
Machines	1	2	3	4	5	6	7
1		1			1		
2	1			1			1
3	1		1			1	
4		1					
5			1			1	
6	1						1

TABLE 3.6 • Reordered Matrix

	Parts						
Machines	7	4	1	3	6	2	5
6	1						
2	1	1	1				
3			1	1	1		
5				1	1		
1						1	1
4						1	

Cell 1 — machines 6, 2 (parts 7, 4, 1); Cell 2 — machines 3, 5 (parts 3, 6); Cell 3 — machines 1, 4 (parts 2, 5)

Note that it is acceptable for an output not to use every resource in a cell and for a resource not to process every output. However, no output should interact with a resource *outside* of its cell. Thus, in Table 3.6, part 1 is listed as needing machine 3, but this is problematic. In this case, if we could duplicate machine 3, we could put it in both cell 1 and cell 2. Or we might consider putting machine 3 in cell 2 and sending component 1 to cell 2 after it is finished in cell 1 (but this violates our desire to produce cell-complete parts). Or we could remove part 1 from the families and put it in a remainder cell (if there are other components and machines not listed in Table 3.5 within the facility).

The general guidelines for reordering the matrix by PFA are as follows:

- Incompatible resources should be in separate cells.
- Each output should be produced in only one cell.
- Any investment in duplicate resources should be minimized.
- The cells should be limited to a reasonable size.

Another, less common method of cell formation is *classification and coding*. With classification and coding, an alphanumeric code is assigned to each part on the basis of design characteristics, processing requirements, or both. Parts with similar codes can be identified and grouped into families.

Project Operations

Project operations are of large scale and finite duration; also, they are nonrepetitive, consisting of multiple, and often simultaneous, tasks that are highly interdependent. However, the primary characteristics of the tasks are their limited duration and, if the output is a physical product, their immobility during processing. Generally, staff, materials, and equipment are brought to the output and located in a nearby *staging area* until needed. Projects have particularly limited lives. Resources are brought together for the duration of the project: Some are consumed, and others, such as equipment and personnel, are deployed to other uses at the conclusion of the project. Typically, the output is unique (a dam, product development, a presidential campaign, a trial).

In designing a processing system, a number of considerations may indicate that the project form is appropriate. One of these is the rate of change in the organization's outputs. If one department must keep current on a number of markets that are rapidly changing, the typical organization would quickly fall behind its competition. The project form offers extremely short reaction times to environmental or internal changes and would thus be called for. In addition, if the tasks are for a limited duration only, the project form is indicated. Finally, the project form is chosen when the output is of a very large scale with multiple, interdependent activities requiring close coordination. During the project, coordination is achieved through frequent meetings of the representatives of the various functional areas on the project team.

One of the advantages of the project form, as noted earlier, is its ability to perform under time and cost constraints. Therefore, if meeting a due date or staying within budget is crucial, the project form is most appropriate. However, a disadvantage of the project form with its mixed personnel from different functional areas (an engineer, a scientist, a businessperson, a technician, etc.), is that it has less depth in any one technical area compared to functional organization by technical specialty. In that case, a number of specialists can be brought together to solve a problem. In addition, specialized resources (e.g. technical equipment) often cannot be justified for a project because of its low utilization; hence, generalized resources must be used instead. The project form of transformation processes is discussed in more detail in Chapter 11.

SELECTION OF A TRANSFORMATION SYSTEM

This section addresses the issue of selecting the appropriate transformation system, or mix of systems, to produce an output. From the preceding discussion, it should be clear that the five transformation systems are somewhat simplified extremes of what is likely to be observed in practice. Few organizations use one of the five forms in a pure sense; most combine two or more forms in what we call a **hybrid** shop. For example, in manufacturing computer keyboards, some parts and sub-assemblies are produced in job shops or cells but then feed into a flow shop at the final assembly line, where a batch of one model is produced. Then the line is modified to produce a batch of another model. Even in "custom" work, jobs are often handled in groups of generally common items throughout most of their processing, leaving minor finishing details such as the fabric on a couch or the facade of a house to give the impression of customizing.

Although services typically take the form of a job shop, the emphasis has recently been on trying to mass-produce them (using cells or flow shops) so as to increase volume and reduce unit costs. Some examples are fast-food outlets, multiphasic medical screening, and group life insurance. Even with services, we often find combined forms of process design: McDonald's prepares batches of Big Macs but will accept individual custom orders. Burger King uses a conveyor assembly line for its Whoppers but advertises its ability to customize its burgers to suit any taste.

The problem for the operations manager is to decide what processing form(s) is most appropriate for the organization, considering long-run efficiency, effectiveness, lead time, capacity, quality, and flexibility. Selection may be even more difficult because, as mentioned previously, it is possible to combine processing forms to attain efficiency in some portions of the production process and flexibility in other portions. It is clear that the tradeoffs must be well understood by the manager, and the expected benefits and costs must be well known.

Unfortunately, most plants do not have the luxury of time for completely reorganizing their processes. As a result, they often grow into a hodge-podge of machines and processes scattered somewhat randomly around the plant, barely resembling any of the above five forms, even if they started out with one of them.

Considerations of Volume and Variety

One of the most important factors in the design of a transformation system is establishing the volume and variety of outputs the organization will produce. High volumes tend to indicate that highly automated mass production will be necessary. High variety, on the other hand, implies the use of skilled labor and general-purpose tools and facilities.

A related consideration here is whether the output will be make-to-stock or make-to-order. A ***make-to-stock*** item is produced in batches of some size that is economical (for the firm) and then stocked (in a warehouse, on shelves, etc.). As customers purchase them, the items are withdrawn from stock. A ***make-to-order*** item is usually produced in a batch of a size set by the customer (sometimes just one) and is delivered to the customer upon its completion. Generally, make-to-stock items are produced in large volumes with low variety, whereas make-to-order items are produced in low volumes with high variety. (Quite often, *every* item is different.)

Clearly, services will not normally be of a type that can be stocked, even if every service is identical (e.g., a physical examination). Also, exceptions to these generalizations are abundant. Automobiles, for example, are made to order, but are produced in high volume and with high variety. (However, autos are really *assembled* to order; the assembly components are produced to stock.) And general-purpose machine shops often produce high volumes of low-variety items for specific customers.

Figure 3.9*a*, based on the *product-process matrix* developed by Bob Hayes and Steve Wheelwright of Harvard, illustrates these points as they relate to the various transformation systems. The horizontal axis shows volume, as measured by the batch size, and the left vertical axis shows the variety of outputs. Organizations making a single unit of output that varies each time (such as dams and custom-built machines) use the project form or sometimes the job shop. Some services also fall into this region, as indicated by the upper left tip of the oval. Job shop and cellular systems, however, are mainly used when a considerable variety of outputs are required in relatively small batches. This is particularly characteristic of services. When the size of a batch increases significantly, with a corresponding decrease in variety, then a flow shop is appropriate. Some services also fall into this category. Last, when all the output is the same and the batch is extremely large (or essentially infinite, as in the ore, petrochemical, and food and drink industries), the continuous process is appropriate. Very few services exist here.

Note that the standard, viable transformation forms lie on the diagonal of the product-process matrix. Operating at some point off this diagonal can be dangerous for the organization unless done carefully as a well-planned strategy. Essentially, no organizations operate in the upper right or lower left segments of this grid. The lower left does, however, represent manufacturing 200 years ago. If you wanted four identical dressers, say, for your four children, they were made one at a time by hand (whether identical or all different, for that matter). Today, however, it is simply too expensive to produce items this way; if the items are all identical, they are made in a large batch and then sold separately. In some cases, it is almost impossible to buy a single unit of some items, such as common tenpenny nails—you have to buy a blister-pack of ten or so. Similarly, the upper right may represent manufacturing in the future, when advanced technology can turn out great masses of completely customized products as cheaply as standard items. Currently, however, we have trouble doing this (in spite of such popular concepts as "mass customization"). Some products, however, lend themselves to approximations to this goal through such specialized techniques as assembly-to-order: fast food, Internet-purchased based computers, and so on. These firms have developed strategies, and the production techniques to accompany them, for successfully using "off-diagonal" transformation processes.

Note the overlap in the different forms. This means, for example, that on occasion some organizations will use a flow shop for outputs with smaller batches or larger variety, or both, than the outputs of organizations using a job shop. There are many possible reasons for this, including economic and historical factors. The organization may also simply be using an inappropriate transformation system. The point is that the categories are not rigid, and many variations do occur. Many organizations also use hybrids or combinations of systems, such as producing components to stock but assembling finished products to order, as in the auto industry.

Note in Figure 3.9*b* the general breakdown of make-to-order and make-to-stock with output variety and size of batch. Project forms (high variety, unit batch size) are almost always make-to-order, and continuous processing forms (no variety, infinite batch size) are almost always make-to-stock, though exceptions occasionally occur.

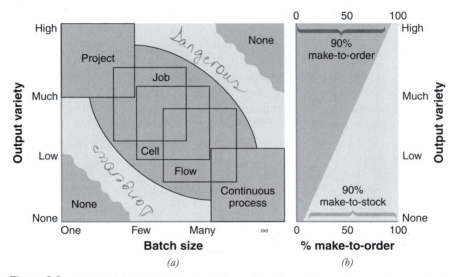

Figure 3.9   Effect of output characteristics on transformation systems—the product-process matrix.

Product and Process Life Cycle

In Chapter 2 we described the life cycle of an output: how long it takes to develop, bring to market, and catch on; how quickly it grows in popularity; how different versions are developed for different market segments; how the output reaches market saturation; how price competition emerges. A similar life cycle occurs in the production system for an output. As a result, a project form of transformation system may be used for the development of a new output, may evolve into a job shop or cellular layout as a market develops, and finally may evolve into a flow shop as full standardization and high volumes develop. (We assume here that a continuous process is not appropriate for the output.) We briefly elaborate on this production life cycle.

In the R&D stage, many variations are investigated during the development of a product. As the output is being developed, prototypes are made in small volumes in a relatively inefficient, uncoordinated manner typically in a job shop.

As demand grows and competitors enter the market, price competition begins and a cellular or flow system, with its high volume and low variable costs, becomes preferred. At the peak of the cycle, demand may increase to the point where such a system is justified.

This progress is illustrated in Figure 3.10, which presents a breakeven analysis for each of four transformation systems. The dark bold line illustrates the lowest-cost system for each stage of the life cycle. At the stage of project development and initiation (R&D and initial production), the cost of fixed equipment is nil, and labor is the predominant contributor to high variable costs. In the expansion stage, the job shop allows some tradeoff of equipment for labor with a corresponding reduction in variable unit costs, thus leading, at these volumes, to a reduction in overall unit costs. Finally, at high volumes characterizing maturity, a nearly complete replacement of expensive labor with equipment is possible, using cellular form and the flow shop.

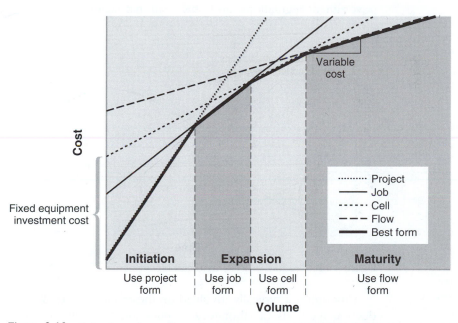

Figure 3.10   Selection of transformation systems by stage of life cycle.

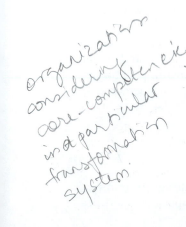

Be advised, however, that not all outputs can or should follow this sequence. The point is that the transformation system should evolve as the market and output evolve. But many organizations see their strength in operating a particular transformation system, such as R&D or low-cost production of large volumes. If their outputs evolve into another stage of the life cycle in which a different transformation system form is preferable, they drop the output (or license it to someone else) and switch to another output more appropriate to their strengths.

Failing to maintain this focus in the organization's production system can quickly result in a "white elephant"—a facility built to be efficient at one task but being inefficiently used for something else. This can also happen if the organization, in an attempt to please every customer, mixes the production of outputs that require different transformation systems. Japanese plants are very carefully planned to maintain one strong focus in each plant. If an output requiring a different process is to be produced, a new plant is acquired or built.

From the previous discussion it is clear that there is a close relationship between the design of a product or service and the design of the production system. Actually, the link is even closer than it seems. Figure 3.11 illustrates the relationship between the innovations throughout the life cycle of a product or service and innovations throughout the life cycle of its production system. At the left, when the product or service is introduced, innovations and changes in its design are frequent. At this point, the production system is more of the project or modeling/job shop form since the design is still changing (the number of *product* innovations is high). Toward the middle, the product design has largely stabilized, and cost competition is forcing innovations in the production process, particularly the substitution of cellular or flow shop machinery for labor (the number of *process* innovations is high). At the right, this phenomenon has subsided and innovations in production methods are primarily the result of competitors' actions, government regulations, and other external factors.

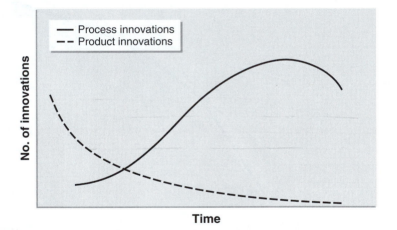

Figure 3.11   Product-process innovations over time.

Although not typically involved on the research side of such innovations in production methods (a laboratory engineering function), the operations manager is intimately involved in *applying* these developments in day-to-day production. The possible tradeoffs in such applications are many and complex. The new production system might be more expensive but might produce a higher-quality output (and thus, the repeat volume may be higher, or perhaps the price can be increased). Or the new production system might be more expensive and might produce a lower-quality output but be simpler and easier to maintain, resulting in a lower total cost and, ultimately, higher profits. Clearly, many considerations—labor, maintenance, quality, materials, capital investment, and so on—are involved in the successful application of research to operations.

Service Processes

As with the design of transformation systems for products, the design of transformation systems for services depends heavily on knowing exactly what characteristics of the service need to be emphasized: its explicit and implicit benefits, its cost, its time duration, its location, and accessibility. Knowing the importance of each of these allows the designer to make the necessary tradeoffs in costs and benefits to offer an effective yet reasonably priced service.

Unfortunately, service transformation systems are frequently implemented with little development or pretesting, which is also a major reason why so many of them fail. Consider the extensive development and testing of the McDonald's fast-food production system, of airline reservations systems, and of many life insurance policies. Each of these also illustrate the many hours of training required to use equipment and procedures properly and efficiently. Yet most new service firms frequently fail to train their personnel adequately, again inviting failure.

In most cases, the various forms and layouts of manufacturing transformation processes apply equally well to services. Flow shops are seen in fast food restaurants, job shops are seen in banks and hospitals, and projects are seen in individual services such as salons and house construction. Chapter 5 includes an example of a *service blueprint* that is commonly used for process flow and capacity analysis purposes, but also may be helpful when designing the service up front.

However, one important service element that is usually missing from manufacturing transformation design is the extensive customer contact during delivery of the service. This presents both problems and also opportunities. For one thing, the customer will often add new inputs to the delivery system or make new demands on it that were not anticipated when it was designed. In addition, customers do not arrive at smooth, even increments of time but instead tend to bunch up, as during lunch periods, and then complain when they have to wait for service. Furthermore, the customers' biased perception of the server, and the server's skills, can often influence their satisfaction with the quality of the service. Obviously, this can either be beneficial or harmful, depending on the circumstances.

On the other hand, having the customer involved in the delivery of a service can also present opportunities to improve it. Since customers know their own needs best, it is wise to let them aid in the preparation or delivery of the service—as with automatic teller machines, salad bars, and pay-at-pump gas stations. In addition to improving the quality of the service, this can save the firm money by making it unnecessary to hire additional servers. However, the customer can also negligently—and quickly—ruin a machine or a tool, and may even sue if injured by it, so the service firm must carefully consider how much self-service it is willing to let the customer perform.

Professor Richard Chase of the University of Southern California (Chase and Tansik 1983) devised a helpful way to view this customer contact when designing service delivery systems. Chase's suggestion is to evaluate whether the service is, in general, high contact or low contact, and what portions of the service, in particular, are each. The value of this analysis is that the service can be made both more efficient and more effective by separating these two portions and designing them differently. For example, the high-contact portions of the service should be handled by workers who are skilled at social interaction, whereas the low-contact portion should employ more technical workers and take advantage of labor-saving equipment. For example, a bank might have a back office where checks are encoded separately from the front office, where customers deposit them. In this back office, equipment and efficiency are the critical job elements, whereas in the front office, interpersonal skills and friendliness are critical.

Whenever possible, the low-contact portion of a service should be decoupled from the high-contact portion so that it may be conducted with efficiency, whereas the high-contact portion is conducted with grace and friendliness. Close analysis of the service tasks may also reveal opportunities for decreasing contact with the customer—through, for example, automated teller machines, phone service, self-service, or the Web, if this is appropriate—with a concomitant opportunity for improving both the efficiency and level of service. In particular, allowing customers to use the Web to obtain service (e.g., obtain account information, place orders) offers them convenient access, 24 hours per day, 365 days per year, and immediate attention (i.e., no longer being placed on hold for the next available representative).

Similarly, there may be some opportunities for increasing the amount of customer contact, such as phone or mail follow-ups after service, which should be exploited to improve the overall service and its image. The service provider should thoroughly investigate these opportunities.

Service Process Design

Like the product-process matrix for manufacturing, Schmenner has developed a similar matrix for services that not only classifies four major and quite different types of services but gives some insights on how to design the best service system. The service matrix is shown in Figure 3.12. Service systems are divided into those with high versus low contact intensity customization (similar to Chase), and whether they are capital intensive or labor intensive. Schmenner names each of the quadrants with an easily understood identifier that captures the essence of that quadrant: service factory, service shop, mass service, and professional service.

Each of the quadrants represents a unique service transformation process, with unique managerial challenges and having unique characteristics. Those services at the high contact side of the matrix have low volumes with high customization and must attain their profitability through high prices. Those on the other side with low contact and customization attain profitability through high volumes. The investment axis identifies whether the service provider puts their resources into expensive equipment or into labor. Thus, one axis is a combination of customer variety and volume (like the product-process matrix) and the other axis is based on the inputs to conduct the service. Examples of typical services in each quadrant are given in the figure.

The matrix is also useful in identifying the managerial challenges for each of the quadrants. In the low contact left end, the managerial challenge is making the service appear warm and friendly so as to attract high volumes. If the level of contact is high, the managerial challenge is trying to be optimally efficient in using capital and labor resources, while keeping prices high. If the service is equipment intensive, the challenge is to keep capital investment costs low. If instead the service is labor intensive, the challenge is to minimize wages and time spent on each customer.

The matrix is also useful in redesigning a service. For example, a firm may decide to move from one quadrant to another to better use their resources or environment. For example, a tax preparation service may start as a high-priced professional service but then move either toward a more automated service shop through computer preparation of the forms, or a less-personalized mass service using less skilled tax preparers.

low cost

	Customer contact intensity	
	Low	**High**
Capital Intensive	**Service factory** Airlines Package/postal services Hotels Recreation	**Service shop** Hospitals Computer dating Repair services Travel agencies
Labor Intensive	**Mass service** Sporting events School classes Retailing Fast food	**Professional service** Legal services Physicians Interior decorators Tax preparers

High price

High price

Figure 3.12 The service matrix.

low cost

Service Gaps

For designing services, it can be useful to inspect the service design and delivery for potential "gaps" between what the customer/client needs and what the service provider is offering (Parasuraman et al. 1988). By identifying the possible gaps in the service process, a service provider can better control the quality, productivity, cost, and performance of their service offering, thereby resulting in greater profit and market share. It can also help identify service industries where better service may offer a competitive advantage.

Figure 3.13 illustrates the concept. Essentially, there is commonly a gap between what the customer/client actually needs and what is delivered that involves gaps throughout the selection, design, and delivery process. We start with gap 1, the reasonable difference between the ideal service that the customer actually needs and what the customer expects. This gap is often influenced heavily by advertising and other communications from the service provider. Gap 2 is the imbalance between what the customer expected and his/her perception of what was actually received. Gap 3 is the final gap on the customer's side; it represents the difference between what was actually delivered and the customer's perception of that reality.

The seven remaining gaps are all on the provider's side. Gap 4 is the misperception by the service provider of what the customer truly needs. Gap 5 is the difference between that misperception and what the provider chooses to offer (the selected service). Gap 6 is the discrepancy between the service that was selected and the service that was designed. Gap 7 concerns marketing and sales and is the disparity between the designed service and what these functions understand it to be. Continuing this path, gap 8 concerns the difference between what the provider is attempting to communicate to the customer and what the customer actually understands. Then returning to the service delivery process, the last two gaps concern the contrast between what was designed and: what was perceived as delivered (gap 9), and what was actually delivered (gap 10).

Clearly, with nine possible opportunities for the service provider to not meet the customer's expectations, not to mention the customer's needs (gap 1), there are a lot of ways to fail in the service provision process. It behooves every service (and product) provider to carefully examine each of these potential failure points in their own business to see if they can improve their service provision process, especially before someone else discovers the opportunity and moves to close the gaps.

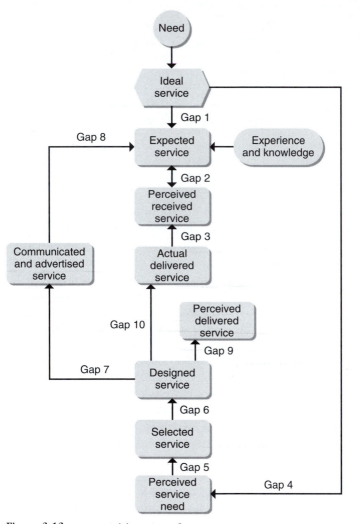

Figure 3.13 Potential locations for service gaps.

Service Guarantees and Fail Safing

Service guarantees are increasingly common among service providers who have confidence they can meet them, and who desire a competitive advantage in their industry. Package transportation companies were among the first to use them, and since then have been adopted by hotels, restaurants, and others in those service businesses that have extensive contact with the public but a reputation for poor service.

There are four major elements of a service guarantee:

1. It must be meaningful to the customer in the sense that it in fact repays the customer for the failure of the service to meet his or her expectations. A guarantee with a trivial payoff that does not satisfy the customer will just increase the customer's dissatisfaction and negate the purpose of the guarantee program in the first place.

2. The guarantee must be unconditional. Again, if there are "exceptions" that exclude the common reasons why the service might fail, the customer will only be more dissatisfied.

3. The guarantee must be easy to communicate and for the customer (and employees) to understand. If the guarantee is complex or complicated to explain, it will not serve to attract customers to the service provider. And employees who are charged with making good on the guarantee also need to fully understand it and be able to execute the guarantee provisions.

4. The guarantee must be easy to "use" in the sense of immediately invoking it when a service failure occurs. If the customer has to return home, mail in a coupon, and wait for satisfaction, the guarantee program will not achieve its purpose.

The information technology field is a leader in the development and use of formalized service guarantees, referring to them as service level agreements (SLAs). Here, a SLA is a written contract between an information technology provider and the user of the technology specifying the level of service that will be provided, typically in measurable terms. In addition to using SLAs to specify the levels of service that will be provided by external organizations, it is also becoming increasingly common for internal information system departments to develop SLAs for the other departments they support within the enterprise. Representative SLA metrics for information technology providers include the percentage of uptime, help desk response times, and the timely reporting of usage statistics.

One approach organizations use to help guarantee their service is a concept called *fail-safing*, which anticipates where a service failure might occur and installs preventive measures. The service blueprint in Chapter 5, mentioned earlier, includes potential failure points in the service process that should be considered for fail-safing. As an example of fail-safing, fast-food playgrounds are ubiquitous these days, but children who are too large can be a danger on the equipment for smaller children (or to themselves), hence the "maximum height" signs at their entrance. And outpatient health clinics give vibrating beepers to patients who sign in so they aren't "lost" in the system.

But it is not only the customer who needs fail-safing; the service providers also need their systems designed to force them into doing the service correctly. A familiar example to both service providers and customers is computer screens that disallow entries in on-line forms that don't match the protocol, or when required fields are inadvertently left empty. Another is McDonald's now-famous french-fry scoop that picks up, straightens, and optimally sizes the amount of fries for the bag, all without human contact. And when using dangerous equipment, it can't be activated unless the operator's hands and body are sensed to be out of danger.

In large part, the emergence of the concepts of service guarantees and fail-safing reflect the tremendous growth and availability of services in our economy, and the increasingly poor record of satisfactory service being provided by so many of these new services. Examples abound: telephone answering systems with unending menus that keep customers from reaching a real person who can fix their problem, airline cancellations/delays/lost baggage, and so on. Although technology is often helpful in solving our problems, it can also multiply them. We discuss the role of a variety of transformation technologies next.

NEW TRANSFORMATION TECHNOLOGIES AND REENGINEERING

Many new technologies, materials, and production methods are revolutionizing service and manufacturing operations. We are constantly bombarded with terms and concepts related to the "factory of the future" and the "office of the future." Most of these systems (though not all) are, of course, due to the advent of the computer and its inexpensive power. Organizations must be careful, however, not to use this new tool simply to automate their existing manual procedures. One of the main advantages of computerization is its ability to aid in the execution of tasks that at one time could be done only inefficiently. If operations are not reorganized to use the computer's power and flexibility efficiently, most of that advantage will be lost. It is commonly said, "Simplify and systemize before you computerize." For example, a manufacturer of helicopter engines that we are familiar with was having a problem controlling its inventory. Its solution to the problem was to purchase expensive automated equipment to store and handle the inventory. Unfortunately, the new automated equipment created more problems than it solved. After reflecting on its predicament, company managers commented that they would have been better off had they improved the efficiency of the operation by eliminating inventory in the first place and not simply thrown technology at the problem.

Taking this concept one step further, many companies are formally designing their business processes. With business process design (BPD), also known as reengineering, companies first determine their customers' needs. Then, on the basis of these needs and the capabilities offered by new technologies, the organization develops work processes to meet the needs. It is somewhat surprising that many organizations have never questioned the appropriateness of their processes, even though the technology available today is vastly different from the technology that was available when these processes were first developed.

A study by Battelle Laboratories of firms that achieve a return of more than 50 percent on investment found that the primary tangible factor common to these firms was a significant technological advantage over their competitors. The importance of technology may come as a surprise, since what we hear about success in business usually involves advertising or financial manipulation. In the next three subsections we describe some of these technologies, first for services, then for products, and last, for reengineering.

Office and Service Technologies

The computer has had a dramatic effect on the service industries, probably even more than in the manufacturing industries. As general examples, consider the optical scanner at the grocery checkout counter, the electronic cash transfer systems in the banks, the mail-sorting systems at the post office, or the energy control systems in buildings that regulate heat, water, and air conditioning.

As true as this may be for services in general, it is particularly true of services that are information intensive. Here the computer has wrought a veritable revolution in the way of doing business. The impact of the computer has perhaps been greatest in the banking industry, with its automatic teller machines and electronic transfers of funds. However, the operations of other information-intense businesses have also been dramatically altered. Examples here would include Web-based reservations systems for hotels, airlines, rental cars, and so on; security systems; telecommunications systems based on voice-over IP (VoIP); multiphasic screening; electronic classrooms; and on and on.

One tool that is, of course, having a tremendous impact is the Web. However, in addition to the public Internet, organizations are adopting the technology to create similar private networks within their own organizations, called *intranets*. Because intranets allow data to be searched for and exchanged freely among all users with access to the network, regardless of whether they are using Windows-based PCs, Apple Macintoshes, or UNIX workstations, intranets solve a number of problems for information managers.

There is little doubt that the Internet revolution has profoundly changed the way business is conducted. It is widely acknowledged that the Web offers organizations enormous opportunities to dramatically improve both efficiency and effectiveness. For example, organizations can update promotional and pricing materials instantaneously when these materials are stored electronically on a Web server. This is not typically possible with printed materials. Furthermore, providing access to promotional materials via the Web can greatly reduce the costs of distribution and printing while at the same time increasing international exposure. Finally, these promotional materials can be greatly enhanced by the inclusion of hypertext links and even audiovisual material such as streaming video.

Beyond email, perhaps the most common use of the Web is searching for information. Here, organizations can use the Web to identify suppliers, do competitive analysis, research new market opportunities, and so on. The ability to identify relevant information on the Web is based largely on the capabilities of search engines. Fortunately, the capabilities of search engines continue to improve both in terms of the quantity of information that is indexed as well as their ability to evaluate the relevance of the results returned from a given query. In fact, Google® recently adopted its search engine technology so that individuals can now search their own personal computer's files, including archives of their email messages.

As one example of an organization that makes extensive use of the Web, Federal Express originally set up a Web server for its customers in late 1994. By early 1996, 12,000 customers each day were using this service to access FedEx's package-tracking database. By 2005, FedEx's Web site was handling an average of 60 million tracking requests per month. In addition to providing its customers with a much higher level of service (they no longer have to wait for the next available customer service representative), the Web-based tracking service saves FedEx substantial amounts of money. For example, FedEx estimates that it saves $1.87 for every caller that is diverted to its website. Looking at it another way, FedEx estimates that it would cost almost $1.4 billion per year to handle the 60 million monthly tracking requests via a call center versus the $21.6 million that is currently spent processing them via the Web (or 3 cents per Web query).

In more sophisticated applications, a manager may query a database through a **decision support system** (DSS) to obtain specific information or a printed report. The DSS may use **artificial intelligence** (AI) or an **expert system** (ES) to analyze preexisting data, collect and process external data, or network to another database through telecommunications.

Artificial intelligence is the part of the field of computer science that focuses on making computers behave like, or emulate, humans. To emulate humans, AI systems manipulate symbols rather than data. In addition, they use networks, rules, and processing procedures rather than algorithms. By using such relationships, AI systems can represent and manipulate abstract ideas and activities. With these abilities, AI systems can make assumptions when needed and can reason inductively, correcting their mistakes as they go by changing their rule systems. This makes them excellent for relatively straightforward decisions in which the data may change but the process is constant. AI will become especially useful in services where single decisions are relatively frequent but not extremely complex, such as repairing autos or handling paperwork. AI can also act as an interpreter between workers and other computerized systems, telling the human what the computerized system needs and acting as a general interface and facilitator.

Expert systems comprise one type of artificial intelligence and have, to date, received most of the attention in this area. These systems are individually designed to capture the expertise of particular individuals or groups with respect to one task or field. Thus, an expert system allows less experienced workers to have the expertise needed to help them make decisions. Quite a few expert systems have been devised for design, testing, repair, and automation.

What will be the effect of all this technology on jobs and the work force? It is clear that the technology will eliminate the simpler role jobs, just as it is now doing in manufacturing. New technologies also open up new jobs, however. A hundred years ago, if we had told the farmers that, by 1990, only one person in a thousand would work on a farm, they too would have asked what the unemployed farmers would do. Obviously, the standard of living rose, new jobs opened up, the work week was reduced, and other such changes accommodated the exodus from the farm. Undoubtedly, that will happen again.

Manufacturing Technologies

Computer-Aided Manufacturing (CAM) was originally the specification by a computer of the machining instructions to produce a product, but has now been expanded to include a wide array of computerized technologies used by engineers, planners, and designers for product design and production planning, as well as manufacturing.

For example, in *computer-aided design* (CAD), the engineer forms a drawing on the computer screen with the keyboard, a light pen, or a mouse and pad. Lines can be specified through coordinates, or the points can be "spotted" on the screen or pad and the computer will draw the line between the points. As the engineer designs the part, the CAD systems can be instructed to enlarge certain portions for a closer examination, rotate the design to show it from different angles, and so on. In addition, the CAD software can automatically check designs, such as the fit of parts that will be assembled together. And once a part is completed and stored, if the engineer needs to design a new part, the stored design of a similar part can be retrieved and changes to the design made right on the computer screen. This saves considerable time, because the engineer doesn't have to develop each new design from scratch.

In addition, many marketing, R&D, and manufacturing activities are facilitated through the use of the electronic database on the parts. For example, the CAD database of parts can be used to obtain the bill of materials or the dimensions of critical parts. And computer-aided engineering (CAE) software uses CAD designs but then subjects them to stress, loads, and vibrations to determine their strength and reliability. And *computer-aided process planning* (CAPP) will turn a part design into a manufacturing production plan, including routings, operations, inspections, and times. Such a system is invaluable in overcoming problems that frequently occur at the interface between engineering and manufacturing.

The capabilities of these systems have been growing tremendously in the last few years, while the prices of the software have fallen just as fast. For example, many excellent microcomputer CAD packages are now available. Productivity increases on the order of 300 and 400 percent are typical. In addition to being used for designing parts and products, CAD is used by architects to design buildings and bridges; designers to create new children's toys; automobile stylists to design futuristic cars; fire analysts to study the historical pattern of fires in a city and design new routes for fire engines and emergency vehicles; jewelers to design rings and other jewelry; and physicians to develop replacements for degenerated or irreparably injured bones.

Numerical control (NC) is one of the oldest technologies available in manufacturing. NC allows a machine to operate automatically through coded numerical instructions. Previously, these instructions were on punched paper tape, which directed the operations of a machine (e.g., a player piano) in the same way that an operator would. When the punched tape was replaced by a computer system attached to the machine, the operation—called *computer numerical control* (CNC)—was much more efficient. More recently, larger computers have been directing the activities of multiple machines through *direct numerical control* (DNC) and material-handling systems such as robots and carts as well, orchestrating their functions and movements to produce the desired parts and goods in much less time. One might think that to justify the expense of these systems, relatively high volumes of standard products would need to be made on them. However, this is directly contrary to their purpose, which is to capitalize on their flexibility and produce *small* batches of a high variety of products. (Nevertheless, the net result of producing a large amount of goods to pay for the expensive equipment is still the goal; it is simply done through greater variety.)

Robots have come of age. Initially used for fairly simple tasks such as welding and spray-painting, these machines have increased tremendously in ability in the last few years. They have much more sophisticated sensors and can perform very complex and difficult tasks, not only in production but also in assembly. A wide variety of robots have been developed to perform a number of highly varied tasks: painting, welding, positioning, lifting, assembly, handling materials, and drilling.

They are particularly valuable for jobs that are either uncomfortable for a human to perform (too hot, too dirty, and so forth) or too dangerous (because of nuclear contamination, corrosive chemicals, poisonous fumes, or the like). When augmented by a *vision* system, a robot can perform an even broader array of tasks such as sorting through parts to select the proper one, picking up a randomly oriented part without damaging it, or inspecting a part for dimensional accuracy or flaws. Clearly, when one technology is wedded to another, such as robots to vision, tremendous increases in capability are possible.

Flexible manufacturing systems (FMSs) are virtually unmanned manufacturing. These systems include a series of machining centers, an automated materials-handling system, and other possible peripherals such as a wash station, coordinate measuring machine, grinder, storage racks, robots, and/or loading and unloading stations. The materials management system is typically a series of automated guided vehicles (carts) for transporting pallets of materials, guided by an embedded wire in the floor. The carts, machines, cranes, and robots are programmed and supervised by a host computer, which interfaces with the plant computer when it needs additional data or is feeding data back.

The advantages of the FMS are those of cellular production (e.g., less space, faster response, low variable costs), as well as those of NC (e.g., consistency, quality, minimal labor expense, preprogrammed machining instructions (no blueprint reading). In spite of their name, FMSs are "flexible" only in a limited sense. For example, most of them are machining systems. None of them could produce toasters or motorcycles. Thus, their flexibility is only relative to what is normally produced with such machines. Although FMSs have given significant improvements in productivity, quality, space requirements, labor, and capacity, the cost of these systems is extremely high—in the millions of dollars—and not all of them have been successful. Therefore, to make them productive in any firm, planning is essential.

Business Process Design (Reengineering)

In addition to formally designing transformation systems, many organizations are now formally designing all their important business processes. It is perhaps most commonly referred to as ***reengineering***, but a wide variety of other names are also frequently used, such as *business process reengineering, business process engineering, business process innovation,* and *business process design* (BPD) or *redesign*. To compound the confusion, often managers incorrectly use terms such as *downsizing* and *restructuring* interchangeably with BPD.

To help put BPD in perspective, consider that the roots of the functional organization date back to the late 1700s, when Adam Smith proposed his concept of the division of labor in *An Inquiry into the Nature and Causes of the Wealth of Nations* (1776). Referring to the 17 operations required to produce a pin, Smith argued that assigning one task to each of 17 workers would be more efficient and would produce more pins than having 17 workers each autonomously perform all 17 tasks.

Although there have been dramatic advances in technology since Smith first proposed the division of labor, it is only recently that organizations have begun to challenge the concept and look for better ways to organize and integrate work.

Indeed, if you were to compare how companies are organized today and how they were organized 20 or 30 years ago, you would find that little has changed in their organizational structures. This is true despite technological advances such as personal computers, fax machines, cellular phones, laser printers, the World Wide Web, compact disks, spreadsheets, word processors, client–server computing, groupware, e-mail, and cable modems, to name a few.

Initially, when these technologies were first adopted by organizations, the dramatic improvements in performance that were expected did not materialize. One popular explanation for this is that organizations were not taking advantage of the capabilities the new technologies offered. Rather, companies were simply using technology to speed up and automate existing practices. Clearly, if an activity or a set of activities is not effective to begin with, performing it faster and with less human intervention does not automatically make it effective.

For instance, one major financial institution reported that more than 90 steps were required for an office worker to get office supplies. These steps mostly involved filling out forms and getting the required signatures. Given the capabilities of information technology, it is certainly true that these steps could be automated and speeded up. For example, a computer system could be developed to generate all the forms automatically and then automatically E-mail them to the appropriate person for authorization. However, is automating all these steps the best solution? Might it not make more sense to eliminate most of them? Consider that even if the forms are generated and dispatched faster, valuable managerial time is still being used to examine and approve these requests every time an employee needs a pad of paper or ballpoint pen. Indeed, when the cost of the controls is weighed against the benefits, it might be much more effective to give employees access to the supply cabinet to retrieve their own supplies as needed. Dr. Hammer uses the term *paving cow paths* to describe organizations that simply adopt a new technology without considering the capabilities it offers to perform work in entirely new and better ways.

The Nynex example at the beginning of this chapter provides a glimpse of several major themes associated with BPD. First, BPD's primary objective is improved customer service. This was clearly illustrated by Nynex's four core processes, as each began with the word *customer*. This brings us to a second theme associated with BPD, a concern with making *quantum* improvements in performance rather than small, *incremental* improvements. Nynex's goal to lower its operating expenses by 35 to 40 percent certainly represents a quantum improvement, as does its expected 1025 percent internal rate of return.

A third important theme of BPD is the central role of technology. When many of the new information technologies were initially adopted by companies, the expected improvements in organizational efficiency and effectiveness often did not materialize. On closer examination, it was discovered that many companies were adapting new technology to fit current business practices rather than attempting to take advantage of the capabilities offered by the technology to perform activities in perhaps entirely different and better ways. The early 1990s marked the beginning of the reengineering movement—companies started to consider the capabilities that technology offered in relationship to the way work was performed and organized.

Michael Hammer and Steven Stanton, in their book *The Reengineering Revolution* (New York: Harper Business, 1995), define reengineering as "the fundamental rethinking and **radical redesign** of business **processes** to bring about **dramatic**

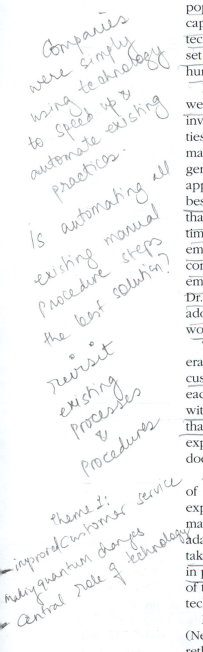

Companies were simply using technology to speed up & automate existing practices.

Is automating all existing manual procedure steps the best solution?

revisit existing processes & procedures

theme 1: improved customer service

making quantum changes

central role of technology

improvements in performance" (p. 3). The keywords *radical, redesign, process,* and *dramatic* are particularly important to understanding the concept of reengineering or BPD. The word **radical** is used to signify that the purpose of BPD is to *profoundly* change the way work is performed, not to make *superficial* changes. It has to do with understanding the foundation upon which work is based and eliminating old ways that no longer make sense. In other words, it refers to *reinventing* the way work is performed and organized, not simply improving it. Radically changing work is often best accomplished by starting with a clean slate and making no assumptions about how work activities are performed.

The second keyword, **redesign**, denotes the fact that BPD is concerned with the design of work. Typically people think of design as being primarily applicable to products. However, the way work is accomplished can also be designed. In fact, Hammer and Stanton point out that having intelligent, capable, well-trained, motivated employees is of little value if work is badly designed to begin with.

The third keyword is **process**. Although all organizations perform processes, it was not until recently that they began organizing work on the basis of these processes. Partly as a result of total quality management (TQM, discussed in Chapter 4), companies began to focus more on meeting customers' needs. As they did this, they soon realized that customers are not particularly interested in the individual activities that are performed to create a product or service. Rather, they are more concerned about the final result of these activities. Of course, because companies were not organized on the basis of their processes, they were not managed on the basis of processes either. Therefore, no one was assigned responsibility for the entire process that created the results of interest to the customer. Using the scenario of product design, a typical company would have departmental managers to oversee market research, manufacturing, and customer service. However, there was no manager responsible for ensuring that the results of all these activities were meeting customers' requirements. We use the term **process-centered** to refer to companies that have organized their work activities on the basis of specific value-creating processes.

The last keyword is **dramatic**. BPD is concerned with making quantum improvements in performance, not small or incremental improvements. Thus, BPD focuses on achieving breakthroughs in performance. A company that lowers its lead time by 10 percent from the previous year does not exemplify a dramatic improvement. On the other hand, a company that reduces its lead time from three weeks to three days does.

To illustrate these concepts, consider the experiences of IBM Credit Corporation. IBM Credit is in the business of financing purchases of IBM office equipment. Numerous companies—including General Motors, Ford, Chrysler, and General Electric—are in the lending business. These companies have found that operating financial units can be extremely profitable in addition to offering customers a higher level of service.

Originally, IBM Credit was organized into functional departments. The steps involved in processing a credit request are shown in Figure 3.14. The process began when an IBM sales rep closed a deal and the customer wanted to finance the purchase through IBM Credit. In this case the sales rep would relay the pertinent information to one of 14 order loggers at IBM Credit. The order loggers sat in a conference room and manually wrote down on pieces of paper the information supplied by the sales reps. Periodically during the day, the pieces of paper were

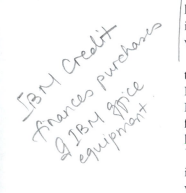

carted upstairs to the credit department. Employees in the credit department entered the pertinent information into a computer to check the borrower's creditworthiness. The results of this check were then recorded on another piece of paper.

Next, the documents would be transferred to the business practices department. This department would modify the standard loan covenant in response to specific requests by customers. The business practices department used its own computer system. After being processed in the business practices department, the documents were transported to the pricing department, where pricers entered the data into a program running on a personal computer to determine the appropriate interest rate. Finally, the entire dossier was transported to an administrator, who converted all the information into a "quote letter." The quote letter was then sent by Federal Express to the field sales rep.

The sales reps were extremely dissatisfied with this process. First of all, the entire process took an average of 6 days and sometimes as long as two weeks. What salesperson wants to give his or her customers two weeks to think over a purchase? On top of this, when a sales rep called to check on the status of a customer's credit request, often the request could not even be located.

As a result of complaints from the sales reps, a manager at IBM Credit decided to investigate the problem. The first thing this manager wanted to determine was how much work time actually went into processing a credit request. To determine this, the manager walked an actual request through the entire process. First, he recorded the time it took to log an actual order. Then, he took the order that was just called in and personally carried it to the credit department. Arriving at the credit department, he selected a worker at random and told the worker to stop what he or she was currently working on and perform the credit check. After repeating this in the other departments, the manager determined that the actual processing time of a credit request was about 90 minutes. Thus, out of an average of six days, each application was being processed only about 90 minutes, indicating a significant opportunity for improvement.

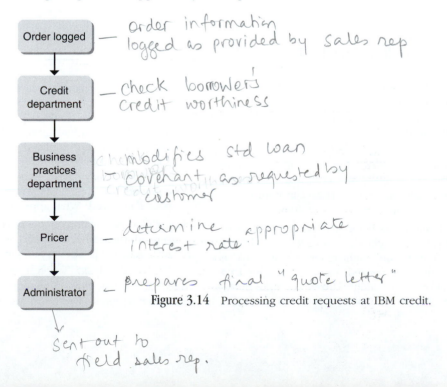

Figure 3.14   Processing credit requests at IBM credit.

IBM Credit's approach to improving this process was to combine all these activities into one job called a *deal structurer.* Thus, one worker handled all the activities required to process a credit request, from logging the information to writing the quote letter. As a result of using deal structurers, turnaround times were reduced to an average of four hours. Furthermore, with a small reduction in head count, the number of deals processed by IBM Credit increased 100 times (not 100 percent). Do these results qualify as dramatic?

Given these results, you may wonder why IBM Credit had ever adopted a functional organizational structure in the first place. To answer this, let's put ourselves in the shoes of a manager at IBM Credit. Suppose we were asked to develop an organization to process credit requests. One requirement that might occur to us is that the process should be able to handle any possible type of credit request. Given this requirement, if you look again at Figure 3.14, you will see that IBM Credit's original functional arrangement accomplishes this objective. For example, no matter how difficult checking a particular borrower's creditworthiness might be, the process could handle it, because everyone in the credit department was a highly trained specialist. The same is true of all the other departments. However, another important question is: How often will this specialized knowledge be needed? In other words, what percent of the credit requests are relatively routine and what percent require deep, specialized knowledge? As IBM found out, the vast majority of credit requests could be handled relatively routinely.

Another explanation for why IBM Credit originally created a functional organization relates to the technology that was available at the time. A key ingredient that allowed IBM Credit to move to the deal-structurer model was advances in technology. For example, spreadsheets, databases, and other decision support tools were adopted so that the deal structurers could quickly check interest rates, access standard clauses, and check the creditworthiness of the borrowers. In effect, the new technology allowed the deal structurers, who had only general knowledge, to function as though they had the specialized knowledge of an expert in a particular discipline.

EXPAND YOUR UNDERSTANDING

1. When a line cannot be perfectly balanced, some people will have more work time than others within each cycle. What might be a solution for this situation?

2. A current sociological trend is to move away from paced lines. Yet increasing automation is pushing workers to match their work pace to that of machines and computers. How can both of these trends be happening at the same time?

3. If a job shop was being laid out in a third-world country, how might the procedure be different? What other factors might enter in that would not exist in an industrialized country? Might the layout also differ among industrialized countries such as Europe and Japan? How about a flow shop?

4. In highly automated facilities, firms frequently increase the job responsibilities of the skilled workers who remain after automation has replaced the manual laborers, although there is less potential for applying their skills. Workers complain that they are under increased pressure to perform but have less control over the automated equipment. Is this ethical on the part of the companies involved? What approach would be better?

5. Cellular production is often conducted in a U-shaped (horseshoe-shaped) cell, rather than the rectangular cells shown in Figure 3.7*b.* What might be the advantages of this U shape?

6. What benefits would a virtual cell obtain, and not obtain, compared with a physical cell?

7. A number of firms are moving toward mini-factories. What advantages might this offer over straight cellular production?

8. If efficiency, variety, and so on are the important measures of the low-contact, or no-contact portion of a service, what are the important measures of the high-contact portion?

9. As the process life cycle changes with the product life cycle, should a firm change along with it or move into new products more appropriate to its existing process? What factors must be considered in this decision?

10. In Figure 3.9, showing the five transformation systems, why don't firms operate in the regions marked "none"?

11. Identify the similarities in Figures 3.9 and 3.12. Also, the differences.

APPLY YOUR UNDERSTANDING
Paradise State University

Paradise State University (PSU) is a medium-sized private university offering both undergraduate and graduate degrees. Students typically choose Paradise State because of its emphasis on high levels of interaction and relatively small classes. University policy prohibits classes with more than 75 students (unless special permission is obtained from the provost), and the target class size is 25 students. All courses are taught by tenure-track faculty members with appropriate terminal degrees. Faculty members teach two courses each semester.

The Business School at PSU offers only an MBA degree in one of six areas of concentration: accounting, finance, general management, management information systems (MIS), marketing, and operations management (OM). The MBA program is a one-year (two-semester) lockstep program. Since the Business School does not offer undergraduate business courses, students entering the program are required to have completed all the undergraduate business prerequisites from an accredited university. The faculty is organized into six functional departments. The table below lists the number of faculty members in each department and the average number of students each year who choose a particular concentration. Students are not permitted to have double concentrations, and PSU does not offer minors at the graduate level.

Department	Faculty	Number of Students per Year
Accounting	8	100
Finance	6	40
General Management	7	70
MIS	10	150
Marketing	6	50
OM	10	30

The number of courses required by each concentration in each department are listed in the table below. For example, a student concentrating in accounting is required to take four accounting classes, one finance class, one management class, one MIS course, one marketing class, and two OM classes.

Concentration	Accounting	Finance	Management	MIS	Marketing	OM
Accounting	4	1	1	1	1	2
Finance	1	4	1	1	1	2
General Management	1	1	4	1	1	2
MIS	1	1	1	4	1	2
Marketing	1	1	1	1	4	2
OM	1	1	1	1	1	5

Questions

1. How many student semesters must each department teach each semester? Given the target class size—25 students—are there enough faculty members?
2. Conceptually, how could the cellular production approach be applied to the Business School?
3. What would be the advantages and disadvantages of adopting a cellular approach at the Business School? As a student, would you prefer a functional organization or a cellular organization? As a faculty member, what would you prefer?
4. On the basis of the information given, develop a rough plan detailing how the Business School faculty might be assigned to cells.

Valley County Medical Clinic

Valley County operates a walk-in medical clinic (VCMC) to meet the nonacute medical needs of its approximately 15,000 citizens. Patients arriving at the clinic are served on a first-come, first-served basis.

As part of a new total quality management program, VCMC conducted an in-depth, four-month study of its current operations. A key component of the study was a survey, distributed to all county citizens. The purpose of the survey was to identify and prioritize areas most in need of improvement. An impressive 44 percent of the surveys were returned and deemed usable. Follow-up analysis indicated that the people who responded were representative of the population served by the clinic. After the results were tabulated, it was determined that the walk-in medical clinic was located near the bottom of the rankings, indicating a great deal of dissatisfaction with the clinic. Preliminary analysis of the respondents' comments indicated that people were reasonably satisfied with the treatment they received at the clinic but were very dissatisfied with the amount of time they had to wait to see a caregiver.

Upon arriving at the clinic, patients receive a form from the receptionist requesting basic biographical information and the nature of the medical condition for which treatment is being sought. Completing the form typically requires two to three minutes. After the form is returned to the receptionist, it is time-stamped and placed in a tray. Clerks collect the forms and retrieve the corresponding patients' files from the basement. The forms typically remain in the tray for about five minutes before being picked up, and it takes the clerk approximately 12 minutes to retrieve the files. After a patient's file is retrieved, the form describing the medical problem is attached to it with a paper clip, and it is placed in a stack with other files. The stack of files is ordered according to the time stamps on the forms.

When the nurse practitioners finish with their current patient, they select the next file from the stack and escort that patient to one of the treatment rooms. On average, files remain in the stack for ten minutes, but this varies considerably depending on the time of day and the day of the week. On Monday mornings, for example, it is common for files to remain in the stack for 30 minutes or more.

Once in the treatment room, the nurse practitioner reads over the form describing the patient's ailment. Next, the nurse discusses the problem with the patient while taking some standard measurements such as blood pressure and temperature. The nurse practitioner then makes a rough diagnosis, based on the measurements and symptoms, to determine if the ailment is one of the 20 that state law permits nurse practitioners to treat. If the condition is treatable by the nurse practitioner, a more thorough diagnosis is undertaken and treatment is prescribed. It typically takes about five minutes for the nurse practitioners to make the rough diagnosis and another 20 minutes to complete the detailed diagnosis and discuss the treatment with the patient. If the condition (as roughly diagnosed) is not treatable by the nurse practitioner, the patient's file is placed in the stack for the on-duty MD. Because of the higher cost of MDs versus nurse practitioners, there is typically only one MD on duty at any time.

Thus, patients wait an average of 25 minutes for the MD. On the other hand, because of their higher training and skill, the MDs are able to diagnose and treat the patients in 15 minutes, despite the fact that they deal with the more difficult and less routine cases. Incidentally, an expert system for nurse practitioners is being tested at another clinic that—if shown to be effective—would initially double the number of ailments treatable by nurse practitioners and over time would probably increase the list even more, as the tool continued to be improved.

Questions

1. Develop a flow chart for the medical clinic that shows the times of the various activities. Is the patients' dissatisfaction with the clinic justified?
2. What probably are the patients' key requirements for the clinic?
3. What assumptions are being made about the way work is performed and treatment administered at the clinic?
4. Redesign the process of treating patients at the clinic using technologies you are familiar with, to better meet the patients' needs as listed in question 2.

X-Opoly, Inc.

X-Opoly, Inc., was founded by two first-year college students to produce a knockoff real estate board game similar to the popular Parker Brothers' game Monopoly®. Initially, the partners started the company just to produce a board game based on popular local landmarks in their small college town, as a way to help pay for their college expenses. However, the game was a big success and because they enjoyed running their own business, they decided to pursue the business full-time after graduation.

X-Opoly has grown rapidly over the last couple of years, designing and producing custom real estate trading games for universities, municipalities, chambers of commerce, and lately even some businesses. Orders range from a couple of hundred games to an occasional order for several thousand. This year X-Opoly expects to sell 50,000 units and projects that its sales will grow 25 percent annually for the next five years.

X-Opoly's orders are either for a new game board that has not been produced before, or repeat orders for a game that was previously produced. If the order is for a new game, the client first meets with a graphic designer from X-Opoly's art department and the actual game board is designed. The design of the board can take anywhere from a few hours to several weeks, depending on how much the client has thought about the game before the meeting. All design work is done on personal computers.

After the design is approved by the client, a copy of the computer file containing the design is transferred electronically to the printing department. Workers in the printing department load the file onto their own personal computers and print out the board design on special decals, 19.25 inches by 19.25 inches, using high-quality color inkjet printers. The side of the decal that is printed on is usually light gray, and the other side contains an adhesive that is covered by a removable backing.

The printing department is also responsible for printing the property cards, game cards, and money. The money is printed on colored paper using standard laser printers. Ten copies of a particular denomination are printed on each 8.5-inch by 11-inch piece of paper. The money is then moved to the cutting department, where it is cut into individual bills. The property cards and game cards are produced similarly, the major difference being that they are printed on material resembling posterboard.

In addition to cutting the money, game cards, and property cards, the cutting department also cuts the cardboard that serves as the substrate for the actual game board. The game board consists of two boards created by cutting a single 19-inch by 19.25-inch piece of cardboard in half, yielding two boards each measuring 19.25 inches by 9.5 inches. After being cut, game boards, money, and cards are stored in totes in a work-in-process area and delivered to the appropriate station on the assembly line as needed.

Because of its explosive growth, X-Opoly's assembly line was never formally planned. It simply evolved into the 19 stations shown in the following table.

Station Number	Task(s) Performed at Station	Time to Perform Task
1	Get box bottom and place plastic money tray in box bottom. Take two dice from bin and place in box bottom in area not taken up by tray.	10 seconds
2	Count out 35 plastic houses and place in box bottom.	35 seconds
3	Count out 15 plastic hotels and place in box bottom.	15 seconds
4	Take one game piece from each of eight bins and place them in box bottom.	15 seconds
5	Take one property card from each of 28 bins. Place rubber band around property cards and place cards in box bottom.	40 seconds
6	Take one orange card from each of 15 bins. Place rubber band around cards and place cards in box bottom.	20 seconds
7	Take one yellow card from each of 15 bins. Take orange cards from box and remove rubber band. Place yellow cards on top of orange cards. Place rubber band around yellow and orange cards and place cards in box bottom.	35 seconds
8	Count out 25 $500 bills and attach to cardboard strip with rubber band. Place money in box bottom.	30 seconds
9	Count out 25 $100 bills. Take $500 bills from box bottom and remove rubber band. Place $100 bills on top of $500 bills. Attach rubber band around money and place in box bottom.	40 seconds
10	Count out 25 $50 bills. Take $500 and $100 bills from box bottom and remove rubber band. Place $50 bills on top. Attach rubber band around money and place in box bottom.	40 seconds
11	Count out 50 $20 bills. Take money in box and remove rubber band. Place $20 bills on top. Attach rubber band around money and place in box bottom.	55 seconds
12	Count out 40 $10 bills. Take money in box and remove rubber band. Place $10 bills on top. Attach rubber band around money and place in box bottom.	45 seconds
13	Count out 40 $5 bills. Take money in box and remove rubber band. Place $5 bills on top. Attach rubber band around money and place in box bottom.	45 seconds
14	Count out 40 $1 bills. Take money in box and remove rubber band. Place $1 bills on top. Attach rubber band around money and place in box bottom.	45 seconds
15	Take money and remove rubber band. Shrink wrap money and place back in box bottom.	20 seconds
16	Take houses, hotels, dice, and game pieces and place in bag. Seal bag and place bag in box.	30 seconds
17	Place two cardboard game board halves in fixture so that they are separated by $\frac{1}{4}$ in. Peel backing off of printed game board decal. Align decal over board halves and lower it down. Remove board from fixture and flip it over. Attach solid blue backing decal. Flip game board over again and fold blue backing over front of game board, creating a $\frac{1}{4}$-in. border. Fold game board in half and place in box covering money tray, game pieces, and cards.	90 seconds
18	Place game instructions in box. Place box top on box bottom. Shrink wrap entire box.	30 seconds
19	Place completed box in carton.	10 seconds

Questions

1. What kind(s) of transformation system(s) does X-Opoly use?
2. What would be involved in switching the assembly line over from the production of one game to the production of another?
3. What is the cycle time of the 19-station line? What is its efficiency?
4. What is the line's maximum capacity per day, assuming that it is operated for one 8-hour shift less two 15-minute breaks? Assuming that X-Opoly operates 200 days per year, what is its annual capacity? How does its capacity compare with its projected demand?

5. On the basis of the task descriptions, develop a precedence graph for the assembly tasks. (Assume that tasks performed in the 19 stations cannot be further divided.) Using these precedence relationships, develop a list of recommendations for rebalancing the line in order to improve its performance.

6. What would be the impact on the line's capacity and efficiency if your recommendations were implemented?

EXERCISES

1. Given the following machine-component matrix, form cells using PFA.

Components

Machines	1	2	3	4	5	6	7
1	1				1		
2				1		1	
3			1	1			
4		1			1		1
5	1						1

2. a. Given the following load matrix of a DVD player factory in Nagoya, Japan, find the best layout and its cost based on rectangular distances.

Department

Department	1	2	3	4	5	6
1	—	4	6	2	0	7
2		—	3	5	1	3
3				2	6	5
4				—	5	2
5					—	3

b. Resolve part a if the rates are ¥4 from odd to even departments, ¥5 from even to odd, ¥6 from odd to odd, and ¥7 from even to even.

3. An insurance office in London is laid out as in the following table. The office manager is considering switching departments 2 and 6 to reduce transport costs. Should this be done? (Use rectangular (rather than shortest) distances. Assume that offices are 10 feet on a side.) What is the difference in annual cost, assuming a 250-day work year?

1	2	3
4	5	6

Daily Trip Matrix

From	To 1	2	3	4	5	6
1	x	40	x	x	x	40
2	30	x	20	30	60	0
3	x	70	x	x	x	20
4	x	0	x	x	x	30
5	x	10	x	x	x	0
6	40	50	20	0	10	x

Trip Cost (to any department) per foot from

1	2	3	4	5	6
£0.02	£0.03	£0.01	£0.03	£0.02	£0.02

4. Re-layout the office in Exercise 3 given the following desired closeness ratings.

Department	1	2	3	4	5	6
1		I	A	X	O	U
2			X	E	I	O
3				O	X	I
4					I	E
5						A
6						

5. Demand for a certain subassembly in a toy manufacturing facility at the North Pole is 96 items per 8-hour shift of elves. The following six tasks are required to produce one subassembly.

Task	Time Required (minutes)	Predecessor Tasks
a	4	—
b	5	a
c	3	a
d	2	b
e	1	b,c
f	5	d,e

What is the required cycle time? Theoretically, how many stations will be required? Balance the line. What is the line's efficiency?

6. An assembly line has the following tasks (times shown in minutes).

   a. Six assemblies are required per hour. Balance the line.

   b. What is the efficiency of the line?

   c. Rebalance the line if task e has a time of 1 minute instead of 3.

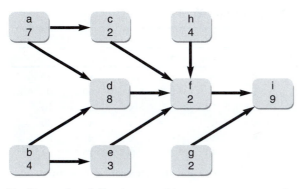

7. Given the following machine-component matrix, form cells using PFA.

Machines	\multicolumn{5}{c}{Components}				
	1	2	3	4	5
1				1	1
2			1		
3	1	1			
4				1	1
5			1	1	
6					1
7		1			
8	1				

8. Kobenhavn Fine Products wishes to balance its line to meet a daily demand of 240 units. Kobenhavn works an 8-hour day on the following tasks:

Task	Time (mins)	Preceding Tasks
1	0.4	none
2	0.3	1
3	1.1	1
4	0.2	3
5	0.5	2
6	0.3	3
7	0.6	5
8	0.6	4, 6, 7

   a. Find the cycle time, efficiency, and minimum number of stations. Balance the line.

   b. Rebalance the line if task 8 requires 0.7 minutes.

9. If the times in Problem 8 were normally distributed, how might Crystal Ball be useful in solving the problem?

BIBLIOGRAPHY

Anupindi, R., S. Chopra, S. D. Deshmukh, J. A. van Mieghem, and E. Zemel. *Managing Business Process Flows*, Upper Saddle River, NJ: Prentice Hall, 1999.

Bradley, T. "Fender Blenders." *1988–1989 Guitar Buyers' Guide*. 129–133.

"He's Gutsy, Brilliant, and Carries an Ax." *Business Week*. (May 9, 1994): 62–66.

Bylinski, G. "The Digital Factory." *Fortune* (November 14, 1994): 92–107.

Chase, R. B., and S. Dasu. "Want to Perfect Your Company's Service? Use Behavioral Science." *Harvard Business Review* (June 2001): 78–84.

Chase, R. B., and D. M. Stewart. "Make Your Service Fail-Safe." *Sloan Management Review* (Spring 1994): 35–44.

Chase, R. B., and D. A. Tansik. "The Customer Contact Model for Organization Design." *Management Science*, 29 (September 1983): 1037–1050.

Davis, T. R. V. "Different Service Firms, Different Core Competencies." *Business Horizons* (September–October 1999): 23–33.

Dennis, D., and J. Meredith. "An Empirical Analysis of Process Industry Transformation Systems." *Management Science*, 46 (August 2000): 1085–1099.

Ferras, L. "Continuous Improvements in Electronics Manufacturing." *Production and Inventory Management Journal* (Second Quarter 1994): 1–5.

Firnstahl, T. W. "My Employees Are My Service Guarantee." *Harvard Business Review* (July–August 1999): 28–32.

Fitzsimmons, J. A., and M. J. Fitzsimmons. *Service Management: Operations, Strategy, and Information Technology*, 3rd ed. New York: Irwin/McGraw-Hill, 2001.

Francis, R. L., L. F. McGinnis, Jr., and J. A. White. *Facility Layout and Location: An Analytical Approach*, 2nd ed. Englewood Cliffs, N.J.: Prentice-Hall, 1998.

Gage, D. "FedEx: Personal Touch," www.baselinemage.com, January 13, 2005.

Hammer, M. *Beyond Reengineering*. New York: Harper Business, 1996.

Hartvigsen, D. *SimQuick: Process Simulation with Excel*. 2nd ed. Upper Saddle River, NJ: Prentice Hall, 2004.

Hayes, R. H., and S. C. Wheelwright. "Link Manufacturing Process and Product Life Cycles." *Harvard Business Review* (January–February 1979): 133–140.

Heskett, J. L., W. E. Sasser, Jr., and L. A. Schlesinger. *The Service Profit Chain*. New York: Free Press, 1997.

Hyer, N. L., and K. H. Brown. "The Discipline of Real Cells." *Journal of Operations Management*, Vol. 17 (1999): 557–574.

Khurana, A. "Managing Complex Production Processes." *Sloan Management Review*, 40 (Winter 1999): 85–98.

Metters, R., K. King-Metters, and M. Pullman. *Successful Service Operations Management*. Mason, OH: South-Western, 2003.

Parasuraman, A., V. A. Zeithaml, and L. L. Berry. "SERVQUAL: A Multiple-Item Scale for Measuring Consumer Perceptions of Service Quality." *Journal of Retailing*, 64 (1988): 12–40.

Rohleder, T. R., and E. A. Silver. "A Tutorial on Business Process Improvement." *Journal of Operations Management*, 15 (May 1997): 139–154.

Spear, S., and H. K. Bowen. "Decoding the DNA of the Toyota Production System." *Harvard Business Review* (September–October 1999): 95–106.

Stoner, D. L., K. J. Tice, and J. E. Ashton. "Simple and Effective Cellular Approach to a Job Machine Shop." *Manufacturing Review*, 2 (June 1989): 119–128.

Verity, J. W. "A Company That's 100% Virtual." *Business Week* (November 21, 1994): 85.

CHAPTER 4

Six Sigma for Process and Quality Improvement

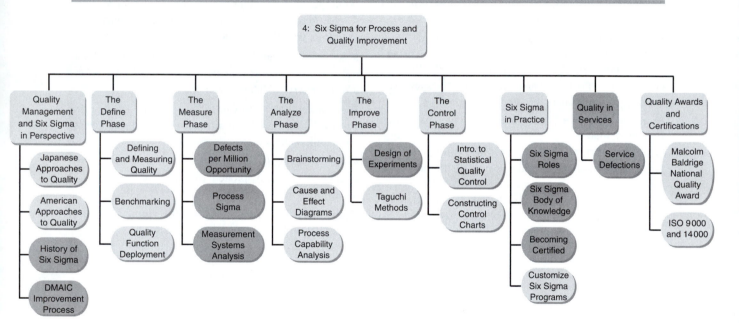

4: Six Sigma for Process and Quality Improvement

Quality Management and Six Sigma in Perspective
- Japanese Approaches to Quality
- American Approaches to Quality
- History of Six Sigma
- DMAIC Improvement Process

The Define Phase
- Defining and Measuring Quality
- Benchmarking
- Quality Function Deployment

The Measure Phase
- Defects per Million Opportunity
- Process Sigma
- Measurement Systems Analysis

The Analyze Phase
- Brainstorming
- Cause and Effect Diagrams
- Process Capability Analysis

The Improve Phase
- Design of Experiments
- Taguchi Methods

The Control Phase
- Intro. to Statistical Quality Control
- Constructing Control Charts

Six Sigma in Practice
- Six Sigma Roles
- Six Sigma Body of Knowledge
- Becoming Certified
- Customize Six Sigma Programs

Quality in Services
- Service Defections

Quality Awards and Certifications
- Malcolm Baldrige National Quality Award
- ISO 9000 and 14000

*More heavily shaded sections indicate especially timely topics.

CHAPTER IN PERSPECTIVE

This chapter discusses one of the most important ways operational activities support the business strategy and enhance competitiveness: the continuous improvement of business processes. Delivering quality products and services has taken on a strategic role in contemporary organizations; being able to deliver with quality is now assumed, and if lacking, that organization is commonly dropped from the list of suppliers. To put our discussion in perspective, we begin our introduction in the next section with a brief history of quality management and Six Sigma. The introduction continues with an overview of the Define,

Measure, Analyze, Improve, and Control (DMAIC) methodology. Next, each phase in the DMAIC approach is discussed in more detail including illustrating the use of representative Six Sigma tools in each phase. The chapter continues with a discussion of Six Sigma in practice. Here we discuss the various roles associated with Six Sigma, becoming certified, and the need for organizations to customize their approach to Six Sigma training and implementation. Finally, the chapter concludes with a discussion of the importance of quality in services and a description of various quality awards/certifications.

INTRODUCTION

- Error prone and inefficient, Bank of America (B of A) was paying a price in terms of both money and customer dissatisfaction. As one example, on a ten-point scale, only 40 percent of B of A's customers rated their experience with the company at the top, that is, a nine or ten. Internally, hundreds of thousands of defects were being created per million opportunities.

  Ken Lewis, the company's new CEO, decided in 2001 that a change in strategy was needed. This entailed a shift from fueling growth by mergers and acquisitions toward more organic growth based on retaining and deepening the relationship with existing customers. Thus, in 2001 the company embarked on its quality journey. Based on his belief that the company needed a more disciplined and comprehensive approach to process improvement, Lewis turned to Six Sigma. A new senior manager reporting directly to Lewis was hired to oversee Quality and Productivity.

  Being a financial services organization, it was to be expected that many in the organization would be skeptical of the applicability of an approach that was developed for factories. One way CEO Lewis addressed this concern was by being among the first to personally complete a Green Belt project and further requiring all of his direct reports to complete projects as well. Each of these projects was a success, providing benefits such as improved customer satisfaction with problem resolution, significantly reduced travel expenses, and increased employee retention.

  If you ask executives at B of A, they will tell you Six Sigma is not a fad but the way we conduct business. To get its Six Sigma initiative off the ground, B of A recruited Black Belts and Master Black Belts from leading Six Sigma organizations such as General Electric, Motorola, and Honeywell—a practice it continues today.

In fact, in early 2004 B of A estimated that there were over 100 open senior leadership positions requiring a background in Six Sigma. One senior executive at B of A has gone so far as to speculate that Black Belt certification will be a mandatory qualification for leadership roles at B of A. To date, B of A has trained in excess of 10,000 employees in the use of Six Sigma tools to support the DMAIC methodology. But perhaps the most compelling statistics relate to the overall benefits B of A has received as a result of its Six Sigma initiatives. More specifically, B of A estimates that it has obtained benefits in excess of $2 billion in less than three years while at the same time increasing its customer delight by 25% (Jones 2004).

- In 2002, the nuclear medicine department of Southside Hospital, a not-for-profit community hospital located in Bayshore, NY, was receiving numerous complaints regarding the turnaround times for stress tests. The turnaround time for a stress test is measured as the elapsed time from when the stress test was ordered by a physician until the results were signed off by a radiologist in the nuclear medicine department. Delays in receiving the results from stress tests impacted the timeliness of treating the patients, which in turn could affect the length of time a patient was required to stay in the hospital. To address the problem associated with excessive turnaround times, hospital administrators decided to test Six Sigma's define, measure, analyze, improve, and control (DMAIC) approach to assess its applicability to healthcare operations. To execute the project, a team consisting of one Black Belt and Three Green Belts was created. In the course of completing the project, the team utilized many traditional Six Sigma tools including voice of the customer, "critical to quality" trees, process mapping, stakeholder analysis, defects per million opportunities, cause and effect diagrams, regression analysis, and Pareto analysis. In the end, the team was able to reduce the turnaround times for stress tests by over 50 percent, from 68 hours to 32 hours (the standard deviation was also reduced from 32 hours to nine hours). In addition, the team was able to increase the process sigma level (discussed later in this chapter) from less than 0.1 to 2. Finally, the project resulted in an overall increase in capacity with no additional cost. In fact, costs actually decreased by $34,000 stemming from savings in salaries. In the end, hospital administrators acknowledged the extent to which such a data-driven approach enhanced the ultimate success of the project (Godin, Raven, Sweetapple, and Del Giudice 2004).

- One of the tasks performed by TRW's corporate law department is the registration of trademarks. The company estimates that it costs an average of $1,200 (not including processing costs) to renew a trademark worldwide. To evaluate the trademark renewal process, a team utilized many traditional Six Sigma tools including voice of the customer, determining the critical to quality characteristics, logistic regression analysis, and value-added process mapping to evaluate the process. One finding from the project was that in numerous cases trademarks were being renewed more out of a sense of history and nostalgia as opposed to providing value to the business. In the end, the project produced hard savings of $1.8 million by eliminating the renewal of entire classes of trademarks. Numerous process improvements in the trademark renewal process were also identified, producing additional soft savings. Finally, by clearly defining defects in the trademark renewal process, the project team was able to establish a baseline process sigma level of 2.18, which can be used to assess the impact of future process improvements (Das, Colello, and Davidson 2004).

As these examples illustrate, Six Sigma is a particularly timely topic in business. As a result, people with a background in Six Sigma are presently in high demand. In fact, at 3M, 25 percent of the 1000 employees who completed Six Sigma training have been promoted two levels or more! To further illustrate the point, a search in early 2005 at Monster.com using the keyword "six sigma" yielded over 3100 hits across virtually all industries, including manufacturing, consulting, technology, financial services, insurance, healthcare, and retail.

As further evidence of the value industry is currently placing on individuals with Six Sigma experience, consider the following quote taken from the letter to shareholders in GE's 2000 annual report whose co-authors included Chairman and CEO Jack Welch and President and Chairman-Elect Jeffrey Immelt (p. 6):

> It is reasonable to guess that the next CEO of this Company, decades down the road, is probably a Six Sigma Black Belt or Master Black Belt somewhere in GE right now, or on the verge of being offered—as all our early-career (3-5 years) top 20% performers will be —a two- to three-year Black Belt assignment. The generic nature of a Black Belt assignment, in addition to its rigorous process discipline and relentless customer focus, makes Six Sigma the perfect training for growing 21st century GE leadership.

A question that naturally arises is, What is driving industry's growing interest in Six Sigma? Perhaps the primary reason driving the current popularity of Six Sigma is that it works as exemplified by the significant benefits several high profile organizations have reported from their Six Sigma initiatives. For example, in the three years ending in 2001, GE estimated that it saved $8 billion as a result of its Six Sigma initiatives. In the following year, GE budgeted $600 million for Six Sigma projects and targeted an additional $2.5 billion in savings. In total, 1 to 2 percent of GE employees are full-time Black Belts, and 40% of executive bonuses are based on achieving Six Sigma goals.

Chapter 2 included a brief discussion of quality as a factor in international competitiveness. Because of its direct link to competitiveness, quality management in general and Six Sigma in particular are among the most timely topics in business today, as the introduction illustrates. Furthermore, quality management and Six Sigma are applicable to all organizations, whether or not a tangible output is produced and whether they exist to make a profit (B of A) or are nonprofit organizations (Southside Hospital).

To put our discussion in perspective, we begin with a brief introduction to quality management and Six Sigma. Here we overview the Japanese and American approaches to quality, the history of Six Sigma, and the Define, Measure, Analyze, Improve, and Control (DMAIC) methodology. Next, each phase in the DMAIC approach is discussed in more detail and representative Six Sigma tools are overviewed. We then focus our attention on Six Sigma in practice and address the various roles associated with Six Sigma and how to become individually certified.

Finally, the chapter concludes with discussions of quality in services and an overview of organizational quality awards/certifications.

QUALITY MANAGEMENT AND SIX SIGMA IN PERSPECTIVE

An often neglected point of significant importance in marketing is that customers are frequently willing to pay for excellent quality. In the traditional view it was thought that products and services of excellent quality would translate into higher costs. Of course this view neglects the negative consequences of gaining a reputation for producing shoddy outputs. Also, the Japanese have demonstrated across numerous industries that it is often possible to improve quality and lower costs at the same time. One explanation for this phenomenon is that it is simply cheaper to do a job right the first time than to try to fix it or rework it later. Philip B. Crosby, an author and expert on quality, expressed this view in the title of a book, *Quality Is Free* (1979), which sold approximately 1 million copies.

Two primary sets of costs are involved in quality: control costs and failure costs. The aggregate of these costs runs between 15 and 35 percent of sales for many U.S. firms. Traditionally, these costs are broken down into four categories, as shown in Table 4.1: prevention costs, appraisal costs, internal costs of defects, and external costs of defects. The first two costs are incurred in attempting to control quality, and the last two are the costs of failing to control quality. Costs of defects (or nonconformance) can run from 50 to 90 percent of the total cost of quality.

We overview Six Sigma as a general methodology for improving the efficiency and effectiveness of business processes, which includes improving their overall quality as well. Before doing so, however, let us first look more closely at the difference between traditional attitudes toward quality in American and Japanese management.

Japanese Approaches to Quality

Although you might think that "made in Japan" signifies a product of superior quality, it may surprise you to learn that many of the techniques and philosophies Japanese companies employ today were actually developed in the United States, usually around the end of World War II. Unfortunately, the sentiment among U.S. manufacturers at the end of World War II was that they already produced the highest-quality products in the world at the lowest cost. Thus, they were not particularly interested in or concerned with improving quality.

Japan was an entirely different story. Its products had a reputation for poor quality, and after it lost the war its economy was a shambles. As a result, Japanese manufacturers were eager for help related to quality improvement. In 1950 the Japanese government invited W. Edwards Deming (then a professor at New York University) to give a series of lectures on quality control to help Japanese engineers reindustrialize the country. But Deming insisted that the heads of the companies attend the talks too. As a result, the top Japanese managers were also invited, and they all showed up.

$\mathcal{T}$ABLE 4.1 • Four Categories of Quality Costs

Category 1: Prevention costs. These costs are incurred in the process of trying to prevent defects and errors from occurring. They consist of such elements as:
- Planning the quality control process
- Training for quality
- Educating the firm's suppliers
- Designing the product for quality
- Designing the production system for quality
- Preventive maintenance

Category 2: Appraisal costs. These are the costs of determining the current quality of the process. They consist of factors such as:
- Measuring and testing parts and materials
- Running special test laboratories
- Acquiring special testing equipment
- Conducting statistical process control programs
- Receiving inspection
- Reporting on quality

Category 3: Internal costs of defects. These costs are incurred when defects and errors are found before shipment or delivery to the customer. They consist of elements such as:
- Labor and materials that go into scrap
- Reworking and retesting to correct defects
- Lost profits on downgraded products and services
- Lost yield from malfunctioning equipment or improperly trained workers
- Downtime of equipment and labor sitting idle while waiting for repairs
- Expediting to get orders of appropriate quality delivered on time

Category 4: External costs of defects. These are the costs of trying to correct defects and errors after receipt by the customer. They include items such as:
- Quick response to complaints
- Adjustments to correct the problem
- Lost goodwill
- Recalls to correct the problem for other customers
- Warranties, insurance, and settlements of lawsuits

According to Deming (1986), the major cause of poor quality is *variation*. Thus, a key tenet of Deming's approach is to reduce variability in the process. Deming stressed that improving quality was the responsibility of top management. However, he also believed that all employees should be trained in the use of problem-solving tools and especially statistical techniques. Perhaps the contribution that Deming is most associated with is his *14 Points*, summarized and illustrated in Table 4.2.

Deming believed that improvements in quality created a chain reaction. Accordingly, improved quality leads to lower costs, which then translate into higher productivity. The resulting better quality and lower prices lead to increased market share. Higher market share means that the company can stay in business and create more jobs.

$\mathcal{T}$ABLE   4.2 • Application of Deming's 14 Points to Services

This table illustrates how the West Babylon school district and a law firm applied Deming's 14 Points to their operations. Not only do these examples illustrate the applicability of Deming's 14 Points to service-oriented organizations, but they also illustrate the applicability of the points to nonprofit organizations.

Deming's 14 Points	School District	Law Firm
1. Create a constancy of purpose toward improvement of product and service, with a plan to become competitive, stay in business, and provide jobs.	Developed a mission statement for the school district.	Committed to quality for long term.
2. Adopt the new philosophy. We can no longer live with commonly accepted levels of delays, mistakes, defective materials, and defective workmanship.	Cross-functional teams set up as quality circles.	Recognized a need for better management.
3. Cease dependence on mass inspection. Require, instead, statistical evidence that quality is built in to eliminate the need for inspection on a mass basis.	Less emphasis on exams.	Emphasized quality of inputs (e.g., staff) and improved processes (e.g., research, filing, billing).
4. End the practice of awarding business on the basis of price tags. Instead, depend on meaningful measures of quality, along with price.	Suppliers who delivered poor quality were taken off list of bidders.	Applied this to purchases of computer systems and office supplies.
5. Improve constantly and forever the system of production and service, to improve quality and productivity, and thus constantly decrease costs.	Quality circles continued to work toward improving the delivery of services.	Improved all processes, measured them by maintaining records, and reduced variation.
6. Institute modern methods of training.	Quality circle used to help select training materials. Teachers trained in use of new classroom technologies.	Improved training material and facilities. Reduced amount of job training by coworkers.
7. Institute modern methods of supervision.	All supervisors received training five times a year on advanced techniques in cooperative supervision. Emphasis was that leading means helping others do their jobs better.	Managed more by coaching and mentoring.
8. Drive out fear so that everyone may work effectively for the company.	Developed new solutions and encouraged experimentation.	Made staff feel secure. Didn't manage by fear.

$\mathcal{T}$ABLE 4.2 • (continued)

Deming's 14 Points	School District	Law Firm
9. Break down organization barriers—everyone must work as a team to foresee and solve problems.	Superintendent's quality council created with representatives from personnel, student services, testing, finance, transportation, and lunch programs.	Created teams of partners, associates, secretaries, and support staff.
10. Eliminate arbitrary numerical goals, posters, and slogans for the work force, which seek new levels of productivity without providing the methods	Transportation staff was given responsibility for reducing waste and accidents.	Provided employees with the means, including training and equipment, to do the job.
11. Eliminate work standards and numerical quotas.	Bell-shaped curve was not used to force grade distribution.	Placed less emphasis on billable hours. Rewarded employees for client services.
12. Remove barriers that rob employees of pride of workmanship.	Focused on how to prevent defects, not fix them after the fact.	Improved communications. Recognized that staff wanted to do a good job.
13. Institute a vigorous program of education and training.	Teachers received regular training in computer technology and multimedia technology.	Emphasized education and training. Trained staff on teamwork and problem solving.
14. Create a structure that will push 13 prior points every day.	Each semester, employees developed one to three goals and a plan to accomplish these goals.	Management pushed plans and vision.

Sources: Deming, W. Edwards. *Quality, Productivity, and Competitive Position* (Cambridge, Mass.: MIT, Center for Advanced Engineering Study, 1982), pp. 16–17. R. Manley and J. Manley, "Sharing the Wealth: TQM Spreads from Business to Education." *Quality Progress* (June 1996), pp. 51–55. Blodget, N. "Law Firm Pioneers Explore New Territory." *Quality Progress* (August 1996), pp. 90–94.

Deming promised the Japanese that if they followed his advice, they would be able to compete with the West within just a few years. They did! Now the most prestigious industrial quality award given in Japan each year is named the Deming Prize.

But the Japanese did not stop there. They tied the concept of quality control directly into their production system—and now they have even tied it into their entire economy through inspections to guarantee the quality of exports. The natural inclinations of Japanese culture and traditions were exploited in this quality crusade. After nearly two decades of a national emphasis on quality, Japan's reputation for producing shoddy goods was totally reversed. And, when high quality is combined with competitive pricing—another strength of the Japanese system—the result is extremely strong competition for existing producers.

American Approaches to Quality

A number of programs and awards, some successful and some unsuccessful, have been instituted in the United States over the years to help improve quality. Typical of such programs is "zero defects," a program developed in the aerospace industry in 1962. This program attempted to prevent errors by eliminating their cause, rather than remedying them after they had been made.

In fact, Philip Crosby, of *Quality is Free* (1979) fame, suggests that zero defects was the only meaningful performance standard and the cost of quality (including the cost of nonconformance) the only performance measure. To Crosby, quality meant not elegance but conformance to requirements. He believed that a problem with quality did not exist per se, but, rather, that the organization had functional problems. Crosby also argued that it was always more cost-effective to perform an activity right the first time. In contrast to Deming, Crosby focused more on management, organizational processes, and changing corporate culture than on the use of statistical techniques.

DILBERT: ©Scott Adams/Dist. by United Feature Syndicate, Inc.

A more recent concept, similar to zero defects that the Japanese and some American firms have embraced, is called *total quality management* (TQM) or *total quality control* (TQC). The basic idea of TQM is that it is extremely expensive to "inspect" quality into a company's outputs and much more efficient and effective to produce them right in the first place. As a result, responsibility for quality has been taken away from the quality control department and placed where it belongs—with the workers who produce the parts or provide the service in the first place. This is called *quality at the source*. It is the heart of *statistical quality control* (SQC), sometimes called *statistical process control* (SPC).

The beginning of TQM dates back to the 1930s, when Dr. W. A. Shewhart began using statistical control at the Bell Institute. In 1951 Juran wrote the *Quality Control Handbook*, which was considered by many to be the "bible" of quality and continues to be a useful reference to this day (Juran and Gryna 1993). In 1954, Juran made his first trip to Japan. In 1956 Japan adopted quality as its national slogan. Both Juran and Deming were students of Shewhart's.

In contrast to Deming, Juran tended to work more within the existing system rather than trying to effect major cultural changes. Also, at the top management level, Juran focused more on quality cost accounting than on statistical techniques of process control. Finally, Juran's definition of quality was "fitness for use," whereas Deming never offered a specific definition.

Just as Deming is probably best remembered for his 14 points, Juran is probably best remembered for his *quality trilogy*.

1. ***Quality planning.*** This is the process of preparing to meet quality goals. During this process customers are identified and products that meet their needs are developed.

2. ***Quality control.*** This is the process of meeting quality goals during operations. Quality control involves five steps: (1) deciding what should be controlled, (2) deciding on the units of measure, (3) developing performance standards, (4) measuring performance, and (5) taking appropriate actions based on an analysis of the gap between actual and standard performance.

3. ***Quality improvement.*** This encompasses the activities directed toward achieving higher levels of performance.

Juran suggested that organizations typically progress through four quality phases. In the first phase, organizations seek to minimize their prevention and appraisal costs. However, because a large number of defects are produced, these organizations incur large external failure costs. To alleviate this problem, the organization increases its appraisal costs in the second phase. This effectively lowers the shipment of defects but increases internal failure costs because defects are discovered earlier. Typically, however, overall total quality costs decrease. In the third phase the organization introduces process control, thereby increasing its appraisal costs but lowering internal and external failure costs even more. Finally, in the fourth phase, the organization increases prevention costs in an effort to decrease total quality costs once again.

Although organizations that implemented TQM programs tended to develop their own unique definition of TQM, most definitions included the notion that all employees were responsible for *continuously* improving the quality of the organization's products and services. Thus, the word *total* is meant to signify that the quality of the organization's outputs is the concern of all employees. Furthermore, because competition is a moving target, continuous improvement programs that provide a steady stream of incremental improvements to the current business processes are an important component of TQM. In general, TQM typically includes the following five steps:

1. Determining what the customers want.

2. Developing products and services that meet or exceed what the customers want (and even "delight" the customers).

3. Developing a process that permits doing the job right the first time.

4. Monitoring the system and using the accumulated data to improve the system.

5. Including customers and suppliers in this process.

A Brief History of Six Sigma

The Six Sigma concept was developed by Bill Smith, a senior engineer at Motorola, in 1986 as a way to standardize the way defects were tallied. As you probably already know, sigma is the Greek symbol used in statistics to refer to standard deviation which is a measure of variation. Adding "six" to "sigma" combines a measure of process performance (*sigma*) with the goal of nearly perfect quality (*six*). More specifically, to some the term Six Sigma literally translates into making no more than 3.4 mistakes (defects) per 1 million opportunities to make a mistake (defect).

While Six Sigma's original definition of 3.4 defects per million opportunities is a rather narrow measure of quality, Six Sigma itself has evolved and now encompasses a broad methodology for designing and improving business processes. In fact, many organizations (e.g., B of A and GE) view Six Sigma as an integral part of their overall business strategy. In the popular book *The Six Sigma Way*, Six Sigma is defined as:

> a comprehensive and flexible system for achieving, sustaining and maximizing business success. Six Sigma is uniquely driven by close understanding of customer needs, disciplined use of facts, data, and statistical analysis, and diligent attention to managing, improving, and reinventing business processes. (p. xi)

At Motorola, Six Sigma is defined as "a business improvement process that focuses an organization on customer requirements, process alignment, analytical rigor, and timely execution".[1] While numerous additional definitions of Six Sigma could be cited, we remark that common themes tend to emerge across the range of suggested definitions, including rigorous (often statistical) analysis, customer focus, data driven, and improving overall business performance. Likewise, a number of benefits are commonly associated with Six Sigma initiatives, including increased profitability, improved quality, improved employee morale, lower costs, higher productivity, market share growth, improved levels of customer retention and satisfaction, and shorter lead times. Interestingly, Motorola became the first company to win the Malcolm Baldrige National Quality Award in 1988. Furthermore, Motorola estimates that in the 18 years Six Sigma has been deployed, it has saved in excess of over $16 billion—which translates into almost $1 billion per year!

The DMAIC Improvement Process

We now turn our attention to the mechanics of using Six Sigma to improve business processes. Arguably, one reason for the success of Six Sigma programs where others have failed is that Six Sigma provides a structured, logical, and disciplined approach to problem solving. More specifically, as shown in Figure 4.1, Six Sigma projects generally follow a well-defined process consisting of five phases. The phases are **d**efine, **m**easure, **a**nalyze, **i**mprove, and **c**ontrol which are collectively referred to as *DMAIC* (pronounced dey-MAY-ihk). As the names of the phases suggest, the DMAIC improvement process can be thought of as an adaptation of the scientific method to process improvement.

Before discussing the DMAIC phases in more detail, a couple of comments are in order. First, as shown in Figure 4.1, the phases in a DMAIC project often serve as project milestones and thus used as gateways to the next phase in the project.

---

[1] www.motorola.com/content/0,,2409-4904,00.html, September, 20, 2004.

In particular, the progress and outcomes associated with the project are evaluated at the end of each phase to assess the merits of permitting the project to move on to the next phase. The extent to which organizational resources will continue to be allocated to the project is typically assessed at these milestones as well.

Second, there are large numbers of standard Six Sigma tools and methodologies that are used at various phases in a DMAIC project. Table 4.3 summarizes some of the more commonly used Six Sigma tools and methodologies in terms of which phase the tool/methodology is most commonly used. We now turn our attention to discussing each DMAIC phase in more detail.

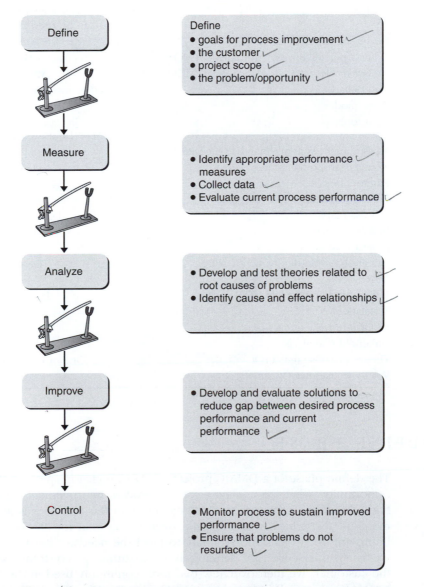

Figure 4.1 The Six Sigma DMAIC approach for process improvement.

$\mathcal{T}$ABLE   4.3 • Common Tools and Methodologies in the Six Sigma Toolset

Six Sigma Tool/Methodology	DMAIC Phase(s) Most Commonly Used in
Affinity diagram	D, A
Benchmarking	D, M
Brainstorming	A, I
Business case	D
Cause and effect diagrams	M, A
Control charts	M, A, I, C
Critical to quality tree	D
Data collection forms	M, A, I, C
Data mining	M
Design for Six Sigma (DFSS)	An entire collection of tools/methodologies that can be used across all phases
Design of experiments (DOE)	A, I
Defects per million opportunities (DPMO)	M
Failure modes and effects analysis (FMEA)	M, I, C
Gantt chart	Tool used to manage entire DMAIC project
Kano model	D, M
Lean tools	An entire collection of tools/methodologies that can be used across all phases
Measurement systems analysis (gage R&R)	M
Nominal group technique	D, M
Pareto analysis	D, M, A, I
Process capability	M, A, I
Process maps	D, M, A, I C
Process sigma	M, I
Project charter	D
Quality function deployment (QFD)	D, M
Regression	A
Rolled throughput yield (RTY)	D, M, A
Simulation	A, I
SIPOC	D
Stakeholder analysis	D, I
Theory of constraints (TOC)	One of the lean tools
Voice of customer (VOC)	D

$\mathcal{T}$HE DEFINE PHASE

The define phase of a DMAIC project focuses on clearly specifying the problem or opportunity, what the goals are for the process improvement project, and identifying the scope of the project. Identifying who the customer is and their requirements is also critical given that the overarching goal for all Six Sigma projects is improving the organization's ability to meet the needs of its customers. Therefore, we begin this section by defining and measuring quality from the perspective of the customer. We then overview two tools commonly used in the Define phase of a DMAIC project: Benchmarking and Quality Function Deployment (QFD).

Defining and Measuring Quality

Quality is a relative term, meaning different things to different people at different times. Richard J. Schonberger has compiled a list of 12 dimensions that customers perceive as associated with products and services:

1. ***Conformance to specifications.*** Conformance to specifications is the extent to which the actual product matches the design specifications. An example of nonconformance would be a pizza delivery operation that consistently required 35 minutes or more to make and deliver pizzas when the company advertised that pizzas would be delivered in 30 minutes or less.

2. ***Performance.*** Surveys suggest that customers most frequently equate the quality of products and services with their performance.[2] Examples of performance include how quickly a sports car accelerates from 0 to 60 miles per hour, how good a steak tastes at a restaurant, and the range and clarity of a wireless phone.

3. ***Quick response.*** Quick response is associated with the amount of time required to react to customers' demands. Examples of quick responses include cell phone carriers that can activate a phone at time of purchase, online retailers that ship from inventory overnight, automobile manufacturers that can design a new model in less than three years, and fire and rescue services that are on the scene within minutes of a 911 call.

4. ***Quick-change expertise.*** Examples of quick-change expertise include a 10-minute oil change, a motorcycle assembly line that can switch over and make any model with little or no delay, and costume and set changes in the theater.

5. ***Features.*** Features are the attributes that a product or service offers. Examples of features include a cell phone with a built-in digital camera, side impact airbags in automobiles, and a salad bar with more than 50 ingredients.

6. ***Reliability.*** Reliability is the probability that a product or service will perform as intended on any given trial or the probability that a product will continue to perform for some period of time. Examples of reliability are the probability that a car will start on any given morning, and the probability that a car will not break down in less than four years.

7. ***Durability.*** Durability refers to how tough a product is. Examples of durability include a notebook computer that still functions after being dropped, watches that are waterproof 100 meters underwater, and a knife that can cut through steel and not need sharpening.

8. ***Serviceability.*** Serviceability refers to the ease with which maintenance or a repair can be performed. A product for which serviceability is important is a copier machine. (Have you ever been in an office when the copier was down?)

---

[2]Spencer Hutches, Jr., "What Customers Want: Results of ASQC/Gallop Survey," *Quality Progress* (February 1989), pp. 33–35.

9. **Aesthetics.** Aesthetics are factors that appeal to human senses. Aesthetic factors associated with an automobile, for instance, include its shape, its color, and the sound of its engine.

10. **Perceived quality.** Quality is not an absolute but, rather, is based on customers' perceptions. Customers' impressions can be influenced by a number of factors, including brand loyalty and an organization's reputation.

11. **Humanity.** Humanity has to do with how the customer is treated. An example of humanity is a private university that maintains small classes so students are not treated like numbers by the professors.

12. **Value.** The value of a product or service relates to how much of the preceding 11 dimensions of quality customers get relative to what they pay. The value dimension of quality suggests that enhancing one or more of the dimensions of quality does not automatically lead to perceived higher quality. Rather, enhancements of quality are evaluated by customers relative to their effect on cost.

It is worth noting that not all the dimensions of quality are relevant to all products and services. Thus, organizations need to identify the dimensions of quality that are relevant to the products and services they offer. Market research about customers' needs is the primary input for determining which dimensions are important. Once the important dimensions have been determined, how the organization and its competitors rate on these dimensions should be assessed. If an organization rates lower on a given dimension than the competition, it can either try to improve on that dimension or attempt to shift customers' attitudes so that the customers will place more emphasis on the dimensions the organization rates highest on. Of course, measuring the quality of a service can often be more difficult than measuring the quality of a product or facilitating good. However, the dimensions of quality apply to both.

Benchmarking

In conjunction with their efforts to improve their products and processes, many organizations are engaging in an activity called **benchmarking**. Essentially, benchmarking involves comparing an organization's processes with the best practices to be found. Benchmarking is used for a variety of purposes, including:

- Comparing an organization's processes with the best organization's processes. When used in this way, benchmarking activities should not be restricted to other organizations in the same industry. Rather, the companies that are best in the world at performing a particular activity, *regardless of industry*, should be studied. For example, Xerox used L.L. Bean to benchmark the order fulfillment process.

- Comparing an organization's products and services with those of other organizations.

- Identifying the best practices to implement.

- Projecting trends in order to be able to respond proactively to future challenges and opportunities.

Benchmarking generally involves three steps. The first step is concerned with preparing for the benchmarking study. In this phase it is important to get the support of senior management and its input on what should be benchmarked. Problem areas, activities related to serving the customer better, and activities related to the mission of the organization are all appropriate candidates for inclusion in the benchmarking study.

The second phase of benchmarking consists of collecting data. There are two general sources of benchmarking data. One source is *published data*. These are often available from universities, financial filings (e.g., 10k reports), consultants, periodicals, trade journals, and books. The other source of data is *original research* conducted by the organization itself. If this approach is employed, a list of organizations to benchmark might include companies that have recently received quality awards or other business awards, are top-rated by industry analysts, have been the subject of recent business articles, or have a track record of superior financial performance. Once the companies have been identified, data can be collected in a variety of ways including interviews, site visits, and surveys.

The third and final phase of benchmarking involves using what has been learned to improve organizational performance. Once the second phase has been completed, identified gaps in performance can be used to set challenging but realistic goals (often called *stretch goals*). Also, the results of the benchmarking study can be used to overcome and eliminate complacency within the organization.

Quality Function Deployment

Arguably, two key drivers of an organization's long-term competitive success are the extent to which its new products or services meet customers' needs, and having the organizational capabilities to develop and deliver such new products and services. Clearly, no amount of clever advertising and no degree of production efficiency will entice customers to continue to purchase products or services that do not meet their needs. Likewise, it serves no purpose for an organization to design new products or services that it does not have the capability to produce or deliver. To illustrate, it would make little sense for a local phone company to market a new service that offers *voice over the Internet (VoIP)* calling if the firm did not have the infrastructure to deliver this type of service. Even if the phone company was able to work out the bugs for such calling, it could still take years to install the necessary hardware that is necessary to deliver this type of service on a large scale. Of course, the desire to offer new products and services can serve as the impetus for acquiring additional process capabilities; however, organizations typically seek to develop new products and services that capitalize on their existing capabilities.

Quality function deployment (QFD) is a powerful tool for helping translate customer requirements into process capabilities. In effect, the use of QFD ensures that newly designed or improved products and services satisfy market requirements and are ultimately producible by the firm. As Figure 4.2 illustrates, the QFD methodology utilizes a series of tables to maintain links between customer requirements, technical requirements, component requirements, process requirements, and ultimately specific process activities. Because of their shape, these tables are often referred to as the *houses of quality*. Before discussing the contents of a house of quality in detail, we first broadly overview the QFD process and discuss the links between the four houses of quality.

Broad Overview of QFD

QFD begins by using *voice of the customer (VOC)* data to specify the customer requirements in the rows of the first house, the Output Planning Matrix, shown in Figure 4.2. The name VOC stems from the fact that the customer's own language is used to capture these requirements. As examples, a sample of mountain bike riders might offer responses regarding their preferences for a new bike such as "the bike should shift effortlessly," "there should be no bob on climbs," "the bike should climb, descend, and handle great," "the bike should suck up the bumps," and "I like a bike that is well balanced with a low center of gravity."

Next, based on the customer requirements listed in the rows, the technical requirements for the product or service are generated and listed in the columns of this house. While the customer requirements are expressed in the customer's own language, the technical requirements are often expressed in a more specialized language such as that used by engineers. Thus, technical requirements for a product might be expressed in terms of dimensions, weights, performance, tensile strength, and compression.

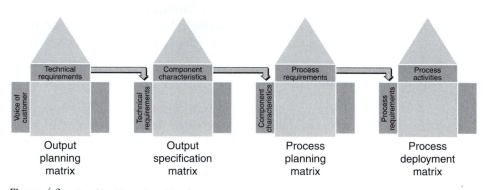

Figure 4.2   Quality Function Deployment process.

Once the rows and columns are generated for the Output Planning Matrix, the relationship matrix in the middle of the house is completed. The cells in the relationship matrix correspond to the intersection of a particular customer requirement and technical requirement. In each cell the strength of the relationship between the corresponding customer requirement and technical requirement is evaluated. An important use of the relationship matrix is to ensure that each customer requirement is addressed by one or more technical requirements. Likewise, the relationship matrix can be used to ensure that designers do not add technical requirements to the product or service that do not address specific customer requirements. Designers who do not specifically consider customers' requirements run the risk of adding a number of "bells and whistles" that the customer may not be interested in. In these cases the designers are simply adding to the cost of the final product or service without proportionally increasing its value. For example, it might be an interesting challenge for an engineer to design a five-speed motor for garage doors. However, since customers would most likely operate it at only its fastest speed, adding the extra controls for additional speeds would not add value for the typical customer.

In the next house of quality, referred to as the Output Specification Matrix in Figure 4.2, the technical requirements which were the columns in the previous house of quality now become the rows. Thus, in the Output Specification Matrix the task now becomes generating a list of the elemental or component characteristics for the product or service which will become the columns in this house of quality. Then, once the columns are specified, the relationship matrix is completed to ensure that: (1) each technical requirement is addressed by one or more component pieces of the product or service, and (2) component requirements that are not related to specific technical requirements are not added.

In the third house shown in Figure 4.2, the Process Planning Matrix, component requirements listed in the columns of the previous house now become the rows of the new house. Next, process requirements are generated based on the component requirements listed in the rows and entered in the columns of the new house. Following this, the relationship matrix is completed for this house to ensure that each component requirement is matched to specific process requirements, and that each process requirement is linked to specific component requirements. The former result ensures that the organization has the capability to produce or deliver the components; the latter result ensures that the organization does not attempt to develop process capabilities that are not related to the component requirements.

Finally, in the Process Deployment Matrix, the process requirements from the columns of the previous house become the rows and specific process activities are generated for each process requirement. Then in a similar fashion to the other houses, the relationship matrix is completed and checks are performed to ensure that all process requirements are addressed by one or more process activities and that no process activities are added that do not address at least one process requirement.

Thus, we see that QFD provides a logical and straightforward approach for ensuring that designs for new or improved products and services meet customers' requirements and are ultimately producible. This is accomplished by first translating the voice of the customer into the technical language of engineers and other specialists. Next, these technical requirements are translated into specific requirements for the components of the new product or service. The component requirements are subsequently translated into specific process requirements, which in turn are translated into specific process activities. In the end, however, it is the customer requirements that drive the entire QFD process.

House of Quality Details

With this general overview of QFD and its four houses of quality, we now turn our attention to the specific information listed in each house of quality. A summary of the general structure of a house of quality is shown in Figure 4.3. Constructing a house of quality begins by listing what it is we are trying to accomplish in the rows at the far left of the house. In the first house, these "Whats," as they are generally called, are the customer requirements or the voice of the customer. After specifying what it is we would like to accomplish, the next task is to think about how to meet these requirements. Thus, the "Hows," as they are called, are listed in the columns of the house. In the case of the first house of quality, the Hows are the technical requirements of the product or service given the customer requirements listed in the rows. The intersection of each What (row) and How (column) is a cell in the relationship matrix. In this relationship matrix, the strength of the relationship between each What and How is evaluated. Likewise, the roof of the house corresponds to a triangular correlation table where the correlations between the technical requirements are assessed. This assessment helps identify those technical requirements that are synergistic with each other and which conflict with one another and therefore where a tradeoff may exist. At the far right of the house, customer importance ratings and the results of a competitive evaluation are summarized. Finally, at the bottom of the house, target values, a competitive evaluation, and importance weights are summarized for each How.

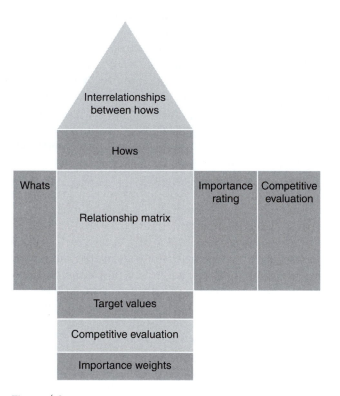

Figure 4.3   The House of Quality.

To illustrate the QFD process, consider a fast-food restaurant chain that is interested in improving its offerings. Figure 4.4 provides the completed Output Planning Matrix for the chain. At the far left of the house, the voice of the customer data is listed and includes customer statements such as "food that tastes good" and "get what I ordered." Based on these customer requirements, a list of technical requirements was generated and listed in the columns. In the relationship matrix, the relationship between each customer requirement and technical requirement was assessed. Thus we see that that there is a strong relationship between the taste of the food and the use of fresh ingredients, while there is only a medium relationship between the taste of the food and the time it takes to make and deliver it to the customer. In the roof of the house the correlations between each of the technical requirements are evaluated and listed. In our example we note that the requirements of "fresh ingredients" and "quality ingredients" are consistent with one another while a tradeoff exists between "limiting the fat and carbohydrate content of the food" and "keeping meal price down." At the far right, customer importance ratings and a competitive evaluation are summarized. Thus we see that good taste, nutrition, and accuracy of the order are the most important aspects of the service to the customers surveyed. On these three dimensions we see that the organization in question has the best tasting food, has the second most nutritional offerings, and has the highest order accuracy. At the bottom of the house, target values and a competitive evaluation are listed for each How. For example, in terms of using fresh ingredients, the chain in question has set a goal of achieving a score of 90 on this dimension and estimates that Competitors A and B score 70 and 75, respectively, on this dimension. Finally, the importance weight or priority for each How is listed at the very bottom of the house.

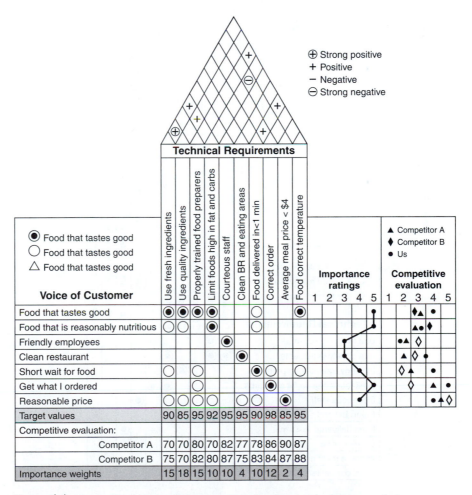

Figure 4.4 Example Output Planning matrix for fast-food restaurant chain.

This can help in making tradeoffs when conflicts are discovered in the roof of the house. In the present case the most important technical requirement is the use of quality ingredients.

Without going into as much detail, Figure 4.5 illustrates how the columns in the first house become the rows in the second house. Likewise, Figures 4.6 and 4.7 continue the example for the remaining houses.

One key advantage of QFD is that it is a visual tool. Through the use of QFD a firm can analyze its outputs in terms of customers' desires, compare its outputs with competitors' outputs, determine what it takes to better meet each customer's requirements, and figure out how to do it. In addition, it provides a means of linking these customer requirements through the entire planning process, ending with the specification of detailed process activities. A number of firms such as Toyota and Hewlett-Packard have adopted QFD and found that it cut their product development time by one-third to one-half and their costs by up to 60 percent (while improving quality).

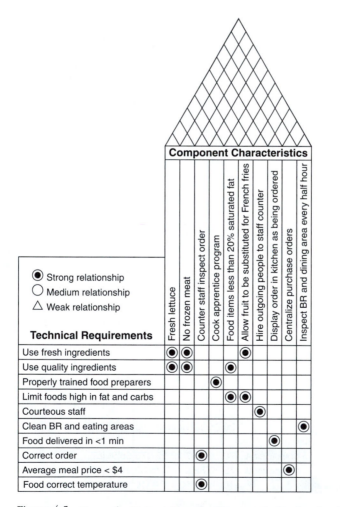

Figure 4.5 Example Output Specification matrix for fast-food restaurant chain

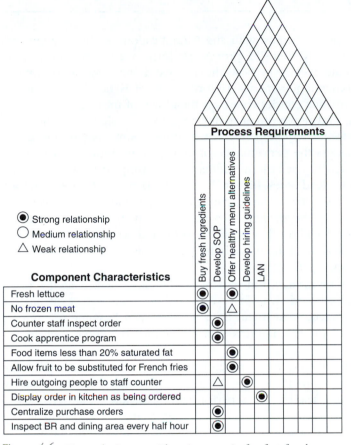

Figure 4.6   Example Process Planning matrix for fast-food restaurant chain.

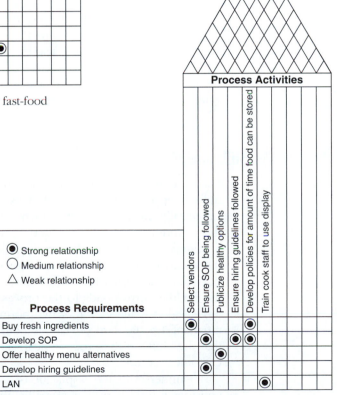

Figure 4.7   Example Process Deployment matrix for fast-food restaurant chain.

THE MEASURE PHASE

Typically the measure phase begins with the identification of the key process performance metrics. Correctly choosing process performance metrics is critical in order to have an accurate picture of how the process is actually performing in terms of meeting customer requirements. Unfortunately, it is not uncommon for analysts to select performance metrics based on their ease of measurement and/or the availability of data, and not on their ability to provide insights into how the process is meeting customer requirements. For example, some organizations use machine utilization to assess the performance of their manufacturing processes. In reality, machine utilization has at best an indirect relationship to what really matters to customers—shorter lead times, higher quality, the percent of orders shipped on time, and so on. As a service example, consider a call center. In this case, performance measures such as the percent of calls answered by the third ring, the percent of calls processed without having to be escalated, and the average hold time are all better indicators of how well the process is performing than, for example, labor utilization.

Once the key process performance metrics have been specified, related process and customer data are collected. One early use of these data is to evaluate the process's current performance, which can then be used as a baseline to evaluate the benefits of potential process improvements that are identified later in the project.

As shown in Table 4.3, there are a variety of tools in the Six Sigma toolkit that are useful during the Measure Phase. We begin our discussion of the Measure Phase with two commonly used process performance measures, namely, *Defects per Million Opportunities (DPMO)* and *Process Sigma*. We then conclude our discussion of the Measure Phase with a brief overview of Measurement Systems Analysis.

Defects Per Million Opportunities

Earlier it was noted that a literal interpretation of Six Sigma is 3.4 defects per million opportunities (DPMO). This may have caused some confusion for more statistically inclined readers, which we shall now attempt to reconcile. To reconcile this difference, we need to discuss an important assumption Motorola made when it originally developed the Six Sigma concept. Specifically, Motorola assumed that the mean of a process can shift (or drift) over time by as much as 1.5 standard deviations, as is illustrated in Figure 4.8. In Figure 4.8, the bold normal curve in the middle corresponds to the process mean when it is perfectly aligned with the target value while the other two normal curves correspond to shifts in the process mean of 1.5 standard deviations both up and down. Note also that it is assumed that the shifts in the process mean do not affect the process standard deviation or customer requirements.

To understand the implications associated with a shift in the process mean, consider a restaurant that offers hamburgers with a target weight of 4 ounces and the process standard deviation is 0.1 ounces. According to Motorola's assumption, the average weight of a hamburger could change over time. More specifically, as shown in Figure 4.9, the average weight of a hamburger could drop to as low as 3.85 ounces or increase to 4.15 ounces. Note that we are referring to the average weight of all hamburgers produced by the process at a particular point in time, not to the weight of individual hamburgers. Also, recall that we assume that the process standard deviation and customer requirements are not affected by a shift in the process mean.

To see the impact that results from a shift in the process mean, let's assume that the customer requirements for hamburgers are right at plus or minus Six Sigma, as shown in Figure 4.9. In this case customers would consider a hamburger acceptable as long as it weighed between 3.4 and 4.6 ounces. It can be easily verified that the area in one tail beyond Six Sigma is 0.0000001%, which yields a combined area of 0.0000002% in both tails. Multiplying this by 1 million yields .002 DPMO, which is considerably less than 3.4 DPMO commonly associated with Six Sigma.

To reconcile this difference, we need to consider the implications associated with a shift in the process mean. For example, what happens when the process mean

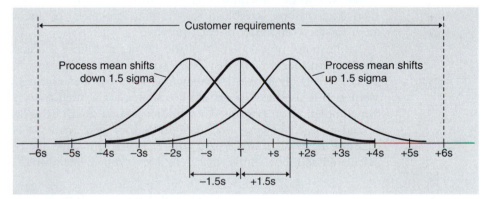

Figure 4.8   Motorola's assumption that the process mean can shift by as much as 1.5 standard deviations.

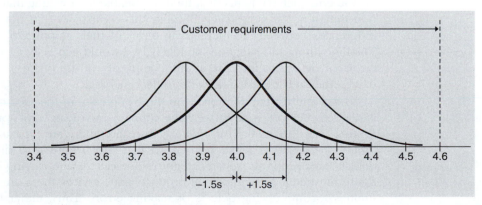

Figure 4.9   Shift in distribution of hamburger weights (after cooking) at a restaurant.

increases by 1.5 standard deviations while the process standard deviation and the customer requirements stay the same? Referring to Figure 4.8, we observe that now the upper tail beyond the customers' requirements would be 4.5 standard deviations above the new process mean while the lower tail would be 7.5 standard deviations below the new process mean. For the normal distribution, the area in the tail beyond 4.5 standard deviations is 0.00034%, which works out to 3.4 DPMO while the area beyond 7.5 standard deviations is 0.0000000000032%, which is less than 1 in a trillion and for practical purposes is zero. Therefore we observe that when the process mean shifts by 1.5 standard deviations, the combined area in the tails is approximately 0.00034%, which is equivalent to 3.4 DPMO. Because the normal distribution is symmetrical, the same results are obtained in cases where the process mean shifts down by 1.5 standard deviations. The only difference is that the areas in the two tails are reversed. Finally, note that the 3.4 DPMO represents the worst possible performance because it corresponds to the largest shift in the process mean. Smaller shifts in the process mean yield lower DPMO values.

An important advantage of using DPMO as a measure of process performance is that it provides a standard measure of process performance. As such, it provides a mechanism for comparing the performance across a range of processes that otherwise would be difficult to compare. In fact, as we now illustrate, DPMO makes such comparisons possible across varying processes by incorporating an adjustment for the complexity of each process.

To illustrate the calculation of the DPMO and how it adjusts for process complexity, consider a bank that processes two types of loans. Method A is used to process relatively simple loans such as for a car and consists of five steps, while Method B is used to process more complex loans such as mortgages and requires the completion of 25 steps. Let's further assume that of the last 10,000 loans processed by each process, a total of 100 errors were made in each method. In this case the number of *defects per unit (DPU)* is the same for both methods and is calculated as follows (note that here a loan represents a unit):

$$\text{DPU} = \frac{\text{Number of defects}}{\text{Number of units}} = \frac{100}{10,000} = 0.01$$

This result suggests that each method is averaging 0.01 errors (or defects) per loan, or one error per 100 loans. Is it then reasonable to conclude that both methods are performing at the same level? Because this comparison has not accounted for the differences between the methods in terms of their complexity, the answer is no. Thinking about this situation intuitively, we would generally expect the number of errors or defects to increase as the complexity of the process increases. Unfortunately, the DPU measure does not reflect this logic.

To account for the differences in the complexity of the methods, an adjustment is needed. Up to this point we have counted each loan (unit) processed as representing one opportunity for a defect. In reality, there are typically multiple opportunities to create a defect (error). To illustrate, Figure 4.10 displays 33 specific defects organized into seven categories associated with staying at a hotel. As this figure illustrates, for virtually all products and services there are numerous opportunities for introducing defects or making errors. Thus, rather than treating each unit or customer as a single opportunity for a defect, an alternative approach is to develop a preliminary list of all the opportunities for creating a defect for a given product or service. Then, the *number of defects per opportunity (DPO)* can be calculated as follows:

$$DPO = \frac{Number\ of\ Defects}{Number\ of\ Units\ (Customers) \times Number\ of\ Opportunities}$$

An important issue that must be addressed in using the DPO measure relates to developing the list of opportunities. In particular, it is possible to make it appear that performance is better than it actually is by padding the list with additional opportunities. To illustrate, in Figure 4.10 there are 33 specific opportunities for defects listed in seven categories. Let's assume that a survey of 100 customers revealed 200 occurrences of the 33 items listed in the figure. Based on this, if we consider each of these 33 items as a valid opportunity for a defect, then the DPO works out to be

$$\frac{200}{100 \times 33} = 0.06$$

Alternatively, if we consider each stage in the service delivery process (i.e., the seven categories listed in Figure 4.10) as an opportunity for a defect, then the DPO increases to

$$\frac{200}{100 \times 7} = 0.29$$

Thus we see that increasing the number of opportunities considered can make the performance look better. Along these lines then, a less than honest manager or supplier could inflate the list of opportunities for defects by including some opportunities that in reality never occur. Besides being unethical, pursuing this strategy greatly undermines the value of using DPO as a standardized measure of process performance. In the end, there are no firm rules for what to include and what not to include. As a general rule of thumb, however, it is suggested that only those defects that are meaningful to the customer be included. One strategy for determining the list of opportunities is to simply treat each stage as representing one opportunity for a defect. Based on this approach, there would be seven opportunities for a defect per hotel customer (of course some of these defects could be repeated over a multiple-day stay). Thus, a hotel customer whose reservation was lost and who experienced an excessive wait for check-in would count as one check-in defect as opposed to two defects.

Based on this logic and returning to our original objective of comparing loan Methods A and B, we determine that Method A has five opportunities to create a defect while Method B has 25. Then, based on the data collected indicating that 100 errors were made in both methods out of the last 10,000 loans processed, we can calculate the DPO for both methods as follows:

$$DPO_A = \frac{100}{10,000 \times 5} = 0.002$$

$$DPO_B = \frac{100}{10,000 \times 25} = 0.0004$$

In contrast to our earlier analysis based on the DPU measure, we now observe a significant difference in the performance of the two processes. This difference is now observable because we have adjusted the performance measure to account for the complexity of the processes. In particular we see that Method A produces an average of 0.002 defect per opportunity while Method B only produces an average of 0.0004 defect per opportunity. Because it is somewhat cumbersome to deal with such small numbers, it is common to multiply the DPO measure by 1 million to yield the DPMO measure discussed earlier. In this case, the DPMOs for methods A and B are 2000 and 400, respectively. Thus, it is expected that Method A would make 2000 mistakes per 1 million opportunities to make a mistake while Method B would make only 400 mistakes per million opportunities.

Hotel reservation	• Name entered incorrectly
	• Wrong date of arrival entered
	• Wrong departure date entered
	• Error entering credit card number or expiration date
	• Wrong address entered
	• Incorrect number of people staying in room entered
	• Wrong room reserved (e.g., smoking versus nonsmoking, number of beds)
	• Incorrect number of baby cribs reserved
	• Wrong room rate entered
Check-in	• Lost reservation
	• Excessive wait
	• Defective or wrong room key
	• Desk staff not courteous
	• No baggage carts available
Room cleaning	• Dirty shower
	• Dirty linens
	• Dirty sink
	• Carpet not vacuumed
	• Trash cans not emptied
Room supplies	• No clean towels
	• No toilet paper
	• No shampoo/hand soap
TV	• Cable out
	• No remote control/remote control defective
Room Service	• Late food order
	• Missing items
	• Billed incorrectly
	• Food not prepared properly
	• Food is cold
Checkout	• Incorrect charge for room service
	• Incorrect telephone charges
	• Excessive wait for desk clerk
	• Excessive wait for bell captain

Figure 4.10   Defect opportunities associated with a stay at a hotel.

Process Sigma

Regarding the term Six Sigma, it was noted earlier that *sigma* corresponds to a measure of process performance. Having clarified why Six Sigma translates into 3.4 DPMO positions us to now examine how *sigma* itself can be used to measure the performance of a process. We now know that when customers consider an output to be of acceptable quality as long as it is within plus or minus six standard deviations from the target value and the process mean can shift by as much as 1.5 standard deviations, the process itself will produce 3.4 DPMO. In effect then, the inherent variability of the process itself relative to the customer requirements provides a measure of the capability of the process to meet the customers' requirements. In other words, one way to measure the performance of a process is to calculate the number of standard deviations the customer requirements are from the process mean or target value. According to this measure, called ***process sigma***, a higher value corresponds to higher process performance. In the examples at the beginning of the chapter, it was noted that Southside Hospital was able to increase its process sigma from 0.1 to 2 while TRW's legal department established a baseline process sigma level of 2.18.

To see why a higher process sigma corresponds to higher process performance, refer to Figure 4.11. In particular, two levels of process sigma are shown in the figure. The normal curve drawn with the thin line corresponds to a process where the customer requirements are aligned at plus or minus three of the process's standard deviations from the target value (3 sigma) and the normal curve drawn with the thick, bold line corresponds to a process where customer requirements are aligned at plus or minus six of the process's standard deviations from the target value (6 sigma). From this figure we observe that the 3 sigma process exhibits more variation and therefore has more area in its tails beyond the customer requirements. This greater amount of area in the tails corresponds to a higher probability of producing an outcome that is not acceptable to the customer.

Table 4.4 examines the impact on process performance for a range of process sigma values for two levels of process drift. Referring back to Figure 4.11, we see from the middle column in Table 4.4, which assumes the process mean can shift by as much as 1.5 standard deviations, that a 3 sigma process produces 66,811 DPMO while a Six Sigma process produces 3.4 DPMO. Note that we are defining a defect rather broadly here in terms of the entire unit of output being either defective or not defective.

The last column of Table 4.4 examines the impact of process stability on process performance. Specifically, while the DPMO values listed in the middle column of the table are based on Motorola's original assumption of shifts in the process mean of as much as 1.5 standard deviations, the last column is based on a process shift of no more than one standard deviation. As can be seen in comparing these two columns, the number of defects produced by a process can be significantly reduced by increasing the stability of the process. For example, at three sigma, a process produces 66,811 DPMO when the process mean shifts by as much as 1.5 standard deviations. If the process's stability is increased so that the process mean shifts by no more than one standard deviation, the DPMO drops by 66 percent to 22,782 DPMO. Based on the results shown in the table, we point out that another way to achieve the target value of 3.4 DPMO is to operate a process at 5.5 sigma while ensuring that the process mean shifts by no more than one standard deviation.

As another example, 3.4 DPMO would be achieved in cases where the process operated at 5 sigma and the process mean shifted by no more than half a standard deviation. This discussion illustrates that there are three drivers of process sigma: the actual customer requirements, the variation in the process as measured by the process standard deviation, and the stability of the process as measured by how much it can shift over time. Thus, the sigma of a process can be increased by widening the customer requirements surrounding the target value, reducing the variation of the process, and/or increasing the stability of the process.

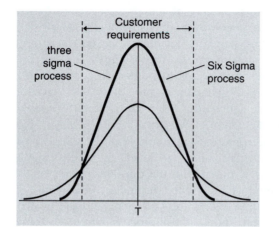

Figure 4.11   Comparison of three sigma process and Six Sigma process.

$\mathcal{T}$ABLE   4.4 • **DPMO for Alternative Process Sigma Levels**

Process Sigma	DPMO (Based on Process Mean Shifting by up to 1.5 Standard Deviations)	DPMO (Based on Process Mean Shifting by up to 1.0 Standard Deviations)
1.0	697,672	522,751
1.5	501,350	314,747
2.0	308,770	160,005
2.5	158,687	67,040
3.0	66,811	22,782
3.5	22,750	6,213
4.0	6,210	1,350
4.5	1,350	233
5.0	233	32
5.5	32	3.4
6.0	3.4	0.3

Measurement Systems Analysis

Whenever we deal with data that were collected via measurement, measures of variation like the standard deviation and variance may not accurately reflect the true variation in the sample or population of interest. In particular, measurement errors may introduce another source of variation. For example, measuring a person's blood pressure manually requires both good eyesight and hearing. It also requires that the dial gauges be properly recalibrated over time.

As an example, consider the 10 systolic blood pressure values shown in Table 4.5 for a random sample of male diabetic patients. In particular we note that the average systolic blood pressure for this sample of patients was 130.5 with a standard deviation of 21 and variance of 442.9. As you may recall from an earlier statistics course, the purpose for measures like the standard deviation and variance is to provide a sense of how much variation or dispersion there is across the population of interest or, in the present case, how much variation there is across male diabetics' systolic blood pressure.

$\mathcal{T}_{ABLE}$ 4.5 • Systolic Blood Pressure Values
for Sample of Male Diabetic Patients

Patient	Systolic Blood Pressure
S. Jones	123
K. Smith	106
T. Carter	136
F. Lance	145
J. Porter	153
L. Davis	157
H. Johnson	101
R. Jones	124
G. Scott	152
B. Regan	108
Average	130.5
Std. Dev.	21.0
Variance	442.9

Figure 4.12 illustrates that the measurement system contributes to the total variance that is actually calculated. More specifically, we note that a calculated or observed value of variation can be broken down into two major components: the actual variation in the process and the variation introduced by the measurement system itself. Based on this insight and referring back to our blood pressure example, we observe that the total calculated variance of 442.9 is the result of the actual differences in the patients' blood pressure (process variation) and perhaps errors made in measuring the patients' blood pressure (measurement system variation). Mathematically this can be expressed as follows:

$$\sigma_T^2 = \sigma_p^2 + \sigma_m^2$$

where:

$\sigma_T^2 =$ the total observed or calculated variation,

$\sigma_p^2 =$ the actual variation inherent in the process and commonly referred to as the part-to-part variation (or, in our example, patient-to-patient variation)

$\sigma_m^2 =$ variation introduced by the measurement system.

Recall from basic statistics that calculating the total variation arising from multiple sources requires summing the variances from each source, not their standard deviations. Therefore, the total observed standard deviation, σ_T, is calculated as

$$\sigma_T = \sqrt{\sigma_p^2 + \sigma_m^2}$$

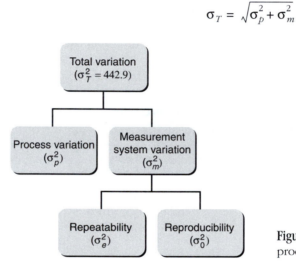

Figure 4.12 Components of total process variation.

The variance introduced by the measurement system can be further broken down into two sources: repeatability and reproducibility. Repeatability corresponds to the ability of the person doing the measuring to get consistent measurement results when measuring a given item. Ideally, a person would obtain the same measurement results when the same item is measured using the same measurement instrument at different points in time. In our blood pressure example, repeatability corresponds to the ability of a given technician to get the same blood pressure reading for a given patient (assuming the patient's blood pressure has not changed) using the same sphygmomanometer. In contrast, reproducibility corresponds to the consistency in the measurement readings when different people measure a particular item using the same measurement instrument. Ideally, different people would obtain the same measurement result when the same item is measured using a common measurement instrument. In the blood pressure example, reproducibility corresponds to the extent to which different technicians get the same blood pressure reading when they take the blood pressure of a given patient (again assuming the patient's blood pressure has not changed) using a common sphygmomanometer. Mathematically, the variation introduced by the measurement system can be expressed as

$$\sigma_m^2 = \sigma_e^2 + \sigma_o^2$$

where:

σ_e^2 =   repeatability or the variation introduced when the same person measures the same item *at different points in time* using the same measuring instrument and obtains different results across the trials

σ_o^2 =   reproducibility or the variation introduced when *different people* measure the same item using the same measuring instrument

The measurement standard deviation is calculated as:

$$\sigma_m = \sqrt{\sigma_e^2 + \sigma_o^2}$$

To assess the variation introduced by the measurement system, a ***Measurement Systems Analysis*** study (or a Gage R&R, for repeatability and reproducibility, study as it is more commonly called) is conducted. The purpose of a Gage R&R study is to assess what percent of the observed variation is being introduced by the measurement system itself and what percent represents the actual underlying variation in the process. Generally speaking, the smaller the percentage of variation introduced by the measurement system, the better.

Performing a Measurement Systems Analysis requires having two or more workers take repeated measurements of multiple test units with known standard values. For example, a Measurement Systems Analysis for taking blood pressure could be done by selecting two or more nurses and having the nurses rotate across multiple patients, taking a patient's blood pressure one time and then moving on to the next patient. Once a nurse finished taking the blood pressure of all patients, the process would be repeated one or more times so that each nurse took each patient's blood pressure two or more times. Prior to the study, the patients could be required to lie down in order to stabilize their blood pressure and remain lying down throughout the study in order to maintain a constant blood pressure. Furthermore, each patient's blood pressure would need to be taken both at the beginning of the study and the end of the study using a digital blood pressure monitor to establish the patient's true blood pressure and ensure that the patient's blood pressure did not change during the study. If it were discovered that one or more of the patients' blood pressures changed during the study, the study would need to be repeated for these patients. Once the data are collected from a Measurement Systems Analysis study, they are analyzed and the total observed variation is partitioned into its constituent parts using analysis of variance (ANOVA) or other similar techniques.

Both the repeatability and reproducibility of a measurement system relate to the impact the measurement system has on the observed variation. In addition to considering the impact the measurement system has on the variation of observed values, it is also important to consider the impact the measurement system has on the mean (or location) of the observed values. To access the impact the measurement system has on the mean of observed values, three additional measurement system metrics are employed:

1. ***Bias*** represents the difference between the average of a number of observations and the true value. For example, assume a nurse takes the systolic blood pressure of a patient three times and observes the following

blood pressures: 126, 128, and 127. Further, assume that it was known at the time the patient's blood pressure was taken that the patient had an actual blood pressure of 125. In this case we can average the three nurse readings and calculate an average blood pressure value of 127. Based on this, the bias would be 2 (i.e., 127 − 125), suggesting that the nurse tends to overestimate a patient's blood pressure by 2. Thus, bias is a measure of the tendency of the measurement system to under- or overestimate the measurement value of interest, perhaps due to a defective instrument, such as the sphygmomanometer. While there may be errors made in taking individual measurements, ideally these errors should cancel out over time and the average should be close to the true value, which would in turn yield a bias of approximately zero.

2. **Linearity** of a measurement system corresponds to the accuracy of the measurement system across the entire range of possible entities to be measured. Ideally, a measurement system's accuracy should not be impacted by an entity's position in the range of possible values. Thus, a blood pressure measuring system that is more accurate for people with a blood pressure of 115 than for people with a blood pressure of 155 does not possess the characteristic of linearity.

3. **Stability** of a measurement system corresponds to the ability of the measurement system to get consistent results over time. For example, assuming a patient's blood pressure remains constant over time, the results of taking the patient's blood pressure at his or her annual physical should yield similar results.

THE ANALYZE PHASE

Having first defined the problem/opportunity, the customer, and the goals for the Six Sigma project and then subsequently considered appropriate performance measures, collected the relevant data, and evaluated the process' current performance, we are now ready to begin the Analyze Phase. In this phase of the project, our objective is to utilize the data that have been collected to develop and test theories related to the root causes of existing gaps between the process's current and desired performance. Ultimately, our goal is to identify key cause and effect relationships that can be leveraged to improve the overall performance of the process.

Referring to Table 4.3 again, there are a number of tools in the Six Sigma toolset that are useful in the Analyze Phase. In this section we will overview three of these tools: (1) brainstorming, (2) cause and effect diagrams, and (3) process capability analysis. Because design of experiments is equally applicable to the improve phase, we defer our discussion of it until the next section.

Brainstorming

Brainstorming is among the most, if not the most, widely used techniques in business to stimulate and foster creativity. It was originally developed by Alex Osborn, an advertising executive, in the 1950s. The basis for brainstorming was Osborn's belief that while on the one hand there can be a synergistic effect associated with having people work in teams (i.e., two heads are better than one), the team's overall creativity and effectiveness is often limited by a tendency to prematurely evaluate ideas as they are being generated. In an effort to capitalize on the strengths of working in teams while at the same time eliminating the drawbacks, Osborn developed the brainstorming approach which includes the following four guidelines:

1. Do not criticize ideas during the brainstorming session.
2. Express all ideas no matter how radical, bizarre, unconventional, ridiculous, or impractical they may seem.
3. Generate as many ideas as possible.
4. Combine, extend, and/or improve on one another's ideas.

As you can see, brainstorming focuses more on the quantity of ideas generated rather than the quality. This is intentional, the point being that there will be ample opportunity to critically evaluate the ideas after the brainstorming session has ended. Therefore, the temptation to criticize or judge ideas early in the process should be avoided so as to not stifle the creativity of the participants during the brainstorming session.

It is interesting to note that despite the wide acceptance and use of brainstorming in industry, much of the research in the area questions its effectiveness. As one example, Diehl and Stroebe (1987) compared both the quantity and quality of ideas generated by people working in teams and individually. In this study, they found that the teams generated an average number of 28 ideas while the same number of people working individually generated an average of 74.5 ideas. Furthermore, when the ideas were evaluated by experts, only 8.9% of the ideas generated by the teams on average were considered "good ideas" compared with 12.7% of the ideas generated by the people working independently. Based on these results and the results of other studies, Professor Leigh Thompson identified four threats to team creativity:

1. *Social loafing.* When working in teams, people may feel they will not get credit for their ideas and therefore may not work as hard in groups compared with the amount of effort they would invest if working individually.
2. *Conformity.* When working in teams, people may be overly conservative with what they are willing to share with the team because of concerns they may have about the reaction of others.
3. *Production blocking.* There are physical limitations that can restrict the productivity of a team. For example, only one person can speak at a time. Likewise, people cannot listen and concentrate on what others are saying and simultaneously generate their own new ideas. When working alone, there are likely to be fewer distractions interrupting a person's train of thought.
4. *Downward norm setting.* Research on teams suggests that individuals working in a team environment tend to match the productivity of the least productive team member.

Fortunately, in addition to identifying these threats to team creativity, Professor Thompson also identified a number of specific actions that can be used to mitigate the threats and actually enhance team creativity. These actions include:

- *Create diversified teams.* Teams consisting of members with a variety of different skills, experiences, training, and so on will position the team to view a problem from multiple perspectives.

- *Use analogical reasoning.* With analogical reasoning, concepts from one discipline or area are applied to other areas. For example, Dr. Eliyahu Goldratt originally developed the Theory of Constraints (discussed in Chapter 10) as a way to improve the efficiency of a factory. More recently, his theory has been extended and applied to the field of project management.

- *Use brainwriting.* Brainwriting involves having the participants in a brainstorming session take periodic breaks to write down their own ideas silently. A key benefit of brainwriting is that it can greatly eliminate production blocking.

- *Use the Nominal Group Technique.* The Nominal Group Technique (NGT) is often included as part of the Six Sigma toolkit as shown in Table 4.3. With the NGT, team members first work independently for perhaps five to ten minutes generating a list of ideas. The team members then share their ideas with the team, often in a round-robin fashion, and the ideas are listed. After all the ideas are listed, the team moves on to discussing, clarifying, and extending them. At the end of the discussion, team members individually rank order the ideas. Depending on the number of ideas, the team may rank order each idea or alternatively select their five or ten favorite ideas and then rank order this subset. The team then evaluates the results, perhaps considering the scores of the ideas or the frequency with which an idea was selected.

- *Record team ideas.* Recording ideas can help a team utilize its time together more effectively by eliminating repetitive discussions and ensuring that ideas are not forgotten.

- *Use trained facilitators to run the brainstorming session.* As experts in brainstorming, trained facilitators can ensure the rules are followed and that the discussion stays on task.

- *Set high standards.* In some cases, a team's lack of performance may be the result of misunderstandings of what is expected or even possible. For example, feedback regarding how many ideas the team has generated in comparison to the number of ideas other teams have generated after similar durations may help increase the quantity of ideas generated.

- *Change the composition of the team.* Research supports that periodically replacing team members helps increase both the quantity of ideas generated by the team as well as the number of different types of ideas generated.

- *Use electronic brainstorming.* With electronic brainstorming, team members are seated in a room with individual computer workstations for each team member. The team members work individually and enter their ideas into the computer. A computer screen located at the front of the room anonymously displays all ideas generated. Thus, the participants are able to build off of one another's ideas without the constraint that only one person can speak at a time or without the interruptions of having to listen to someone else while trying to think independently.

- *Make the workplace a playground.* Creativity can be fostered by making simple changes to the work environment. While the possibilities are endless, the common denominator is to make the environment fun. Some ideas include placing toys that foster creativity at each seat (e.g., Play-Doh, Legos, building blocks), painting a conference room in nontraditional colors, and changing the name of the room from "the conference room" to "the innovation zone."

Cause and Effect Diagrams

Cause and effect diagrams are another widely used Six Sigma tool. In fact, developing a cause and effect diagram often goes hand-in-hand with brainstorming. For example, a cause and effect diagram provides an effective way to organize the ideas that are generated in a brainstorming session addressing the causes of a particular problem. Alternatively, a brainstorming session may be held to develop the cause and effect diagram.

As an example, Figure 4.13 provides a simplified version of the cause and effect diagram developed at the West Babylon School District in Long Island, NY. In particular, there was a common perception by the teachers that insufficient time was being spent covering the curriculum. To better help understand the problem and analyze it, a cause and effect diagram was developed.

Creating cause and effect diagrams is a fairly straightforward process. First, a box summarizing the problem is drawn at the far right of the workspace and a horizontal line with an arrow terminating at the box is added. Next, the major causes of the problem are identified and connected to the original horizontal line. Referring to Figure 4.13, four major causes were identified regarding the problem associated with a lack of teaching time in the fifth grade: (1) scheduling, (2) staffing, (3) no priority given for classroom instruction time, and (4) state mandates. The process of creating a cause and effect diagram continues by attempting to break down each major cause into more detailed causes and then possibly breaking down these detailed causes even further. For example, according to Figure 4.13, we observe that issues related to shared staffing and lack of funding contribute to the staffing problem.

Not only can cause and effect diagrams be developed quickly, they provide an intuitive approach for better understanding problems. Furthermore, important insights are often obtained through the process of creating the diagram, as well as from the diagram itself. However, it should also be noted that, while the cause and effect diagram is well structured, the process of creating one is usually not. It is typical to bounce around from the detailed analysis of a particular cause to adding one or more additional major causes. Furthermore, as additional ideas are generated, it may be decided to eliminate, move, combine, and/or rename the major causes or the more detailed causes. Finally, note that because of its appearance, cause and effect diagrams are often referred to as "fishbone" diagrams.

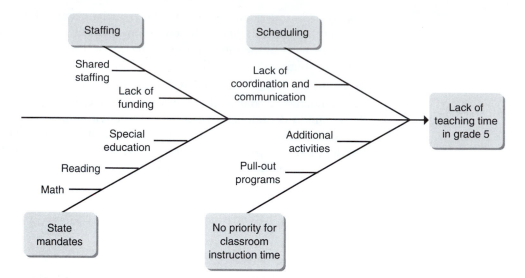

Figure 4.13 Fishbone diagram to analyze the problem of insufficent time being spent covering the curriculum. *Source:* Adapted from R. Manley and J. Manley. "Sharing the Wealth: TQM Spreads from Business to Education." *Quality Progress* (June 1996), pp. 51–55.

Process Capability Analysis

With the advent of total quality management programs and their emphasis on "making it right the first time," organizations are becoming increasingly concerned with the ability of their production processes and service delivery processes to meet customer requirements. Process Capability Analysis allows an organization to measure the extent to which its processes can meet its customer requirements or the design specifications for the product or service. As shown in Figure 4.14, process capability depends on:

1. Location of the process mean.
2. Natural variability inherent in the process.
3. Stability of the process.
4. Product's design requirements.

In Figure 4.14*a* the natural variation inherent in the process and the product's design specifications are well matched, resulting in a production system that is consistently capable of meeting the design requirements. However, in Figure 4.14*b* the natural variation in the production system is greater than the product's design requirements. This will lead to the production of a large amount of product that does not meet the requirements: The production system simply does not have the necessary ability. Options in this situation include improving the production system, relaxing the design requirements, or producing a large quantity of product that is unfit for use.

In Figure 4.14*c* the situation is reversed: The product has wider design specifications than the natural variation inherent in the production system. In this case the production system is easily able to meet the design specifications, and the organization may choose to investigate more economical production systems in order to lower costs. Finally, although the widths of design specifications and process variation are equal in Figure 4.14*d*, their means are out of sync. Thus, this system will produce a fair amount of output above the upper specification limit (USL). In this situation the solution would be to shift the process mean to the left so that it is better aligned with the design specifications.

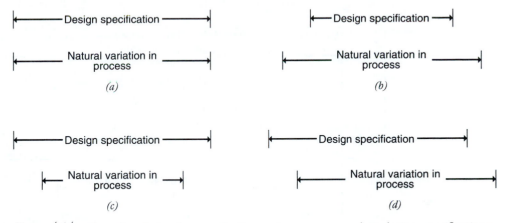

Figure 4.14   Natural variation in a production system versus product design specifications.

More formally, the relationship between the natural variation in the production system and the product's design specifications can be quantified using a ***process capability index***. The process capability index (C_p) is typically defined as the ratio of the width of the product's design specification to six standard deviations of the production system. Six standard deviations for the production system is used because three standard deviations above and below the production system's process mean will include 99.7 percent of the possible production outcomes, assuming that the output of the production system can be approximated with a normal distribution. Mathematically, the process capability index is calculated as

$$C_P = \frac{\text{product's design specification range}}{6 \text{ standard deviations of the production system}} = \frac{\text{USL} - \text{LSL}}{6\sigma}$$

where LSL and USL are a product's lower and upper design specification limits, respectively, and σ is the standard deviation of the production system.

According to this index, a C_p of less than 1 indicates that a particular process is not capable of consistently meeting design specifications; a C_p greater than 1 indicates that the production process is capable of consistently meeting the requirements. As a rule of thumb, many organizations desire a C_p index of at least 1.5 (Evans and Lindsay 1999). Achieving *Six Sigma quality* with no more than 3.4 defective parts per million provides a C_p index of 2.0 (assuming the process mean can shift by as much as 1.5 standard deviations).

Figure 4.15 illustrates the effect that changes in the natural variation of the production system have on the C_p index for fixed product design specifications. In Figure 4.15*a* the natural variation in the process is much less than the product's design specification range, yielding a C_p index greater than 1. In contrast, in Figure

4.15*b* the natural variation in the process is larger than the product's design specifications, yielding a C_p index less than 1. Finally, in Figure 4.15*c* the natural process variation and the design specifications are equal, yielding a C_p index equal to 1.

One limitation of the process capability index is that it only compares the magnitudes of the product's design specification range and the process's natural variation. It does not consider the degree to which these ranges are actually aligned.

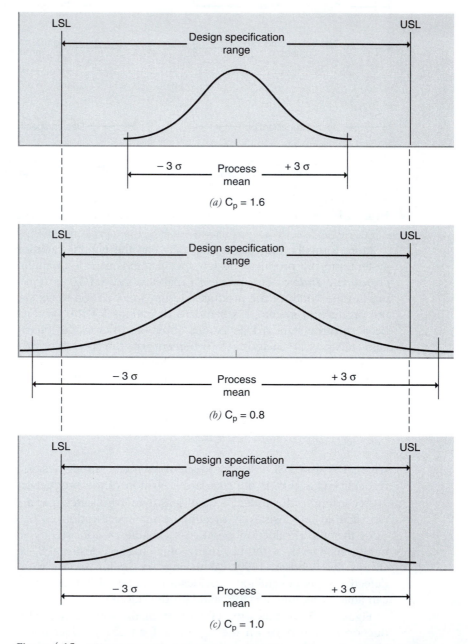

Figure 4.15 Effect of production system variability on process capability index. (*a*) C_p = 1.6; (*b*) C_p = 0.8; (*c*) C_p = 1.0.

For example, the situations shown in Figure 4.14*a* and Figure 4.14*d* both yield a C_p index of 1. However, as was pointed out earlier, a considerable amount of defective product would be produced in the situation shown in Figure 4.14*d*, owing to the lack of alignment between the design specifications and the process mean. The most common way to evaluate the extent to which the process mean is centered within the product's design specification range is to calculate a one-sided process capability index C_{pk}, as follows:

$$C_{pu} = \frac{\text{USL} - \text{process mean}}{3\sigma}$$

$$C_{pl} = \frac{\text{process mean} - \text{LSL}}{3\sigma}$$

$$C_{pk} = \min(C_{pl}, C_{pk})$$

$\mathcal{T}$HE IMPROVE PHASE

Having defined the problem, measured the process's current performance, and analyzed the process, we are now in a position to identify and test options for improving the process. In the remainder of this section, our focus will be on the use of Design of Experiments (DOE) as a process improvement tool.

Design of Experiments

Perhaps the most common approach to analyzing problems is to investigate one factor at a time (aka OFAT and 1FAT). Unfortunately, the one factor at a time approach suffers from several important shortcomings. To illustrate these short-comings, consider the operation of a financial institution's call center for its credit cards. A representative performance measure would be the time it takes the call center's customer service reps (CSRs) to process an incoming call. Factors or variables that might initially be identified as having an impact on the time to process a call include the nature of the call, the time of day, and the CSR that handles the call.

The first shortcoming with OFAT is that it is not typically possible to test one factor at a time and hold all the other factors constant. For example, assume that processing time data were collected for two CSRs over some period of time and it was determined that CSR A averaged five minutes per call while CSR B averaged seven minutes per call. Based on these data, can we conclude that CSR A is more efficient than CSR B? The answer is no because the impact of other variables has not been accounted for. In this case it could be that CSR B's calls were of a more difficult nature to handle. Or perhaps the data for CSR A were collected around lunch time when there was a high volume of calls and numerous callers on hold while the data from CSR B were collected early in the morning when the call volume was lower and there were virtually no callers on hold. The point is that when one variable is studied at a time and the values of other variables are not controlled or otherwise accounted for, it is difficult, if not impossible, to draw valid conclusions about the impact of a single variable.

Another shortcoming associated with the OFAT approach is that it is not possible to account for interactions or joint variation between variables. To illustrate the concept of interaction, consider the interaction plots shown in Figure 4.16. Interaction plots are used to help evaluate the separate effects of the independent variables (or main effects), as well as possible joint or interaction effects among the independent variables. In the plots shown in Figure 4.16, there are two independent variables (i.e., the CSR and the nature of the call) and one dependent or response variable (call duration). Furthermore, data for each of the dependent variables were collected at two levels. The two levels for the nature of the call are calls related to canceling an account and calls related to address changes. The two levels for CSR were data collected for calls handled by CSR A and those handled by CSR B. Had a third CSR been included in the study, the CSR variable would have had three levels. Also note that in the interaction plot the dependent variable is plotted on the vertical axis (call duration in our example), one independent variable is plotted on the horizontal axis (CSR), and then a line is added for each level of the remaining independent variable (nature of the call).

Referring to Figure 4.16a, we observe that no definitive statements can be made about either independent variable. In other words, we cannot say definitely that change of address calls take longer than calls to cancel an account nor can we say definitely that CSR A takes longer than CSR B. Rather, the impact the two independent variables have on call duration depends jointly on their respective levels. Thus, we see that CSR A cancels accounts faster than CSR B, while CSR B processes address changes faster than CSR A. In other words, the duration of a call depends on both which CSR takes the call as well as the nature of the call. In this particular case, where no definitive statements can be made about either independent variable, we say that there is no main effect and only a joint or interaction effect.

Figure 4.16b illustrates the opposite end of the spectrum, where there is only a main effect and no interaction. In analyzing Figure 4.16b, we can definitely say that change of address calls take longer than calls to cancel an account. In addition, we can say definitely that CSR B takes longer to process a call than CSR A. Note that because the lines are parallel in Figure 4.16b, there is no interaction effect and only main effects. Thus we note that the amount of extra time it takes to process a change of address compared with canceling an account is the same for both CSRs A and B.

Finally, Figure 4.16c illustrates a situation where there are both main and interaction effects. In terms of main effects, we can say that CSR B takes longer than CSR A regardless of the call type and that changing an address takes longer than canceling an account regardless of the CSR. However, because the lines are not perfectly parallel, there is also an interaction effect. In this case the interaction requires that we qualify our conclusions. Specifically, we observe that while changing an address takes longer than canceling an account, the extra time it takes CSR B to change an address compared to canceling an account is greater than the extra time CSR A requires.

In comparing Figures 4.16a–4.16c, a couple of observations are in order. First, the more parallel the lines are to one another in the interaction plot, the more significant the main effects are relative to the interaction effects. In contrast, the more the lines are perpendicular to one another, the more significant the interaction effects are relative to the main effects.

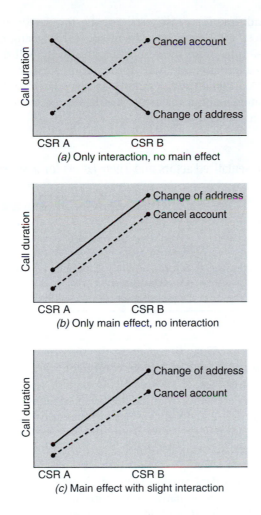

Figure 4.16   Types of interaction between two variables.

One approach to overcoming the shortcomings associated with the OFAT approach is to use design of experiments (DOE) techniques. DOE techniques utilize the principles of statistics to design experiments to investigate multiple process variables simultaneously. With DOE techniques, multiple factors are varied and therefore studied simultaneously, and repeated measurements are typically taken for each combination of factor level settings.

Some major considerations associated with DOE include:

- *Determining which factors to include in the experiment.* Interviewing subject matter experts (SME) is one way to identify relevant factors. Work in the previous phases of the Six Sigma project may also provide important insights into relevant factors. Along these lines, cause and effect diagrams are often particularly helpful for identifying relevant factors.

- *Specifying the levels for each factor.* Once the factors are identified, the levels of each factor must be specified. For example, referring to the Southside Hospital example from the beginning of the chapter, Table 4.6 summarizes an experiment that investigates four factors that are hypothesized to have an impact on the lead time for stress tests. For the first factor, method used to order the stress test, two levels have been specified—using either a fax machine or the Web to order the test. Thus, the study will investigate the impact these two alternative methods for ordering stress tests has on the overall stress test lead time. Notice that the factor related to the method used to educate the patients about the stress test has three levels, while each of the other factors has two levels.

$\mathcal{T}$ABLE   4.6 • Representative Factors and Their Levels for a Stress Test Study

Factor	Levels
Method used to order stress test	Fax, Web
Method used to schedule patient appointments	Fixed time appointments; patients given a time window
Method used to educate patients about stress test	Information sheet; phone call from nurse; in-person meeting with nurse
Dictation technology	Tape recorder and transcriber; speech recognition

- *Determining how much data to collect*. In the experimental design listed in Table 4.6 there are a total of 24 treatment combinations (2 levels of the method used to order the stress test × 2 levels of the patient scheduling method × 3 levels of the patient education method × 2 levels of the dictation technology). Therefore, 24 patients are needed in order to obtain one observation for each possible treatment combination. Of course, to have confidence in the results of a study, it is necessary to collect more than one observation. In DOE terminology, we refer to multiple observations for a treatment combination as replication. If historical data are available, preliminary calculations may be performed to determine how many replications are needed in order to obtain a specified level of statistical confidence. In other cases, limitations such as the time available to complete the study, personnel, or money may dictate the number of replications possible.

- *Determining the type of experimental design*. Fundamentally, there are two types of experimental designs. A full factorial experiment corresponds to a study where data are collected for all possible treatment combinations. A fractional factorial experiment corresponds to a study where data are collected for only a subset of all possible treatment combinations. Fractional factorial experiments are used when the number of treatment combinations is so large that it is not practical to collect data for each treatment combination. For example, a study with seven factors, each with three levels, would have 2187 treatment combinations (3^7). In many cases, investigating 2187 treatment combinations is not practical. Fortunately, in these cases fractional factorial designs can be developed that reduce the number of treatment combinations while at the same time still providing the most relevant information. In effect, DOE techniques utilize statistical principles to maximize the amount of information that can be obtained from a given number of treatment combinations. Because the calculations are quite complex, the design of fractional factorial experiments is typically done with the aid of specialized computer software or published experimental design catalogues.

Taguchi Methods

Among the more popular approaches used to design experiments are Taguchi methods, named after Genichi Taguchi. According to Taguchi, most of the quality of products and services are determined at the design stage, and therefore the production system can affect quality only slightly. Taguchi focused on this fact to develop an approach to designing quality into outputs. Rather than trying to constantly control equipment and workers to stay within specifications—sizes, finishes, times—he has devised a procedure for statistical testing to determine the best combination of product and process design to make the output relatively independent of normal fluctuations in the production system. To do this, statistical experimentation is conducted to determine what product and process designs produce outputs with the highest uniformity at lowest cost.

$\mathcal{T}$HE CONTROL PHASE

As the Six Sigma project nears completion, the focus in the final phase shifts to the development of procedures to monitor the process. Here our purpose is to ensure that the process's new higher level of performance is maintained and that previous problems do not resurface. In the remainder of this section, we discuss the use of control charts—the most commonly used control tool.

Introduction to Statistical Quality Control

One of management's most difficult decisions in quality control centers on whether an activity needs adjustment. This requires some form of inspection, either *measuring* something or simply determining the *existence* of a characteristic. Measuring, called *inspection for variables*, usually relates to weight, length, temperature, diameter, or some other variable that can be *scaled*. Identifying a characteristic, called *inspection of attributes*, can also examine scaled variables but usually considers *dichotomous* variables such as right–wrong, acceptable–defective, black–white, timely–late, and other such characteristics that either cannot be measured or do not *need* to be measured with any more precision than yes–no.

Walter A. Shewhart developed the concept of statistical **control charts** in the 1920s to distinguish between *chance variation* in a system and variation caused by the system's being out of control—*assignable variation*. Should a process go out of control, that must first be detected, then the assignable cause must be identified, and finally the appropriate action or adjustment must be performed. The control chart is used to detect when a process has gone out of control.

A repetitive operation will seldom produce *exactly* the same quality, size, and so on; rather, with each repetition the operation will generate variation around some average. This variation is particularly characteristic of a sampling process where random samples are taken and a sample mean is calculated, as in quality control.

Because this variation usually has a large number of small, uncontrollable sources, the pattern of variability is often well described by a standard frequency distribution such as the *normal distribution*, shown plotted against the vertical scale in Figure 4.17.

The succession of measures that results from the continued repetition of some process can thus be thought of as a *population* of numbers, normally distributed, with some mean and standard deviation. As long as the distribution remains the same, the process is considered to be in control and simply exhibiting chance variation. One way to determine if the distribution is staying the same is to keep checking the mean of the distribution—if it changes to some other value, the operation may be considered out of control. The problem, however, is that it is too expensive for organizations to keep constantly checking operations. Therefore, *samples* of the output are checked instead.

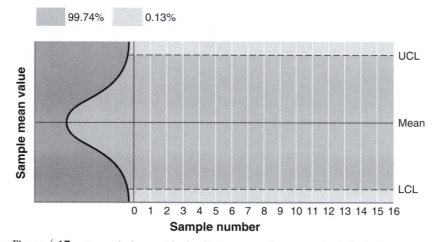

Figure 4.17   Control chart with the limits set at three standard deviations.

In sampling output for inspection, it is imperative that the sample fully *represent* the population being checked; therefore, a *random sample* should be used. But when checks are made only of sample averages, rather than 100 percent of the output, there is always a chance of selecting a sample with an unusually high or low mean. The problem facing the operations manager is thus to decide what is *too high* or *too low* and therefore should be considered out of control. Also, the manager must consider the fact that the more samples eventually taken, the higher the likelihood of accidentally selecting a sample with too high (or too low) a mean *when the process is actually still under control.*

The values of the sample mean that are too high or low are called the **upper control limit** (UCL) and the **lower control limit** (LCL), respectively. These limits generally allow an approach to control that is known as *management by exception*, because, theoretically, the manager need take no action unless a *sample mean* exceeds the control limits. The control limits most commonly used in organizations are plus and minus *three standard deviations*. We know from statistics that the chance that a sample mean will exceed three standard deviations, in either direction, due simply to chance variation, is less than 0.3 percent (i.e., 3 times per 1000 samples). Thus, the chance that a sample will fall above the UCL or below the LCL because of natural random causes is so small that this occurrence is strong evidence of assignable variation. Figure 4.17 illustrates the use of control limits set at three standard deviations. Of course, using the higher limit values (3 or more) increases the risk of not detecting a process that is only slightly out of control.

An even better approach is to use control charts to predict when an out-of-control situation is likely to occur rather than waiting for a process to actually go out of control. If only chance variation is present in the process, the points plotted on a control chart will not typically exhibit any pattern. On the other hand, if the points exhibit some systematic pattern, this is an indication that assignable variation may be present and corrective action should be taken.

The control chart, though originally developed for quality control in manufacturing, is applicable to all sorts of repetitive activities in any kind of organization. Thus, it can be used for services as well as products, for people or machines, for cost or quality, and so on.

For the control of variables—that is, measured characteristics—two control charts are required:

1. Chart of the *sample means*.
2. Chart of the *range* (*R*) of values in each sample (largest value in sample minus smallest value in sample).

It is important to use two control charts for variables because of the way in which control of process quality can be lost. To illustrate this phenomenon, we will use the data supplied in Table 4.7, which correspond to weights of tacos made at a fast-food restaurant. Three samples are taken each day: one during the lunch-hour rush, one during the dinner-hour rush, and one a couple of hours before the restaurant is closed. Each sample consists of three tacos randomly selected from a bin that stores completed tacos waiting to be sold to customers.

$\mathscr{T}$ABLE 4.7 ● Sample Data of Weights of Tacos (ounces)

Sample	Scenario 1	Scenario 2
1	4, 5, 6	5, 4, 6
2	6, 7, 8	3, 5, 7
3	7, 9, 8	8, 2, 5

Referring to scenario 1, we can easily determine that the average of sample 1 is 5 ounces and the range is 2 ounces ($\overline{X}_1 = 5$, $R_1 = 2$). Similarly, $\overline{X}_2 = 7$, $R_2 = 2$, $\overline{X}_3 = 8$, and $R_3 = 2$. If we consider only the ranges of the samples, no problem is indicated, because all three samples have a range of 2 (assuming that a range of 2 ounces is acceptable to management). On the other hand, the behavior of the process means shows evidence of a problem. Specifically, the process means (weights) have increased throughout the day from an average of 5 ounces to an average of 8 ounces. Thus, for the data listed in scenario 1, the sample ranges indicate acceptable process performance while the sample means indicate unacceptable process performance.

The sample statistics can be calculated in the same way for scenario 2: $\overline{X}_1 = 5$, $R_1 = 2$, $\overline{X}_2 = 5$, $R_2 = 4$, $\overline{X}_3 = 5$, and $R_3 = 6$. In contrast to scenario 1, the sample means show acceptable performance while the sample ranges show possibly unacceptable performance. Thus, we see the necessity of monitoring both the mean and the variability of a process.

Figure 4.18 illustrates these two patterns of change in the distribution of process values more formally. These changes might be due to boredom, tool wear, improper training, the weather, fatigue, or any other such influence. In Figure 4.18*a* the variability in the process remains the same but the mean changes (scenario 1); this effect would be seen in the means ($\overline{X}$) chart but not in the range (R) chart. In Figure 4.18*b* the mean remains the same, but the variability tends to increase (scenario 2 above); this would be seen in the range (R) chart but not the means ($\overline{X}$) chart.

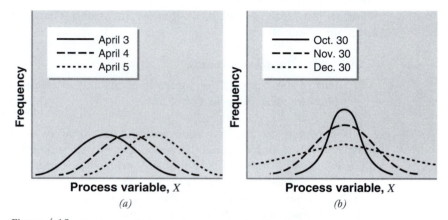

Figure 4.18   Patterns of change in process distributions.

In terms of quality of the output, either type of change could result in lower quality, depending on the situation. Regarding control limits, the lower control limit (LCL) for the means chart may be negative, depending on the variable being measured. For example, variables such as profit and temperature can be negative, but variables such as length, diameter, and weight cannot. Since (by definition) the range can *never* be negative, if calculations indicate a negative LCL for the range chart, it should simply be set to zero.

As indicated earlier, control limits for the means chart are usually set at plus and minus three standard deviations. But if a range chart is also being used, these limits for the means chart can be found by using the average range, which is directly related to the standard deviation, in the following equations (where $\overline{\overline{X}}$ is the average of the sample means):

$$\text{UCL}_{\overline{x}} = \overline{\overline{X}} + A_2\,\overline{R}$$

$$\text{LCL}_{\overline{x}} = \overline{\overline{X}} - A_2\,\overline{R}$$

Similarly, control limits for the range chart are found from

$$\text{UCL}_R = D_4\overline{R}$$

$$\text{LCL}_R = D_3\overline{R}$$

The factors A_2, D_3, and D_4 vary with the sample size and are tabulated in Table 4.8.

$\mathcal{T}_{\text{ABLE}}$ 4.8 • Control Chart Factors to Determine Control Limits

Sample Size, n	A_2	D_3	D_4
2	1.880	0	3.267
3	1.023	0	2.575
4	0.729	0	2.282
5	0.577	0	2.115
6	0.483	0	2.004
7	0.419	0.076	1.924
8	0.373	0.136	1.864
9	0.337	0.184	1.816
10	0.308	0.223	1.777
12	0.266	0.284	1.716
14	0.235	0.329	1.671
16	0.212	0.364	1.636
18	0.194	0.392	1.608
20	0.180	0.414	1.586
22	0.167	0.434	1.566
24	0.157	0.452	1.548

Constructing Control Charts

The best way to illustrate the construction of control charts is by example. Assume that a chain of 10 ice cream stores is interested in monitoring the age of the ice cream served at its stores. To maintain a continuing check on this quality, one could select stores at random from the chain each day and note the age of the ice cream served. To set up the control charts, initial samples need to be taken. These data will, if considered representative by management, be used to set standards (i.e., control limits) for future ice cream inventory. For our example, we assume that a sample of $n = 4$ of the 10 stores each day will give the best control for the trouble involved.

The mean age and range in ages for the initial samples were entered into the spreadsheet shown in Table 4.9. Note that each sample mean and sample range shown in Table 4.9 is based on data collected by randomly visiting four stores. The grand mean $\overline{\overline{X}}$, and the average range ($\overline{R}$) were also calculated (cells B23 and C23, respectively). The grand mean is then simply the average of all the daily means:

$$\overline{\overline{X}} = \frac{\sum \overline{X}}{N}$$

where N is 20 days of samples and the average range is

$$\overline{R} = \frac{\sum R}{N}$$

$\mathcal{T}$ABLE   4.9 • Mean and Range
of Ages of Ice Cream

	A	B	C
1		**Sample**	**Sample**
2	**Date**	**Mean**	**Range**
3	June 1	10	18
4	June 2	13	13
5	June 3	11	15
6	June 4	14	14
7	June 5	9	14
8	June 6	11	10
9	June 7	8	15
10	June 8	12	17
11	June 9	13	9
12	June 10	10	16
13	June 11	13	12
14	June 12	12	14
15	June 13	8	13
16	June 14	11	15
17	June 15	11	11
18	June 16	9	14
19	June 17	10	13
20	June 18	9	19
21	June 19	12	14
22	June 20	14	14
23	**Average**	**11**	**14**

The data in Table 4.9 can now be used to construct control charts that will indicate to management any sudden change, for better or worse, in the quality (age) of the ice cream. Both a chart of means, to check the age of the ice cream being served, and a chart of ranges, to check consistency among stores should be used.

The grand mean and average range will give the center line on these charts, respectively. The values of A_2, D_3, and D_4 are obtained from Table 4.8 for $n = 4$, resulting in the following control limits:

$$\text{UCL}_{\bar{x}} = 11 + 0.729(14) = 21.206$$

$$\text{LCL}_{\bar{x}} = 11 - 0.729(14) = 0.794$$

$$\text{UCL}_R = 2.282(14) = 31.948$$

$$\text{LCL}_R = 0(14) = 0$$

The control charts for this example were developed using a spreadsheet and are shown in Figures 4.19 and 4.20. In addition, the data in Table 4.9 are graphed on the charts. As seen in Figure 4.19, no pattern is apparent from the data; the points appear to fall randomly around the grand mean (centerline) and thus are considered by management to be representative.

The range chart, Figure 4.20, again shows no apparent pattern and is also acceptable to management. Each day, as a new sample is taken, $\bar{X}$ and R will be calculated and plotted on the two charts. If either $\bar{X}$ or R is outside the LCL or UCL, management must then undertake to find the assignable cause for the variation.

Control charts can also be used for controlling attributes of the output. The most common of these charts are the *fraction-defective p chart* and the *number-of-defects c chart*. As with the range chart, the lower control limit for attribute charts can never be negative.

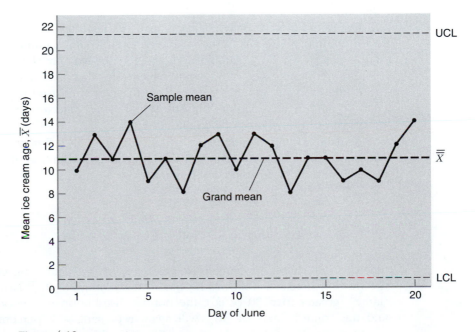

Figure 4.19   Mean ice cream age.

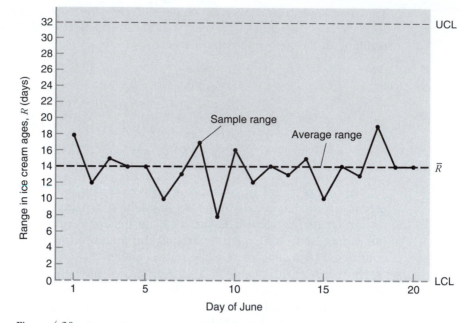

Figure 4.20   Range in ice cream age.

The fraction-defective p chart can be used for any two-state (*dichotomous*) process such as heavy versus light, acceptable versus unacceptable, on-time versus late, or placed properly versus misplaced. The control chart for p is constructed in much the same way as the control chart for $\overline{X}$. First, a large sample of historical data is gathered, and the fraction (percent) having the characteristic in question (e.g., too light, defective, misplaced), $\overline{p}$, is computed on the entire set of data as a whole.

Large samples are usually taken because the fraction of interest is typically small and the number of items in the samples should be large enough to include some of the defectives. For example, a fraction defective may be 3 percent or less. Therefore, a sample size of 33 would have to be taken (i.e., $1/0.03 = 33$) to expect to include even one defective item. Note that the data used to *derive* the control chart do not have to use the same size sample as is collected to use the chart. *Any* set of data can be used to determine $\overline{p}$.

Since the fraction defective follows a *binomial* distribution (bi means "two": either an item is or it is not) rather than a normal distribution, the standard deviation may be calculated directly from $\overline{p}$ as

$$\sigma_p = \sqrt{\frac{\overline{p}(1-\overline{p})}{n}}$$

where n is the uniform sample size to be used for controlling quality. Although the fraction defective follows the binomial distribution, if $\overline{p}$ is near 0.5, or n is "large" (greater than 30 or so), the normal distribution is a good approximation and the control limits of $3\sigma_p$ will again represent 99.7 percent of the sample observations. Again, the LCL cannot be negative.

The number-of-defects c chart is used for a single situation in which any number of incidents may occur, each with a small probability. Typical of such incidents are scratches in tables, fire alarms in a city, typesetting errors in a newspaper, and the number of improper autoinsertions per printed circuit board. An average number of incidents, $\bar{c}$, is determined from combined past data by dividing the total number of incidents observed by the number of items inspected. The distribution of such incidents is known to follow the *Poisson distribution* with a standard deviation of

$$\sigma_c = \sqrt{c}$$

Again, the normal distribution is used as an approximation to derive control limits with a minimum LCL of zero.

$\mathcal{S}$IX SIGMA IN PRACTICE

To conclude our introduction to Six Sigma, we now turn our attention to issues related to employing Six Sigma to improve business processes and performance. Here our focus will be on the various roles played in Six Sigma initiatives, the Six Sigma body of knowledge, becoming certified in Six Sigma, and the need for each organization to customize its Six Sigma program to its unique needs.

Six Sigma Roles

One aspect that differentiates Six Sigma from other earlier process improvement programs including total quality management and reengineering is that with Six Sigma, specific roles and titles for these roles have been defined and generally accepted. The central roles to Six Sigma include:

- *Master Black Belts*. Master Black Belts combine an advanced knowledge of the Six Sigma toolkit with a deep understanding of the business. The primary roles of Master Black Belts are to develop and execute Six Sigma training programs and to work with senior management to ensure that Six Sigma initiatives are being best leveraged to help the organization achieve its strategic goals.
- *Black Belts*. With a solid background in the Six Sigma toolkit, the two primary roles of Black Belts are conducting Six Sigma training and leading Six Sigma projects. Both Black Belt and Master Black Belt positions tend to be full-time positions.
- *Green Belts*. Green belts have broad knowledge of the Six Sigma toolkit, but not nearly as much depth in the tools as Black Belts and Master Black Belts. The majority of the work of Six Sigma projects is typically completed by Green Belts under the guidance and direction of Black Belts and, on occasion, Master Black Belts. Usually, Green Belts split their time between their work on Six Sigma projects and other work responsibilities.

- *Yellow Belts.* Although not as common as Master Black Belts, Black Belts, and Green Belts, some organizations have added the Yellow Belt rank as a designation for those employees that have completed Six Sigma awareness training.

In addition to these central roles, there are also a number of important supporting roles including:

- *Champions/Sponsors.* Champions are senior managers that support and promote Six Sigma projects. The employees working on a Six Sigma project rely on the champion's senior position within the organization to help them obtain the needed resources to successfully complete the project as well as to remove hurdles that might otherwise derail the successful completion of the project.

- *Process owners.* Although process owners are the managers with end-to-end responsibility for a particular business process, typically they do not direct Six Sigma projects. Rather, they are best viewed as being the customers of Six Sigma projects.

The Six Sigma Body of Knowledge

Another aspect that differentiates Six Sigma from earlier process improvement programs is that there is a well-defined Six Sigma body of knowledge (BOK). Thus, despite the large number of organizations that offer Six Sigma training and the wide variety of organizations that have adopted Six Sigma, there is a high degree of consensus among practitioners regarding the composition of the Six Sigma BOK. Contributing to this was the American Society for Quality (ASQ), a well-respected professional society with over 100,000 members, developing a standard for the Six Sigma BOK.

ASQ has divided the Six Sigma BOK into ten major categories. Five of these categories correspond to the Define-Measure-Analyze-Improve-Control (DMAIC) framework commonly utilized in Six Sigma projects. The following is a brief overview of the ten categories comprising ASQ's BOK, including the number of questions on ASQ's Six Sigma Black Belt exam that are taken from each category. For additional information, the interested reader is referred to the *Certified Six Sigma Black Belt* brochure available for download at www.asq.org.

- *Enterprise Deployment (9 questions).* This category includes topics related to understanding the value of Six Sigma to an organization, the Six Sigma philosophy and its goals, and understanding the various organizational roles in Six Sigma. Enterprise Deployment is further divided into the following four subcategories: (1) Enterprise View, (2) Leadership, (3) Organizational Goals and Objectives, and (4) History of Organizational Improvement/Foundations of Six Sigma.

- *Business Process Management (9 questions).* The Business Process Management category consists of three subcategories: (1) Process versus Functional View, (2) Voice of the Customer, and (3) Business Results.

As these subcategories suggest, Business Process Management focuses on issues related to understanding a process, including its components, boundaries, owners, customers, and performance.

- *Project Management (15 questions).* Given the project nature of Six Sigma initiatives, in-depth knowledge of project management is a critical skill for the Six Sigma Black Belt. The Project Management category includes subcategories on the Project Charter and Plan, Team Leadership, Team Dynamics and Performance, Change Agent, and Management and Planning Tools. It is interesting to note that the first and last subcategories address what are typically considered to be traditional project management topics while the remaining topics are perhaps more closely associated with organizational behavior.

- *Six Sigma Improvement Methodology and Tools—Define (9 questions).* The define phase of Six Sigma project focuses on defining the project scope, the customer requirements, appropriate performance metrics, and the problem statement.

- *Six Sigma Improvement Methodology and Tools—Measure (30 questions).* The largest number of questions on ASQ's Six Sigma Black Belt exam are drawn from the Measure category. Measure is further divided into six subcategories: (1) Process Analysis and Documentation, (2) Probability and Statistics, (3) Collecting and Summarizing Data, (4) Properties and Applications of Probability Distributions, (5) Measurement Systems, and (6) Analyzing Process Capability.

- *Six Sigma Improvement Methodology and Tools—Analyze (23 questions).* This category focuses primarily on exploratory data analysis and hypothesis testing. Topics in this category include regression analysis, correlation, point and interval estimation, ANOVA, paired-comparison tests, goodness-of-fit tests, and type I and II errors.

- *Six Sigma Improvement Methodology and Tools—Improve (22 questions).* This is one of the more technical areas in the BOK and includes subcategories on the Design of Experiments, Response Surface Methodology, and Evolutionary Operations.

- *Six Sigma Improvement Methodology and Tools—Control (15 questions).* This category emphasizes statistical process control and the use of lean tools for control.

- *Lean Enterprise (9 questions).* This category's topics include the theory of constraints, cycle time reduction, and continuous flow manufacturing. This category also includes subcategories on Lean Tools and Total Productive Maintenance.

- *Design for Six Sigma (DFSS) (9 questions).* Like the previous category on the Lean Enterprise, the DFSS category could be considered a complete discipline in its own right. In ASQ's BOK, this category is further divided into five subcategories: (1) Quality Function Deployment (QFD), (2) Robust Design and Process, (3) Failure Mode and Effects Analysis, (4) Design for X (DFX), and (5) Special Design Tools.

Becoming Certified

In addition to having well-defined roles, another aspect that differentiates Six Sigma from earlier programs is that accompanying each of the central Six Sigma roles is a certification process. Along these lines, it is a common practice for organizations to make a distinction between employees who are Six Sigma trained at a certain level and those who are certified at the level. In these organizations, becoming certified at a given level entails meeting additional requirements beyond receiving the training, such as passing an examination and/or successfully completing one or more Six Sigma projects.

Generally speaking, there are four alternative ways of obtaining Black Belt certification. Perhaps the most common approach is for employees to be trained and certified internally by their current employer. In fact, based on their success with Six Sigma, some organizations actually open their training programs to people outside their organizations. Two notable examples are Motorola University (www.motorola.com/motorolauniversity) and Rockwell Automation's PowerLean certification program (www.dodge-reliance.com/power_services/preform/power-lean.html).

A second approach for obtaining certification is through numerous consulting organizations that offer both training and certification programs. These organizations can be easily found by doing a search of the Web using a search string such as "six sigma certification." Third, a number of universities have begun offering training and in some cases certification programs. Several universities even offer this training and certification through online distance education programs. Finally, individuals can obtain certification through professional societies, perhaps most commonly through ASQ.

Given the wide range of options for becoming certified, it is somewhat surprising to observe the extent to which these varied certification programs are standardized both in terms of duration and content. For example, it appears that the standard for Black Belt training is a four-month program during which students receive one week of formal in-class training each month and use the remaining time to complete a Black Belt project.

The Need to Customize Six Sigma Programs

Although there is a fair amount of consensus related to the roles, BOK, and training practices surrounding Six Sigma programs, organizations that have succeeded with their Six Sigma programs also recognize the need to tailor their Six Sigma approach to their unique needs. ScottishPower, an electric and gas provider to more than 5 million customers in the United States and United Kingdom, serves as an excellent example of this. In May 2001, ScottishPower brought in an external consultant to begin training its first wave of 20 full-time Black Belts. Because of the limited data that were available and the relatively generic nature of the external consultant's training program, ScottishPower emphasized the use of the more simple tools in its early Six Sigma projects including process mapping, Pareto analysis, cause and effect diagrams, and stakeholder analysis. Six months after the first wave of Black Belt training, a second group of 20 employees was selected for full-time Black Belt training. Based on their experience from the first round, ScottishPower identified the need to better use statistical analysis to identify the root causes of problems.

Thus the second wave of training, which was performed by ScottishPower's own Black Belts that were trained in the first wave, emphasized statistical techniques such as the use of t-tests, ANOVA, correlation, regression, and DOE. Based on a desire to gain additional value from the data that were being collected, Scottish-Power began emphasizing additional techniques in subsequent waves including chi-square tests, nonparametric tests such as Mann-Whitney and Kruskall-Wallis, and Box-Cox transformations. ScottishPower's experience and success with Six Sigma highlights the importance of customizing a Six Sigma program to the organization's unique needs and adopting the training as the organization becomes more sophisticated in both its ability to collect and analyze data.

QUALITY IN SERVICES

transformed into data & into more tangible measures of performance like financial measurements

Measuring the quality of the service portion of an output is often more difficult than measuring the quality of the facilitating good for a variety of reasons—including the service portion being abstract rather than concrete, transient rather than permanent, and psychological rather than physical. One way to cope with these difficulties is to use customer satisfaction surveys. For example, J.D. Power and Associates makes extensive use of customer satisfaction surveys to rate airlines, hotel chains, and rental car companies.[3] For example, its ratings of airlines in 2000 was based on over 6000 flight evaluations supplied by a national survey of frequent flyers. According to these travelers, on-time performance is the single most important factor, accounting for 25 percent of overall satisfaction with a flight. Other important factors include the airport check-in process (11%), courtesy of flight attendants (11%), and seating area and comfort (11%). In 2000, Continental Airlines received the highest ranking in both the long (more than 500 miles) and short flight categories.

J.D. Power ranks hotel chains and rental car companies in a similar fashion. For example, in 2000, J.D. Power ranked the overall satisfaction of 52 upscale hotels on the basis of over 10,000 individual evaluations of these hotels. According to J.D. Power, the primary factors impacting hotel customer satisfaction are satisfaction with the guest room, the reservation and check-in process, the departure process (including accuracy of the bill), guest services, and food and beverages. In 2000, Omni Hotels was the highest ranked upscale hotel. In terms of rental car companies, the key factors that contribute to customer satisfaction included the the car pick-up process, the car return process, rental rates, the rental car's condition, and the reservation process. In 2000, Enterprise was the highest ranked rental car company.

A common approach to improving the quality of services is to methodically train the employees in standard procedures and to use equipment that reinforces this training. The ultimate example is McDonald's Hamburger University, where managers, in particular, are intensively trained in the McDonald's system of food preparation and delivery. Not only is training intensive, but follow-up checkups are continuous, and incentives and rewards are given for continuing to pay attention

---

[3]Source: www.jdpower.com, February 15, 2001.

to quality. Furthermore, the equipment is designed to reinforce the quality process taught to the employee, and to discourage sloppy habits that lead to lesser quality.

The value of better quality is becoming known in office processes as well (Berstein 1991). For example, University Microfilms Inc. (UMI) of Ann Arbor, Michigan, was facing a growing backlog of requests for theses: 8000. Upon investigation, UMI found that the average thesis waits 150 days for processing but is processed only for a total time of two hours; much of the time is spent waiting for the author to reply to questions. By working on the quality of its editing and processing techniques, UMI cut the time in half within six months; it is now down to 60 days. As a result, customers' complaints were reduced by 17 percent and output increased by almost 50 percent with the same people.

Financial services can also benefit from better quality. Several years ago, First National Bank of Chicago noticed that its requests for letters of credit were handled by nine different employees who conducted dozens of steps, a process that consumed four days. By retraining its employees so that each would be able to process a customer's request through all the steps, First Chicago was able to let each customer deal with only one employee, who could complete the process within a day. Now each time a letter of credit is ordered, the customer is placed back with the same employee. As a result, the department involved has been able to double its output of letters of credit using the services of 49 percent fewer employees.

By paying attention to the quality delivered to customers, American Express was able to cut the processing time for new credit applications from 22 days to 11 days, thereby more than doubling the revenue per employee in its credit card division. It had previously tracked errors and processing time internally but had ignored the impacts on the customer. When it began focusing on the customer, it suddenly found that speed in the credit department was often immaterial in shortening the customer's waiting time for credit approval, because four more departments still had to process every new application.

Service Defections

When a tangible product is produced, quality is often measured in terms of defects. In services, the analogy to a product defect is a defecting customer—that is, a customer who takes his or her business elsewhere. Thus, service defections can be measured in a variety of ways, such as the percent of customers that do not renew their membership (health clubs), percent of sales from new versus repeat customers (office supply store), and the number of customers that cancel their service (long-distance phone companies). Of course, the concept of a defecting customer is equally applicable to organizations that produce tangible outputs.

Organizations should monitor their defecting customers for a number of reasons. First, research suggests that long-time customers offer organizations a number of benefits. For example, the longer a customer has a relationship with an organization, the more likely that customer is to purchase additional products and services and the less price-sensitive they are. In addition, no advertising is necessary to get the business of long-term customers. In fact, long-term customers may actually be a source of free advertising for the company. One study published in the *Harvard Business Review* concluded that cutting defections in half more than doubles the average company's rate of growth. Likewise, improving customer retention rates by 5 percent can double profits.

Defections by customers can provide a variety of useful information. First, feedback obtained from defecting customers can be used to identify areas that need improvement. Also, the feedback can be used to determine what can be done to win these customers back. Finally, increases in the defection rate can be used as an early warning signal.

QUALITY AWARDS AND CERTIFICATIONS

The Deming Prize was established in 1950 and is still administered by the Japanese Union of Scientists and Engineers (JUSE). The prize, which is actually a medal, recognizes organizations that have excelled in total quality management. It is open to all organizations regardless of their national origin. In the remainder of this section, the Baldrige National Quality Award and two ISO certifications are briefly overviewed.

The Malcolm Baldrige National Quality Award

In response to Japan's Deming Prize, in 1987 the United States established the Malcolm Baldrige National Quality Award. In 2004, four organizations won the award: The Bama Companies (manufacturing category), Texas Nameplate Company (small business category), the Kenneth W. Monfort College of Business (education category) and the Robert Wood Johnson University Hospital (health care category). The 2005 criteria for the award are summarized in Table 4.10.

ISO 9000 and 14000

Unlike the Deming Prize or the Baldrige Award, ISO 9000 is not an award for which companies must compete. Rather, ISO 9000 was developed as a guideline for designing, manufacturing, selling, and servicing products. In fact, in contrast to the Deming Prize and the Baldrige Award, which recognize organizations for excellent performance, ISO 9000 is intended as more of a checklist of good business practices. Thus, the intent of the ISO 9000 standard is that, if an organization selects a supplier that is ISO 9000-certified, it has some assurance that the supplier follows accepted business practices in the areas specified in the standard. However, one criticism of ISO 9000 is that it does not require any specific actions, and therefore each organization determines how it can best meet the requirements of the standard.

ISO 9000 was developed by the International Organization for Standardization and first issued in March 1987. A major revision to ISO 9000 was completed in December 2000, and the new standard is commonly referred to as ISO 9000:2000. Since its introduction, ISO 9000 has become the most widely recognized standard in the world. To illustrate its importance, in 1993 the European Community required that companies in several industries become certified as a condition of conducting business in Europe. In fact, over 630,000 organizations in 152 countries have implemented ISO 9000 and/or ISO 14000.[4]

ISO 14000 is a series of standards covering environmental management systems, environmental auditing, evaluation of environmental performance, environmental labeling, and life-cycle assessment. Like ISO 9000, ISO 14001 (a subset of the ISO 14000 series) is a standard in which organizations can become certified. The focus of ISO 14001 is on an organization's environmental management system. However, like ISO 9000, ISO 14001 does not prescribe specific standards for performance or levels of improvement. Rather, its intent is to help organizations improve their environmental performance through documentation control, operational control, control of records, training, statistical techniques, and corrective and preventive actions.

$\mathcal{T}$ABLE   4.10 • Criteria for the Malcolm Baldrige Award of 2005

Category	Items	Point	Values
1	**Leadership**		**120**
1.1	Senior Leadership	70	
1.2	Governance and Social Responsibilities	50	
2	**Strategic Planning**		**85**
2.1	Strategy Development	40	
2.2	Strategy Deployment	45	
3	**Customer and Market Focus**		**85**
3.1	Customer and Market Knowledge	40	
3.2	Customer Relationships and Satisfaction	45	
4	**Measurement, Analysis, and Knowledge Management**		**90**
4.1	Measurement, Analysis, and Review of Organizational Performance	45	
4.2	Information and Knowledge Management	45	
5	**Human Resource Focus**		**85**
5.1	Work Systems	35	
5.2	Employee Learning and Motivation	25	
5.3	Employee Well-Being and Satisfaction	25	
6	**Process Management**		**85**
6.1	Value Creation Processes	45	
6.2	Support Processes and Operational Planning	40	
7	**Business Results**		**450**
7.1	Product and Service Outcomes	100	
7.2	Customer-Focused Results	70	
7.3	Financial and Market Results	70	
7.4	Human Resource Results	70	
7.5	Organizational Effectiveness Results	70	
7.6	Leadership and Social Responsibility Results	70	
	TOTAL POINTS		**1000**

Source: http://www.quality.nist.gov, April 30, 2005.

---

[4]www.iso.org.iso/en/iso9000-14000.index.html, April 30, 2005

EXPAND YOUR UNDERSTANDING

1. Contrast Six Sigma with earlier initiatives such as total quality management and reengineering.

2. Is there any relationship between process sigma, DPMO, and process capability?

3. Measurement Systems Analysis focuses primarily on the variation introduced into the measurement system by human operators. Can you think of other sources of variation introduced by the measurement system beyond the human operators?

4. Under what kinds of circumstances might an organization wish to use control limits of two standard deviations or even one standard deviation? What should it bear in mind when using these lower limits?

5. Why are two control charts not necessary in controlling for attributes? Might not the variability of the fraction defective or the number of defects also be going out of control?

6. It is generally not appropriate to apply control charts to the same data that were used to derive the mean and limits. Why? What are the two possible outcomes if this is done, how likely is each, and what are the appropriate interpretations?

7. In deriving the p chart, why can the sample size vary? What must be remembered if the p chart is applied to a different sample size each time?

8. Firms regularly employ a taster for drinkable food products. What is the purpose of this taster?

9. How is quality handled differently in service firms and product firms? Does quality mean something different in a service firm?

10. Is the DMAIC approach more applicable to projects focusing on incremental change or radical change? Why?

11. Are there any limitations you see associated with QFD? Benchmarking?

APPLY YOUR UNDERSTANDING
Paint Tint

Late last month, Jim Runnels, a sales representative for the Paint Tint Corporation, was called to the plant of Townhouse Paint Company, one of his largest accounts. The purchasing agent for Townhouse Paint was complaining that the tubes of paint tint it had received over the last couple of weeks were not within the specified range of 4.9 to 5.1 ounces.

The off-weight tubes had not been detected by Townhouse's receiving clerks and had not been weighed or otherwise checked by their quality control staff. The problem arose when Townhouse began to use the tubes of tinting agent and found that the paint colors were not matching the specifications. The mixing charts used by the salespeople in Townhouse's retail stores were based on 5-ounce tubes of tinting agent. Overfilled or underfilled tubes would result in improper paint mixes, and therefore in colors that did not meet customers' expectations.

In consequence, Townhouse had to issue special instructions to all of its retail people that would allow them to compensate for the off-weight tubes. The Townhouse purchasing agent made it clear that a new supplier would be sought if this problem recurred. Paint Tint's quality control department was immediately summoned to assist in determining the cause of the problem.

Paint Tint's quality manager, Ronald Wilson, speculated that the cause of the problem was with the second shift. To analyze the problem, he entered into a spreadsheet the data from all the previous samples taken over the last two months. As it turned out, 15 random samples had been taken over the two-month period for both the first and the second shifts. Samples always consisted of 10 randomly selected tubes of paint tint. Also, separate sampling schedules were used for the first and second shifts so that the second shift would not automatically assume that it would be subject to a random sample just because the first shift had been earlier in the day.

After entering the sample weight data of the tubes into the following spreadsheet and calculating the sample means, Ronald was quite puzzled. There did not seem to be any noticeable difference in the average weights across the two shifts. Furthermore, although the lines were running at less than full capacity during the first six samples, there still did not seem to be any change in either line after reaching full production.

	A	B	C	D	E	F	G	H	I	J	K	L	M	N	O	P
1	**First Shift**															
2		**Sample Number**														
3	**Observation**	**1**	**2**	**3**	**4**	**5**	**6**	**7**	**8**	**9**	**10**	**11**	**12**	**13**	**14**	**15**
4	**1**	4.90	5.05	4.96	4.92	4.96	5.03	4.99	5.00	5.02	5.03	5.01	4.95	5.02	4.96	5.06
5	**2**	5.03	5.04	4.96	5.00	5.00	4.99	5.03	5.01	5.05	4.90	4.94	4.95	4.95	4.97	4.97
6	**3**	5.00	5.00	4.92	5.05	5.03	4.98	5.01	4.95	5.00	4.95	5.00	5.06	5.00	4.93	5.00
7	**4**	5.03	5.11	5.01	5.03	4.98	4.99	5.02	5.01	5.01	5.01	5.00	5.02	4.98	5.01	5.00
8	**5**	5.02	4.94	4.98	5.01	5.00	4.98	5.01	4.99	5.03	5.01	4.96	4.94	5.04	5.00	5.03
9	**6**	4.92	5.02	5.00	5.02	5.02	5.01	4.99	4.98	5.00	4.94	4.98	4.99	5.02	5.04	5.08
10	**7**	5.04	5.03	4.98	5.02	5.00	4.99	5.06	4.96	5.01	4.98	5.01	4.97	4.99	4.98	4.97
11	**8**	4.92	5.00	5.00	4.96	5.01	5.01	5.05	5.00	4.97	4.98	4.97	4.97	5.05	5.08	4.98
12	**9**	4.95	4.95	4.94	5.02	4.95	4.98	4.97	4.94	5.07	5.00	5.00	4.96	5.02	4.94	5.00
13	**10**	5.02	4.99	5.08	4.94	5.00	4.95	5.04	4.98	5.02	5.01	4.98	5.02	5.06	5.02	4.97
14	**Average**	**4.98**	**5.01**	**4.98**	**5.00**	**5.00**	**4.99**	**5.02**	**4.98**	**5.02**	**4.98**	**4.99**	**4.98**	**5.01**	**4.99**	**5.01**
15																
16																
17	**Second Shift**															
18		**Sample Number**														
19	**Observation**	**1**	**2**	**3**	**4**	**5**	**6**	**7**	**8**	**9**	**10**	**11**	**12**	**13**	**14**	**15**
20	**1**	5.03	5.02	4.99	4.96	5.03	5.02	5.08	5.10	5.16	5.00	4.97	5.11	5.11	4.90	5.02
21	**2**	4.90	4.95	4.97	4.97	4.98	5.03	4.97	4.93	4.92	4.97	4.91	5.05	4.98	4.92	4.98
22	**3**	5.02	4.94	5.04	4.98	5.00	4.98	4.93	4.92	4.99	5.08	5.15	4.93	5.13	4.97	4.86
23	**4**	4.98	5.05	5.02	5.00	4.97	5.06	4.84	4.93	5.00	5.07	4.96	5.15	5.15	4.92	4.94
24	**5**	5.01	4.95	5.02	5.02	4.98	5.04	5.07	5.03	4.98	4.94	4.91	4.98	5.10	5.04	4.93
25	**6**	4.99	4.99	4.99	5.03	5.00	5.04	4.95	4.96	4.99	4.96	5.07	4.88	5.12	5.03	4.97
26	**7**	4.99	4.97	5.00	4.98	4.99	4.99	4.93	4.86	5.01	5.13	5.15	4.74	5.01	4.91	5.05
27	**8**	5.02	5.00	5.00	4.96	4.98	4.98	4.99	5.08	5.07	4.93	4.95	4.90	4.93	4.95	4.97
28	**9**	5.01	5.00	5.05	5.02	5.03	4.97	4.82	4.96	4.93	4.96	4.91	5.03	5.04	4.98	5.03
29	**10**	4.97	4.99	4.95	5.03	5.00	4.99	5.05	5.14	5.03	4.91	5.11	5.04	5.03	5.08	4.92
30	**Average**	**4.99**	**4.99**	**5.00**	**5.00**	**5.00**	**5.01**	**4.96**	**4.99**	**5.01**	**5.00**	**5.01**	**4.98**	**5.06**	**4.97**	**4.97**

Questions

1. Can you identify any difference between the first and second shifts that explains the weight problem? If so, when is this difference first detectable?
2. How would you rate the ability of Paint Tint's production process to meet Townhouse Paint's requirements? What are the implications of your evaluation?

KoalaTech, Ltd.

KoalaTech, Ltd., of Sydney, Australia, produces office equipment for small businesses and home offices. Several months ago it launched its PFS 1000, a single unit that functions as a color printer, color scanner, color copier, and fax machine. The PFS 1000 won rave reviews for its functionality, affordable price, and innovative design. This, coupled with KoalaTech's reputation for producing highly reliable products, quickly led to a severe backlog. KoalaTech's plant simply could not keep up with demand.

Initially, KoalaTech's President, Nancy Samuelson, was extremely concerned about the backlog and put a great deal of pressure on the plant manager, George Johnson, to increase production. However, Nancy abruptly shifted gears when a new report indicated that returns and complaints for the PFS 1000 were running four times higher than the usual industry rate. Because KoalaTech's reputation was on the line, Nancy decided that the problem required immediate attention. She also decided that the quickest way to diagnose the problem and to avoid the usual mentality of "blaming it on the other department" would be to bring in an outside consultant with expertise in these matters.

Nancy hired Ken Cathey to investigate the problem. Nancy and Ken agreed that Ken should spend his first week interviewing key personnel in an effort to learn as much about the problem as possible. Because of the urgency of the problem, Nancy promised Ken that he would have complete access to—and the cooperation of—all employees. Nancy would send out a memo immediately informing all employees that they were expected to cooperate and assist Ken in any way they could.

The next morning, Ken decided to begin his investigation by discussing the quality problem with several of the production supervisors. He began with the supervisor of the final assembly area, Todd Allision. Todd commented:

> I received Nancy's memo yesterday, and frankly, the problem with the PFS 1000 does not surprise me. One of the problems we've had in final assembly is with the casing. Basically, the case is composed of a top and a bottom. The problem that we are having is that these pieces rarely fit together, so we typically have to force them together. I'm sure this is adding a lot of extra stress on the cases. I haven't seen a breakdown on what the problems with quality are, but it wouldn't surprise me if one of the problems was cracked cases or cases that are coming apart. I should also mention that we never had this problem with our old supplier. However, when purchasing determined that we could save over $A1 per unit, we switched to a new supplier for the cases.

The meeting with Todd lasted for about 1 1/2 hours, and Ken decided that rather than meet with someone else, he would be better off reviewing the notes he had taken and filling in any gaps while the conversation was still fresh in his mind. Then he would break for lunch and meet with one or two additional people in the afternoon.

After returning from lunch, Ken stopped by to talk with Steve Morgan, the production supervisor for the printed circuit boards. Ken found Steve and an equipment operator staring at one of the auto-insertion machines used to place components such as integrated circuits, capacitors, and resistors on the printed circuit board before wave soldering. Arriving, Ken introduced himself to Steve and asked, "What's up?" Steve responded:

> We are having an extremely difficult time making the printed circuit boards for the PFS 1000. The designers placed the components closer together than this generation of equipment was designed to handle. As a result, the leads of the components are constantly being bent. I doubt that more

than 25 percent of the boards have all their components installed properly. As a result, we are spending a great deal of time inspecting all the boards and reworking the ones with problems. Also, because of the huge backlog for these boards and the large number that must be reworked, we have been trying to operate the equipment 20 percent faster than its normal operating rate. This has caused the machine to break down much more frequently. I estimate that on a given eight-hour shift, the machine is down one to two hours.

In terms of your job—to determine the cause of the problems with quality—faulty circuit boards are very likely a key contributor. We are doing our best to find and correct all the defects, but inspecting and reworking the boards is a very tedious process, and the employees are putting in a lot of extra hours. In addition, we are under enormous pressure to get the boards to final assembly. My biggest regret is that I didn't have more input when they were building the prototypes of the PFS 1000. The prototypes are all built by highly trained technicians using primarily a manual process. Unfortunately, the prototypes are built only to give the engineers feedback on their designs. Had they shown some people in production the prototypes, we could have made suggestions on changes that would have made the design easier to produce.

Ken decided to end the day by talking to the plant manager, Harvey Michaels. Harvey was in complete agreement with Todd and Steve and discussed at length the enormous pressure he was under to get product out the door: "The bottom line is that no one cooperates. Purchasing changes suppliers to save a few bucks, and we end up with components that can't be used. Then our own engineers design products that we can't produce. We need to work together."

On his second day, Ken decided to follow up on the information he had gathered the day before. He first visited the director of purchasing, Marilyn Reagan. When asked about the problem of the cases that did not fit together, Marilyn responded:

The fact of the matter is that switching suppliers for the cases saved $A1.04 per unit. That may not sound like a lot, but multiply that by the 125,000 units we are expecting to sell this year, and it turns out to be pretty significant. Those guys in production think the world revolves around them. I am, however, sympathetic to their problems, and I plan on discussing the problem with the supplier the next time we meet. That should be some time next month.

After wrapping up the meeting with Marilyn, Ken decided he would next talk to the director of engineering. On the way, he recognized a person at a vending machine as the worker who had been standing next to Steve at the auto-insertion machine. Ken introduced himself and decided to talk with the worker for a few minutes. The worker introduced himself as Jim and discussed how he had been working in the shipping department just two weeks ago. The operator before Jim had quit because of the pressure. Jim hadn't received any formal training in operating the new equipment, but he said that Steve tried to check on him a couple of times a day to see how things were going. Jim appreciated Steve's efforts, but the quality inspectors made him nervous and he felt that they were always looking over his shoulder.

Ken thanked Jim for his input and then headed off to meet with the director of engineering, Jack Carel. After introducing himself, Ken took a seat in front of Jack's desk. Jack began:

So you are here to investigate our little quality snafu. The pressure that we are under here in engineering is the need to shrink things down. Two years ago fax machines, printers, scanners, and copiers were all separate pieces of equipment. Now, with the introduction of the PFS 1000, all this functionality is included in one piece of equipment not much larger than the original printer. That means design tolerances are going to be a lot tighter and the product is going to be more difficult to manufacture. But the fact of the matter is that manufacturing is going to have to get its act together if we are going to survive. The engineering department did its job. We designed a state-of-the-art piece of office equipment, and the prototypes we built proved that the design works. It's now up to the manufacturing guys to figure out how to produce it. We have done all that we can and should be expected to do.

To end his second day, Ken decided to meet with the director of quality assurance, Debbie Lynn. Debbie commented:

> My biggest challenge as director of quality assurance is trying to convince the rest of the organization the importance quality plays. Sure everyone gives lip-service to the importance of quality, but as the end of the month approaches, getting the product out the door is always the highest priority. Also, while I am officially held accountable for quality, I have no formal authority over the production workers. The quality inspectors that report to me do little more than inspect product and tag it if it doesn't meet the specifications so that it is sent to the rework area. In all honesty, I am quite optimistic about Nancy's current concern for quality and very much welcome the opportunity to work closely with you to improve Officetech's quality initiatives.

Questions

1. Which departments at KoalaTech have the most impact on quality? What role should each department play in helping KoalaTech improve overall quality?
2. Draw a fishbone chart to help explain how the other functional areas are creating problems for manufacturing—which ultimately may be the causes of the excessive complaints and returns.
3. What recommendations would you make to Nancy concerning KoalaTech's problem with quality? What role should the quality assurance department play?

EXERCISES

1. A call center has determined there are five types of defects that can occur in processing customer calls: the customer spends too long on hold, the customer is given the wrong information, the customer rep handles the call in an unprofessional way, the customer is transferred to the wrong destination, and the customer is disconnected. A total of 468 calls were subject to a quality audit last month and the results obtained from the audit are summarized in the lists below. What is the DPMO for the call center?

Number of Defects/Call	Frequency
1	73
2	13
3	3
4	1
5	0

2. Over the last quarter, 742 shots were administered at a walk-in clinic. To be treated properly, patients must be given the correct dosage of the correct medication. During the quarter in question, it was determined that one patient received the incorrect dosage of the correct medication, another patient received the wrong medication, and a third patient received both the wrong medication and the wrong dosage given her age and weight. What is the DPMO and process sigma level for the clinic?

3. A silk screening company prints 6000 decals per month. A random sample of 150 decals is taken every week and inspected based on four characteristics. The data for the last four weeks is summarized in the table below. Assuming the data in the table are representative of the process, what is the DPMO and process sigma level for the silk screening process?

Decal Characteristic	Number of Defects Observed
Color accuracy	10
Image alignment	7
Color consistency	8
Image sharpness	3

4. A hospital made 225 medication errors last year. Of these errors, 30 percent were the result of an error with the prescription while 70 percent were from errors made while dispensing the medication. The hospital admitted 8465 patients last year, and the patients received an average of 4.8 prescriptions per hospital stay. Medications are dispensed at the time they are needed and each medication is dispensed four times per day on average. The average patient stay at the hospital is 3.5 days. Compute the DPMO and process sigma level for the patient medicine process. What assumptions, if any, were needed to calculate the DPMO?

5. In the chapter it was noted that when the process mean can shift by as much as 1.5 standard deviations, a C_p of 2.0 is needed in order to achieve 3.4 million defective parts per million. What C_p is needed in order to achieve the same 3.4 defective parts per million assuming the process is perfectly stable and its mean does not shift?

6. Top management of the Royal Scottish Bank monitors the volume of activity at 38 branch banks with control charts. If deposit volume (or any of perhaps a dozen other volume indicators) at a branch falls below the LCL, there is apparently some problem with the branch's market share. If, on the other hand, the volume exceeds the UCL, it means the branch should be considered for expansion or that a new branch might be opened in an adjacent neighborhood.

Given the 10-day samples for each of the six months below, prepare an $\overline{X}$ chart for monthly deposit volume (in hundreds of thousands of dollars) for the Kilmarnock branch. Use control limits of ±3σ. The average range of the six samples was found to be £85,260.

	Average of 10-Day Deposits (£100,000)
June	0.93
July	1.05
August	1.21
September	0.91
October	0.89
November	1.13

7. Using the following weekly demand data for a new soft drink, determine the upper and lower control limits that can be used in recognizing a change in demand patterns. Use ±3σ control limits.

Week	Demand (6-packs)
1	3500
2	4100
3	3750
4	4300
5	4000
6	3650

8. A control chart has a mean of 50 and two-sigma control limits of 40 and 60. The following data are plotted on the chart: 38, 55, 58, 42, 64, 49, 51, 58, 61, 46, 44, 50. Should action be taken?

9. Given the following data, construct a 3σ range control chart.

Day of Sample	Sample Values
Saturday	22, 19, 20
Sunday	21, 20, 17
Monday	16, 17, 18
Tuesday	20, 16, 21
Wednesday	23. 20, 20
Thursday	19, 16, 21

a. If Friday's results are 15, 14, and 21, is the process in control?

b. Construct a 3σ means control chart and determine if the process is still in control on Friday.

10. Customers of Dough Boy Ltd. have specified that pizza crusts they order should be 28–32 centimeters in diameter. Sample data recently collected indicate that Dough Boy's crusts average 30 centimeters in diameter, with a standard deviation of 1.1 centimeters. Is Dough Boy's pizza crust production system capable of meeting its customers' requirements? If not, what options does Dough Boy have to rectify this situation?

11. Design specifications for a bottled product are that it should contain 350–363 milliliters. Sample data indicate that the bottles contain an average of 355 milliliters, with a standard deviation of 2 milliliters. Is the filling operation capable of meeting the design specifications? Why or why not?

12. a. Using the following data, prepare a p chart for the control of picking accuracy in a wholesale food warehouse. Sample size is expected to be 100 cases.

Day	Number of Cases Picked	Number of Incorrect Picks
1	4700	38
2	5100	49
3	3800	27
4	4100	31
5	4500	42
6	5200	48

b. Determine if days 7, 8, and 9 are under control.

Day	Number of Cases Picked	Number of Incorrect Picks
7	100	1
8	100	2
9	100	4

13. A new machine for making nails produced 25 defective nails on Monday, 36 on Tuesday, 17 on Wednesday, and 47 on Thursday. Construct an $\overline{X}$ chart, p chart, and c chart based on the results for Monday through Wednesday and determine if Thursday's production was in control. The machine produces 1 million or so nails a day. Which is the proper chart to use?

14. Construct a p chart using 2σ limits based on the results of 20 samples of size 400 in Table A.

15. Twenty samples of 100 were taken, with the following number of defectives: 8, 5, 3, 9, 4, 5, 8, 5, 3, 6, 4, 3, 5, 6, 2, 5, 0, 3, 4, 2. Construct a 3σ p chart.

16. Sheets of Styrofoam are being inspected for flaws. The first day's results from a new machine that produced five sheets are 17, 28, 9, 21, 14. Design a control chart for future production.

17. Solve Problem 11 with Crystal Ball, What percent of the bottles will be properly filled?

18. Assume in Problem 10 that the crusts must only *exceed* 28 cm. What mean crust diameter will result in 99 percent of the crusts meeting the minimum specification? Verify your results with Crystal Ball.

Table A

Sample Number	Number of Defects
1	2
2	0
3	8
4	5
5	8
6	4
7	4
8	2
9	9
10	2
11	3
12	0
13	5
14	6
15	7
16	1
17	5
18	8
19	2
20	1

BIBLIOGRAPHY

Alwan, L. *Statistical Process Analysis*. New York: Irwin/McGraw-Hill, 2000.

Arndt, M. "Quality Isn't Just for Widgets; Six Sigma, the Quality-Control and Cost-Cutting Power Tool, Is Proving Its Worth on the Service Side," *Business Week*, (July 22, 2002): 72.

Berstein, A. "Quality Is Becoming Job One in the Office, Too." *Business Week* (April 29, 1991): 52–54.

Besterfield, D. H. *Quality Control*, 6th ed. Upper Saddle River, NJ: Prentice Hall, 2001.

Breyfogel III, F. W., *Implementing Six Sigma*, 2nd ed. New York: Wiley, 2003.

Crosby, P. B. *Quality Is Free: The Art of Making Quality Certain*. New York: McGraw-Hill, 1979.

Das, R., S. Colello, and H. Davidson, "Six Sigma in Corporate Law." *Six Sigma Forum* (November 2004): 30–36.

Deming, W. E. *Out of Crisis*. Cambridge, MA: MIT Press, 1986.

Diehl, M., and W. Stroebe, "Productivity Loss in Brainstorming Groups: Towards a Solution of a Riddle," *Journal of Personality and Social Psychology*, 53 (1987): 497–509.

Evans, J. R., and W. M. Lindsay. *The Management and Control of Quality*. Cincinnati: South-Western, 1999.

Foster, T. A. *Managing Quality: An Integrative Approach*. Upper Saddle River, NJ: Prentice Hall, 2001.

Godin, E., D. Raven, C. Sweetapple, and F. R. Del Giudice, "Faster Test Results," *Quality Progress* (January 2004): 33–39.

Goetsch, D. L., and S. B. Davis. *Quality Management: Introduction to Total Quality Management for Production, Processing, and Services*, 3rd ed. Upper Saddle River, NJ: Prentice Hall, 2000.

Harrington, H. J., and J. S. Harrington. *High Performance Benchmarking*. New York: McGraw-Hill, 1996.

Harvey, J. "Service Quality: A Tutorial." *Journal of Operations Management*, 16 (1998): 583–597.

Jones Jr., M. H., "Six Sigma ... at a Bank?" *Six Sigma Forum Magazine* (February 2004): 13–17.

Jones, T. O., and W. E. Sasser, Jr. "Why Satisfied Customers Defect." *Harvard Business Review* (November–December 1995): 89–99.

Juran, J. M., and F. M. Gryna, Jr. *Quality Planning and Analysis*, 3rd ed. New York: McGraw-Hill, 1993.

Ledolter, J., and C. Burrill. *Statistical Quality Control: Strategies and Tools for Continual Improvement*. New York: John Wiley and Sons, 1999.

Montgomery, D. C. *Introduction to Statistical Quality Control*, 4th ed. New York: Wiley, 2001.

Ott, E., E. G. Schilling, and D. Neubauer. *Process Quality Control*. New York: McGraw-Hill, 2000.

Pande, P. S., R. P. Neuman, and R. R. Cavanagh. *The Six Sigma Way*. New York: McGraw-Hill, 2000.

Peace, G. S. *Taguchi Methods: A Hands-On Approach*. Reading, MA: Addison-Wesley, 1993.

Pyzdek, T. *The Six Sigma Handbook,* rev. ed. New York: McGraw Hill, 2003.

Rath & Strong. *Rath & Strong's Six Sigma Pocket Guide.* Rath & Strong, Inc., 2000.

Reichheld, F. F. "Learning from Customer Defections." *Harvard Business Review* (March–April 1996): 56–69.

Salegna, G., and F. Fazel. "Obstacles to Implementing Quality." *Quality Progress* (July 2000): 53-57.

Sester, D. "Motorola: A Tradition of Quality." *Quality* (October 2001): 30–34.

Shafer, S. M. "Karate in Business School? This is Not Your Father's Black Belt," *Quality Management Journal*, 12 (No. 2, 2005): 47–56.

Summers, D. *Quality*, 2nd ed. Upper Saddle River, NJ: Prentice Hall, 2000.

Thompson, L., "Improving the Creativity of Organizational Work Groups," *Academy of Management Executive*, 17 (2003): 96–111.

Wortman, B., W. R. Richardson, G. Gee, M. Williams, T. Pearson, F. Bensley, J. P. Patel, J. DeSimone, and D. R. Carlson, *CSSBB Primer*. West Terre Haute, IN: Quality Council of Indiana, 2001.

Zeithhaml, V. A., A. Parasuraman, and L. L. Berry. *Delivering Quality Service and Balancing Customer Expectations*. New York: The Free Press, 1990.

CHAPTER 5

Capacity and Location Planning

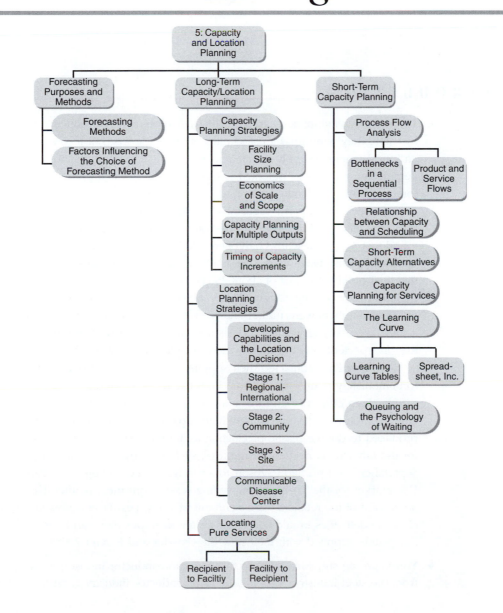

- **5: Capacity and Location Planning**
  - **Forecasting Purposes and Methods**
    - Forecasting Methods
    - Factors Influencing the Choice of Forecasting Method
  - **Long-Term Capacity/Location Planning**
    - Capacity Planning Strategies
      - Facility Size Planning
      - Economics of Scale and Scope
      - Capacity Planning for Multiple Outputs
      - Timing of Capacity Increments
    - Location Planning Strategies
      - Developing Capabilities and the Location Decision
      - Stage 1: Regional-International
      - Stage 2: Community
      - Stage 3: Site
      - Communicable Disease Center
    - Locating Pure Services
      - Recipient to Faciltiy
      - Facility to Recipient
  - **Short-Term Capacity Planning**
    - Process Flow Analysis
      - Bottlenecks in a Sequential Process
      - Product and Service Flows
    - Relationship between Capacity and Scheduling
    - Short-Term Capacity Alternatives
    - Capacity Planning for Services
    - The Learning Curve
      - Learning Curve Tables
      - Spread-sheet, Inc.
    - Queuing and the Psychology of Waiting

CHAPTER IN PERSPECTIVE

In this chapter our attention turns to translating the forecast of demand into capacity requirements for the organization's various resources. Having adequate capacity and being properly located has become critical for dependability and speed, while having excess capacity will impair costs, all strategic competitive factors. After a brief overview of the purposes and methods of forecasting, the chapter discusses various measures of capacity.

Next, we discuss issues related to long-term capacity planning including size, timing, and location planning strategies. This is followed by a discussion of short-term capacity planning including process flow analysis, the relationship between capacity and scheduling, and how humans' ability to learn affects capacity planning. The chapter concludes with a discussion of the theory and psychology of waiting lines.

INTRODUCTION

- The holiday retail market can be highly dangerous to toy producers. If forecasts are too high, they wind up with stockpiles of unsold losers, but if forecasts are too low and they cannot resupply stores quickly, they will have huge shortages of a hot item, losing millions of potential sales dollars. This puts a premium on accurate forecasts and flexible capacity.

  One weekend in early August 2003, LeapFrog introduced a new $35 educational toy to the infant/toddler market: LittleTouch LeapPads. On Monday morning, analysts found that 360 of these toys had been sold in stores around the United States. Based on their forecasting software, this small number, if not due to some anomaly, implied that their holiday forecast of about 350,000 units was much too low and they needed to double their shipments immediately. Before putting in an expedite order, however, the sales numbers were further analyzed by four separate software programs to see if there were any anomalies such as special sales or advertising that could explain this unexpectedly high number—there wasn't, the toy was a hit!

  Next, LeapFrog contacted their supplier in China to find out what it would take to immediately double production. Fortunately, their supplier was expert in supply-chain efficiency and manufacturing capacity flexibility. With special authorization from LeapFrog, new high-capacity dies were quickly designed and produced to double plastic production and additional vendors were quickly found for the other parts needed for the toys, such as baby-drool resistant paper. By September, the firm had to resort to air freight to get enough LeapPads to the U.S. market for the Thanksgiving selling season, but the day after Thanksgiving, 30 percent of the retailers were again out of stock. LeapFrog is now adding fast boat (14 day) deliveries in addition to air freight in hopes they can keep retailers adequately supplied with their new hit. (Fowler and Pereira 2003)

- You might be surprised to learn that the semiconductor industry is taking a lesson from the steel industry. After all, the semiconductor industry is on the leading edge of technology, whereas the steel industry is decidedly mature. However, these industries have an important characteristic in common: Both tend to require factories that are large and expensive (i.e., in excess of $1 billion). However, in the late 1980s steelmakers began to abandon economies of scale as a rationale for building large factories and began to develop smaller production facilities called minimills.

Now chip makers are adopting a similar approach: they are constructing smaller and more automated wafer fabrication factories. One reason for this is that shorter product life cycles will make it virtually impossible to recoup the costs to build a conventional wafer fab. It takes 22 to 30 months to recapture the investment in a conventional wafer fabrication facility, but it is projected that it will take only 10 months to recoup the development costs of a so-called minifab. Another important benefit associated with the minifabs is that because equipment can be grouped in clusters, the time required to complete the 200 processing steps can be reduced from the current 60 to 90 days to 7 days. This is particularly important because studies indicate that getting a new chip to market a few months earlier can result in as much as $1 billion in added revenues (Port 1994).

- In the early 1990s, Mercedes-Benz began investigating the feasibility of producing a luxury sports-utility vehicle, referred to as the *Multi-Purpose Vehicle* (MPV). Faced with increasing international competition, Mercedes deviated from its established procedures and staffed the project team with young product planners, engineers, and marketers. The team was charged with finding a site outside of Germany to build the MPV (up to this time, all Mercedes automobiles had been built in Germany). The team initially narrowed the search for the new facility to North America, because the combined costs of labor, shipping, and components would be lowest in this region. Costs were particularly important since the MPV was to be priced about the same as a fully loaded Jeep Grand Cherokee, yet Mercedes would operate its plant at a much lower volume than producers such as Chrysler.

  After further analysis, the team decided to limit the search to sites in the United States in order to be close to the primary market and to avoid the penalties associated with currency fluctuations. The team identified 100 possible sites in 35 states. As it began analyzing the sites, its primary concern was the cost of transportation. Since the MPV was going to be built only in the United States and half of its output would be exported, the team focused on sites near Atlantic or Gulf seaports, major highways, and rail lines. Also, workers' ages and mix of skills were considered.

  Eventually, the original list of sites was pared down to three sites in North Carolina, South Carolina, and Alabama. All three finalists were evaluated as relatively equal in terms of business climate, education levels, transportation, and long-term operating costs. According to the managing director, the decision to locate the new facility in Alabama came down to a perception on the part of Mercedes that Alabama was the most dedicated to the project (Woodruff and Templeman 1993).

- A *geographic information system* (GIS) is used to view and analyze data on digital maps as opposed to analyzing the same data printed out in massive tables that require reams of paper. One upscale clothing retailer with stores in Eau Claire and Green Bay, Wisconsin, analyzed its sales data on a map of the central part of the state. The map showed that each store drew the majority of its customers from a 20-mile radius.

The map also highlighted an area between Eau Claire and Green Bay where only 15 percent of the potential customers had actually visited either store. Management's conclusion was that a new store in Wausau was needed to reach this untapped market. To take another example, at Super Valu (one of the nation's largest supermarket wholesalers), analysts would spread out paper maps and compare them with demographic data. Now, using a GIS, the same information is displayed on the screen of a personal computer, making it much easier to read and analyze (Tetzeli 1993).

- In industries such as fashion, which are characterized by highly volatile demand, the combined costs of stockouts and markdowns can be greater than total manufacturing costs. One approach to forecasting in these highly volatile industries is to determine what can and cannot be predicted well. Products in the "predictable" category are made farthest in advance, saving manufacturing capacity for the "unpredictable" products so that they can be produced closer to their actual selling season. Using this approach, Sport Obermeyer, a producer of fashionable skiwear, increased its profits between 50 percent and 100 percent over a three-year period in the early 1990s (Fisher, Hammond, Obermeyer, and Raman 1994).

As we will discuss in more detail throughout this chapter, **_capacity_** represents the rate at which a transformation system can create outputs. Capacity planning is as important to service organizations as it is to manufacturing organizations. For example, the transformation process at Burger King is designed so that capacity can be quickly adjusted to match a highly variable demand rate throughout the day. And in manufacturing, semiconductor firms incur enormous costs associated with expanding capacity. To further complicate matters for manufacturing businesses, shorter product life cycles mean that they have less time to recoup their investment, especially when the next generation of products makes their current products obsolete.

Clearly, capacity and location are important elements of a firm's competitive strategy, and in fact play a major role in the Sand Cone competitive dimensions described earlier in Chapter 2: quality, delivery dependability, speed, and cost. For example, if capacity is insufficient for demand peaks, then confusion and errors will result when attempting to meet excessive demand, lowering the quality of the firm's outputs. And without capacity and a convenient location, customers cannot depend on the availability of the output and may turn to competitors. In terms of speed, sufficient capacity and a convenient location allow the organization to meet demand quickly, whenever and wherever it arises. And finally, if the firm has insufficient capacity, it will cost considerably more to engage the extra resources to meet unexpected demand whether the resources are additional labor in the form of overtime or hiring, subcontracting out a portion of the demand, or storing inventory to meet demand peaks.

In this chapter we first briefly discuss the role of forecasting, not only for long-term capacity planning but also in terms of short-term capacity needs, and then go into detail about long-term capacity/location strategies. Over the long term, capacity and location are interwoven considerations, as will be described more extensively in the supply chain management discussion in Chapter 7. Following the long-term discussion, we move into a description of short-term capacity alternatives, but here we are largely past the point of making a location decision. In this section, we also discuss process flow analysis, the learning curve, and issues specifically relevant to service capacity requirements.

FORECASTING PURPOSES AND METHODS

There is usually a close relationship between competing successfully and being able to predict key aspects of the future accurately. Clearly, it is not practical to try to plan without some prediction of the future. Even planning a simple party requires predicting how many people will show up, how much they will eat and drink, what kind of snacks and beverages they will enjoy, and how long they will stay. A business introducing a new service needs to predict the demand for the service, how prices and advertising will affect this demand, how competitors will respond, and so on.

Thus, we see that an accurate estimate of demand for the output is crucial to the efficient operation of the production system and, hence, to managing the organization's resources. For example, a supermarket chain that is contemplating the addition of a new store must have a reasonable estimate of demand in order to determine how big the store and the parking lot should be, what ancillary departments (such as a bakery, pharmacy, deli, and bank) should be included, and how many shopping carts and checkout lanes should be specified in the plans. Once the facility is constructed, a more specific, perhaps weekly, forecast of demand will be needed so that the manager will be able to schedule workers and order merchandise. The same is true for decisions about capacity, scheduling, and staffing in a product organization. Capacity (obtaining the proper level of resources) and scheduling (the timing of resource usage) both require forecasting, whether or not it be a formal procedure.

As an aside, it is worth noting that it is not only demand for the output that can be forecast. The tools of forecasting can also be used to predict the development of new technology, national and international economic conditions, and even many factors internal to the organization such as changes in lead time, scrap rates, cost trends, personnel growth, and departmental productivity. Here, however, we will restrict our discussion to the uses of forecasting for long- and short-term capacity planning.

Forecasts are used in organizations for four primary purposes, the first two of which are strategic and long range, and the last two of which are more tactical and short range.

1. To decide whether demand is sufficient to justify entering the market. If demand exists but at too low a price to cover the costs that an organization will incur in producing an output, then the organization should reject the opportunity.

2. To determine long-term (2- to 5-year) capacity needed, in order to design facilities. An overall projection of demand for a number of years in the future serves as the basis for decisions related to expanding, or contracting, capacity to meet the demand. Since there is competition, even in the not-for-profit sector, an organization is courting disaster if it produces inefficiently, because of excess idle capacity, or insufficiently to meet demand, because of too little capacity.

3. To determine midterm (3-month to 18-month) fluctuations in demand, in order to avoid shortsighted decisions that will hurt the company in the long run. To illustrate, if a company planned its staffing solely on the basis of its

weekly forecast, each week it might adjust the level on the basis of a forecast for the coming week. Thus, in some weeks it might lay off workers only to rehire them in the following week. Such weekly adjustments would most likely lower morale and productivity. A better approach is to base staffing on a longer-term perspective.

4. To ascertain short-term (1-week to 3-month) fluctuations in demand for the purposes of production planning, work force scheduling, materials planning, and other such needs. These forecasts support a number of operational activities and can have a significant effect on organizational productivity, bottlenecks, master schedules, meeting promised delivery dates, and other such issues of concern to top management and to the organization as a whole.

Forecasting Methods

Forecasting methods can be grouped in several ways. One classification, illustrated in Figure 5.1, distinguishes between formal forecasting techniques and informal approaches such as intuition, spur-of-the-moment guesses, and seat-of-the-pants predictions. Our attention here will obviously be directed to the formal methods.

In general, qualitative forecasting methods are often used for long-range forecasts, especially when external factors (e.g., an especially cold winter) may play a significant role. They are also of use when historical data are very limited or nonexistent, as in the introduction of a new product or service.

Some of the most significant decisions made by organizations, frequently strategic decisions, are made on the basis of *qualitative* forecasts. These often concern either a new product or service or long-range changes in the nature of the organization's outputs. In both cases, relevant historical data on demand are typically not available.

Qualitative forecasts are made using information such as telephone or mail surveys of consumers' attitudes and intentions, consumer panels, test marketing in limited areas, expert opinion and panels, and analyses of historical demand for similar products or services—a method known as *historical analogy*. One example of historical analogy would be the use of demand data for CD-ROMs to predict the demand curve for DVDs, or Broadway shows to predict the demand for movies.

A special type of expert panel uses what is called the *Delphi* method. The RAND Corporation developed the Delphi method as a group technique for forecasting the demand for new or contemplated products or services. The intent was to eliminate the undesirable effects of interaction between members of the group (such as loud and dominating individuals) while retaining the benefits of their broad experience and knowledge. The method begins by having each member provide individual written forecasts, along with any supporting arguments and assumptions. These forecasts are submitted to a Delphi researcher, who edits, clarifies, and summarizes the data. These data are then provided as feedback to the members, along with a second round of questions. This procedure continues, usually for about four rounds, when a consensus among panel members can often be reached on some of the issues.

Another qualitative device often used in forecasting is called *life-cycle analysis*. Experienced managers who have introduced several new products are often able to estimate how long a product will remain in each stage of its life cycle. This forecast, coupled with other market information, can produce reasonably accurate estimates of demand in the medium to long range.

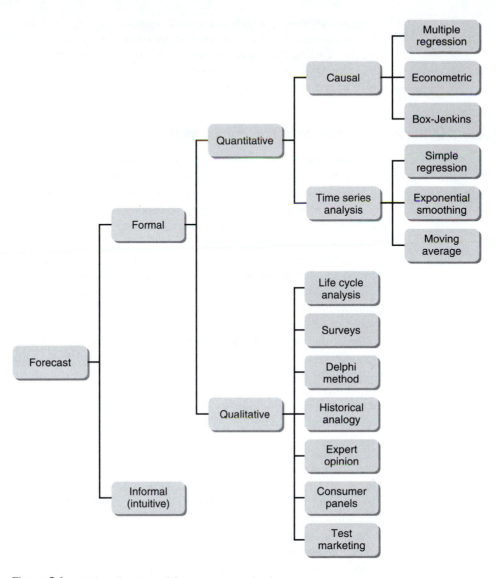

Figure 5.1 A classification of forecasting methods.

Quantitative forecasting methods are generally divided between methods that simply project the past history or behavior of the variable into the future (*time series analysis*) and those that also include external data (*causal*). Time series analysis is the simpler of the two and ranges from just using an average of the past data to using regression analysis corrected for seasonality in the data. Simple projection techniques are obviously limited to, and primarily used for, very short-term forecasting. Such approaches often work well in a stable environment but cannot react to changing industry factors or changes in the national economy. The Wiley website for this text (see the Preface for the URL) includes descriptions and examples of some of the more common time series forecasting techniques.

Causal methods, which are usually quite complex, include histories of external factors and employ sophisticated statistical techniques. Many "canned" computerized forecasting packages are available for the quantitative techniques, both time series analysis and causal. Check the bibliography at the end of the chapter for more information about these sophisticated techniques.

Factors Influencing the Choice of Forecasting Method

What method is chosen to prepare a demand forecast depends on a number of factors. First, long-range (2- to 5-year) forecasts typically require the least accuracy and are only for general (or aggregate) planning, whereas short-range forecasts require greater accuracy and are for detailed operations. Thus, the most accurate methods are usually used for short-term needs and, fortunately, the data in the near term is usually the most accurate.

Second, if the data are available, one of the quantitative forecasting methods can be used. Otherwise, nonquantitative techniques are required. Attempting to forecast without a demand history is almost as hard as using a crystal ball. The demand history need not be long or complete, but some historical data should be used if at all possible.

Third, the greater the limitation on time or money available for forecasting, the more likely it is that an unsophisticated method will have to be used. In general, management wants to use a forecasting method that minimizes not only the cost of making the forecast but also the cost of an *inaccurate* forecast; that is, management's goal is to minimize the total forecasting costs. Costs of inaccurate forecasting include the cost of over- or understocking an item, the costs of under- or overstaffing, and the intangible and opportunity costs associated with loss of goodwill because a demanded item is not available.

Fourth, with the advent of computers, the cost of statistical forecasts based on historical data and the time required to make such forecasts have been reduced significantly. It has therefore become more cost-effective for organizations to conduct sophisticated forecasts.

Once a forecast of demand has been developed, it is translated into capacity requirements for the organization's various resources. Thus, the demand forecast is an important input to both long-term and short-term capacity planning. We discuss these topics in turn in the remainder of this chapter.

$\mathcal{L}$ONG-TERM CAPACITY/LOCATION PLANNING _____

Capacity and location decisions are highly strategic because they are very expensive investments and, once made, are not easily changed or reversed. Hence, they must be carefully and thoroughly analyzed beforehand, using all available tools at management's disposal. **Capacity** is generally taken to mean the maximum *rate* at which a transformation system produces outputs or processes inputs, though the rate may be "all at once." Table 5.1 lists measures of capacity for a number of production systems. Notice that since capacity is defined as a rate, measures should be clear about the *time dimension*. For instance, how meaningful is it to know that a hospital can perform 25 surgeries? Without knowing whether this is simultaneously, per day, per week, or possibly per month, the number is relatively meaningless.

As illustrated in Table 5.1, airlines often measure their capacity in *available seat miles* (ASMs) per year. One ASM is one seat available for one passenger for 1 mile. Clearly, the number of planes an airline has, their size, how often they are flown, and the route structure of the airline all affect its ASMs, or capacity. However, we may also talk about the capacity of a single plane, such as a 550-seat jumbo, and here we clearly mean "all at once." Nevertheless, this capacity measure is not very useful without knowing to what use the plane may be put, such as constantly being in the air generating ASMs or used as an occasional backup. Similarly, an elementary measure of a hospital's capacity is often simply the number of beds it has (for the full year is implied). Thus, a 50-bed hospital is "small" and a 1000-bed hospital is "large." And a restaurant may measure its capacity in tables (per hour), a hotel in rooms (per night), and a public service agency in family contacts (per weekday).

$\mathcal{T}$ABLE 5.1 • Examples of Measures of Capacity

Production System	Measure of Capacity in Terms of Outputs Produced	Measure of Capacity in Terms of Inputs Processed
Airline	available seat miles per year	reservation calls handled per day
Hospital	babies delivered per month	patients admitted per week
Supermarket	customers checked out per hour	cartons unloaded per hour
Post Office	packages delivered per day	letters sorted per hour
University	graduates per quarter	students admitted per year
Automobile Assembly Plant	autos assembled per year	deliveries of parts per day

Notice that these measures of capacity do not recognize the multiple types of outputs with which an organization may, in reality, be concerned. ASMs say nothing about the freight capacity of an airline, but freight may be a major contributor to profits. Similarly, number of beds says nothing about outpatient treatment, ambulance rescues, and other services provided by a hospital. Thus, capacity planning must often consider the capacity to produce multiple outputs. Unfortunately, some of the outputs may require the same organizational resources, as well as some very specialized resources.

The provision of adequate capacity is clearly a generic problem, common to all types of organizations, but in pure service organizations capacity is a special problem because the output cannot normally be stored for later use. A utility, for example, must have capacity available to meet peak power demands, yet the *average* power demand may be much, much lower. Where the provision of the service is by human labor, low productivity is a danger when staffing is provided to meet the demand peaks.

Another characteristic of capacity is that, frequently, a variety of restrictions can limit it. For example, the capacity of a fast-food restaurant may be limited not only by the number of order-takers on duty but also by the number of cooks, the number of machines to prepare the food, the amount of food in stock, the space in the restaurant, and even the number of parking spaces outside. Any one of these factors can become a **bottleneck** (discussed in a later section of the chapter) that limits the restaurant's normal operating capacity to something less than its theoretical or design capacity.

In addition, during the production process there are often natural losses, waste (avoidable), scrap (unavoidable), defects, errors, and so on that again limit the capacity of a system. These losses are considered in a measure known as the **yield** of the process: the amount of output of acceptable quality emerging from a production system compared with the amount that entered it. **Yield management**, also known as **revenue management**, is a somewhat different topic but of high interest these days, particularly in services. However, it is more related to schedule management and is thus deferred to our discussion in Chapter 6.

In the process of trying to forecast the long-run capacity needs for the organization, the issue of location of the facility, or facilities, cannot be ignored because the demand may well be a function of *where* the facility is located. And if there are multiple facilities, the capacity needs for any one will certainly depend on how many others are serving the same geographic needs. Moreover, transportation may also be a factor if there is a facilitating good, or product, involved, as well as inventories, warehouses, and other such matters that concern **supply chain management**. In these days of intense worldwide competition, supply chain management is taking on significantly more importance, as it accounts for a greater and greater proportion of the total cost of all outputs. Although we discuss the interplay between capacity and location in this chapter, we defer the larger discussion of supply chain management to Chapter 7.

Capacity Planning Strategies

Issues of capacity planning over the long run relate primarily to the strategic issues of initiating, expanding, and contracting the major facilities used in producing the output. Note the interdependence of the capacity decision with the location decision. Every capacity decision requires a corresponding location decision. For example, expanding an existing facility defines the location of the new capacity to be an existing facility. This section covers capacity planning strategies in terms of facility size, economies of scale and scope, timing of capacity increments, and capacity for multiple outputs. The following section covers the location aspects and relationships.

Facility Size Planning

Figure 5.2 illustrates the issue of facility size in terms of capacity and unit cost. Product cost curves are shown for five sizes of production facilities. When plants are operated at their lowest-cost production level (A, B, or C), the larger facilities will generally have the lowest costs, a phenomenon known as *economies of scale*. However, if production levels must be set at a value other than the lowest-cost level, the advantage of a larger facility may be lost. For example, point D is characterized by congestion and excessive overtime, and point E by idle labor and low equipment utilization. Points F and G illustrate some of the diseconomies of scale, as described next.

Economies of Scale and Scope

Obtaining lower unit costs through the use of larger facilities is known as **economies of scale**. Primarily, the economy comes from spreading the required fixed costs—land, administration, sales force, facilities, and such other factors—over a larger volume of products or services, although there are also economies obtained through stronger purchasing power and learning curve effects (discussed in a later section). However, as illustrated by points F and G in Figure 5.2, there is a limit to the benefits that can be obtained, because the inherent inefficiencies of large facilities begin to counter their economic benefits. This occurs through increased bureaucracy, poor communication, long lines of responsibility and authority, and the like. Many manufacturers now have a corporate policy that no plant will be larger than 200 to 250 workers, often considered an optimum size.

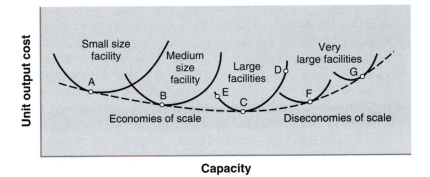

Figure 5.2 Envelope of lowest unit output costs with facility size.

Managers frequently think in terms of economies of scale when making decisions about where to produce new products or services, or whether or not to extend their line of products and services. However, the focus lost through adding these new production requirements can jeopardize the competitive strength of a firm. Managers would be well advised to examine more closely where the economies are expected to come from: sometimes it is from higher volumes, sometimes from the use of common technology, sometimes from availability of off-peak capacity. If the source of the economy results in offsetting diseconomies of scale, as a result of loss of focus or for other reasons, the firm should not proceed.

An allied concept related to the use of many of the advanced, flexible technologies such as programmable robots is called **economies of scope**. The phrase implies that economies can also be obtained with flexibility by offering variety instead of volume. However, upon closer examination it is not clear why being flexible offers any particular economies. The real reason for economies of scope derives from the same economies as those of scale—spreading fixed costs among more products or services—but the scale is now obtained over many small batches of a wide variety of outputs, rather than large batches of only a few standard outputs.

Capacity Planning for Multiple Outputs

Realistically, organizations are not always expanding their capacity. We usually focus on this issue because we are studying firms in the process of growth, but even successful organizations often reduce their capacity. Major ways of contracting capacity are to divest the firm of operations, lay off workers, outsourcing, and sell or lease equipment and facilities. Most organizations, however, try to contract only capacity that is inefficient or inappropriate for their circumstances, owing in part to a felt responsibility to the community. If it appears that organizational resources are going to be excessively idle in the future, organizations often attempt to add new outputs to their current output mix rather than contracting capacity (the latter frequently being done at a loss). This entails an analysis of the candidate output's life and seasonal demand cycles.

It is traditional in fire departments to use the slack months for building inspections, conducting fire prevention programs, giving talks on safety, and other such activities. The large investment in labor and equipment is thus more effectively utilized throughout the year by adoption of an *anticyclic* output (an output counter to the fire cycle)—fire prevention. For many of the same reasons, many fire departments have been given the responsibility for the city or county's medical rescue service (although rescue alarms are not entirely anticyclic to fire alarms).

Clearly, many organizations, such as the makers of greeting cards, fur coats, swimming pool equipment, and fireworks, face this cyclic difficulty. A classic case of **seasonality** is that of furnace dealers. For the last 100 years all their business typically was in the late autumn and winter, as illustrated in Figure 5.3. With the rapid acceptance of air conditioning in the 1950s and 1960s, many furnace dealers eagerly added this product to their output mix. Not only was it conceptually along the same lines (environmental comfort) and often physically interconnected with the home furnace but, most important, it was almost completely anticyclic to the seasonal heating cycle. As shown in Figure 5.3, the addition of air conditioning considerably leveled dealers' sales throughout the year in comparison with furnace sales alone.

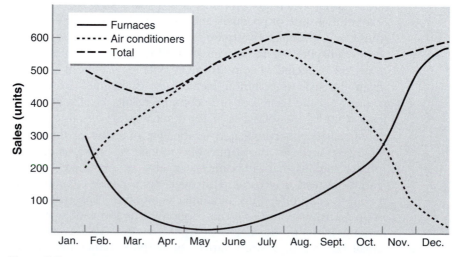

Figure 5.3   Anticyclic product sales.

In a similar manner, and for much the same reasons, organizations add to their mix outputs that are anticyclic to existing output *life cycles*. Figure 5.4 illustrates the expected life cycles of an organization's current and projected outputs. Total required capacity is found by adding together the separate capacities of each of the required outputs. Note the projected dip in required capacity five years in the future, and, of course, beyond the 8-year R&D planning horizon.

The message of Figure 5.4 should be clear to the organization—an output with a three-year life cycle (appearing similar to the shaded area) is needed between years 4 and 7 in order to maintain efficient utilization of the organization's available capacity. A priority output development program will have to be instituted immediately. At this point it is probably too late to develop something through R&D; a more effective strategy, especially in light of the relatively low volume and short life cycle, might be an extension of an existing output.

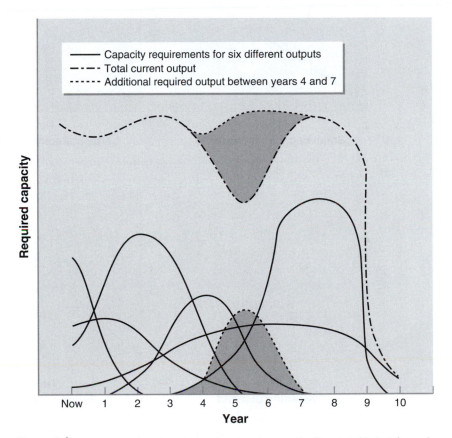

Figure 5.4 Forecast of required organizational capacity from multiple life cycles.

Timing of Capacity Increments

Once the best alternative for obtaining the desired capacity has been determined, the timing and manner must still be chosen. A number of approaches are illustrated in Figure 5.5. Sometimes there is an opportunity to add capacity in small increments (Figure 5.5*a*) rather than as one large chunk (Figure 5.5*b*), such as an entire plant.

Clearly, small increments are less risky, but they do not offer an opportunity to upgrade the entire production system at one time, as a single chunk does. Other choices are to add capacity before the demand has arisen (Figure 5.5c) or after (Figure 5.5d). Adding capacity before demand occurs upstages the competition and enhances customers' loyalty but risks the cost of the capacity if the expected demand never materializes. Adding capacity after demand arises will encourage the competition to move into the market and take away part of your share. Clearly, the most appropriate strategy must be carefully evaluated for the situation at hand.

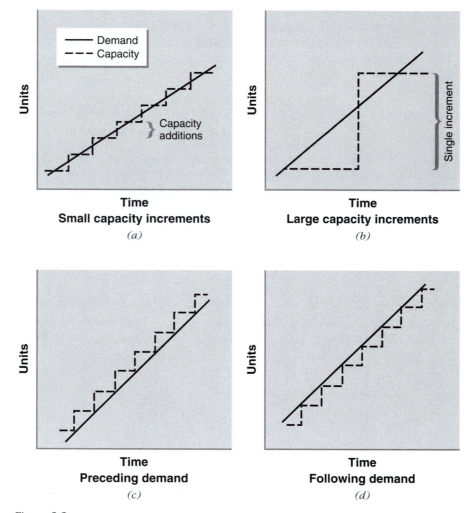

Figure 5.5 Methods of adding fixed capacity.

Location Planning Strategies

Having determined capacity requirements, we next discuss the most economical way to obtain the inputs needed to produce and deliver the output to the customer. This includes determining the location of the facility relative to suppliers and potential customers. Although we are discussing capacity and location planning sequentially, as noted earlier, these decisions are typically considered simultaneously since every capacity decision requires a location decision (e.g., where to add the new capacity or which plant should be closed).

In general, the decision about location is divided into three stages: regional (including international), community, and site. Sources of information for these stages are chambers of commerce, realtors, utilities, banks, suppliers, transportation companies, savings and loan associations, government agencies, and management consultants who specialize in relocation. For some pure service organizations (e.g., physicians), only the site selection stage may be relevant because they are already focused on a specific region and community. Before discussing these stages in detail, however, we first highlight the relationship between the location decision and the development of core capabilities.

Developing Capabilities and the Location Decision

In examining the rationale offered by organizations regarding their decisions to relocate existing facilities or open new ones, it often appears that these decisions are being driven primarily by short-term considerations such as differentials in wage rates and fluctuations in exchange rates. In addition to having the appearance of being more band-aid solutions than addressing how to improve long-term competitiveness, these decisions are often dominated by operational factors such as wage rates and transportation costs. The problem with such static and one-dimensional analyses is that conditions change. For example, if one competitor chooses a location based on low wage rates, there is very little to prevent its competitors from locating in the same region. Furthermore, the benefit of low wages is likely to be short-lived as the demand for labor will increase when more organizations locate in the region.

An alternative approach to the location decision is to consider the impact these decisions have on the development of key organizational capabilities. In Chapter 2 we defined core capabilities as the organizational practices and business processes that distinguish an organization from its competition. Clearly, the way various organizational units are located relative to one another can have a significant impact on interactions between these units, which in turn impacts the development of core capabilities.

In order to leverage the location decision to enhance the development of long-term capabilities, Bartmess and Cerny (1993) suggest the following six-step process:

1. Identify the sources of value the company will deliver to its customers. In effect, this translates into identifying the order winners discussed in Chapter 2.

2. Once the order winners have been defined, the organization needs to identify the key organizational capabilities needed in order to have a competitive advantage.

3. Based on the capabilities identified, implications for the location of organizational units should be assessed. For example, if the company determines that a rapid product development capability is needed, then it follows that design needs to be in close contact with manufacturing and leading edge customers. Alternatively, if operational flexibility is needed, then it follows that manufacturing needs to be in close proximity to design, customers, marketing, and management information systems.

4. Identify potential locations.

5. Evaluate the sites in terms of their impact on the development of capabilities, as well as on financial and operational criteria.

6. Develop a strategy for building an appropriate network of locations.

Having highlighted the relationship between choosing a location and the development of capabilities, we next turn our attention to the actual stages that location decisions typically progress through.

Stage 1: Regional–International

In the regional–international stage, an organization focuses on what part of the world (e.g., North America, Europe, Pacific rim) or perhaps in what region of a country (e.g., Southwest, Midwest, Northeast) it wants to locate its new facility. For example, when Mercedes-Benz needed a new facility to produce its new multi-purpose vehicle (MPV), it initially decided that its new facility should be located in North America and subsequently further narrowed the region to sites in the southeastern United States. There are four major considerations in selecting a national or overseas region for a facility: *proximity, labor supply, availability of inputs*, and *environment*.

To minimize transportation costs and provide acceptable service to customers, the facility should be located in a region in close *proximity* to customers and suppliers. Although methods of finding the location with the minimum transportation costs will be presented later in this chapter, a common rule of thumb within the United States is that the facility should be within 200 miles of major industrial and commercial customers and suppliers. Beyond this range, transportation costs begin to rise quickly.

The region should have the proper *supply of labor* available and in the correct proportions of required skills. One important reason for the past expansion of American firms abroad, particularly to Japan in the 1980s, was the availability of labor there at wage rates much lower than rates at home. Currently, this disparity has been eliminated because of Japan's increased wages. However, the real consideration should not be wage rates, but rather the productivity of domestic labor relative to productivity abroad. This comparison would thus involve level of skills, use of equipment, wage rates, and even work ethics (which differ even between regions within the United States) to determine the most favorable labor supply in terms of output per dollar of wages and capital investment. The organization of the labor pool should also be given consideration—that is, whether all the skills are unionized or whether there is an open shop. Some states have passed *right-to-work laws* that forbid any requirement that all employees join a union in order to work in an organization. Often, these laws result in significantly lower wage rates in these states.

The region selected for location of the facility should have the necessary *inputs* available. For example, supplies that are difficult, expensive, or time-consuming to ship and those that are necessary to the organization (i.e., no reasonable substitutes exist) should be readily available. The proper type (rail, water, highway, air) and supply of transportation; sufficient quantities of basic resources such as water, electricity, gas, coal, and oil; and appropriate communication facilities should also be available. Obviously, many American industries are located abroad in order to use raw materials (oil, copper, etc.) available there.

The regional *environment* should be conducive to the work of the organization. Not only should the weather be appropriate, but the political, legal, and social climate should also be favorable. The following matters should be considered:

1. Regional taxes
2. Regional regulations on operations (pollution, hiring, etc.)
3. Barriers to imports or exports
4. Political stability (nationalization policies, kidnappings)
5. Cultural and economic peculiarities (e.g., restrictions on working women)

These factors are especially critical in locating in a foreign country, particularly an underdeveloped country. Firms locating in such regions should not be surprised to find large differences in the way things are done. For example, in some countries governmental decisions tend to move slowly, with extreme centralization of authority. Very little planning seems to occur. Events appear to occur by "God's will" or by default. The pace of work is unhurried, and at times discipline, especially among managers, seems totally absent. Corruption and payoffs often seem to be normal ways of doing business, and accounting systems are highly suspect. Living conditions for the workers, especially in urbanized areas, are depressing. Transportation and communication systems (roads, ports, phone service) can be incomplete and notoriously unreliable. Attempting to achieve something under such conditions can, understandably, be very discouraging. When locating in such countries, a firm should allow for such difficulties and unexpected problems. In such an environment, Murphy's law thrives.

With the escalating use of outsourcing, and especially offshoring, the roles of location and capacity in the competitive elements of a firm's strategy take on increased importance. By subcontracting production to another firm, an organization can often save substantially on labor costs (especially when offshoring) and at the same time reduce their own asset base tremendously, thereby increasing both their profit margins and their return on assets (ROA). Contract manufacturers such as Flextronics, Selectron, and Jabil Circuit are quick to point out these advantages and others, such as leaving the organization free to concentrate on their strengths such as design, brand building, marketing, and strategy. There are, however, also disadvantages in both outsourcing and offshoring. One is the loss of control of the product. Another is a probable reduction in speed of response to customers. A third, which is especially sensitive in communities and is increasingly publicized by the media, is the loss of domestic jobs when the company outsources its work. And outsourcing production is always a dangerous action, first because engineering and then design typically must follow production overseas, meaning the additional loss of these capabilities within the organization. And second, there is the increased potential that the firm is simply training a powerful competitor (especially if engineering and design have also been outsourced), thereby "hollowing itself out." In the 1980s, many firms in the television and video cassette recording industries outsourced all their production overseas, simply slapping on their own logo to sell their product domestically. Then the foreign producers started introducing their own brands and all the formerly domestic producers went out of business, losing the entire industry to foreign competition.

A model to help make the regional–national location decision is the CVD model we described for helping with the job shop layout in Chapter 3. In this case, we are interested in the total of all the supply costs into the facility and all the distribution costs out to customers. The procedure is to select some initial site for the facility that appears to be good and then sum the products of the transportation rate (C), the volume or weights (V), and the distance (D) over all the locations. Then we can simply consider placing the facility in another site and see if the cost is less, and so on. If all the sites are prespecified, then the site with the lowest cost is deemed best (at least on this one measure).

Stage 2: Community

After the region of a new facility has been selected, candidate communities within the region are identified for further analysis. Many of the considerations made at the regional–international stage should also be considered at this next stage. For example, the availability of acceptable sites, attitudes of the local government, regulations, zoning, taxes, labor supply, the size and characteristics of the market, and the weather would again be considered. In addition, the availability of local financing, monetary inducements (such as tax incentives) for establishing operations there, and the community's attitude toward the organization itself would be additional factors of interest to the organization.

Last, the preferences of the organization's staff should play a role in selecting a community. These would probably be influenced by the amenities available in the community such as homes, religious congregations, shopping centers, schools and universities, medical care, fire and police protection, and entertainment, as well as local tax rates and other costs. Upper-level educational institutions may also be of interest to the organization in terms of opportunity for relevant research and development. For example, it was no coincidence that major IBM plants were located in Lexington, Kentucky, Denver, Colorado, and Austin, Texas, which are also sites of major state universities.

The standard "breakeven" or "cost-volume-profit" model can be helpful for this stage of the location decision, except that there is no revenue line and there are multiple costs lines, each representing a different community's costs. We assume that the problem is to choose from among a set of predetermined communities, on the basis of a range of fixed and variable costs rather than just distribution cost, as calculated by the CVD model just given. That is, distribution cost may be considered, but it is only one factor (perhaps fixed, perhaps variable with output volume) among many that need to be considered to make a decision. Although the relevant *factors* for comparison between the communities may be known (e.g., labor costs, taxes, utility charges), their values may be uncertain, particularly if they are a function of the output rate of the facility being located. The various alternatives for location are then compared by graphing total operating costs for each alternative at different levels of demand, as in Figure 5.6.

This is accomplished by dividing the total operating cost into two components— fixed costs that do not vary with the demand for the output (e.g., land, buildings, equipment, property taxes, insurance) and variable costs such as labor, materials, and transportation—and plotting them on the axes of a graph. At the demand point E (the intersection of the two lines) the costs for the two alternatives are the same; for demand levels in excess of E, community 2 is best, and for levels less than E, community 1 is best. Thus, if the range of uncertainty concerning the output volume is entirely *above* point E, the manager need not be concerned about which community to choose—community 2 is best. Similar reasoning holds for any uncertainty existing entirely *below* point E—community 1 is best.

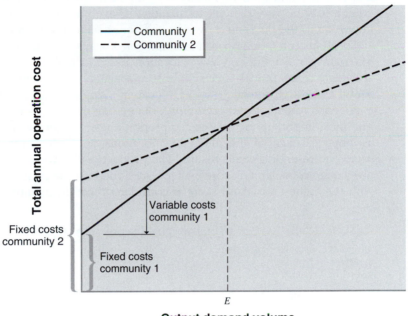

Figure 5.6 Breakeven location model

If the range of uncertainty is closely restricted to point E, then either community may be selected because the costs will be approximately the same in either case. However, if the range of uncertainty is broad and varies considerably from point E in both directions, then the breakeven chart will indicate to the manager the extra costs that will be incurred by choosing the wrong community. Before selecting either community, the manager should probably attempt to gather more information, to reduce the range of uncertainty in demand.

Stage 3: Site

After a list of candidate communities is developed, specific sites within them are identified. The *site*—the actual location of the facility—should be appropriate to the nature of the operation. Such matters as size; adjoining land; zoning; community attitudes; drainage; soil; the availability of water, sewers, and utilities; waste disposal; transportation; the size of the local market; and the costs of development are considered. The development of industrial parks in some communities has alleviated many of the difficulties involved in choosing a site, since the developer automatically takes care of most of these matters. Before any final decision is made, a cash-flow analysis is conducted for each of the candidate sites; this includes the cost of labor, land, taxes, utilities, transportation, and so on.

A model that can help with the site selection is the *weighted score model*. This approach can combine cost measures, profit measures, other quantitative measures, and qualitative measures to help analyze multiple locations (as well as any other multi-criteria decision). Deciding on a location, whether for products or services, is complicated by the existence of multiple criteria such as executives' preferences, maximization of facility use, and customers' attitudes. These and other criteria may be very difficult to quantify, or even measure qualitatively; if they are important to the decision, however, they must be included in the location analysis.

Locations can be compared in a number of ways. The most common is probably just managerial intuition: which location best satisfies the important criteria? The weighted score model is a simple formalization of this intuitive process that is useful as a rough screening tool for locating a single facility. In this model a weight is assigned to each factor (*criterion*), depending on its importance to the manager. The most important factors receive proportionately higher weights. Then a score is assigned to each of the alternative locations on each factor, again with higher scores representing better results. The product of the weights and the scores then gives a set of weighted scores, which are added up for each location. The location with the highest weighted score is considered best. In quantitative terms:

$$\text{Total weighted score} = \sum_i W_i S_i$$

where

i = index for factors
W_i = weight of factor i
S_i = score of the location being evaluated on factor i

The following example illustrates the method.

Communicable Disease Center

A province health department is investigating three possible locations for a specialized control clinic that will monitor acquired immune deficiency syndrome (AIDS) and other sexually transmitted diseases (STDs). The director of public health for the province is particularly concerned with four factors.

1. The most important consideration in the treatment of STDs is ease of access for those infected. Since they are generally disinclined to recognize and seek treatment, it is foolish to locate a clinic where it is not easily accessible to as many patients as possible. This aspect of location is probably as much as 50 percent more important than the lease cost of the building.

2. Still, the annual cost of the lease is not a minor consideration. Unfortunately, the health department is limited to a very tight budget, and any extra cost for the lease will mean that less equipment and staff are available to the clinic.

3. For some patients it is of the utmost importance that confidentiality be maintained. Thus, although the clinic must be easily accessible, it must also be relatively inconspicuous. This factor is probably just as important as the cost of the lease.

4. The director also wants to consider the convenience of the location for the staff, since many of the physicians will be donating their time to the clinic. This consideration is the least important of all, perhaps only half as important as the cost of the lease.

The three locations being considered are a relatively accessible building on Adams Avenue, an inconspicuous office complex near the downtown bus terminal, and a group of public offices in the Civic Center, which would be almost rent-free.

The director has decided to evaluate (score) each of these alternative locations on each of the four factors. He has decided to use a 4-point scale on which 1 represents "poor" and 4 represents "excellent." His scores and the weights (derived from the relative importance of the four factors) are shown in Table 5.2. The problem now is somehow to use this information to determine the best location for the clinic.

To determine the weighted score for each location, we multiply each score by the weight for that factor and then the sum over all factors for each location, as illustrated in Table 5.3. Since higher scores indicate better ratings, the location with the largest score—B, the office near the bus terminal—is best, followed by C, the Civic Center.

$\mathcal{T}$ABLE 5.2 • Potential Clinic Sites

		Potential Locations		
W: Weight	F: Factor	A: Adams Avenue	B: Bus Terminal Complex	C: Civic Center
2	1. Annual lease cost	1	3	4
3	2. Accessibility for patients	3	3	2
2	3. Inconspicuousness	2	4	2
1	4. Accessibility for personnel	4	1	2

Note: Factor scoring scale: 1, poor; 2, acceptable; 3, good; 4, excellent.

$\mathcal{T}$ABLE 5.3 • Comparison of Site Factors by the Weighted Score Method

		Sites:		
Factor	Weight	A	B	C
1	2	$2 \times 1 = 2$	$2 \times 3 = 6$	$2 \times 4 = 8$
2	3	$3 \times 3 = 9$	$3 \times 3 = 9$	$3 \times 2 = 6$
3	2	$2 \times 2 = 4$	$2 \times 4 = 8$	$2 \times 2 = 4$
4	1	$1 \times 4 = 4$	$1 \times 1 = 1$	$1 \times 2 = 2$
Total		19	24	20

Quebec City, Canada, provides a good example of almost exactly this process (Price and Turcotte 1986). The Red Cross Blood Donor Clinic and Transfusion Center of Quebec City in Canada was located in a confined spot in the downtown area and wanted to expand in another location. The center's main activities affecting the choice of a new location were receiving donors, delivering blood and blood products throughout the community and the province of Quebec, and holding blood donor clinics over the same region.

Accordingly, the criteria for a site were identified as

- Highway access for both clinics and blood deliveries
- Ability to attract more donors as a result of improved accessibility and visibility
- Convenience to both public and private transportation
- Ease of travel for employees
- Internal floor space
- Lot size
- Acceptability of the site to management and governmental authorities involved in the decision

The analysis of the problem was very complicated, owing to conflicting requirements and the unavailability of data. Nevertheless, five sites were finally identified and evaluated on the basis of four final criteria. The five sites were then ranked on each of these criteria, and a scoring model was constructed to help management determine the best location. The weights were to be determined by management, and they could be modified to determine if changing them would have any effect on the best location. The final scores and rankings, assuming equal weights across the four criteria, are shown in Table 5.4.

$\mathcal{T}$ABLE   5.4 • Comparison of Quebec City's Site Factors

Site	Road Access	Bus Access	Proximity	Availability	Rank
1	0.4	0.0	0.4	0.7	1
2	0.2	0.2	0.3	0.7	2
3	0.3	0.3	0.2	0.0	4
4	0.0	0.4	0.1	0.0	5
5	0.1	0.1	0.0	0.7	3

Locating Pure Services

Although all the material presented so far applies equally to services and product firms, some situations unique to service organizations are worth noting. Two that we will look at in detail here involve the recipient coming to the facility, as in retailing, and the facility going to the recipient, as with "alarm" services.

Recipient to Facility

In recipient-to-facility situations, the facility draws customers or recipients from an area surrounding it, possibly in competition with other, similar facilities. Research has found that under these circumstances the drawing power of retail facilities is proportional to the size of the facility and inversely proportional to the square (or cube, in some cases) of the average recipient's travel time. This assumes that all other factors—such as price and quality—are equivalent or insignificant. This type of relationship is known as a *gravity* method because, like gravity, it operates by drawing nearby objects in.

Next, consider the situation of public services such as health clinics, libraries, and colleges. Apart from the difficulty of framing a location model is the probably more significant problem of choosing a measure, or measures, of service: number of recipients served (a "surrogate" measure), change in the recipient's condition (a direct measure of benefit), quantity of services offered (another surrogate), and so on. Some measures recommended in the literature on health clinics, which can be used for trial-and-error procedures, are:

1. *Facility utilization.* Maximize the number of visits to the facilities.
2. *Travel distance per citizen.* Minimize the average distance per person in the region to the nearest clinic.
3. *Travel distance per visit.* Minimize the average distance per visit to the nearest clinic. No one measure has been found to work best for all cases of deciding on a location.

Facility to Recipient

Facility-to-recipient situations are common among the urban "alarm" services: fire, police, and ambulance. Again, the problem of measuring a service appropriately involves such factors as number of recipients served, average waiting time for service, value of property saved, and number of service facilities. Two general cases are encountered in this problem, whether a single- or multiple-facility service is being located:

1. High-density demand for services where multiple vehicles are located in the same facility and vehicles are often dispatched from one alarm directly to another
2. Widely distributed demand for services where extreme travel distances require additional facilities

Typical of situation 1 are fire companies and ambulances. Results in these cases have been basically the same. There is a significant drop-off in the returns to scale as more units are added to the system. Typically, the first three or four will improve all measures by up to 80 percent of the maximum improvement. Each additional unit gains less. A second common finding is that optimally located facilities yield only about a 15 percent improvement over existing or evenly dispersed facilities. Last, incremental approaches to selecting additional locations provide slightly poorer service than a total relocation analysis of all the facilities.

SHORT-TERM CAPACITY PLANNING

In the short term, capacity planning is primarily related to issues of scheduling, labor shifts, balancing of resource capacities, and other such issues instead of location decisions. We will look into a variety of such approaches in this section.

DILBERT: ©Scott Adams/Dist. by United Feature Syndicate, Inc.

Process-Flow Analysis

Earlier, we discussed some factors that might limit the output of a production system, such as bottlenecks in the system and yield considerations like scrap and defects. Here we will introduce some other terms relating to the use of a production system. One capacity measure that is commonly used is **utilization**, which is simply the actual output relative to some expected, designed, or normal output rate. For example, if a machine runs 4 hours a day in an American plant and the maintenance and setup time are usually 2 hours a day, the utilization for that day might be reported as 4/6 = 67%, which is considered to be fairly high utilization for a machine in a job shop. However, if the machine was in a Japanese plant, the utilization would probably be reported as 4/24 = 17%, since the machine could, in theory, have been used for all 24 hours in the day!

Clearly, utilization figures do not mean much unless one knows what the "normal" or expected output rate is based on. (When labor utilization measures are used for wage payment plans, this "normal" definition is often a heated subject of union negotiations. For example, should mandated "breaks" be included in the base or not? Should sick time be included? Lunch? Inactivity due to lack of materials to work on? And so on.) An advantage of basing the utilization on 24 hours is that this shows how much more could be done with the resource if it were needed. On the other hand, most managers would not like hearing that their expensive machinery was only being 17 percent utilized!

Bottlenecks in a Sequential Process

Another, major concept in operations is that of *efficiency versus capacity (output rate)*. **Efficiency** is defined as output divided by input. Here we measure output as minutes of work embodied in the item being produced, and input as minutes of resource time spent overall in producing the item. It is important to understand what production situations are amenable to simple capacity improvements by adding capital resources and what production situations are not. Normally, we expect that the amount of productive capacity and the capital investment to gain this capacity will be about proportional. Suppose blood samples are being analyzed in a spectroscope run by one nurse (and both spectroscope and nurse are constantly busy with this task) at the rate of 10 per hour, and a capacity of 100 per hour is required. Then the resource investment translates directly—10 spectroscopes and 10 nurses will be needed.

However, if the production process is *sequential*, the resource investment may not translate so directly into the required output. Normally, many workers and machines are required to produce an output. In that case, the direct capacity-investment correspondence may not exist because of **bottlenecks** in the production process. Bottlenecks are places (there may be more than one) in the production process where production slows down because of a slow, or insufficient number of, machine(s), or perhaps because of a slow worker, or because the product needs to spend time drying. Fixing such bottlenecks usually only marginally improves the capacity of the system, however, because a new bottleneck arises somewhere else in the production process (this common problem is called "floating bottlenecks"). The following examples illustrate how this happens. For ease of understanding, we use a machine to illustrate the bottleneck, but any kind of service operation could also be a bottleneck, and often is in most services, but is less obvious.

Assume that King Sports Products produces a variety of tennis rackets *sequentially* on four machines, and the times required on each machine for one typical racket are as shown in Figure 5.7. Note in this figure that the work embodied in each finished tennis racket is 4 + 3 + 10 + 2 = 19 minutes, which is also the ***throughput time*** for a racket if there are no other rackets being made—that is, the system is not busy. However, during a busy production day, this throughput time will increase, as we will see next.

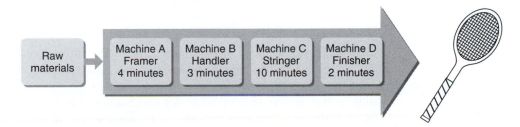

Figure 5.7   King Sports product process.

To minimize the cost of equipment, King could use one of each machine. The resulting capacity or output rate will then be based on the *slowest* machine's processing time of 10 minutes, resulting in 6 units per hour. That is, since every item must go through *each* of the machines, in order, every racket must wait for machine C, the bottleneck, to finish before it can proceed. During this wait, the first, second, and fourth machines will be idle 6, 7, and 8 minutes, respectively, out of every 10-minute cycle.

(Also, the throughput time during such a busy period now becomes 10 + 10 + 10 + 2 = 32 minutes. The racket need not wait at the last machine to exit but the machine must wait 8 minutes for the next racket.) Since the output in this process embodies 19 minutes of work, whereas the input consists of four machines that spend 10 minutes each during every cycle that produces an item (not all of which is necessarily productive), this gives an overall efficiency of only 47.5 percent:

$$\text{efficiency} = \frac{\text{output}}{\text{input}} = \frac{4+3+10+2}{4(10)} = \frac{19}{40} = 47.5\%$$

Note that it does not matter whether the bottleneck is at the end of the sequence, at the beginning, or in the middle. The process is still slowed, on average, to the output rate of the slowest machine. The capacity of this process is thus six units per hour, and the **cycle time of the process** is 10 minutes, or 1/6 of an hour—the output rate and the cycle time are always reciprocals. The process cycle time can be visualized as the time between items coming off the end of the production line, whereas the throughput time can be visualized as the time you would spend in the production process if you attached yourself to the item being produced and rode along through the production process—there is often no relationship between them! And the final output work time is the productive time the item spends in the process.

If King is willing to invest in another, fifth machine, it should purchase another machine of type C, since that is the bottleneck. Then it could run machines C1 and C2 concurrently and put out two units every 10 minutes, obtaining an "effective" machine C processing time of 5 minutes for the machines by staggering their production. Note that machine C is still the bottleneck in the production process, so this effective 5-minute machine processing time is once again the cycle time for the system. The effect of this single investment would be to *double* the capacity/output rate to 12 units per hour (5-min cycle time) and increase the system efficiency to

$$\frac{4+3+10+2}{5(5)} = \frac{19}{25} = 76\%$$

Note in this efficiency calculation that the work output per racket is always 19 minutes, regardless of the number of machines; only the input changes. Now the input is five machines running at a 5-minute cycle time. Continuing in this manner results in the data shown in Table 5.5 and sketched in Figure 5.8. In developing Table 5.5, the next machine added was always the machine that currently had the longest machine time. For example, when there were six machines, machine A had the longest machine time. Thus, the seventh machine added was a machine A.

Note from the table and figure that efficiency of production does not always increase when machines are added, although the general trend is upward. This is because some systems are fairly well "balanced" to begin with. (For example, the cycles across the machines are quite even with seven machines, 2, 3, 3.33, 2; and even more-so at 10 machines. Also note that the addition of only one extra machine at such points does not pay for itself.) If points of high efficiency are reached "early" (as machines are added), these points will tend to be natural operating solutions. For example, a tremendous gain in efficiency (and in output percentage) is reaped by adding a fifth machine to the system. Further additions do not gain much. The next largest gain occurs when the tenth machine is added to the system.

$\mathscr{T}$ABLE 5.5 • Return to King for Using More Machines

Number of Machines	Type of Next Machine	Machine Times (min)				Cycle Time (min)	Total Hourly Output	Efficiency (%)
		A	B	C	D			
4	—	4	3	10	2	10	6	47.5
5	C	4	3	5	2	5	12	76.0
6	C	4	3	3.33	2	4	15	79.2
7	A	2	3	3.33	2	3.33	18	81.4
8	C	2	3	2.5	2	3	20	79.2
9	B	2	1.5	2.5	2	2.5	24	84.4
10	C	2	1.5	2	2	2	30	95.0
11	D	2	1.5	2	1	2	30	86.0
12	A	1.33	1.5	2	1	2	30	79.2
13	C	1.33	1.5	1.67	1	1.67	36	87.5
14	C	1.33	1.5	1.43	1	1.5	40	90.5

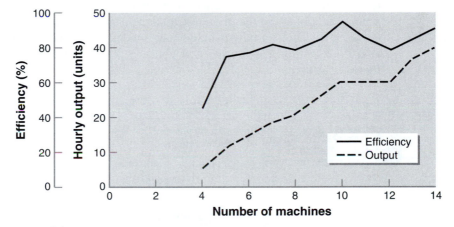

Figure 5.8   Efficiency and output increase when machines are being added.

Although this analysis describes the general tradeoffs of the system, no mention has been made of demand. Suppose that demand is 14 units per hour. Then, to minimize risk but still keep an efficient system, King might use five machines and either work overtime, undersupply the market, or use a number of other strategies, as will be discussed later. Similarly, for a demand of 25 to 35 per hour, the use of 10 machines would be appropriate.

Product and Service Flows

With the role of a bottleneck in a production process in mind, let us now consider the more general procedure of conducting a process-flow analysis, also known in service systems as "mapping" or "blueprinting." The purpose of conducting a process flow analysis is normally to identify bottlenecks, inventory buildup points, and time delays in a production process, crucially important in determining the capacity capability of the process. Standard nomenclature is to use rectangles for tasks/activities, triangles for storage or waiting points, diamonds for decision points, and arrows for flows. An activity changes the characteristics of a product or service, whereas a flow simply indicates the next step in the process, which may involve a change in position.

A simplified process-flow diagram for a manufactured unit composed of two purchased parts and one fabricated 25-pound component is shown in Figure 5.9. Demand is currently 120 units per 8-hour day or 15 units per hour, for an effective process cycle time of one unit every 60/15 = 4 minutes. The inputs, on the left, consist of 1.5 tons (i.e., 3000 lbs) of raw materials delivered by a two-ton capacity truck once a day and 240 parts delivered by a 300-part capacity truck once a day, both of which immediately go into different storage facilities (with different capacities, as shown). The capacities of each stage in the production process are as labeled. Fabrication of the 15 hourly 25-pound components will require 15 × 25 = 375 pounds per hour of raw material from the storage facility. The fabricated components will then flow into Assembly, along with 30 parts withdrawn per hour from the parts storage facility. Assembly then produces the 15 units per hour, which flow into two separate packaging lines with different processing times due to their age. New line A packages 10 units each hour while old line B packages 5 units an hour, for the required total demand. Although the output demand is currently 120 units a day, management anticipates an increase of perhaps as much as a third in the near future; their concern is whether the system can handle this increase in demand.

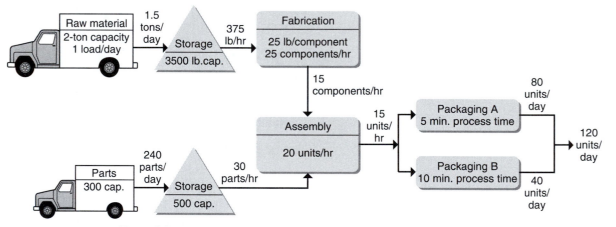

Figure 5.9 Process flow for manufactured unit.

As we see from the diagram, there is currently excess capacity throughout the production system, but is there enough at each stage and process to handle the additional 0.333 × 120 = 40 units a day? Assembly, at 20 units per hour, could just handle the anticipated demand of 120 + 40 = 160 units a day: 20 × 8 = 160. However, the raw material storage facility, which can only hold 3500 pounds (enough to produce only 3500/25 = 140 units a day), is a bottleneck in the system, since we need 160 × 25 pounds/unit = 4000 pounds of storage (the limit of the delivery truck's capacity). Perhaps we could change our system to deliver a portion of the truckload directly to fabrication, or run out 500 pounds to fabrication as the raw material is unloaded from the truck so there is enough space for the full required 2-ton delivery. Note that any activity, resources or storage, could have been the bottleneck in the process. What's more, even if we increase the capacity of the storage facility, the bottleneck will shift to the packaging machines, being able to produce only 12 units per hour from A and another six per hour from B, for a total of 18 per hour, or 144 units a day. And if their capacity is increased, the bottleneck will shift to the 300-part truck delivery because we will need $160 \times 2 = 320$ parts delivered each day. As you can see, the bottleneck shifts around the facility as we solve one problem after another. However, the process-flow diagram allows us to *anticipate* such shifts and head them off before they become real problems.

In a similar manner, Figure 5.10 presents a flow diagram for a simple photocopy service. When used for a service process, the process flow diagram also typically

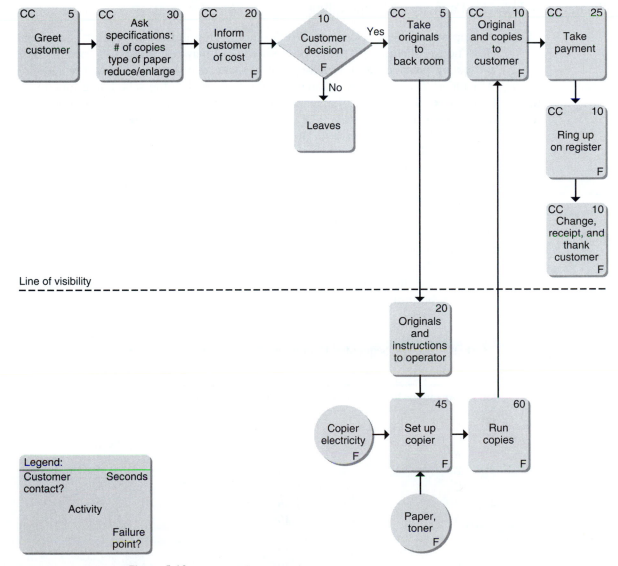

Figure 5.10 Process-flow map for a service.

illustrates potential failure points in the process and the *line of visibility* that divides those activities a customer perceives from those that are conducted out of the customer's sight (the "backroom," as in an auto repair shop, where operations can be conducted with efficiency). Since products are not usually produced in a service, the diagram is called a service "map" or "blueprint," as noted earlier, and shows the process times more prominently instead. Note the potential failure points in the photocopy service diagram, and the "line of visibility" that divides what the customer sees from the backroom operations. Although Figure 5.10 illustrates a simple service process for illustration purposes, service processes are frequently as complex as Figure 5.9, or even more so, and also involve bottlenecks and combined operations.

Relationship between Capacity and Scheduling

An important aspect of capacity worth emphasizing in the earlier discussions is its close tie to scheduling. That is, poor scheduling may result in what appears to be a capacity problem, and a shortage of capacity may lead to constant scheduling difficulties. Thus, capacity planning is closely related to the scheduling function, a topic to be discussed in Chapter 6. The difference is that capacity is oriented primarily toward the *acquisition* of productive resources, whereas scheduling concerns the *timing* of their use. However, it is often difficult to separate the two, especially where human resources are involved, such as in the use of overtime or the overlapping of shifts.

As a simple example, suppose that an organization has to complete within 2 weeks the two customers' jobs shown in Table 5.6. The table shows the sequential processing operations still to be completed and the times required. (The operations resources may be of any form—a facility, a piece of equipment, or an especially skilled worker.) In total, 60 hours of resource A are needed, 45 hours of B, and 25 hours of C. It would appear that 2 weeks (80 hours) of capacity on each of these three resources would be sufficient, and additional capacity would, therefore, be unnecessary.

$\mathcal{T}$ABLE 5.6 • Sequential Operations Required for Two Jobs

Job	Operations Resource Needed	Time Required (hours)
1	A	10
	C	10
	A	30
	B	20
	C	5
2	B	15
	A	10
	C	10
	A	10
	B	10

Figure 5.11 shows the resource requirements of the two jobs plotted along a time scale. Such a chart is called a **Gantt chart** and can be used to show time schedules and capacities of facilities, workers, jobs, activities, machines, and so forth. In Figure 5.11*a*, each job was scheduled on the required resource as soon as it finished on the previous resource, whether or not the new resource was occupied with the other job. This infeasible schedule is called **infinite loading** because work is scheduled on the resource as if it had infinite capacity to handle any and all jobs. Note that in this way capacity conflicts and possible resolutions can be easily visualized. Shifting the jobs to avoid such conflicts—this is called **finite loading**—gives the longer but feasible schedule shown in Figure 5.11*b*.

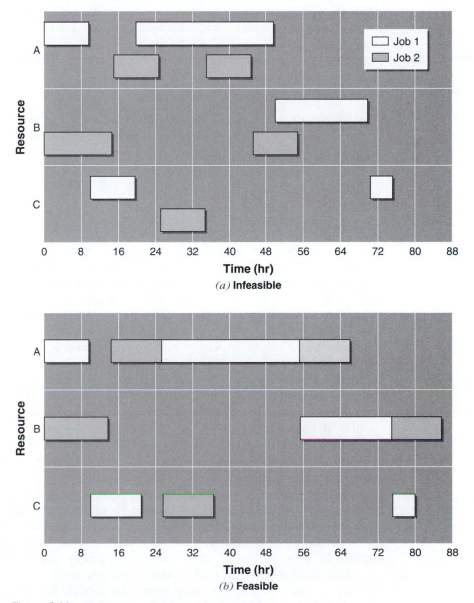

Figure 5.11   Gantt charts for capacity planning and scheduling.

The first resource conflict in Figure 5.11*a* occurs at 20 hours, when job 1 finishes on resource C and next requires resource A, which is still working on job 2. The second conflict, again at A, occurs at 35 hours, and the third, on B, at 50 hours. It is quickly found that deferring one job for the other has drastic consequences for conflicts of resources later (sometimes adding conflicts and sometimes avoiding them) as well as for job completion times. Another consideration, not specified here, is whether an operation can be stopped for awhile and then restarted (called *operation splitting*), for example to let another job pass through (called *preemption*), or, once started, must be worked on until completion. If splitting were allowed for job 2, we could have stopped work at resource A on job 2 at 20 hours to let job 1 begin and then finished the work starting at time 50 when job 1 was finished on resource A. Such operation splitting allows flexibility for rush work but hurts productivity because machines must be taken down and set up multiple times for the same job.

Short-term Capacity Alternatives

The problem of short-term capacity is to handle unexpected but imminent actual demand, either less than or more than expected, in an economic manner. It is known, of course, that the forecast will not be perfect; thus, managers of resources must plan what short-term capacity alternatives to use in either case. Such considerations are usually limited to, at most, the next 6 months, and usually much less, such as the next few days or hours.

Some alternatives for obtaining short-run capacity are categorized in Table 5.7. Each of the techniques in the table has advantages and disadvantages. The first set of alternatives concerns simply trying to increase the resource base. The use of overtime is expensive (time and a half), and productivity after 8 hours of work often declines. It is a simple and easily invoked approach, however, that does not require additional investment, so overtime is one of the most common alternatives. The use of extra shifts requires hiring but no extra facilities. However, productivity of second and third shifts is often lower than that of the first shift. Part-time hiring can be expensive and is usually feasible for only low or unskilled work. Floating workers are flexible and very useful, but of course also cost extra. Leasing facilities and workers is often a good approach, but the extra cost reduces the profit, and these external resources may not be available during the high-demand periods when they are most seriously needed. Subcontracting may require a long lead time, is considerable trouble to implement, and may leave little, if any, profit.

The second set of techniques involves attempts to find ways to improve the utilization of existing resources. For daily demand peaks (seen especially in services, as discussed in the next section), shifts can be overlapped to provide extra capacity at peak times, or staggered to adjust to changes in demand loads. Cross-training the workers to substitute for each other can effectively increase labor flexibility. And there may be other ways to make labor and other resources adjustable also. A similar alternative is to simply share resources whenever possible. Especially for services, appointment and reservation systems, if feasible, can significantly smooth out daily demand peaks. If the output can be stocked ahead of time, as with a product, this is an excellent and very common approach to meeting capacity needs. If recipients are willing, the backlogging of demand to be met later during slack periods is an excellent strategy; a less-accurate forecast is needed, and investment in finished goods is nil. However, this may be an open invitation to competition.

$\mathcal{T}$ABLE 5.7 • Techniques for Increasing Short-run Capacity

I. Increase resources
  1. Use overtime
  2. Add shifts
  3. Employ part-time workers
  4. Use floating workers
  5. Lease workers and facilities
  6. Subcontract

II. Improve resource use
  7. Overlap or stagger shifts
  8. Cross-train the workers
  9. Create adjustable resources
  10. Share resources
  11. Schedule appointments/reservations
  12. Inventory output (if feasible) ahead of demand
  13. Backlog or queue demand

III. Modify the output
  14. Standardize the output
  15. Offer complimentary services
  16. Have the recipient do part of the work
  17. Transform service operations into inventoriable product operations
  18. Cut back on quality

IV. Modify the demand
  19. Partition the demand
  20. Change the price
  21. Change the promotion
  22. Initiate a yield/revenue management system

V. Do not meet demand
  23. Do not supply all the demand

Modifying the output is a creative approach. Doing less customization, allowing fewer variants, offering complimentary services, and encouraging recipients to do some assembly or finishing tasks themselves (as at self-service gasoline stations and check-out lines), perhaps with a small price incentive, are frequently employed and are excellent alternatives.

Attempting to alter the demand, partition it, or shift it to a different period is another creative approach. Running promotions or price differentials ("off-peak" pricing), or both, for slack periods is an excellent method for leveling demand, especially in utilities, telephones, and similar services. Prices are not easily increased above normal in high-demand periods, however. One formal method of partitioning both the demand and the resource supply is known as yield or revenue management, a subject we will discuss in more detail in Chapter 6. Last, the manager may simply decide not to meet the market demand—again, however, at the cost of inviting competition.

In actuality, many of these alternatives are not feasible except in certain types of organizations or in particular circumstances. For example, when demand is high, subcontractors are full, outside facilities and staff are already overbooked, second-shift workers are employed elsewhere, and marketing promotion is already low key. Thus, of the many possible alternatives, most firms tend to rely on only a few, such as overtime and, for product firms, stocking up ahead of demand.

So far we have primarily discussed increasing capacity in the short run, but firms also have a need to *decrease* short-run capacity. This is more difficult, however, and most such capacity simply goes unused. If the output involves a product, some inventory buildup may be allowed in order to make use of the available capacity; otherwise, system maintenance may be done (cleaning, fixing, preprocessing, and so on).

Capacity Planning for Services

Capacity planning is often much more difficult for pure service operations than for products, and with a service there is a clearer distinction between long- and short-run capacity planning. For services, the more difficult aspects of providing capacity occur in the short run, usually because the demand for a service is subject to daily peaks and valleys, and the output cannot be stored ahead of time to buffer this fluctuation. For example, doctors' offices see demand peaks at 9 A.M. and 1 P.M., and college classes see it at 10 A.M. Or there may be weekly peaks, monthly peaks, or yearly peaks, such as Friday's demand on banks to deposit (or cash) paychecks, and the first-of-the-month demand on restaurants when social security checks arrive in the mail. Some services, such as fire departments, experience multiple peaks, as illustrated in Figure 5.12a, which shows the regular *daily* cycle of fire alarms, with a peak from 3 to 7 P.M.; and Figure 5.12b, which shows the *yearly* cycle of fire alarms, with a peak in April.

As noted earlier with regard to products, frequently it is not clear whether a problem is a matter of scheduling or capacity; this is particularly true with services. The primary problem is matching availability of staff to demand in terms of timing and skills, both on a daily basis and over the longer term (such as weekly and monthly). Service organizations have developed many novel approaches to this problem as just briefly described: split shifts, overlapping shifts, duty tours (e.g., 48 or 72 hrs for firefighters), part-time help, overbooking, appointment systems, and on-call staff. Some of these approaches will be considered in more detail in Chapter 6. However, for services, a favorite alternative is to share capacity with neighboring units by pooling resources such as generators, police patrols, or hotel rooms. When one organization is temporarily overloaded, the neighbor absorbs the excess demand. Another favorite approach for some services that has even been too successful is that of shifting the demand to off-peak periods. When AT&T offered lower phone rates after 5 P.M., it found that it had to raise the Sunday night 5–11 P.M. rate owing to excessive shifted demand.

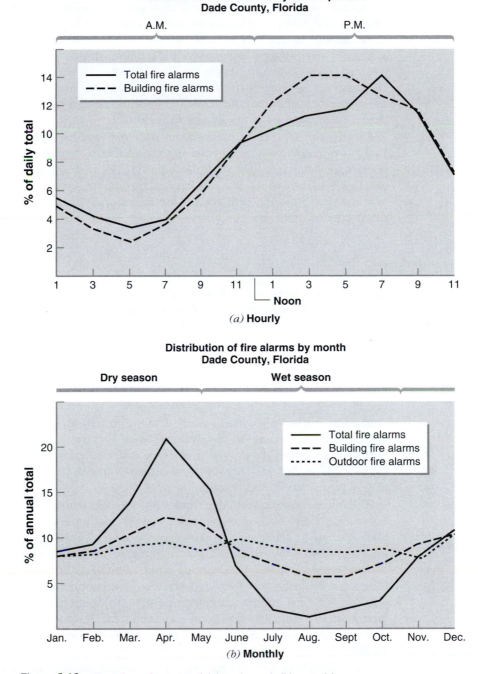

Figure 5.12   Fire alarm histories (*a*) hourly and (*b*) monthly.

In many situations, it is almost impossible to measure an organization's capacity to produce a service, because the service is so abstract. Thus, a more common approach is to measure *inputs* rather than outputs, and assume (perhaps with regular checkups) that the production system is successful at transforming the inputs into acceptable services (outputs). For example, organizations that offer plays, art exhibits, and other such intangible services do not measure their patrons' pleasure or relaxation; rather, they measure number of performances, number of actors and actresses, and number of paintings (or painting days, since many exhibits have a rotating travel schedule). Even fire departments do not attempt to measure their capacity by the number of fires they can extinguish; instead, they use the number of engines or companies they can offer in response to a call, the service or response time, or the number of firefighters responding.

Clearly, this manner of measuring service capacity can leave a lot to be desired. Do more paintings give greater satisfaction? Do higher-quality paintings give greater satisfaction? Might there be other factors that are equally or more important, such as the crowd, the parking facilities, or the lighting on the paintings? Is a hospital where more deaths occur providing worse service? Is a hospital with more physicians on staff providing better service?

The Learning Curve

An extremely important aspect of capacity planning, and an important operations concept in and of itself, is the **learning curve** effect—the ability of humans to increase their productive capacity through "learning." This issue is particularly important in the short-term start-up of new and unfamiliar processes such as those involving new technologies (e.g., learning to use a new software program), and always occurs in the production ramp-up of new models of automobiles, planes, computers, etc. Thus, the characteristic of slow, possibly error-prone output initially, followed by better, faster production, should be of major concern to marketing and sales—which are often trying to market the output or have promised a certain volume to a customer by a set date; to accounting—which is checking productivity and yield rates in order to determine a fair cost for the output; and to finance—which is concerned with the timing of cash flows related to purchases, labor, and revenues.

The improvement with experience is not necessarily due to learning alone, however. Better tools, improvements in work methods, upgraded output designs, and other such factors also help increase productivity. Hence, such curves are also known as *improvement curves, production progress functions, performance curves*, and *experience curves*. The learning curve effect, from this viewpoint, also affects long-term capacity and should be factored into longer-term planning processes, another issue of interest to marketing and accounting, as well as finance. The Japanese, in particular, count on increasing the long-term capacity of a facility through the workers' development of better work methods and improvements in tools.

The derivation of the learning curve began in the airframe manufacturing industry during the 1930s, when it was found that the labor-hours needed to build each successive airplane decreased relatively smoothly. In particular, the learning curve law was found to be

Each time the output doubles, the labor hours decrease to a fixed percentage of their previous value.

In the case of plane production, this percentage was found to be 80 percent. Thus, when the first plane of a series required 100,000 labor-hours to produce, the second took 80,000 labor hours, the fourth took 80,000 × 0.80 = 64,000, the eighth 64,000 × 0.80 = 51,200, and so on. This type of mathematical relationship is described by the *negative exponential function*[1], illustrated for airplanes in Figure 5.13.

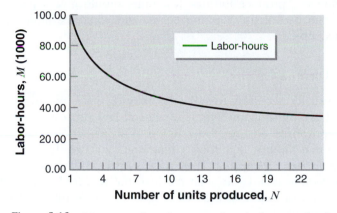

Figure 5.13   80 percent learning curve for airplane production.

A number of factors affect the learning curve rate, but the most important are the complexity of the task and the percentage of human, compared with mechanical, input. The greatest learning—sometimes at a rate as much as 60 percent (lower rates meaning greater learning)—occurs for highly complex tasks consisting primarily of human inputs. A task that is highly machine-automated clearly leaves little opportunity for learning. (Thus, a rate close to 100 percent would apply, because only the human can learn.) In airframe manufacturing the proportion of human effort is about 75 percent, and an 80 percent learning rate applies. For similar work of the same complexity and ratio of human-to-machine input, approximately the same rate will apply.

---

[1]The function is as follows:

$$M = mN^r$$

where

M = labor-hours for the Nth unit
m = labor hours for first unit
N = number of units produced
r = exponent of curve corresponding to learning rate
   = log(learning rate)/0.693

Two forms of the learning curve relationship are used in the literature. In one form M corresponds to the cumulative average labor-hours of all N units, and in the other form M corresponds to the actual labor-hours to produce the Nth unit. The second interpretation is more useful for capacity planning and will be used here. For example, then, a learning rate of 90 percent would mean that each time production doubled from, say, N_1 to N_2, unit N_2 would require 90 percent of the labor hours that N_1 required. The log here is the "natural" log (the base e), and 0.693 is the natural log of 2.0. But base 10, or any other base, may be used if divided by the log of 2.0 to the same base. That is, r = log(learning rate)/log 2.0.

But learning curves are not limited to manufacturing, or even to product-oriented organizations. These curves apply just as well to hairdressing, selling, finding a parking space, and preparing pizza. As indicated, they also apply to *groups* of individuals, and *systems* that include people and machines, as well as to individuals.

The primary question, of course, is what learning rate to apply. If previous experience is available, this may give some indication; if not, a close watch of the time it takes to produce the first few units should give a good indication. Let us illustrate the use of the learning curve, and some learning curve tables, with a simple example.

Learning Curve Tables

It is not usually necessary to solve the learning curve equation every time you run across a learning situation. First, the general law already stated will usually suffice for most purposes. Second, the solution to the equation for various learning rates, assuming that the first item took 1 time unit, has already been calculated and tabulated in Tables 5.8 and 5.9. These tables provide the percentage of time the Nth unit will require relative to what the first unit required (Table 5.8) and the cumulative amount of time that the first N units will take relative to what the first unit took (Table 5.9).

To use Tables 5.8 and 5.9, you multiply the values given in these tables by the labor-hours actually required for the first unit in your situation to get the time for the Nth unit, or the cumulative time for units 1 through N, respectively. Returning to our example—the 80 percent learning curve for airplanes—we see in Table 5.8 that unit 2 (left-hand column) under "80%" will require 0.8 of what unit 1 required (100,000 labor-hours), that unit 4 will require 0.64, that unit 8 will take 0.512, and so forth. In addition, we also see that unit 3 will take 0.7021 and unit 6, for example, 0.5617 (i.e., 0.5617 × 100,000 or 56,170 labor-hours). The *total* labor-hours to produce two, four, or eight planes can be found by adding the necessary values together, or by looking at Table 5.9, where this has already been done. Again, reading under "80%" for 2, 4, and 8 units, we get 1.8, 3.142, and 5.346 × 100,000, respectively, for 180,000, 314,200, and 534,600 labor-hours, cumulative. We next illustrate the use of the learning curve tables with a simple example, followed by a more complex example.

Following the engineering specifications for the assembly of a new motor, a production team was able to assemble the first (prototype) motor in 3.6 hours. After more practice on the second and third motors, the team was able to assemble the fourth motor in 1.76 hours. What is the team's learning rate, and how long will the next motor probably take?

Here the actual individual assembly times are given, so we can use Table 5.8, which tabulates *the ratio of what the Nth unit took relative to the first unit*. First, we need to find the ratio from the given data and then locate that value somewhere in the table. Our ratio for the fourth motor would be: 1.76/3.6 = 0.49. Next, we turn to Table 5.8 and scan across row "4" under the "Units" column. We find the value 0.49 under "70%," so this is our learning rate for the team (which is pretty good, by the way).

To find out how long the next (fifth) motor will take, we drop down the "70%" column to the next row that corresponds to the fifth unit. (*Note*: The rows are not always in increments of 1. For example, at 10 they jump by 2, and at 100 by 20.)

$\mathcal{T}$ABLE 5.8 • Unit Values of the Learning Curve

Example: Unit 1 took 10 hours, 80% learning rate. What will unit 5 require?
Solution: Unit 5 row, 80% column value = 0.5956. Thus, unit 5 will take 10 (0.5956) = 5.956 hours.

	Improvement Ratios							
Units	60%	65%	70%	75%	80%	85%	90%	95%
1	1.0000	1.0000	1.0000	1.0000	1.0000	1.0000	1.0000	1.0000
2	0.6000	0.6500	0.7000	0.7500	0.8000	0.8500	0.9000	0.9500
3	0.4450	0.5052	0.5682	0.6338	0.7021	0.7729	0.8462	0.9219
4	0.3600	0.4225	0.4900	0.5625	0.6400	0.7225	0.8100	0.9025
5	0.3054	0.3678	0.4368	0.5127	0.5956	0.6857	0.7830	0.8877
6	0.2670	0.3284	0.3977	0.4754	0.5617	0.6570	0.7616	0.8758
7	0.2383	0.2984	0.3674	0.4459	0.5345	0.6337	0.7439	0.8659
8	0.2160	0.2746	0.3430	0.4219	0.5120	0.6141	0.7290	0.8574
9	0.1980	0.2552	0.3228	0.4017	0.4930	0.5974	0.7161	0.8499
10	0.1832	0.2391	0.3058	0.3846	0.4765	0.5828	0.7047	0.8433
12	0.1602	0.2135	0.2784	0.3565	0.4493	0.5584	0.6854	0.8320
14	0.1430	0.1940	0.2572	0.3344	0.4276	0.5386	0.6696	0.8226
16	0.1296	0.1785	0.2401	0.3164	0.4096	0.5220	0.6561	0.8145
18	0.1188	0.1659	0.2260	0.3013	0.3944	0.5078	0.6445	0.8074
20	0.1099	0.1554	0.2141	0.2884	0.3812	0.4954	0.6342	0.8012
22	0.1025	0.1465	0.2038	0.2772	0.3697	0.4844	0.6251	0.7955
24	0.0961	0.1387	0.1949	0.2674	0.3595	0.4747	0.6169	0.7904
25	0.0933	0.1353	0.1908	0.2629	0.3548	0.4701	0.6131	0.7880
30	0.0815	0.1208	0.1737	0.2437	0.3346	0.4505	0.5963	0.7775
35	0.0728	0.1097	0.1605	0.2286	0.3184	0.4345	0.5825	0.7687
40	0.0660	0.1010	0.1498	0.2163	0.3050	0.4211	0.5708	0.7611
45	0.0605	0.0939	0.1410	0.2060	0.2936	0.4096	0.5607	0.7545
50	0.0560	0.0879	0.1336	0.1972	0.2838	0.3996	0.5518	0.7486
60	0.0489	0.0785	0.1216	0.1828	0.2676	0.3829	0.5367	0.7386
70	0.0437	0.0713	0.1123	0.1715	0.2547	0.3693	0.5243	0.7302
80	0.0396	0.0657	0.1049	0.1622	0.2440	0.3579	0.5137	0.7231
90	0.0363	0.0610	0.0987	0.1545	0.2349	0.3482	0.5046	0.7168
100	0.0336	0.0572	0.0935	0.1479	0.2271	0.3397	0.4966	0.7112
120	0.0294	0.0510	0.0851	0.1371	0.2141	0.3255	0.4830	0.7017
140	0.0262	0.0464	0.0786	0.1287	0.2038	0.3139	0.4718	0.6937
160	0.0237	0.0427	0.0734	0.1217	0.1952	0.3042	0.4623	0.6869
180	0.0218	0.0397	0.0691	0.1159	0.1879	0.2959	0.4541	0.6809
200	0.0201	0.0371	0.0655	0.1109	0.1816	0.2887	0.4469	0.6757
250	0.0171	0.0323	0.0584	0.1011	0.1691	0.2740	0.4320	0.6646
300	0.0149	0.0289	0.0531	0.0937	0.1594	0.2625	0.4202	0.6557
350	0.0133	0.0262	0.0491	0.0879	0.1517	0.2532	0.4105	0.6482
400	0.0121	0.0241	0.0458	0.0832	0.1453	0.2454	0.4022	0.6419
450	0.0111	0.0224	0.0431	0.0792	0.1399	0.2387	0.3951	0.6363
500	0.0103	0.0210	0.0408	0.0758	0.1352	0.2329	0.3888	0.6314

Source: Albert N. Schreiber, Richard A. Johnson, Robert C. Meier, William T. Newell, and Henry C. Fischer, *Cases in Manufacturing Management* (New York: McGraw-Hill, 1965), p. 464. Reprinted by permission of McGraw-Hill, © 1965.

$\mathscr{T}$ABLE   5.9 • Cumulative Values of the Learning Curve

Example: Unit 1 took 10 hours, 80% learning rate. What will be
the total hours required to produce the first five units?
Solution: Unit 5 row, 80% column: value = 3.738. Thus, the first five
units will require 10 (3.738) = 37.38 hours.

	Improvement Ratios							
Units	60%	65%	70%	75%	80%	85%	90%	95%
1	1.000	1.000	1.000	1.000	1.000	1.000	1.000	1.000
2	1.600	1.650	1.700	1.750	1.800	1.850	1.900	1.950
3	2.045	2.155	2.268	2.384	2.502	2.623	2.746	2.872
4	2.405	2.578	2.758	2.946	3.142	3.345	3.556	3.774
5	2.710	2.946	3.195	3.459	3.738	4.031	4.339	4.662
6	2.977	3.274	3.593	3.934	4.299	4.688	5.101	5.538
7	3.216	3.572	3.960	4.380	4.834	5.322	5.845	6.404
8	3.432	3.847	4.303	4.802	5.346	5.936	6.574	7.261
9	3.630	4.102	4.626	5.204	5.839	6.533	7.290	8.111
10	3.813	4.341	4.931	5.589	6.315	7.116	7.994	8.955
12	4.144	4.780	5.501	6.315	7.227	8.244	9.374	10.62
14	4.438	5.177	6.026	6.994	8.092	9.331	10.72	12.27
16	4.704	5.541	6.514	7.635	8.920	10.38	12.04	13.91
18	4.946	5.879	6.972	8.245	9.716	11.41	13.33	15.52
20	5.171	6.195	7.407	8.828	10.48	12.40	14.61	17.13
22	5.379	6.492	7.819	9.388	11.23	13.38	15.86	18.72
24	5.574	6.773	8.213	9.928	11.95	14.33	17.10	20.31
25	5.668	6.909	8.404	10.19	12.31	14.80	17.71	21.10
30	6.097	7.540	9.305	11.45	14.02	17.09	20.73	25.00
35	6.478	8.109	10.13	12.72	15.64	19.29	23.67	28.86
40	6.821	8.631	10.90	13.72	17.19	21.43	26.54	32.68
45	7.134	9.114	11.62	14.77	18.68	23.50	29.37	36.47
50	7.422	9.565	12.31	15.78	20.12	25.51	32.14	40.22
60	7.941	10.39	13.57	17.67	22.87	29.41	37.57	47.65
70	8.401	11.13	14.74	19.43	25.47	33.17	42.87	54.99
80	8.814	11.82	15.82	21.09	27.96	36.80	48.05	62.25
90	9.191	12.45	16.83	22.67	30.35	40.32	53.14	69.45
100	9.539	13.03	17.79	24.18	32.65	43.75	58.14	76.59
120	10.16	14.11	19.57	27.02	37.05	50.39	67.93	90.71
140	10.72	15.08	21.20	29.67	41.22	56.78	77.46	104.7
160	11.21	15.97	22.72	32.17	45.20	62.95	86.80	118.5
180	11.67	16.79	24.14	34.54	49.03	68.95	95.96	132.1
200	12.09	17.55	25.48	36.80	52.72	74.79	105.0	145.7
250	13.01	19.28	28.56	42.08	61.47	88.83	126.9	179.2
300	13.81	20.81	31.34	46.94	69.66	102.2	148.2	212.2
350	14.51	22.18	33.89	51.48	77.43	115.1	169.0	244.8
400	15.14	23.44	36.26	55.75	84.85	127.6	189.3	277.0
450	15.72	24.60	38.48	59.80	91.97	139.7	209.2	309.0
500	16.26	25.68	40.58	63.68	98.851	51.5	228.8	340.6

Source: Albert N. Schreiber, Richard A. Johnson, Robert C. Meier, William T.
Newell, and Henry C. Fischer, *Cases in Manufacturing Management* (New York:
McGraw-Hill, 1965), p. 465. Reprinted by permission of McGraw-Hill, © 1965.

At the fifth row the value is 0.4368, which, when multiplied by what the first unit took (3.6 hours), gives: 0.4368 × 3.6 = 1.57 hours. Remember: The tabulated values assume that the first unit took only 1 hour (or min., or day, or whatever the measure), so if the first unit took something other than "1," you need to multiply the table value by the actual time it took to produce the first unit.

Next, let us consider a more complex, real-life problem that also requires the use of the cumulative table, Table 5.9.

Spreadsheet, Inc.

Spreadsheet, Inc., has just entered the growing software training market with a contract from a financial organization to teach spreadsheet modeling techniques to the organization's 10 managers, for purposes of financial and pension planning. The lesson for the last manager has just ended, and the organization, considering the first 10 lessons highly successful, has engaged Spreadsheet to give the same lessons to its staff of 150 agents. The lesson for the first manager was highly experimental, requiring 100 hours in all, but careful analysis and refinement of the techniques have gradually decreased this time to the point where the average time for all 10 initial lessons was just under half that value, 49 hours each. To properly staff, schedule, plan, and cost out the work for the 150 lessons, Spreadsheet needs to know how many hours of lessons will be required.

To begin, we can use Table 5.9 to determine the learning rate: the average of 49 hours each, times 10 managers, gives 490 hours, cumulative. This is 4.9 times what the first manager required (490 hours/100 hours). Finding the value 4.9 in Table 5.9 for 10 units will then give the learning curve rate applying to these complex lessons. Reading across the 10-unit row, we find 4.931 (close enough) under the "70%" column. (On occasion, interpolation between columns may be necessary, or alternatively the exact quantities can be calculated directly using the formula. Spreadsheets can greatly facilitate the task of manually calculating time estimates based on the learning curve formula.)

Assuming that the lessons are continuous and the teaching techniques are not forgotten (an important assumption), we can look further down the "70%" column in Table 5.9 to find the value corresponding to the *total* number of lessons to be given: 10 + 150 = 160. This value, 22.72, is then multiplied by the amount of time required for the first lesson (100 hours) to give a grand total of 2272 hours for the 160 lessons. Since the initial 10 managers required a total of 490 hours by themselves, the second group, consisting of the agents, will require 2272 − 490 = 1782 hours. The time phasing of this 1782 hours is also available, if desired, from Table 5.8.

The learning curve is only a theoretical construct, of course, and therefore only approximates actual learning. A more realistic, and typical, learning pattern is illustrated in Figure 5.14. Initially, actual labor hours per unit vary around the theoretical curve until a "learning plateau" is reached at, perhaps, the tenth unit. At this plateau no significant learning appears to occur, until there is a breakthrough. Learning typically involves a number of such plateaus and breakthroughs. At about 30 units, production is halted for a period of time and "forgetting" occurs, rapidly at first but then trailing off. When production is resumed, relearning occurs very quickly (as when someone relearns to ride a bicycle after 40 years) until the original efficiency is reached (at about 33 units). If the conditions are the same at this time as for the initial part of the curve, the original learning curve rate will then hold.

After sufficient time passes, the improvement due to learning becomes trivial in comparison with natural variability in efficiency, and at that point we say learning has ceased.

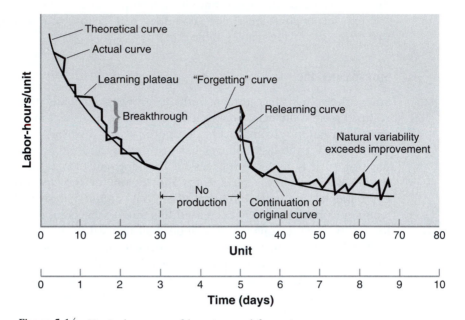

Figure 5.14 Typical pattern of learning and forgetting.

Queuing and the Psychology of Waiting

An important element in evaluating the capacity of operations to produce either products or services concerns the waiting lines, backlogs, or *queues*, that tend to build up in front of the operations. Queuing theory provides a mechanism to determine several key performance measure of an operating system based on the rate of arrivals to the system and the system's capacity (specified as the system's service rate). With an unpaced production line, for example, buffer inventory between operations builds up at some times and disappears at other times, owing to natural variability in the difficulty of the operations. The Wiley website for this text (see Preface for URL) includes a discussion of the theory, equations, and some example calculations of queuing.

In the production of services, this variability is even greater because of both the amount of highly variable human *input* and the variable *requirements* for services. What is more, the "items" in queue are often people, who tend to complain and make trouble if kept waiting too long. Thus, it behooves the operations manager to provide adequate service to keep long queues from forming. This costs more money for service facilities and staffs. But long queues cost money also, in the form of in-process inventory, unfinished orders, lost sales, and ill will. Figure 5.15 conceptually illustrates, as a function of the capacity of the service facility, the tradeoffs in these two costs.

1. *Cost of waiting.* In-process inventory, ill will, lost sales. This cost decreases with service capacity.

2. *Cost of service facilities.* Equipment, supplies, and staff. This cost increases with service capacity.

At some point the total of the two costs in Figure 5.15 is minimized, and it is at this point that managers typically wish to operate. However, before investing resources in adding expensive service facilities, the manager may find it worth-while trying to reduce the cost of waiting instead. Given that perceptions and expectations may have more to do with customer satisfaction than actual waiting time, David Maister (1984) has formulated eight insightful "principles" of waiting, which, if addressed carefully, may be more effective in reducing the overall cost of waiting to the organization than adding service facilities.

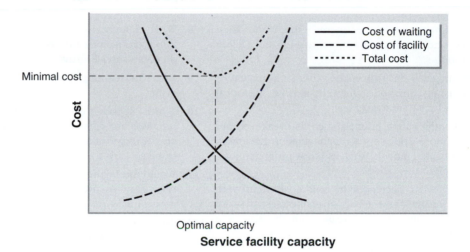

Figure 5.15   The relevant queuing costs.

1. ***Unoccupied time feels longer than occupied time.*** Give customers something to do while waiting, hopefully something that will facilitate the service that is to come. An example is having customers key in their Social Security number while waiting on the phone so the representative will have their file on screen as they answer the call.

2. ***Pre-service waiting feels longer than in-service waiting.*** Using staging areas to complete portions of the service, such as taking a patient's temperature and blood pressure, communicates to them that the service has begun.

3. ***Anxiety makes waiting seem longer.*** Offer information to relieve anxiety, or distracters (even music, mirrors) to allay anxiety.

4. ***Uncertain waiting is longer than known, finite waiting.*** Provide cues, or direct announcements, to indicate how soon the service will be coming or finishing (especially in the case of a painful procedure).

5. ***Unexplained waiting is longer than explained waiting.*** Keep customers informed about why they are being delayed, and how long it will be before they can be serviced.

6. ***Unfair waiting is longer than fair waiting.*** Make sure that priority or express customers are handled in a manner transparent to other customers, and treated out of sight, if possible.

7. ***Solo waiting is longer than group waiting.*** In part this reflects principles 1 (someone else to talk to), 3 (seeing and talking to others can reduce anxiety), and 5 (other waiting customers may communicate reasons for the waiting), as well as the general principle that there is more security in groups.

8. ***The more valuable the service, the longer it is worth waiting for.*** The use of marketing and other means to increase the perception of the value of the service will reduce the impatience with waiting.

EXPAND YOUR UNDERSTANDING

1. What impact might the Internet, the World Wide Web, and intranets have on using the Delphi method?

2. Why might a decision maker choose a qualitative forecasting method when extensive historical demand data are available?

3. Frequently, simple models such as breakeven are much more appealing to management than more sophisticated models (such as linear programming). Why might this be so?

4. Exactly what decreases in unit cost occur with larger facilities as a result of economies of scale? Might any unit costs increase with the size of a facility?

5. Why has the concept of economies of scope never arisen before? List where the economies come from.

6. How ethical is it for airlines, hotels, and other service providers to overbook their limited-capacity facilities intentionally, knowing that at some point they will have to turn away a customer with a "guaranteed" reservation?

7. Describe how the concept of bottlenecks would apply to services as well as products. Give some examples from your experience.

8. What elements would be measured if a product firm were to measure its capacity by its inputs, as do some service firms?

9. Does the learning curve continue downward forever?

10. Which measures used to locate pure service organizations are direct measures of benefit and which are surrogate measures of benefit? Can you think of better direct measures? Why aren't they used?

11. Would the failure points, line of visibility, and processing times used in service maps be useful in process flow diagrams for products?

12. When might an organization not use all three stages of the location selection process described here?

13. Might the breakeven model be used for the national or site stage of location? Might the weighted score model be useful in the national or community stage of location? What factors would be used in these models at other stages?

14. Are the principles of waiting captured in the 23 capacity techniques of Table 5.7? Which ones?

15. Would a firm that simply expanded their current product line gain economies of scope? Might highly flexible and proficient labor also offer economies of scope?

APPLY YOUR UNDERSTANDING
Bangalore Training Services (BTS)

BTS was an entrepreneurial startup developed by Deepa Anand and Monisha Patel, two recent MBA graduates from the United States who had served internships in the summer with a U. S. call center who was considering setting up operations in India but was unsure how to find suitable employees. Their plan was to offer training to Indian men and women in call center activities such as sales, service, and trouble-shooting for electronic goods of all sorts, and then match those employees to the needs of foreign firms looking to set up call centers. The training consisted of a dozen sessions covering culture, speaking fluency, electronic awareness, buying and service behaviors, and other such basic matters that all call centers required.

Questions

Discuss how the following topics from this chapter might be of relevance to Deepa and Monisha in setting up their new firm:
1. Capacity planning
2. Learning curve
3. Bottlenecks
4. Psychology of waiting
5. Scheduling
6. Service map/blueprint

Exit Manufacturing Company

The planning committee of Exit Manufacturing Company (made up of the vice presidents of marketing, finance, and production) was discussing the plans for a new factory to be located outside of Atlanta, Georgia, U.S.A. The factory would produce exterior doors consisting of prehung metal over Styrofoam insulation. The doors would be made in a standard format, with 15 different insert panels that could be added by retailers after manufacture. The standardization of construction was expected to create numerous production efficiencies over competitors' factories that produced multidimensional doors. Atlanta was felt to be an ideal site because of its location—in the heart of the sunbelt, with its growing construction industry. By locating close to these growing sunbelt states, Exit would minimize distribution costs.

The capital cost for the factory was expected to be $14 million. Annual maintenance expenses were projected to total 5 percent of capital. Fuel and utility costs were expected to be $500,000 per year. An analysis of the area's labor market indicated that a wage rate of $10 per hour could be expected. It was estimated that producing a door in the new facility would require 1.5 labor-hours. Fringe benefits paid to the operating labor were expected to equal 15 percent of direct labor costs. Supervisory, clerical, technical, and managerial salaries were forecast to total $350,000 per year. Taxes and insurance would cost $200,000 per year. Other miscellaneous expenses were expected to total $250,000 per year. Depreciation was based on a 30-year life with use of the straight-line method and a $4 million salvage value. Sheet metal, Styrofoam, adhesive for the doors, and frames were projected to cost $12 per door. Paint, hinges, doorknobs, and accessories were estimated to total $7.80 per door. Crating and shipping supplies were expected to cost $2.50 per door.

Exit's marketing manager prepared the following price-demand chart for the distribution area of the new plant. Through analysis of these data, the committee members felt that they could verify their expectation of an increase from 15 to 25 percent in the current market share, owing to the cost advantage of standardization.

Average Sales Price ($/door)	Area Sales (in units)
$90	40,000
$103	38,000
$115	31,000
$135	22,000

Questions

Develop a breakeven capacity analysis for Exit's new door and determine:
a. Best price, production rate, and profit.
b. Breakeven production rate with the price in a.
c. Breakeven price with the production rate in a.
d. Sensitivity of profits to variable cost, price, and production rate.

Stafford Chemical, Inc.

Stafford Chemical, Inc. is a privately held company that produces a range of specialty chemicals. Currently, its most important product line is paint pigments used by the automobile industry. Stafford Chemical was founded more than 60 years ago by Phillip Stafford in a small town north of Cincinnati, Ohio, U.S.A., and is currently run by Phillip's grandson, George Stafford. Stafford has more than 150 employees, and approximately three-quarters of them work on the shop floor. Stafford Chemical operates out of the same plant Phillip built when he founded the company; however, it has undergone several expansions over the years.

Recently, a Japanese competitor of Stafford Chemical by the name of Ozawa Industries announced plans to expand its operations to the United States. Ozawa, a subsidiary of a large industrial Japanese company, decided to locate a new facility in the United States to better serve some of its customers: Japanese automobile manufacturers who have built assembly plants in the U.S.A.

The governor of Ohio has been particularly aggressive in trying to persuade Ozawa Industries to locate in a new industrial park located about 30 miles from Stafford's current plant. She has expressed a willingness to negotiate special tax rates, to subsidize workers' training, and to expand the existing highway to meet Ozawa's needs. In a recent newspaper article, she was quoted as saying:

Making the concessions I have proposed to get Ozawa to locate within our state is a good business decision and a good investment in our state. The plant will provide high-paying jobs for 400 of our citizens. Furthermore, over the long run, the income taxes that these 400 individuals will pay will more than offset the concessions I have proposed. Since several other states have indicated a willingness to make similar concessions, it is unlikely that Ozawa would choose our state without them.

George Stafford was outraged after being shown the governor's comments. I can't believe this. Stafford Chemical has operated in this state for over 60 years. I am the third generation of Staffords to run this business. Many of our employees' parents and grandparents worked here. We have taken pride in being an exemplary corporate citizen. And now our governor wants to help one of our major competitors drive us out of business. How are we supposed to compete with such a large industrial giant? We should be the ones who are getting the tax break and help with workers' training. Doesn't 60 years of paying taxes and employing workers count for something? Where is the governor's loyalty? It seems to me that the state should be loyal to its long-term citizens, the ones who care about the state and community they operate in—not some large industrial giant looking to save a buck.

Questions

1. How valid is George Stafford's argument? How valid is the governor's argument? Is Stafford Chemical being punished because it was already located within the state?
2. How ethical is it for states and local governments to offer incentives to attract new businesses to their localities? Are federal laws needed to keep states from competing with one another?
3. Does the fact that Ozawa is a foreign company alter the ethical nature of the governor's actions? What about Ozawa's size?
4. What are George's options?

EXERCISES

1. Three professors are grading a combined final exam. Each is grading different questions on the test. One professor requires 3 minutes to finish her portion, another takes 6 minutes, and the third takes 2 minutes. Assume there is no learning curve effect.

   a. What will be their hourly output?

   b. If there are 45 tests to grade, how long will the grading take?

   c. If each professor were to grade the exams separately in 18 minutes, how long would it take to grade the 45 tests? How long if another professor (who also required 18 min) joined them?

   d. If another professor pitches in just to help the second professor, how long will it take the four of them to grade the tests?

   e. If a fifth professor offers to help, what might happen?

2. A toy firm produces drums sequentially on three machines A, B, and C with cycle times of 3, 4, and 6 minutes, respectively.

   a. Determine the optimum efficiency and output rates for adding one, two, . . . , six more machines.

   b. Assume now that two identical lines are operating, each with machines A, B, and C. If new machines can be shared between the lines, how should one, two, and then three new machines be added? What are the resulting efficiencies and outputs of the two lines? Is it always best to equally share extra machines between the two lines?

3. If the production system for a product has a utilization of 80 percent, and a yield of 75 percent, what capacity is needed to produce 1000 units a year?

4. If unit 1 requires 6 labor hours and unit 5 requires 1.8324, what is the learning rate? What will unit 6 require? What have the first five units required in total?

5. A production lot of 25 units required 103.6 hours of effort. Accounting records show that the first unit took 7 hours. What was the learning rate?

6. If unit 1 required 200 hours to produce and the labor records for an Air Force contract of 50 units indicate an average labor content of 63.1 hours per unit, what was the learning rate? What total additional number of labor-hours would be required for another Air Force contract of 50 units? What would be the average labor content of this second contract? Of both contracts combined? If labor costs the vendor $10 per hour on this second Air Force contract and the price to the Air Force is fixed at $550 each, what can you say about the profitability of the first and second contracts, and hence the bidding process in general?

7. All the reports you wrote for one class had three sections: introduction, analysis, conclusion. The times required to complete these sections (including typing, etc.) are shown below in hours.

Report	Introduction	Analysis	Conclusion
1	1.5	6	2
2	—	(lost data)	—
3	1	3	0.8

   The class requires five reports in all. You are now starting report 4 and, although you are working faster, you can afford to spend only 1 hour a day on these reports. Report 5 is due in one week (7 days). Will you be done in time?

8. Use the CVD model to evaluate the following three locations in terms of access to five destinations. Site I is located 313, 245, 188, 36, and 89 feet, respectively, from the five destinations; site II, 221, 376, 92, 124, and 22 feet; and site III, 78, 102, 445, 123, and 208 feet.

9. Reevaluate exercise 8 if the number of trips to each of the destinations is, respectively, 15, 6, 12, 33, and 21.

10. The location subcommittee's final report to the board has focused on three acceptable communities. Table 15b in the appendix to the report indicates that the cost of locating in communities 1, 2, and 3 is approximately €400,000, €500,000, and €600,000 per year (respectively), mortgaged over 30 years. Paragraph 2 on page 39 of the report indicates that the variable cost per unit of product will increase 15 percent in community 1 but decrease 15 percent in community 3, owing to differences in labor rates. As plant manager, you know that variable costs to date have averaged about €3.05 per unit and sales for the next decade are expected to average 20 percent more than the last 10 years, during which annual sales varied between 40,000 and 80,000 units. Which location would you recommend?

11. Nina is trying to decide in which of four shopping centers to locate her new boutique. Some cater to a higher class of clientele than others, some are in an indoor mall, some have a much greater volume

than others, and, of course, rent varies considerably. Because of the nature of her store, she has decided that the class of clientele is the most important consideration. Following this, however, she must pay attention to her expenses; and rent is a major item—probably 90 percent as important as clientele. An indoor, temperature-controlled mall is a big help, however, for stores such as hers, where 70 percent of sales are from passersby slowly strolling and window-shopping. Thus, she rates this as about 95 percent as important as rent. Last, a higher volume of shoppers means more potential sales; she thus rates this factor as 80 percent as important as rent. As an aid in visualizing her location alternatives, she has constructed the following table. "Good" is scored as 3, "fair" as 2, and "poor" as 1. Use a weighted score model to help Nina come to a decision.

	Location			
	1	2	3	4
Class of clientele	Fair	Good	Poor	Good
Rent	Good	Fair	Poor	Good
Indoor mall	Good	Poor	Good	Poor
Volume	Good	Fair	Good	Poor

12. What was the design capacity of a production system that produces 753 good units a year with a utilization of 90 percent and yield of 85 percent?

13. A defense contractor is bidding on a military contract for 100 radar units. The contractor employs 30 machine operators who work 165 hours a month each. The first radar unit required 1145 operator-hours, and the learning curve for this type of work is known to be 75 percent. It takes a month to order and receive raw material components, which cost $500 per radar unit. The material is then paid for in the month it is received. Fixed costs include a month to tool up, which costs $10,000, and then $5000 per month for every month of production. Direct labor and variable overhead are $8 per hour. The contractor can deliver only completed units and is paid the following month. Profit is set at 10 percent of the bid price. Find the bid price, derive the production schedule, and calculate the cash flow schedule.

14. Is Clarton or Uppingham the best location for a production volume of 600 services? The fixed costs of Clarton total £6000 (pounds, United Kingdom) per year, while those of Uppingham total only £4500. However, the variable costs of Clarton are £8, while those of Uppingham are £10.

15. The head of the Campus Computing Center is faced with locating a new centralized computer center at one of three possible locations on the campus. The decision is to be based on the number of users in each department and the distance of the various departments from each possible location. Which location should be chosen?

Department	Number of Users	Distance by Location		
		1	2	3
1	25	0	3	5
2	30	5	4	3
3	10	2	0	1
4	5	3	2	0
5	14	6	2	3

16. A new product involves the following costs associated with three possible locations. If demand is forecast to be 3900 units a year, which location should be selected?

	Location		
	A	B	C
Annual cost	$10,000	40,000	25,000
Unit variable cost	$10.00	2.50	6.30

17. Resolve Problem 14 using Crystal Ball assuming the fixed costs are uniformly distributed between 4000 and 8000 for Clarton and 4000 and 5000 for Uppingham and the variable costs are normally distributed with a standard deviation of 1 for Clarton and 2 for Uppingham.

BIBLIOGRAPHY

Armstrong, J. S. *Long Range Forecasting: From Crystal Ball to Computer.* New York: John Wiley and Sons, Inc., 1995.

Ballou, R. H. *Business Logistics Management*, 4th ed. Upper Saddle River, NJ: Prentice Hall, 1998.

Bartmess, A., and K. Cerny. "Building Competitive Advantage through a Global Network of Capabilities." *California Management Review*, 35 (1993): 78–103.

Belkaoui, A. *The Learning Curve.* Westport, CT: Quorum Books, 1986.

Blackstone, J. H. *Capacity Management.* Cincinnati, OH: South-Western, 1989.

Crandall, R. E., and R. E. Markland. "Demand Management—Today's Challenge for Service Industries." *Production and Operations Management,* 5 (Summer 1996): 106–120.

Drezner, Z. and H. Hamacher. *Facility Location: Applications and Theory.* Berlin: Springer Verlag, 2002.

Durrande-Moreau, A., and J.-C. Usunier. "Time Styles and the Waiting Experience: An Exploratory Study." *Journal of Service Research,* 2 (November 1999): 173–186.

Ferdows, K. "Making the Most of Foreign Factories." *Fortune* (March–April 1997): 73–88.

Filley, R. D. "Putting the 'Fast' in Fast Foods: Burger King." *Industrial Engineering* (January 1983): 44–47.

Fisher, M. L., J. H. Hammond, W. R. Obermeyer, and A. Raman. "Making Supply Meet Demand in an Uncertain World." *Harvard Business Review,* 72 (May–June 1994): 83–93.

Fitzsimmons, J. A., and M. J. Fitzsimmons. *Service Management: Operations, Strategy, and Information Technology.* New York: Irwin/McGraw-Hill, 2001.

Fowler, G. A. and J. Pereira. "Behind Hit Toy, A Race to Tap Seasonal Surge." *Wall Street Journal,* 18 December 2003: A1, A12.

Francis, R. L., L. F. McGinnis, Jr., and J. A. White. *Layout and Location: An Analytical Approach,* 2nd ed. Upper Saddle River, NJ: Prentice-Hall, 1998.

Hartvigsen, D. *SimQuick: Process Simulation with Excel.* 2nd ed. Upper Saddle River, NJ: Prentice-Hall, 2004.

Heskett, J. "Note on Service Mapping." Harvard Reprint No. 9-693-065, November 1992.

Hunt, V. D. *Process Mapping.* New York: John Wiley and Sons, Inc., 1996.

Johnson, J. C., and D. F. Wood. *Contemporary Logistics,* 6th ed. Upper Saddle River, NJ: Prentice Hall, 1996.

Klassen, K. J., and T. R. Rohleder. "Combining Operations and Marketing to Manage Capacity and Demand in Services." *The Service Industries Journal,* vol. 21, no. 2 (2001): 1–30.

Kurana, A. "Managing Complex Production Processes," *Sloan Management Review,* 40 (Winter 1999): 85–98.

MacCormick, A. D., L. J. Newman III, and D. B. Rosenfield. "The New Dynamics of Global Manufacturing Site Location." *Sloan Management Review* (Summer 1994): 69–77.

Maister, D. H. "The Psychology of Waiting Lines." Harvard Reprint No. 9-684-064, May 1984.

Marshall, P. W. "A Note on Process Analysis (Abridged)." Harvard Reprint No. 9-689-032, September 1994.

Niebel, B., and A. Freivalds. *Methods, Standards, and Work Design,* 10th ed. New York: McGraw-Hill, 1999.

Port, O. "Huh? Chipmakers Copying Steelmakers?" *Business Week* (August 15, 1994): 97–98.

Price, W. L., and M. Turcotte. "Locating a Blood Bank." *Interfaces* (September-October 1986) 17-26.

Pullman, M. E., J. C. Goodale, and R. Verma. "Service Capacity Design with an Integrated Market Utility-Based Method." In J. A. Fitzsimmons and M. J. Fitzsimmons (eds.), *New Service Development.* Thousand Oaks, CA: Sage, 2000: 111–137.

Radas, S., and S. M. Shugan. "Managing Service Demand: Shifting and Bundling." *Journal of Service Research,* 1 (August 1998): 47–64.

Rahman, S. "Theory of Constraints—A Review of the Philosophy and its Applications." *International Journal of Operations and Production Management,* 18 (1998): 336–355.

Sale, D. R. *Manufacturing Facilities: Location, Planning and Design.* Boston: PWS Publishing, 1994.

Sanders, N. R., and L. P. Ritzman. "Bringing Judgment into Combination Forecasts." *Journal of Operations Management.* 13 (1995): 311–321.

Sanders, N. R., and K. B. Manrodt. "Forecasting Practices in U.S. Corporations: Survey Results." *Interfaces,* 24 (March–April 1994): 91–100.

Schmenner, R. W. "The Location Decisions of New Services." In J. A. Fitzsimmons and M. J. Fitzsimmons (eds.), *New Service Development.* Thousand Oaks, CA: Sage, 2000: 216–238.

Silver, E. A., D. F. Pyke, and R. Peterson. *Inventory Management, Production Planning, and Scheduling,* 3rd ed. New York, John Wiley and Sons, Inc., 1998.

Sipper, D., and R. Bulfin. *Production: Planning, Control, and Integration.* New York: McGraw-Hill (1997).

Teplitz, C. J. *The Learning Curve Deskbook.* Westport, CT: Greenwood Publishing Group, 1991.

CHAPTER 6

Schedule Management

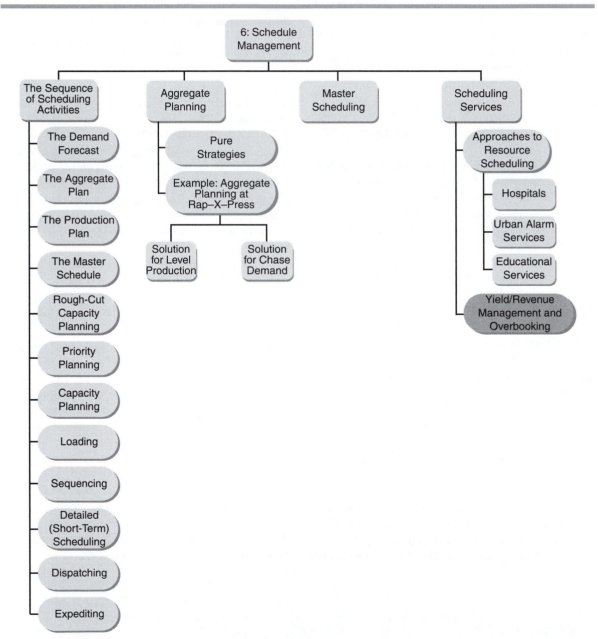

In this chapter we add the dimension of time to our previously static picture of the organization, transforming it into a running, operating set of activities that are producing and supplying outputs to live, demanding customers. Here we are concerned with scheduling to ensure that the right tasks are conducted at the right time on the right items to produce and deliver the output to the customer in a dependable and cost-effective manner, strategic factors described in Chapter 2. We begin the chapter with a broad overview of the sequence of scheduling activities and then discuss the topics of aggregate planning and master scheduling in more detail. The chapter concludes with a discussion of scheduling services including the topic of yield/revenue management and overbooking.

INTRODUCTION

- At the Henry Ford Hospital, the aggregate scheduling problem is to match available capital, workers, and supplies to a highly variable pattern of demand. The hospital has 903 beds arranged into 30 nursing units, with each nursing unit containing 8 to 44 beds. For purposes of planning, each of the nursing units is treated as an independent production facility. However, a number of factors complicate the aggregate planning process at the hospital. First, as noted, demand exhibits a high degree of variability. For example, while the average number of occupied beds in 1991 was 770, in one 8-week period it was 861 and in another it was 660. A second complicating factor is the large penalty incurred by the hospital for HMO patients who require care but cannot be admitted because a bed is not available. In these cases, not only does the hospital lose the revenue from the patient, but it must also pay another hospital for the patient's stay. A third complication is the tight labor market for registered nurses, making it difficult and expensive to change the rate of production. On average, it takes the hospital 12 to 16 weeks to recruit and train each nurse, at a cost of approximately $7,600 per nurse. A final complication is the high costs associated with idle facilities. The hospital estimates that the cost of one eight-bed patient module exceeds $35,000 per month (Schramm and Freund 1993).

- Package Products, in Pittsburgh, Pennsylvania, produces folding carton packing for the bakery and deli industries. A key aspect of Package Products' strategy is to be recognized by its customers for quality, reliability, and service. Significant growth during the 1990s greatly complicated the task of managing the company's operations. In addition, its customers were becoming more demanding, and the marketplace was becoming more competitive. To gain better control over its operations, Package Products implemented a finite capacity scheduling (FCS) software package. Before it acquired the FCS system, a Gantt chart was maintained manually to schedule jobs. Problems with the manual system included chronic capacity shortages and the fact that key data resided in the heads of people who were scattered throughout the organization. Two criteria used for selecting the FCS software package were that it should work with the company's existing business system and that it should not be a "black box," claiming to provide optimal schedules that no one could really understand. Through the use of the FCS program, overtime has been substantially reduced, on-time delivery has been improved by 32 percent, and backorders have been reduced by 53 percent. Additionally, customer service can now respond to customers' inquiries in an average of 22 seconds—versus taking overnight previously (Trail 1996).

There are many considerations and complications associated with developing aggregate and detailed production plans and schedules. Developing an aggregate production plan is important because without taking a sufficiently long-term view of the organization, we may end up making short-run decisions that adversely affect the organization in the long run. For example, during one period at the Henry Ford Hospital, a decision was made to reduce the staff. However, shortly after the staff was reduced, it was determined that more staff was needed, and thus new staff members were recruited. The net result was that the hospital incurred both the costs associated with reducing its staff and the costs associated with recruiting and training a new staff a short time later. A better approach would have been to compare the costs of reducing and hiring staff with the costs of having too large a staff for a short time period. Of course, this requires being able to look far enough into the future (forecasting) to estimate if and when demand will pick up again.

Problems with productivity are often attributable, in large part, to poor schedule management: ensuring that the *right* tasks are conducted at the *right* time on the *right* items to produce the output. Scheduling is also an important component of the overall product supply chain that addresses issues managers must face on a daily basis: where each input (material, machine, worker) must be, when it must be there, what form it must be in, how many must be available, and many other such details.

Scheduling for continuous process and flow shops is much easier than for job shops. This is because scheduling is largely *built into* the continuous or flow transformation process when the facility is designed and therefore need not (in fact *cannot*) be constantly changed. To reschedule these facilities, beyond just slightly increasing or decreasing the rate of input, requires a rebalancing of the entire flow through the production system. At the other extreme, the scheduling of project operations is probably the most important single planning activity in the successful management of projects. Because of the extent of the topic of project scheduling, we defer its treatment to Chapter 11.

In this chapter we begin with a look at the generic sequence of the scheduling activities in product firms, since these functions are better developed and more common in product firms than in service organizations. Following this, we look at the first major activity in the sequence of activities: aggregate planning. The aggregate plan forms the foundation for all other scheduling and materials management. Two pure strategies—level production and chase demand—are described and illustrated with an example. Next, we consider the major task of master scheduling and discuss its purpose, procedures, and results, briefly noting the role of rough-cut capacity planning in validating the feasibility of the master production schedule. Finally, we consider the problem of detailed scheduling for services and the common procedure of overbooking to reduce the opportunity costs of the expensive resources.

$\mathscr{T}$HE SEQUENCE OF SCHEDULING ACTIVITIES _____

In most organizations a department (or an individual) is specifically responsible for scheduling operations. In product organizations, this function is frequently called production planning and control, or some similar name. The breadth of this department's responsibility varies considerably; for example, it may consist only of planning gross output levels or may include all the scheduling activities illustrated in Figure 6.1.

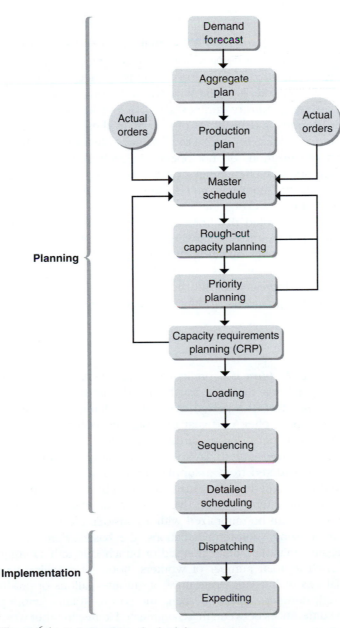

Figure 6.1   Relationship of scheduling activities.

This figure does not describe a *standardized* scheduling system, such as might exist in an available computer package; rather, it shows a complex set of activities and terms that are often grouped under *scheduling*. Many of these have become major activities only since the advent of computerized scheduling. Before that, they were simply a matter of individual judgment (as some of them still are). Let us look at the scheduling activities in Figure 6.1 and their interrelationships; in the following sections of the chapter, we will then look more intensively at some of the major activities and describe some approaches to dealing with them.

The Demand Forecast

As we described in Chapter 5, the foundation that supports scheduling is, in most cases, the forecast of demand for the upcoming planning horizon. In some industries, however, only minimal forecasting is needed because customers place orders a year or more ahead of the time when the output will be needed. For example, in the airframe industry, airlines may place orders years ahead of time because of long lead times and backlogs of orders. In these situations, organizational operations are scheduled on the basis of actual orders instead of forecasted demand.

Most organizations do not operate in such a favorable environment, however, and their success often hinges on the accuracy of their forecasts of demand. In these cases the concepts and techniques of forecasting briefly overviewed in Chapter 5 are especially relevant for scheduling.

It might be noted that forecasts over different periods are used for different purposes. For example, long-range forecasts (i.e., 2–5 years) are used more for facility and capacity planning than for any scheduling function. In the range of 3 to 18 months, forecasts are used for aggregate planning, as described later, and detailed forecasts for the next few months are particularly crucial in near-term scheduling such as loading and sequencing.

The Aggregate Plan

The **aggregate plan** is a preliminary, approximate schedule of an organization's overall operations that will satisfy the demand forecast at minimum cost. The *planning horizon*, the period over which changes and demands are taken into consideration, is often one year or more and is broken into monthly or quarterly periods. This is because one of the purposes of aggregate planning is to minimize the effects of shortsighted, day-to-day scheduling, in which small amounts of material may be ordered from a supplier and workers laid off one week, only to be followed by reordering more material and rehiring the workers the next week. By taking a longer-term perspective on use of resources, short-term changes in requirements can be minimized with a considerable saving in costs.

In minimizing short-term variations, the basic approach is to work only with "aggregate" units (i.e., units grouped or bunched together). Aggregate resources are used, such as total number of workers, hours of machine time, and tons of raw materials, as well as aggregate units of output—gallons of product, hours of service delivered, number of patients seen, and so on—totally ignoring the fact that there may be differences between these aggregated items. In other words, neither resources nor outputs are broken down into more specific categories; that occurs at a later stage.

On occasion, the units of aggregation are somewhat difficult to determine, especially if the variation in output is extreme (as when a manufacturer produces dishwashers, clothes washers, and dryers). In such cases, *equivalent units* are usually determined; these are based on value, cost, worker-hours, or some similar measure. For the appliance manufacturer, the aggregate plan might be: January 5000 "appliances"; February 4000 "appliances"; and so on.

The resulting problem in aggregate planning is to minimize the long-run costs of meeting forecasted demand. The relevant costs include hiring and laying off workers, storing finished goods (if a product is involved), paying wages and overtime, covering the expense of shortages and *back orders*, and subcontracting. As it turns out, the use of inventory to buffer production against variations in demand is an extremely important managerial option. In service organizations this option is usually not available, since services—such as plane trips and patient care—cannot be inventoried. The result is an increased cost of producing the service, with an increase in its price. Aggregate planning is discussed in considerably more detail later in this chapter.

The Production Plan

The result of managerial iteration and changes to the aggregate plan is the organization's formal **production plan** for the planning horizon used by the organization (e.g., 1 year). Sometimes this plan is broken down (i.e., *disaggregated*) one level into major output groups (still aggregated)—for example, by models but not by colors. In either case, the production plan shows the resources required and changes in output over the future: requirements for hiring, limitations on capacity, relative increases and decreases in inventories of materials, and output rate of goods or services.

The Master Schedule

The driving force behind scheduling is the master schedule, also known in industry as the **master production schedule** (MPS). There are two reasons for this:

1. It is at this point that *actual* orders are incorporated into the scheduling system.
2. This is also the stage where aggregate planned outputs are broken down into individual scheduled items that customers actually want (called **level zero items**). These items are then checked for feasibility against lead time (time to produce or ship the items) and operational capacity (if there is enough equipment, labor, etc.).

The actual scheduling is usually iterative, with a preliminary schedule being drawn up, checked for problems, and then revised. After a schedule has been determined, the following points are checked:

- Does the schedule meet the production plan?
- Does the schedule meet the end item demand forecasts?

- Are there conflicts in the schedule involving priority or capacity? (See the next two scheduling activities.) "Rough-cut capacity planning" (discussed next), based on the MPS, derives weekly work-center loads and compares them with capacities available.
- Does the schedule violate any other constraints regarding equipment, lead times, supplies, facilities, and so forth?
- Does the schedule conform to organizational policy?
- Does the schedule violate any legal regulations or organizational or union rules?
- Does the schedule provide for flexibility and backups?

Problems in any one of these areas may force a revision of the schedule and a repeat of the previous steps. The result is that the master schedule then specifies *what end items* are to be *produced in what periods* to *minimize costs* and gives some measure of assurance that such a plan is *feasible*. Clearly, such a document is of major importance to any organization—it is, in a sense, a blueprint for future operations. Master scheduling is discussed in more detail later in this chapter.

Rough-Cut Capacity Planning

As a part of checking the feasibility of the master schedule, a simple type of **rough-cut capacity planning** is conducted. One way of doing this, among many, is as follows. Historical ratios of workloads per unit of each type of product are used to determine the loads placed on the work centers by all the products being made in any one period. Then the loads are assumed to fall on the work centers in the same period as the demands; that is, the lead times are not used to offset the loads. If a work center's capacities are not overloaded (underloads are also checked), it is assumed that sufficient capacity exists to handle the master schedule, and it is accepted for production. Capacity planning was discussed in Chapter 5, but will be brought up again in Chapter 9.

Priority Planning

The term *priority planning* relates not to giving priorities to jobs (a topic included under *sequencing*), but rather to determining *what material* is needed *when*. For a master production schedule to be feasible, the proper raw materials, purchased materials, and manufactured or purchased subassemblies must be available when needed, with the top priority going to immediate needs. The key to production planning is the "needed" date. Years ago, scheduling concentrated on *launching orders*, that is, on when to *place* the order. Priority planning concentrates on when the order is actually needed and schedules *backward* from that date. For example, if an item is needed on June 18 and requires a 2-week lead time, then the order is released on June 4 and not before. Why store inventory needlessly?

The systems that have been devised for accomplishing this task are inventory control systems based on lead times and expected demands. The classic order-point inventory systems are most appropriate for organizations *producing to stock* (e.g., flow shops). These are called *order-point systems* because new orders for materials are sent out when the inventory on hand reaches a certain low point. For organizations that *produce to order* (e.g., many job shops), requirements for materials are known with near-certainty because they are tied to specified outputs. For example, every car requires four wheel covers—the number of wheel covers depends only on the number of cars. Computerized **materials requirements planning** (MRP) systems anticipate needs, consider lead times, release purchase orders, and schedule production in accord with the master schedule. If insufficient lead time exists to produce or obtain the necessary materials, or other problems arise, the master schedule must be revised or other arrangements made. These inventory systems are discussed in greater detail in Chapter 9.

Capacity Planning

The inventory control system and master schedule drive the **capacity requirements planning** (CRP) system. This system projects job orders and demands for materials into requirements for equipment, work force, and facility and finds the total required capacity of each over the planning horizon. That is, during a given week, how many nurses will be required, how many hours of a kidney machine, how many hours in operating rooms?

This may or may not exceed *available* capacity. If it is within the limits of capacity, then the master schedule is finalized, work orders are released according to schedule, orders for materials are released by the priority planning system, and *load reports* are sent to work centers, listing the work facing each area on the basis of the CRP system. Note that external lead times (often longer than internal lead times) from suppliers have already been checked at the stage of priority planning, so the master schedule can indeed now be finalized.

If the limits of capacity are exceeded, however, something must be changed. Some jobs must be delayed, or a less demanding schedule must be devised, or extra capacity must be obtained elsewhere (e.g., by hiring more workers or using overtime). It is the task of production planning and control to solve this problem.

Loading

Loading means deciding which jobs to assign to which work centers. Although the capacity planning system determines that sufficient gross capacity exists to meet the master schedule, *no actual* assignment of jobs to work centers is made. Some equipment will generally be superior for certain jobs, and some equipment will be less heavily loaded than other equipment. Thus, there is often a "best" (fastest or least costly) assignment of jobs to work centers.

Sequencing

Even after jobs have been assigned to work centers, the *order* in which to process the jobs—their **sequencing**—must still be determined. Unfortunately, even this seemingly small final step can have major repercussions on the organization's workload capacity and on whether or not jobs are completed on time. A number of priority rules have been researched, and some interesting results are available in the literature.

Detailed (Short-Term) Scheduling

Once all this has been specified, detailed schedules itemizing specific jobs, times, materials, and workers can be drawn up. This is usually done only a few days in advance, however, since changes are always occurring and detailed schedules become outdated quickly. It is the responsibility of production planning and control to ensure that when a job is ready to be worked on, all the items, equipment, facilities, and information (blueprints, operations sheets, etc.) are available as scheduled. This topic is also discussed later.

Dispatching

All the previous activities constitute schedule *planning;* no production per se has taken place yet. **Dispatching** is the physical *release* of a work order from the production planning and control department to operations. The release may be manual—from the *dead load file*, as it is called—or through a computerized master scheduling system.

Expediting

Once production planning and control has released a job to operations (or the *shop floor*, as it is sometimes called), the department usually has no more responsibility for it, and it is the production manager's task to get the job done on time. This task is known as **expediting**. When jobs fall behind schedule, managers have historically tended to use expediters to help push these "hot" jobs through the operations. Of course, expediting can be done more proactively, by monitoring the progress of jobs to ensure that they stay on schedule.

Before computerized scheduling techniques were available, extensive use of expediters was common (and it still is in many organizations). The problem was the impossibility of the scheduling task facing production planning and control. Not only could it not determine a good production schedule; it often could not even tell when insufficient capacity existed. Production managers thus relied heavily on expediters to gather all the necessary materials together (often cannibalizing parts from other jobs) in order to get important jobs completed. Of course, this further delayed the remaining jobs, so that more and more jobs tended to become "hot."

Commonly, yellow tags were used to label "hot" jobs until, pretty soon, all the jobs had yellow tags. To identify "especially hot" jobs, then, red tags were used. After a while the operations area resembled a rainbow, whereupon no new orders were accepted, the backlog was worked off, and the cycle started from scratch.

It may be presumed that a clear indication of the failure of a scheduling system is the existence of a great many expediters. One problem with the informal scheduling system, of course, was a lack of *de-expediting* (delaying jobs that had dropped in priority) to reflect changes in required due dates and thus, in priorities and schedules. Deexpediting has now been built into the computerized manufacturing resource planning (MRP II) and scheduling systems that are now so common in industry.

AGGREGATE PLANNING

The problem of aggregate planning arises in the following context. Managers have a month-to-month forecast of total demand for all outputs (combined) for the next year or so. They are expected to capitalize on this demand by supplying whatever portion of it will maximize long-run profitability. That is, not all the demand need be satisfied if attempting to fill it will result in lower overall profits. But a loss of market share might result, which, in turn, may reduce long-run profitability.

The managers have a set of productive facilities and workers with some maximum capacity to supply demand. There may also be some finished output available in inventory to help meet the demand, but there may, as well, be backorders of unsatisfied demand. They must decide how to employ the resources at their disposal to best meet the demand. If excess capacity is available, they may lease it out, sell it, or lay off workers. If insufficient capacity is available, but only for a short time in the future, they may employ overtime or part-time workers, subcontract work, or simply not meet the demand.

As discussed in Chapter 5, there are a number of ways of changing the capacity available to a manager to meet demand at minimum cost, such as:

1. Overtime
2. Additional or fewer shifts
3. Hiring or laying off workers (including part-time)
4. Subcontracting
5. Building up inventories during slack periods
6. Leasing facilities or workers, or both
7. Backlogging demand
8. Changing demand through marketing promotions or pricing
9. Undersupplying the market

Each strategy has advantages and disadvantages and perhaps certain restrictions on its use (such as legal or union regulations, or limitations on a public facility). The managers must plan their strategy carefully, because a shortsighted strategy, such as laying off workers when they will be needed again later, can be very expensive to rectify. However, an excessively long-range perspective may also be incorrect: a worker may be kept idle for a year when it would be much cheaper to lay off and then rehire the worker. Note that some of these alternatives (e.g., overtime, hiring, and layoffs) assume that equipment and facilities are already available and that there are not three shifts working 7 days a week. If this is not the case, then additional facilities and equipment may also need to be acquired.

Pure Strategies

There are two aggregate planning strategies, known as *pure strategies*, which, though rarely used in practice because of their expense, give managers a starting point to improve upon and also a feel for some upper limits on cost:

1. ***Level production.*** With a level production strategy, the same amount of output is produced each period. Inventories of finished goods (or backlogged demand) are used to meet variations in demand, at the cost of investment in inventory or the expense of a shortage (stockout). The advantage is steady employment with no work force expenses. Since service outputs cannot generally be inventoried, this strategy, for a service firm, normally results in a constant but poorly utilized work force (e.g., repair crews, firefighters) of a size large enough to meet peak demand. If the service firm uses a smaller work force, it risks losing some demand to a competitor.

2. ***Chase demand.*** In this strategy, production is identical to the expected demand for the period in question. This is typically obtained either through overtime or hiring and laying off. (Again, this assumes sufficient equipment and facilities.) The advantage of this policy is that there are no costs entailed by inventories of finished goods, except perhaps for buffer stock (also called *safety stock*, as discussed in Chapter 8), and no shortage costs, including loss of goodwill. Service firms use this strategy by making use of overtime, split shifts, overlapping shifts, call-in workers, part-time workers, and so on.

The vast majority of firms often achieve lower costs than the costs of these two pure strategies by using *hybrid* (mixed) strategies that include overtime, hiring and layoffs, subcontracting, and the like. Product firms also have the option of trading off investment in inventories of finished goods for changes in capacity level or vice versa. (For example, a product firm can build up inventory ahead of demand rather than acquiring all the capacity needed to meet peak demand.) We demonstrate with an example.

Example: Aggregate Planning at Rap-X-Press

Rap-X-Press is a new local express pickup and delivery business. Sarah Primes is responsible for determining and acquiring the personnel Rap-X-Press will need in the coming year. Sarah has determined the firm's needs for each quarter in each of the three major personnel categories shown in Figure 6.2. The sum of the three categories gives the aggregate personnel needs.

In trying to determine a hiring schedule for next year, Sarah must make a judgment concerning whether the increased need for personnel is simply seasonal or, instead, represents permanent growth in the market. Essentially, will the number of drivers needed in the first quarter of the year following that shown in Figure 6.2 drop back to 10, or will it remain at 18? If the need will decrease, Sarah might want to use overtime, or temporary drivers and sorters, in quarters 3 and 4, for example. However, if the growth in demand is permanent, she may decide to hire permanent workers.

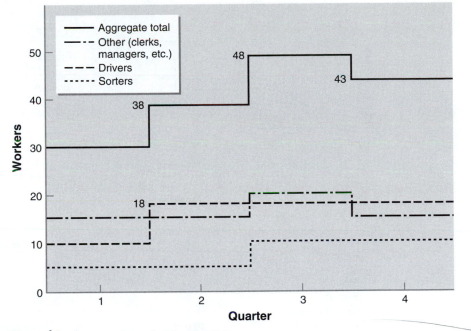

Figure 6.2   Personnel needed by Rap-X-Press.

Suppose the average salary for Rap-X-Press is $5,000 per quarter per employee, but the cost of lost sales, including goodwill, when there are insufficient employees is estimated to be $6,000 per quarter per employee. The cost of using overtime in place of hiring a worker is $8,000 per quarter. What would be the total annual cost for a level production strategy of 40 workers? What would be the cost for a chase demand strategy employing 30 workers? 40 workers?

Solution for Level Production

The analysis for the level production strategy at 40 workers is given in Figure 6.3. Two sets of costs are incurred: the cost of having excess workers in the first two periods (totaling $60,000), and the cost of being short in the last two periods (totaling $66,000), for a grand total over the year of $126,000. Note that if the level of starting workers is raised (to, say, 45) or lowered (to, say, 35), the two costs will change, giving a different total annual cost. Thus, with a level production strategy in a simplistic setting such as this, there may be an optimal number of employees to keep on the payroll.

Solution for Chase Demand

Table 6.1 gives the cost calculations for the chase demand strategy using overtime with 30 workers. As can be seen, there is no excess employee cost, but the overtime cost is overwhelming: $312,000 total for the year. In Table 6.2, overtime is used, assuming a starting work force of 40. In this case, an excess employee cost is incurred, but the required overtime is so much less that the total cost for the year drops to $148,000. Although chase demand is a much better strategy with 40 workers than with 30, it is not as cheap as level production.

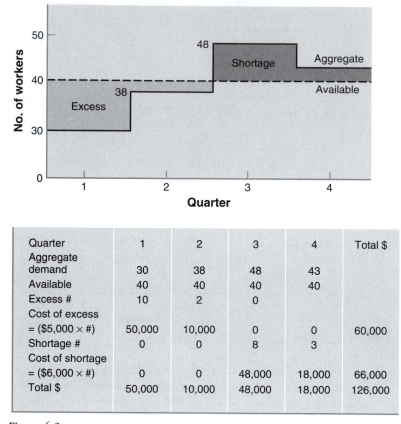

Figure 6.3 Level production at 40 workers.

Quarter	1	2	3	4	Total $
Aggregate demand	30	38	48	43	
Available	40	40	40	40	
Excess #	10	2	0		
Cost of excess = ($5,000 × #)	50,000	10,000	0	0	60,000
Shortage #	0	0	8	3	
Cost of shortage = ($6,000 × #)	0	0	48,000	18,000	66,000
Total $	50,000	10,000	48,000	18,000	126,000

$\mathcal{T}$ABLE   6.1 • Cost of Chase Demand with 30 Workers

Quarter	1	2	3	4	Total $
Aggregate demand	30	38	48	43	
Available	30	30	30	30	
Overtime #	0	8	18	13	
Overtime cost = ($8,000 × #)	0	64,000	144,000	104,000	312,000

The point of all these calculations is to show the potential complexity of the problem. The best solution for any firm depends on the costs of overtime, shortage, ill will, excess staffing, hiring and layoffs (which were not considered here), and the other alternatives open to the firm (such as subcontracting). But the best solution depends not only on the set of costs facing a firm, but also on the expected (and actual) demand rates over the year. Given the risk that demand forecasts may be in error, managers may choose a staffing strategy that is more expensive relative to the forecast in order to protect themselves against the risk of being in error (such as having inadequate staff to handle a potential explosion in demand).

$\mathcal{T}$ABLE   6.2 ● Cost of Chase Demand with 40 Workers

Quarter	1	2	3	4	Total $
Aggregate demand	30	38	48	43	
Available	40	40	40	40	
Overtime #	0	0	8	3	
Overtime cost = ($8,000 × #)	0	0	64,000	24,000	88,000
Excess #	10	2	0	0	
Cost of excess = ($5,000 × #)	50,000	10,000	0	0	60,000
Total Cost					148,000

Ohio National Bank (ONB), one of the largest banks in Ohio at the time, employed 1800 people who provided a full range of banking services. (ONB is now integrated into BanOhio National Bank.) The management of ONB was seeking ways to better schedule its full- and part-time encoders while reducing the number of unencoded checks at the end of each day (Krajewski and Ritzman 1980). Existing methods of scheduling were unable to give an accurate estimate of either the number of encoders needed at any given time or the time when a set of encoders would finish the day's work. As a result, some checks went unencoded at the end of the work day, increasing the bank's float costs, or last-minute overtime was required to complete the encoding, which irritated the encoders, increased turnover and personnel costs, and reduced productivity and morale.

ONB's existing schedule consisted of 33 full-time encoders from 11 A.M. to 8 P.M., two part-time encoders from 12 noon to 5 P.M., and two more part-time encoders from 5 P.M. to 10 P.M. every day of the week. This fixed schedule did not accommodate variability in the volume of checks arriving, and the full-time encoders frequently had to work overtime to complete all the work. It was clearly necessary to do a better job of matching the work force to the expected volumes.

This was done by designing a computer program to schedule the encoders' shifts. It consisted of two primary models. The first model used simple linear regression to predict expected hourly volumes on the basis of past data about arrivals by hour of the day, day of the week, day of the month, and month of the year. The second model used linear programming to determine the optimal number of full- and part-time encoders to schedule for each shift to minimize the sum of weekly regular-time wages, overtime wages, and float costs. The major data required for this second model are definitions of shifts, volumes of checks, encoder productivities, costs, number of encoding machines, and any limits on the number of encoders and the amount of overtime. The output consisted of three reports: shift assignments, hourly clerks on hand, and the costs of the schedule.

The general solution for ONB was to use two full-time encoders from 11 A.M. to 8 P.M. and 33 part-time encoders from 1 to 6 P.M. all week, plus 27 part-time encoders from 6 to 10 P.M. on Mondays, Tuesdays, and Fridays. This schedule was estimated to save ONB almost $80,000 per year. Regular use of the program indicated that the encoding was completed by 10 P.M. about 98 percent of the time, whereas it had rarely been achieved in the past. Moreover, unexpected overtime and poorly defined work schedules ceased to be a significant cause of turnover.

MASTER SCHEDULING

As briefly described earlier, aggregate planning leads to the firm's production plan. Disaggregating the production plan into individual end items results in the master production schedule (MPS). The master production schedule shows how many of what end items (or assemblies, in the case of a make-to-order firm) to produce when. If the production plan is stated in dollars or kilos or some other such measure, it will have to be converted into units of production in the MPS.

Because it is the final word about what the company will actually build and when, the MPS also acts as upper management's "handle" on the production system. By altering the MPS, management can alter inventory levels, lead times, capacity demands, and so on. Such power is a two-edged sword, however. If management attempts to overload the MPS in order to produce more output than can realistically be made, the shop will jam up with work to be done and will not get anything out. In creating the MPS, limits on capacity must be carefully observed; they cannot be ignored by using a master schedule that is only top management's "wish list."

In the traditional functional organization, the main players in creating the master schedule are sales and operations, each representing one of two primary objectives of master scheduling:

1. **Sales:** To schedule finished goods to meet delivery needs
2. **Operations:** To maintain efficient utilization of work centers by not overloading or underloading them

If these objectives cannot be met—because of, say, a capacity limitation in a work center—then the production plan may have to be revised.

In addition to limiting work to what can realistically be done, the MPS also includes other functions. First, it buffers the forecast by "smoothing" demand over time, reducing capacity-constrained peaks, and raising low-demand idle periods. It also subtracts existing inventories of products from the forecasts so that the shop doesn't make products that already exist in inventory. And it "batches" demands over time into convenient and economical groups for production so that scarce facilities and equipment aren't wasted.

As noted earlier, the MPS is based both on firm orders, received through salespersons or directly from the customer, and on end item forecasts of future demand for which orders have not yet been received. In addition to the forecast demands, extra demands, such as demand for spare parts, are added to the MPS. Then these requirements are all summed by the delivery time period to make up the total demand facing the organization over the planning horizon. As more firm orders come in, they continue to replace or "consume" the forecasted orders, as shown in Figure 6.4. The items still remaining in the forecast that have not been replaced by firm orders are considered *available to promise* by sales.

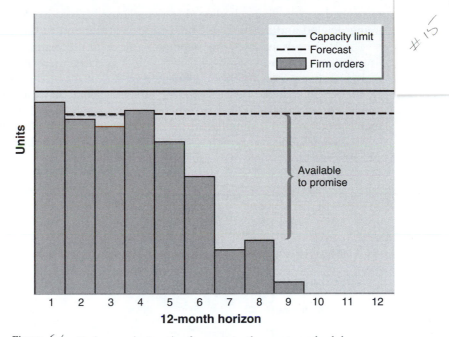

Figure 6.4   Orders replacing the forecast in the master schedule.

The MPS is usually stated in terms of weekly periods, or *buckets*, as they are called. Some firms use days, and some even use hours. Nevertheless, the disaggregation of the quarterly, or monthly, production plan into MPS buckets is still the same. The planning horizon may extend for a year or more, but it must extend at least as long as the longest lead time item in the product. Otherwise, the demands cannot be placed on the schedule. For example, if you maintained a 12-month MPS and had a component that took 15 months to obtain, you wouldn't be able to schedule the delivery of orders taken today (and due to be delivered in 16 months or so).

In some situations (such as make-to-order firms), final products are assembled to order from existing components, modules, or assemblies that have been produced at some earlier time. That is, the assemblies are produced to stock and scheduled on the MPS, but the final products are produced to order and scheduled on a separate final assembly schedule. This is shown in Figure 6.5. Note that the final demands total to the MPS, but the specific *combination* of components was unknown until the actual orders arrived. Automobiles, some computers, and pre-fabricated homes are made this way. And some restaurants prepare meals in this way, to meet peak demand periods with only one cook or only a few workers.

An MPS is needed for both job shops and flow shops, although the detailed issues of scheduling are different, as will be seen later. That is, both require a production schedule that satisfies customers' demands but doesn't exceed the limits of capacity. Nevertheless, just because aggregate capacity may be satisfied for a workstation or facility, certain scheduling aspects may limit the use of that capacity and thereby pose another problem for the MPS, if not the entire production plan. We will discuss these kinds of problems later.

Although we appear to discuss master scheduling as a static process, in reality it is very dynamic, changing continually and being reworked weekly. It is best visualized as a rolling schedule that is replanned every week, the previous week being deleted and a new week being added at the end of the planning horizon.

The MPS itself includes four separate periods in the planning horizon that serve four unique purposes, as shown in Figure 6.6. First, there is usually an immediately upcoming *frozen* period, delineated by a *time fence*, during which orders can no longer be changed because critical subcomponents have already been ordered, produced, or installed. This frozen period is usually stated as 1 month because many products are assembled in the last two or three weeks before delivery. Up until assembly, the components are still being made in the shop, and changes may still be possible in their manufacture or assembly.

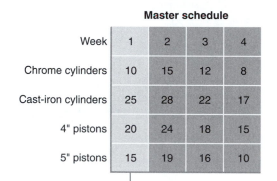

Master schedule

Week	1	2	3	4
Chrome cylinders	10	15	12	8
Cast-iron cylinders	25	28	22	17
4" pistons	20	24	18	15
5" pistons	15	19	16	10

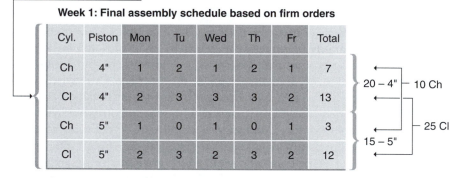

Week 1: Final assembly schedule based on firm orders

Cyl.	Piston	Mon	Tu	Wed	Th	Fr	Total
Ch	4"	1	2	1	2	1	7
CI	4"	2	3	3	3	2	13
Ch	5"	1	0	1	0	1	3
CI	5"	2	3	2	3	2	12

20 – 4" ⌐ 10 Ch

15 – 5" └ 25 CI

Figure 6.5 Master and final assembly schedules: custom pumps division.

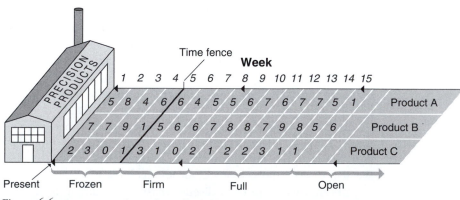

Figure 6.6 Four periods in the rolling MPS.

Following this time is a *firm* period of just a few weeks when changes may be taken, but only if they are exceptional. These changes may require approval from a senior manager. The next period is called *full* because the forecast has been fully consumed, so no more orders can be taken. However, changes may be taken in existing orders. Last is the *open* period, when there are still items available to promise.

$\mathscr{S}$CHEDULING SERVICES

In this section we consider the scheduling of pure services. Much of what was said previously applies to the scheduling of services as well as products, but here we consider some scheduling issues of particular relevance to services.

Up to now we have dealt primarily with situations where the jobs (or recipients) were the items to be loaded, sequenced, or scheduled. There are, however, many operations for which scheduling of the jobs themselves is either inappropriate or impossible, and it is necessary to concentrate instead on scheduling one or more of the input resources. Therefore, the staff, the materials, or the facilities are scheduled to correspond, as closely as possible, with the expected arrival of the jobs. Such situations are common in service systems such as supermarkets, hospitals, urban alarm services, colleges, restaurants, and airlines.

In the scheduling of jobs we were primarily interested in minimizing the number of late jobs, minimizing the rejects, maximizing the throughput, and maximizing the utilization of available resources. In the scheduling of resources, however, there may be considerably more criteria of interest, especially when one of the resources being scheduled is staff. The desires of the staff regarding shifts, holidays, and work schedules become critically important when work schedules are variable and not all employees are on the same schedule. In these situations there usually exist schedules that will displease everyone and schedules that will satisfy most of the staff's more important priorities—and it is crucial that one of the latter be chosen rather than one of the former.

Approaches to Resource Scheduling

The primary approach to the scheduling of resources is to match availability to demand (e.g., 7 P.M.–12 A.M. is the high period for fire alarms). By so doing, we are not required to provide a continuing high level of resources that are poorly utilized the great majority of the time. However, this requires that a good forecast of demand be available for the proper scheduling of resources. If demand cannot be accurately predicted, the resulting service with variable resources might be worse than using a constant level of resources.

Methods of increasing resources for peak demand include using overtime and part-time help and leasing equipment and facilities. Also, if multiple areas within an organization tend to experience varying demand, it is often helpful to use *floating* workers or combine departments to minimize variability. On occasion, new technologies, such as 24-hour automated tellers, 24-hour order entry via the Web, and paying bills by telephone, can aid the organization.

As mentioned previously, the use of promotion and advertising to shift *demand* for resources is highly practical in many situations. Thus, we see *off-peak pricing* in the utilities and communication industries, summer sales of snowblowers in retailing, and cut rates for transportation and tours both in off-peak seasons (fall, winter) and at off-peak times (weekends, nights). Let us now consider how some specific service organizations approach their scheduling problems.

Hospitals

There are multiple needs for scheduling in hospitals. Although arrivals of patients (the jobs) are in part uncontrollable (e.g., emergencies), they are to some extent controllable through selective admissions for hernia operations, some maternity cases, in-hospital observation, and so on. With selective admissions, the hospital administrator can smooth the demand faced by the hospital and thereby improve service and increase the utilization of the hospital's limited resources.

Very specialized, expensive equipment such as a kidney machine is also carefully scheduled to allow other hospitals access to it, thus maximizing its utilization. By sharing such expensive equipment among a number of hospitals, more hospitals have access to modern technology for their patients at a reasonable level of investment.

Of all the scheduling in hospitals, the most crucial is probably the scheduling of nurses, as illustrated in the following example describing Harper Hospital (Filley 1983). This is because (1) it is mandatory, given the nature of hospitals, that nurses always be available; (2) nursing resources are a large expense for a hospital; and (3) there are a number of constraints on the scheduling of nurses, such as number of days per week, hours per day, weeks per year, and hours during the day.

Like many other hospitals, Harper Hospital of Detroit was under heavy pressure from Blue Cross, Medicare, and Medicaid to provide more health care at less cost. In addition, it needed to achieve more economies of scale from a merger that had taken place some years before. It also desired to improve its patient care. One target to help achieve these goals was a better system for scheduling nurses.

Previously, nurses were scheduled on the basis of strict bed counts, problems with inadequate staffing during the prior day, and requests for extra help. What was developed was a *patient classification system* (PCS) that incorporated labor standards to determine what levels of nursing were needed. At the end of each shift, designated nurses evaluated each area's patients by their condition and assigned them to a "care level" ranging from minimal to intensive. An hour before the next shift begins, the patients' needs for care are added up—accounting for new admissions, checkouts, and returns from surgery—to determine the total levels of care required. Given the levels in each area, nursing labor standards are used to determine how many nurses are needed on the next shift.

As a result of the new system, both the quality of patient care and the nurses' satisfaction went up. Annual labor savings from the new system were estimated as exceeding $600,000. Harper has further fine-tuned the PCS system and now recalibrates its standards every 2 years.

Urban Alarm Services

In urban services that respond to alarms—such as police, fire, and rescue services—the jobs (alarms) appear randomly and must be quickly serviced with sufficient resources. Otherwise, extreme loss of life or property may result. In many ways this problem is similar to that of a hospital, since the cost of staffing personnel is a major expense, but floating fire companies and police SWAT units may be utilized where needed, and some services (such as fire inspection) can be scheduled to help *smooth* demand.

Sometimes a major difference vastly complicates some of these services (particularly fire): **_duty tours_** of extended duration, as opposed to regular shifts, run over multiple days. These tours vary from 24 to 48 hours in teams of two to four members. Common schedules for such services are "two (days) on and three off" and "one on and two off," with every fifth tour or so off as well (for a running time off, every 3 weeks, of perhaps 3 + 2 + 3 = 8 days). Because living and sleeping-in are considered part of the job requirements, the standard workweek is in excess of 40 hours—common values are 50 and 54 hours. Clearly, the scheduling of such duty tours is a complex problem, not only because of the unusual duration of the tours but also because of the implications concerning overtime, temptations of "moonlighting," and other such issues.

Educational Services

Colleges and universities have scheduling requirements for all types of transformations: intermittent (such as counseling), continuous (English 1), batch (field trips), and project (regional conferences). In some of these situations the jobs (students) are scheduled; in some the staff (faculty, administrators) are scheduled; and in others the facilities (classrooms, convention centers) are scheduled.

The primary problem, however, involves the scheduling of classes, assignment of students, and allocation of facilities and faculty resources to these classes. To obtain a manageable schedule, three difficult elements must be coordinated in this process:

1. Accurate forecast of students' demand for classes
2. Limitations on available classroom space
3. Multiple needs and desires of the faculty, such as
   - Number of "preparations"
   - Number of classes
   - Timing of classes
   - Level of classes
   - Leave requirements (sabbatical, maternity, etc.)
   - Release requirements (research, projects, administration)

Because of the number of objectives in such scheduling problems, a variety of multicriteria approaches have been used to aid in finding acceptable schedules, including simulation, goal programming, and interactive modeling.

In summary, the approach to scheduling services is usually to match resources and forecasted demand. Since demand cannot be controlled, it is impossible to build up inventory ahead of time, and backordering is usually not feasible. Careful scheduling of staff, facilities, and materials is done instead, with (limited) flexibility achieved through floating part-time and overtime labor and off-peak rates to encourage leveling of demand. The best schedule is often not the one that optimizes the use of resources or minimizes lateness for the expected demand, but rather the one that gives acceptable results under all likely operating conditions. As described in Chapter 5, an important aspect of scheduling services is the queues that tend to build up if capacity is inadequate. Here, queuing theory and psychology concerning waiting can be profitably applied.

Yield/Revenue Management and Overbooking

Yield management, also sometimes called *revenue management*, is the attempt to allocate the fixed capacity of a service (although the process is now being used by retailers and manufacturers, also) to match the highest revenue demand in the marketplace. It appears that American Airlines was one of the first to develop this technique, but its use has spread to hotels, cruise lines, and other services who hold a fixed capacity for revenue-producing customers, jobs, items, and so on. As described by Kimes (1989), yield management is most appropriate under the following circumstances.

1. *Fixed capacity.* There is only a limited, indivisible number of capacity openings available for the period. There is no flexibility in either dividing up the capacity or in finding additional capacity.

2. *Perishable capacity.* Once the period passes, the capacity can no longer be used for that period. There is essentially no salvage value for the capacity.

3. *Segmentable market.* The demand for the capacity must be segmentable into different revenue/profit classes, such as business versus pleasure, Saturday night stayover or not, deluxe and budget, and so on.

4. *Capacity sold in advance.* The capacity is sold by reservation. Using yield management techniques, certain classes of capacity are held back for certain, more profitable classes of reservations or periods of the season. If the profitable classes fail to fill by a certain time point, some of the capacity is then released for the next lowest profit class. This procedure cascades down through both reservation classes and time points as the period in question approaches.

5. *Uncertain demand.* Although demand for each of the reservation classes may be forecast, the actual demand experienced in each of the classes for each of the time periods is uncertain.

6. *Low marginal sales cost, high marginal capacity addition cost.* The cost to add a unit of capacity is extremely high but the cost to sell (rent) a unit of it for the period in question is low.

The technique used to determine how to allocate capacity among the different classes is similar to that used for *overbooking*. Overbooking is an attempt to reduce costs through better schedule management, as illustrated by Scandinavian Airlines (Alstrup et al. 1989). Scandinavian Airlines (SAS) operates a fleet of DC-9 aircraft with 110 seats each. If SAS accepts reservations for only these 110 seats, "no-shows" (passengers who fail to show up for a flight) will refuse to pay for their reservations and SAS can lose from 5 to 30 percent of the available seats.

If there are 100 flights every day, these no-shows can cost the airline as much as $50 million a year. To avoid this loss, all airlines overbook flights by accepting a fixed percentage of reservations in excess of what is actually available.

The management of SAS decided to develop an automated overbooking system to include such factors as class, destination, days before departure, current reservations, and existing cancellations. The objective of the system was to determine an optimal overbooking policy for the different classes on each flight, considering the costs of ill will, alternative flight arrangements, empty seats, and upgrading or downgrading a passenger's reserved class.

A number of interesting findings were made in the process of conducting the study. For example, an early finding was that the probability that a reservation would be canceled was independent of the time the reservation was made. When the system was completed, it was tested against the heuristics used by experienced employees who had a good "feel" for what the overbooking rate should be. It was found that the automated system would increase SAS's net revenue by about $2 million a year.

To better understand the situation and demonstrate the solution approach, let us assume that the number of seats on a plane is fixed at 28. How many reservations should the airline accept, given the chances described in Table 6.3 of no-shows? For example, if 32 reservations are accepted, the probability that only 30 passengers show up is 35 percent.

Suppose that a profit of $50 is made for each passenger carried, but a cost is incurred if a passenger with a reservation has to be turned away. This cost could be a free ticket, ill will, passage on another airline, or whatever. If the cost is low—say, less than the profit—then it will be to the airline's advantage to overbook quite a bit (although possibly not all the way to 32, since there would then be a 90 percent chance of having an overbooking cost). On the other hand, suppose that the cost is very high—much more than the profit. Then the airline would be very reluctant to overbook much at all, out of fear of having to pay one or more costs of overbooking. Table 6.4 gives the probabilities of demand for each set of overbookings accepted, as specified in the previous paragraph. Assume that turning a passenger away costs the airline $20, how many reservations should be accepted? Suppose the cost is $100.

Using the probabilities of no-shows (shown in Table 6.3), we can calculate the costs and profits according to Table 6.5. (There is no sense in accepting more than 32 reservations, because this will definitely fill the plane.) Here we see that the total profit is $1,359. The process is repeated for 31 reservations, and the calculations

$\mathcal{T}$ABLE 6.3 • Demand for Flights

No. of No-Shows	Relative Frequency
4	0.10
3	0.20
2	0.35
1	0.25
0	0.10
	1.00

are given in Table 6.6. Continuing with 30, 29, and 28 reservations (it makes no sense to accept fewer than 28 reservations), we get the values shown in Table 6.7. Clearly, the maximum profit is obtained with 31 reservations. If the turnaway cost is raised to $100, the results are shown in Table 6.8. Now the highest profit is obtained with 29 reservations.

Table 6.4 • Demand Probabilities with Reservations (from Table 6.3)

Relative Frequency	Reservations				
	28	29	30	31	32
0.10	24	25	26	27	28
0.20	25	26	27	28	29
0.35	26	27	28	29	30
0.25	27	28	29	30	31
0.10	28	29	30	31	32
1.00					

Table 6.5 • Expected Profit with 32 Reservations

	Demand					
	28	29	30	31	32	Total
Probabilities	0.10	0.20	0.35	0.25	0.10	
Seats filled (S)	28	28	28	28	28	
Profit: $50 S	1400	1400	1400	1400	1400	
Turnaways (T)	0	1	2	3	4	
Cost: $20 T	0	20	40	60	80	
Net profit	1400	1380	1360	1340	1320	
Expected net profit	140	276	476	335	132	$1359

Table 6.6 • Expected Profit with 32 Reservations

	Demand					
	27	28	29	30	31	Total
Probabilities	0.10	0.20	0.35	0.25	0.10	
Seats filled (S)	27	28	28	28	28	
Profit: $50 S	1350	1400	1400	1400	1400	
Turnaways (T)	0	0	1	2	3	
Cost: $20 T	0	0	20	40	60	
Net profit	1350	1400	1380	1360	1340	
Expected net profit	135	280	483	340	134	$1372

$\mathscr{T}$ABLE 6.7 • Expected Profit
   at $20 Turnaway Cost

Reservations	Expected Profits
32	$1359
31	$1372 (best)
30	$1371
29	$1345.5
28	$1302.5

$\mathscr{T}$ABLE 6.8 • Expected Profit
   at $100 Turnaway Cost

Reservations	Expected Profits
32	$1195
31	$1280
30	$1335
29	$1337.5 (best)
28	$1302.5

EXPAND YOUR UNDERSTANDING

1. Why go through the process of aggregating fore-casts to produce an aggregate plan, which is then disaggregated into the actual product or service master schedule? Why not just use the individual forecasts to produce the master schedule?

2. Describe the role of sales in setting the master schedule. Is its only concern to get as much produced as possible? What else may sales be concerned about when it helps set the schedule?

3. A lot of scheduling seems to be the straightforward manipulation of data, applying ratios, batching lots, meeting deadlines, converting pounds to units, and so on. Couldn't all this be done by computer? What would be hard to do by computer?

4. Describe any of your experiences with level production or chase demand. Do these concepts apply only to businesses? Where else might you see them?

5. Suppose you are a production scheduler and receive a notice from sales that a customer has canceled an order that was in the frozen portion of the master schedule. Would you go ahead and build the product anyway because the schedule is frozen? Or would you immediately stop work on the order? If you stopped work, what good is having a frozen schedule that really is not frozen?

6. In what way is rough-cut capacity planning actually "rough"? What does it ignore?

7. How ethical is it to overbook (and guarantee) limited service capacity in a restaurant? What about a hospital, where lack of service could have serious, perhaps fatal, consequences?

8. Many services, such as airlines, conduct their scheduling in two stages. First, an overall macro schedule is constructed and optimized for costs and service to the customer. This schedule is then considered to be the baseline for detailed scheduling to attempt to achieve. The second, detailed stage is then a real-time schedule to adjust the macro schedule for any necessary changes, emergencies, and so on. Describe how this might work for airlines, hospitals, schools, and urban alarm services. What serious problems might arise with this approach?

9. Referring to the Revenue Management section, why might an early reservation be cancelled? A late reservation?

APPLY YOUR UNDERSTANDING
Grassboy, Ltd.

Grassboy, Ltd. produces a line of Canadian lawn mowers for both domestic sales and export to the U.S.A. The mowers come in a variety of engine sizes and cutting widths. In an effort to deal with the highly seasonal nature of its demand, Grassboy forecasts demand for the next eight quarters. The forecast for the next eight quarters is given in the following table.

Quarter	Demand Forecast
1	5000
2	7500
3	15,000
4	5000
5	6000
6	8000
7	16,000
8	5500

Grassboy has a single production line that can assemble 7000 units per quarter per shift using regular time and can assemble an additional 25 percent using overtime. The assembly line can be operated for either one or two shifts; however, the union contract permits making changes to the number of shifts only at the beginning of a quarter. The company is permitted to send the workers home early without pay if its plans call for producing less than 7000 units in a given quarter. The cost of adding a shift is $C7500 (Canadian dollars), and the cost of eliminating a shift is $C14,000. Grassboy also has identified several overseas manufacturers that can produce as many of its lawn mowers as needed as subcontractors.

On average, the cost of producing a single lawn mower is $C25 per mower using regular time and $C33 using overtime. The delivered cost of mowers produced by subcontractors is $C49. Grassboy's cost of holding a lawn mower in inventory for one quarter is $C4, and the cost of backordering a unit is $C12 per quarter. Inventory costs are calculated on the basis of average inventory held during the quarter (i.e., the average of the quarter's beginning and ending inventory). Backorder costs are calculated on the basis of the ending backorder position in a given quarter.

Grassboy was operating with one shift in the quarter just ending and expects to end the quarter with 750 units in inventory.

Questions

1. Develop an aggregate plan that calls for a constant level of employment that meets the fluctuations in demand by using inventory, backorders, overtime, subcontracting, or some combination of these. Assume that all demand must be met by the eighth quarter.
2. Develop an aggregate plan that meets the fluctuations in demand by adjusting the number of shifts.
3. What are the advantages and disadvantages of the aggregate schedules you developed? Which one would you recommend to Grassboy's management?

EXERCISES

1. How many workers are needed with level production to meet quarterly demands of 45, 65, 50, and 40 if each worker can produce five units each quarter? Recalculate your answer if there are already 20 units in inventory. Recalculate again assuming that there are 20 inventory units but also that 10 units are required as safety stock.

2. In a particular French factory, two workers can each produce 10 pumps a quarter. Find the long-run average annual cost of using overtime (at €20/unit) and undertime (at €10/unit) to chase quarterly demands of 40, 60, 30, and 20.

3. Use the same data as in Exercise 2 but use hiring and layoffs, at a cost of €30 each, to chase demand.

4. Find the costs of inventory and backordering in Wales with level production to meet quarterly demands of 20, 50, 30, and 40. Inventory costs £10/unit/quarter, and backordering costs £15/unit/quarter.

5. Demand forecasts for your product for each quarter of the year are 120, 140, 110, and 90, with this pattern repeating in the future as far as can be told. The current workforce is 11, and each worker can produce 10 units in a quarter. Inventory costs are

$10 per unit per quarter, whereas shortage costs with backordering are $13 per unit per quarter. Hiring and layoff costs $100 per worker, but idle workers cost $150 a quarter. Cost to produce units on overtime is an additional $15 each. Find the best long-term production plan if all demand must be met.

6. A fancy Swiss restaurant has 30 tables. If it accepts N reservations, the probability that N will arrive is 0.1; $N-1$ is 0.2; $N-2$ is 0.3; and $N-3$ is 0.4. If each unfilled table costs F20 (Swiss francs) but a customer turned away costs F10, find how many reservations to accept. Solve again, assuming that a customer turned away costs F25.

7. The Arms Hotel in South Africa has only 56 rooms. An unfilled room represents R500 (rands) a night in lost profit, whereas every turnaway due to a filled room costs R300 in ill will. If N reservations are accepted, the probability of N, $N-1$, and $N-2$ guests actually showing up is 0.2, 0.5, 0.3, respectively. How many reservations should be accepted?

8. Use Crystal Ball to solve Problem 7. How does the simulation compare to the calculated answer?

BIBLIOGRAPHY

Alstrup, J., S. E. Andersson, S. Boas, O. B. G. Madsen, and R. V. V. Vidal. "Booking Control Increases Profit at Scandinavian Airlines." *Interfaces* (July–August 1989): 10–19.

Brandimarte, P., and A. Villa (eds.). *Modeling Manufacturing Systems: From Aggregate Planning to Real-Time Control.* New York: Springer, 1999.

Filley, R. D. "Cost Effective Patient Care: Harper-Grace Hospitals." *Industrial Engineering* (January 1983): 48–52.

Fisher, M. L., J. H. Hammond, W. R. Obermeyer, and A. Raman. "Making Supply Meet Demand in an Uncertain World." *Harvard Business Review*, 72 (May–June 1994): 83–93.

Fitzsimmons, J. A., and M. J. Fitzsimmons. *Service Management: Operations, Strategy, and Information Technology.* New York: Irwin/McGraw-Hill, 2001.

Goldratt, E. Y., and J. Cox. *The Goal: A Process of On-Going Improvement.* Croton-on-Hudson, NY: North River, 1984.

Haksever, C., B. Render, and R. Russell. *Service Management and Operations*, 2nd ed. Upper Saddle River, NJ: Prentice Hall, 2000.

Kimes, S. E. "Yield Management: A Tool for Capacity-Constrained Service Firms." *Journal of Operations Management*, vol. 8, no. 4 (October 1989): 348–363.

Kimes, S. E., and R. B. Chase. "The Strategic Levers of Yield Management." *Journal of Service Research*, 1 (November 1998): 156–166.

Kirchmier, B. and G. I. Plenert. *Finite Capacity Scheduling.* New York: John Wiley and Sons, Inc., 2002.

Krajewski, L. J., and, L. P. Ritzman. "Shift Scheduling in Banking Operations: A Case Application." *Interfaces* (April 1980): 1–7.

LaForge, R. L., and C. W. Craighead. "Computer-Based Scheduling in Manufacturing Firms: Some Indicators of Successful Practice." *Production and Inventory Management Journal* (1st Qtr., 2000): 29-34.

Metters, R., and V. Vargus. "Yield Management for the Nonprofit Sector." *Journal of Service Research*, 1 (February 1999): 215–226.

Metters, R., and V. Vargus. "A Comparison of Production Scheduling Policies on Costs, Service Levels, and Schedule Changes." *Production and Operations Management*, 17 (Fall 1999): 76–91.

Pinedo, M. *Scheduling: Theory, Algorithms, and Systems*, 2nd ed. Upper Saddle River, NJ: Prentice-Hall, 2001.

Pinedo, M., and X. Chao. *Operations Scheduling with Applications in Manufacturing and Services*. Boston: McGraw-Hill/Irwin, 1998.

Radas, S., and S. M. Shugan. "Managing Service Demand: Shifting and Bundling." *Journal of Service Research*, 1 (August 1998): 47–64.

Ramani, K. V. "Scheduling Doctors' Activities at a Large Teaching Hospital." *Production and Inventory Management Journal* (1st/2nd Qtr., 2002): 56-62.

Schmenner, R. W. *Service Operations Management*. Upper Saddle River, NJ: Prentice-Hall, 1995.

Schramm, W. R., and Freund, L. E. "Application of Economic Control Charts by a Nursing Modeling Team." *Industrial Engineering* (April 1993): 27–31.

Silver, E. A., D. F. Pyke, and R. Peterson. *Inventory Management, Production Planning, and Scheduling*, 3rd ed. New York, John Wiley and Sons, Inc., 1998.

Sipper, D., and R. Bulfin. *Production: Planning, Control, and Integration*. New York: McGraw-Hill, 1997.

Smith, B. C., J. F. Leimkuhler, and R. M. Darrow. "Yield Management at American Airlines." *Interfaces*, 22 (January–February 1992): 8–31.

Sule, D. R. *Industrial Scheduling*. Boston: PWS Publishing, 1997.

Trail, D. T. "Package Products Capitalizes on Data." *APICS—The Performance Advantage* (August 1996): 38–41.

Vollmann, T. E., W. L. Berry, and D. C. Whybark. *Manufacturing Planning and Control Systems*, 4th ed. Homewood, IL: Irwin, 1997.

CHAPTER 7

Supply Chain Management

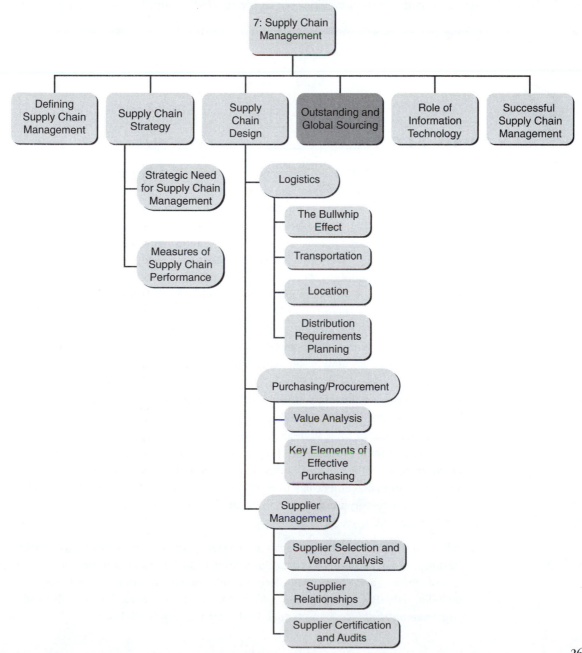

$\mathscr{C}$HAPTER IN PERSPECTIVE

In this chapter we move from the topics of planning for capacity and production to designing the supply chain, a strategic consideration involving such topical issues as restructuring the value chain, outsourcing, and e-commerce. Competent management of the supply chain has major impacts on all the strategic sand cone factors described in Chapter 2: quality, dependability, speed, and cost. We first define the concept of supply chains and discuss their strategic importance. We then describe the many elements involved in their design, such as logistics, purchasing, and supplier management. From this we move to the issues of global sourcing, the role of information technology, and conclude with guidelines for successful supply chain management.

$\mathscr{I}$NTRODUCTION

- During the year 2000, Palm Inc. was selling every PDA (computerized Personal Digital Assistant) they could make and, as expected, their sourcing processes were largely tactical: How soon could they receive the components they needed?

  In the last few years, Palm has developed a strategic supply chain management function, including a Strategic Sourcing organization. As a result, they have gone from doing business with hundreds of suppliers to developing deep relationships with only a few suppliers. For example, in 2001 about 150 suppliers accounted for about 80 percent of Palm's purchasing expenditures. Now they have 50.

  One example of the advantages of developing such deep relationships with suppliers has been the success of their Zire PDA, introduced with the surprisingly low price of $99 when most new PDAs cost over $400. The secret to driving the cost so low was working closely with their suppliers to hit tight cost targets for the display, the processor, the memory, the battery, and the mechanicals. As a result, the Zire became Palm's fastest selling PDA in their history, with 90 percent of the buyers being first-time PDA users.

  One outcome of their strategic sourcing strategy has been that Palm now makes 95 percent of their products in China with two original design manufacturers and Flextronics, a contract manufacturer. The result of their new strategic emphasis on supply chain management has been a 27 percent reduction in overall costs, an increase in inventory turns from 3 to 22, and a 30 percent increase in profit margins (Carbone 2003).

- When the Internet revolution began, a number of organizations rushed to establish B2B online marketplaces for entire industries including steel, automobile manufacturing, and electronics. More recently, however, a number of firms including HP, IBM, and Wal-Mart created their own *private exchanges* (also called *corporate marketplaces*). In contrast to the original public B2B online marketplaces, these private exchanges provide links between a particular organization and only invited suppliers and other partners via the Web. For example, HP uses its private exchange to allow its suppliers to view the entire supply chain at all times.

Ace Hardware's motivation for the development of its system was the desire to manage its inventory more efficiently and be able to collaborate with suppliers in real time. To achieve these objectives, Ace used its supply chain management software to link its 14 distribution centers with nine suppliers. With this system, managers at Ace are able to check their inventory levels and at the same time check the inventory levels of their suppliers. Prior to adopting the new system, managers at Ace relied on faxes and EDI to communicate orders to their suppliers, a process that typically required 7 to 10 days.

As a final example, IBM's system provides links to over 20,000 of its suppliers. By the year 2000, IBM estimated that approximately 94% of its invoices, or 400,000 per month, were handled electronically via its private exchange. IBM further estimates that it realized almost $400 million in savings that year due to the increased efficiency of its Web-based procurement system (Harris 2001).

- Liz Claiborne used to have 250 suppliers in 35 countries spread around the globe, from Mexico to Cambodia. With the expiration of 30-year-old international apparel quotas on January 1, 2005, Liz Claiborne is considering how much of their clothing production to consolidate at Luen Thai Holdings Ltd. in Dongguan, southern China. This is where a new "supply chain city" is being created that includes a 2-million square foot factory, dormitories for 4000 workers, and all the supporting infrastructure required to consolidate design, production, and shipment of clothing across the globe. Liz Claiborne estimates they will be able to eliminate 40 percent of some clothing labor costs through this consolidation, and cut their concept-to-shipment time from 90 to 60 days (Kahn 2004).

- Dell Computer is a classic case in supply chain management. Established in 1984, Dell experienced supply problems in 1993 and thereupon completely redesigned its supply chain process along the lines of what its founder, Michael Dell, called the "direct" model. Between 1993 and 1998, Dell's earnings subsequently grew at 65 percent per year. Dell's supply chain redesign was based on the following elements.

First, Dell sells directly to customers, eliminating the costs and delays of wholesalers and retailers. This also gives Dell direct access to their final customers so they can segment their customer markets and fulfill each segment's needs more completely, providing better value to their customers and higher profitability. It also allows them to anticipate and forecast each segment's demands better, and offer Web pages customized to their needs.

Second, Dell also takes advantage of new information technologies in their communications with suppliers who can access Dell's component inventories, production plans, and forecasts in real time and thus keep their production precisely matched to Dell's needs. With component levels matched to Dell's production rate, Dell can minimize its own inventory levels.

Third, Dell deliberately maintains absolute minimum inventory levels at every stage of production, averaging 4 days overall (Dignan 2002) compared to competitors' 80–100 days, and in component inventory, only hours worth. With such low levels of inventory, not only is cash conserved but improved parts can be immediately put into production and if a flaw is detected in a product, only minimal amounts of defective products must be scrapped. For some component parts, such as monitors, Dell maintains no inventory at all, arranging for the delivery contractor to pick up the needed items from the suppliers, match them to the order, and deliver the entire batch to the customer in a single delivery.

Last, Dell also manages its cash flow very carefully, collecting payments from customers *before* having to pay its own suppliers, thereby gaining interest on the float. In 1998, this time difference (called their *cash conversion cycle*) amounted to about 9 days; by 2005, it had increased to about 37 days, or basically over an entire month's worth of interest on the value of their annual sales (Dignan 2002; Magretta 1998)!

The concept of supply chain management has taken on the nature of a crusade in U.S. industry, in part because of the tremendous benefits that accrue to firms participating in a well-managed supply chain. It is worth noting that, although the benefits of superior supply chain management are clear for manufacturing and distribution firms, even service organizations benefit from good supply chain management. This is because services not only use supplies and facilitating goods in the delivery of their service (as noted in Chapter 1), but also because they, too, outsource many of their internal functions, such as information technology, accounting, and human resource management, just like manufacturers do. Thus, the provision of these services becomes part of another supply chain, a chain of services rather than goods, but nonetheless one requiring the same attention to strategy, purchasing, logistics, and management oversight, just like for goods.

We begin the chapter with some definitions of the supply chain and supply chain management. As with any new concept, not everyone envisions supply chain management in the same way. We then discuss some of the important strategic advantages that accrue to wise management of the supply chain. From this overview, we then consider the elements of the supply chain in depth, including purchasing/procurement, logistics, transportation, resource planning, and supplier management. Next, we revisit the issue of offshoring in terms of global sourcing in the supply chain. An important element of global sourcing is the critical role of information technology as a major catalyst in the supply chain movement. We conclude with some guidelines for successful supply chain management.

DEFINING SUPPLY CHAIN MANAGEMENT

The term **supply chain** generally refers to all the activities involved in supplying an end user with a product or service. The perception of each organization that is involved—the ore refiners, the transporters, the component producers, the manufacturer, the wholesaler, the retailer, and the customer—being a link in the process makes the analogy of a chain quite appropriate. In Figure 7.1, we show the position of a typical company (A) in the chain, with its suppliers to the left of it, all the way "upstream" (as it is often called) to the raw materials, and its customers to the right, all the way "downstream" to the ultimate consumer. However, company C in the chain (a downstream "customer" as far as company A is considered) sees the same thing as company A, with its suppliers (including upstream supplier company A) to its left and its customers to its right. And as is seen, company B in the middle is the customer of one firm and the supplier to another firm, as is the situation of almost all the companies in the chain.

Of course, all these companies need multiple materials and services, typically, to serve their immediate customer in the chain, so there is really a bunch of upstream supplier company links connected on the left side of each link in the chain (only shown with links for company A, arrows for all others). And most firms typically sell to more than one customer, so there are also multiple downstream customer links connected on the right side of each link in the chain (again shown only for company A). Clearly, managing all these links, that is, suppliers and customers, even if only those directly connected to your company, is a major task!

Given such a lengthy process, it may behoove companies to store inventories of their outputs (if feasible) for immediate delivery. Moreover, it must be remembered that it is not just goods that are flowing along the chain but also information, funds, paper, people, and other such items, and they are flowing in *both* directions along the chain. In addition, the green revolution encourages recycling, recovery, and reuse of products so even the used product may be flowing back up the chain. In addition, the supply chain also involves other functional areas and activities such as product/service design, finance, accounting, marketing, human resources, and engineering. Thus, instead of a chain, we should probably think of the supply process as more of a network, with everyone communicating with, and passing monies and items between, everyone else.

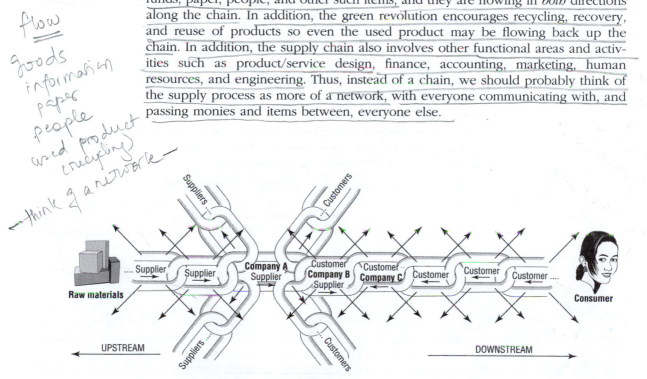

Figure 7.1   The supply chain.

Supply chain management (SCM) then concerns the process of trying to manage this entire chain from initial receipt of the ultimate consumer's order all the way back to the raw materials providers and then ultimate delivery back to the consumer. Note that SCM is not restricted to managing only the links that connect with your company's position in the chain, but *all* the links along the chain, so that savings (or increased value) in any part of the chain can be shared or leveraged by other companies along the chain. For example, Toyota is famous for teaching their suppliers how to install and operate their famed Toyota Production System (also known as ***lean manufacturing***). But the teaching doesn't stop there, since Toyota's first tier suppliers can gain additional improvements by teaching their suppliers, the second tier, and so on up the supply chain. Supply chain management has exploded in interest primarily because of the development of new information technologies such as intranets, e-mail, EDI (electronic data interchange), and of course, the Internet. These technologies, in conjunction with greater global competition, have fostered an interest and ability in improving processes along the entire supply chain, resulting in better performance at reduced cost.

SCM also can be considered to include a number of other managerial thrusts, such as quality management (Chapter 4), inventory management (Chapter 8), enterprise resource planning (ERP, Chapter 9), and lean production (including just-in-time, Chapter 10). But it is even more comprehensive than that. For example, it includes marketing aspects in terms of communication with the customer, engineering issues involved in product/service design, financial aspects in terms of payments and float, purchasing elements such as sole-sourcing, and of course, technological initiatives such as the omnipresent Internet. To a large extent, this breakthrough in conceptualizing the potential for improvement in customer value by including all elements of the value chain is due to the development of advanced information technologies, such as the Internet.

Other definitions of SCM include the following points (Walker and Alber 1999):

- SCM coordinates and integrates all the supply chain activities into a seamless process and links all of the partners in the chain, including departments within an organization as well as the external suppliers, carriers, third-party companies, and information system providers.

- SCM enables manufacturers to actively plan and collaborate across a distributed supply chain, to ensure all parties are aware of commitments, schedules, and expedites. By actively collaborating as a virtual corporation, manufacturers and their suppliers can source, produce, and deliver products with minimal lead time and expense.

- The goal of SCM is to optimally deliver the right product to the right place at the right time, while yielding the greatest possible profit.

The SCM objective of attempting to manage activities that lie outside a manager's normal realm of internal responsibility (that is, managing 2nd- or 3rd-tier suppliers, or downstream customers) is to reduce the costs of delivering a product or service to a user and improve its value. Sometimes a distinction is made between a "value" chain, a "demand" chain, and a narrowly defined supply chain that simply manages suppliers to obtain the lowest cost. The conceptualization of

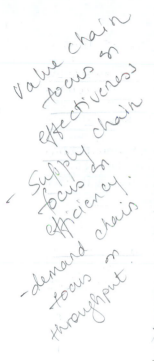

the ***value chain*** is that it considers other important aspects of customer value besides cost such as timeliness, quality, and functionality. That is, where the supply chain tends to focus on efficiency, the value chain focuses on effectiveness. These important issues will be discussed in more detail in the next section.

Also, as many are now pointing out (e.g., Lummus and Vokurka 1999), the current conceptualization of the supply chain still has many elements of the old "push" system of production. The newer "pull" systems, consisting of just-in-time deliveries (JIT), lean manufacturing, and so on, dictate a different view of the value chain, called a ***demand chain***. In this conceptualization, a customer order *pulls* the product through the chain on demand, thereby further improving costs and benefits. Of course, acting after the fact rather than anticipating demand will put even further stress on the ability of the value chain to respond in a timely manner.

Attempts to reduce the costs of supply (previously considered as "purchasing" or "procurement") have been ongoing for decades, of course. However, management has also realized that there are costs other than strict materials and production costs in the supply chain that can be reduced with better information sharing and tighter management, and these costs are at the forefront of attention in supply chain management. For example, costs of multiple shipments, costs of inappropriate functionality, costs of low quality, costs of late delivery—these are all costs that can be eliminated with better information sharing and managerial oversight.

SUPPLY CHAIN STRATEGY

The concept of the value chain was mentioned earlier, and it should be emphasized that an organization's supply chain strategy needs to be tailored to meet the needs of its customers, which isn't always the lowest cost. In fashion goods, for example, fast response to short fashion seasons is much more important than lowest cost. And in high technology, new functionality (or reliability, or security) may be more important than cost. Thus, the strategy for building an organization's supply chain should focus on maximizing the value to their customers, where value can be considered to be benefits received for the price paid, or benefits/cost.

In situations where the goods are basic commodities with standard benefits (food, home supplies, standard clothing), then cost reduction will be the focus. But in fashion goods, timeliness should be the focus of the supply chain, meaning quick deliveries, stockpiling of long lead time items, and so on. In new notebook computers, the focus might be on identifying firms that offer new functionality; in telecom the focus might be on reliability; in music the focus might be on flexibility to meet quickly changing tastes or talent. Thus, the supply chain needs to be carefully matched to the firm's market and needs. Where the firm operates in multiple markets, or appeals to multiple needs within the same market, it may find it necessary to operate different supply chains for each focus. Although most of the remaining discussion in this chapter is directed toward the traditional supply chain strategy of minimizing costs, which is always an important consideration and probably the major focus of most supply chains today, the other possible strategic purposes should be kept in mind also.

The broader concept of the supply chain includes the supply, storage, & movement of materials, information, personnel, equipment, & finished goods within the organization & between it & its environment.

274   Chapter 7: Supply Chain Management

Strategic Need for Supply Chain Management

To understand the potential for obtaining strategic advantage from better management of the supply chain, it is useful to realize that total supply chain costs represent better than half, and in some cases three-quarters, of the total operating expenses for most organizations (Quinn 1997). To understand these values, bear in mind that the broader concept of the supply chain includes the supply, storage, and movement of materials, information, personnel, equipment, and finished goods within the organization and between it and its environment. The objective of supply chain management is to integrate the entire process of satisfying the customer's needs all along the supply chain. This includes procuring different groups of raw materials from multiple sources (often through purchasing or recycling or recovery), transporting them to various processing and assembly facilities, and distributing them through appropriate distributors or retailers to the final consumer. Within this process are a great variety of activities such as packaging, schedule coordination, credit establishment, inventory management, warehousing, maintenance, purchasing, order processing, and supplier selection and management.

As organizations have continued to adopt more efficient production techniques such as lean manufacturing, total quality management, inventory reduction techniques to reduce costs and improve the quality, functionality, and speed of delivery of their products and services to customers, the costs and delays of *procuring* the requisite inputs and *distributing* the resulting goods and services are taking a greater and greater fraction of the total cost and time. For example, the cost of just physical distribution itself is now up to 30 percent of sales in the food industry. To achieve quick response with quality goods that accurately satisfy the need at the lowest possible cost requires taking a broad, long-range, integrated perspective of the entire customer fulfillment process instead of focusing on the little segments and pieces of the chain.

For instance, if each segment of the supply chain is acting in a way to optimize its own value, there will be discontinuities at the interfaces and unnecessary costs will result. If an integrated view is taken instead, there may be opportunities in the supply chain where additional expense or time in one segment can save tremendous expense or time in another segment. If a broad enough view is then taken, the savings in the one segment could be shared with the losing segment, so everyone would be further ahead. This broad, integrated view of the supply chain is more feasible these days due to the recent capabilities of advanced information technology and computer processing (e.g., bar codes, computerized manufacturing, the Internet, enterprise resource planning systems, electronic funds transfer).

Other factors are also driving the need to better manage the supply chain:

- **Increasing global competition.** In addition to increased pressure on cost from global competitors who have lower labor rates, they also frequently offer better quality, functionality, and customer responsiveness. This is pressuring firms to look globally for better or cheaper suppliers, resulting in increased outsourcing and off-shoring.

- **Outsourcing.** Since more organizations are outsourcing and thereby increasing the need for transportation, this has pushed up transportation costs.

- **E-commerce.** The advent of e-commerce and other electronic technologies has made it easier and cheaper to outsource, either domestically or even globally.

- **Shorter life cycles.** Customers are demanding greater variety, faster response, higher quality, and cheaper prices. One result of these demands is shorter product life cycles, which means constantly changing supply chains, and more chains over the same period of time.

- **Greater supply chain complexity.** Finally, simply the increased complexity of the supply chains requires much more attention and better management of these chains. For example, in early 2001 when the bottom fell out of the telecom market, Solectron Corp., the world's biggest electronics contract manufacturer, was holding $4.7 billion of inventory from its 4000 suppliers to fill firm orders from Cisco, Ericsson, Lucent, and other telecoms. But when the telecoms cancelled their orders, no one knew who owned all that inventory (Engardio 2001)!

Implementing supply chain management has brought significant documented benefits to many companies. Ferguson (2000) reports, for example, that compared to their competitors, such firms enjoy a 45 percent supply chain cost advantage, an order-cycle time and inventory days of supply 50 percent lower, and finished product delivery 17 percent faster. Lummus et al. (1998) note that these firms operate with 36 percent lower logistics costs which, by itself, translates into a 4 percent increase in net profit margins. One firm reported a 25–50 percent reduction in finished product inventories, a 10 percent reduction in cost, and a 10–25 percent improvement in production process reliability.

Of course, these are primarily the cost aspects of the SCM process, which are more easily measured than the qualitative benefits such as more loyal customers and a larger market share. In fact, considering the Dell example discussed earlier, it would appear that the cost savings are probably the lesser of Dell's SCM benefits and that the major benefits are its impact on revenues due to the delivery of greater overall value to the consumer. There are also significant effects on other important aspects of an organization, such as its ability to learn new procedures and ways of operating, the morale of its employees, and the ability to change direction quickly.

Measures of Supply Chain Performance

Better supply chain performance will show up in a number of standard financial measures of a company's health. Lower inventories, normally considered an asset, will be reflected in less need for *working capital* (WC) and a higher *return on asset* (ROA) ratio (since assets are reduced). And the lower cost to carry these inventories (as well as other reduced costs in the supply chain) will be seen in a reduced *cost of goods sold* (CGS), and thus a higher *contribution margin, return on sales* (ROS), and *operating income.* Moreover, if the supply chain is also better managed to provide other benefits to the consumer, as mentioned earlier, the effect should be seen in higher *total revenue* since the consumer will be willing to pay more. Lower costs, if used to reduce prices, will also result in higher volumes, which will further increase revenues.

Beyond these standard financial measures, however, we can also look at some more operations-oriented measures that we typically use to see how well operations is performing, such as defect rates, lead times, inventory turns, productivity ratios, and so on. Since one of the major cost savings in SCM is the cost of inventories, it is worthwhile to examine some performance measures related to inventory reduction. One such measure to track is the percent of the firm's assets represented by inventory. First we calculate the aggregate inventory value (at cost) on average for the year (AAIV):

$$\text{AAIV} = \text{raw materials} + \text{work-in-process} + \text{finished goods}$$
$$\text{\% Assets in Inventories} = \text{AAIV/total assets}$$

Another inventory measure is the inventory turnover (or "turns," as it is sometimes called):

$$\text{Inventory turnover ("turns")} = \text{annual cost of goods sold/AAIV}$$

Note that the inventory turnover is based on the same items that make up total annual revenues, but is based on their cost instead of their price. Turnover essentially represents how often the inventory is replenished to obtain the total sales for the year. Like ROA, the more the inventory and assets can be reduced and still maintain the same sales, the better! Inverting the equation for turns gives us the same information but through a measure of the proportion of the year's sales we are holding in inventory. This is usually expressed in daily (or weekly) periods:

$$\text{Days of supply} = \text{AAIV/daily CGS}$$

In some firms that have achieved supply chain excellence, they measure their supply in *hours* instead of days. Dell Computer is one of these firms (Dignan 2002; Magretta 1998) due to the outstanding job they have done on fine-honing their supply chains. Moreover, they have reduced their supply time so much that they actually receive payment from the customer *before* (known as *float*, another financial term) they have to pay their suppliers for the parts that make up the customer's product! In 1998 this amounted to 9 days of float; by 2005 it had grown to over a month's worth of revenues for Dell to invest wherever they wanted.

SUPPLY CHAIN DESIGN

As shown in Figure 7.2, the supply chain consists of the network of organizations that supply inputs to the business unit, the business unit itself, and the customer network. Note that the supplier network can include both internal suppliers (i.e., other operating divisions of the same organization) and external suppliers (i.e., operating divisions of separate organizations). Also, note how design activities cut across the supplier network and the business unit, and how distribution activities cut across the business unit and the customer network. This broader view of the entire process of serving customer needs provides numerous benefits. For example, it focuses management attention on the entire process that creates value for the customer, not the individual activities. When viewed in this way, information is more freely shared up and down the supply chain, keeping all parties informed of one another's needs. Furthermore, activities can be performed at the point in the supply chain where they make the most sense. To illustrate, instead of providing Johnson Controls with detailed specifications for car seats, Chrysler provides broad specifications and relies on Johnson Controls' expertise to design and manufacture its car seats.

In this section we will look at each of the major elements of the supply chain to better understand how they operate and interact to deliver value to the final customer. The major elements we consider here are logistics (including the "bull-whip" effect, transportation, location, and distribution requirements planning), purchasing/procurement, and supplier management. And obviously, materials management and scheduling are also important elements of the value chain, but these topics will be considered in more detail in later chapters.

Logistics

Logistics can be defined as planning and controlling efficient, effective flows of goods, services, and information from one point to another. As such, it consists of inventories, distribution networks, storage and warehousing, transportation, information processing, and even production—a rather all-enveloping term. Here we will deal with logistics in general, and in terms of its tradeoffs with transportation. In later subsections we deal with the subcomponents concerning transportation, distribution, and production.

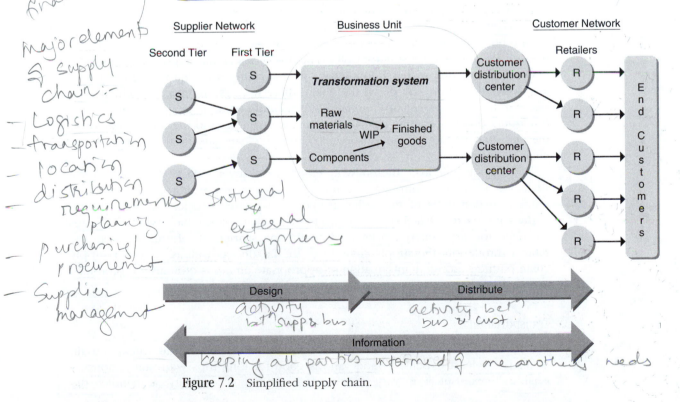

Figure 7.2 Simplified supply chain.

In these days of intense worldwide competition, international production in supply chains, and global distribution, logistics is taking on tremendous importance. Labor cost is dropping as a proportion of total output cost, as are manufacturing costs in general, but the costs of acquisition and distribution have remained about the same and now account, as noted above, for up to 30 percent of sales. Moreover, as quality and functionality become more standardized, speed of response and cost are becoming particularly important in the final selection of a supplier.

The Bullwhip Effect

An important logistical effect that is now better understood is known as the **bullwhip effect**, named after the action of a whip where each segment further down the whip goes faster than that above it. The same effect occurs in a supply chain, but in reverse order, and has been well documented. What happens is that a small percentage increase in a retailer's orders results in the wholesaler increasing his orders by an amount greater than that of the retailer—a safety stock—just to be covered in case demand is increasing. Then the distribution center sees this greater demand from its wholesalers and increases its orders by some safety percentage, also to be safe. The end result is that the factory sees a huge jump in demand. As it orders more equipment, labor, and materials to satisfy this big increase, too much is fed into the pipeline and the retailer cuts back, with the wholesaler and distribution center likewise cutting back even more. The factory then sees a tremendous drop in demand and reverses the cycle, cutting excessively into production and initiating another round of excessive demand. This boom-bust cycle is particularly prevalent in some industries, such as commercial building. Obviously, both overproduction and underproduction are expensive and drive up supply chain costs.

The bullwhip effect can occur whenever any one of three conditions is extreme enough to cause the boom–bust cycle. The first condition is simply long lead times between the stages of the supply chain, so that changes in demand requirements are slow moving up and down the chain, thereby allowing excessive changes to occur in the other stages of the chain. The second condition is large lot sizes with infrequent orders, resulting again in lags in information. And the third condition is the sole transmission of information occurring by handoffs from one link of the chain to the next.

The ways to eliminate the bullwhip effect are to reverse these three conditions. Reducing lead times through just-in-time programs, for example, will result in immediate deliveries of the ordered amounts so safety stocks are unnecessary. Reducing lot sizes means smaller, more frequent deliveries, which again eliminates the need for large safety stocks. And finally, the sharing of information from the retailer throughout the supply chain gives the factory, as well as the other supply chain partners, accurate information so appropriate amounts of items are produced and delivered.

Transportation

The four major **transportation modes** are, historically, water, rail, truck, and air. Water is the least expensive mode and is good for long trips with bulky, nonperishable items. But it is very slow and of limited accessibility. It handles the

measure

majority of ton-miles of traffic. However, railroads handle the most total tons of traffic and are thus used for shorter hauls than water. They have many advantages: ability to handle small as well as large items, good accessibility, specialized services (e.g., refrigeration, liquids, cattle), and still a relatively low cost.

Trucking holds more advantages for short hauls with small volumes to specialized locations. Truck transport has grown at the expense of rail for several reasons, such as growth of the national highway system, better equipment, and liberalized regulations.

Air transport is used for small, high-value, or perishable items such as electronic components, lobsters, optical instruments, and important paperwork. Its main advantage is speed of delivery over long distances. Thus, for the appropriate products, it can significantly reduce inventory and warehousing costs, with a corresponding improvement in customer service.

Taking all the pros and cons of each mode of transportation into consideration in planning is a complex task. Table 7.1 lists the major considerations that should be factored into the decision. Each particular situation may have additional factors to consider.

Independent of the specific mode of transport are additional transportation problems involving such considerations as the *number* of transporting vehicles, their capacities, and the *routes* that each vehicle will take. In general, these interrelated problems are frequently included as part of the *routing problem*. Solving the routing problem involves finding the best number of vehicles and their routes to deliver the organization's output to a group of geographically dispersed recipients. When only one vehicle is serving all the recipients, the problem is known as the *traveling salesman problem*. In this problem, a number of possible routes exist between the organization and all the recipients, but only a few or perhaps just one of these routes will minimize the total cost of delivery. In the routing and traveling salesman problems, certain procedures are available to minimize either the distance traveled or the cost, but quite often there are other considerations, such as balancing workloads among vehicles or minimizing idle or delay time.

truck transportation
– growth of national hwy
– better equipment
– liberalized regulations

$\mathcal{T}$ABLE   7.1 • **Factors to Consider in Transportation Decisions**

- Cost per unit shipped
- Ability to fill the transporting vehicle
- Total shipment cost
- Protection of contents from theft, weather, and the like
- Shipping time
- Availability of insurance on contents, delivery, and so forth
- Difficulty of arranging shipment (governmental regulations, transportation to shipment site, etc.)
- Delivery accommodations (to customer's site, transfer to another transportation mode, extra charges)
- Seasonal considerations: weather, holidays, and so on
- Consolidation possibilities (among multiple products)
- Risk (to contents, to delivery promises, to cost, etc.)
- Size of product being shipped
- Perishability of product during shipment

Schneider Intl.

Location

Besides distributing outputs to customers by transporting them, if there is a facilitating good, we can also locate where our customers can easily obtain them. Since service outputs without a facilitating good are generally difficult, expensive, or even impossible to transport, service organizations distribute their output primarily by locating in the vicinity of their recipients. Examples of this approach include medical clinics, churches, playgrounds, restaurants, and beauty shops.

Advances in information and telecommunications technology have allowed some pure service organizations (i.e., those without a facilitating good) to reach their recipients through phone, cable, the Internet, or microwave links. Thus, stockbrokers, banks, and other such service providers may locate in areas removed from their customers or recipients but more economical in other respects, such as proximity to the stock exchange or the downtown business district.

Some pure service organizations, however, do attempt to transport their services, although frequently with a great deal of trouble. These instances occur when the nature of the service (a traveling carnival, a home show) makes it impractical to remain in one fixed location for an extended duration or, more commonly, when the service (mobile X-ray, blood donor vehicle, bookmobile) is deemed very important to the public but may otherwise be inaccessible.

Product organizations, on the other hand, can generally trade transportation costs for location costs more easily and, therefore, can usually minimize their logistics costs. This allows goods producers to locate in the best global locations for each stage in their supply chains. In some instances, however, even product organizations are forced into fixed locations. One of these instances concerns the nature of the firm's inputs, and the other concerns its outputs.

Processing Natural Resources—Organizations that process natural or basic resources as raw materials or other essential inputs to obtain their outputs will locate near their resource if one of the following conditions holds:

1. There is a large loss in size or weight during processing.
2. High economies of scale exist for the product. That is, the operating cost of one large plant with the same total capacity as two smaller plants is significantly less than the combined operating costs of the two small plants.
3. The raw material is perishable (as in fish processing and canning) and cannot be shipped long distances before being processed.

Examples of these types of industries include mining, canning, beer production, and lumber. In these cases the natural inputs (raw materials) are either voluminous or perishable, and the final product is much reduced in size, thus greatly reducing the cost of transportation to the recipients (either final users or further processors).

Immobile Outputs—The outputs of some organizations may be relatively immobile, such as dams, roads, buildings, and bridges. In these cases (referred to as *projects*) the organization locates itself at the construction site and transports all required inputs to that location. The home office is frequently little more than one room with a phone, secretary, files, and billing and record-keeping facilities.

Product organizations may also locate close to their market, not necessarily to minimize transportation costs of distribution, but to improve customer service.

retailers.

Being close to the market makes it easier for the recipient to contact the organization and also allows the organization to respond to changes in demand (involving both quantity and variety) from current and new recipients. As in war, the people on the front line are closest to the action and are able to respond to changing situations faster than those far away, simply because information about changes is available sooner and is generally more accurate.

Distribution Requirements Planning

DRP

The concept of **distribution requirements planning** (DRP) follows naturally from our logistics discussion. The distribution process is illustrated in Figure 7.3, where retailers order from local warehouses, the warehouses are supplied from regional centers, and the regional centers draw from the central distribution facility, which gets its inventory directly from the factory.

main key:-
- time lags
- based off
ROP
stor capacity
safety stock

Clearly, there are time lags in each chain of this process. Also, each distribution point has its own standard reorder quantity, storage capacity, safety stock level, and so on. Without planning by the factory or central distribution facility, orders can often bunch up, requiring high stocking levels to avoid shortages or stockouts. This is, of course, true throughout the system, so high inventory levels are held by each of the distribution points in the entire system. The solution is to apply MRP to the distribution function, as will be illustrated in Chapter 9.

apply
MRP
(materials resource planning)

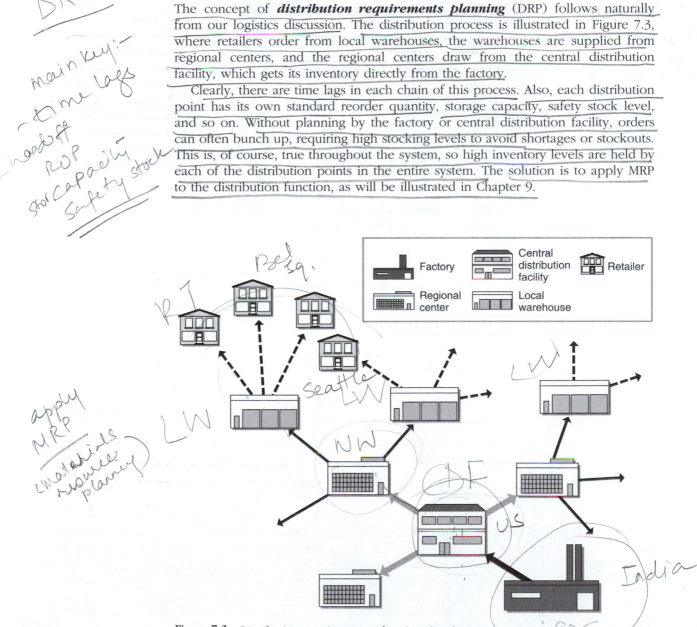

Figure 7.3   Distribution requirements planning situation.

Purchasing/Procurement

Organizations depend heavily on purchasing activities to help them achieve their supply chain strategy by obtaining quality materials and services at the right cost when they are needed. Purchasing is expected to be able to quickly identify and qualify suppliers, negotiate contracts for the best price, arrange for transportation, and then continue to oversee and manage these suppliers. Lately, purchasing has been given the added responsibility in many organizations for also supplying major services to the organization, such as information technology, accounting, human resources, and other previously internal functions.

Another common term for the purchasing function is **procurement**. Whereas "purchasing" implies a *monetary* transaction, "procurement" is the responsibility for acquiring the goods and services the organization needs, by any means. Thus, it may include, for example, scrap and recycled, as well as purchased materials. Procurement thus allows the consideration of environmental aspects of obtaining and distributing products. For example, there is often the possibility of recovering certain materials through recycling, reuse, or scrap purchases. And remanufacturing of goods is an inexpensive alternative to virgin production. On the distribution side, the concept of *reverse logistics* is being practiced in Germany, where packaging must reverse the logistics chain and flow back to the producer who originated it, for disposal or reuse.

The purchasing area has a major potential for lowering costs and increasing profits—perhaps the most powerful within the organization. Consider the following data concerning a simple manufacturing organization.

$$
\begin{aligned}
\text{Total sales} &= \$10,000,000 \\
\text{Purchased materials} &= 7,000,000 \\
\text{Labor and salaries} &= 2,000,000 \\
\text{Overhead} &= 500,000 \\
\text{Profit} &= 500,000
\end{aligned}
$$

To double profits to $1 million, one or a combination of the following five actions could be taken.

1. Increase sales by 100 percent
2. Increase selling price by 5 percent (same volume)
3. Decrease labor and salaries by 25 percent
4. Decrease overhead by 100 percent
5. Decrease purchase costs by 7.1 percent

Although action 2 may appear easiest, it may well be impossible, since competitors and the market often set prices. Moreover, raising prices almost always reduces the sales volume. In fact, raising prices often decreases the total profit (through lower volume). Alternative 5 is thus particularly appealing. Decreasing the cost of purchased material provides significant profit leverage. In the previous example, every 1 percent decrease in the cost of purchases results in a 14 percent increase in profits. This potential is often neglected in both business and public organizations.

Furthermore, this logic is also applicable to service organizations. For example, investment firms typically spend 15 percent of their revenues on purchases. However, manufacturing firms spend about 55 percent of their revenues for outside materials and services (Tully 1995)! And with factory automation and outsourcing increasing, the percentage of expenditures on purchases is increasing even more. In addition, with lean and JIT programs at so many firms (discussed in greater detail in Chapter 10), "just-in-time purchasing" is even further increasing the importance of the purchasing and procurement, since delays in the receipt of materials, or receiving the wrong materials, will stop a JIT program dead in its tracks.

SCM programs are putting ever greater emphasis on the purchasing function. Thus, we are seeing multiple new initiatives for cutting purchasing costs, including reverse auctions and joint venture websites by organizations who are normally competitors. Reverse auctions use a website to list the items a company wants to buy and bidders make proposals to supply them, the lowest qualified bidder typically winning the auction. Joint venture websites are typically for the same purpose but combine the purchasing power of multiple large players in an industry— automobile manufacturing, aerospace, health care, for example—in order to obtain even bigger cost savings. Such sites are virtual online bazaars, including all the goods and services the joint partners wish to outsource. But the range and volumes are massive, considering that the big three auto companies each spends close to $80 billion a year on such purchases.

Value Analysis

A special responsibility of purchasing, or purchasing working jointly with engineering/design and operations (and sometimes even the supplier), is to regularly evaluate the *function* of purchased items or services, especially those that are expensive or used in high volumes. The goal is to either reduce the cost of the item or improve its performance. This is called "value analysis" because the task is to investigate the total value of the item to see if the item can be eliminated, redesigned for reduced cost, replaced with a less expensive or more beneficial item, or even if the specifications can be relaxed. Other aspects are investigated, too, such as the packaging, the lead time, the transportation mode, the materials the item is made from, whether the part can be combined with another part or parts, and so on.

Recent efforts in this area have extended the reach further up the supply chain to involve second and third tier suppliers, and even bringing them in before the product is designed in order to improve its value up front, called *early supplier involvement*. Value analysis should be a continuing effort to improve supply chain performance and increase its value to the ultimate consumer.

Key Elements of Effective Purchasing

Organizations that are highly effective in SCM purchasing seem to follow three practices:

1. **They leverage their buying power.** The advantages associated with decentralization are typically not achieved when it comes to purchasing.

For example, Columbia/HCA combines the purchases of its 200-plus hospitals to increase its overall purchasing power. By combining all of its purchases for supplies ranging from cotton swabs to IV solution, for instance, it was able to reduce purchasing costs by $200 million and boost profits by 15 percent.

2. *They commit to a small number of dependable suppliers.* Leading suppliers are invited to compete for an organization's business on the basis of set requirements, such as state-of-the-art products, financial condition, reliable delivery, and commitment to continuous improvement. The best one-to-three suppliers are selected from the field of bidders on the basis of the specified requirements. Typically, 1- to 5-year contracts are awarded to the selected suppliers. These contracts provide the supplier with the opportunity to demonstrate its commitment to the partnership. The customer shares information and technology with the supplier, and the supplier responds in turn. If a supplier is able to consistently improve its performance, the organization reciprocates by increasing the volume of business awarded to that supplier and extending the contract.

3. *They work with and help their suppliers reduce total cost.* Often, organizations will send their own production people to a supplier's plant to help the supplier improve its operating efficiency, improve its quality, and reduce waste. Additionally, an organization may benchmark key aspects of a supplier's operation such as prices, costs, and technologies. If it is discovered that a supplier has slipped relative to the competition, the organization can try to help the supplier regain its lead. If the supplier is unable or unwilling to take the steps necessary to regain its leadership position, the organization may need to find a new partner.

Supplier Management

Our discussion of the management of an organization's suppliers will focus on three areas: (1) selecting the suppliers, (2) contemporary relationships with suppliers, and (3) certification and auditing of ongoing suppliers.

Supplier Selection and Vendor Analysis

The general characteristics of a good supplier are:

- Deliveries are made on time and are of the quality and in the quantity specified.
- Prices are fair, and efforts are made to hold or reduce the price.
- Supplier is able to react to unforeseen changes such as an increase or decrease in demand, quality, specifications, or delivery schedules—all frequent occurrences.
- Supplier continually improves products and services.
- Supplier is willing to share information and be an important link in the supply chain.

However, these are not the only factors considered in selecting a supplier. Additional considerations involve the supplier's reputation/reliability, having a nearby location (especially important for JIT delivery), their financial strength, the strength of their management, and even what other customers and suppliers are involved with the supplier. For example, if we are a relatively small customer, we might be more at risk of not getting a delivery if a larger customer experiences a problem and needs our supplier's immediate help. Or if our supplier has weak or unreliable second or third tier suppliers, we might encounter a problem getting our supplies through no fault of our direct supplier.

Supplier Relationships

In these days of intense global competition and supply chain management, the relationship between customers and suppliers has changed significantly. In the past, most customers purchased from the lowest bidders who could meet their quality and delivery needs, often maintaining at least two or three suppliers in case one was suddenly unable to meet their needs due to a wildcat strike or delivery problem. As pressure mounted to reduce costs, they often pressured their suppliers to cut costs by promising larger volumes to those who had the lowest costs and smaller amounts to the others.

To implement SCM, customers are seeking a closer, more cooperative relationship with their suppliers. They are cutting back the total number of their suppliers by a factor of 10 or 20 and combining their purchases, with those remaining getting the overwhelming volume of all their business. They are also asking suppliers to do a greater portion of assembly, such as with automobile seats and other automotive components, which can then simply be installed as a package rather than assembled first and then installed. Not only does the reduced assembly labor save them cost but in return for the higher volumes, they are expecting even further reductions in cost from their reduced number of suppliers.

DILBERT: ©Scott Adams/Dist. by United Feature Syndicate, Inc.

Supplier Certification and Audits

As can be seen, these **sole-sourcing** arrangements are becoming virtual partnerships, with the customer asking the supplier to become more involved even at the design stage, and asking for smaller, more frequent JIT deliveries of higher-quality items. This means longer-term relationships, help with each other's problems, joint planning, sharing of information, and so on. To do this, suppliers are being *certified* or *qualified* so that their shipments do not need to be inspected by the customer—the items go directly to the production line. This is often referred to as **stockless purchasing**, because the items do not sit in the stockroom costing capital for holding and securing them. To ensure that the contracted supplies will be available when needed, the customers periodically conduct **supplier audits** of their vendors, checking for potential production or delivery problems, quality assurance, design competence, process improvement procedures, and the management of corrective actions. Some customers rely on standard industry certifications such as ISO 9000 rather than incurring the time and expense of conducting their own certification. Such certified suppliers are sometimes known as *world-class* suppliers.

Of course, most of the benefits of this partnership accrue to the customer rather than the supplier. The main immediate benefit to the supplier is that they stay in business, and even grow. If managed properly, they should even become more profitable. However, with the help of their customers, their production processes should improve substantially, both in quality and efficiency, resulting in cost reductions that are shared between the partners. Toyota is known for helping their suppliers, and even their second and third tier suppliers, in this kind of fashion.

In the not-too-distant past, when just-in-time (JIT) production was still novel, customers were using sole-sourcing as a way to put pressure on their suppliers, forcing the supplier to stock inventories of items for immediate delivery rather than holding the stock themselves. Singing the praises of JIT—and insisting that the supplier implement JIT so that its deliveries could be made in smaller, more frequent batches—was often just a ploy to accommodate the customers' own sloppy schedules, because they never knew from week to week what they were going to need the following week. Today, firms are moving to Lean/JIT (described in detail in Chapter 10) and bringing their suppliers along with them. In many cases, the customer, like Toyota, is teaching the supplier how to implement effective Lean/JIT programs in their own organizations.

OUTSOURCING AND GLOBAL SOURCING

Outsourcing is the process of contracting with external suppliers for goods and services that were formally provided internally, and offers an important benefit for SCM. Global sourcing is an important aspect of supply chain outsourcing strategy and we see it occurring more and more. In the news, we read and hear about the meetings of GATT (General Agreement on Tariffs and Trade), the latest accords of the G-7 major trading nations, the dangers of NAFTA (North American Free Trade Agreement), the job losses due to overseas outsourcing (furniture manufacturers closing U.S. plants and sourcing from Asia, call centers being relocated to India), and so on. When asked on the Lou Dobbs show for the reasons all this outsourcing is occurring now, the economist Paul Craig Roberts responded that two primary factors were responsible: (1) The fall of communism and the economic insulation it had maintained; and (2) the advent of telecommunications and computer technology that physically allowed work that previously had to be done locally or regionally to now be conducted overseas.

The classic example of global outsourcing has been Nike, where the shoes were designed in the United States but all the production was done overseas. The strategic appeal of this lean model of business to other manufacturing and consumer firms is multiple. First, overseas production offers the promise of much cheaper labor costs, clearly a strategic benefit. But equally attractive to many firms that are outsourcing, whether globally or domestically, is the ability to dump a large portion of their capital-intensive production assets and staff, thus giving a big boost to their balance sheets, especially their return on assets. In addition, not being burdened with fixed, unchangeable capital production assets allows the firm to be more flexible and responsive to their customers' changing needs.

There is a danger to outsourcing however, particularly overseas outsourcing, and that is the possibility of being *hollowed out*, as noted in Chapter 2. To summarize, this is the situation where the supplier has been trained to produce, and even sometimes design, the customer's product so well that they can simply sell the product under their own brand and compete successfully against their former customer. In many cases, the customer has gone so long without designing or producing their own product—simply slapping their logo on the foreign-produced item—that they have lost the knowledge and skills to even compete in the market. This happened in the 1980s when American manufacturers trained foreign firms in how to produce television sets and other electronic goods, and lost those entire industries. Clearly, decisions about outsourcing at this level are strategic ones for the organization, involving both great potential benefits but also great risks, and should be deliberated thoroughly.

A more recent phenomenon is the trend toward outsourcing the entire production process to third-party **contract manufacturers**. In this case, the firms often conclude that their core competency is not in manufacturing, per se, but rather in system innovation or design. In the electronics industry, this is becoming a major element of SCM strategy for firms like Cisco, Dell, IBM, and many others. Cisco, for example, hardly makes any products itself. The big players in this growing industry are Solectron, Jabil Circuit, Venture, Flextronics, and SCI Systems. In fact, in the electronics sector, contract manufacturing was growing faster than the rate of growth of electronics itself in the late 1990s. In spite of the provision of products, these contract manufacturers consider themselves manufacturing *service* providers, and indeed, this is a major service they offer their customers. However, in addition to the major impacts outsourcing involves for operations, it also has major impacts on other functional areas of the organization such as marketing, finance, R&D, and human resource management. Moreover, to use this approach successfully requires that the firm maintain a strong, perhaps even core, competence in outsourcing. Many failures have resulted when firms jumped into outsourcing but didn't have the skills to manage it properly.

Outsourcing in general is a major strategic element of SCM these days, not just for production materials but for a wide range of services as well. For example, organizations are coming to realize that many of the activities they perform internally, such as accounting, human resources, R&D, and even product design and information systems, are not part of their *core competencies* and can be performed more efficiently and effectively by third-party providers, often at a fraction of the cost of in-house workers. There is thus a growing movement toward increasing the span of SCM to include the acquisition of these services in their responsibility.

ROLE OF INFORMATION TECHNOLOGY

In the not-too-distant past, the primary means of communication between members of a supply chain was paper. Unfortunately, communicating via paper-based transactions is slow, often unreliable, and prone to errors. For example, Campbell Soup Company estimated that 60 percent of the fax and phone orders it received contained errors (Verity 1996). As a result, salespeople often spent 40 percent of their time correcting these errors rather than making additional sales. To correct this problem, Campbell invested $30 million in the electronic redesign of its order-processing system. The company expected the new system to increase the percentage of paperless orders it received to 80 percent. Managers estimated the system would reduce costs by $18 million annually while at the same time reducing delivery times.

Some problems with paper-based systems have been the time and money that are wasted rekeying the same information into different computer systems. And, of course, the more times the same information is entered, the more opportunities there are for making mistakes. Some analysts estimate that the use of information technology has reduced the cost of processing a purchase order from $150 to $25.

As Campbell Soup illustrates, electronic information technology is a key element and the primary enabler of effective supply chain management. In today's highly competitive environment, the effective use of information technology helps organizations reduce cycle times, adopt more responsive cross-functional organizational structures, capture more timely information, and reduce errors and costs. The ultimate goal of such information systems is to make available to all participants in the supply chain all the information needed at the time it is needed. Such information includes the status of orders, product availabilities, delivery schedules, and other such supply chain data.

Everyone knows that computers are everywhere these days, and embedded in all kinds of products that one would not have expected. But why is this, and why now? Professor Richard Chase of the University of Southern California believes that the answer lies in two esoteric laws—one about physical goods and the other about abstract information. The first is the better known of the two: Moore's law, which states that computing power doubles every 18–24 months. The unstated surprise about Moore's law is that this doubling of power comes at the same or lower cost as before the doubling. Clearly, with enough money our big computer companies could double computing power every 18 (or 12 or 6) months, but the size of the computers would grow enormously, as well as their costs. Yet this law implies that the cost and size does *not* increase. As a result, more and more computing power is becoming available for less and less money; hence it is becoming omnipresent, appearing everywhere we go and in everything we buy.

The second law is less familiar to the public but derives from the fact that information assets, like knowledge, tend to grow with use rather than dwindle, as with physical assets. This second law is called Metcalfe's law, which says that the value of a network increases with the square of the number of elements (or users) connected to the network. This is why Amazon and Microsoft and eBay have been so successful—with more people in a network, the value of the network to the user is enhanced, so more people join this network. And competing networks, with fewer users, are of less value and hence fade away.

As a result of these two laws, the growth of computers, which support networks, and networks that support people's needs (business transactions, communication, blogging, etc.), has exploded. This phenomenon has been particularly prevalent in business, where it has contributed to both increased value (and thus revenues) and reduced costs, thereby having a double impact on increased profits. Next we will look at some particular types of information technology that are commonly used in business, especially to support supply chain management.

Electronic business (**e-business**) is the use of electronic information technology to help various groups of business people communicate and conduct business transactions. Its three primary advantages are enhanced productivity and reduced costs, speed, and the creation of new value opportunities. The primary enablers of e-business have been electronic data interchange (EDI), e-commerce, intranets and extranets, groupware applications, customer relationship management (CRM) systems, and enterprise resource planning (ERP) systems.

One early approach to e-business was **electronic data interchange** (EDI)—the ability of one organization's computer to communicate with another's computer. With EDI, business documents such as purchase orders and invoices are transferred between the computers of different organizations in a standard format. The benefits of EDI include faster access to information, reduced paperwork, less redundancy, improved customer service, and better order tracing. And, of course, the costs of paper transactions, both physical (paper handling, mailing, printing, etc.) and quality (errors), are reduced substantially.

Electronic commerce (**e-commerce**) is the term used to describe the execution of business transactions in a paperless environment, primarily through the Internet. In essence, this consists of two major parts: an Internet portal, such as a website (discussed a bit later) for information and communication, and the fulfillment transactions to deliver the product or service. These, in turn, include the use of bar coding and scanning, radio frequency identification (RFID), databases, point of sale (POS) terminals, e-mail, electronic funds transfer, the Internet, and websites and hubs. **Bar coding** and **scanning** technologies permit the rapid collection and dissemination of information throughout the supply chain. For example, Wal-Mart is well known for making available the **point-of-sale** (**POS**) information it collects at its check-out terminals to its supply chain partners. Federal Express uses the same technology to provide its customers with up-to-date tracking information on their packages. Firms also use bar coding and scanning within their production facilities to correctly produce and process items, and to keep track of different stock-keeping units (SKUs).

Most people are familiar with bar codes and scanning, but the new **RFID** tags/transponders are much less familiar. Wal-Mart has also become known for initiating the retail use of this new technology through their suppliers in order to better track their products. RFID tags provide much more information than bar codes and come in two versions, passive and active. The passive tags are as small as the head of a pin and as thin as a sheet of paper; readers can interrogate them as they pass by, typically within about 20 feet. Active tags broadcast their information and can be read from much greater distances. However, the main difficulty with employing these technologies has been the cost of the tags, running about $0.25/apiece as of 2005, but the industry goal is to get the price down to $0.05 in the years ahead.

Arguably the most significant information technology development for supply chain management is the **Internet**, and more specifically, its graphical component known as the **World Wide Web** (Web). Without a doubt, the Web offers enormous opportunities for members of a supply chain to share information. Companies such as IBM, General Electric, Dun & Bradstreet, and Microsoft are rapidly developing products and services that will help make the Web the global infrastructure for electronic commerce (Verity 1996).

For example, as noted earlier in the purchasing discussion, the Web will allow various forms of purchasing fulfillment to take place, from placing electronic catalogues on a website to holding joint purchasing bazaars, exchanges, and auction marketplaces involving massive amounts of materials. Bazaars and reverse auctions (one buyer, multiple sellers) were discussed earlier, but exchanges are for information transfer (often hosted by third parties, such as mySAP.com), and auction marketplaces (one seller, multiple buyers) are primarily for selling commodities or near-commodities at low prices. Of course, the costs of initiating and executing these forms of purchasing will be almost trivial compared to their paper-based predecessors. For example, updating an electronic catalogue can be done instantaneously, rather than waiting until next year's printing. In addition, password-protected customized catalogues reflecting negotiated prices can also be placed on a firm's website for use by individual customers.

Intranets are web-based networks that allow all employees of a firm to intercommunicate. They are usually firewall protected and use existing Internet technologies to create portals for company-specific information and communication, such as newsletters, training, human resource information and forms, product information, and so on. **Extranets** are private networks to allow the organization to securely interact with external parties. They use Internet protocols and public telecommunication systems to work with external vendors, suppliers, dealers, customers, and so on. Clearly, the extranet would be a major element of a firm's supply chain information system.

Groupware simply refers to any of the various systems, either internal or commercial, that facilitate the work of groups or teams in the organization. Their purpose is for communication, collaboration, and coordination (of schedules, workflow, etc.). Most groupware systems these days are web based. The major commercial systems are Lotus Notes, Novell Groupwise, and Microsoft Exchange and Netmeeting.

Customer relationship management (**CRM**) systems are designed to collect and interpret customer-based data (Ragins and Greco 2003). This could be from internal sources such as marketing, sales, or customer support services or from external sources like market research or the customer. The aim is to develop a process for improving the firm's response to their customers' needs, especially the most profitable customers. CRM systems thus provide comprehensive customer data so the firm can provide better customer service and design and offer the most appropriate products and services for them.

Enterprise resource planning (**ERP**) systems greatly facilitate communication throughout the supply chain and over the Internet. The ERP system embodies much more than just the supply chain, however; it also includes all the electronic information concerning the various parts of the firm. These massive systems can not only reduce costs and allow instant access to the entire firm's database but can also help increase revenues, by up to 25 percent in some cases (Mabert 2001, p. 50). The topic of enterprise resource management is extensive and will be described in detail in Chapter 9.

SUCCESSFUL SUPPLY CHAIN MANAGEMENT

[handwritten margin note: Basic requirements for successful supply chain mgmt. 1) trustworthy partners 2) good communication 3) appropriate performance measures 4) competent managers with vision.]

The basic requirements for successful supply chain management are trustworthy partners, good communication, appropriate performance measures, and competent managers with vision. Innovation to suit the particular situation of the individual organization is particularly desirable. Some examples of visionary SCM innovations that have been developed are:

- Dell's "direct model" and Palm's "strategic sourcing," as described earlier.
- Wal-Mart's "**cross-docking**" technique of off-loading goods from incoming trucks at a warehouse directly into outbound distribution trucks instead of being placed into inventory.
- The relatively common approach used by Dell and many others of "**delayed differentiation**" where final modules are either inventoried for last-minute assembly to customer order, or differentiating features are added to the final product upon receipt of the customer's order.
- Sport Obermeyer's and Hewlett-Packard's "**postponement**" approach to delayed differentiation where variety and customization are delayed until as late in the production process as possible, sometimes even arranging with the carrier to perform the final customization (called **channel assembly**). In Sport Obermeyer's (Fisher et al. 1994) version, those product lines where demand is better known are produced first, while customer demand volume information is being collected on less easily forecast lines whose production has thus been postponed. Similarly, Hewlett-Packard ships generic DeskJet printers to regional centers around the globe, where local workers add country-specific power supplies, power cords, and local language instructions. Another variant of postponement was mentioned in the Dell example cited earlier, where *drop shipping* arrangements are made with the carrier to deliver third-party supplied elements of the product (e.g., monitors) to the customer at the same time that the main product is being delivered.

EXPAND YOUR UNDERSTANDING

1. Why is supply chain management such a topic of interest lately, especially multifacility distribution? Why wasn't it previously?
2. Will all production eventually reside in China? What exceptions might exist?
3. What appears to be the primary "secret" of successful supply chain management?
4. Given that the current conceptualization of the supply chain includes JIT and lean manufacturing, what other elements of SCM need to be changed to move toward the idea of a *demand* chain?
5. In what way can contract manufacturers consider themselves service providers? Hasn't Nike been doing this for years? What's the difference?
6. To date it appears that purchasing has been the primary beneficiary of supply chain management. Why do you think this is so? What do you expect will happen in the future?
7. The bullwhip effect is often blamed for the boom and bust cycles in our national economy. Which of the remedies for eliminating this effect in a supply chain might also benefit the national economy?

8. How does postponement differ from assemble to order?

9. Why does the Internet rather than the older EDI now seem to be the information foundation for SCM?

10. Why do you think Wal-Mart has been the pioneer of RFID technology?

11. E-commerce has been supplanted by e-business. What is the basic difference between the two?

12. Contrast SCM systems with ERP systems. Which do you suspect are larger and more costly?

13. What additional information might a retailer such as Wal-Mart be interested in putting on an RFID tag, beyond the basic product identification that a bar code communicates?

APPLY YOUR UNDERSTANDING
Dart's Parts, Inc.

Z. "Dart" Mitchell leaned forward in his chair to read the e-mail that had just arrived from one of his major customers, Avery Machine Corp. It read as follows:

"To all our preferred suppliers—

Due to our commitments to our primary customer, Globus Enterprises, we will in the future be doing all of our supply chain business by way of the Internet, e-mail, and EDI. This includes order preparation, bidding, forecasting, production scheduling, delivery monitoring, cost control, accounts payable and receivable, credit and financing, market and advertising planning, human resource acquisition, engineering specifications, and so on. To maintain compatibility with our systems, you will have to invest in a specific set of EDI hardware and software, available from GoingBust.com on the Web. Although the hardware and software are expensive, we anticipate that the cost savings and increased business this will provide over the coming years can more than offset the additional cost. Please let us know if we can continue to count on you as one of our preferred suppliers as we move our supply chain into the information age.

J. R. Avery, Chairman
Avery Machine Corp."

Dart's Parts had been founded in 1974, when the country was coming out of the 1973–74 recession and the need for machine part fabricators was great. Over the years, Dart had built up the business to where it now had a solid base of major customers and a comfortable backlog of orders. Dart had increased the capacity of the plant substantially over the years, moving from a small rented facility to its own 200,000 square foot plant, with a separate 50,000 square foot warehouse located adjacent to the main plant. Although not a "first adopter" when it came to new technology, Dart's embraced proven advanced technologies both on the plant floor, such as robots and numerically controlled machine tools, as well as in the office with computers, digital copiers, and other such office equipment.

Dart Mitchell had been reading industry magazines about some of these new technologies and had to admit they sounded promising. However, he had read about some horror stories too, when the much-advertised features turned into a nightmare. In one case, a customer had forced its suppliers to obtain production schedules off their website. Initially responding to high growth in a new product line, the firm had put their component needs on their website but when a major order was cancelled, they were late changing the Web production schedule. As a result, the suppliers were stuck with hundreds of unneeded components and the company wouldn't reimburse them. In another case, a manufacturer had made a bid for electronic parts on a Web auction and won. However, when they received the parts, they were too large to fit in the standard-sized enclosure they were using and they all had to be scrapped.

Dart believed that this new technology was indeed the future of the industry, but was concerned about getting in too early and being stuck with the wrong equipment. Learning about the new supply chain technology would undoubtedly open avenues to increased business, and might also cut a number of costs. Of course, it would also save their reputation with Avery, a major customer. However, obtaining the EDI system would be a major financial investment for the firm, particularly if Avery later dropped this approach and went to an all-Internet ERP system like some customers had been talking about doing. At this point, Dart wasn't sure what to do.

Questions

1. Identify the trade-offs facing Dart's Parts.
2. What are the pros and cons of each alternative?
3. What additional information would be useful to have?
4. What recommendations would you make to Dart Mitchell?

BIBLIOGRAPHY

Ballou, R. H. *Business Logistics Management.* Upper Saddle River, NJ: Prentice-Hall, 1999.

Bender, P. S. "Debunking 5 Supply Chain Myths." *Supply Chain Management Review* (March 2000): 52–58.

Blackwell, R. D., and K. Blackwell. "The Century of the Consumer: Converting Supply Chains into Demand Chains." *Supply Chain Management Review* (Fall 1999): 22–32.

Bowersox, D. J., D. J. Closs, and M. B. Cooper. *Supply Chain Logistics Management.* New York: Irwin/McGraw-Hill, 2002.

Burt, D. N., D. W. Dobler, and S. L. Starling. *World Class Supply Managment^{SM}: The Key to Supply Chain Management,* 7th ed. New York: McGraw-Hill/Irwin, 2003.

Carbone, J. "Strategic Sourcing is Palm's Pilot." *Purchasing*, April 17, 2003.

Champion, D. "Mastering the Value Chain." *Harvard Business Review* (June 2001): 109–115.

Chopra, S., and P. Meindl. *Supply Chain Management: Strategy, Planning, and Operation.* Upper Saddle River, NJ: Prentice-Hall, 2001.

Clark, T., and J. Hammond. "Reengineering Channel Reordering Processes to Improve Total Supply Chain Performance." *Production and Operations Management*, 6 (1997): 248–265.

Cooper, M., D. M. Lambert, and J. D. Pagh. "Supply Chain Management: More than a New Name for Logistics." *The International Journal of Logistics Management*, vol. 8, no. 1 (1997): 1–14.

Coyle, J. J., E. J. Bardi, and R. A. Novack. *Transportation.* Cincinnati: South-Western, 2000.

Cross, G. J. "How E-Business is Transforming Supply Chain Management." *Engineering Management Review*, 28 (Third Quarter 2000): 17–19.

Dignan, L. "Is Dell Hitting the Efficiency Wall?" MSNBC News.Com, July 29, 2002, pp. 1–5.

Ellram, L. M., and B. Liu. "The Financial Impact of Supply Management." *Supply Chain Management Review* (November–December 2002): 30–37.

Engardio, P. "Why the Supply Chain Broke Down." *Business Week* (March 19, 2001), p. 41.

Evans, P., and T. S. Wurster. "Getting Real about Virtual Commerce." *Harvard Business Review* (November–December 1999): 84–94.

Ferdows, K. "Making the Most of Foreign Factories." *Harvard Business Review* (March–April 1997): 73–88.

Ferguson, B. R. "Implementing Supply Chain Management." *Production and Inventory Management Journal*, 41 (Second Quarter 2000): 64–67.

Fisher, M. L., J. H. Hammond, W.R. Obermeyer, and A. Raman. "Making Supply Meet Demand in an Uncertain World." *Harvard Business Review* (May–June 1994): 83–93.

Fisher, M. L. "What Is the Right Supply Chain for Your Product?" *Harvard Business Review* (March–April 1997): 105–116.

Frohlich, M. T., and R. Westbrook. "Arcs of Integration: An International Study of Supply Chain Strategies." *Journal of Operations Management*, 19 (2001): 185–200.

Ferguson, B. R. "Implementing Supply Chain Management." *Production and Inventory Management Journal*, 40 (Second Quarter 2000): 64–67.

Gray, C. D. "Does Your Supply Chain System Measure Up?" *APICS—The Performance Advantage*, 9 (January 1999): 56.

Hammer, M. "The Superefficient Company." *Harvard Business Review* (Sept. 2001): 82-91.

Handfield, R. B., and E. L. Nichols, Jr. *Introduction to Supply Chain Management*. Upper Saddle River, NJ: Prentice-Hall, 1999.

Harris, N. " 'Private Exchanges' May Allow B-to-B Commerce to Thrive After All." *The Wall Street Journal*, (March 16, 2001): B1, B4.

Kahn, G. "Making Labels for Less: Supply-Chain City Transforms Apparel Industry." *Wall Street Journal* (August 13, 2004): B1, B3.

Kanakamedala, K., G. Ramsdell, and V. Srivatsan. "Getting Supply Chain Software Right." *The McKinsey Quarterly*, no. 1 (2003).

Kanet, J. J., and A. R. Cannon. "Implementing Supply Chain Management: Lessons Learned at Becton Dickinson." *Production and Inventory Management Journal*, 41 (Second Quarter 2000): 33–40.

Kaplan, S., and M. Sawhney. "E-Hubs: The New B2B Marketplaces." *Harvard Business Review* (May–June 2000): 97–103.

Levy, D. L. "Lean Production in an International Supply Chain." *Sloan Management Review*, 38 (Winter 1997): 94–101.

Lewis, J. D. *The Connected Corporations: How Leading Companies Win Through Customer-Supplier Alliances*. New York: Free Press, 1996.

Lummus, R. R., and R. J. Vokurka. "Managing the Demand Chain Through Managing the Information Flow: Capturing 'Moments of Information'." *Production and Inventory Management Journal*, 40 (First Quarter 1999): 16–20.

Lummus, R. R., and R. J. Vokurka. "Strategic Supply Chain Planning." *Production and Inventory Management Journal*, 39 (Third Quarter 1998): 49–58.

Mabert, V. A., A. Soni, and M. A. Venkataramanan. "Enterprise Resource Planning: Measuring Value." *Production and Inventory Management Journal*, 42 (Third/Fourth Quarter 2001): 46–51.

Magretta, J. "The Power of Virtual Integration: An Interview with Dell Computer's Michael Dell." *Harvard Business Review* (March–April 1998): 72–84.

Maloni, M., and W. C. Benton. "Power Influences in the Supply Chain." *Journal of Business Logistics*, vol. 21 (2000): 49–73.

Monczka, R., K. J. Petersen, R. B. Handfield, and G. L. Ragatz. "Success Factors in Strategic Supplier Alliances." *Decision Sciences*, 29 (Summer 1998): 553–577.

Monczka, R., R. Trent, and R. Handfield. *Purchasing and Supply Chain Management*. Cincinnati: South-Western, 1997.

Quinn, F. J. "What's the Buzz? Supply Chain Management; Part 1." *Logistics Management*, 36 (February 1997), 43.

Ragins, E. J., and A. J. Greco. "Customer Relationship Management and E-Business: More Than a Software Solution." *Review of Business*, Winter, 2003, 25–30.

Ross, D. F. *Competing Through Supply Chain Management*. New York: Chapman and Hall, 1998.

Simchi-Levi, D., P. Kaminsky, and E. Simchi-Levi. *Designing and Managing the Supply Chain: Concepts, Strategies, and Case Studies*. New York: Irwin/McGraw-Hill, 2000.

Simchi-Levi, D., P. Kaminsky, and E. Simchi-Levi. *Supply Chain Management*, 2nd ed. New York: McGraw-Hill, 2003.

Shapiro, C., and H. R. Varian. *Information Rules: A Strategic Guide to the Network Economy*. Boston: Harvard Business School Press, 1999.

Tully, S. "Purchasing's New Muscle." *Fortune* (February 20, 1995): 75–83.

Turban, E., J. Lee, D. King, and H. M. Chung. *Electronic Commerce: A Managerial Perspective*. Upper Saddle River, NJ: Prentice Hall, 2000.

Verity, J. W. "Invoice? What's an Invoice?" *Business Week* (June 10, 1996): 110–112.

Walker, W. T., and K. L. Alber. "Understanding Supply Chain Management." *APICS—The Performance Advantage*, 9 (January 1999), 38–43.

The Beer Game[1]

The *Beer Game* has become a staple of the operations management course in MBA programs across the country. In effect, the game simulates material and information flows in a simplified supply chain. As shown in Figure 7S.1, the supply chain consists of four stages. Moving from the factory downstream, the supply chain consists of a factory, wholesaler, distributor, and retailer. Accordingly, each stage in the supply chain is required to manage its inventory levels given the receipt of orders from its downstream customer through the placement of orders with its upstream supplier. The only exceptions to this are that the retailer's demand comes from the final consumer and the factory schedules production requests as opposed to placing an order from an upstream supplier.

There is a 2-week delay between the retailer, wholesaler, and distributor. Thus, orders from the retailer to the wholesaler in a given week arrive 2 weeks after the wholesaler ships them. Likewise, orders from the wholesaler to the distributor in a particular week arrive two weeks after the distributor ships it. Production orders at the factory are available to ship three weeks after the production requests.

Your objective in playing the game is to minimize the sum of your total weekly costs. Weekly costs consist of two components: an inventory cost and a backlog cost. More specifically, weekly inventory cost is calculated at the rate of $.50/keg of beer in inventory at the end of the week, while backlog costs are calculated at the rate of $1.00/keg on backlog at the end of the week. Obviously, only one of these costs can be positive in any given week (although it is possible that they both could be zero in a particular week).

Because a supply chain for the beer industry in reality would likely be characterized by multiple factories, dozens of distributors, hundreds of wholesalers, and tens of thousands of retailers, it is often the case that the only information shared between a supplier and its customer is order information. Therefore, in the game, the only communication you may have with your upstream supplier is the placement of your order.

In terms of the initial conditions, as it turns out, the demand at the retailer stage has been quite stable at four kegs per week for the last several weeks. Therefore, every order placed throughout the entire supply chain has been for four kegs over this period. Furthermore, each stage has maintained an inventory level of 12 kegs or the equivalent of three weeks of demand. However, as the weather turns warmer in the near future, demand is expected to increase. Also, it is expected that there will be one or more promotions over the coming months.

---

[1]Adapted from J. Sterman "Instructions for Running the Beer Distribution Game, Massachusetts Institute of Technology, October 1894; J. H. Hammond. "The Beer Game: Description of Exercise," Harvard Business School, 9-964-104.

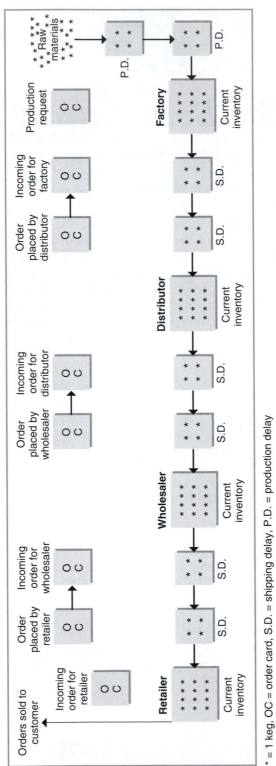

* = 1 keg, OC = order card, S.D. = shipping delay, P.D. = production delay

Figure 7S.1 The beer game board and initial conditions.

In playing the game, you will be assigned to one of the four stages in the supply chain. During each week of simulated time, you will be required to perform the following five tasks. It is important that these tasks be completed in the order listed below and that each stage in the supply chain complete the task simultaneously with the other stages. Note that only the final task requires you to make a decision.

1. Deliver your beer and advance shipments. Move the beer in the **Shipping Delay** box (on the right, adjacent to your **Current Inventory** box) into the **Current Inventory** box. Next, move beer in the other **Shipping Delay** box to the right to the now empty **Shipping Delay** box. [Factories move the inventory from the **Production Delay** box directly to the right of the **Current Inventory** box into the **Current Inventory** box. Then move inventory from the top **Production Delay** box to the bottom **Production Delay** box.]

2. Pick up the incoming order from your downstream customer in your **Incoming Order** box at your top left (retailers read incoming order from the consumer). Fill as much of the order as you can from your current inventory by placing the appropriate quantity of kegs in the **Shipping Delay** box directly to the left of your **Current Inventory** box. Quantities ordered above your current inventory level become part of your current backlog. More specifically, the amount to ship this week is calculated as follows:

$$\text{Quantity to Ship} = \text{Incoming Order This Week} + \text{Previous Week's Backlog}$$

3. Calculate and record in Figure 7S.2 your ending inventory or backlog position (as a negative number.) Count the number of kegs remaining in your current inventory after the shipment for the week has been made. If you get into a backlog situation, the backlog must be accumulated from week to week since quantities ordered but not shipped must be made up. The week's ending backlog position is calculated as follows:

$$\text{Current Week's Backlog} = \text{Previous Week's Backlog} + \text{Incoming Order} - \text{Shipments Received this Week}$$

4. Advance your order cards. (Factories fill their production requests.) Advance the order from the **Order Placed** box to the **Incoming Order** box (or, for the factory, read the **Production Request** and fill the **Production Delay** box from the raw materials inventory). Make sure to keep the order cards face down as you move them.

5. Decide how much to order, write it down on your order card (and in Figure 7S.2), and place the card face down in the **Orders Placed** box. Factories decide how much to schedule for production, write it down on your order, and place the card face down in the **Production Request** box.

6. Repeat steps 1–5.

Most likely, your instructor will have the class complete one or more practice runs or go through the first couple of weeks at a slow pace.

Week	Inventory	Order Placed	Week	Inventory	Order Placed
1			26		
2			27		
3			28		
4			29		
5			30		
6			31		
7			32		
8			33		
9			34		
10			35		
11			36		
12			37		
13			38		
14			39		
15			40		
16			41		
17			42		
18			43		
19			44		
20			45		
21			46		
22			47		
23			48		
24			49		
25			50		

Figure 7S.2   Data sheet.

CHAPTER 8

Inventory Management

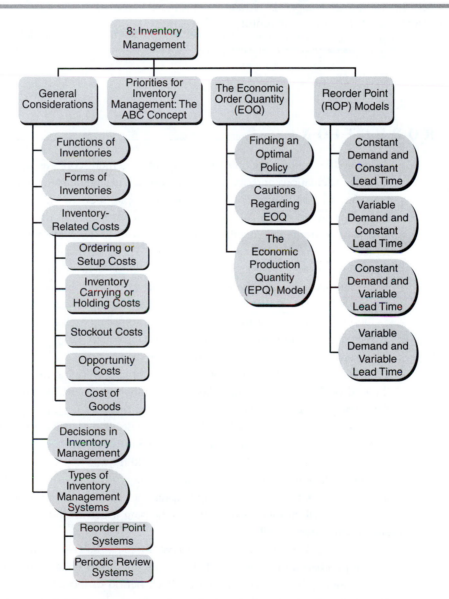

8: Inventory Management

- General Considerations
  - Functions of Inventories
  - Forms of Inventories
  - Inventory-Related Costs
    - Ordering or Setup Costs
    - Inventory Carrying or Holding Costs
    - Stockout Costs
    - Opportunity Costs
    - Cost of Goods
  - Decisions in Inventory Management
  - Types of Inventory Management Systems
    - Reorder Point Systems
    - Periodic Review Systems
- Priorities for Inventory Management: The ABC Concept
- The Economic Order Quantity (EOQ)
  - Finding an Optimal Policy
  - Cautions Regarding EOQ
  - The Economic Production Quantity (EPQ) Model
- Reorder Point (ROP) Models
  - Constant Demand and Constant Lead Time
  - Variable Demand and Constant Lead Time
  - Constant Demand and Variable Lead Time
  - Variable Demand and Variable Lead Time

CHAPTER IN PERSPECTIVE

Inventory management deals with determining how much and when to order to support the production plan and is a crucial element of the supply chain. Excess inventories incur extra cost while insufficient inventories can ruin the schedule, hurting both the strategic value elements of delivery dependability and speed. After discussing the functions and forms of inventory, inventory-related costs, and types of inventory management systems, the ABC classification system for prioritizing inventory items is overviewed. Next, the *economic order quantity* (EOQ) model is discussed for independent demand items. The chapter concludes with some cautions regarding the use of the EOQ.

INTRODUCTION

- To many, the mere mention of inventory management conjures up images of detailed calculations and analysis. However, while inventory management is often considered to be a rather bland and narrow topic, there are a number of areas related to inventory management that are generating significant interest. One such area is radio frequency identification (RFID). With RFID, conventional bar codes are replaced with computer chips or smart tags. These smart tags use wireless technology to track inventory. In addition to labor savings, the RFID allows organizations to manage their inventory more effectively. In 2005, spending on RFID had already reached $1 billion and is projected to increase to $4.6 billion by 2007.

  One early adopter of RFID is Wal-Mart, a company well known for its investments in supply chain technology. By January 2005, 53 of its top 100 suppliers were sending RFID-tagged goods to its three distribution centers in the Dallas, Texas area. Wal-Mart's goal is to have all top 100 suppliers shipping RFID-tagged goods by the end of February 2005 in addition to 37 other suppliers. In subsequent waves, Wal-Mart plans to have the next 200 suppliers onboard by January of 2006 and its entire supplier base onboard by the end of 2006. Wal-Mart itself has installed RFID readers in 104 of its Wal-Mart stores and 36 Sam's Clubs.

  The impetus for Wal-Mart's investment in RFID was the lack of visibility it had into its backroom storage areas. Better visibility would translate into better information with which to base replenishment orders which in turn would provide a better overall customer experience by helping it get inventory onto the store shelves in a more timely manner.

  The major drawback to RFID is its cost. In 2005, the cost of smart tags was $0.25 each if purchased in volume, and $0.75 if purchased in smaller quantities. For many organizations, this translates into a payback period of more than two years. However, the stated goal in the industry is to get the price of smart tags down to $.05, which would make adopting RFID more appealing and economical for many organizations. (Lacy 2004; Blanchard 2005)

- Vendor-managed inventory (VMI) is another inventory management topic that is generating a significant amount of interest. With VMI, suppliers are given responsibility for managing the inventory carried by their retail or wholesale customers. The customers still own the inventory; however, the suppliers are given the responsibility for managing it. Using point-of-sale data, suppliers determine the timing and quantity of inventory replenishment orders.

  Rich Products, a $2 billion family-owned food company headquartered in Buffalo, has a partnership with IBM to provide VMI services to the grocery industry for its frozen food items. With this service, grocery customers provide information daily to IBM electronically about inventory withdrawals and inventory balances. Rich accesses this information and then uses its customers' own purchasing systems to generate replenishment orders based on service performance agreements. These purchase orders are then sent to Rich electronically. Through the use of VMI, retailers hope to increase their inventory turnover while at the same time reducing the occurrence of stockouts. (Richardson 2004)

In Chapter 7, we discussed the management of supply chains. In this chapter, we continue our discussion of supply chains by looking at the uses of inventories, and the means of determining the best levels of inventories to hold. The chapter considers both purchased and internally produced inventories. Although we describe various functions of inventories, the material in the chapter focuses largely on cycle inventories that are replenished on a regular basis in "lots" or batches—that is, where the production of the materials is not produced by a continuous or flow process.

From Chapter 7, as well as the earlier examples, it is clear that the supply chain and inventory management systems must fit closely with the scheduling systems. In fact, such systems are typically known as *production and inventory control systems*. This tie has become closer with the development of computerized production planning and control systems, because the management of tremendous quantities and varieties of materials is not the problem for computers that it was for manual systems. This has allowed the two systems to be joined, for both substantial savings in costs and significant improvement in the control of materials and operations, thereby resulting in higher productivity, adherence to promised due dates, and other such benefits.

GENERAL CONSIDERATIONS

Although inventory is inanimate, the topic of inventory and inventory control can arouse completely different sentiments in the minds of people in various departments within an organization. The salespeople generally prefer large quantities of inventory to be on hand. In this way they can meet customers' requests without having to wait. Customer service is their primary concern. The accounting and financial personnel see inventory in a different light. High inventories do not translate into high customer service in the accountant's language; rather, they translate into large amounts of tied-up capital that could otherwise be used to reduce debt or for other more economically advantageous purposes. From the viewpoint of the operations manager, inventories are a tool that can be used to promote efficient operation of the production facilities. Neither high inventories nor low inventories, per se, are desirable; inventories are simply allowed to fluctuate so that production can be adjusted to its most efficient level. And top management's concern is with the "bottom line"—what advantages the inventories are providing versus their costs.

Functions of Inventories

There are many purposes for holding inventory, but, in general, inventories have five basic functions. Be aware that inventories will not generally be identified and segregated within the organization by these functions and that not all functions will be represented in all organizations.

1. ***Transit inventories***. Transit inventories exist because materials must be moved from one location to another. (These are also known as ***pipeline inventories***.) A truckload of merchandise from a retailer's regional warehouse to one of its retail stores is an example of transit inventory. This inventory results because of the transportation time required.

2. ***Buffer inventories***. Another purpose of inventories is to protect against the uncertainties of supply and demand. Buffer inventories—or, as they are sometimes called, ***safety stocks***—serve to cushion the effect of unpredictable events. The amount of inventory over and above the average demand requirement is considered to be buffer stock held to meet any demand in excess of the average. The higher the level of inventory, the better the customer service—that is, the fewer the ***stockouts*** and ***backorders***. A stockout exists when a customer's order for an item cannot be filled because the inventory of that item has run out. If there is a stockout, the firm will usually backorder the item immediately, rather than wait until the next regular ordering period.

3. ***Anticipation inventories***. An anticipated future event such as a price increase, a strike, or a seasonal increase in demand is the reason for holding anticipation inventories. For example, rather than operating with excessive overtime in one period and then allowing the productive system to be idle or shut down because of insufficient demand in another period, inventories can be allowed to build up before an event to be consumed during or after the event. Manufacturers, wholesalers, and retailers build anticipation inventories before occasions such as Christmas and Halloween, when demand for specialized products will be high.

4. ***Decoupling inventories***. It would be a rare production system in which all equipment and personnel operated at exactly the same rate. Yet if you were to take an inspection tour through a production facility, you would notice that most of the equipment and people were producing. Products move smoothly even though one machine can process parts five times as fast as the one before or after it. An inventory of parts between machines, or fluid in a vat, known as decoupling inventory, acts to disengage the production system. That is, inventories act as shock absorbers, or cushions, increasing and decreasing in size as parts are added to and used up from the stock.

Even if a preceding machine were to break down, the following machines could still produce (at least for a while), since an in-process inventory of parts would be waiting for production. The more inventories management carries between stages in the manufacturing and distribution system, the less coordination is needed to keep the system running smoothly. Clearly, there is an optimum balance between inventory level and coordination in the operations system. Without decoupling inventories, each operation in the plant would have to produce at an identical rate (a paced line) to keep the production flowing smoothly, and when one operation broke down, the entire plant would come to a standstill.

5. **Cycle inventories**. Cycle inventories—or, as they are sometimes called, *lot-size* inventories—exist for a different reason from the others just discussed. Each of the previous types of inventories serves one of the major purposes for holding inventory. Cycle inventories, on the other hand, result from management's attempt to minimize the total cost of carrying and ordering inventory. If the annual demand for a particular part is 12,000 units, management could decide to place one order for 12,000 units and maintain a rather large inventory throughout the year or place 12 orders of 1000 each and maintain a lower level of inventory. But the costs associated with ordering and receiving would increase. Cycle inventories are the inventories that result from ordering in batches or "lots" rather than as needed.

Forms of Inventories

Inventories are usually classified into four forms, some of which correspond directly with the previous inventory functions but some of which do not.

1. *Raw materials*. Raw materials are objects, commodities, elements, and items that are received (usually purchased) from outside the organization to be used directly in the production of the final output. When we think of raw materials, we think of such things as sheet metal, flour, paint, structural steel, chemicals, and other basic materials. But nuts and bolts, hydraulic cylinders, pizza crusts, syringes, engines, frames, integrated circuits, and other assemblies purchased from outside the organization would also be considered part of the raw materials inventory.

2. *Maintenance, repair, and operating supplies*. Maintenance, repair, and operating (MRO) supplies are items used to support and maintain the operation, including spares, supplies, and stores. Spares are sometimes produced by the organization itself rather than purchased. These are usually machine parts or supplies that are crucial to production. The term *supplies* is often used synonymously with *inventories*. The general convention, and the one that we will adopt in this book, is that supplies are stocks of items used (consumed) in the production of goods or services but are not directly a part of the finished product. Examples are copier paper, staples, pencils, and packing material. Stores commonly include both supplies and raw materials that are kept in stock or on shelves in a special location.

3. *Work-in-process.* **Work-in-process** (WIP) inventory consists of all the materials, parts, and assemblies that are being worked on or are waiting to be processed within the operations system. Decoupling inventories are an example of work-in-process. That is, they are all the items that have left the raw materials inventory but have not yet been converted or assembled into a final product.

4. *Finished goods.* The **finished goods** inventory is the stock of completed products. Goods, once completed, are transferred out of work-in-process inventory and into the finished goods inventory. From here they can be sent to distribution centers, sold to wholesalers, or sold directly to retailers or final customers.

DILBERT: ©Scott Adams/Dist. by United Feature Syndicate, Inc.

As you can see from this discussion, the inventory system and the operations system within an organization are strongly interrelated. Inventories affect customer service, utilization of facilities and equipment, capacity, and efficiency of labor. Therefore, the plans concerning the acquisition and storage of materials, or "inventories," are vital to the production system.

The ultimate objective of any inventory system is to make decisions regarding the level of inventory that will result in a good balance between the purposes for holding inventories and the costs associated with them. Typically, we hear inventory management practitioners and researchers speaking of *total cost minimization* as the objective of an inventory system. If we were able to place dollar costs on interruptions in the smooth flow of goods through the operations system, on not meeting customers' demands, or on failures to provide the other purposes for which inventories exist, then minimization of total costs would be a reasonable objective. But since we are unable to assign costs to many of these subjective factors, we must be satisfied with obtaining a good balance between the costs and the functions of inventories.

Inventory-Related Costs

There are essentially five broad categories of costs associated with inventory systems: ordering or setup costs, inventory carrying or holding costs, stockout costs, opportunity costs, and cost of goods. This section looks at these costs in turn.

Ordering or Setup Costs

Ordering costs are costs associated with outside procurement of material, and *setup costs* are costs associated with internal procurement (i.e., internal manufacture) of parts of material. Ordering costs include writing the order, processing the order through the purchasing system, postage, processing invoices, processing accounts payable, and the work of the receiving department, such as handling, testing, inspection, and transporting. Setup costs also include writing orders and processing for the internal production system, setup labor, machine downtime due to a new setup (e.g., cost of an idle, nonproducing machine), parts damaged during setup (e.g., actual parts are often used for tests during setup), and costs associated with employees' learning curve (e.g., the cost of early production spoilage and low productivity immediately after a new production run is started).

Inventory Carrying or Holding Costs

Inventory *carrying* or *holding* costs have the following major components:

- Capital costs
- Storage costs
- Risk costs

Capital costs include interest on money invested in inventory and in the land, buildings, and equipment necessary to hold and maintain the inventory, an item of special interest to both financial and top management. These rates often exceed 20 percent of the cost of the goods. If these investments were not required, the organization could invest the capital in an alternative that would earn some return on investment.

Storage costs include rent, taxes, and insurance on buildings; depreciation of buildings; maintenance and repairs; heat, power, and light; salaries of security personnel; taxes on the inventory; labor costs for handling inventory; clerical costs for keeping records; taxes and insurance on equipment; depreciation of equipment; fuel and energy for equipment; and repairs and maintenance. Some of these costs are variable, some fixed, and some "semifixed."

Risk costs include the costs of obsolete inventory, insurance on inventory, physical deterioration of the inventory, and losses from pilferage.

Even though some of these costs are relatively small, the total costs of carrying items in inventory can be quite large. Studies have found that for a typical manufacturing firm, the cost is frequently as large as 35 percent of the cost of the inventoried items. A large portion of this is the cost of the invested capital.

Stockout Costs

If inventory is unavailable when customers request it, a situation that marketing detests, or when it is needed for production, a stockout occurs. Several costs are associated with each type of stockout. A stockout of an item demanded by a customer or client can result in lost sales or demand, lost goodwill (which is very difficult to estimate), and costs associated with processing back orders (such as extra paperwork, expediting, special handling, and higher shipping costs). A stockout of an item needed for production results in costs for rescheduling production, costs of down time and delays caused by the shortage, the cost of "rush" shipping of needed parts, and possibly the cost of substituting a more expensive part or material.

Opportunity Costs

Often capacity and inventory costs can be traded off for one another. For example, capacity costs can be incurred because a change in productive capacity is necessary or because there is a temporary shortage of or excess in capacity. Why would capacity be too great or too small? If, for example, a company tried to meet seasonal demand (or any fluctuations in demand) by changing the level of production rather than by allowing the level of inventory to rise or fall, capacity would have to be increased during high-demand periods and lie idle during low-demand periods. Also, capacity problems are often due to scheduling conflicts. These commonly arise when multiple products have to be produced on the same set of facilities.

Opportunity costs include the overtime required to increase capacity; the human resource management costs of hiring, training, and terminating employees; the cost of using less-skilled workers during peak periods; and the cost of idle time if capacity is *not* reduced during periods when demand decreases. The tradeoffs in these costs were considered earlier, in Chapter 6, with regard to aggregate planning.

Cost of Goods

Last, the goods themselves must be paid for. Although they must be acquired sooner or later anyway, *when* they are acquired can influence their cost considerably, as through quantity discounts.

Decisions in Inventory Management

The objective of an inventory management system is to make decisions regarding the appropriate level of inventory and changes in the level of inventory. To maintain the appropriate level of inventory, decision rules are needed to answer two basic questions:

1. When should an order be placed to replenish the inventory?
2. How much should be ordered?

The decision rules guide the inventory manager or computerized materials management system in evaluating the current state of the inventory and deciding if some action, such as replenishment, is required. Various types of inventory management systems incorporate different rules to decide "when" and "how much." Some depend on time and others on the level of inventory, but the essential decisions are the same. Even when complexities, such as uncertainty in demand and delivery times, are introduced, deciding "how many" and "when to order" still remains the basis of sound inventory management.

Types of Inventory Management Systems

All inventory systems can be classified as one of three varieties, based on the approach taken to deciding "when to order":

1. Reorder point systems
2. Periodic review systems
3. Materials requirements planning (MRP) systems (see Chapter 9)

Before we discuss these three systems, let us consider a simplified inventory management situation, to provide a background.

Consider a distributor of bottled water imported from a spring in the Swiss Alps. The distributor sells 1000 5-gallon bottles per month to residential customers in the southeast. Demand for the 5-gallon bottles is constant throughout the year. Suppose that the distributor has a policy of ordering 2000 bottles per order and that it has just received a shipment of 2000, bringing its inventory level to 2000.

The distributor sells 1000 5-gallon bottles per month, and therefore the beginning inventory of 2000 units will be depleted by the end of the second month. To avoid "stocking out," an order must be placed and shipment received before the end of the second month. To keep the costs of carrying inventory as low as possible, it is desirable to schedule receipt of the order at the time that the previous inventory is exhausted. Assuming this perfect scheduling and "instantaneous replenishment" (the entire order quantity is received when the inventory level reaches zero), we can graph the inventory level as it changes over time as in Figure 8.1. We will return to this example later.

Inventory is used at the rate of 1000 per month, and orders are received so that the inventory level is replenished before a stockout can occur. No stockouts occur, and the inventory level never exceeds the order quantity of 2000. While beyond the scope of this book, we note that more sophisticated models are not dependent on the unrealistic assumptions of constant demand and instantaneous replenishment. For now, let us turn to a discussion of the three types of inventory control systems.

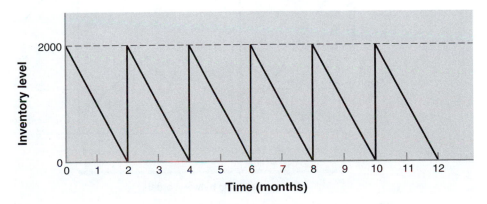

Figure 8.1   Fluctuations in inventory.

Reorder Point Systems

In reorder point systems an inventory *level* is specified at which a replenishment order for a fixed quantity of the inventory item is to be placed. Whenever the inventory on hand reaches the predetermined inventory level—the **reorder point**—an order may be placed for a prespecified amount if there are no current outstanding orders, as illustrated in Figure 8.2. Note in the figure that the demand rates between cycles are not necessarily the same, which is true in general for any time period. The reorder point is established so that the inventory on hand at the time an order is placed is sufficient to meet demand during the **lead time** (i.e., the time between placement of an order and receipt of the shipment). The quantity of inventory to be ordered is often based on the **economic order quantity** (EOQ) (one answer to the question "how much to order"), an approach illustrated later in this chapter. But other rules for deciding "how much," such as ordering a "six-week supply," are also used in reorder point systems.

A simplified and much-used variation of the reorder point system is the **two-bin** system, in which parts are stored in two bins—one large and one small. The small bin usually holds sufficient parts to satisfy demand during the replenishment lead time. Parts are used from only the large bin, until it is empty. At that time, a replenishment order is placed, and parts from the small bin are used until the replenishment order is received.

Many variations of two-bin systems have been developed. In some systems it is simply the responsibility of the employee who removes the last item from the large bin to place a requisition for materials with the purchasing department or with the supervisor. In others, a completed requisition is placed at the bottom of the larger bin and needs to be picked up and submitted only when the last item is removed. In others, a card is affixed to a wrapped quantity of items in the small bin. When these items are opened, the card is removed and sent to data processing to generate an order. The advantage of the two-bin system is that no detailed real-time

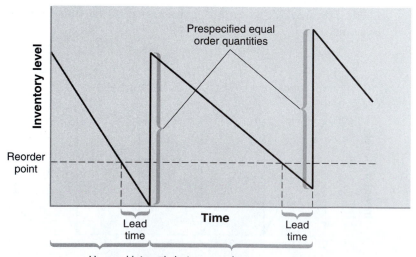

Figure 8.2 A reorder point system.

records of inventory use (a ***perpetual inventory system***) must be kept, and inventory need not be continually recounted to determine whether or not a reorder should be placed.

This latter point is important. A perpetual inventory system requires either a manual card system or a computerized system to keep track of daily usage and daily stock levels. Also, each day the cards or the computer file must be "searched" to find all items that have fallen to or below the reorder point. Note that these clerical functions remove the burden of assessing proper inventory levels from the people who use the inventory. Perpetual systems run into problems when those who use the inventory fail to report its use. Management controls over the inventory system must be fairly rigid to ensure that perpetual records remain accurate and, in turn, result in the proper placement of orders for inventory. This also requires a regular physical check of the inventory to be sure that the records are accurate. A reorder point system could not perform adequately without either a two-bin system or perpetual inventory control. Without one of these, someone would have to record the inventory balances for all items each day in order to have accurate counts and, therefore, to know when to order. The recent development of real-time inventory control systems that include computerized order entry and invoicing has greatly eased the difficulties of the perpetual system and reduced the need for two-bin systems. For example, inventory records at grocery stores can be instantaneously updated as items are scanned at the cash registers. Of course, actual inventory may still not be what is expected due to shrinkage (theft), spoilage, damage, and such.

Periodic Review Systems

In ***periodic review systems*** the inventory level is reviewed at equal time intervals, and at each review a reorder may be placed to bring the level up to a desired quantity. Such a system is especially appropriate for retailers ordering families of goods. The amount of the reorder is based on a maximum level established for each inventory item. The quantity that should be reordered is the amount necessary to bring the *on-hand* inventory plus the *on-order* quantity, less the expected demand over the lead time, up to the maximum level:

Reorder quantity = maximum level − on-hand inventory − on-order quantity
+ demand over lead time

The on-hand inventory is the amount actually in stock. If the system allows backorders, then on-hand could be negative, at least in theory. If backorders are not used, then a stockout simply results in a zero on-hand quantity.

The on-order amount is the quantity for which purchase orders have been issued, but delivery has not yet been made. We deduct the on-order quantity (Q) to ensure that an order is not placed for the same goods. Figure 8.3 illustrates such an occurrence. Suppose that at review point A an order is simply placed for Q_A. At review point B, the first order has not arrived, so an order for Q_B is placed. No attention was paid to the on-order quantity. Now, sometime later, Q_A is received, and then Q_B. At review point C, inventory exceeds the desired maximum.

In periodic review systems the *review period* (and therefore the *reorder period*) is fixed, and the *order quantity varies* (see Figure 8.4) according to the rule just given. This system is more appropriate when it is difficult to keep track of inventory levels and the cost of stockouts or safety stock is not excessive. Since inventory is not continuously tracked, there is a significant chance of stocking out. This possibility can be avoided by using safety stock.

In reorder point systems the *order quantity is fixed*, and the *reorder period varies* (see Figure 8.2). This system is best where a continuing watch of inventory levels is feasible and stockouts or safety stock would be expensive. If demand increases during the period, the reorder point system would simply place an order sooner than normal. The periodic review system would review and place an order

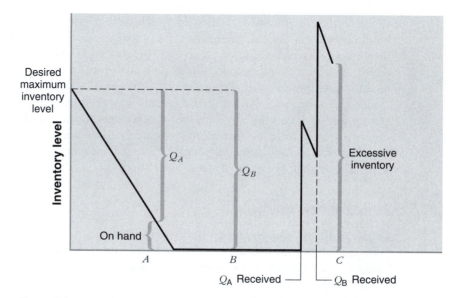

Figure 8.3   Periodic review system without considering on-order quantity.

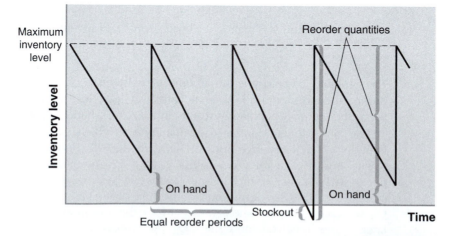

Figure 8.4   Periodic review system (assumes none on order at time of reorder).

at the regularly scheduled time but for a quantity larger than normal. However, in both systems there is a risk of a stockout because the demand during the lead time may be greater than the amount on hand at the time the order is placed. As we will see, there are ways to compensate for this risk.

Note that it is not unusual for some organizations to use a reorder point system for some inventory items and a periodic review system for other items. For example, large grocery chains often carry inventories of some items such as canned vegetables in their own regional warehouses and rely on third-party distributors for other products such as cosmetics. For the items available in the chain's own regional warehouse, orders are automatically submitted to the warehouse based on a reorder point system as items are scanned at the checkout. For the items supplied by the third-party distributors, orders are submitted at fixed times (e.g., once a week or once every other week) based on a physical count of what is actually on the store's shelves, what is already on order, and any special promotions that may be run.

Another type of periodic review inventory situation is that of the single-period, minimal-salvage-value problem. This situation is faced by vendors who stock a certain amount of material for an upcoming period of uncertain demand and then must resupply for the next period, a situation commonly known as the **newsboy problem**. More specifically, a semiperishable commodity is purchased in some order size before demand is known and is then either sold or scrapped, depending on the demand level. If an insufficient amount was ordered, the vendor loses the opportunity to have made additional profits. If too much was ordered, the vendor takes a loss (either a total loss or, if there is some salvage value, a partial loss) on the excess.

However, this problem is almost identical to that of the overbooking situation discussed in Chapter 6, except these products are ordered ahead of time instead of reservations taken for the upcoming period. Nevertheless, the same type of solution approach is used: assuming one stocking/reservation level is chosen and then working out the expected value of the profits, trying the next level, and so on. Hence, we will not repeat the procedure here.

PRIORITIES FOR INVENTORY MANAGEMENT: THE ABC CONCEPT

In practice, not all inventories need be controlled with equal attention. Some inventories are simply too small or too unimportant to warrant intensive monitoring and control. In addition, in implementing new inventory management systems, priorities must be developed to allow management to decide the order in which to include the inventoried items in the control system. One simple procedure that has been widely and successfully used is the ABC classification system.

The **ABC classification system** is based on the annual dollar purchases of an inventoried item. As can be seen from Table 8.1, a relatively small proportion of the total items in an inventory account for a relatively large proportion of the total annual dollar volume, and a large proportion of the items account for a small proportion of the dollars. This phenomenon is often found in systems in which large numbers of different items are maintained. It is also in evidence in marketing, where a small number of customers represent the bulk of the sales; in complaint departments, where a large volume of complaints come from a relatively small group; and so forth.

The three classifications used in the ABC system are:

- A. *High-value items*. The 15 to 20 percent[1] of the items that account for 75 to 80 percent of the total annual inventory value.

- B. *Medium-value items*. The 30 to 40 percent of the items that account for approximately 15 percent of the total annual inventory value.

- C. *Low-value items*. The 40 to 50 percent of the items that account for 10 to 15 percent of the annual inventory value.

The classification is shown in Figure 8.5, which gives the cumulative distribution of the dollar value of inventory items. In practice, the A items are identified first, then the C items, and what is left is usually considered to represent the B items. Of course, at times it may be appropriate to reclassify an item on the basis of other criteria. For example, a B item that has especially long lead times or is considered critical can be elevated to category A. A common misconception is that the ABC classification is based on the dollar value of the individual items. In actuality, relatively costly items can still be classified as C if annual usage is low enough.

The ABC classification is management's guide to the priorities of inventory items. The A items should be subject to the tightest control, with detailed inventory records and accurate, updated values of order quantities and reorder points. B items are subject to normal control, with order quantities set by EOQ (as shown in the next section) but with less frequent updating of records and review of order quantities and reorder points. C items are subject to little control; orders are placed for a six-month to one-year supply so that relatively little control must be exercised and inventory records can be kept simple. Essentially, the time and effort saved by not controlling C items is used to tighten control of A items.

$\mathcal{T}$ABLE 8.1 • Inventory Value by Item

Annual Quantity Used	Percentage of Total Items	Annual Dollar Purchases	Percentage of Total Purchases
521	4.8	$15,400,000	50.7
574	5.3	6,200,000	20.4
1023	9.4	3,600,000	11.8
1145	10.5	2,300,000	7.6
3754	34.0	1,800,000	5.9
3906	36.0	1,100,000	3.6
10,923	100.0	$30,400,000	100.0

[1]The percentages are somewhat arbitrary and vary to suit individual needs.

Johnson & Johnson's Devro Division uses very expensive, complex machinery in a 24-hour, seven-day continuous process to produce sausage casings for food processors in the United States, England, Australia, Canada, and Germany (Flowers and O'Neill 1978). To keep the equipment working and quickly repair any breakdowns, Devro maintains a large, expensive stock of more than 1000 spare parts. Previously, parts were ordered from a routine check of the stock-room, which resulted in excesses of some parts and shortages of others. For the shortages, air freight was used to expedite the deliveries, since normal lead times were too long.

To gain better control over these parts, Devro implemented a more formal inventory control, based on the ABC approach. To initiate the study, data were collected on each of the 1337 spare parts and a standard ABC analysis was conducted. The result was that 33 items were identified as class A (representing about 50 percent of total annual dollar usage), 330 items as class B (representing 35 percent of usage), and the remaining 974 items as class C.

The A and B items were placed on perpetual inventory cards, and traveling requisitions were prepared for them beforehand. For traveling requisitions, departmental approval was required only once a year, so the requisition could go directly to purchasing for ordering.

The result has been a reduction in air freight charges of 46 percent and item-ordering time from three days to one day. The frequency of ordering the wrong part has also been reduced, and since all the necessary information is on the requisition, the crib room attendant is saving an hour a day. Last, owing to the consolidation of information, parts are now being ordered from the lowest-cost supplier and competitive bids are being sought on the items most frequently used.

The ABC concept is not only used for inventory control but is also frequently used to determine priorities for customer service and to decide on levels of safety stock. The concept is also known by other names, such as the *80–20 rule* and the *Pareto principle* (after the economist who discovered the effect).

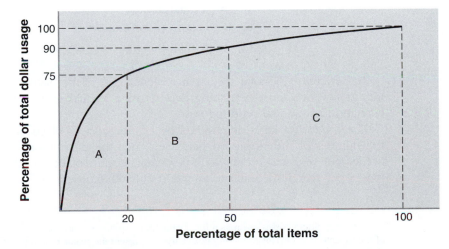

Figure 8.5 ABC inventory categories.

$\mathcal{T}$HE ECONOMIC ORDER QUANTITY (EOQ) _____

The concept of *economic order quantity* (EOQ) applies to inventory items that are replenished in *batches* or *orders* and are not produced and delivered continuously. Although we have identified a number of costs associated with inventory decisions, only two categories, carrying cost and ordering cost, are considered in the basic EOQ model. Shortage costs and opportunity costs are not relevant because shortages and changes in capacity should not occur if demand is constant, as we assume in this basic case. The cost of the goods is considered to be fixed and, hence, does not alter the decisions as to *when* inventory should be reordered or *how much* should be ordered.

More specifically, we assume the following in the basic EOQ model:

1. Rate of demand is constant (e.g., 50 units per day).

2. Shortages are not allowed.

3. Lead times are known with certainty, so stock replenishment can be scheduled to arrive exactly when the inventory drops to zero.

4. Purchase price, ordering cost, and per-unit holding cost are independent of quantity ordered.

5. Items are ordered independently of each other.

Let us return to the water distributor example discussed earlier, which sells 1000 5-gallon bottles per month (30 days) and purchases in quantities of 2000 per order. Lead time for the receipt of an order is six days. The cost accounting department has analyzed inventory costs and has determined that the cost of placing an order is $60 and the annual cost of holding one 5-gallon bottle in inventory is $10.[2]

Under its current policy of ordering 2000 per order, what is the water distributor's total annual inventory cost? Its inventory pattern is represented by the "sawtooth" curve of Figure 8.6. For simplicity, let

$$
\begin{aligned}
Q &= \text{order quantity} \\
U &= \text{annual usage} \\
C_O &= \text{cost to place one order} \\
C_H &= \text{annual holding cost per unit}
\end{aligned}
$$

To determine the total annual incremental cost of the distributor's current inventory policy, we must determine two separate annual costs: total annual holding cost and total annual ordering cost.

The *ordering* cost is determined by C_O, the cost to place one order ($60), and the number of orders placed per year. Since the distributor sells 12,000 5-gallon bottles per year and orders 2000 per order, it must place six (that is, 12,000/2000) orders per year, for a total ordering cost of $360 (6 orders per year $\times$ $60 per order).

_____

[2]Sometimes holding cost is given as a fixed value per year and other times as a percentage of the value of the inventory, especially when interest charges represent the major holding costs. Then holding cost $C_H = iC$, where C is the cost of the inventory item and i is the interest rate.

Using our notation, we write the annual ordering cost as

$$\text{annual ordering cost} = \frac{U}{Q} \times C_O$$

The annual holding cost is determined by C_H, the cost of holding one five-gallon bottle for one year ($10), and the number of bottles held as "cycle stock." Notice that the inventory level is constantly changing and that no single bottle ever remains in inventory for an entire year. On average, however, there are 1000 bottles in the inventory. Consider one cycle of the distributor's inventory graph, as shown in Figure 8.7. The inventory level begins at 2000 units and falls to 0 units before the next cycle begins. Since the rate of decline in inventory is constant (i.e., 1000 per month), the average level is 1000 units, or simply the arithmetic average of the two levels: $(2000 + 0)/2 = 1000$.

If, on the average, there are 1000 bottles in inventory over the entire year, then the annual inventory holding cost is $10,000 ($10 per unit × 1000 units). Or, in our general notation,

$$\text{annual holding cost} = \frac{Q}{2} \times C_H$$

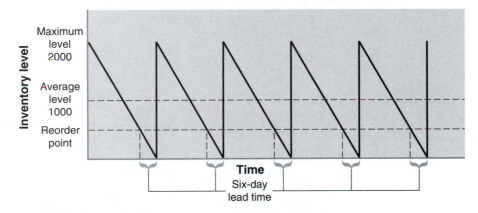

Figure 8.6   Water distributor's inventory pattern.

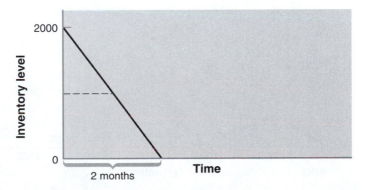

Figure 8.7   Water distributor's inventory graph.

Adding annual ordering cost and annual holding cost gives the following equation for total annual cost (TAC):

$$\text{TAC} = \left(\frac{U}{Q}\right) C_O + \left(\frac{Q}{2}\right) C_H$$

For the water distributor, TAC is \$360 + \$10,000 = \$10,360. Thus, its current inventory policy of ordering quantities of 2000 bottles is costing \$10,360 per year. Is this the best policy, or can it be improved?

Finding an Optimal Policy

We can graph annual holding cost and annual ordering cost as a function of the order quantity, as shown in Figure 8.8. Since the annual holding cost is $(Q/2)C_H$, which can be written $(C_H/2)Q$, we see that holding cost is linear and increasing with respect to Q. Annual order cost is $(U/Q)C_O$, which can be rewritten as $(UC_O)/Q$. We can see that ordering cost is nonlinear with respect to Q and decreases as Q increases.

Now, if we add the two graphed quantities for all values of Q, we have the TAC curve shown in Figure 8.8. Note that TAC first decreases as ordering cost decreases but then starts to increase quickly. The point at which TAC is minimized is the optimal order quantity; that is, it gives the quantity Q that provides the least total

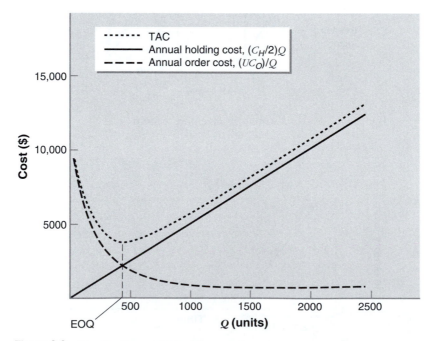

Figure 8.8   Graph of annual inventory costs.

annual inventory cost. This point is called the *economic order quantity* (EOQ), and for this inventory problem it happens to occur where the order cost curve intersects the holding cost curve. (The minimum point is not *always* where two curves intersect; it just happens to be so in the case of EOQ.) From Figure 8.8 we can see that EOQ is approximately 400 bottles per order.

We can compute an accurate value algebraically by noting that the value of Q at the point of intersection of the two cost lines is the EOQ. We can find an equation for EOQ by setting the two costs equal to one another and solving for the value of Q:

$$EOQ = \sqrt{\frac{2UC_O}{C_H}}$$

For the water distributor, we can compute EOQ as

$$EOQ = \sqrt{\frac{2(12,000)60}{10}} = \sqrt{144,000} = 379.6$$

Obviously, since we cannot order a fraction of a bottle, the order quantity would be rounded to 380 units.

The total annual cost (TAC) of this policy would be

$$TAC = \left(\frac{12,000}{380}\right)60 + \frac{380}{2}\,10 = 1894.74 + 1900 = \$3794.74$$

Note that this is an improvement in total annual cost of $6,565.26 over the present policy of ordering 2000. Actual inventory situations often exhibit relative "insensitivity" to changes in quantity in the vicinity of EOQ. To the inventory manager, what this means is added flexibility in order quantities. If, for example, shipping and handling was more convenient or economical in quantities of 500 (perhaps the items are shipped on pallets in quantities of 250), the additional 120 units per order would cost the organization only an extra $145.26 per year.

Cautions Regarding EOQ

The EOQ is a computed minimum-cost order quantity. As with any model or formula, the GIGO rule (garbage in, garbage out) applies. If the values used in computing EOQ are inaccurate, then EOQ will be inaccurate—though, as mentioned previously, a slight error will not increase costs significantly. EOQ relies heavily on two variables that are subject to considerable misinterpretation. These are the two cost elements: holding cost (C_H) and order cost (C_O). In the derivation of EOQ, we assumed that by ordering fewer units per order, the cost of holding inventory would be reduced. Similarly, it was assumed that by reducing the number of orders placed each year the cost of ordering could be proportionately reduced. Both assumptions must be thoroughly questioned in looking at each cost element that is included in both C_H and C_O.

For example, if a single purchasing agent is employed by the firm, and orders are reduced from 3000 per year to 2000 per year, does it stand to reason that the purchasing expense will be reduced by one-third? Unless the person is paid on a piecework basis, the answer is clearly no. Similarly, suppose we rent a warehouse that will hold 100,000 items and that we currently keep it full. If the order sizes are reduced so that the warehouse is only 65 percent occupied, can we persuade the owners to charge us only 65 percent of the rental price? Again, the answer is no. Clearly, then, when costs are determined for computations, only real, out-of-pocket costs should be used. Costs that are committed or "sunk," no matter what the inventory level or number of orders is, should be excluded.

Note also that C_H and C_O are *controllable* costs. That is, they can be reduced, if this is advantageous. This is exactly what the Japanese recognized. The problems they saw with holding inventory were:

- Product defects become hidden in the inventory, thereby increasing scrap and rework later in the production system, when defects are harder to repair. Just as important, the problem in the system that led to the defective part cannot be tracked down so easily later.

- Storage space takes up precious room and separates all the company's functions and equipment, thereby increasing problems with communication. Space itself is extremely expensive in Japan (directly increasing the variable C_H).

- More inventory in the plant means that more control is needed, more planning is required, larger systems are required to move all that stock, and in general more "hassle" is created, which leads to errors, defects, missed deliveries, long lead times, and more difficulty in product changeovers.

Rarely do U.S. firms consider these real costs in the EOQ formula. More typically, these costs are considered part of the indirect, overhead, or "burden" costs that are assumed to be uncontrollable. Again, the message is: Be very careful about the values used in the EOQ formula.

Also, it should be noted that very small EOQ values (e.g., 2) will not usually be valid, because the cost functions are questionable for such small orders. Last, EOQ reorder sizes should not be followed blindly. There may not be enough cash just now to pay for an EOQ, or storage space may be insufficient.

The Economic Production Quantity (EPQ) Model

The **economic production quantity** (EPQ) model is used when the replenishment does not arrive exactly as the inventory drops to zero. Rather, in these cases the inventory level is built up gradually as the product is produced internally. Thus, with its assumption of instantaneous replenishment, the EOQ model is more appropriate for situations in which the product is purchased, whereas the EPQ model is appropriate for situatuions in which the product is made in-house. With internal products, the inventory level is gradually increased as additional units of the product are completed. Also, with internally produced items, an equipment setup cost (C_S) is incurred as oposed to an ordering cost (C_O). The inventory pattern is shown in Figure 8.9.

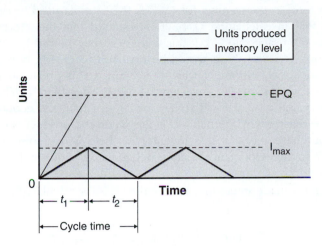

Figure 8.9   Inventory pattern for internally produced items.

Notice in Figure 8.9 that in the EPQ model the maximum level of inventory (I_{max}) is less than the production quantity, because the product is being used to meet customers' demand as it is being produced. In the basic EOQ model, I_{max} is equal to the EOQ, since the order arrives all at once just as the inventory level drops to zero.

In Figure 8.9, one inventory cycle takes $t_1 + t_2$ time units. This cycle consists of two parts: the period when the product is being made (i.e., from time 0 to time t_1), and the period from time t_1 to time $t_1 + t_2$ when production has ceased and inventory is being used to meet demand. The length of t_1 and t_2 depends on the production rate (P) and usage rate (U). In the formulas below we use Q_{EPQ} to distinguish the EPQ from the economic order quantity Q.

$$t_1 = \frac{Q_{EPQ}}{P}$$

$$t_2 = \frac{I_{max}}{U}$$

$$\text{Cycle time} = t_1 + t_2 = \frac{Q_{EPQ}}{U}$$

In summary, t_1 is the time required to produce Q_{EPQ} units given a production rate of P; t_2 is the time it takes to use up the accumulated inventory given a usage rate U; and cycle time ($t_1 + t_2$) is the time it takes to use up the Q_{EPQ} units produced. Note that t_1 is often referred to as the *run time*.

To use these formulas, we need Q_{EPQ} and I_{max}. Here we simply present the formulas for the EPQ and I_{max} and note that they can be derived using elementary calculus and geometry.

$$Q_{EPQ} = \sqrt{\frac{2UC_S}{C_H}}\sqrt{\frac{P}{P-U}}, \text{ and}$$

$$I_{max} = \frac{Q_{EPQ}}{P}(P-U)$$

The first term in the formula for Q_{EPQ} is the formula used to calculate the EOQ. Also, note that in calculating Q_{EPQ}, it is assumed that the production rate (P) is greater than the usage rate (U). If this were not true, the product would have to be produced nonstop and there would be no need to decide how much should be produced once the equipment was set up. Since P is greater than U, the second term in the formula for Q_{EPQ} will always be greater than 1. Thus the economic production quantity (Q_{EPQ}) will always be greater than the economic order quantity (Q). The reason why the batch is larger when the product is made, as opposed to being purchased, is that less inventory is held, since some of the product is being used to meet demand as it is being made. Thus it is less expensive to produce more.

For products made internally, total annual cost is calculated as

$$\text{TAC} = \left(\frac{I_{max}}{2} \right) C_H + \left(\frac{U}{Q_{EPQ}} \right) C_S$$

$\mathcal{R}$EORDER POINT (ROP) MODELS

The EOQ and EPQ models address the second fundamental question about inventory: how much to order. We now focus our attention on the first fundamental question and consider the issue of when to place an order. More specifically, in this section we overview reorder point (ROP) models that address the issue of when to order in situations where there is uncertain demand over multiple periods.

Before we present the reorder point model, the concepts of safety stock and service level must be addressed. Safety stocks are inventories maintained to reduce the chances of a stockout. Safety stocks are needed because demand during the lead time (DDLT) can vary, as can the lead time itself; thus there is a chance of exhausting the inventory while waiting for it to be resupplied.

Service level is the portion of demand that is met with on-hand inventory. Service level can be measured in a variety of ways, such as the *percentage of orders* that can be filled with on-hand inventory or the *percentage of demanded items* that are shipped from on-hand inventory. There is an important relationship between safety stock and service level: Safety stock is held to achieve the desired service level set by management.

Figure 8.10 illustrates the ROP model. The expected demand during lead time is Q_1 units. At time A, on-hand inventory is equal to Q_1 plus the safety stock. The safety stock is carried only as an insurance policy against unexpected high demand during the lead time or unexpected delays in the lead time. Thus, we don't expect to use any of it. Since we are not expecting to use any of the safety stock, point A represents the ROP because the amount of inventory on-hand is equal to the expected demand during lead time. In other words, if we place a replenishment order when the on-hand inventory reaches Q_1 plus the safety stock, then the replenishment order should arrive just as Q_1 units are used up and only the safety stock remains. In Figure 8.10, the replenishment order arrives at time B. The expected lead time is the amount of time between points A and B.

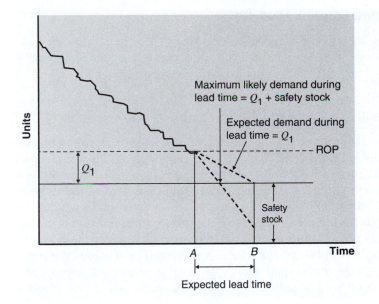

Figure 8.10 Reorder point (ROP) model.

For the purpose of discussing ROP models, it is helpful to distinguish four scenarios as follows:

	Constant lead time	Variable lead time
Constant demand	scenario 1	scenario 3
Variable demand	scenario 2	scenario 4

The following notation will be used:

u = demand rate when demand is constant

$\bar{\mu}$ = average demand rate when demand can vary

σ_u = standard deviation of demand when demand varies

LT = lead time when lead time is constant

$\overline{LT}$ = average lead time when lead time can vary

σ_{LT} = standard deviation of lead time when lead time varies

In general, ROP is calculated as:

ROP = expected demand during lead time + safety stock
    = usage rate × lead time + safety stock

Constant Demand and Constant Lead Time

In situations where both demand and lead time are constant, there is no uncertainty and therefore no need to carry safety stock. Thus, ROP is calculated as

$$\text{ROP} = \text{usage rate} \times \text{lead time} = u(LT)$$

Variable Demand and Constant Lead Time

In situations where the demand rate varies, inventory can be carried over and above the expected demand during lead time to guard against unexpectedly high demand during this period. As we discussed earlier, such inventory is referred to as safety stock. Often, the demand during lead time is assumed to be normally distributed, as shown in Figure 8.11. Given this distribution of demand, management must determine a desired service level. The service level represents the probability of meeting all demand during lead time. Since the area under the normal curve sums up to 1, the probability of stockout is represented by 1 minus the service level.

Once the desired service level is specified, an appropriate value of z can be found from a standard normal table such as the one given in Appendix A. For example, suppose management desires a 97 percent service level. Using the table in Appendix A, we find a value as close as possible to 0.97 and then determine the z-value for it. The number closest to 0.97 is 0.9699, which corresponds to a z-value of 1.88. In essence, a z-value of 1.88 means that to provide a 97 percent service level, we must carry an extra 1.88 standard deviations of demand in safety stock.

On the basis of this intuition, the ROP for situations with variable demand and constant lead time is calculated as

$$\text{ROP} = \bar{u}LT + z\sqrt{LT}\,(\sigma_u)$$

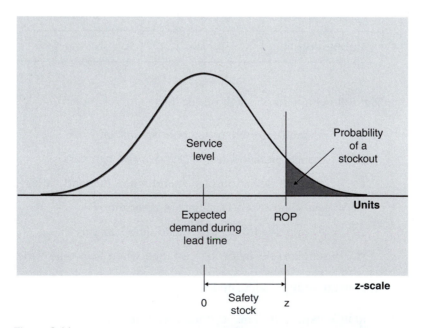

Figure 8.11   Determining ROP assuming normal distribution for demand during lead time.

In this equation, the first term represents the expected demand during lead time. The second represents the safety stock. Note that $\sqrt{LT}\,(\sigma_u)$ is the standard deviation of demand during lead time. Thus, when this quantity is multiplied by the appropriate z-value, the safety stock represents z standard deviations of demand during lead time.

Constant Demand and Variable Lead Time

In scenario 2, demand varied while lead time was assumed to be constant. In these cases, safety stock can be held to guard against unexpectedly high demand during the lead time. In scenario 3, we reverse our previous assumptions and assume that demand is constant but the lead time varies. Here, safety stock can be held to guard against extended lead times, that is, unexpected delays in the receipt of a replenishment order. When demand is constant and lead time varies, the ROP is calculated as

$$\text{ROP} = u(\overline{LT}) + z(\mu)\sigma_{LT}$$

Variable Demand and Variable Lead Time

Perhaps most realistic are situations in which both demand and lead time can vary. In these cases both sources of variation have to be "pooled" together to get a single measure of overall variation in demand during lead time (DDLT). Without going into detail, we simply note that the formula for calculating the overall variation of demand during lead time in this situation is based on the product of two independent variables (demand and lead time). The overall standard deviation of demand during lead time is calculated as

$$\sigma_{DDLT} = \sqrt{\overline{LT}\sigma_\mu^2 + \bar{\mu}^2\sigma_{LT}^2}$$

On this basis, the ROP for situations in which both demand and lead time vary is calculated as

$$\text{ROP} = \bar{\mu}(\overline{LT}) + z(\sigma_{DDLT})$$

EXPAND YOUR UNDERSTANDING

1. Do any of the five functions and four forms of inventories exist in service firms? If so, which ones, and why? If not, how are the functions served?

2. Contrast the functions and forms of inventories. Does every form exist for each function and vice versa, or are some more common?

3. How do you make the actual decision about identifying A and B items when you have the list of total annual inventory values? How do you decide where to draw the line? Is the process different from deciding between grades of A or B in a university class?

4. Suppose you determine an EOQ for a situation but you know the value is too low to last until the next time supplies arrive. What should you do? Should you order two EOQs?

5. What inflexibilities are forced on service organizations as a result of their inability to inventory their output? Which of the five inventory costs are avoided?

6. What costs go up if buffer and decoupling inventories (and their costs) are eliminated? What steps can be taken to control these additional costs?

7. Why is the largest cost in inventory—the cost of the goods themselves—not considered in the EOQ model?

8. Discuss the limitations of the EOQ model. Is certainty in demand and lead time a reasonable assumption?

9. Grocery stores have traditionally used periodic review for inventory control. What type of system can be maintained with the automatic sensing equipment at checkout counters?

10. What is the major difference between the EOQ and EPQ models?

11. What way of measuring service level do you think management would prefer?

APPLY YOUR UNDERSTANDING
Delta Products Inc.

Delta Products, of Groningen, The Netherlands, makes a line of door hardware including doorknob sets and deadbolts. Its product line is particularly well known for excellent quality, a high level of security, and ease of installation.

Delta hired Nikki Scott, a first-year MBA concentrating in operations management, for one of its summer internships. Her task was to spend the summer analyzing the operation and usage of the large transfer press, the plant's current bottleneck machine. The transfer press stamps out the doorknobs used in Delta's door hardware and is available 2000 hours per year for this task. At the end of the summer, in a report to the department manager and plant manager, Nikki was to submit her recommendations for improving the operation of the transfer press.

Nikki spent the first week familiarizing herself with the operation of the transfer press by observing and questioning the machine operator. By the end of the first week, she determined that Delta uses six unique doorknobs in its door hardware.

She decided that her next task was to get an estimate of the annual demand for the knobs. She studied Delta's product catalogs and determined which products each knob was used in. Next, she got from the sales manager a copy of a spreadsheet that contained the complete sales figures for each product over the last 3 years. After casually looking over the data, she observed that the sales were remarkably stable over the 3-year period. Nikki added formulas to the spreadsheet to average the sales data over the 3-year period and to calculate the number of knobs of each type that were used.

With her analysis of the demand for knobs completed, Nikki turned her attention to the actual production of the knobs. She spent the next couple of weeks collecting data on the individual processing times of the knobs on the transfer press, the time required to set up the press to produce a new batch of knobs, and the production batch sizes currently being used. She also worked closely with the cost accountant to determine the cost of holding knobs in inventory, and she found that machine operators are paid €15 per hour, including fringe benefits. Nikki summarized the information for her report in the following spreadsheet.

	A	B	C	D	E	F
1			Unit	Setup	Annual	
2		Annual	Processing	time	Holding Cost	Current
3	Item	Demand	Time (hours)	(hours)	(€/unit)	Batch Size
4	Knob A	6000	0.0500	6.2	3.25	1500
5	Knob B	3000	0.0420	4.6	3.85	1500
6	Knob C	7000	0.0400	7.2	2.75	1500
7	Knob D	10,000	0.0380	5.4	3.70	2000
8	Knob E	8400	0.0375	3.8	4.20	1500
9	Knob F	9400	0.0480	6.8	2.25	2000

Her next task was to analyze the information she had compiled and look for ways to improve the operation. Given the information she had available, she began by developing a spreadsheet to calculate the *economic order quantity* (EOQ). She then developed another spreadsheet to compare the *total annual cost* (TAC) of using the current batch sizes with the economic order quantities she calculated. Nikki was extremely pleased when she realized she could save Delta almost €7000 per year in just one department if it adopted her recommended economic order quantities. After rechecking her calculations, she was convinced of the validity of her analysis and couldn't wait to see the plant manager's reaction to her report. She was actually hoping that the plant manager would be impressed enough with her work to offer her a full-time position upon graduation. The final spreadsheet she developed to summarize the potential savings to Delta is shown next.

	A	B	C	D	E
1				TAC	
2		Current	Economic	Current	
3		Batch	Order	Batch	TAC
4	Item	Size	Quantity	Size	EOQ
5	Knob A	1500	586	2810	1904
6	Knob B	1500	328	3026	1262
7	Knob C	1500	741	2567	2039
8	Knob D	2000	662	4105	2448
9	Knob E	1500	477	3469	2005
10	Knob F	2000	923	2729	2077
11					
12	Total			18,705.1	11,736.98
13					
14	Annual Savings			€6,968.12	

On the Monday of her last week, Nikki met with the plant manager, Joe Thomas, and the press department manager, Mike Willis. After complimenting Nikki on a very thorough and well-written report, Joe asked Mike what his reaction was. Mike commented:

> I also was very impressed with the thoroughness of Nikki's analysis. The data that she collected on setup times, production times, and holding costs are the best data we have ever had about our operations. Unfortunately, while I have not had a chance to thoroughly run the numbers, I think there is a problem with Nikki's analysis. Her analysis requires significant reductions in our batch sizes. While I agree that we could save money by cutting the batch sizes, the fact of the matter is that the transfer press she analyzed is one of our major bottlenecks. We are currently using every second of the 2000 hours we have available on the machine. Cutting the lot sizes as Nikki has suggested will require more setups, and we simply don't have the time for additional setups.

Nikki was quite distraught by the outcome of the meeting. She still had a week left in her internship, and she desperately wanted to salvage the work she had spent an entire summer working on. She was determined to spend her final week finding a way to save Delta money while at the same time not exceeding its available capacity.

Questions

1. Verify Nikki's calculations of the economic order quantity and total annual cost.
2. Is Mike's intuition correct—that using Nikki's economic order quantities will exceed the 2000 hours of capacity available on the transfer press?
3. Are there any opportunities for Delta to save money without exceeding its available capacity?
4. Does the fact that the doorknobs are produced internally versus being purchased from an outside supplier have any impact on the optimal course of action in this situation?

EXERCISES

1. Categorize the following inventory-related expenses as to cost type and probable relevance in an inventory model to determine the best order size: postage, warehouse rent, purchase order forms, secretarial labor (writing orders), warehouse guard, interest cost of money, costs of the goods, distribution cost per unit, receiving cost for raw materials, ill will for lost sales, warehouse heating, advertising, expediting costs to meet due dates, president's salary, fire insurance on finished goods.

2. Categorize the following inventory items as type A, B, or C.

Unit Cost ($)	Annual Usage (units)
10,000	4
7000	1
4000	13
1200	5
700	500
300	20
250	45
60	5000
27	400
17	4000
9	1000
7	8000
3	750
2	4000
1	12,000

3. Frame-Up, a self-service picture framing shop for tourists in Sevilla, Spain, orders 3000 meters of a certain molding every month. The order cost is €40 and the holding cost is €0.05 per meter per year. What is the current annual inventory cost? What is the maximum inventory level? What is the EOQ?

4. The Corner Convenient Store (CCS) in northern Chicago, USA receives orders from its distributor in three days from the time an order is placed. Light Cola sells at the rate of 860 cans per day. (It can sell 250 days of the year.) A six-pack of Light Cola costs CCS $1.20. Annual holding cost is 10 percent of the cost of the cola. Order cost is $25.00. What is CCS's EOQ, and what is the reorder point?

5. It is time to consider reordering material in a periodic review inventory system. The inventory on hand is 100 units, maximum desired level of inventory is 250 units, usage rate is 10 units a day, reorder period is every two weeks (10 working days), lead time for resupply is 15 days, and amount on order is 250 units. How much should be ordered?

6. A Liverpool, England camera supplies wholesaler purchases £1 million worth of camera equipment each year. It costs £100 to place and receive an order, and the annual holding cost per item is 20 percent of the item's value.
   a. What is the £ value of the EOQ?
   b. How many months' supply is the EOQ?
   c. How often should orders be placed?
   d. How much will the annual holding cost change if the company orders monthly? How much will the annual ordering cost change?
   e. What should the £ value of the EOQ be if the wholesaler doubles its annual purchases? What should it be if (instead) the ordering cost doubles? What should it be if the holding cost drops to 10 percent?

7. Wing Computer Corporation of Xiamen, China uses 15,000 keyboards each year in the production of computer terminals for major computer manufacturers headquartered in Taiwan. Order cost for the keyboards is 50 renminbi and the holding cost for one keyboard is 1.5 renminbi per unit per year. What is the EOQ? If Wing orders 1250 per month, what will be the total annual cost? What is the average inventory level?

8. Gaming, Inc., has the capacity to produce 25,000 slot machines per year. Demand has been stable over the last few years at about 10,000 slot machines per year. It costs the company $250 to set up its production line to produce the slot machines and $35 to hold one slot machine in

inventory for a year. What batch size should be used to produce the slot machine?

9. In Exercise 8, how much would Gaming save annually if it used your batch quantity versus a batch quantity of 750 slot machines?

10. In Exercise 8, what is the maximum inventory level of slot machines that Gaming would accumulate? What are the run and cycle times? Plot the inventory pattern for Gaming.

11. A firm maintains a maximum inventory level of 55 units, has a reorder point of 35 units, and is currently at 15 units with an outstanding order of 30 units. How many units should it order? Suppose its current inventory was 30 units? Assume that demand over the lead time is 5 units.

12. Given: yearly demand = 12,000; carrying cost/unit/year = $1; ordering cost = $15; lead time = 5 days; safety stock = 200; price = $0.10 each. Find the total annual cost of the inventory system under an optimal ordering policy.

13. A law office purchases copier paper from a local office supply company. The lead time is always one day. The law office uses an average of 10 reams of paper a day, with a standard deviation of 1.5 reams. What reorder point should the law

office use if it is willing to accept only a 2.5 percent chance of a stockout?

14. Sam's Song Electronics has a contract to supply the Korean government with 25 computer motherboards each month, with a guaranteed 99 percent service level. The lead time for the boards averages 5 days, with a standard deviation of 0.72 day. What reorder point should be used for the display units?

15. Quarry Company places orders for blasting caps once each month. The order quantity is 500 per month. The purchasing agent has just learned of the EOQ model and wants to try it out. He or she determines that order costs are $1.50 and that holding cost is $8 per cap per year. What is the EOQ? Should the company change its order quantity to the EOQ? Base your answer on economic and practical grounds.

16. Solve Problem 13 using Crystal Ball. How do the results compare?

17. Solve Problem 14 using Crystal Ball. How do the results compare?

18. Resolve Problem 13 assuming the lead time is normally distributed with a standard deviation of 0.5 days. Solve again using Crystal Ball and compare your results.

BIBLIOGRAPHY

Blanchard, D. "RFID is Off and Running at Wal-Mart," *Logistics Today*, 46 (February 2005): pp. 1–2.

Bowers, M. R., and A. Agarwal. "Lower In-Process Inventories and Better On-Time Performance at Tanner Companies, Inc." *Interfaces*, 25 (July–August 1995): 30–43.

Fisher, M. L., J. H. Hammond, W. R. Obermeyer, and A. Raman. "Making Supply Meet Demand in an Uncertain World." *Harvard Business Review*, 72 (May–June 1994): 83–93.

Flowers, A. D., and J. B. O'Neill II. "An Application of Classical Inventory Analysis to a Spare Parts Inventory." *Interfaces* (February 1978): 76–79.

Greene, J. H. *Production and Inventory Control Handbook*, 3rd ed. New York: McGraw-Hill, 1997.

Johnson, J. C., and D. F. Wood. *Contemporary Logistics*, 6th ed. Upper Saddle River, NJ: Prentice Hall, 1996.

Lacy, S. "Inching Toward the RFID Revolution," *Business Week Online*, August 31, 2004.

Landvater, D. V. *World Class Production and Inventory Management*. Newburg, NH: Oliver Wight Publications, 1997.

Lee, H. L., and C. Billington. "Managing Supply Chain Inventory: Pitfalls and Opportunities." *Sloan Management Review*, 33 (Spring 1992): 65–73.

Lieberman, M. B., S. Helper, and L. Dmeester. "The Empirical Determinants of Inventory Levels in High-Volume Manufacturing." *Production and Operations Management*, 8 (Spring 1999): 44–55.

Richardson, H. L., "The Ins & Outs of VMI," *Logistics Today*, 45 (March 2004): 19—21.

Silver, E. A., D. F. Pyke, and R. Peterson. *Inventory Management, Production Planning, and Scheduling*, 3rd ed. New York, Wiley, 1998.

Sipper, D., and R. Bulfin. *Production: Planning, Control, and Integration*. New York: McGraw-Hill (1997).

Vollmann, T. E., W. L. Berry, and D. C. Whybark. *Manufacturing Planning and Control Systems*, 4th ed. Homewood, IL.: Irwin, 1997.

Wild, T. *Best Practices in Inventory Management*. New York: Wiley, 1998.

Zipkin, P. H. *Foundations of Inventory Management*. New York: Irwin/McGraw-Hill, 2000.

CHAPTER 9

Enterprise Resource Planning

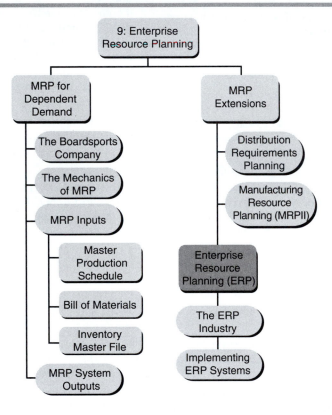

CHAPTER IN PERSPECTIVE

Enterprise resource planning (ERP) systems are the latest innovation in the evolution of systems for coordinating production decisions between different functions within the firm, as well as across functions outside the firm such as those of suppliers and customers. Clearly, ERP systems are a major aspect of the information network required for efficient supply chains and thus have a strategic effect on the organization's ability to deliver value to the customer. The first step in this evolution, however, started with material requirements planning (MRP) systems, which is where we begin our discussion. MRP applies to items that are used to create finished products whose demand is known or can be accurately forecast. As opposed to inventory management, which concerns items whose demand is independent of other items, MRP is used for *dependent* demand items. Although we commonly think of MRP having been created for complex products consisting of many parts and components, it is noteworthy that MRP has been highly effective in services also, including hospitals, hotels, and even NASA. The chapter thus begins with how MRP systems work, the inputs they require, and the outputs they deliver. Following this, the extensions to material requirements planning are discussed, including distribution requirements planning (DRP), manufacturing resource planning (MRP II), and enterprise resource planning (ERP). The chapter concludes with a discussion of the implementation of ERP systems.

INTRODUCTION

- Elf Aquitaine is a diversified French company with interests in petroleum products, chemicals, and pharmaceuticals. After a series of mergers and acquisitions, its Elf Atochem North America chemical subsidiary, a $2 billion company, was experiencing problems with the flow of critical information across and within its 12 business units. In particular, a number of its systems such as ordering and production, and sales forecasting and budgeting were not integrated with one another. Compounding the problem, each of the 12 business units developed a unique approach for tracking and reporting financial data. The result of the poor information flows was that decision makers were not getting the information they needed to make timely business decisions. Furthermore, because its customers often did business with multiple business units, the lack of integration was a frustration to customers as they had to deal with each unit separately—placing separate orders and paying separate invoices, even though from their perspective Elf Atochem was a single company.

  Inside the company, things were not much better. For example, processing an order required seven handoffs between departments. Lack of planning required the frequent shutdown of the production lines to accommodate changes to the production schedule and the need to write off more than $6 million in inventory each year. Sales were lost because representatives could not promise delivery dates, given the lack of integration between the ordering and production systems.

329

To address these problems and better integrate the flows of data, Elf Atochem decided to implement SAP's R/3 ERP system. However, rather than viewing the software rather narrowly as a solution to their current problems, they viewed the software from the perspective of the capabilities it offered, and considered these capabilities in developing the organization's strategy and structure. For example, the accounts receivable and credit departments were combined. In another break from conventional wisdom, Elf Atochem chose to focus on four key processes:
(1) materials management, (2) production planning, (3) order management, and (4) financial reporting, rather than trying to implement ERP across the entire organization.

In terms of actually implementing its ERP system, Elf Atochem decided to implement the system in one business unit at a time. In addition to making the implementation more manageable, key insights were gained in each phase that could be incorporated in later stages. Using this phased implementation approach, Elf Atochem was able to roll out its ERP system ahead of schedule and under budget.

The primary benefit Elf Atochem has achieved is that it now has the real-time information needed to link sales and production planning. However, in addition to operating more effectively, the organization's overall efficiency has also been enhanced. In particular, inventory, labor costs, and distribution expenses have all been reduced. These improvements are expected to translate into operating cost savings in the tens of millions of dollars range (Davenport 1998).

- Ulrich Seif, National Semiconductor's CIO, has a rather nontraditional view of the role of IT. Rather than viewing IT as a support function, Seif views IT as the part of the business that creates technology solutions that in turn position the company to capitalize on business opportunities. According to Seif, technology solutions are needed that provide National with the flexibility to rapidly create new business processes given the current business environment, which requires closer communication and coordination with external business partners. However, until recently, the variety of systems National had in place actually hindered rather than helped the IT department's ability to develop strategic solutions. For example, the time and money being spent maintaining the existing legacy systems left little time or money for new systems development.

To address this problem Seif developed a strategy to replace National's outdated legacy systems. Seif also set a directive that the payback for any new system had to be less than one year. Given this directive, National decided to focus its efforts on three key areas: purchasing, inventory management, and maintenance management. These processes were chosen in part because of the belief that unnecessary costs were being incurred in these areas as a result of each manufacturing plant using a different system. While National considered adopting SAP's R/3 system, and actually ran it on a pilot basis in one plant, Seif felt that the program was too complex. In Seif's own words "The SAP system was a Cadillac, and we found that the plants only needed a Camry." In the end, National chose IFS as its ERP vendor. However, National does use SAP to manage its corporate, financial, and human resource functions.

With the one year payback goal, National decided that the best approach for implementing its ERP system was one plant at a time. The first plant chosen for implementation was in the U.K., and the project was completed in nine months. Next, the ERP system was implemented in a plant in Texas in six months. The system was implemented in three months in the third plant in Maine. Mohammad Ibrahim, director of manufacturing systems, estimated that each of the three plants achieved $1 million in annual savings. Contributing to these savings was replacing a number of outdated legacy systems with a new integrated system, increased uptime on critical equipment due to better maintenance management, and the ability to pool purchase orders across plants, leading to better prices. In addition to these cost savings, decision makers have better visibility of the plant-level operations.

It is also worth noting that National has integrated its IFS ERP system with Workstream, a manufacturing execution system developed by Applied Materials, a purchasing system from Ariba, and i2 Technologies software for demand and production planning. Integrating these packages required the development of middleware to link these systems together. In effect, the middleware allowed the users to get any data they needed. As Seif notes, "Users simply enter a request for data or a request to perform a transaction, and [the middleware] sends that request to the appropriate systems and pulls the appropriate data. All of this cut-and-paste is done in the background, and users are not aware of it. For them, any piece of data is only three seconds away." (Hill 2003).

In this chapter, we continue our discussion of the supply chain in terms of managing the production and supply of dependent-demand items across multiple organizations in the supply chain, and especially the critical information requirements. *Dependent-demand* items are so named because their demand is derived from (depends on) the demand for independent-demand items (usually finished goods). Although the calculations involved in managing dependent-demand items are not very complicated, the quantity of data can be overwhelming. Therefore, materials management systems for dependent-demand items typically require substantial computer resources, especially when the items are being produced across multiple entities, a common application of enterprise resource planning (ERP) systems. We begin our discussion of ERP systems with the predecessor of these systems—material requirements planning (MRP) systems.

MRP systems have been around now for decades and are often embodied in more sophisticated computerized control and information systems such as MRP II systems and enterprise resource planning (ERP) and management systems. The benefits of MRP have been well proven in many kinds of organizations ranging from manufacturers to hospitals to NASA—the space agency.

The biggest benefit of MRP systems is in meeting due dates since they accurately time-phase the acquisition and production of long lead time items needed to assemble or construct the final output. But in the process, they automatically provide information concerning capacity and financial requirements for upcoming periods, and update this information when final demand needs change, hence the evolution to ERP systems. Moreover, they also eliminate waste, improve productivity, and foster higher quality—all highly desirable outcomes in and of themselves.

$\mathscr{MRP}$ FOR DEPENDENT DEMAND _____

Many items, particularly *finished products* such as automobiles, televisions, and cartons of ice cream, are said to experience independent demand. That is, the demand for these items is unrelated to the demand for other items. For instance, in general there is no product that creates a demand for an automobile. However, every time an automobile is demanded, a demand for one steering wheel is created. Thus, the demand for steering wheels depends on and is derived from the demand for automobiles.

Independent demand appears to be random—that is, caused by chance events. Most *raw materials, components*, and *subassemblies* are dependent on demands for these finished goods and other assemblies and subassemblies. Furthermore, independent demand may occur at a constant rate over an inventory cycle. However, these items are usually produced or ordered in batches based on the economic order quantity model. Therefore, when a lot is ordered for production in the factory, all materials and components needed for production are ordered at the same time, creating a "lump" in demand for the dependent-demand items.

Examples of constant and lumpy demands are shown in Figure 9.1. In the case of constant demand, demand varies around the average (shown by the dashed line). Materials requirements planning (MRP) is a system designed specifically for the situation when "lumps" in demand are known about beforehand, typically because the demands are "dependent." For example, in a facility that produces wooden doors, reorders of (finished) doors may be based on a reorder point system. When the number of finished doors on hand reaches a prespecified reorder point, then an order is placed into production on the shop floor. Figure 9.2*a* illustrates this inventory time pattern where the demand for finished doors is relatively constant.

If a reorder point system similar to the one used in managing the inventory of finished doors was used in managing the inventory of lumber used to produce the doors, the pattern shown in Figure 9.2*b* would result. Notice that in Figure 9.2*b* the normal inventory level is X units; when the inventory of finished doors in

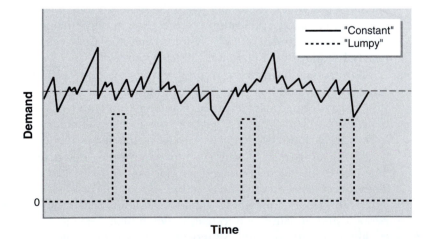

Figure 9.1 Constant and lumpy demands.

Figure 9.2*a* reaches its reorder point and a production order is released to the shop, a requisition for the required quantity of lumber is made against that inventory. The inventory level will drop by the quantity used in producing the lot, thus causing the raw materials inventory to fall below its reorder point. This triggers a reorder for a quantity of lumber, resulting in replenishment of the inventory after its purchase lead time.

As you can see, the average inventory level for the lumber is quite high, and most of this inventory is being held for long periods of time without being used. A logical approach to help lower this level is to anticipate the timing and quantities of demands on the lumber inventory and then schedule purchases to meet this requirement. Figure 9.3 illustrates the results of this anticipation of demand. Figure 9.3*a* illustrates the same pattern of finished-product inventory as Figure 9.2*a*. Figure 9.3*b* depicts the scheduling of receipts of lumber just before the time when it is needed. The impact on average inventory level is obvious. All reorder point systems assume (even though implicitly) that demand for each item in inventory is independent of the demand for other items in the inventory. These systems work well when the assumption holds but work rather poorly for items whose demand is dependent on higher-level items. Materials requirements planning is one method used for dependent inventory items.

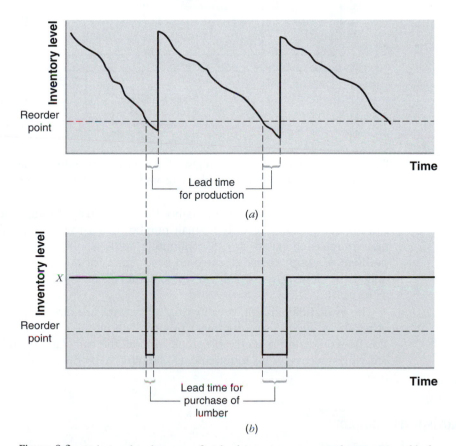

Figure 9.2   Relationship between finished item inventory and raw material/subassembly item inventory—reorder point approach: (*a*) finished doors, (*b*) lumber.

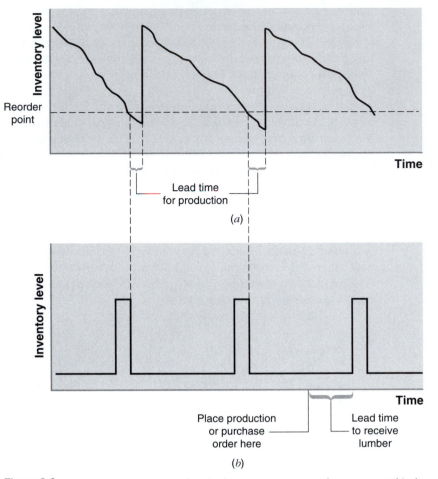

Figure 9.3 Relationship between finished item inventory and raw material/subassembly item inventories—a requirements planning approach: (*a*) finished doors, (*b*) lumber.

However, dependent demand is not the only cause of lumpy demand. Demand can appear in lumps if only a small number of customers exist for the item and their purchasing habits are discontinuous. MRP is not a solution to the general problem of lumpy demand, since no basis exists for developing the materials plan unless the demand is *dependent* on something that a planner can either measure or forecast.

The availability and practicality of MRP systems are directly related to the advent of relatively inexpensive computer power. Without the computer, inventory professionals would simply be unable to perform all the calculations and maintain all the schedules necessary for requirements planning. A simple example will illustrate this point.

The Boardsports Company

The Boardsports Company produces a skateboard known as the Sidewalk Special. Its major components are one fiberglass board and two wheel assemblies. The lead time (measured to the end of the period) to assemble a Special from its two major components is one week. The first component, the board, is purchased and has a 3-week delivery lead time. The second component, the wheel assembly, is assembled by Boardsports. Each wheel assembly is made up (with a 1-week lead time) of one wheel mounting stand (manufactured by Boardsports with a 4-week lead time), two wheels (purchased with a 1-week lead time), one spindle (manufactured by Boardsports with a 2-week lead time), and two chrome-plated locknuts (purchased with a 1-week lead time). The product structure (or **product tree**) is shown in Figure 9.4.

To produce an order for 50 Specials, the material requirements are computed as follows.

$$\text{Fiberglass boards: } 1 \times \text{number (no.) of Specials} = 1 \times 50 = 50$$

$$\text{Wheel assemblies: } 2 \times \text{no. of Specials} = 2 \times 50 = 100$$

$$\text{Wheels: } 2 \times \text{no. of wheel assemblies} = 2 \times 100 = 200$$

$$\text{Spindles: } 1 \times \text{no. of wheel assemblies} = 1 \times 100 = 100$$

$$\text{Wheel mount stand: } 1 \times \text{no. of wheel assemblies} = 1 \times 100 = 100$$

$$\text{Locknut: } 2 \times \text{no. of wheel assemblies} = 2 \times 100 = 200$$

Assume that according to the master schedule, an order for 50 Specials is due to be delivered in 10 weeks. The calendar in Table 9.1 illustrates the timing of due dates and the necessary order dates (assuming the lead times stated earlier) that must be met in order to deliver in the tenth week.

Note that MRP is a highly *logical* system. Knowing that 50 Specials must be shipped at the end of week 10 means that 50 boards must be placed on order for outside procurement at the end of week 6, that an order for 100 mounting stands must be placed in the shop at the end of week 4, and so forth. This is illustrated in the time-scaled assembly chart in Figure 9.5. (In essence, this is the product tree of Figure 9.4 laid on its side, with its components time-scaled to show their lead times.) Ordering in each week what will be needed rather than, say, an EOQ amount, is called **lot-for-lot** ordering.

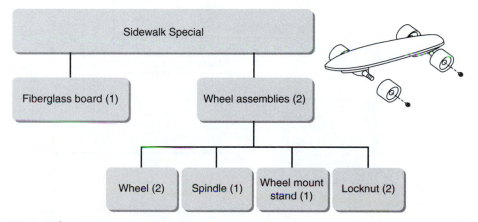

Figure 9.4   Skateboard product tree.

$\mathcal{T}$ABLE   9.1   •   Demand for Sidewalk Specials

| | | \multicolumn{10}{c}{Week} |
		1	2	3	4	5	6	7	8	9	10
Sidewalk Specials											50
Boards	Date needed										50
	Order date							50			
Wheel assembly	Date needed									100	
	Order date							100			
Wheels	Date needed								200		
	Order date						200				
Spindles	Date needed								100		
	Order date					100					
Mounting stands	Date needed								100		
	Order date			100							
Locknuts	Date needed								200		
	Order date						200				

(Boards: 3-week lead time — arrow from Date needed 50 to Order date 50)

Ordering later than these dates would result in late shipment (or working over-time and otherwise expediting the order), and ordering earlier would result in having inventory available (and occupying space, requiring paperwork, and incurring other holding costs) before it is needed (though perhaps at a savings in order costs). MRP looks at each end product and the dates when each is needed. From these due dates, needed dates for all lower-level items are computed, and from these due dates starting or order dates are determined.

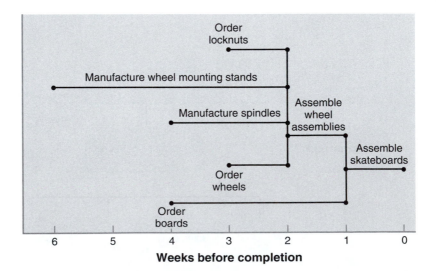

Figure 9.5   Time-scaled assembly chart for skateboard.

The overall idea is simple, but consider the extreme complexity of operating an MRP system manually. In this simple example, with only one end product, the calculations and record keeping are straightforward. But for a large firm that manufactures hundreds of end items with thousands of intermediate components, only a computer can keep up with the processing volume.

This is an important point because MRP is not a revolutionary idea. The basic idea has been around for some time. It is and has been practiced for construction projects (from a single house to a mammoth skyscraper) that are scheduled according to a philosophy of having "the right materials to the right place at the right time." MRP has come of age in manufacturing and assembly operations because large-scale and relatively inexpensive computer power is available.

The Mechanics of MRP

Materials requirements planning is a management system for production and inventory. As such, it requires information about both production and inventory in order to produce its primary output—a schedule or plan for orders, both released and pending, which specifies actions to be taken now and in the future. Figure 9.6 illustrates the flows of information within an MRP system and indicates three primary inputs to the MRP system:

1. Master production schedule
2. Bill of materials file
3. Inventory master file

A major output from the MRP computer system is the planned order release report, although other reports—on changes, exceptions, and deexpediting—are also outputs.

Figure 9.6 shows in detail a portion of Figure 6.1. Here we are not concerned with the aggregate plan or the production plan, and the demand forecast is passed right through the master production schedule, which feeds the MRP system. However, MRP also requires other inputs that are not related to the major scheduling

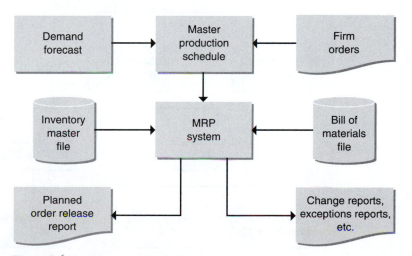

Figure 9.6   Schematic of MRP system.

functions shown in Figure 6.1, such as current inventory levels and bills of material for the products. The MRP output reports shown in Figure 9.6 are, then, the inputs to the capacity planning function shown in Figure 6.1.

The relationship between materials planning and operations scheduling is, of necessity, intimate. Any attempts to design these two systems so that they operate independently will either fail outright or, at best, be grossly inefficient.

MRP Inputs

As already indicated, the MRP inputs are the master production schedule, the bill of materials file, and the inventory master file.

Master Production Schedule

As discussed in Chapter 6, the master production schedule is based on actual customer orders and predicted demand. This schedule indicates exactly when each end item will be produced to meet the firm and predicted demand. That is, it is a time-phased production plan for all end items.

Bill of Materials

For each item in the master production schedule, there is a **bill of materials** (BOM). The bill of materials file indicates all the raw materials, components, subassemblies, and assemblies required to produce an item. The MRP computer system accesses the bill of materials file to determine exactly what items, and in what quantities, are required to complete an order for a given item.

Rather than simply listing all the parts necessary to produce one finished product, the BOM shows the way a finished product is put together from individual items, components, and subassemblies. For example, the product structure illustrated in Figure 9.7 would generate the BOM illustrated in Figure 9.8.

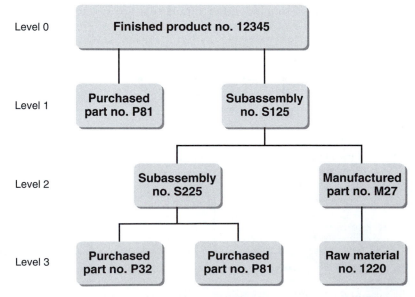

Figure 9.7 Product tree structure.

Level 1 Parts	Level 2 Parts	Level 3 Parts	Description	Quantity	Source
No. P81				1	Purchased
No. S125				1	Manufactured
	No. S225			1	Manufactured
		No. P32		1	Purchased
		No. P81		2	Purchased
	No. M27			1	Manufactured
		No. 1220		3	Purchased

Figure 9.8 Bill of materials (BOM) for a three-level product.

This BOM shows the finished product (sometimes called the ***parent item***) at the highest, or *zero*, level. Subassemblies and parts that go directly into the assembly of the finished product are called level 1 components, parts and subassemblies that go into level 1 components are shown as level 2, and so on. Thus, when a master production schedule shows a requirement for a given quantity of finished products for a certain due date, production planners can ***explode*** the BOM for that finished product to determine the number, due dates, and necessary order dates of subcomponents.

Exploding a BOM simply means stepping down through all its levels and determining the quantity and lead time for each item required to make up the item at that level. Note that if some items are manufactured internally, their lead time will be a function of the number of items to be produced rather than a fixed period, possibly requiring an adjustment to the MRP inputs. The result of exploding a BOM for a given product is a time-phased requirement for specific quantities of each item necessary to make the finished product. In some cases, it may happen that when the BOM is exploded we will find out that the lead time to obtain the needed components is so long that we are already behind schedule in ordering the parts. Then, if we are to meet the demand, we must expedite or take some other action to meet the demands at the various levels. We exploded an order for skateboards earlier in Table 9.1, although we had not formally introduced the notion of a bill of materials. If the mounting stands in the table had an 8-week lead time instead of 4 weeks, we would not be able to meet the demand for 50 Sidewalk Specials in week 10. A great deal of the time required to implement an MRP system is spent restructuring BOMs (so that they can be exploded properly) and verifying their accuracy. Clearly, exploding incorrect BOMs will only cause trouble further downstream.

Note in Figures 9.7 and 9.8 that purchased part No. P81 is used as both a level 1 and a level 3 component and is specifically identified in both locations in the product tree and bill of materials. Purchased part No. P81 could perhaps be a stainless steel nut and bolt assembly used to produce subassembly No. S225 and to complete the assembly of the finished product 12345 by being put together with subassembly No. S125. We do not aggregate the number of P81s used to produce a single finished product (i.e., we do not show part No. P81 as requiring 3 to produce finished product No. 12345), because aggregating would not allow us to identify the specific number of P81s necessary to produce a lot of S225 subassemblies. It would also preclude knowing how many P81s would be necessary to complete final assembly of S125 subassemblies into finished products.

Inventory Master File

The inventory master file contains detailed information regarding the number or quantity of each item on hand, on order, and committed to use in various time periods. The MRP system accesses the inventory master computer file to determine the quantity available for use in a given time period, and if enough are available to meet the needs of the order, it commits these for use during the time period by updating the inventory record. If sufficient items are not available, the system includes this item, as well as the usual lot size, on the planned order release report.

MRP System Outputs

Three specific outputs of the MRP system constitute the plan of action for released and pending orders:

1. Order action report
2. Open orders report
3. Planned-order release report

The *order action report* indicates which orders are to be released during the current time period and which orders are to be canceled. The *open orders report* shows which orders are to be expedited or deexpedited. This report is an exception report, listing only those open orders for which action is necessary. The *planned-order release report* is the time-phased plan for orders to be released in future time periods. It is this report, along with the open orders report, that determines whether or not a master production schedule is feasible. As noted earlier, it may happen that the lead time offsets back up past the current point in time, indicating that the schedule is infeasible and expediting or some other action will be necessary to satisfy the MRP demands.

$\mathcal{MRP}$ EXTENSIONS _____

Next, let us look at some derivatives of the MRP procedure.

Distribution Requirements Planning

The concept of **distribution requirements planning** (DRP) was discussed earlier in Chapter 7 and illustrated in Figure 7.3, where retailers order from local warehouses, and so on. By applying MRP to the distribution function, these demands are anticipated and orders are released ahead of time to avoid stockouts and their resultant high follow-on inventories. As with MRP, when we offset the multiple lead times of the various levels, we may find that the factory order date is already in the past and, hence, we are going to have a stockout unless we expedite or take other action. This offsetting process is shown in Table 9.2; note how on-hand inventory is handled in the DRP (and MRP also) process. In the appropriate distribution environment, factory orders are built up from lower levels in the distribution network, which provides significant advantages in scheduling and coordination. The DRP process is, however, vulnerable to poor forecasts at the

$\mathscr{T}_{\text{ABLE}}$ 9.2 • The DRP Process

Local warehouse A				Local warehouse B				

Week	11	12	13	14	15	16	17	18	19	
Carton requirements			83	16		17				
On hand	90	90	90	7	21	21	4	4	4	Regional center I
Net requirement				9						(1 week lead time
Planned receipts				30						Order size: 30)
Planned releases			30							

									Regional centre II

Week	11	12	13	14	15	16	17	18	19	
Carton requirements			30			60				Central distribution
On hand	10	10	10	30	30	30	20	20	20	facility
Net requirement			20			30				(1 week lead time
Planned receipts			50			50				Order size: 50)
Planned releases		50			50					

Week	11	12	13	14	15	16	17	18	19	
Carton requirements		50			50					Factory
On hand	90	90	40	40	40	190	190	190	190	(2 week lead time
Net requirement					10					Order size: 200)
Planned receipts					200					
Planned releases			200							

lower levels. If local forecasts are incorrect, then demands placed on the factory will also be incorrect, and either excess stock, at an unnecessary cost, or shortages will result.

Manufacturing Resource Planning (MRP II)

When the scheduling activities illustrated in Figure 6.1 are computerized and tied in with purchasing, accounting, sales, engineering, and other such functional areas, the result is known as *manufacturing resource planning* (MRP II). A typical MRP II system is illustrated in Figure 9.9. The forecast and actual customer orders come into the master schedule, which drives the production system. Another major input to the production system is the engineering database, which includes bills of materials, engineering designs, drawings, and other such information required to manufacture and assemble the product.

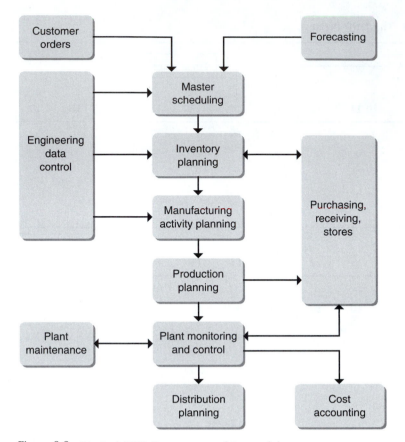

Figure 9.9 Typical MRP II systems and its modules.

At the bottom of Figure 9.9 is the actual build stage, where plant monitoring and control operates. This function receives additional information and gives information to plant maintenance. Cost accounting data are also collected at this stage. The process is completed with distribution requirements planning.

Clearly, all other company functions can also be tied to this system. Finance, knowing when items will be purchased and when products will be delivered, can properly project cash flows. Human resources (personnel) can similarly project requirements for hiring (and layoffs). And marketing can determine up-to-date customer delivery times, lead times, and so on.

A number of MRP II software packages are available, for all sizes of computers. Many, such as Micro-MRP, now run on microcomputers. Each package operates in basically the same manner. First, it takes the sales forecast and basic engineering data for each product and, using an MRP subsystem, develops the time-phased materials requirements. Once this information is available, the purchasing, capacity planning, and operations scheduling modules take over to produce purchase-order requirements, route the product through operations, generate capacity requirements by individual operations, and load and schedule operations for production.

Requirements-based scheduling systems such as MRP II require a computer system for implementation because of their relatively large scale and complexity. The role of the computer is extremely important here. Again, the concept of requirements-based scheduling is not novel; it simply was previously too cumbersome to pursue in a clerically oriented system. Construction management has for years recognized the need for detailed requirements planning and scheduling. If material, labor, or equipment was at the job site in the wrong sequence or at the wrong time, not only would bottlenecks be unending, but wasted time and material losses from weather damage and theft would raise the cost of construction to unreasonable levels.

The computer has simply allowed all this clerical data processing and file handling to be accomplished more efficiently. Hence, what once was conceptually feasible but technically infeasible is now both technically and conceptually possible. And because of the speed of the computer, managers can perform as many simulations and "what-if" experiments as they wish, in order to determine the best decision. The system simulates the impacts of the decision throughout the organization, predicting the results in terms of customer orders and due dates.

MRP has even been applied to services. For example, when NASA was planning on perhaps as many as 30 shuttle launches a year, it became aware that many scheduling conflicts were possible, given its limited, and expensive, resources (Steinberg, Lee, and Khumawala 1980). To handle the extensive demands of each launch, it had to design a flight operations planning schedule (FOPS), or calendar of resource readiness. The resource demands of different flights, of which there are eight varieties, had to be coordinated with the perhaps self-conflicting demands of individual flights. The approach taken to address this problem was a variant of MRP, called requirements planning.

To use the requirements planning approach for FOPS, a bill of requirements based on component activities needed for each flight was identified. Since some activities cannot proceed until other activities have been completed, a dependent-demand element is directly analogous to MRP, even though there are no inventories of materials to consider. It is also necessary to check how much "load" each activity places on the different departments in NASA in each time period. The schedule can be constructed either through infinite loading (not worrying about exceeding departmental capacities) or through finite loading, where excessive loads are shifted either earlier or later in time to remain within departmental capacities.

The flight schedule file represents the master production schedule in MRP because it identifies final "products" (launches) that must be completed without delays. Activities are scheduled backward from the flight schedule file as each is required. This gives the resulting schedule for all activities to support each flight. If there is a conflict for scarce resources, the earliest scheduled flight takes priority. Two primary resources are checked: labor and equipment. Each department must identify whether it is labor-constrained or equipment-constrained for the system to check. Each department then receives a weekly load profile summary that indicates its planned activities to support each launch. It also receives a summary of the required activities over the coming weeks. Through the use of the FOPS system, NASA has been able to effectively manage multiple, simultaneous schedules for its space shuttle launches.

ENTERPRISE RESOURCE PLANNING (ERP)

As we just discussed, MRP II extends MRP systems to share information with a variety of other functional departments outside the operations area, including engineering, purchasing, customer-order entry, plant maintenance, and cost accounting. Thus, a key component of MRP II is storing operational information centrally and providing access to those departments that need it. Before MRP II systems, it was not uncommon for each functional department to maintain its own computer system. With these separate systems, the same information would be reentered and stored in several different databases throughout an organization. Aside from the added cost of reentering the same information, another more fundamental problem with this approach is that it is difficult to update information consistently when it is stored in multiple locations. Indeed, it was frequently not even known how many different databases held a particular piece of information. Further compounding the problem, it is common for the same information to have different values in each database. For example, the cost to produce a particular item would often have different values in the engineering, production, sales, and accounting databases. Not surprisingly, fragmented databases and information systems lead to fragmented businesses which are less acceptable in today's highly competitive marketplace.

The next stage in the evolution of information systems has been directed toward integrating all the business activities and processes throughout an entire organization, as well as with external plants and even suppliers and customers in the supply chain. These information systems are commonly referred to as **enterprise resource planning** (ERP) systems or simply **enterprise systems** (ES). As the name suggests, the objective of these systems is to provide seamless, real-time information to all employees who need it, throughout the entire organization (or enterprise), and to those outside the organization. In many cases, business process design (BPD, discussed in Chapter 5) has served as the impetus for developing and implementing these ERP systems.

Figure 9.10 provides a broad overview of SAP's MySAP ERP system. MySAP, announced in 2003, represents the latest evolution of SAP's ERP system. SAP introduced its R/2 system in 1979, which was an ERP system that ran on mainframe computers and its R/3 system for client server computing environments in 1992. MySAP takes the evolution one step further and is based on service-oriented architecture (SOA) whereby organizations will be able to access the SAP software via the Internet and thereby have access to the full functionality of the software without having to actually install and deploy the software throughout the enterprise. With the introduction of MySAP, SAP has announced that they will no longer continue to develop R/3.

As shown in Figure 9.10, an ERP system consists of a number of modules that provide the functionality to support a variety of organizational processes. These modules all access data from the central database, and changes made via these modules update the central database. In comparison to MRP II, ERP extends the idea of a central shared database to all areas within, and even outside, the organization. Thus ERP may include not only MRP (production) and MRP II (purchasing, order entry, shipping, etc.) systems but also accounting, sales, product design, finance, quality, and human resource systems and databases, plus electronic data interchange (EDI) or use of the Internet with other plants, suppliers, and customers. Using ERP, each area interacts with a centralized database and servers so suppliers can check on the latest demands and customers can determine the status of their order or available capacity for new orders. ERP can also handle international complications such as differences in taxes, currency, accounting rules, and language. Figure 9.11 provides additional details about the functionality offered by each MySAP module.

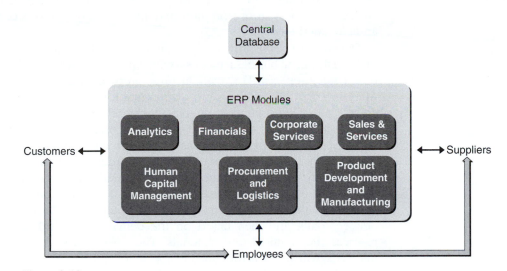

Figure 9.10   SAP's MySAP ERP system.

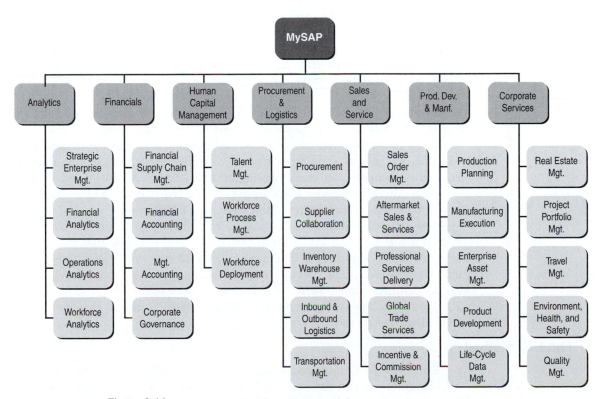

Figure 9.11   Detailed view of MySAP's modules.

With the ERP approach, information is entered once at the source and made available to all stakeholders needing it. Clearly, this approach eliminates the incompatibility created when different functional departments use different systems, and it also eliminates the need for people in different parts of the organization to reenter the same information over and over again into separate computer systems. Although ERP ties all these areas together, the actual implementation of an ERP system in an organization may include only portions of these modules on an as-needed basis.

Davenport (1998) provides an example that illustrates the opportunity to automate tasks in a business process with an ERP system. In the example, a Paris-based sales rep of a U.S. manufacturer prepares a quote for a customer in Paris. After entering the customer information into a notebook computer, the ERP system creates the sales contract in French. Included in the sales contract are important details of the order such as the product's configuration, quantity ordered, price, delivery date, and payment terms. When the customer agrees to the terms of the quote, the sales rep submits the order electronically with a single keystroke. The system then automatically checks the customer's credit and accepts the order if it is within the customer's credit limit. Upon accepting the order, the ERP system then schedules the shipment of the completed order based on the agreed-upon delivery date, and then based on the delivery date and appropriate lead times reserves the required raw materials. The system also determines if the required materials will be available and, if not, automatically generates the orders for the needed materials from suppliers. Next, the ERP system schedules the actual assembly of the order in one of the organization's Asian facilities. In addition, sales and production forecasts are updated, the commission due the rep is calculated and credited to his or her account (in French francs), and the profitability of the order in U.S. dollars computed. Finally, the business units and corporate financial statements such as balance sheets, accounts-payable, accounts-receivable, cash flows, and so on are immediately updated.

As this example illustrates, the integration offered by ERP systems provides organizations with the potential to achieve dramatic improvements in the execution of their business processes. Owens Corning achieved this integration by replacing 211 legacy systems with one ERP system. Much of the benefit associated with this integration stems from having real-time access to operating and financial data. For example, after implementing an ERP system, Autodesk reduced the time it took to deliver an order from an average of two weeks to shipping 98% of its orders within 24 hours. Before implementing an ERP system, it took IBM's Storage Systems division 5 days to reprice all of its products. After implementing an ERP system it was able to accomplish the same task in 5 minutes. IBM also reduced the time required to ship replacement parts from 22 days to 3 days, and reduced the time to perform credit checks from 20 minutes to 3 seconds! Fujitsu Microelectronics achieved similar benefits, reducing its order fulfillment time from 18 days to less than two days and reducing the time required to close its financial books from eight days to four days.

The ERP Industry

Forrester Research (Hamerman and Wang 2005) estimates that the overall market for ERP software and services was $21 billion in 2004. Of this $21 billion, approximately $6.2 billion was spent on licensing fees, $8.2 billion on maintenance, and

$6.6 billion on services. Forrester projects that while overall spending on ERP systems will increase 4.2% annually through 2008, spending on maintenance will increase at almost double this rate, or 7% annually through 2008. Over the last couple of years, there has been considerable consolidation of large ERP software vendors. Notable mergers and acquisitions include Peoplesoft's purchase of J.D. Edwards, Oracle's purchase of Peoplesoft, and SSA Global's purchase of Baan. Figure 9.12 shows the market share (based on 2004 revenues) of the five largest ERP vendors. SAP, the market leader, claims 12 million users and 91,500 installations.

Implementing ERP Systems

According to the Forrester report, ERP was the top IT spending priority in 2005. The key drivers for the strong interest in ERP include:

- The desire to standardize and improve business processes.
- The desire to integrate the organization's existing information systems.
- The need for better and more timely information.
- The need to comply with Sarbanes-Oxley.

Typically, it requires an organization one to three years to implement an ERP system and the cost can run as high as two to three percent of sales. It should also be noted that the cost of implementing an ERP system typically ranges from three to 10 times the cost of the software. The actual costs of implementing an ERP are driven by a number of factors including:

- The number of employees that will be using the system (commonly referred to as the number of seats).
- The number of modules that will be implemented.
- The extent to which the organization attempts to integrate its ERP system with an internal intranet.
- How much the organization's processes must be modified to conform with the ERP system.
- The amount of consulting and training required.
- The extent to which the organization's existing data must be converted to conform to the data requirements of the new ERP system.

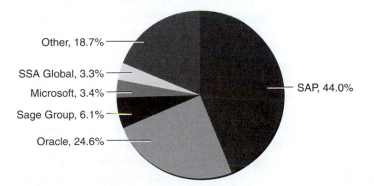

Figure 9.12 Market share (based on 2004 revenues) of five top ERP vendors.

Many of these costs, such as consulting, training, process redesign, and data conversion, are not obvious and as a result are not adequately budgeted for. A recent study of firms known to have implemented ERP found that 55.5 percent of the firms reported that the cost of implementing the ERP system exceeded the original budget and for these firms the budget was exceeded by an average of almost 61 per cent (Mabert et al. 2001).

In terms of the actual implementation of an ERP system, organizations tend to follow one of three general approaches:

- *The "Big Bang" approach*. With this approach, organizations implement the new ERP system all at once and scrap their existing legacy systems. This approach is by far the most ambitious approach and the most difficult. Originally, it was the most frequently used approach, but is now rarely used.

- *The "United Federation" approach*. With this approach, business units/ divisions are free to implement independent systems but common processes such as financial reporting are linked across the enterprise. This is currently the most commonly used approach.

- *The "Test the Waters" approach*. The focus of this approach is on a few key processes. Typically, a subset of the available modules is implemented to support these key processes. Because of the limited scope, neither the overall business processes nor the way work activities are performed is drastically changed. Overall, this approach limits the risk associated with implementing ERP, but by the same token has a limited payoff. This approach is commonly utilized by smaller organizations.

According to the Forrester report (2005), organizations have had the greatest success implementing finance and HR applications. Organizations have had less success with modules that support production and product/service delivery. As a result, Forrester projects that ERP vendors will be expanding the functionality of ERP systems into customer relationship management (CRM) and supply chain management.

In terms of the challenges organizations face in implementing ERP systems, perhaps the most significant issue is the difficulty of customizing an ERP system to meet an organization's unique needs and processes. As a result, organizations find that they must change their business processes and the way employees perform their work activities to conform to the software. In effect then, ERP systems can be thought of as not simply a software package but rather a way of doing business. Thus, organizations that have had the greatest success implementing ERP tend to view the decision broadly, from a more strategic perspective, as opposed to the rather narrow perspectives of technology or systems. It should also be noted that ERP vendors counter the drawback associated with the difficulty to customize ERP systems by emphasizing the fact that their ERP systems are based on best practices and are continuously updated to reflect the current state of the art in best practices.

In evaluating and implementing ERP systems, organizations may discover gaps between the functionality offered by the software and the organization's unique business needs. In these cases, organizations have two basic choices: change their practices to conform to the software or customize the software. For organizations that choose to conform to the software, a basic question then becomes how do you differentiate yourself from the competition? For organizations not willing to change their processes to conform to the ERP system, the cost of customizing the software represents about one-third of the cost of implementing the ERP system. In addition to the cost associated with customizing the software, another drawback is that the ERP vendor may no longer support the ERP system after it is customized.

Another significant challenge associated with ERP systems is the high maintenance costs. Typically, organizations spend 20 to 30 percent of the total implementation cost annually maintaining the system. On a per-user basis, this can translate into over $50,000 per year. Large organizations face the additional challenge of often having to integrate systems from multiple ERP vendors. This challenge often results from mergers and acquisitions where the previously separate corporations used different ERP vendors. The problem also arises in organizations that operated on a more decentralized basis.

A final challenge related to implementing ERP systems relates to configuring the software. In configuring the software, thousands of configuration switches that define how the software will operate and how the processes are executed must be set. For example, SAP's R/3 system has more than 3000 configuration tables. As you can imagine, a great deal of expertise is needed in order to set the configuration switches properly.

The bottom line is that while there is tremendous value in integrating systems across the enterprise, doing so is an extremely complex activity. The organizations that have had the greatest success with ERP are the ones that view it strategically, not from a systems or technology perspective.

EXPAND YOUR UNDERSTANDING _____

1. Why are accurate records, particularly regarding bills of material and inventories, important for MRP?

2. Comparing Figures 9.2 and 9.3, what percentage of inventory reduction would you estimate has occurred? If this firm holds $1 million worth of lumber before MRP and values its capital at 20 percent, how much is the MRP conversion worth to it?

3. Another way to do lot sizing is to use the EOQ. Why not just do this, since it gives an optimal answer?

4. How might MRP be applied to services? Are the same inputs required? Will the outputs be the same?

5. MRP II and ERP are relatively new applications of computer technology. How difficult do you think each would be to implement in the typical firm? What aspects of these technologies might make them difficult? How long might each take to implement?

6. In many of today's firms, the customer's computer is tied to the supplier's computer so that purchase orders go directly into the supplier's planning system. What are the implications of this close relationship?

7. Since MRP II is meant to be an integrated planning process, where do top management's control and influence come in? Shouldn't there be some direction to such an integrated plan?

8. Why is the choice of an ERP system best viewed as a strategic decision as opposed to a technology or information systems decision?

9. Discuss the relative merits of customizing versus not customizing an ERP system from the perspective of an organization you are familiar with. What would you recommend the organization do?

10. Discuss the pros and cons of relying on outside expertise in the selection and implementation of an ERP system.

11. In what ways can an ERP system enhance an organization's competitive position? In what ways might an ERP system erode an organization's competitive position?

APPLY YOUR UNDERSTANDING
Antonio Jorge da Coria

The firm of Antonio Jorge da Coria (AJC), S.A. began operations in Salvadore, on the east coast of Brazil some 15 years ago. Initially producing home humidifiers, AJC now employs approximately 280 people in the manufacture of a number of add-on appliances for residential heating and air conditioning units, primarily dehumidifiers and air purifiers. AJC currently produces 30 different models, but because of heavy competition, engineering changes are constantly taking place and the product line is often changing. Each model is made up of between 40 and several hundred different parts, which range from purchased nuts and bolts and prefabricated subassemblies to internally manufactured components.

AJC purchases over 2500 parts and manufactures over 1000 parts and assemblies of its own. Many of the parts are used in several different models, and some parts—such as nuts and bolts—are used in over 75 percent of the finished products.

The finished goods inventory is kept relatively small. Sales are forecast on a month-to-month basis, and production is scheduled according to actual sales orders and the sales forecast. For this reason, production lots placed in the final assembly line are usually for relatively small quantities.

Rather than producing manufactured parts and subcomponents and purchasing other parts according to the sales forecast, parts, subassemblies, and purchased items are ordered on the basis of reorder point and economic order quantity. Since it is imperative to maintain accurate control of these raw materials and subassembly items, all parts and materials stored in the main supply area are controlled with the use of perpetual inventory cards, which are maintained by the scheduling department. Each card contains the reorder point, the economic order quantity, and the lead time for outside procurement or internal manufacture. Both receipt of new inventory into the main supply room and use of items from the supply room are recorded on the inventory card.

The scheduling department is responsible for checking the availability of inventory on the inventory cards. Approximately three weeks before a final assembly order is to be placed on the floor, the scheduler checks all the cards for parts needed in that assembly to determine whether issuing the number required to complete the assembly will reduce the inventory below the reorder point. If the scheduler determines that the projected final assembly order will result in hitting the reorder point, a production order or a purchase order is issued.

Physical inventories are taken every quarter, and usually a substantial number of small adjustments must be made. The quarterly physical inventory was suggested after a series of major inventory shortages occurred several years ago. The company's current policy allows any worker to enter the main supply area to remove needed parts. The workers are to fill out materials requisitions and to sign for all parts removed, but they are frequently in a rush and fail to complete the inventory requisitions accurately. There have been several cases in which parts staged for final assembly of one product were removed and used on the assembly of another item.

To adjust for many of these problems, the production schedulers often add a safety factor to the reorder point when placing orders and they have typically increased the order quantity from 10 to 25 percent over the economic order quantity. Their justification is that "it is less expensive to carry a little extra inventory than to shut down the production facility waiting for a rush order."

Questions

1. Evaluate and critique the existing system used by AJC.
2. How might MRP work in a situation like this?
3. Beyond implementing a computerized MRP system, what other suggestions would you make to help alleviate AJC's problems?

EXERCISES

1. A customer service (A) is made up of 1 B, 1 C, and 1 D subservices. Each B is made up of 1 C and 1 E. C's are made from 1 G. E's are made from 1 C and 1 I. D's consist of 1 F and 1 H. Each F is made from 1 I and 1 J. Each H is made from 1 J and 1 K.

(a) Develop a service tree for end service A.

(b) How many of each of the component services are required to complete 80 A's?

2. Product 101 consists of three 202 subassemblies and one 204 subassembly. The 202 subassembly consists of one 617, one 324 subassembly, and one 401. A 204 subassembly consists of one 500 and one 401. The 324 subassembly consists of one 617 and one 515.

(a) Prepare a product tree.

(b) Prepare an indented bill of materials.

(c) Determine the number of each subassembly or component required to produce fifty 101s.

3. Complete the MRP for item No. 6606 below. (*Hint:* See Table 9.2.)

Week	5	6	7	8	9	10	11	12	13	14	15	16	17
Gross requirement				100			50	30			80		
On hand 100													
Net requirement													
Planned-order receipts													
Planned-order releases													
Lead time = 3 weeks													

4. Wooden pencils are made in 1 week out of four kinds of parts: two wooden halves, the graphite, the metal cap, and the rubber eraser. Construct an MRP explosion for orders of 10 dozen in week 2, 30 dozen in week 3, and 15 dozen in week 5. There are currently 500 wooden halves on hand, 300 graphite rods, and 1500 metal caps, but no rubber erasers. All items are purchased with a 1-week lead time except the graphite, which takes 2 weeks. Create a schedule of releases for the wooden halves and graphite. Use lot-for-lot ordering. (*Hint:* See Table 9.2.)

5. Given the following, how many No. 1342 items should be purchased and when?

Item	Lead Times (weeks)	On Hand	Demand in Week				
			11	12	13	14	15
19	1	100	100	0	100	200	0
1342	2	200	0	500	0	0	0
102	1	0	50	0	0	0	0
312	2	0	0	0	0	10	0

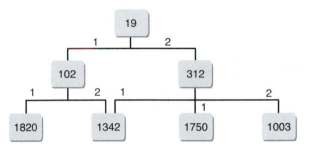

BIBLIOGRAPHY

Bancroft, N., H. Seip, and A. Spungel. *Implementing SAP R/3*. Greenwich, CT: Manning, 1998.

Curran, T., and G. Keller. *SAP/3 Business Blueprint*. Upper Saddle River, NJ: Prentice Hall, 1998.

Davenport, T. "Putting the Enterprise into the Enterprise System." *Harvard Business Review* (July–August 1998): 121–131.

Davenport, T. *Mission Critical: Realizing the Promise of Enterprise Systems*. Boston: Harvard Business School Press, 2000.

Dinnin, M., and E. W. Shuster. "Fighting Friction: Using Low-Cost Passive Tags, Auto-ID Technology Seeks to Speed Up the Flow of Goods." *APICS-The Performance Advantage*, (February 2003): 27–31.

Earl, M., and M. M. Bensaou. "The Right Mind-Set of Managing Information Technology." *Harvard Business Review* (September–October 1998): 119–129.

Hamerman, P., and R. Wang. "ERP Applications—The Technology and Industry Battle Heats Up." Forrester Research, Inc. Report, June 9, 2005.

Hill Jr., S. "This CIO Means Business: National Semiconductor Uses Modified Best-of-Breed Approach to Achieve Goals." www.manufacturingsystems.com, August 1, 2003.

Hoy, P. A. "The Changing Role of MRP II." *APICS—The Performance Advantage* (June 1996): 50–53.

Jacobs, E. R., and D. C. Whybark. *Why ERP? A Primer on SAP Implementation.* New York: Irwin/McGraw-Hill, 2000.

Jordan, W. G., and K. R. Krumweide. "ERP Implementors, Beware!" *Cost Management Update* (March 1999): 1–4.

Kanet, J., and V. Sridharan. "The Value of Using Scheduling Information in Planning Material Requirements." *Decision Sciences*, 29 (Spring 1998): 479–498.

Kapp, K. M., B. Latham, and H.-F. Latham. *Integrated Learning for ERP Success.* Boca Raton, FL: St Lucie Press, 1999.

Koch, C., D. Slater, and E. Baatz. "The ABC's of ERP," CIO.com, December 22, 1999.

Mabert, V. A., A. Soni, and M. A. Venkataramanan. "Enterprise Resource Planning Survey of U.S. Manufacturing Firms." *Production and Inventory Management Journal*, 41 (Second Quarter 2000): 52–58.

Mabert, V. A., A. Soni, and M. A. Venkataramanan. "Enterprise Resource Planning: Measuring Value." *Production and Inventory Management Journal* (Third/Fourth Quarter 2001): 46–51.

Malis, E. "ERP for Electronic Commerce." *Manufacturing Systems* (April 1999): 26–27.

META Group. "ERP Implementation Study Reveals Costs, Benefits." *APICS—The Performance Advantage* (October 1999): 7.

Norris, G. *E-Business and ERP: Transforming the Enterprise.* New York, Wiley, 2000.

Ptak, C. *MRP and Beyond.* Homewood, IL: Irwin Professional Publications, 1996.

Ptak, C. A., and E. Schragenheim. *ERP: Tools, Techniques, and Applications for Integrating the Supply Chain.* Boca Raton, FL: St Lucie Press, 1999.

SAP, "mySAP ERP Solution Overview." www.sap.com/solutions/business-suite/erp/pdf/BWP_mySAP_ERP_Overview.pdf, June 26, 2005.

Scalle, C. X., and M. J. Cotteleer. *Enterprise Resource Planning (ERP).* Boston, MA: Harvard Business School Publishing, 1999.

Sheikh, K. *Manufacturing Resource Planning (MRP II) with Introduction to ERP, SCM, and CRM.* New York: McGraw-Hill, 2002.

Shtub, A. *Enterprise Resource Planning: The Dynamics of Operations Management.* Boston: Kluwer, 1999.

Steinberg, E. E., W. B. Lee, and B. Khumawala. "A Requirements Planning System for the Space Shuttle Operations Schedule." *Journal of Operations Management,* vol. 1, no. 2 (November 1980): 69–76.

Vollmann, T. E., W. L. Berry, and D. C. Whybark. *Manufacturing Planning and Control Systems*, 4th ed. Homewood, IL: Irwin, 1997.

Wallace, T. F., and M. H. Kremzar. *ERP: Making it Happen: The Implementer's Guide to Success with Enterprise Resource Planning.* New York: Wiley, 2001.

CHAPTER 10

Lean Management

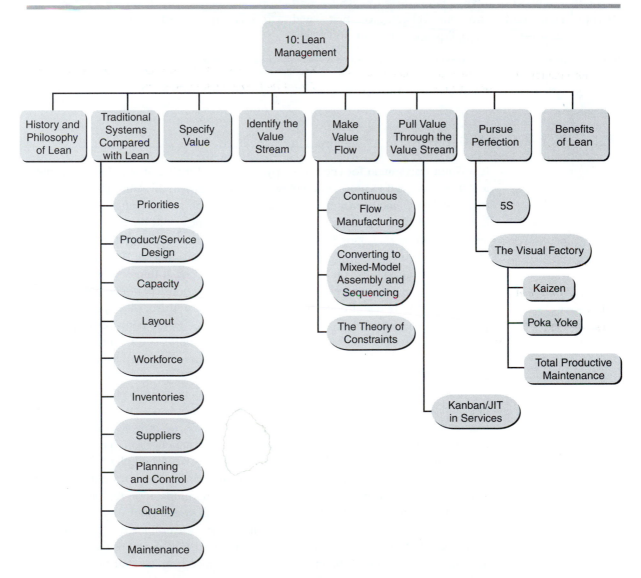

CHAPTER IN PERSPECTIVE

In this chapter, we discuss the role of lean production for minimizing costs while enhancing the strategic value factors of quality, dependability, and speed. Although not a strategy per se, lean management has taken on the aura of a global competitive philosophy because so many firms that embrace it have been so successful: Toyota, Dell, and numerous others. We first address the history and philosophy of lean and then make a comparison between traditional production systems and lean. Following this, we continue with a discussion of five lean principles: (1) specify value from the customer's point of view, (2) identify the value stream, (3) make value flow, (4) have the customer pull value, and (5) pursue perfection. The chapter concludes with a discussion of the benefits associated with lean.

[Handwritten margin note: Lean: minimize costs while enhancing the strategic value factors of quality, dependability, & speed.]

INTRODUCTION

- It was not uncommon for chemotherapy patients at Virginia Mason Medical Center, a 350-bed hospital located in downtown Seattle, to spend an entire day receiving their weekly chemotherapy treatment. To illustrate the process, after arriving at 8:00 A.M. and checking in on the first floor, the patient would be asked to go to the laboratory for blood testing located on the sixth floor. After having the blood drawn, the patient would then wait for the results to be sent to the oncologist and then eventually meet with the oncologist on the second floor. If things progressed smoothly, the patient would begin receiving the intravenous chemotherapy treatment by noon in an open and noisy room that was shared with six other patients.

To improve this process, Virginia Mason has turned to the concepts of lean pioneered by Toyota shortly after World War II. Virginia Mason's overarching goal was to improve the patient experience while at the same time increasing the overall efficiency of the process. Using lean concepts, Virginia Mason completely redesigned the process for chemotherapy patients so that everything flows to the patient as opposed to the patient flowing through the process. For example, instead of being located on separate floors, the labs and doctors' offices are now adjacent to private patient treatment rooms. Furthermore, each private treatment room has a flat-screen TV, a computer, nursing supplies, and toilet facilities. A dedicated pharmacy was also added to the cancer treatment center, thereby eliminating delays for patients of up to two hours. Other improvements have reduced the preparation time for chemotherapy treatments from three hours to less than one hour. Across the entire medical center, hospital administrators estimate that its lean initiatives have resulted in savings of $6 million in capital spending, freed up 13,000 square feet, reduced inventory costs by $360,000, and reduced the distance hospital staff walk each day by 34 miles. In addition to these tangible results, the hospital achieved a number of other benefits including improved patient satisfaction, shorter bill collection times, and lower infection rates. To achieve these benefits, the hospital spent approximately $1.5 million, primarily for consultants, travel, and training (Connolly 2005).

[Handwritten margin note: Lean pioneered by Toyota shortly after World War II.]

[Handwritten margin note: Savings of $6 million in capital spending]

Integrating 66 with lean.

- Although Xerox often gets more publicity for its financial difficulties, it does have a long track record in the area of quality management. Xerox's journey began in the early 1980s when it established its Leadership Through Quality Initiative which focused on improving business processes in order to improve customer satisfaction, quality, and productivity. Fast forward to the late 1990s and we see Six Sigma and Lean being adopted by Xerox's manufacturing and supply chain functions. While limited in scope, the Lean and Six Sigma programs help Xerox improve its operating efficiency and effectiveness. Perhaps in part due to the success of these limited initiatives, in mid-2002 Xerox's leadership decided to integrate its Lean and Six Sigma programs across the entire enterprise, naming the initiative Xerox Lean Six Sigma. To support this initiative, Xerox kicked off an intense Black Belt training program in January 2003 which included employees from all functional areas. By August 2004, 400 Black Belts had been trained, 2500 employees had completed or were in the process of completing Green Belt training, 2000 leaders had completed a two-day workshop, and 10,000 employees had completed Yellow Belt awareness training. Furthermore, a total of 700 Lean Six Sigma projects have been completed across all areas of Xerox including product design, supply chain, marketing and sales, customer service, and strategy deployment. Xerox estimates that it achieved an initial $6 million return in 2003 based on a $14 million investment in Lean Six Sigma and expects even bigger gains in the years ahead (Fornari and Maszle 2004).

- Honeywell International, a diversified technology company with 2004 sales in excess of $25 billion, is another company that has successfully integrated its Six Sigma initiatives with its lean initiatives. In particular, Honeywell has combined Six Sigma's traditional emphasis on variation reduction with lean's emphasis on waste reduction to create its Six Sigma Plus program.

  Honeywell competes in four major industry segments: (1) Aerospace, (2) Automation and Control Solutions, (3) Specialty Materials, and (4) Transportation Systems. The business unit for each of these industry segments is headed by a group president. Reporting to each group president is a Six Sigma Plus Leader (SSPL) that is responsible for developing the strategic plans and deploying these plans for Six Sigma Plus initiatives within the group. Reporting to the SSPL is a team composed of Master Black Belts (MBBs), Lean Masters (LMs), Black Belts (BBs), and Lean Experts (LEs). MBBs and LMs, also referred to as Honeywell Masters (HMs), work on projects that have more than a $1 million financial impact and are also responsible for training, mentoring, and certifying BBs and LEs. BBs and LEs work on projects that have a financial impact in the range of $200,000 to $250,000 and train, mentor, and certify Green Belts. In 2002, two HM training waves, five LE waves, 15 BB waves, and 15 BBL training waves, each with 20 to 30 employees, were conducted in North America and additional waves were conducted in Europe and Asia. The HM waves consist of five weeks of training while the BB and LE waves consist of four weeks of training. The BBL training supplements the core BB training with additional lean topics.

  In addition to the SSPLs in each business unit, Honeywell has a Vice President of Six Sigma that reports directly to the CEO. This VP chairs the Six Sigma Plus Executive Council which in turn oversees all training and ensures a common

[handwritten margin notes:]
Initiative: Xerox Lean Six Sigma

Honeywell International, Inc. → a diversified technology company

curriculum is used company wide. In 2002, Honeywell reported productivity improvement gains of $1.2 billion. Looking to the future, Honeywell's 2004 Annual Report announced the introduction of the Honeywell Operating System (HOS). The HOS is based on the Toyota Production System and will be used to provide a roadmap to further integrate Six Sigma and lean tools (Hill and Kearney 2003).

- The hospital patient discharge process is often associated with substantial patient dissatisfaction. However, in addition to frustrating patients, delays in the discharge process can create problems in other areas of the hospital such as admitting and the emergency department, as these areas must wait for the rooms vacated by discharged patients. To address the inefficiencies often associated with the patient discharge process, Valley Baptist Hospital in Harlingen, Texas utilized Lean, Six Sigma, and change management techniques. One specific goal of this project was to reduce the time from when a patient discharge order was entered into the computer until the time the patient was transported from the room to 45 minutes.

The process improvement team began by mapping the current patient discharge process. In mapping the process, the team discovered that the there was little consistency across the nurses in terms of their approaches to discharging patients. Further analysis of the process map was undertaken to identify the activities in the discharge process that were not adding value or, in this case, helping discharge patients faster. In the end, all activities were classified as either value-added, nonvalue-added, or value enabler. The team further enhanced the process map to show rework loops, communication flows among the staff, and physical movements. Key performance metrics were also added to the process map which highlighted a substantial amount of nonvalue-added time.

As the team further embellished and analyzed the process map, it was able to identify several primary drivers of waste in the patient discharge process. For example, the team discovered that in 21% of the cases, nurses required clarification from a doctor before the discharge order could be entered into the computer. The need to clarify an order added an average of 33 minutes to the discharge process. As another example, the team discovered that in some cases the primary nurse took the patient's vital signs while in other cases a second nurse took the vital signs, which were then reported to the primary nurse. Having the primary nurse take the vital signs himself or herself reduced the elapsed time by an average of 64 minutes.

Based on these insights and others, the process improvement team developed a new standard operating procedure consisting of six steps for the patient discharge process. After adopting the new process, the mean time to discharge a patient was reduced by 74%, from 185 minutes to 48 minutes. Furthermore, the standard deviation of discharge times also decreased by 71%, from 128.7 minutes to 37.2 minutes. Finally, the percentage of discharged patients that vacated their rooms in 45 minutes or less increased from 6.9% to 61.7% (DeBusk and Rangel 2005).

As these examples illustrate, **_Lean_** is a philosophy that seeks to eliminate all types of waste whether it be excessive delays in treating patients, excessive lead times, carrying excessive levels of inventory, workers or parts traveling excessive distances,

a strong customer orientation is central to lean.

spending too much time setting up equipment, unneeded space, reworking defective products, clarifying patient orders, idle facilities, and scrap. The examples also illustrate several other important themes associated with lean. First, since waste can be thought of as those activities and outcomes that do not add value for the customer, a strong customer orientation is central to lean. This was illustrated in the Virginia Mason example where the chemotherapy process was redesigned so that the treatment process flowed to the patient as opposed to the patient flowing through the process. In fact, Virginia Mason made additional changes not mentioned in the example to improve the customer experience, including allocating the best rooms with windows to patients, adding a waterfall and meditation room to help ease patient stress, and adding an Internet café. A second theme relates to the large payoff that can be achieved through lean initiatives. This is exemplified by Honeywell's $1.2 billion in productivity gains, Virginia Mason's cost, space, and travel savings, and Valley Baptist's 74% reduction in patient discharge time. Finally, a third theme that emerges from the examples is the trend for organizations to merge their Six Sigma (discussed in Chapter 4) programs with their Lean programs. This trend reflects the complementary nature of these two programs: Six Sigma's focus on variation reduction and lean's focus on eliminating waste. Clearly, a process with little variation but lots of waste would not be desirable and vice versa.

6σ focuses on variation reduction. Lean focuses on waste reduction. (Toyota) apply lean first & then refine process using 6σ (motrola)

In essence, the goal of lean is to accomplish more with fewer resources; less workers, inventory, space, equipment, time, scrap, and so on. To accomplish this goal, Womack and Jones, in their book *Lean Thinking*, identify five lean principles:

5 Lean principles

1. Specify value from the customer's point of view.
2. Identify the value stream, the complete set of activities required to create the output valued by the customer.
3. Make value flow through the value stream by eliminating nonvalue added activities and streamlining the remaining value-added steps.
4. Have the customer pull value through the value stream.
5. Pursue perfection. →apply 6σ

Lean cannot be reduced to a "formula," and therefore every firm must apply the philosophy differently. In the remainder of this chapter, we discuss these five lean principles in more detail. However, before discussing these principles in detail, we begin our discussion with an overview of the lean philosophy to put it in proper context.

HISTORY AND PHILOSOPHY OF LEAN _____

Lean: synchronous manufacturing Imp

Lean production (also known as **synchronous manufacturing** or simply **lean**) is the name given to the Toyota Production System. Toyota began developing its approach to manufacturing shortly after World War II. The Toyota system is known for its minimal use of resources and elimination of all forms of waste, including time. Thus, for example, just-in-time (JIT) is a substantial portion of the Toyota system. Similarly, lean production is an integral element of supply chain management as it is currently envisioned. As such, it requires identifying and eliminating

JIT   Imp

istances,

all forms of nonvalue-added activities throughout the entire supply chain. Teams of multiskilled workers are employed at all levels of the organization to root out inefficiency and waste. To understand why lean was developed, it is important to understand a little about the history and culture of Japan.

Japan is a small country with minimal resources and a large population. Thus, the Japanese have always been careful not to waste resources, including space (especially land), as well as time and labor. Waste is abhorrent because the country has so little space and so few natural resources to begin with. Therefore, the Japanese have been motivated to maximize the gain or yield from the few resources available. It has also been necessary for them to maintain their respect for each other in order to work and live together smoothly and effectively in such a densely populated space. As a result, their work systems tend to be based on three primary tenets:

1. Minimizing waste in all forms
2. Continually improving processes and systems
3. Maintaining respect for all workers

During production, the Japanese studiously avoid waste of materials, space, and labor. They therefore pay significant attention to identifying and correcting problems that could potentially lead to such waste. Moreover, operations and procedures are constantly being improved and fine-tuned to increase productivity and yield, further eliminating waste. Equal respect is paid to all workers, and the trappings of status are minimized so that respect among all can be maintained.

Although low cost and consistent quality are important goals when a firm adopts lean, many other benefits also have accrued in those firms where it has been implemented. Examples include reduced inventories of all types (and thus less need for the space they require), greater productivity among both labor and staff, shorter lead times, improved processes, increased equipment productivity and utilization, better quality, fewer errors, and higher morale among the workforce and managers. Because of its broad nature and wide range of benefits, lean has become for many companies a major element in their competitive strategy as the Xerox example at the beginning of the chapter illustrated.

The second tenet of Japanese work systems is continuous improvement which corresponds to the lean principle of pursuing perfection. Accordingly, lean is not considered simply a one-time event to streamline the transformation system from a sloppy, wasteful form to an efficient, competitive form. Rather it is an ongoing journey that seeks to make continuing improvements throughout the system to keep the firm competitive and profitable in the future.

Perhaps the most important of the three tenets is the third, maintaining respect for all workers. Unfortunately, U.S. industry seems to be moving more slowly in this direction, and U.S. firms seem far behind the Japanese in obtaining respect and loyalty from their workers. This is probably because these firms and industries do not show respect for and loyalty to their employees in the first place.

Initially, in the early 1980s, the Japanese approach to production was greeted with a great deal of ambivalence in the United States. Typical of the sentiment at this time was, "It will never work here." However, this view abruptly changed when a number of domestic companies such as Hewlett-Packard and Harley-

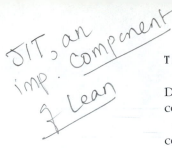
JIT, an imp. component of lean

Davidson began demonstrating the significant benefits of JIT, an important component of lean.

Next, we describe the most common characteristics of lean systems and compare them with the more traditional systems.

TRADITIONAL SYSTEMS COMPARED WITH LEAN

differences range from philosophy to culture to standard op. procedures

Table 10.1 presents a dozen characteristics of lean systems that tend to distinguish them from the more traditional systems historically used in U.S. industry. These characteristics range from philosophy and culture to standard operating procedures. Several of the contrasts summarized in Table 10.1 are elaborated on in the remainder of this section.

Priorities

Imp

Know which customers you "do not" want

Traditionally, most firms want to accept all customer orders, or at least provide a large number of options from which customers may order. However, this confuses the production task, increases the chance of errors, and increases costs. With lean, the target market is usually limited and the options are also limited. A wise lean firm knows which customers it does *not* want.

Thus, we see that right from the start the overall priorities of lean firms are different from those of the traditional firm. This perspective is reflected in the approach lean firms take to each of the other characteristics as well. In one sense, their "strategy" for competing is different from that of the traditional firm, and this strategy permeates their production system.

Product/Service Design

incrementally improve each design

eliminate wasted time

In line with the priorities, engineering in the lean firm designs standard outputs and incrementally improves each design. The parts and subassemblies that make up each output are also standardized; over time they are further simplified and improved. More traditionally, engineers attempt to design custom outputs to satisfy unique customers, starting from scratch each time and designing new parts and subassemblies. The reason for the new parts and subassemblies is often that the engineers change and do not know what their predecessors have already designed. Yet even if the same engineers are doing the design work, they often design new parts when a previously designed, tested, and proven part would do—because they cannot afford the time to find the previous design.

DFM DFA

Furthermore, designers in lean organizations usually include considerations about the manufacturability of the part or product. This is called ***design for manufacturability*** (DFM) or ***design for assembly*** (DFA). Too often, the traditional firm whips up an engineering design as quickly as it can (since it has had to start from scratch) and then passes the design on to manufacturing without giving a thought to how it can be made (sometimes it cannot). With this approach, poor quality and high costs often result and cannot be improved on the shop floor, since they were designed in from the start. If the product or part absolutely cannot be made, or perhaps cannot be assembled, then the design is sent back to engineering to modify, taking more time and costing more in engineering hours.

*T*ABLE   10.1 • Comparison of Traditional Systems and Lean

Characteristic	Traditional	Lean
Priorities	Accept all orders	Limited market
	Many options	Few options
		Low cost, high quality
Product/Service design	Customized outputs	Standardized outputs
	Design from scratch	Incremental design
		Simplify, design for manufacturing
Capacity	Highly utilized	Moderately utilized
	Inflexible	Flexible
Transformation system	Job shop	Flow shops, cellular manufacturing
Layout	Large space	Small space
	Materials handling equipment	Close, manual transfer
Work force	Narrow skills	Broad skills
	Specialized	Flexible
	Individualized	Work teams
	Competitive attitude	Cooperative attitude
	Change by edict	Change by consensus
	Easy pace	Hard pace
	Status: symbols, pay, privilege	No status differentials
Scheduling	Long setups	Quick changeovers
	Long runs	Mixed-model runs
Inventories	Large WIP buffers	Small WIP buffers
	Stores, cribs, stockrooms	Floor stock
Suppliers	Many	Few or single-sourced
	Competitive	Cooperative, network
	Deliveries to central receiving area	Deliveries directly to assembly line
	Independent forecasts	Shared forecasts
Planning and control	Planning-oriented	Control-oriented
	Complex	Simple
	Computerized	Visual
Quality	Via inspection	At the source
	Critical points	Continuous
	Acceptance sampling	Statistical process control
Maintenance	Corrective	Preventive
	By experts	By operator
	Run equipment fast	Run equipment slowly
	Run one shift	Run 24 hours

Capacity

[handwritten annotation: excess capacities are kept to the minimum to avoid inherent waste, particularly WIP inventories]

In terms of capacity, traditional firms tend to design extra capacities of all kinds into the system ***just-in-case*** a problem arises and they are needed. These capacities may consist of extra equipment, overtime, partial shifts, and frequently, large work-in-process (WIP) inventories. All of them cost extra money to acquire and maintain, which eventually increases the cost of the product.

[handwritten annotation: respect in work →]

In lean organizations, excess capacities are kept to a minimum to avoid inherent waste, particularly the WIP inventories, as will be discussed in more detail later. In place of the excess capacities, tighter control is exerted over the production system so that conditions do not arise where significant additional capacity is needed in the first place.

Layout

[handwritten annotation: use of Cells]

The traditional method of layout follows the job-shop approach of using widely spread-out equipment with space for stockrooms, tool cribs, and work-in-process inventories between the equipment. To handle and move all this inventory, automated or semiautomated equipment such as conveyors, carousels, and forklifts is also required, which takes even more space.

With lean, equipment is moved as close together as possible so that parts can be actually handed from one worker or machine to the next. The use of cells and flow lines permits the production of parts in small lots with minimal work-in-process and material moving equipment. The cells are often U-shaped so that one worker can easily access all the machines without moving very far, and finished products will exit at the same point where raw materials enter the cell.

It is not unusual for the work flows in a traditional job shop to look like a plate of spaghetti when traced on a diagram of the shop. In fact, creating such a diagram where the physical flows of the parts are mapped onto the shop floor is referred to as a ***spaghetti chart*** and is a commonly used lean tool. In particular, spaghetti charts can be used to identify excessive travel distances, backtracking, and other sources of waste. Based on the insights gained from creating and analyzing a spaghetti chart, ideas for shortening work flows and making them more direct with fewer major part-family flow streams can be identified and implemented. In service-oriented and transactional processes, spaghetti charts can be created by having a person assume the role of the part and actually walking through the process as would a patient or invoice.

Workforce

[handwritten annotation: Create a smarter workforce... — one that is smarter than the machines]

A key element of lean is the role of the work force as a means of uncovering and solving problems. Rather than considering the workers as the traditional cogs in the great plant machine, each with its own tasks, skills, and narrow responsibilities, lean strives for a broadly skilled, flexible worker who will look for and solve production problems wherever they appear.

In the traditional shop, much of the employees' time is nonworking time: looking for parts, moving materials, setting up machines, getting instructions, and so on. Thus, when actually working, the employees tend to work fast, producing

[handwritten annotation at bottom: Lean strives for a broadly skilled, flexible worker who will look & solve production problems wherever they appear.]

parts at a rapid pace whether or not the parts are needed. (This, of course, results in errors, scrap, and machine breakdowns, which again provide a reason to stop working.) The outcome is a stop-and-go situation that, overall, results in a relatively inefficient, ineffective pace for most workers.

Conversely, with lean, the workers produce only when the next worker is ready. The pace is steady and fast, although never frantic. In spite of the built-in rule that workers should be idle if work is not needed, the focus on smooth flows, short setups, and other such simplifications means that workers are rarely idle. (Of course, if they *are* idle; that is an immediate signal to the system designers that work is not progressing smoothly through the plant and adjustments need to be made.)

Inventories

In Japan, inventory is seen as an evil in itself. It is a resource sitting idle, wasting money. But, more important, inventory tends to hide problems. In the traditional plant, inventories are used to buffer operations so that problems at one stage don't affect the next stage. However, inventories also hide problems, such as defective parts, until the inventory is needed and then is found to be defective. For example, in a plant with lots of work-in-process inventory, a worker who discovers a batch of defective parts can simply put them aside and work on something else. By the time the worker returns to the defective batch, if ever, so much time has elapsed since the batch was processed upstream that the cause of the problem is unlikely to be discovered and corrected to prevent a recurrence. In contrast, in an environment where there is little or no buffer inventory, a worker who discovers a defective batch has no choice but to work on the batch. Furthermore, the worker can then notify upstream operations of the problem so they can correct it and ensure that it does not occur in the future.

The Japanese liken inventory, and the money it represents, to the water in a lake. They see problems as boulders and obstacles under the water, as shown in Figure 10.1. To expose the problems, they reduce the inventories, also shown in Figure 10.1, and then solve the problems. Then they lower the inventory more, exposing more problems, and solve those, too. They continue this until all the problems are solved and the inventory investment is practically gone. The result is a greatly improved and smoother production system.

In the traditional plant, almost the opposite happens. Because managers know that their plant produces, say, 15 percent defective products, they produce 15 percent extra, which goes into inventory. That's the wrong way to handle the

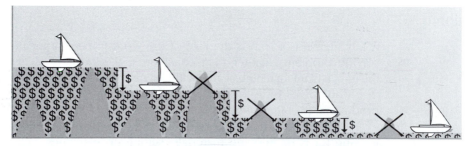

Figure 10.1   Lowering inventory investment to expose problems.

problem—they should fix the problem in the first place, not cover it up with expensive inventory.

All types of inventories are considered liabilities: work-in-process, raw materials, finished goods, component parts, and so on. By eliminating storage space, not only do we save space, but we also disallow inventories where defectives can be hidden until no one knows who made them. And by eliminating queues of work waiting for machines, we facilitate automatic inspection by workers of hand-passed parts, thereby identifying problems when they begin rather than after 1000 units have been made incorrectly.

If the space saved when operations are moved closer to each other—frequently 33 percent of the original space—is immediately used for something else, then inventory can't be dumped there. This facilitates reducing simultaneously the lead time, smoothing the workload, and reducing the inventory.

Last, with minimal or no inventory, control of materials is much easier and less expensive. Parts don't get lost, don't have to be moved, don't have to be labeled, and don't have to be held in computer memory or inventory records. Basically, discipline and quality are much improved and cost is reduced, simultaneously.

In Chapter 8, the economic order quantity (EOQ) was presented as the optimal order quantity, given the tradeoff between inventory carrying cost and setup or ordering cost. The EOQ model also demonstrates the relationship between setup cost and average inventory levels: order quantities, and consequently average inventory levels, increase as setup time and cost increase. Knowing that the EOQ minimized total costs, managers in the United States simply plugged values into the EOQ formula to determine optimal order quantities. However, use of the EOQ model assumes that its inputs are fixed. In contrast to their American counterparts, managers in Japan did not assume that these inputs were fixed. In fact, they invested significant amounts of time and other resources in finding ways to reduce equipment setup times. These efforts led to substantial reductions in setup times and therefore in setup costs, and ultimately to much smaller batch sizes, which became the basis of the JIT system.

As discussed in Chapter 3, one approach to reducing setup times is to adopt cellular manufacturing. Another approach, if the equipment is available and utilization rates are not a problem, is to use multiple machines that have already been set up for the new task. Alternatively, some of the more advanced and automated equipment will automatically reset itself. In the remaining cases, the setup task can be made much more efficient through a number of techniques that have been largely identified and catalogued by the Japanese. Some of these are described next.

One lean tool used to reduce setup times is SMED, which stands for single minute exchange of die. SMED was developed by Shigeo Shingo, and is an important component of the Toyota Production System. While SMED literally translates to a single minute for practical purposes, the goal is to reduce setup times to under 10 minutes (i.e., a single digit, not a single minute). An excellent example of SMED is provided by the CMI factory that is jointly operated by GM and Suzuki, where machine setup times were reduced from 36 hours to 6 minutes.

A key element of SMED is distinguishing between internal setup time, which requires that the machine be turned off, and external setup time, which can be conducted while the machine is still working on the previous part. First, a major effort is directed toward converting internal to external setup time, which is easier to reduce. This is largely done by identifying all the previously internal setup tasks that can either be conducted just as easily as external setup work or, with some changes in the operation, be done externally. Then, the external task times are reduced by such techniques as staging dies, using duplicate fixtures, employing shuttles, and installing roller supports. Last, internal time is reduced by such creative approaches as using hinged bolts, folding brackets, guide pins, or Lazy Susans.

Once the setup times are reduced, the firm gains not only in smoother work flows and shorter lead times, but also in flexibility to any changes in production schedules stemming from accidents, unexpected breakages, customers' problems, and so on. Clearly, this flexibility is immensely valuable.

Suppliers

Traditional practice has been to treat suppliers as adversaries and play them off against each other. Multiple sourcing purportedly keeps prices down and ensures a wide supply of parts. However, multiple sourcing also means that no supplier is getting an important fraction of the order; thus, there is no incentive to work with the firm to meet specifications for quality and delivery.

With lean, the desire is for frequent, smooth deliveries of small lots, with the supplier considered part of the team. As part of the team, the supplier is even expected to help plan and design the purchased parts to be supplied. Schedules must be closely coordinated, and many small deliveries are expected every day. Thus, it is in the supplier's interest to locate a plant or warehouse close to the customer. Clearly then, the supplier must have a large enough order to make this trouble worthwhile; thus, **single-sourcing** for 100 percent of the requirements is common. But with such large orders, the customer can expect the supplier to become more efficient in producing the larger quantities of items, so quantity discounts become available. Moreover, having just one source is also more convenient for a firm that must interact and coordinate closely with the supplier. Companies that develop single-sourcing relationships recognize the mutual dependency of the supplier–customer relationship. Specifically, for the customer to prosper in the marketplace, the supplier must supply high-quality items in the right quantities on time. On the other hand, the more successful the customer, the more business is generated for the supplier.

Perhaps equally significant, there is no incoming inspection of the materials to check their quality—all parts must be of specified quality and guaranteed by the supplier. Again, this requires a cooperative rather than an adversarial approach, with the supplier working with the team. Many lean firms are now establishing a list of "certified" suppliers that they can count on to deliver perfect quality and thus become members of their production teams. In fact, many organizations implementing such programs will purchase products only from suppliers that pass their certification criteria. Often, companies that set up certification programs work with their suppliers to help them become certified.

Single-sourcing also has some disadvantages, however. The largest, of course, is the risk of being totally dependent on one supplier. If the supplier, perhaps through no fault on its part, cannot deliver as needed, the firm is stuck. With the minimal buffers typical of a lean organization, this could mean expensive idled production and large shortages. There is also some question about the supplier's incentive to become more creative in terms of producing higher quality or less expensive parts, because it already has the single-source contract. Yet the Japanese constantly pressure their suppliers to continue reducing prices, expecting that, at the least, the effect of increased learning with higher volumes will result in lower prices.

Planning and Control

In the traditional firm, planning is the focus, and it is typically complex and computerized. MRP is a good example of the level of planning and analysis that goes into the traditional production system. Unfortunately, plans often go astray, but since the firm is focused on planning rather than control, the result is to try to improve planning the next time, and this, in turn, results in ever more complex plans. Thus, these firms spend most of their time planning and replanning and very little time actually executing the plans.

In the lean approach, the focus is on control. Thus, procedures are kept simple, visual, and made as routine as possible. Rather than planning and forecasting for an uncertain future, the firm attempts to respond to what actually happens in real time with flexible, quick operations. Some planning is certainly conducted, but to be even more effective and efficient in responding to actual events, the planning is directed to simple expectations and improvements in the control system.

But is there any way to combine the advantages of the lean JIT approach and MRP? Yes, there is a way. It consists of using MRP to pull the long-lead-time items and purchases *into* the shop, and it then employs JIT once the parts and raw materials have entered the shop. Dover's OPW Division uses this approach, for example. It employs MRP's explosion and lead-time offsetting to identify and order the external parts and raw materials and uses JIT's procedures to run a smooth, efficient plant once the parts and materials arrive. In other cases MRP is used as a planning tool for order releases and final assembly schedules, while JIT is used to execute and implement the plan.

Quality

The traditional approach to quality is to inspect the goods at critical points in the production system to weed out bad items and correct the system. At the least, final inspection on a sample should be conducted before a lot is sent to a customer. If too many defectives are found, the entire lot is inspected and the bad items are replaced with good ones. Scrap rates are tracked so that the firm knows how many to initiate through the production system in order to yield the number of good items desired by the customer.

With lean, the goal is zero defects and perfect quality. A number of approaches are used for this purpose, as described in Chapter 4. But the most important elements are the workers themselves—who check the parts as they hand them to the next worker—and the small lot sizes produced, as described earlier. If a part is bad, it is caught at the time of production, and the error in the production system is corrected immediately.

Maintenance

Corrective Maintenance vs Preventive maintenance

In the traditional approach to production, maintenance has been what is termed ***corrective maintenance***, although ***preventive maintenance*** is also common. Corrective maintenance is repairing a machine when it breaks down, whereas preventive maintenance is conducting maintenance before the machine is expected to fail, or at regular intervals. Corrective maintenance is more acceptable in the traditional firm, because there are queues of material sitting in front of the machines to be worked on so that production can continue undisturbed, at least until the queues are gone.

But in the lean enterprise, if a machine breaks down it will eventually stop all the following *downstream* equipment for lack of work. (It will almost immediately stop all *upstream* equipment as well, through the pull system.) Therefore, in lean organizations, the maintenance function assumes greater responsibility and has greater visibility. To reflect its expanded role, lean organizations refer to the maintenance function as total productive maintenance (TPM). One key aspect of TPM is that instead of employing a "crew" of experts who do nothing but repair broken equipment, the lean enterprise relies much more heavily on the operator for many of the maintenance tasks, especially simple preventive maintenance. We will return to the topic of TPM later in the chapter.

With our comparison of traditional and lean organizations complete, we now turn our attention to the five principles of lean and discuss each in more detail. This discussion will include an overview of representative tools and methodologies commonly used to support each principle.

SPECIFY VALUE

V. V. Imp

Value is ultimately defined by the customer.

At the heart of lean is the concept of value. While producers and service providers seek to create value for their customers, it is important to recognize that value is ultimately defined by the customer. Thus, one way to define value is to consider what and how much a customer is willing to pay for a particular product or service. Of course, related to how much a customer is willing to pay for a product or service is the strength of the customer's desires and needs, and the variety of options available to satisfy these needs.

Imp — less imp — more Imp

Alternatively, another common definition of value is that it is the opposite of waste or ***muda***. Waste can be defined as those activities that consume resources but from the customer's perspective create no value. From this perspective, waste is often classified into one of the following seven categories:

1. *Overproduction.* Creating more of an output than is needed at a particular point in time. Producing more than is needed creates the need for additional space to store the surplus, requires purchasing more raw materials than were needed, and often has a detrimental effect on profit margins as the surplus may need to be disposed of at distressed prices.

2. *Inventory.* Inventory takes a variety of forms, including raw materials, work-in-process, and finished goods. It requires space for its storage, leading to lease and utility expenses. Furthermore, the inventory must be insured, handled, financed, and tracked, further increasing the cost of holding it.

However, despite all these efforts, some portion of inventory will tend to get damaged, some may become obsolete, and some may even be stolen. Unfortunately, most, if not all, of the work related to maintaining inventory is not value added in the eyes of customer.

3. *Waiting.* Waiting relates to delays or events that prevent a worker from performing his or her work. A worker with nothing to work on because of a delay in an upstream activity, a worker who is idle because a piece of equipment broke down, or a worker who is idle while waiting for a piece of equipment to be set up all exemplify the waste of waiting.

4. *Unnecessary transport.* Any time a worker or a part must be moved, it is considered waste. One goal of lean is to seek ways to reduce the distance people or work must travel, as was illustrated by the Virginia Mason Medical Center example at the beginning of the chapter.

5. *Unnecessary processing.* Unnecessary processing relates to extra steps in a process. Examples of unnecessary processing include removing burrs from machined parts, reworking defective parts, and entering the same information into multiple databases. Also, from the lean perspective, inspections are generally considered unnecessary processing.

6. *Unnecessary human motions.* Using the human body efficiently and effectively is not only vital to the health of the workers, but also to the productivity of the organization. Time and motion studies as well as ergonomic studies are used to help design work environments that increase the efficiency, safety, and effectiveness of workers.

7. *Defects.* Parts that must be reworked, or in more extreme cases scrapped, represent the final category of waste. Having to perform rework requires repeating steps that were already performed, while scrapping parts results in extra material and processing charges with no corresponding output to offset these charges. The key to providing outputs that are valued by the customer is developing a solid understanding of customer needs. Establishing the voice of the customer, perhaps through a quality function deployment initiative (see Chapter 4), is one approach commonly used to help identify and better understand customer needs.

Based on a better understanding of how the customer defines value, the next logical task is to define a target cost. Generally speaking, the low-cost producer in an industry has more options available to it than other organizations in the industry. For example, the low-cost producer has the option of matching its competitors' prices and thereby maintaining a higher profit margin. Alternatively, the low-cost provider can offer its products and services at a lower price than the competition in an effort to increase its market share.

IDENTIFY THE VALUE STREAM

Once value has been defined from the customer's perspective and a target cost established, the next step is to identify the set of activities or value stream required to create the customer-valued output. Broadly speaking, the value stream includes all activities (value added and nonvalue added) from the creation of the raw materials to the final delivery of the output to the end consumer. Within the organization, the value stream includes the design of the output, continues through the operations function where raw materials are transformed into finished goods, and ends with the delivery of its output to the customer. However, it should also be pointed out that a properly crafted value stream map should transcend organizational boundaries. Thus, a complete value stream map would include an organization's suppliers, the suppliers to its suppliers, and any distributors, retailers, and so on between the organization and the end consumer.

The activities within a value stream map are often broadly categorized as:

- Value-added (e.g., patient diagnosis)
- Nonvalue-added but necessary (e.g., requiring patients to sign a HIPAA form)
- Nonvalue-added and not necessary (e.g., waiting for the doctor)

The challenge associated with value-added activities is to identify ways to perform these activities in such a way that more value is created and/or less resources consumed. Likewise, the challenge for both types of nonvalue-added activities is to identify opportunities to eliminate them or perhaps transform the activity into something that is valued by the customer.

An example value stream map for a fast-food restaurant is shown in Figure 10.2. To keep the example simple, the value stream map does not include activities beyond the boundary of a single restaurant. However, as noted earlier, a properly crafted value stream map would include interactions between the restaurant and the corporate office as well as interactions between the restaurant and its supplier base and the corporation and the supplier base. We assume that after conducting a market research study, it was determined that the only activities that the customers valued were placing their orders and having their orders prepared. To identify and highlight these activities as value-added, shading has been added to the corresponding boxes in the value stream map. Analysis of the value stream map suggests that of the 255 seconds a drive-through customer is in the process, only 150 seconds are value-added. Analysis of the value stream map also suggests the need to identify opportunities to eliminate or reduce the amount of time customers wait to place their orders as well as streamlining the payment and order delivery tasks.

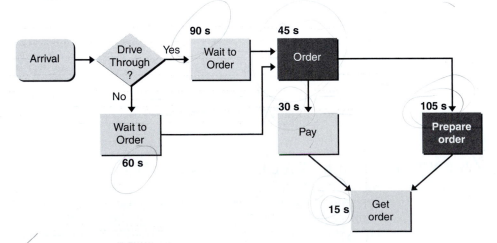

Figure 10.2   Value stream map for fast-food restaurant.

Make Value Flow

Erratic flows in one part of the value stream often become magnified in other parts of the system, not only further down the stream but, because of scheduling, further *up* the line as well. This is due to the formation of queues in the production system, the batching of parts for processing on machines, the lot-sizing rules we use to initiate production, and many other similar policies. These disruptions to the smooth flow of goods are costly to the production system and waste time, materials, and human energy. Thus, having identified the value stream, the next step is to transform it from the traditional batch and wait approach to one where the flow is continuous. This is accomplished by eliminating nonvalue-added activities and streamlining the remaining value-added steps. In fact, many lean organizations make the analogy that goods should "flow like water." A key aspect to achieving such a smooth flow is to master-schedule small lots of final products.

Another obstacle to smooth flows is the traditional functional organization structure. In the functional organization, work is organized based on the similarity of the work performed. Thus, you have accounting departments, marketing departments, radiology units, quality assurance departments, and so on. The problem with organizing work on the basis of the type of work performed is that work must then be handed off from department to department. Such hand-offs inevitably create delays in the process and introduce opportunities for making errors. Therefore, lean organizations have a bias toward organizing work based on the value creating process the work supports, as opposed to organizing work functionally.

It should also be pointed out that early production or delivery is just as inappropriate as late delivery. The goal is *perfect* adherence to schedule—without this, erratic flows are introduced throughout the value stream. With continuous, smooth flows of parts come continuous, level flows of work so there are no peak demands on workers, machines, or other resources. Then, once adequate capacity has been attained it will always be sufficient.

Continuous Flow Manufacturing

An important tenet to making value flow in lean enterprises is continuous flow manufacturing (CFM). According to this tenet, work should flow through the process without interruption, one unit at a time based on the customer's demand rate. Thus, once the processing of a unit has begun, the work should continue uninterrupted until the unit is completed. This is reflected by the phrase, "Don't let the parts touch the floor." To accomplish this, delays associated with setting up equipment, moving work between departments, storing work because a needed resource is unavailable, equipment breakdowns, and so on must be eliminated.

To synchronize the flow of work with the customer's demand rate, the ***takt time*** is calculated (the same as the cycle time, as calculated in Chapter 3). The term takt time, German for the baton used by orchestra conductors, was coined by Toyota and translates the customer demand rate into time. In effect, the takt time defines the rhythm or pace that work must be completed at in order to meet the customer demand rate. More specifically, takt time is calculated as:

$$\text{takt time} = \frac{\text{available work time}}{\text{customer required volume}}$$

To illustrate the concept of takt time, consider an insurance company that operates nine hours per day processing claims. Assume that the employees get two 15-minute breaks and one hour for lunch. Further assume that the company receives 6000 claims per month and that there are 20 working days per month. In this case, the takt time would be calculated as:

$$\text{takt time} = \frac{540 \text{ min} - 30 \text{ min} - 60 \text{ min}}{\dfrac{6000}{20}} = \frac{450}{300} = 1.5 \text{ minutes/claim}$$

In this case, the insurance company must process a claim every 1.5 minutes. But suppose the processing of an application requires 15 minutes of work. Then in this case, 10 employees working in parallel would be needed. In other words, processing 10 applications every 15 minutes is equivalent to processing one application every 1.5 minutes.

Converting to Mixed-Model Assembly and Sequencing

Another approach for enhancing the flow of work is mixed-model assembly and sequencing. With mixed-model assembly, items are produced smoothly throughout the day rather than in large batches of one item, followed by long shutdowns and setups and then by another large batch of another item. Let us demonstrate with an example.

Suppose three different models are being produced in a plant that operates two shifts, and the monthly demands are as given in Table 10.2. Dividing the monthly demand by 20 working days per month and then again by two shifts per day gives the daily production requirements per shift. A common divisor of the required production per shift of 20 A's, 15 B's, and 10 C's is 5. Using 5 as the common divisor means that we would produce five batches of each of these models each shift. Dividing the required production per shift of each model by five batches indicates that on each production cycle, 4 units of A, 3 units of B, and 2 units of C will be produced. Assuming two 15-minute breaks per 8-hour shift (480 minutes), the production rate must be 45 units per 450 minute shift (480 − 15 − 15 = 450), or 10 minutes per unit (450 minutes per shift/45 units per shift). Because one cycle consists of 9 units (4 A's, 3 B's, and 2 C's), the entire cycle will take 90 minutes. Thus, each production cycle of 4 A's, 3 B's, and 2 C's will be repeated five times each shift to produce the required 45 units.

One possible production cycle would be to produce the three models in batches using a sequence such as A-A-A-A-B-B-B-C-C. Alternatively, to smooth the production of the nine units throughout the production cycle, a sequence such as A-B-A-

TABLE 10.2 • Mixed-Model Assembly Cycle

Model	Monthly Demand	Required/Shift	Units/Cycle
A	800	800/(20 × 2) = 20	4
B	600	15	3
C	400	10	2
Total	1800	45	9

B-C-A-B-A-C might be used. Clearly, numerous other sequences are also possible. With daily production of all models, no erratic changes are introduced into the plant through customer demand, because some of every product is always available. When models are produced in traditional batches (such as producing 1000 A's, then 750 B's, followed by 500 C's), one or more batches may well be depleted before the other batches are finished. This then necessitates putting a "rush" order through the plant (in order not to lose a customer for the models that are out of stock), disrupting ongoing work, and adding to the cost of all products—not to mention the frustration involved.

The Theory of Constraints

The **theory of constraints** (Goldratt 1990), offers a systematic way to view and analyze process flows. Key aspects of the theory of constraints (TOC) include identifying the bottlenecks in the process and balancing the work flows in the system. Other names for the same concept are drum-buffer-rope (DBR), goal system, and synchronous manufacturing. TOC is often compared to kanban (discussed later in this chapter) and MRP (Chapter 9) as another way to plan production and schedule operations. Studies comparing these systems seem to show that each has different strengths—MRP to generate time-phased requirements, TOC to plan medium-time-horizon bottleneck facilities, and JIT to maximize throughput—and manufacturers should employ a combination of the three.

The theory of constraints was originally implemented through a proprietary package primarily used in the make-to-order and automotive industries called *optimized production technology* (OPT), which is based on an alternative approach to capacity planning. The basic procedure is first to identify bottleneck workstations in the shop, schedule them to keep them fully utilized, and then schedule the non–bottleneck workstations to keep the bottlenecks busy so that they are never waiting for work. The following ten guidelines capture the essence of the theory:

1. *Flows rather than capacities should be balanced throughout the shop.* The objective is to move material quickly and smoothly through the production system, not to balance capacities or utilization of equipment or human resources.

2. *Fluctuations in a tightly connected, sequence-dependent system add to each other rather than averaging out.*

3. *Utilization of a non–bottleneck is determined by other constraints in the system, such as bottlenecks.* Non–bottleneck resources do not restrict the amount of output that a production system can create. Thus, these resources should be managed to support the operations of those resources (i.e., the bottlenecks) that do constrain the amount of output. Clearly, operating a non–bottleneck resource at a higher rate of output than the bottleneck resource does nothing to increase the output produced by the entire production system.

4. *Utilizing a workstation (producing when material is not yet needed) is not the same as activation.* Traditionally, managers have not made a distinction between "using" a resource and "activating" it. However, according to the theory of constraints, a resource is considered *utilized* only if it is helping the entire system create more output. If a machine is independently

producing more output than the rest of the system, the time the machine is operated to produce outputs over and above what the overall system is producing is considered activation, not utilization.

5. *An hour lost at a bottleneck is an hour lost for the whole shop.* Since the bottleneck resource limits the amount of output the entire system can create, time when this resource is not producing output is a loss to the entire system that cannot be made up. Lost time at a bottleneck resource can result because of down time for maintenance or because the resource was starved for work. For example, if a hair stylist is idle for an hour because no customers arrive, this hour of lost haircuts cannot be made up, even if twice as many customers as usual arrive in the next hour.

6. *An hour saved at a non–bottleneck is a mirage.* Since non–bottlenecks have plenty of capacity and do not limit the output of the production system, saving time at these resources does not increase total output. The implication for managers is that time-saving improvements to the system should be directed at bottleneck resources.

7. *Bottlenecks govern shop throughput and work-in-process inventories.*

8. *The transfer batch need not be the same size as the process batch.* The size of the *process batch* is the size of the batch produced each time a job is run. Often, this size is determined by trading off various costs, as is done with the economic order quantity (EOQ) model discussed in Chapter 8. On the other hand, the size of the *transfer batch* is the size of the batch of parts moved from one work center to another work center. Clearly, parts can be moved in smaller batches than the process batch. Indeed, considerable reductions in batch flow times can often be obtained by using a transfer batch that is smaller than the process batch. For example, assume that a manufacturer produces a part in batches of 10. This part requires three operations, each performed on a different machine. The operation time is 5 minutes per part per operation. Figure 10.3*a* demonstrates the effect on flow time when a process batch of 10 units is reduced to a transfer batch of one unit. Specifically, in Figure 10.3*a* the transfer batch is the same size as the process batch, and a flow time of 150 minutes results. In Figure 10.3*b*, the one-unit transfer batch reduces flow time to 60 minutes. The reason for long flow time with a large transfer batch is that in any batch, the first part must always wait for all the other parts to complete their processing before it is started on the next machine. In Figure 10.3*a*, the first part in the batch has to wait 45 minutes for the other nine parts. When the transfer batch is reduced to one unit, the parts in the batch do not have to wait for the other parts in the process batch.

9. *The size of the process batch should be variable, not fixed.* Because the economics of different resources can vary, the process batch does not need to be the same size at all stages of production. For example, consider an item that is produced on an injection molding machine and then visits a trimming department. Because the time and cost to set up injection molding equipment are likely to be very different from the time and cost to set up the trimming equipment, there is no reason why the batch size should be the same at each of these stages. Thus, batch size at each stage should be determined by the specific economics of that stage.

Time	5	10	15	20	25	30	35	40	45	50	55	60	65	70	75	80	85	90	95	100	105	110	115	120	125	130	135	140	145	150
Opn 1	P1	P2	P3	P4	P5	P6	P7	P8	P9	P10																				
Opn 2											P1	P2	P3	P4	P5	P6	P7	P8	P9	P10										
Opn 3																					P1	P2	P3	P4	P5	P6	P7	P8	P9	P10

(a)

Time	5	10	15	20	25	30	35	40	45	50	55	60
Opn 1	P1	P2	P3	P4	P5	P6	P7	P8	P9	P10		
Opn 2		P1	P2	P3	P4	P5	P6	P7	P8	P9	P10	
Opn 3			P1	P2	P3	P4	P5	P6	P7	P8	P9	P10

(b)

Figure 10.3 Transfer batch size and its effects on flow time. (*a*) Transfer batch size equals process batch size. (*b*) Transfer batch size equals one part.

10. *A shop schedule should be set by examining all the shop constraints simultaneously.* Traditionally, schedules are determined sequentially. First, the batch size is determined. Next, lead times are calculated and priorities set. Finally, schedules are adjusted on the basis of capacity constraints. The theory of constraints advocates considering all constraints simultaneously in developing schedules. The theory also argues that lead times are the result of the schedules and therefore cannot be determined beforehand.

The critical aspect of these guidelines is the focus on bottleneck workstations, not overloading the workstations, and the splitting of batches in order to move items along to the next workstation when desirable. A five-step process is recommended for implementing the theory of constraints:

1. *Identify the system's constraint(s).* Usually the process-flow diagram will help identify the constraints, but the ultimate constraint may in fact be sales representatives' time, capital available for investment, mandated policies such as a single shift, or even demand in the marketplace.

2. *Exploit the constraint.* Find ways to maximize the return per unit of the constraint. An example here would be to use the scarce resource to produce as much of the highest profit item as possible.

3. *Subordinate all else to the constraint.* The objective here is to make sure the constraint is always productive and that something else isn't drawing

resources away from the constraint. For example, perhaps inventories should be built in front of a scarce machine or worker.

4. *Elevate the constraint.* Again, find ways to make the constraint as productive as possible, such as extra maintenance; saving time on the constraint by using other, perhaps less-efficient machines more intensively; or even obtaining more of the constraint.

5. *If the constraint is no longer a bottleneck, find the next constraint and repeat the steps.* Once a bottleneck has been eliminated, something else becomes the bottleneck—perhaps another machine or storage facility, or perhaps the demand in the marketplace.

PULL VALUE THROUGH THE VALUE STREAM

In the traditional firm, long lead times are often thought to allow more time to make decisions and get work performed. But in the lean enterprise, short lead times mean easier, more accurate forecasting and planning. Moreover, a way to capitalize on the increasing strategic importance of fast response to the customer is to minimize all the lead times. If lead times are reduced, there is less time for things to go awry, to get lost, or to be changed. For example, it is quite common for an order placed two months ago to be changed every three weeks until it is delivered: change an option, change the quantity ordered, and so on. However, if the delivery time is one week or less, the customers can place the order when they know exactly what they need and can therefore delay ordering until the week before they need it.

As opposed to the MRP approach of "pushing" materials through a plant, lean enterprises rely on **pull systems** whereby actual customer demand drives the production process. Push systems are planning-based systems that determine when workstations will probably need parts if everything goes according to plan. However, operations rarely go according to plan, and as a result, materials may be either too late or too early. To safeguard against being too late and to make sure that people always have enough work to keep busy, safety stocks are used, even with MRP; these may not even be needed, but they further increase the stocks of materials in the plant. Thus, in a push system we see workers always busy making items and lots of material in the plant.

In comparison, a pull system is a control-based system that signals the requirement for parts as they are needed in reality. The result is that workers may occasionally (and sometimes frequently) be idle because more materials are not needed. This keeps material from being produced when it is not needed (waste). The appearance of a plant using a pull system is quiet and slow, with minimal material around.

To further contrast the differences between push and pull systems, consider the production system shown in Figure 10.4. The system consists of one machine of type A and one machine of type B. Machine A has the capacity to produce 75 units per day, and machine B has the capacity to produce 50 units per day. All products are first produced on machine A and then processed on machine B. Daily demand for the organization is 50 units.

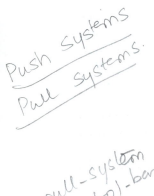

Figure 10.4 Sequential production system with two machines.

In a push system, each work center would work as fast as it could and *push* the product on to work centers downstream, regardless of whether they needed additional materials. In Figure 10.4, after the first day of operation, machine A would produce 75 units, machine B would process 50 of the 75 units it received from machine A, and 25 units would be added to work-in-process inventory. Each day the system operates in this fashion, 25 more units will be added to the work-in-process inventory in front of machine B. This might seem irrational to you, but the only way for inventory not to be built up is for machine A to produce less than it is capable of producing. In this example, we could idle machine A 33 percent of the day and produce and transport only 50 units to machine B. However, if you were the plant manager and you noticed that the worker assigned to machine A was working only 67 percent of the time, what would you think? You might think the worker was goofing off and order him or her to run the machine. Of course, doing this only increases the amount of money tied up in inventory and does nothing to increase the amount of product completed and shipped to the customer.

In a pull system, the worker at machine A would produce only in response to requests for more materials made by the worker at machine B. Furthermore, the worker at machine B is authorized to make additional product only to replenish product that is used to meet actual customer demand. If there is no customer demand, machine B will sit idle. And if machine B sits idle, machine A will be idle. In this way, the production of the entire operation is matched to actual demand.

The signals used in a pull system to authorize production may be of various kinds. Dover Corporation's OPW Division makes gasoline nozzles for gas pumps and uses wire bins as signals. Each bin holds 500 nozzles, and two are used at any time. Raw material is taken out of one bin until it is empty, and then material is drawn from the second bin. A bin collector constantly scouts the plant, looking for empty bins, and returns them to the stockroom where they are refilled and returned to the workstations. In this manner, no more than two bins' worth of material (1000 units) is ever in process.

Hewlett-Packard uses yellow tape to make squares about 1 foot on a side as the signals for its assembly lines. One square lies between every two workers. When workers finish an item, they draw the next unit to work on from the square between them and the previous worker. When the square is empty, this is the signal that another item is needed from the previous worker. Thus there are never more than two items in process per worker.

These two examples are actually modifications of Toyota's original JIT system. Toyota's materials management system is known as ***kanban***, which means "card" in Japanese. The idea behind this system is to authorize materials for production only if there is a need for them. Through the use of kanban authorization cards, production is "pulled" through the system, instead of pushed out before it is needed and then stored. Thus, the MPS authorizes final assembly, which in turn authorizes subassembly production, which in its turn authorizes parts assembly, and so on. If production stops at some point in the system, immediately all downstream production also stops, and soon thereafter all upstream production as well.

Typically, two cards are used—a withdrawal kanban and a production kanban. The cards are very simple, showing only the part number and name, the work centers involved, a storage location, and the container capacity. The approach is illustrated in Figure 10.5.

Assume that work flows from work center (WC) 4 to WC5, and containers are used to transport the output from WC4 to WC5, where they are used as inputs. When WC5 sees that it will be needing more input parts, it takes an empty container and a withdrawal kanban back to WC4. There it leaves the empty container and locates a full one, which has a production kanban with it. WC5's withdrawal kanban authorizes it to remove the full container and put the production kanban in a rack at WC4, thereby authorizing the production of another container of parts. Back at WC5, the withdrawal kanban is placed back in its rack. WC4 cannot initiate production and fill an empty container until it has a production kanban on the rack authorizing additional production. Thus, withdrawal kanbans authorize the acquisition of additional materials from a supplying work center and production kanbans authorize a work center to make additional product.

The advantage of such a system is its simplicity. Being entirely visual in nature, it facilitates smooth production flow, quality inspection, minimization of inventory, and clear control of the production system.

Kanban/JIT in Services

Of course many services, and especially pure services, have no choice but to provide their service exactly when it is demanded. For example, a hair stylist cannot build up inventories of cuts and styles before the actual customers arrive. Now JIT is being adopted in other services that use materials rather extensively. For

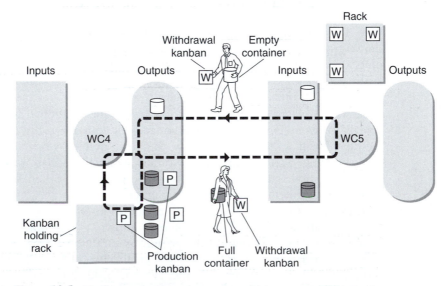

Figure 10.5 Kanban process.

example, professors can choose materials from a wide variety of sources and let a "just-in-time" publisher compile the material into a custom-made book as quickly and cheaply as a standard book. Supermarkets replenish their shelves on a JIT basis as customers withdraw purchases. And everyone is familiar with fast-turnaround operations such as cleaners, automobile oil changes, photo processing, and eyeglass lenses, not to mention fast food.

Many, if not most, of the techniques used in manufacturing to become lean are equally applicable to services such as close supplier ties (food spoils), maintaining a flexible workforce (customization), and using reservation systems and off-peak pricing to keep level loads on the system. In addition, the general advantages that manufacturers accrue through defect-free operations, flexible layouts, minimal inventories, preventive maintenance, advanced technologies, standardized work methods, and other such approaches provide equal advantages to service organizations, and in some cases greater advantages.

PURSUE PERFECTION

At the risk of stating the obvious, competition is a moving target. By the same token, opportunities to improve processes never end. Therefore, it is common for lean enterprises to focus less on meeting the immediate challenges posed by the competition and to focus more on the long-term goal of achieving perfection. In the remainder of this section, we overview five commonly used tools lean organizations turn to in their pursuit of perfection: 5S, the visual factory, kaizen, poka yoke, and total productive maintenance.

5S

A widely used approach for increasing the efficiency of individual work activities is 5S. The approach consists of the following five steps:

1. *Sort*. Distinguish what work must be performed to complete a task from what does not need to be done. Eliminate the unnecessary steps.
2. *Straighten (Set in order)*. A common phrase in industrial engineering is "A place for everything and everything in its place."
3. *Scrub (Shine)*. Maintain a workplace that is clean and free of clutter.
4. *Systemize*. Develop and implement standardized procedures for maintaining an orderly work environment.
5. *Standardize (Sustain)*. Make the previous four steps a habit.

The Visual Factory

With little or no slack to absorb disruptions, successful execution in a lean environment requires that workers and decision makers are constantly up to date with the conditions in the work environment. One way lean organizations accomplish this is through an approach called the visual factory. The objectives of the visual factory are to help make problems visible, help employees stay up to date on current operating conditions, and to communicate process improvement goals. With the visual factory, problems can be made visible through the use of charts displayed throughout the workplace that plot trends related to quality, on time delivery performance, safety, machine downtime, productivity, and so on. Likewise, visual factories make use of production and schedule boards to help employees stay up to date on current conditions. It should be noted that the concept of a visual factory is equally applicable to services. For example, a call center one of the authors recently visited had a board that displayed updated information on the percent of calls that were answered within the desired time frame.

Kaizen   *continuous improvement*

The Japanese word "kaizen" literally translates into continuous improvement. The lean journey in the pursuit of perfection requires a continuous series of incremental improvements. In some cases, a continuous improvement initiative may take a year or longer to implement. However, recently a short-term approach to continuous improvement called the ***kaizen blitz*** (a.k.a. kaizen workshops, kaizen events) is becoming increasingly popular. In a kaizen blitz, a cross-functional team completes a continuous improvement project in under a week. Often the kaizen blitz begins with a day or two of formal training in lean concepts. The training is then followed by the team completing a continuous improvement project. The project requires the team to collect any needed data, analyze the data, and then immediately implement the proposed improvements. Typical goals for a kaizen blitz include one or more of the following: reducing the amount of floor space needed, increasing process flexibility, improving work flows, improving quality, enhancing the safety of the working environment, and reducing or eliminating nonvalue-added activities.

Poka Yoke   *mistake-proof work activities*

The goal of poka yoke is to mistake-proof work activities in a way that prevents errors from being committed in the first place. Examples of poka yoke include supplementing electronic forms with computer code or scripts that check the validity of information entered into fields as it is being entered, designing a machine that requires the operator to press two buttons simultaneously to cycle the machine so that neither hand can be caught in the machine when it is operating, and placing parts in kits based on their assembly sequence.

Total Productive Maintenance

A key driver of waste and therefore an important component of lean is the effective use of equipment. In particular, equipment impacts waste in a number of ways including:

- *Breakdowns.* When a piece of equipment fails, it is no longer creating valued outputs, which can lead to customer dissatisfaction as well as economic repercussions for the firm. Furthermore, workers may be made idle during the breakdown, further adding to the firm's cost without corresponding increases in sales.

- *Setups.* Like breakdowns, a piece of equipment undergoing a setup or changeover is not creating valued outputs. Moreover, during the setup, workers are being paid to make the changeover and if a specialized group performs the setup, the machine operators may be idled during the setup period.

- *Stoppages.* At times, production on a piece of equipment may need to be halted because its output is unacceptable.

- *Reduced speed.* Another potential loss occurs when a piece of equipment is operated at a lower production rate than the rate it was designed to operate at.

- *Yields.* Yield relates to the percent of the total output produced that is acceptable. Lower yields correspond to greater amounts of waste in the form of scrap and rework.

Total productive maintenance (TPM) focuses broadly on the cost of equipment over its entire life cycle and encompasses a variety of tools and techniques to improve equipment maintenance practices as well as to help prevent and predict equipment failures. Key components of a TPM program include:

- Identifying ways to maximize equipment effectiveness.

- Developing a productive maintenance system for maintaining equipment over its entire life cycle.

- Coordinating the work of engineering, operations, and maintenance employees.

- Giving employees the responsibility to maintain the equipment they operate.

A measure of ***overall equipment effectiveness*** is calculated as the product of equipment availability, equipment efficiency, and the rate of quality output. Equipment availability represents the percent of time a piece of equipment is available to produce output. Equipment efficiency is a function of the theoretical cycle time, the actual cycle time, actual processing time, and equipment operating time. The rate of quality output corresponds to the yield on the piece of equipment. An overall effectiveness rating of 85 percent is considered excellent.

BENEFITS OF LEAN

In summary, it appears that lean is not one of the annual fads of American management but rather a philosophy for efficiently and effectively using the resources an organization already has at its disposal. As such, it will not disappear from the scene, though its tenets are increasingly being merged with other programs such as Six Sigma and supply chain management. And in spite of the concerns about the timely physical transportation of goods, a major challenge for the future will be the effective utilization of the many information technologies available to managers, such as the Internet. In too many cases, organizations are relying too much on internal forecasts rather than using the Internet and other information and communications technologies to access their customer's real-time production schedules. In the future, lean organizations will increasingly make use of satellite tracking systems, wireless communication, scanning technology, global positioning systems, two-dimensional bar codes and RFID tags, and paperless documentation across the entire value chain.

As we have seen, lean offers a variety of possible benefits: reduced inventories and space, faster response to customers due to shorter lead times, less scrap, higher quality, increased communication and teamwork, and greater emphasis on identifying and solving problems. In general, there are five primary types of benefits: (1) cost savings, (2) revenue increases, (3) investment savings, (4) workforce improvements, and (5) uncovering problems.

1. *Cost savings.* Costs are saved a number of ways: inventory reductions, reduced scrap, fewer defects, fewer changes due to both customers and engineering, less space, decreased labor hours, less rework, reduced overhead, and other such effects.

2. *Revenue increases.* Revenues are increased primarily through better service and quality to the customer. Short lead times and faster response to customers' needs result in better margins and higher sales. In addition, revenues will be coming in faster on newer products and services.

3. *Investment savings.* Investment is saved through three primary effects. First, less space (about a third) is needed for the same capacity. Second, inventory is reduced to the point that turns run about 50 to 100 a year (compared with 3 or 4, historically). Third, the volume of work produced in the same facility is significantly increased, frequently by as much as 100 percent.

4. *Workforce improvements.* The employees of lean firms are much more satisfied with their work. They prefer the teamwork it demands, and they like the fact that fewer problems arise. They are also better trained for the flexibility and skills needed with lean (e.g., problem solving, maintenance), and they enjoy the growth they experience in their jobs. All this translates into better, more productive work.

5. *Uncovering problems.* One of the unexpected benefits is the greater visibility to problems that lean allows, if management is willing to capitalize on the opportunity to fix these problems. In trying to speed up a process, all types of difficulties are uncovered and most of them are various forms of waste, so not only is response time improved but cost is also.

EXPAND YOUR UNDERSTANDING _____

1. In your opinion, does it make more sense for an organization to merge its lean and Six Sigma programs or keep them separate?

2. Describe how trying to please every customer turns into a "trap" for traditional production. Aren't customization and multiple options the way of the future, particularly for differing national tastes and preferences?

3. The Japanese say that "a defect is a treasure." What way do they mean, and how does this relate to lean?

4. How smooth is a production flow where every item requires a setup? Wouldn't flows be smoother with long runs where no setups were required for days?

5. Does the theory of constraints apply to services as well as to products?

6. One JIT consultant suggests that managers implement JIT by just removing inventories from the floor. What is likely to happen if they do this? What would the Japanese do?

7. With single-sourcing, how does the firm protect itself from price gouging? From strikes or interruptions to supply?

8. How might lean apply to a service like an airline? A retailer? A university?

9. American managers hate to see high-paid workers sitting idle, even maintenance employees. What is the alternative?

10. The theory of constraints distinguishes between process batches and transfer batches. It also recommends that process batches vary according to the economics of efficiency at each stage of production. Considering the effects of order size and size of the preceding process batch, how then should transfer batches be determined?

11. Consider a service you are familiar with. List examples for each of the seven categories of waste for the service.

12. In identifying the value stream, why is it important to go beyond the boundaries of the organization of interest?

APPLY YOUR UNDERSTANDING
J. Galt Lock Ltd.

J. Galt Lock Ltd., located in Sydney, Australia, produces a line of door locksets and hardware for the residential, light commercial, and retail markets. The company's single plant is just over 200,000 square feet and is organized into the following functional departments: screw machines, presses, machining, maintenance, tool and dies, latches, plating, buffing, subassembly, and final assembly. The company employs approximately 375 people, 290 of whom are hourly workers. The largest category of employees—assemblers—accounts for two-thirds of the workforce.

The company uses a proprietary planning and scheduling system that uses both an AS/400 minicomputer and spreadsheet analysis performed on a microcomputer to determine production and purchasing requirements. At any given time, there are 1500 to 3000 open work orders on the shop floor. The average lot size is 50,000 parts, but for some products the size is as high as 250,000 parts.

The planning system creates work orders for each part number in the bills of materials, which are delivered to the various departments. Department supervisors determine the order in which to process the jobs, since the system does not prioritize the work orders. A variety of scheduling methods are used throughout the plant, including kanbans, work orders, and expediters; however, the use of these different methods often creates problems. For example, one production manager commented that although a "kanban pull scheduling system is being used between subassembly and final assembly, frequently the right card is not used at the right time, the correct quantity is not always produced, and there are no predetermined schedules and paths for the pickup and delivery of parts." In fact, it was discovered that work orders were often being superseded by expediters and supervisors, large lag times existed between the decision to produce a batch and the start of actual production, and suppliers were not being included in the "information pipeline." One production supervisor commented:

> We routinely abort the plans generated by our formal planning system because we figure out other ways of pushing product. Although we use Kanban systems in two areas of the plant, in reality everything here is a push system. Everything is based on inventory levels and/or incoming customer orders. We push not just the customer order but all the raw materials and everything that is associated with the product being assembled.

In an effort to improve its operations, Galt Lock hired a consulting company. The consultant determined that 36 percent of the floor space was being used to hold inventory, 25 percent was for work centers, 14 percent for aisles, 7 percent for offices, and 18 percent for nonvalue-adding activities. The production manager commented:

We have an entire department that is dedicated to inventory storage consisting of 10 to 11 aisles of parts. What is bad is that we have all these parts, and none of them are the right ones. Lots of parts, and we still can't build.

The consultant also determined that the upstream "supplying" work centers were often far from the downstream "using" work centers, material flows were discontinuous as the parts were picked up and set down numerous times, and workers and supervisors often spent a considerable amount of time hunting for parts. The production manager commented:

Work-in-process is everywhere. You can find work-in-process at every one of the stations on the shop floor. It is extremely difficult to find materials on the shop floor because of the tremendous amount of inventory on the shop floor. It is also very difficult to tell at what state a customer order is in or the material necessary to make that customer order, because we have such long runs of components and subassemblies.

The plant manager commented:

My biggest concern is consistent delivery to customers. We just started monitoring on-time delivery performance, and it was the first time that measurement had ever been used at this operation. We found out how poorly we are actually doing. It is a matter of routinely trying to chase things down in the factory that will complete customer orders. The challenge of more consistent delivery is compounded by the fact that we have to respond much faster. Our customers used to give us three to six weeks of lead time, but now the big retailers we are starting to deal with give us only two or three days. And if we don't get it out in that short period of time, we lose the customer.

Questions

1. Evaluate and critique the existing operation and the management of J. Galt Lock.
2. How applicable is JIT to a situation like this? Would converting from a functional layout to a cellular layout facilitate the implementation of JIT?
3. Where could the principles of lean production be of value to J. Galt Lock?

EXERCISES

1. The time between patient arrivals to the blood drawing unit of a medical lab averages 2 minutes. The lab is staffed with two nurses that actually draw the patients' blood. The nurses work from 9:00 A.M. to 5:30 P.M. and get two 10-minute breaks and a half-hour for lunch. What is the takt time for drawing patient blood?

2. Referring to Exercise 1, assume that additional analysis was performed and it was determined that an average of 255 patients (with standard deviation of 30) requiring blood work come to the lab each day. It was further determined that the duration of the nurses' breaks ranged between 9 to 13.5 minutes, with all times in the range equally likely and that the time taken for lunch ranged between 28 minutes and 34 minutes, again with all times in the range equally likely. Using Crystal Ball or another simulation package, develop a distribution for the takt time assuming that the number of patients that arrive on a given day is normally distributed. What are the managerial implications of your analysis?

3. The high-speed copier of a printing and document services firm is available 95% of the operating hours. The copier is operated at a rate of three copies per second, although it was designed to make four copies per second. Data suggest that about 3 percent of the copied pages must be scrapped and recopied. What is the overall equipment effectiveness of the high-speed copier?

4. Referring to Exercise 3, assume that the copier availability follows a triangular distribution and that sometimes the copier is available for as few as 2 hours in a 12-hour day, is typically available 10 hours a day, and occasionally is available all 12 hours. Further assume that the rate the copier operates varies based on the type of job, from two copies per second to four copies per second with all rates in this range equally likely. Finally, assume that the scrap rate is normally distributed with a mean of 3 percent and standard deviation of 0.7 percent. Using Crystal Ball or another simulation package, develop the distribution for the copier's overall equipment effectiveness. What are the managerial implications of your analysis?

BIBLIOGRAPHY

Alternburg, K., D. Griscom, J. Hart, F. Smith, and G. Wohler. "Just-in-Time Logistics Support for the Automobile Industry." *Production and Inventory Management Journal*, 40 (Second Quarter 1999): 59–66.

Bowersox, D. J., and D. J. Closs. *Logistical Management: The Integrated Supply Chain Process*. New York: McGraw-Hill, 1996.

Burrows, P. "The Computer Is in the Mail (Really)." *Business Week* (January 23, 1995): 76–77.

Chen, S., and R. Chen. "Manufacturer-Supplier Relationship in a JIT Environment." *Production and Inventory Management Journal*, 38 (First Quarter 1997): 58–64.

Connolly, C. "Hospital takes Page from Toyota," *The Washington Post,* (January 3, 2005): www.msnbc.msn.com/id/8079313/.

DeBusk, C., and A. Rangel Jr. "Creating a Lean Six Sigma Hospital Process," healthcare.isixsigma.com, (May 30, 2005).

Duclos, L. K., S. M. Siha, and R. R. Lummus. "JIT in Services: A Review of Current Practices and Future Directions for Research." *Intr'l. Journal of Service Industry Management*, 6 (Number 5, 1995): 36–52.

Fornari, A., and S. Maszle "Lean Six Sigma Leads Xerox," *Six Sigma Forum Magazine* (August 2004): pp. 11–16.

Goldratt, E. M. *Theory of Constraints*, 2nd rev. ed. Croton-on-Hudson: North River Press, 1990.

Hill, W. J., and W. Kearney "The Honeywell Experience," *Six Sigma Forum Magazine* (February 2003): pp. 34–37.

Hobbs, O. K. "Managing JIT Toward Maturity." *Production and Inventory Management Journal*, 38 (First Quarter 1997): 47–50.

Mascitelli, R. "Lean Thinking: It's about Efficient Value Creation." *Target* (Second Quarter 2000): 22–26.

Monden, Y. *Toyota Production System*, 2nd ed. Atlanta, GA: Industrial Engineering and Management Press, 1993.

Monden, Y. *Toyota Production System: An Integrated Approach to Just-in-Time*. Atlanta, GA: Institute of Industrial Engineers, 1998.

Pyzdek, T. *The Six Sigma Handbook*. New York: McGraw-Hill, 2003.

Richman, T. "Logistics Management: How 20 Best-Practice Companies Do It." *Harvard Business Review* (September–October 1995): 11.

Schniederjans, M. *Topics in Just-in-Time Management*. Boston: Allyn & Bacon, 1993.

Schonberger, R. *World Class Manufacturing: The Next Decade: Building Power, Strength, and Value*. New York: Free Press, 1996.

Swanson, C. A., and W. M. Lankford. "JIT Manufacturing." *Business Process Management Journal*, 4 (1998): 333–341.

Tonkin, L. "System Sensor's Lean Journey." *Target* (Second Quarter 2002): 44–47.

White, R. E., J. N. Pearson, and J. R. Wilson. "JIT Manufacturing: A Survey of Implementations in Small and Large U.S. Manufacturers." *Management Science*, 45 (January 1999): 1–15.

Womack, J. "Lean Thinking for Process Management," Presented at the Decision Sciences Institute Annual Meeting, November 22, 2004.

Womack, J., and D. Jones. *Lean Thinking: Banish Waste and Create Wealth in Your Corporation*. New York: Simon & Schuster, 2003.

Wortman, B., W. R. Richardson, G. Gee, M. Williams, T. Pearson, F. Bensley, J. P. Patel, J. DeSimone, and D. R. Carlson, CSSBB Primer (West Terre Haute, IN: Quality Council of Indiana, 2001).

Zipkin, P. H., *Foundations of Inventory Management*. New York: Irwin/McGraw-Hill, 2000.

CHAPTER 11

Project Management

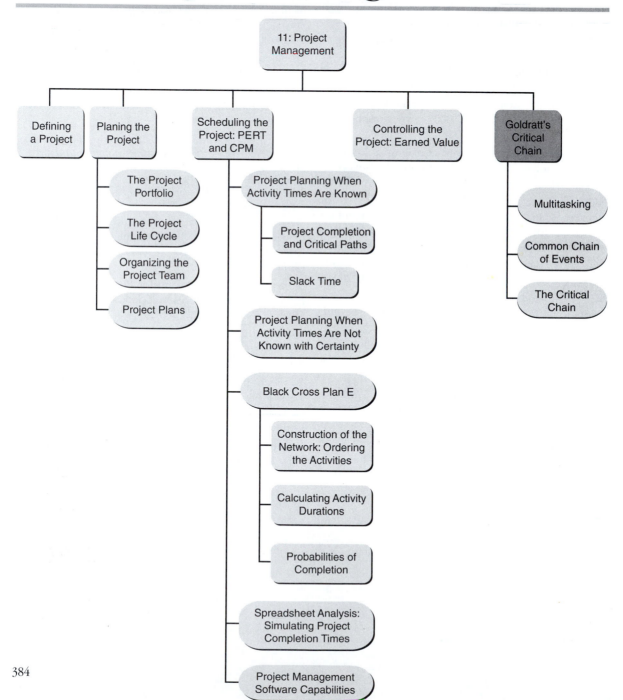

In this chapter, we continue our discussion of scheduling from Chapter 6 but shift our attention to the scheduling of projects. Projects are actually processes that are performed infrequently or ad hoc. They range from simple combinations of tactical tasks to strategic organizational change, and from setting up a party to putting a person on the moon. The chapter begins with a discussion of the crucial topics of project selection, project planning, and organizing the project team. We then move on to an explanation of some project-scheduling techniques for situations where activity times are known, or not known with certainty. Some typical project management software printouts are illustrated. The chapter continues with a discussion of controlling project cost and performance, and then concludes with a description of Goldratt's insights about projects under the topic "critical chain."

INTRODUCTION

- Numerous examples of projects have already been discussed in this book. For example, Chapter 1 described a project for transporting the Olympic Flame to Atlanta. You may recall that two years of planning went into this project, and completing it required coordinating 10,000 runners who carried the Olympic Torch 15,000 miles in 84 days. In another example described in Chapter 5, Mercedes-Benz formed a project team to find a location for its new manufacturing facility.

- At a more detailed level, consider that the team formed to develop the Chrysler Viper had only 3 years to complete the development project from concept to roadster. This included developing an entirely new 8.0-liter V-10 aluminum engine and a high-performance six-speed transmission. Typically, such development projects required 5 years at Chrysler. Thus, from the very beginning of the project, managers at Chrysler recognized the importance of consistent end-to-end project management.

    Team members for the project were hand-picked, and a project management system called Artemis Prestige was selected as a tool to help manage the project. According to managers at Chrysler, the project management system required the ability to track multiple projects concurrently, allow users to use it interactively, provide project personnel with a broad picture of the entire project, and help identify the impact of each activity on the ultimate completion of the project. These capabilities could then be used to perform "what if" analyses to assess the effect of changes in resource allocations and other engineering changes. With these capabilities, personnel could determine the effect of a proposed change before making a commitment to the change. In general, the Artemis software package provided a vital communications network and helped ensure that critical links between different parts of the project were completed according to the plan.

    By most accounts, the Viper project was an overwhelming success and yielded several significant innovations. For example, the first test engine required less than a year to develop. This was particularly important because several other major

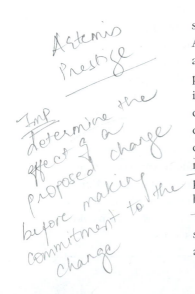

385

components, including the transmission, depended on the engine. The transmission was developed in $1\frac{1}{2}$ years, down from the usual 5 to 6 years. Additionally, many important innovations in the frame, body, and brakes were incorporated into the Viper (O'Keeffe 1994).

- Zeneca Pharmaceuticals U.S. is a unit of the research-intensive pharmaceutical business of Zeneca Group PLC, headquartered in the United Kingdom. The Zeneca Pharmaceuticals mission is to develop new drugs for the medical community. The development of a new drug is a complex project requiring extensive management and guidance over a long duration, typically 10 years. Basically, drug development is the process by which a new chemical entity is synthesized, found to have therapeutic pharmacologic "activity" in living animals, tested in more animals and in humans, and approved by the Food and Drug Administration (FDA) as a "new drug." After approval, the drug is sold to patients, usually by prescription. Unfortunately, in the process that begins with research and ends with approval for market, only about one drug in 10,000 meets with success, due to the many hurdles that must be overcome.

The major steps that the project manager must follow in the development process are as follows. (1) *Preclinical testing* is done in the lab and with animals to determine if the compound is biologically active and safe. (2) Before tests with human subjects can be conducted, an *investigational new drug* (IND) application, giving the test results and describing how the drug is made, must be filed. (3) *Human clinical testing* is conducted—Phase I: Pharmacological profile of a drug's actions; safe dosages; patterns of absorption, distribution, metabolism, and excretion; duration of action from tests on a small sample of healthy subjects. Phase II: Pilot efficacy studies in 200 to 300 volunteer patients to assess effectiveness, which may last two years. Phase III: Extensive clinical trials (in 1000 to 3000 patients) to confirm efficacy and identify low-incidence adverse reactions; this phase may last three years. (4) *New drug application* (NDA): The results of the previous testing must be reported, typically in thousands of pages, in an NDA filed with the FDA. Additional information includes the structure of the drug, its scientific rationale, details of its formulation and production, and the proposed labeling. (5) Following *approval* of the NDA, the company must submit periodic reports to the FDA concerning adverse reactions and production, quality control, and distribution data.

There are some major differences between project management of pharmaceutical R&D and that in other industries. For one thing, the final result here is not so much the physical product, but rather information—reams of paper giving proof that the drug is safe and efficacious. Because of the abstract nature of this "proof," the result may be sufficient at one point in time, or for one drug, but not at another time or for another drug. In addition, the long duration, extreme costs (averaging $250 million per drug), and high chances for failure anywhere along the route to development are generally rare in other projects. Moreover, failure can come from diverse causes, including the success of competing drugs, adverse patient reactions, escalating costs, or insufficient efficacy. The extensive and sophisticated use of project management techniques is the main tool that pharmaceutical R&D firms like Zeneca Pharmaceuticals can use to improve their chances of success.

Project management is concerned with managing organizational activities that result in a single output. For example, in the traditional functional organization, a product development team with representatives from production, finance, marketing, and engineering can be assembled to ensure that new product designs simultaneously meet the requirements of each area. Ensuring that each area's requirements are being met as the new design is developed reduces the likelihood that costly changes will have to be made later in the process. The result is that new products can be developed faster and less expensively, thereby enhancing the firm's overall responsiveness. Perhaps a better product is developed as well, owing to the synergy of including a variety of different perspectives earlier in the design process.

In this chapter, we describe the many activities required in the successful management of projects. We start with the definition of a project and why project management is different from managing functional activities. We then move into the project life cycle activities starting with planning the project, which includes an understanding of the role of the project in the organization's strategy and a description of the two major types of project life cycles and why it is important to be able to tell which is applicable for the project at hand. This is then followed by a discussion about organizing the project team and the various techniques available to the project manager for planning the project activities. Following this, we discuss the major topics of scheduling the project and determining the probability of completing it by its due date. In the process, we describe the capabilities and outputs of some project management software packages. Moving along the project life cycle, we then address the topics of controlling the project's cost and performance. The chapter concludes with a discussion of the "critical chain" concept of project management.

DEFINING A PROJECT

Up to this point, you might not have realized that projects are actually a special type of process. As described in Chapter 3, the term *process* refers to a set of activities that, taken together, creates something of value to customers. Typically, the term process is used to refer to a set of activities that are routinely repeated, such as processing insurance forms, handling customers' complaints, and assembling an MP3 player. The term *project* also refers to a set of activities that, taken together, produces a valued output. However, unlike a typical process, each project is unique and has a clear beginning and end. Therefore, projects are processes that are performed infrequently and ad hoc, with a clear specification of the desired objective.

There are two other typical characteristics of projects which are less obvious. One is that there is a limited budget to attain the unique desired objective. The second is that the objective is extremely important to the organization. If neither of these two characteristics were true, it would be foolish to designate a *special* project team to accomplish the project since, with an unlimited budget, it could be done by regular functional departmental employees doing their routine work.

In Chapter 3, the project form of the transformation process was briefly described. The choice of the project form usually indicates the importance of the project objective to the organization. Thus, top-grade resources, including staff, are often made available for project operations. As a result, project organizations become professionalized and are often managed on that basis. That is, minimal supervision is exercised, administrative routine is minimized, and the professional is given the problem and the required results (cost, performance, deadline). The individual is then given the privacy and freedom to decide *how* to solve his or her portion of the problem.

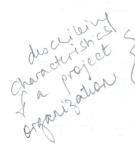

describing characteristics of a project organization

A great many projects require varying emphases during their life cycle. For example, technical performance may be crucial at the beginning, cost overruns in the middle, and on-time completion at the end. The flexibility of making spur-of-the-moment changes in emphasis by trading off one criterion for another is basic to the project design form. This ability results from the close contact of the project manager with the technical staff—there are few, if any, "middle managers."

Following are some examples of projects:

- Constructing highways, bridges, tunnels, and dams
- Building ships, planes, and rockets, or a doghouse
- Erecting skyscrapers, steel mills, homes, and processing plants
- Locating and laying out amusement parks, camping grounds, and refuges
- Organizing conferences, banquets, conventions, and weddings
- Managing R&D projects such as the Manhattan Project (which developed the atomic bomb)
- Running political campaigns, war operations, advertising campaigns, or firefighting operations
- Chairing ad hoc task forces, overseeing planning for government agencies, or conducting corporate audits
- Converting from one computer system to another

As may be noticed in this list, the number of project operations is growing in our economy, probably at about the same rate as services (which many of them are). Some of the reasons for this growth in project operations are as follows:

1. *More sophisticated technology.* An outgrowth of our information age, and its technology, has been increased public awareness of project operations (e.g., Project Apollo) and interest in using the project form to achieve society's goals (Project Head Start).

2. *Better-educated citizens.* People are more aware of the world around them, and of techniques (such as project management) for achieving their objectives.

3. *More leisure time.* People have the time available to follow, and even participate in, projects.

4. *Increased accountability.* Society as a whole has increased its emphasis on the attainment of objectives (affirmative action, environmental protection, better fuel economy) and the evaluation of activities leading toward those objectives.

5. *Higher productivity.* People and organizations are involved in more activities, and are more productive in those activities, than ever before.

6. *Faster response to customers.* Today's intense competition has escalated the importance of quick response to customers' needs, and projects are often more responsive and flexible than bureaucracies or functionally organized firms.

7. *Greater customization for customers.* Intense competition has also increased the importance of better meeting the customer's unique needs in terms of both the service and the facilitating good. Again, as long as a major technical breakthrough isn't required (for which the project form with its reduced functional depth is less suitable), the project form of organizing is more likely to meet this need.

In physical project operations, such as bridge construction, most of the *production* per se is completed elsewhere and brought to the project area at the proper time. As a result, a great many project activities are *assembly* operations. The project design form concentrates resources on the achievement of specific objectives primarily through proper *scheduling* and *control* of activities, many of which are simultaneous. Some of the scheduling considerations in project management are knowing what activities must be completed and in what order, how long they will take, when to increase and decrease the labor force, and when to order materials so that they will not arrive too early (thus requiring storage and being in the way) or too late (thus delaying the project). The control activities include anticipating what can and might go wrong, knowing what resources can be shifted among activities to keep the project on schedule, and so forth.

PLANNING THE PROJECT

In this section, we focus in some detail on the planning of projects. In the area of project management, planning is probably the single most important element in the success of the project and considerable research has been done on the topic. We start with the role of the organization's many projects in achieving its strategy, known as the organization's **project portfolio**. This portfolio evolves over time since projects have a finite life cycle, as discussed in the next section. Following this, we discuss the project team and its tie to the parent organization. Last, we discuss some of the details of the actual project planning tools.

The Project Portfolio

The long-term purpose of projects in the organization is to ultimately achieve the organization's goals. This tie is accomplished through the project portfolio, also known as the organization's **aggregate project plan**, as described in Chapter 2. In making project selection decisions, it is vital to consider the interactions among various projects and to manage the projects as a set. This is in stark contrast to the common practice of simply setting a project budget and specified return on investment (ROI) hurdle rate, then funding projects until either the budget or supply of acceptable projects is exhausted. Organizations that fund all projects that meet

Imp ⇒

their ROI criterion typically end up with significantly more ongoing projects than they can competently manage and thus their contribution to the organization's long-term goals can be lost. Because ROI is an insufficient selection criterion, the set of projects chosen may not be close to an optimal portfolio for achieving their purpose.

What is the optimal portfolio for an organization?

The Project Life Cycle

Stretched - S life cycle form

exponential form (module integrated)

It has been found, for example, that progress in a project is not at all uniform, but instead follows one of two common forms, as shown in Figure 11.1. In the stretched-S life cycle form, illustrated in Figure 11.1*a*, when the project is initiated, progress is slow as responsibilities are assigned and organization takes place. But the project gathers speed during the implementation stage, and much progress is made. As the end of the project draws near, the more difficult tasks that were postponed earlier must now be completed, yet people are being drawn off the project and activity is "winding down," so the end keeps slipping out of reach.

In the exponential form, illustrated in Figure 11.1*b*, after the project is initiated there is continuous activity on numerous aspects of the project, but until all the elemental parts come together at the end, there is no final output. This is typical of projects that require final assembly of components to produce the whole (like a car), or goods (like a cake, which is only glop until it is baked in the oven). It is especially typical of office and other such service work where the final output is a life insurance policy, or ad piece, or perhaps even an MBA degree. Without that last signature, or piece of paper, or earned credit, there is virtually no product.

The reason it is important to contrast these two forms, besides pointing out their difference in managerial needs, is that during the budgeting stage, if there is a flat across-the-board budget cut of, say, 10 percent and the project is of the

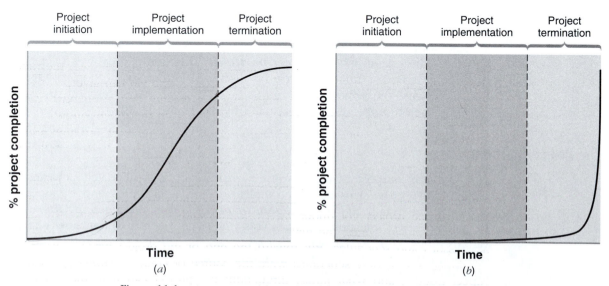

Figure 11.1   Two project life cycles. (*a*) Stretched-S. (*b*) Exponential.

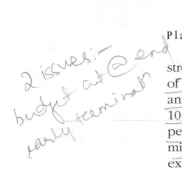

[handwritten margin note: 2 issues:- budget out @ end / early termination]

stretched-S form, then not being able to spend that last 10 percent of the budget is of no urgent matter, since probably 97 percent of the benefits will be achieved anyway. However, if the project is of the exponential form, then missing the last 10 percent is catastrophic because this is where all the value is attained. Another perspective on the same issue is the effect of early termination of the project. Terminating the stretched-S form early will have negligible impact, but terminating the exponential form will be a complete disaster. It is imperative the project manager and top management know which type of project they are working with before taking such actions.

Organizing the Project Team

[handwritten margin notes: Management + consulting firms typify project organization; matrix orgs; weak or ftnal matrix; strong or project matrix]

Projects can be organized in any of a number of ways. There is the ad hoc project form in a functional organization that reports to a senior executive. And there are projects that are just another activity in a project organization that is completely organized in terms of projects. Management consulting firms typify project organizations. There are matrix organizations where projects have both a functional and a program superior. Combinations of these forms are also common, such as the "weak" or functional matrix, and the "strong" or project matrix. Each of these has its own advantages and disadvantages, and what works the best depends largely on the circumstances of the organization and the reason it started a project.

Regardless of the form of the project, a team will be required to run the project. Some members of the team may be directly assigned to the project manager for the duration, while others may have only partial responsibilities for the project and still report to their functional superior. There are three types of team members who should report directly to the project manager (PM), however:

- Those who will be having a long-term relationship with the project
- Those with whom the PM will need to communicate closely or continuously
- Those with rare skills necessary to project success

[handwritten margin note: not a lot of incentives that PM can give to people working on the project]

Yet, even if these people report to the PM, it is still not common for the PM to have the authority to reward these people with pay bonuses, extra vacation, or other such personnel matters—that authority normally still resides with the functional manager. Thus, there are not a lot of incentives the PM can give people for working hard on the project. The main ones are the fun and excitement of the challenge, and doing something that will be important to the organization.

With the pressures that tend to gravitate toward such important and high-profile projects, it may be assumed that there is also a lot of opportunity for conflict to arise. This is true, and not only between the PM and other organizational units, but even between members of the project team. According to Thamhain and Wilemon (1975), at project formation the main sources of conflict were priorities and procedures. As the project got under way, priorities and schedules became the main points of conflict. During the main implementation stage, conflict shifted to technical issues and schedules. But toward the end of the project when timing was becoming crucial, only schedules were the source of conflict. Knowing when to expect trouble, and what kinds, throughout the project can help the PM keep peace within the project team and facilitate smooth project progress.

[handwritten note at bottom: communication a key in Project Management]

Project Plans

[margin note: WBS]

One of the project manager's major responsibilities during the initiation stage is to define all the tasks in as much detail as possible so that they can be scheduled and costed out, and responsibility can be assigned. This set of task descriptions is called the **work breakdown structure** (WBS), and it provides the basis for the project master schedule.

A typical WBS and master schedule are illustrated in Figures 11.2 and 11.3 for a project installing assembly-line robots. Milestone, commitment, and completion points are shown, and actual progress is graphed. The last status update shows that the project is a month behind schedule.

The scheduling of project activities is highly complex because of (1) the number of activities required, (2) the precedence relationships among the activities, and (3) the limited time of the project. Project scheduling is similar to the scheduling discussed earlier in some ways but still differs significantly. For example, the basic network approaches—**program evaluation and review technique** (PERT) and **critical path method** (CPM)—are based on variations of the Gantt chart. Figure 11.3 is, in a sense, a type of Gantt chart but is inadequate for scheduling the multitude of subtasks that compose, for example, task A1. That is, a project schedule has to handle an enormous number of different operations and materials, which must be coordinated in such a way that the subsequent activities can take place and the entire project (job) can be completed by the due date.

[margin note: PERT (Program Evaluation & Review Techniques) & CPM (critical path method) → variations of the Gantt Chart]

The scheduling procedure for project operations must be able not only to identify and handle the variety of tasks that must be done, but also to handle their time sequencing. In addition, it must be able to integrate the performance and timing of all the tasks with the project as a whole so that control can be exercised, for example, by shifting resources from operations with slack (permissible slippage) to other operations whose delay might threaten the project's

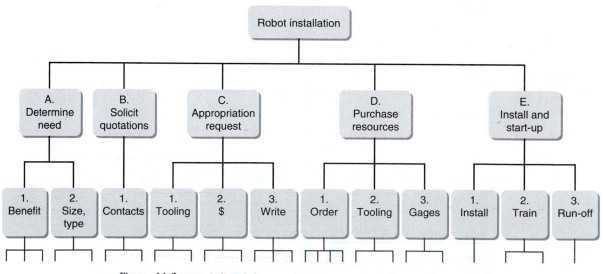

Figure 11.2 Work breakdown structure.

timely completion. The tasks involved in planning and scheduling project operations are:

- *Planning*. Determining what must be done and which tasks must *precede* others
- *Scheduling*. Determining *when* the tasks must be completed; when they *can* and when they *must* be started; which tasks are *critical* to the timely completion of the project; and which tasks have *slack* in their timing and how much

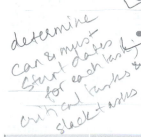

[handwritten margin note: determine can & must start dates for each task, critical tasks & slack tasks]

Subproject	Task		Responsible Dept.	Dependent Dept.	20X4 / 20X5 (J F M A M J J A S O N D J F M A M J J A S O N D)
Determine need	A1	Find operations that benefit most	Industrial engr. (IE)		△ Mar; ▲ (actual)
	A2	Approx. size and type needed	Project engr. (PE)	Industrial engr. (IE)	△ May; ▲ Aug
Solicit quotations	B1	Contact suppliers & review quotes	Project engr. (PE)	Finance, IE, purchasing	○ Jul; △ Sep; ● Nov; ▲ □ Dec
Write appropriation request	C1	Determine tooling costs	Tool design	Industrial engr. (IE)	△ Jan (20X5)
	C2	Determine labor savings	Industrial engr. (IE)	Industrial engr. (IE)	△ Dec; ▲ Nov
	C3	Actual writing	Project engr. (PE)	Tool design, finance, IE	△ / ○ Feb (20X5)
Purchase machine, tooling, and gages	D1	Order robot	Purchasing	Project engr. (PE)	△ Apr (20X5)
	D2	Design and order or manufacture tooling	Tool design	Purchasing, tool making	△ Jun (20X5)
	D3	Specify needed gages and order of manufacturing	Quality control	Tool design, purchasing	△ / ○ Jun (20X5)
Install and start-up	E1	Install robot	Plant layout	Mill-wrights	△ Aug (20X5)
	E2	Train employees	Personnel	Process engr., manufacturing	△ Aug (20X5)
	E3	Run-off	Manufacturing	Quality control	△ / + Nov (20X5)

Legend:
- + Project completion
- □ Contractual commitment
- △ Planned completion
- ▲ Actual completion
- λ Status date
- ○ Milestone planned
- ● Milestone achieved
- – – Planned progress
- —— Actual progress

Note: As of 31 Jan., 20X5 the project is one month behind schedule. This is due mainly to the delay in task C1, which was caused by the late completion of A2.

Figure 11.3 Project master schedule. Reprinted from J. Meredith and S. J. Mantel, Jr., *Project Management: A Managerial Approach*, 3rd ed. New York: Wiley, 1995. Used with permission.

SCHEDULING THE PROJECT: PERT AND CPM

The project scheduling process is based on the activities that must be conducted to achieve the project's goals, the length of time each requires, and the order in which they must be completed. If a number of similar projects must be conducted, sometimes these activities can be structured generically to apply equally well to all the projects.

Two primary techniques have been developed to plan projects consisting of ordered activities: PERT and CPM. Although PERT and CPM originally had some differences in the way activities were determined and laid out, many current approaches to project scheduling minimize these differences and present an integrated view, as we will see here. It will be helpful to define some terms first.

- *Activity*. One of the project operations, or tasks; an activity requires resources and takes some amount of time to complete.

- *Event*. Completion of an activity, or series of activities, at a particular point in time.

- *Network*. Set of all project activities graphically interrelated through precedence relationships. In this text, network lines (or *arcs*) represent activities, connections between the lines (called *nodes*) represent events, and arrows on the arcs represent precedence. (This is typical of the PERT approach; in CPM the nodes represent activities.)

- *Path*. Series of connected activities from the start to the finish of the project.

- *Critical path*. Any path that if delayed will delay the completion of the entire project.

- *Critical activities*. Activities on the critical path or paths.

Project Planning When Activity Times Are Known

The primary inputs to project planning are a list of the activities that must be completed, the *activity completion times* (also called *activity durations*), and precedence relationships among the activities (i.e., what activities must be completed before another activity can be started). In this section, we assume that activity completion times are known with certainty. Later, we relax this assumption and consider situations in which activity completion times are not known with certainty.

Important outputs of project planning include:

- Graphical representation of the entire project, showing all precedence relationships among the activities
- Time it will take to complete the project
- Identification of critical path or paths
- Identification of critical activities
- Slack times for all activities and paths
- Earliest and latest time each activity can be started
- Earliest and latest time each activity can be completed

$\mathcal{T}$ABLE 11.1 • Data for a Seven-Activity Project

Activity	Time (days)	Preceded by
A	10	—
B	7	—
C	5	A
D	13	A
E	4	B, C
F	12	D
G	14	E

Project Completion and Critical Paths

Table 11.1 shows the activity times and precedence for seven activities that must all be finished to complete a project. According to the table, activities A and B can be started at any time. Activities C and D can be started once activity A is completed. Activity E cannot be started until both activities B and C are finished, and so on. The network diagram for this project is shown in Figure 11.4, in which nodes (circles) represent events (i.e., the start or completion of an activity) and arcs (lines) correspond to activities. Each arc is labeled with a letter to identify the corresponding activity. Activity durations are shown in parentheses next to the activity labels. Finally, arrows are used to show precedence relationships among activities. This way of depicting a project is known as "activity-on-arc" (AOA) and is typical of PERT; the CPM alternative, activity-on-node (AON), is also common however, especially in project management software programs (e.g., see Meredith and Mantel 2006).

From Figure 11.4, it can be seen that there are three paths from node 1 to node 6: A–D–F (or 1–2–4–6), A–C–E–G (or 1–2–3–5–6), and B–E–G (or 1–3–5–6). Summing the activity times on a particular path provides the path completion time. For example, the time to complete path A–D–F is 35 (10 + 13 + 12).

To determine the expected completion time of the entire project, *early start times* T_{ES} and *early finish times* T_{EF} can be calculated for each activity, as shown in Figure 11.5. The values of T_{ES} and T_{EF} are calculated moving left to right through the network. Thus, we begin with the leftmost node (node 1) and work our way to the rightmost node (node 6). To illustrate, if the project is started at time zero, then activities A and B can be started as early as time zero, since neither of them is preceded by another activity. Since activity A requires 10 days, if it is started as early as time zero, it can be completed on day 10. Likewise, if activity B is started at time zero, it can be completed as early as day 7. Continuing on, since activity A

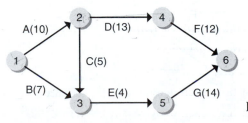

Figure 11.4 Network diagram for project.

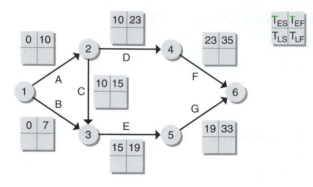

Figure 11.5 Early start and finish times.

can be finished as early as day 10, activity C can start as early as day 10 and finish as early as day 15. Now consider activity E. Activity E cannot be started until activities B and C are *both* completed. Since activity B can be finished as early as day 7 and C can be finished as early as day 15, activity E can be started only as early as day 15 (remember, E cannot start until both activities B and C are completed). If activity E is started as early as day 15, it can finish as early as day 19. The remaining earliest start and finish times are calculated in a similar fashion. After T_{ES} and T_{EF} are calculated for all the activities, we can determine the earliest time that the project can be completed. Since this project cannot be completed until all paths are completed, the earliest it could be completed is day 35.

Once T_{ES} and T_{EF} have been calculated for each activity, the latest times each activity can be started and finished without delaying the completion of the project can be determined. In contrast to T_{ES} and T_{EF}, *latest start time* (T_{LS}) and *latest finish time* (T_{LF}) are calculated by moving backward through the network, from right to left. Times T_{LS} and T_{LF} for this example are shown in Figure 11.6.

In calculating T_{ES} and T_{EF}, we determined that the project could be completed by day 35. If the project is to be completed by day 35, then activities F and G can be completed as late as day 35 without delaying completion of the project. Thus, the latest finish time for activities F and G is 35. Since activity F requires 12 days, it can start as late as 23 (35 – 12) and still finish by day 35. Likewise, activity G can start as late as 21 (35 – 14) and still finish by day 35. Continuing on, since activity F can start as late as day 23, activity D can finish as late as day 23. Since activity D requires 13 days, it can start as late as day 10 (23 – 13) without delaying the entire project. Activity E must finish by 21 so as not to delay activity G and thus can start as late as day 17. To permit activity E to start by day 17, activities B and C must finish by day 17. Activity C can start as late as day 12 and still finish by

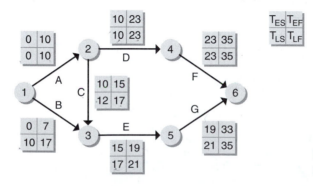

Figure 11.6 Latest start and finish times.

day 17. Activity A precedes both C and D. Activity C can start as late as day 12 and D as late as day 10. Since activity A must be finished before either of these activities is started, A must be finished by day 10. (If A finished later than day 10, then activity D would start later than its latest start time and the entire project would be delayed.)

Slack Time

Times T_{ES}, T_{EF}, T_{LS}, and T_{LF} can be used by the project manager to help plan and develop schedules for the project. For example, if an activity requires a key resource or individual, its earliest and latest start times provide a window during which that resource can be acquired or assigned to the project. Alternatively, if an activity falls behind schedule, the latest completion time provides an indication of whether the slippage will delay the entire project or can simply be absorbed.

Notice in Figure 11.6 that for some activities, T_{ES} is equal to T_{LS} and T_{EF} is equal to T_{LF}. For these activities, there is no flexibility in terms of when they can be started and completed. In other cases, an activity's T_{ES} is less than its T_{LS} and its T_{EF} is less than its T_{LF}. In these cases the project manager can exercise some discretion in terms of when the activity is started and when it is completed. The amount of flexibility the project manager has in terms of starting and completing an activity is referred to as its **slack** (or **float**) and is calculated as

$$\text{Activity slack} = T_{LS} - T_{ES} = T_{LF} - T_{EF}$$

All activities on the critical path have zero slack—that is, there is no room for delay in any activity on the critical path without delaying the entire project. Activities off the critical path may delay up to a point where further delay would delay the entire project. Table 11.2 shows T_{ES}, T_{EF}, T_{LS}, T_{LF}, and slack for our seven-activity project shown earlier in Figure 11.8.

In addition to calculating slack times for individual activities, slack times can be calculated for entire paths. Since all paths must be finished to complete the project, the time to complete the project is the time to complete the path with the longest duration. Thus, the path with the longest duration is critical in the sense that any delay in completing it will delay the completion of the entire project. Path slacks are calculated as

$$\text{Path slack} = \text{duration of critical path} - \text{path duration}$$

$\mathscr{T}$ABLE   11.2 • Event Early and Late Times

Activity	T_{ES}	T_{EF}	T_{LS}	T_{LF}	Slack
A	0	10	0	10	0
B	0	7	10	17	10
C	10	15	12	17	2
D	10	23	10	23	0
E	15	19	17	21	2
F	23	35	23	35	0
G	19	33	21	35	2

Table 11.3 • Calculation of Path Slacks

Path	Duration	Slack	Critical?
A–D–F	35	0 (35–35)	Yes
A–C–E–G	33	2 (35–33)	No
B–E–G	25	10 (35–25)	No

Table 11.3 contains the slack times for the three paths in our example project. Path A–D–F has the longest duration, and therefore its completion determines when the project is completed. The other paths require less than 35 days and therefore have slack. For example, path B–E–G has a slack of 10 days, implying that its completion can be delayed by 10 days without delaying the completion of the entire project.

Before leaving the topic of slack, it is important to point out that the slack times computed for individual activities are not additive. To illustrate, when the slack times were calculated for the individual activities, slack times of 10, 2, and 2 were computed for activities B, E, and G, respectively (see Table 11.2). If these slack times were additive, then path B–E–G would have a slack of 14 days. However, from Table 11.3 we observe that the slack for path B–E–G is only 10 days. The point is that slack times for individual activities are computed on the assumption that only one particular activity is delayed. As an example, activity B's slack of 10 days means that it can be delayed by up to 10 days without delaying the entire project, as long as the other activities on the path (activities E and G) are not delayed. However, if activity B is delayed by 10 days and either activity E or G is delayed by even 1 day, the entire project will be delayed.

Project Planning When Activity Times Are Not Known with Certainty

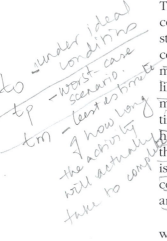

The previous section discussed project planning in situations where the activity completion times were known with certainty before the project was actually started. In reality, however, project activity times are frequently not known with certainty beforehand. In these cases, project managers often develop three estimates for each activity: an optimistic time t_o, a pessimistic time t_p, and a most likely time t_m. The *optimistic time* is the amount of time the project manager estimates it will take to complete the activity under ideal conditions; that is, only one time in a hundred would it take less time than this. The *pessimistic time* refers to how long the activity will take to complete under the worst-case scenario; again, there is only a 1% chance it would ever take longer than this. The *most likely time* is the project manager's best estimate of how long the activity will actually take to complete. In addition to these three time estimates, the precedence relationships among the activities are also needed as inputs to the project planning process.

The primary outputs of project planning when activity times are not known with certainty include:

- Graphical representation of the entire project, showing all precedence relationships among the activities

- Expected activity and path completion times
- Variance of activity and path completion times
- Probability that the project will be completed by a specified time
- That time corresponding to certain probability of the project being complete

variance

We now illustrate project planning in a situation in which activity durations are not known with certainty before the project starts.

Black Cross Plan E

Black Cross is a volunteer service organization recently formed in California to prepare for and respond to "the big one," a major earthquake that has been expected for a decade. Black Cross has developed a single, efficient, uniform response plan (plan E) consisting of 10 major activities for all cities where the earthquake causes major damage. Clearly, completing the project activities as quickly as possible is crucial to saving lives and property and aiding victims in distress. The staff of Black Cross has determined not only the most likely times for each activity but also the fastest time in which each could probably (99% sure) be done (i.e., the *optimistic time*), as well as the slowest time (i.e., *pessimistic time*) that might (again, 99% sure) be encountered by a project team out in the field (if everything went wrong). The project operations and the optimistic, most likely, and pessimistic times, in hours, are listed in Table 11.4, along with the activities that must precede them.

Construction of the Network: Ordering the Activities

The project network illustrating the activities and their interdependence is constructed by first examining Table 11.4 for those activities that have no activities preceding them. These activities—a, b, and c—are all drawn out of a starting node, which, for convenience in Figure 11.7, we have labeled 1.

$\mathcal{T}$ABLE   11.4 • Plan E Activity Times (hours)

Project Activity	Optimistic Time t_o	Most Likely Time t_m	Pessimistic Time t_p	Required Preceding Activities
a	5	11	11	none
b	10	10	10	none
c	2	5	8	none
d	1	7	13	a
e	4	4	10	b, c
f	4	7	10	b, c
g	2	2	2	b, c
h	0	6	6	c
i	2	8	14	g, h
j	1	4	7	d, e

duration is known with certainty

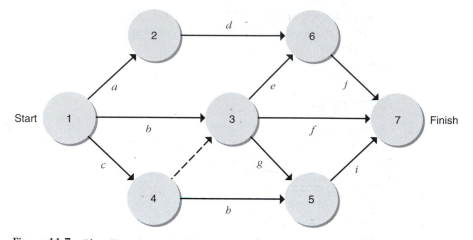

Figure 11.7   Plan E project operations network.

Next, the activity list is scanned for activities that require only that activities a, b, or c be completed. Thus, activities d through h can be drawn in the network next. Activity d can be drawn directly out of node 2, and activity h can be drawn out of node 4. But if node 3 indicates the completion of activity b, how can activities e, f, and g be drawn, since they also depend on the completion of activity c? This is accomplished by the use of a ***dummy activity*** from node 4 to node 3, which indicates that event 3 depends on the accomplishment of activity c (event 4) as well as activity b. The dummy activity, shown as a dashed line in Figure 11.7, requires no time to accomplish, but the link is necessary, so that activities e, f, and g cannot start before both activities b and c are completed.

What if activity e did not require that activity c be completed, whereas f and g did? If this was the case, the diagram would be drawn as shown in Figure 11.8. Care must be taken to ensure that the proper precedence relations are drawn; otherwise, the project might be unnecessarily delayed.

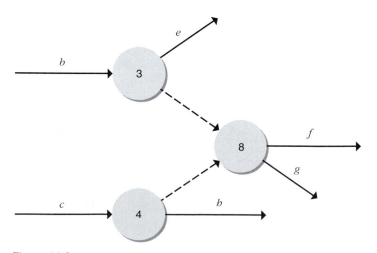

Figure 11.8   Proper use of dummy activities.

The remainder of the diagram is drawn in the same manner. Activity i, which depends on activities g and h, comes out of node 5, which represents the completion of g and h. A similar situation occurs with activity j. All of the remaining activities without completion nodes (f, i, and j) are then directed to the project completion node 7.

Calculating Activity Durations

We have now completed a graphic network representation of the information about precedence shown in Table 11.4. Next we can place the expected activity times on the network to get an indication of which activities should be scheduled first and when they should be completed, in order for the project not to be delayed.

The estimation of the three activity times in Table 11.4 is based on the assumption that the activities are independent of one another. Therefore, an activity that goes wrong will not necessarily affect the other activities, which can still go right. Additionally, it is assumed that the difference between t_o and t_m need *not* be the same as the difference between t_p and t_m. For example, a critical piece of equipment may be wearing out. If it is working well, this equipment can do a task in 2 hours that normally takes 3 hours; but if the equipment is performing poorly, the task may require 10 hours. Thus, we may see nonsymmetrical optimistic and pessimistic task times for project activities, as for activities e and h in Table 11.4. Note also that for some activities, such as b, the durations are known with certainty.

The general form of nonsymmetrical or skewed distribution used in approximating PERT activity times is called the beta distribution and has a mean (expected completion time t_e) and a variance, or uncertainty in this time, σ^2, as given below. The beta distribution is used because it is flexible enough to allow one tail of the distribution to be longer than the other (more things will typically go worse than expected than will go better than expected in a project) and is thus a more appropriate distribution for activity completion times.

$$t_e = \frac{t_o + 4t_m + t_p}{6}$$

$$\sigma^2 = \left(\frac{t_p - t_o}{6}\right)^2$$

The above equation for the expected completion time is simply a weighted average of the three time estimates, with weights of 1, 4, and 1, and the denominator of 6 is, of course, the sum of the weights. The value of 6 in the estimate of the variance, however, comes from a different source, the assumption that the optimistic and pessimistic times are each three standard deviations (3) from the mean. This only applies, however, to estimates made at the 99% sure level. If a manager is reluctant to make estimates at that level and feels that a 95%, or 90%, level is easier to estimate, then the equations for the standard deviation change (the approximation for the mean is still acceptable, however) to:

$$95\% \text{ level: } \sigma = (t_p - t_o)/3.3$$
$$90\% \text{ level: } \sigma = (t_p - t_o)/2.6$$

The results of these calculations (at the 99% level) are listed in Table 11.5 and are indicated on the network in Figure 11.9 in parentheses.

*T*ABLE   11.5 • Expected
Times and Variances
of Activities

Activity	Expected Time t_e	Variance σ^2
a	10	1
b	10	0
c	5	1
d	7	4
e	5	1
f	7	1
g	2	0
h	5	1
i	8	4
j	4	1

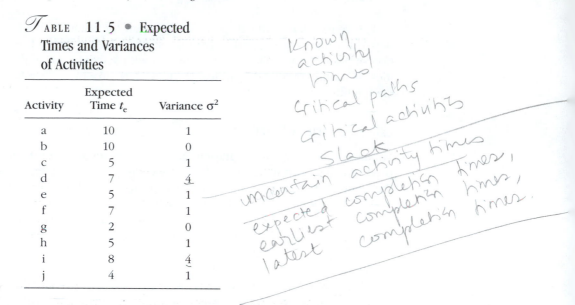

[handwritten margin notes:] Known activity times / critical paths / critical activities / slack / uncertain activity times, / expected completion times, / earliest completion times, / latest completion times.

The discussion of project management with known activity times included critical paths, critical activities, and slack. These concepts are not particularly useful in situations where activity times are not known with certainty. To demonstrate this we will use Table 11.6, where the paths and their expected completion times, earliest completion times, and latest completion times are listed for the network diagram shown in Figure 11.7. To calculate a path's expected completion time, the activity expected times t_e were summed up for all activities on the path. Similarly, times t_o and t_p were summed up for all activities on a given path to determine the path's earliest completion time and latest completion time, respectively.

Referring to Table 11.6, path a–d–j is most likely to take the longest (i.e., 21 hours). However, to see why this path is not considered the critical path, observe that if all the activities go exceptionally well on this path, it can be completed in as few as 7 hours. Referring to the last column in Table 11.6, we can see that it is possible for any of the other paths to take longer than 7 hours. Therefore, without

[handwritten margin note:] Cannot compute critical path here

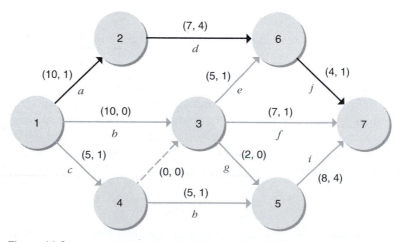

Figure 11.9   Expected times and variances of activities.

Table 11.6 • Expected, Earliest, and Latest Completion Times of Paths

Path	Expected Completion Time (hours)	Earliest Completion Time (hours)	Latest Completion Time (hours)
a–d–j	21	7	31
b–e–j	19	15	27
b–f	17	14	20
b–g–i	20	14	26
c–e–j	14	7	25
c–f	12	6	18
c–g–i	15	6	24
c–h–i	18	4	28

knowing the activity times with certainty, we see that any of the paths has the potential to be the longest path. Furthermore, we will not know which of the paths will take longest to complete until the project is actually completed. And since we cannot determine before the start of the project which path will be critical, we cannot determine how much slack the other paths have.

Probabilities of Completion

When activity times are not known with certainty, we cannot determine how long it will actually take to complete the project. However, using the variance of each activity (the variances in Table 11.5), we can compute the likelihood or probability of completing the project in a given time period, assuming that the activity durations are independent of each other. The distribution of a path's completion time will be approximately normally distributed if the path has a large number of activities on it. (Recall from the central limit theorem in statistics that this is true regardless of the distribution of the activities themselves, beta in our case.) For example, the mean time along path a–d–j was found to be 21 hours. The variance is found by summing the variances of each of the activities on the path. In our example, this would be

$$V_{\text{path a–d–j}} = \sigma_a^2 + \sigma_d^2 + \sigma_j^2$$
$$= 1 + 4 + 1$$
$$= 6$$

The probability of completing this path in, say, 23 hours is then found by calculating the standard normal deviate of the desired completion time less the expected completion time, and using the table of the standard normal probability distribution (inside rear cover) to find the corresponding probability:

$$Z = \frac{\text{desired completion time} - \text{expected completion time}}{\sqrt{V}}$$

$$= \frac{23 - 21}{\sqrt{6}}$$
$$= 0.818$$

which results in a probability (see Figure 11.10) of 79 percent. This can also be found in Excel® using the NORMDIST function with the syntax =NORMDIST(D,t_e,σ,TRUE) where D is the desired time of interest, 23 days in our case. Similarly, we can calculate that completion time by which we would be, say, 90% sure the project would be completed. From Appendix A, we find the standard normal deviate corresponding to 90% as about 1.28, so 21 + (1.28$\sqrt{6}$) = 24.14 hours. Again, this could also be found in Excel® from the NORMINV function with syntax =NORMINV(probability,t_e,σ), which in our case would be =NORMINV(.90,21,2.449) = 24.14 hours.

So far, we have determined only that there is a 79 percent chance that path a–d–j will be completed in 23 hours or less. If we were interested in calculating the probability that the entire project will be completed in 23 hours, we would need to calculate the probability that all paths will be finished within 23 hours. To calculate the probability that all paths will be finished in 23 hours or less, we first calculate the probability that each path will be finished in 23 hours or less, as we just did for path a–d–j. Then we multiply these probabilities together to determine the probability that all paths will be completed by the specified time. The reason we multiply these probabilities together is that we are assuming that path completion times are independent of one another. Of course, if the paths have activities in common, they are not truly independent of one another and a more complex analysis or simulation, illustrated next, is necessary.

To simplify the number of calculations required to compute the probability that a project will be completed by some specified time, for practical purposes it is reasonable to include only those paths whose expected time plus 2.33 standard deviations is more than the specified time. The reason for doing this is that if the sum of a path's expected time and 2.33 of its standard deviations is less than the specified time, then the probability that this path will take longer than the specified time is very small (i.e., less than 1 percent), and therefore we assume that the probability that it will be completed by the specified time is 100 percent. Finally, note that to calculate the probability that a project will take longer than some specified time, we first calculate the probability that it will take less than the specified time and then subtract this value from 1.

Spreadsheet Analysis: Simulating Project Completion Times

When activity times are uncertain, it is usually not possible to know which path will be the critical path before the project is actually completed. In these situations,

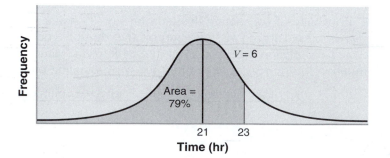

Figure 11.10   Probability distribution of path completion time.

simulation analysis can provide some insights into the range and distribution of project completion times. To illustrate this, we use the following network diagram consisting of six activities labeled A through F.

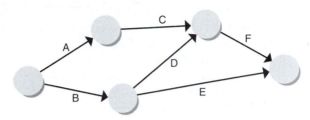

Based on historical data, it has been determined that all the activity times are approximately normally distributed with the means and standard deviations given in the following table.

t_e σ

Activity	Mean (days)	Standard Deviation
A	32.1	1.2
B	24.6	3.1
C	22.2	2.2
D	26.1	5.2
E	34.4	6.2
F	34.5	4.1

Inspection of the network diagram reveals three paths: A–C–F, B–D–F, and B–E.

To simulate the completion of this project using Crystal Ball® (see Appendix B for additional details on Crystal Ball), the following spreadsheet was developed. In the spreadsheet, completing the project is simulated by generating random numbers for the six activities and then adding up the activity times that make up each path to determine how long the paths take to complete. The longest path determines the project completion time.

	A	B	C	D	E	F	G	H	I	J
1	Activity	Activity	Activity	Activity	Activity	Activity	Path	Path	Path	Completion
2	A	B	C	D	E	F	ACF	BDF	BE	Time
3	32.1	24.6	22.2	26.1	34.4	34.5	88.8	85.2	59	88.8
4										
5										
6										
7										
8										
9	Formulae:									
10	Cell G3	= A3 + C3 + F3								
11	Cell H3	= B3 + D3 + F3								
12	Cell I3	= B3 + E3								
13	Cell J3	= MAX (G3:I3)								

Assumption Cells

Forecast Cell

In the spreadsheet, randomly generated activity times from a normal distribution for each activity are generated in cells A3:F3 by defining these cells as assumption cells. For example, cell A3 was defined as an assumption cell with a normal distribution and mean and standard deviation of 32.1 and 1.2, respectively. In column G the time to complete path A–C–F is calculated based on the activity times generated in cells A3:F3. For example, in cell G3, the formula = A3 + C3 + F3 was entered. In a similar fashion, cells H3 and I3 are used to calculate the time to complete paths B–D–F and B–E, respectively.

Cell J3 keeps track of when the project is actually completed on a given replication. Since the longest path determines the time when the project is completed, = MAX(G3:I3) was entered in cell J3.

The results of simulating the project are summarized in the figure below. The results indicate that, on the average, the project required 90.28 days to complete. Furthermore, across the 1000 replications of the project, the fastest project completion time was 75.77 days and the longest was 109.77 days.

Forecast: Project Completion Time

Edit Preferences View Run Help

Cell J3   Statistics

Statistic	Value
Trials	1,000
Mean	90.28
Median	90.11
Mode	---
Standard Deviation	5.24
Variance	27.49
Skewness	0.36
Kurtosis	3.44
Coeff. of Variability	0.06
Range Minimum	75.77
Range Maximum	109.77
Range Width	34.00
Mean Std. Error	0.17

Project Management Software Capabilities

There has been explosive growth in project management software packages and their capabilities. The competition is fierce, and there is a wide range of packages available, depending on the project need and the funds available. The main aspects to consider when selecting a package are the capabilities required and the time and money available to invest in a package. If the project is a very large, complex one, or one that interacts with a number of other projects that must also be managed with the software, then some of the more sophisticated packages are appropriate. However, not only do these cost more, they also take longer to learn and greater computer power to run. On the other hand, if the project is simpler, a less elaborate package that is easier to learn and use may be the best choice.

A yearly survey and analysis of such packages is conducted by the Project Management Institute. These surveys give details on the friendliness of each package, their capabilities (schedules, calendars, budgets, resource diagrams and tables, graphics, their migration capabilities, report generation, tracking capability, etc.), their computer requirements, and their cost.

Probably the most commonly used package these days is Microsoft's Project. This package is fairly sophisticated for the cost and is extremely easy to learn and use. Examples of some of its report capabilities are given in Figures 11.11, 11.12, and 11.13.

CONTROLLING THE PROJECT: EARNED VALUE

One of the control systems most widely used in projects is the cost variance report. Cost standards are determined through engineering estimates or through analysis of past performance. They become the target costs for the project. The

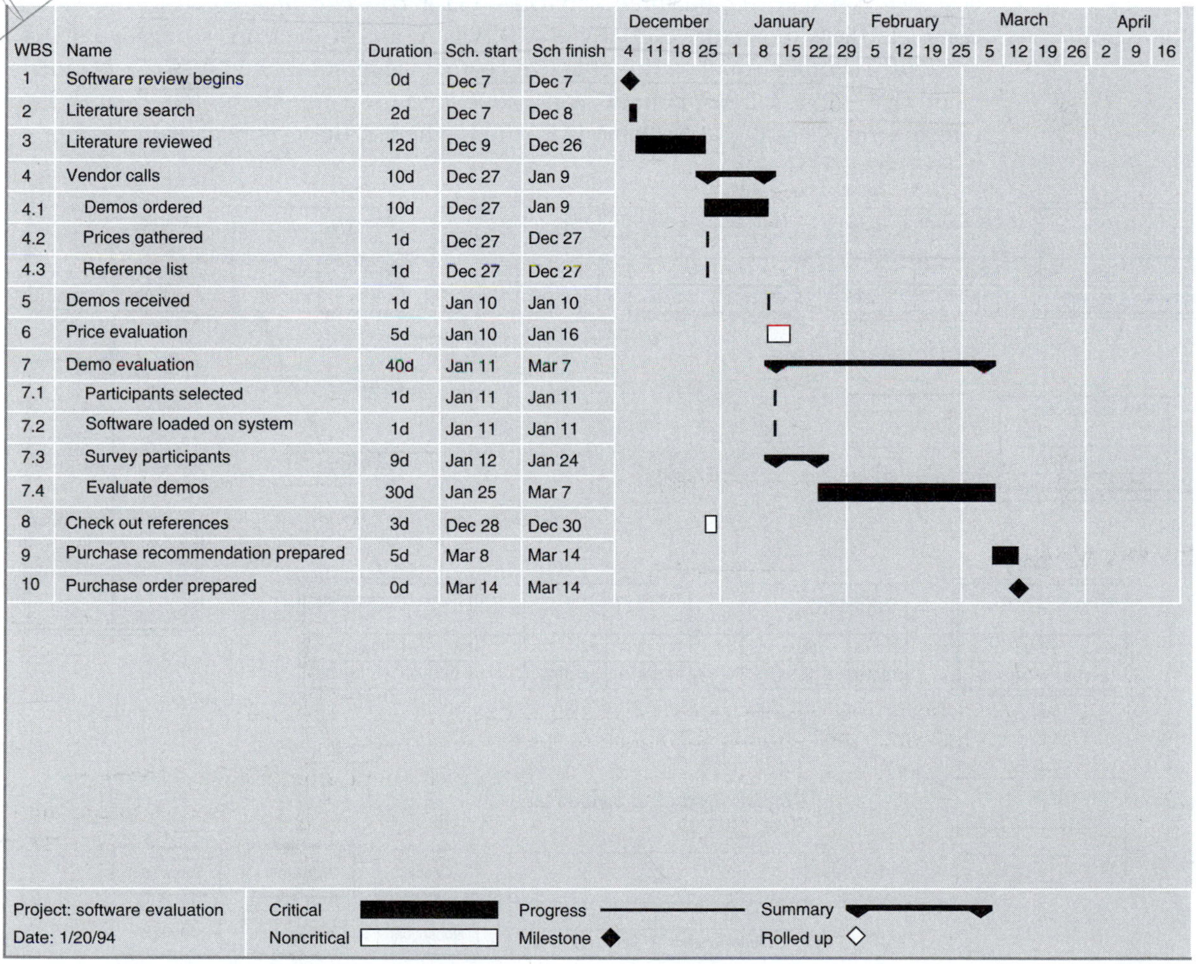

WBS	Name	Duration	Sch. start	Sch finish
1	Software review begins	0d	Dec 7	Dec 7
2	Literature search	2d	Dec 7	Dec 8
3	Literature reviewed	12d	Dec 9	Dec 26
4	Vendor calls	10d	Dec 27	Jan 9
4.1	Demos ordered	10d	Dec 27	Jan 9
4.2	Prices gathered	1d	Dec 27	Dec 27
4.3	Reference list	1d	Dec 27	Dec 27
5	Demos received	1d	Jan 10	Jan 10
6	Price evaluation	5d	Jan 10	Jan 16
7	Demo evaluation	40d	Jan 11	Mar 7
7.1	Participants selected	1d	Jan 11	Jan 11
7.2	Software loaded on system	1d	Jan 11	Jan 11
7.3	Survey participants	9d	Jan 12	Jan 24
7.4	Evaluate demos	30d	Jan 25	Mar 7
8	Check out references	3d	Dec 28	Dec 30
9	Purchase recommendation prepared	5d	Mar 8	Mar 14
10	Purchase order prepared	0d	Mar 14	Mar 14

Project: software evaluation
Date: 1/20/94

Critical ▬ Noncritical ▭ Progress —— Milestone ◆ Summary ▼——▼ Rolled up ◇

Figure 11.11 Microsoft Project's Gantt chart.

actual costs are then monitored by the organization's cost-accounting system and are compared with the cost standard. Feedback is provided to the project manager, who can exert any necessary control if the difference between standard and actual (called a variance) is considered significant.

As an example, consider the cost-schedule charts in Figure 11.14. In Figure 11.14a, actual progress is plotted alongside planned progress, and the "effective" progress time (TE) is noted. Because progress is less than planned, TE is less than the actual time (TA). On the cost chart (Figure 11.14b) we see that the apparent variance between the planned value and actual cost at this time (PV – AC) is quite small, despite the lack of progress (earned value, EV). But this is misleading; the variance should be much more given the lack of progress.

These two graphs are combined for project managers into an **earned value** chart—Figure 11.15—where the planned value (PV), actual cost (AC), and earned value completed (actual earned dollars of progress, EV) are plotted. In this situation (which is different from that in Figure 11.14), the actual cost is greater than the plan, even though progress lags behind the plan (thus, the huge cost variance). Plotted in this manner, one chart will serve to monitor both progress and cost. We can then define three variances: (1) a *cost variance* equal to the value completed less the actual cost (EV – AC), where a cost overrun is negative; (2) a *schedule variance* equal to the effective cost or value completed less the planned value (EV – PV), where "behind" is negative; and (3) a *time variance* equal to the effective time less the actual time (TE – TA), where a delay is negative.

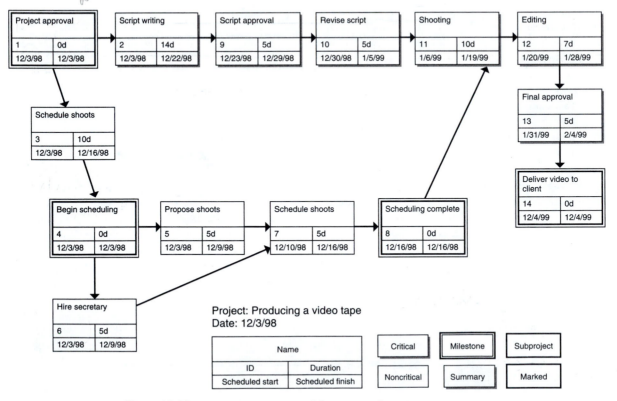

Figure 11.12 PERT chart generated by Microsoft Project.

Software Evaluation						
December						
Sun	Mon	Tue	Wed	Thu	Fri	Sat
				1	2	3
4	5	6	7	8	9	10
11	12	13	14	15	16	17
18	19	20	21	22	23	24
25	26	27	28	29	30	31

Week of Dec 4:
Software review beg...
Literature search, 2d
Literature reviewed, 12d

Week of Dec 11:
Literature reviewed, 12d

Week of Dec 18:
Literature reviewed, 12d

Week of Dec 25:
Reference list, 1d
Prices gathered, 1d
Check out references, 3d
Demos ordered, 10d
Vendor calls, 10d
Literature reviewed, 12d

Figure 11.13 Calendar of activities created by Microsoft Project.

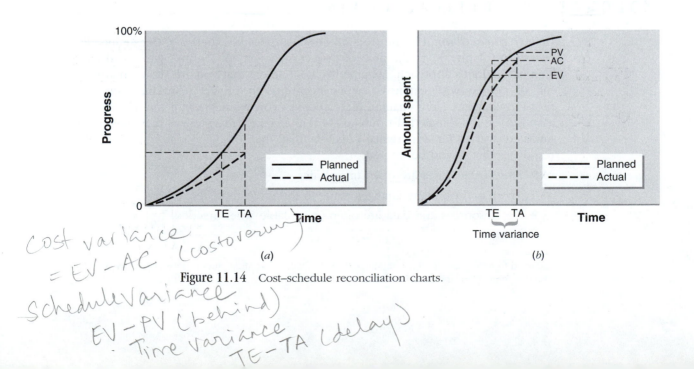

Figure 11.14 Cost–schedule reconciliation charts.

Cost variance
= EV – AC (cost overrun)

Schedule variance
EV – PV (behind)

Time variance
TE – TA (delay)

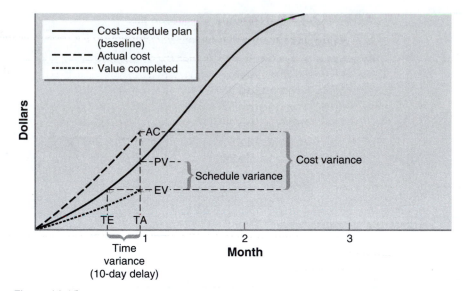

Figure 11.15   Earned value chart.

When these variances are significant, the project manager must identify (or at least attempt to identify) an *assignable cause* for the variance. That is, he or she must study the project to determine why the variance occurred. This is so that the proper remedy can be used to keep the variance from recurring. A corrective action is called for if some inefficiency or change in the prescribed process caused the variance.

Variances can be both favorable and unfavorable. A significant *favorable variance* (e.g., a variance resulting from a large quantity discount on material) will usually not require corrective action, though investigation is still worthwhile so that this better-than-expected performance can be repeated.

GOLDRATT'S CRITICAL CHAIN*

In the *Critical Chain*, Eliyahu Goldratt (1997) applies his Theory of Constraints discussed in Chapter 10 to the field of project management. To motivate our discussion of Goldratt's approach, imagine for the moment that you are sitting in a room full of people with extensive experience as both project team members and project managers. Now imagine the responses you would hear if the group were asked to list the things that troubled them most about the projects they have been involved with. Our experience suggests that the following are typical of the responses that would be offered:

- Project due dates are often unrealistic.
- There are too many changes made in the project's scope.
- Key resources and data are often unavailable when needed.

*Adapted from S. J. Mantel, Jr., J. R. Meredith, S. M. Shafer, and M. M. Sutton, *Project Management in Practice*, John Wiley and Sons Inc., 2001, pp. 191–197.

• The budget is frequently unrealistic and therefore often exceeded.

• It seems like my project is always in competition for resources with other projects.

One interesting observation is that these same issues tend to be raised regardless of the organizational context. Thus we tend to hear strikingly similar complaints regardless of whether the group is referring to a construction project, a software development project, a project to develop an advertising campaign, and so on.

Based on this, is it all that farfetched to conclude that the causes of problems are generic across all types of projects? In our opinion, this is not unlikely at all. Indeed, project management is fundamentally concerned with effectively trading off three primary objectives: performance, cost, and time. Referring back to the earlier list of complaints, it can be seen that each issue deals with one or more of the three primary project objectives.

Given our conclusion that the problems encountered when managing projects tend to be strongly related to the need to trade off one project objective for another, a natural issue that arises is the extent to which these tradeoffs are caused by human decisions and practices. In other words, can more effective project management minimize the occurrence of these problems? To investigate this issue, let's examine the first complaint regarding unrealistic due dates in more detail.

One way to investigate this issue is to see if we can identify any generally accepted practices that would tend to cause the shared perception of many project workers that project due dates are often set too optimistically. To make our discussion more concrete, consider the three network diagrams shown in Figure 11.16. The primary difference between the three diagrams is the degree of interdependence across the paths. In scenario 1, there is only a single path. In scenario 2, the path B–C–D–E is preceded by three activities A1, A2, and A3. Therefore, the completion of path B–C–D–E depends on which of its three preceding tasks takes the longest. In scenario 3 there are two completely independent paths, each consisting of five tasks.

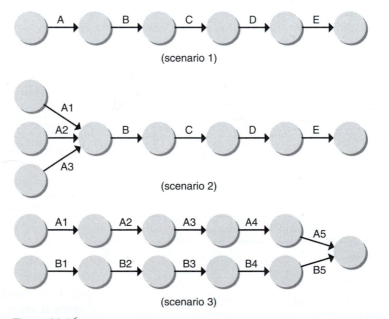

Figure 11.16   Three project scenarios.

Assume that as project manager you are told that all of the tasks in the three network diagrams require 10 days to complete. What completion time would you calculate for each project? If you assume that the activity times are known with certainty, then all three projects would have the same 50-days' duration. If you find this result somewhat unsettling, you are in good company. Thinking about it intuitively, how can a simple project like scenario 1 with a single path and only five activities have the same duration as scenario 2 with three paths and seven activities, or with scenario 3 with two paths and 10 activities?

Perhaps part of the problem is our assumption that the activity times are known with certainty. To investigate this further, let's assume that all activity times are normally distributed with a mean of 10 days and standard deviation of three. The results of simulating the completion of the three projects 200 times each are summarized in Figure 11.17.

As you can see from Figure 11.17, removing the assumption that the activity times are known with certainty leads to quite different results. Scenario 1's average duration was slightly higher than the 50 we calculated earlier under the assumption of deterministic time estimates. To a large extent with this linear structure, activities that take less than the expected time tend to cancel out the variability of activities that take more than the expected time, resulting in an overall average completion time that is close to the expected completion time for the project. Also observe that the more interrelated scenarios 2 and 3, on average, take even longer than scenario 1 and that their minimum times are significantly longer than scenario 1's minimum time.

But perhaps most importantly, note that while the average completion times of the projects are still close to 50, this is simply the average project completion time after simulating the execution of each project 200 times. That is, approximately 50 percent of the time the projects will be completed in less than 50 days and 50 percent of the time the projects will be completed in more than 50 days under the reasonable assumption that the distribution of project completion times follows a symmetrical distribution. (Note that here we are referring to the distribution of project completion times as being symmetrical, not the distribution of project activity times.) In other words, had we estimated the project duration based on the assumption that the activity times are known with certainty, we would incur a greater than 50 percent chance that the actual project duration would exceed this estimate. How would you like to have responsibility for a project that has only a 50 percent chance of being completed on time? This example clearly demonstrates how the commonly made assumption of known activity times in practice can lead to quite unrealistic project deadlines.

	Scenario 1	Scenario 2	Scenario 3
Average	50.4	51.9	53.4
Std. Dev.	7.1	6.3	5.3
Max	69.4	72.7	69.3
Min	30.1	36.1	39.3
Median	50.0	51.8	53.1

Figure 11.17 Summary project completion results after simulating three scenarios 200 times each.

It is important to point out that the results would have been even more dramatic had the activities required some common resources. Similarly, the results would have been more dramatic and realistic had a nonsymmetrical distribution been used to model the activity times. Why, you might ask, would a nonsymmetrical distribution more realistically model the activity times? Suppose you scheduled a status meeting to last 20 minutes. Is there *any* chance the meeting will last 40 minutes longer than expected, or 60 minutes? What about 40 minutes less, or −20 minutes?

Based on the discussion to this point and assuming that project workers have a general desire to be recognized for good performance, what do you imagine project workers do when they are asked to provide time estimates for tasks they will be responsible for? Do you think they give an estimate that they believe provides them with only a 50 percent chance of being met? Or, more likely, do you imagine they inflate or *pad* their estimate to increase the likelihood of successfully completing the task on time? What would you do?

If you are like most of the people we know, you would inflate your time estimate. Unfortunately, inflated time estimates tend to create even more problems. First, inflating the time estimate has no impact on the actual probability distribution of completing the activity. Second, what do you imagine happens in cases where a project team member finishes early? More than likely, the team member believes that it is in his or her best interest to remain silent about completing activities in less than the allotted time so that future time estimates are not automatically discounted by management based on a track record of early task completions. Moreover, there are sometimes penalties for completing early, such as storage of materials. Third, just as things tend to fill available closet and storage space in your home, work tends to fill available time. Thus, the scope of the task may be expanded to fill the available time. Perhaps even more dangerous than the inflated estimate becoming a self-fulfilling prophecy is that, after receiving approval for a task based on an inflated time estimate, workers may perceive that they now have plenty of time to complete the task and therefore *delay starting the task*. Goldratt refers to this as the *student syndrome*, likening it to the way students often delay writing a term paper until the last minute. The problem of delaying the start of a task is that obstacles are frequently not discovered until the task has been underway for some time. By delaying the start of the task, the opportunity to effectively deal with these obstacles and complete the task on time is greatly diminished.

In summary, we observe that the common practice of simply adding up task durations often leads to unrealistic project due dates. This is primarily the result of assuming that task times are known and that paths are independent. A natural consequence of this is that project team members will tend to inflate their time estimates. Inflated time estimates further compound the problem, particularly in cases where the student syndrome comes into play.

Multitasking

Up to this point, our perspective has been a single project. We now investigate another problem created by conventional practice—the practice of assigning people concurrently to multiple projects.

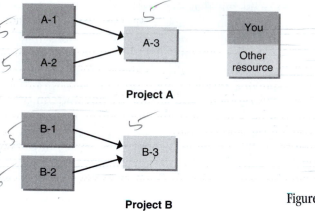

Project A

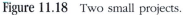

Project B

Figure 11.18   Two small projects.

When project team members are assigned to multiple projects, they have to allocate their time across these projects or *multitask*. Multitasking involves switching from a task associated with one project to another task associated with a different project. To illustrate this, consider the two small projects shown in Figure 11.18. The completion of each of the projects' three tasks requires you and one additional resource. Further, the completion of each task requires 5 days. In Figure 11.19, Gantt charts have been developed for two alternative ways of competing the tasks. In Gantt chart (*a*), you switch between projects after each task is completed, while in Gantt chart (*b*) you complete all of your assigned tasks for Project A before beginning any work on Project B. Since in both of these cases the two projects are finished in 25 days, aren't both sequences equally desirable? The answer is absolutely not. First, while it is true that in both cases Project B is finished by time 25, in the top sequence Project A finishes at time 20, while in the bottom sequence Project A finishes 5 days earlier. Therefore, the sequence shown in the bottom Gantt chart is preferable because it results in Project A finishing 5 days earlier with no penalty to Project B.

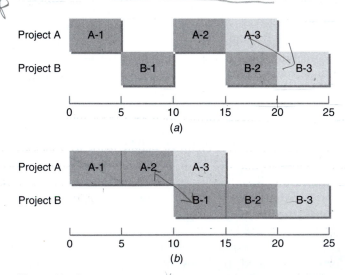

Figure 11.19   Alternative Gantt charts for projects A and B.

Perhaps even more importantly, our analysis overlooks another important factor. Specifically, there is typically a penalty or cost associated with switching from working on one project to another. In your own experience, is it more efficient to complete the assignment for one course and then move on to another course or is it more efficient to complete one project management homework problem, then move on to an accounting problem, then on to a statistics problem, then back to a project management problem, and so on? Obviously each time you switch to a different course, you have to retrieve the appropriate textbook, find the right page, recall where you left off, and (perhaps most significantly) get into the proper frame of mind. Therefore, as this example demonstrates, switching attention from project to project is likely to extend activity times. Eliminating such switching costs further increases the benefits associated with Gantt chart (b) shown in Figure 11.19.

Common Chain of Events

According to Goldratt, the preceding activities lead to the following chain of events:

1. Assuming that activity times are known and that the paths are independent leads to underestimating the actual amount of time needed to complete the project.

2. Because the time needed to complete the project is underestimated, project team members tend to inflate their time estimates.

3. Inflated time estimates leads to work filling available time, workers not reporting that a task has been completed early, and perhaps most importantly, the student syndrome.

4. An important caveat then becomes that safety time is not transparent and is often misused.

5. Misused safety time results in missed deadlines and milestones.

6. Hidden safety time further complicates the task of prioritizing project activities.

7. The lack of clear priorities likely results in poor multitasking.

8. Task durations increase as a result of poor multitasking.

9. Uneven demand on resources—some overloaded and others underloaded—may also occur as a result of poor multitasking.

10. In an effort to fully utilize all resources, more projects will be undertaken to better utilize underloaded resources.

11. Adding more projects further increases poor multitasking.

According to Goldratt, this chain of events leads to a vicious cycle. Specifically, as work continues to pile up, team members are pressured to do more poor multitasking. Increasing the amount of poor multitasking leads to longer activity times. Longer activity times lead to longer project completion times, which ultimately leads to more projects piling up.

It might have occurred to you that one way to reverse this cycle would be to add more resources. According to Goldratt, however, the appropriate response is to reduce the number of projects assigned to each person in an effort to reduce the amount of bad multitasking. Incidentally, a simple way to measure the amount of bad multitasking is to calculate the difference between the time required to do the work for a task and the elapsed time to complete the task.

Determining when to release projects into the system is the primary mechanism for ensuring that the right amount of work is assigned to each person. If projects are started too early, they simply add to the chaos and contribute to poor multitasking. On the other hand, if projects are started too late, key resources may go underutilized and projects will be inevitably delayed.

Consistent with his Theory of Constraints (see Chapter 10), Goldratt suggests that the key to resolving this trade-off is to schedule the start of new projects based on the availability of bottleneck resources. Goldratt further suggests that time buffers be created between resources that feed bottleneck resources and the bottleneck resources.

While properly scheduling the start of new projects does much to address the problems associated with poor multitasking, it does little to address the problem of setting unrealistic project deadlines and the accompanying response of inflated time estimates. Relying on elementary statistics, it can be easily shown that the amount of safety time needed to protect a particular path is less than the sum of the safety times required to protect the individual activities making up the path. The same approach is commonly used in inventory management, where it can be shown that less safety stock is needed at a central warehouse to provide a certain service level than the amount of safety stock that would be required to provide this same service level if carried at multiple distributed locations.

Based on this intuition, Goldratt suggests reducing the amount of safety time added to individual tasks and adding some fraction of the safety time reduced back to be used as a bank of safety buffer for the entire project, called the *project buffer.* The amount of time each task is reduced depends on how much of a reduction is needed to get project team members to change their behavior. For example, the allotted time for tasks should be reduced to the point that the student syndrome is eliminated. To motivate the project team members, Goldratt suggests using activity durations where in fact there is a high probability that the task will not be finished on time.

The Critical Chain

Another limitation associated with traditional approaches to project management is that the dependency between resources and tasks is often ignored. To illustrate this, consider the network diagram shown in Figure 11.20. According to the figure, the activities emanating from node 1 require resource A, while the activities emanating from nodes 2 and 3 require resources C and B, respectively. Using tra-

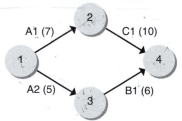

Figure 11.20 Sample network diagram.

ditional approaches to project management, two paths would be identified: A1–C1 with a duration of 17 days and A2–B1 with a duration of 11 days. Taking this approach a step further, we would conclude that path A1–C1 is the critical path.

The problem with this logic is that activities A1 and A2 are not truly independent as the diagram would seem to indicate since their completion requires the same resource. Based on this new insight, we see that if resource A completes activity A1 first, thereby delaying the start of A2 for 7 days, then path A1–C1's duration remains 17 days while path A2–B1's duration increases from 11 to 18 days. Likewise, if resource A completes activity A2 first, then path A1–C1's duration increases from 17 to 22 days while path A2–B1's duration remains 11 days.

To address the need to consider both precedence relationships and resource dependencies, Goldratt proposes thinking in terms of the longest chain of consecutively dependent tasks where such dependencies can arise from a variety of sources, including precedence relationships among the tasks and resource dependencies. Goldratt coined the term *critical chain* to refer to the longest chain of consecutively dependent activities.

Based on this definition of the critical chain, there are two potential sources that can delay the completion of a project. In a similar fashion to the critical path concept, one source of delay is the tasks that make up the critical chain. The project buffer discussed earlier is used to protect against these delays (see Figure 11.21). Tasks external to the critical chain can also delay the completion of the project if these delays end up delaying one or more of the tasks on the critical chain. As shown in Figure 11.21, safety time can be added to these paths as well to ensure that they do not delay tasks on the critical chain. The safety time added to chains other than the critical chain is called a feeding buffer since these paths often feed into the critical chain. Thus, the objective of feeding buffers is to ensure that non-critical chains are completed so that they do not delay tasks on the critical chain.

Clearly, activities on the critical chain should be given the highest priority. Likewise, to ensure that resources are available when needed, they should be contacted at the start of the project. It is also wise to keep these resources updated on the status of the project and to remind them periodically of when their input will be needed. Goldratt suggests reminding these resources 2 weeks before the start of their work, then 3 days prior to their start, and finally the day before they start. Since any delay of an activity on the critical chain can cause a delay of the entire project, it is important that a resource immediately switch to the task on the critical chain when needed.

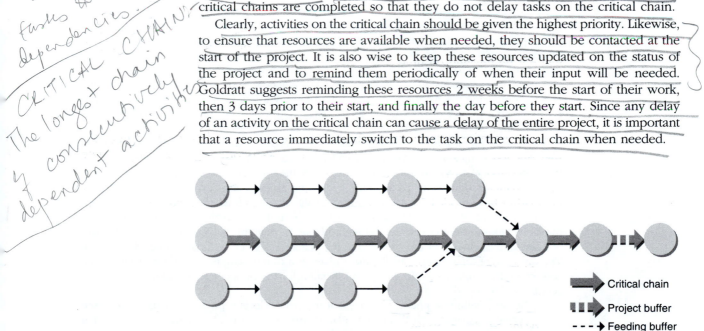

Figure 11.21   Project and feeding buffers.

EXPAND YOUR UNDERSTANDING

1. Frequently, the project's tasks are not well defined, and there is an urge to "get on with the work," since time is critical. How serious is it to minimize the planning effort and get on with the project?

2. Contrast the cost–schedule reconciliation charts with the earned value chart. Which one would a project manager prefer?

3. How would a manager calculate the value completed for an earned value chart?

4. Do you think people's estimates are more accurate for optimistic or pessimistic activity times?

5. Of the reasons discussed for the growth in project operations, which do you think are contributing most?

6. Why doesn't it make sense to think in terms of a critical path when activity times are not known with certainty?

7. In calculating the probability that a project will be finished by some specified time, the probabilities of each path are multiplied together, on the assumption that the paths are independent of one another. How reasonable is this assumption?

8. Is the stretched-S life cycle project form more common or the exponential form? What other aspects of managing a project are affected by the nature of the project form besides budgeting and early termination?

9. What do you think are the reasons for the topics of conflict among the project team in each stage of the project?

10. Given the powerful nature of project management software packages today, why should a project manager have to know how to construct a PERT chart or work breakdown structure?

11. Given the ease of use of simulation software such as Crystal Ball®, what other data used in project management should probably be simulated?

12. Describe how to actually calculate earned value.

13. What does the project portfolio illustrate? How might it be useful to management?

APPLY YOUR UNDERSTANDING
Nutri-Sam

Nutri-Sam produces a line of vitamins and nutritional supplements. It recently introduced its Nutri-Sports Energy Bar, which is based on new scientific findings about the proper balance of macronutrients. The energy bar has become extremely popular among elite athletes and other people who follow the diet. One distinguishing feature of the Nutri-Sports Energy Bar is that each bar contains 50 milligrams of eicosapentaenoic acid (EPA), a substance strongly linked to reducing the risk of cancer but found in only a few foods, such as salmon. Nutri-Sam was able to include EPA in its sports bars because it had previously developed and patented a process to refine EPA for its line of fish-oil capsules.

Because of the success of the Nutri-Sports Energy Bar in the United States, Nutri-Sam is considering offering it in Latin America. With its domestic facility currently operating at capacity, the president of Nutri-Sam has decided to investigate the option of adding approximately 10,000 square feet of production space to its facility in Latin America at a cost of $5 million.

The project to expand the Latin American facility involves four major phases: (1) concept development, (2) definition of the plan, (3) design and construction, and (4) start-up and turnover. During the concept development phase, a program manager is chosen who will oversee all four phases of the project and the manager is given a budget to develop a plan. The outcome of the concept development phase is a rough plan, feasibility estimates for the project, and a rough schedule. Also, a justification for the project and a budget for the next phase are developed.

In the plan definition phase, the program manager selects a project manager to oversee the activities associated with this phase. Plan definition consists of four major activities that are completed more or less concurrently: defining the project scope, developing a broad schedule of activities, developing detailed cost estimates, and developing a plan for staffing.

The output of this phase is a detailed plan and proposal for management specifying how much the project will cost, how long it will take, and what the deliverables are.

If the project gets management's approval and management provides the appropriations, the project progresses to the third phase, design and construction. This phase consists of four major activities: detailed engineering, mobilization of the construction employees, procurement of production equipment, and construction of the facility. Typically, the detailed engineering and the mobilization of the construction employees are done concurrently. Once these activities are completed, construction of the facility and procurement of the production equipment are done concurrently. The outcome of this phase is the physical construction of the facility.

The final phase, start-up and turnover, consists of four major activities: pre-start-up inspection of the facility, recruiting and training the workforce, solving start-up problems, and determining optimal operating parameters (called centerlining). Once the pre-start-up inspection is completed, the workforce is recruited and trained at the same time that start-up problems are solved. Centerlining is initiated upon the completion of these activities. The desired outcome of this phase is a facility operating at design requirements.

The next table provides optimistic, most likely, and pessimistic time estimates for the major activities.

Activity	Optimistic Time (months)	Most Likely Time (months)	Pessimistic Time (months)
Concept Development	3	12	24
Plan Definition			
Define project scope	1	2	12
Develop broad schedule	0.25	0.5	1
Detailed cost estimates	0.2	0.3	0.5
Develop staffing Plan	0.2	0.3	0.6
Design and Construction			
Detailed engineering	2	3	6
Facility construction	8	12	24
Mobilization of employees	0.5	2	4
Procurement of equipment	1	3	12
Start-up and Turnover			
Pre-start-up inspection	0.25	0.5	1
Recruiting and training	0.25	0.5	1
Solving start-up problems	0	1	2
Centerlining	0	1	4

Questions

1. Draw a network diagram for this project. Identify the four most critical paths through the network diagram.
2. Simulate the completion of this project 1000 times assuming that activity times follow a triangular distribution. Estimate the mean and standard deviation of the project completion time.
3. Develop a frequency chart to summarize the results of your simulation.
4. Find the probability that the project can be completed within 30 months. What is the probability that the project will take longer than 40 months? What is the probability that the project will take between 30 and 40 months?

EXERCISES

1. The following PERT chart was prepared at the beginning of a small construction project.

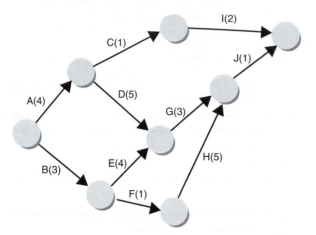

The duration, in days, follows the letter of each activity. What is the critical path? Which activities should be monitored most closely?

At the end of the first week of construction, it was noted that activity A was completed in 2.5 days, but activity B required 4.5 days. What impact does this have on the project? Are the same activities critical?

2. Refer to Exercise 1. Compute the earliest start and finish times, the latest start and finish times, and the slack times for each activity. Also, calculate the slack for each path.

3. Given the following German autobahn repair project, find the probability of completion by 17 weeks; by 24 weeks.

		Times (weeks)	
Activity	Optimistic	Most Likely	Pessimistic
1–2	5	11	11
1–3	10	10	10
1–4	2	5	8
2–6	1	7	13
3–6	4	4	10
3–7	4	7	10
3–5	2	2	2
4–5	0	6	6
5–7	2	8	14
6–7	1	4	7

If the firm can complete the project within 18 weeks, it will receive a bonus of ¤10,000. But if the

project is delayed beyond 22 weeks, it must pay a penalty of ¤5000. If the firm can choose whether or not to bid on this project, what should its decision be if this is normally only a breakeven project?

4. Construct a network for the project below and find its expected completion time.

Activity	t_e (weeks)	Preceding Activities
a	3	None
b	5	a
c	3	a
d	1	c
e	3	b
f	4	b, d
g	2	c
h	3	g, f
i	1	e, h

5. Given the estimated activity times and the network below:

Activity	t_o	t_m	t_p
A	6	7	14
B	8	10	12
C	2	3	4
D	6	7	8
E	5	5.5	9
F	5	7	9
G	4	6	8
H	2.7	3	3.5

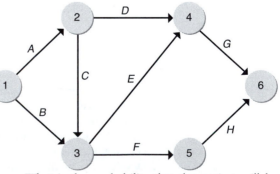

What is the probability that the project will be completed within:

a. 21 days? b. 22 days? c. 25 days?

6. Pusan Iron and Steel, located on the eastern coast of South Korea, is a major supplier of both girder and rolled steel to the emerging construction, appliance, and automobile companies of China. Due to growing sales volumes and the need for faster delivery, Pusan is converting its current single weigh station to a larger, multiple drive-through station. The new drive-through weigh station will consist of a heated, air-conditioned building with a large floor and a small office. The large room will have the scales, a 15-foot counter, and several display cases for its equipment.

Before erection of the building, the project manager evaluated the project using PERT/CPM analysis. The following activities with their corresponding times were recorded.

#	Activity	Opti- mistic	Most Likely	Pessi- mistic	Preced- ing Tasks
1	Lay foundation	8	10	13	—
2	Dig hole for scale	5	6	8	—
3	Insert scale bases	13	15	21	2
4	Erect frame	10	12	14	1, 3
5	Complete building	11	20	30	4
6	Insert scales	4	5	8	5
7	Insert dis- play cases	2	3	4	5
8	Put in office equipment	4	6	10	7
9	Give finishing touches	2	3	4	8, 6

The header "Times" spans the Optimistic, Most Likely, and Pessimistic columns.

Using PERT/CPM analysis, find the expected completion time.

7. As in the situation illustrated in Figure 11.14, an Irish Web-design project at day 70 exhibits only 35 percent progress when 40 percent was planned, for an effective date of 55. Planned value was €17,000 at day 55 and €24,000 at day 70, and actual cost was €20,000 at day 55 and €30,000 at day 70. Find the time variance, cost variance, and schedule variance.

8. As in the situation shown in Figure 11.15, a project at month 2 exhibited an actual cost of $78,000, a planned value of $84,000, and a value completed of $81,000. Find the cost and schedule variances. Estimate time variance.

9. A project at month 5 had an actual cost of $34,000, a planned value of $42,000, and an earned value of $39,000. Find the cost and schedule variances.

10. Referring to the problem solved in the Spreadsheet Analysis: Simulating Project Completion Times, simulate the project 1000 times and determine:

  a. The probability the project is completed in 85 days or less.

  b. The probability the project requires 96 days or more to be completed.

  c. The probability the project is completed in 83 to 97 days.

11. Referring to the problem solved in the Spreadsheet Analysis: Simulating Project Completion Times, enhance the model to calculate the probability that each path is the critical path.

12. Given a PERT network:

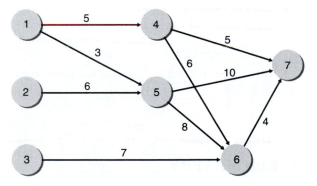

Note that three activities can start immediately. Find:

  a. Critical path.

  b. Earliest time to complete the project.

  c. Slack on activities 4–6, 5–6, and 4–7.

13. The events of the project below are designated 1, 2, and so on.

  a. Draw the PERT network.

  b. Find the critical path.

  c. Find the slacks on all activities.

Activity	Preceding Event	Succeeding Event	T_e (weeks)	Preceding Activities
a	1	2	3	none
b	1	3	6	none
c	1	4	8	none
d	2	5	7	a
e	3	5	5	b
f	4	5	10	c
g	4	6	4	c
h	5	7	5	d, e, f
i	6	7	6	g

a. Draw the PERT diagram.

b. Find the critical path.

c. Find the completion time.

15. In the project network shown in the following figure, the number alongside each activity designates its known duration in weeks. Determine:

a. Earliest and latest start and finish times for each activity.

b. Earliest time that the project can be completed.

c. Slack for activities.

d. Critical events and activities.

e. Critical path.

14.

Activity	Duration
A–B	1
A–C	2
A–D	3
D–C	4
C–B	3
D–E	8
C–F	2
B–F	4
I–J	2
C–E	6
E–F	5
F–G	10
F–H	11
E–H	1
G–H	9
E–J	3
G–I	8
H–J	6

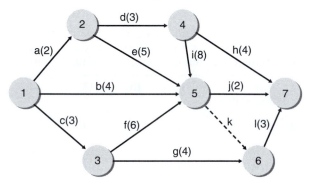

BIBLIOGRAPHY

Angus, R. B., N. A. Gundersen, and T. P. Cullinane. *Planning, Performing, and Controlling Projects: Principles and Applications*, 2nd ed. Upper Saddle River, NJ: Prentice Hall, 2000.

Cleland, D. I. *Project Managers' Portable Handbook.* New York: McGraw-Hill, 2000.

Ghattas, R. G., and S. L. McKee. *Practical Project Management.* Upper Saddle River, NJ: Prentice Hall, 2001.

Gido, J., and J. P. Clements. *Successful Project Management, with Microsoft Project 2005 CD-ROM*, Cincinnati: Thompson/South-Western, 2004.

Goldratt, E. M. *Critical Chain.* Great Barrington, MA: North River Press, 1997.

Graham, R. J., and R. L. Englund. *Creating an Environment for Successful Projects.* San Francisco, CA: Jossey-Bass, 1997.

Gray, C. F., and E. W. Larson. *Project Management: The Managerial Process.* New York: McGraw-Hill/Irwin, 2005.

Ibbs, C. W., and Y.-H. Kwak. "Assessing Project Management Maturity." *Project Management Journal,* March 2000.

Kerzner, H. *Project Management: A Systems Approach to Planning, Scheduling, and Controlling,* 8th ed. New York: Wiley, 2003.

Kerzner, H. *Applied Project Management: Best Practices on Implementation.* New York: Wiley, 2000.

Kolisch, R. "Resource Allocation Capabilities of Commercial Project Management Software Packages." *Interfaces,* 29 (July–August 1999): 19–31.

Lewis, J. P. *Mastering Project Management.* New York: McGraw-Hill, 1998.

Lowery, G., and R. Ferrara. *Managing Projects with Microsoft Project 98.* New York: Van Nostrand Reinhold, 1998.

Meredith, J. R., and S. J. Mantel, Jr. *Project Management: A Managerial Approach,* 6th ed. New York: Wiley, 2006.

Mantel, S. J., Jr., J. R. Meredith, S. M. Shafer, and M. M. Sutton. *Project Management in Practice,* 2nd ed. New York: Wiley, 2005.

Nicholas, J. M. *Project Management for Business and Technology,* 2nd ed. Englewood Cliffs, NJ: Prentice Hall, 2001.

O'Keeffe, S. W. T. "Chrysler and Artemis: Striking Back with the Viper." *Industrial Engineering* (December 1994): 15–17.

Project Management Institute. *A Guide to the Project Management Body of Knowledge,* 3rd ed. Newtown Square, PA: Project Management Institute, 2004.

Spinner, M. P. *Project Management: Principles and Practices.* Upper Saddle River, NJ: Prentice Hall, 2000.

Thamhain, H. J., and D. L. Wilemon. "Conflict Management in Project Life Cycles." *Sloan Management Review* (Summer 1975).

Verma, V. K., and H. J. Thamhain. *Human Resource Skills for the Project Manager.* Upper Darby, PA: Project Management Institute Publications, 1997.

Risk Analysis Using Crystal Ball 2000

The effective management of operations requires the ability to deal with a fair amount of uncertainty. The quality of raw materials, the lead time of inventory replenishment orders, the actions of competitors, the timing of customer arrivals, and the duration of project activities exemplify the uncertainties associated with managing operations. Furthermore, while there are a number of actions that can be taken to reduce the amount of uncertainty, it is quite unlikely that it could ever be completely eliminated. Therefore, in today's turbulent business environment, effective decision making requires an ability to manage the ambiguity that arises in situations with less than perfect information.

One approach that is particularly useful in helping better understand the implications associated with uncertain information is risk analysis. The essence of risk analysis is to make assumptions about the probability distributions associated with key parameters and variables and to use Monte Carlo simulation models based on these distributions to evaluate the desirability of certain managerial decisions. Using this approach, a mathematical model is constructed of the situation and run to see what the outcomes will be under various scenarios. The model is run (or replicated) many, many times based on the probabilities of the variables. Equations in the model are then used to construct a statistical distribution of the outcomes of interest, such as costs, profits, completion dates, or return on investment. The objective is to illustrate to the manager the distribution or *risk profile* of the outcomes associated with the decision. These risk profiles are one factor to be considered when making the decision, along with many others such as strategic concerns, behavioral issues, fit with the organization, and so on.

This appendix illustrates how Crystal Ball, an Excel™ Add-In, can be used to conduct such analyses in the context of project management (see Chapter 11) and thereby obtain a better understanding of the risks associated with managing projects. In particular, the topics of project selection and project budgeting are addressed in the following sections, respectively.

CONSIDERING UNCERTAINTY IN PROJECT SELECTION DECISIONS

To illustrate the value of considering uncertainty in the project selection decision, consider the experience of a fictitious dot-com organization that needs to upgrade its server computers. Company management has identified the following two options: 1) shift to a Windows-based platform from its current Unix-based platform, or 2) stick with a Unix-based platform. The company estimates that if it migrates to Windows, the new server hardware could cost as little as $100,000 or as much as $200,000. The technical group's best estimate is that the hardware costs will be $125,000 if the Windows option is pursued. Likewise, the company's best guess regarding the cost to upgrade and convert its software to Windows is $300,000 with a range of $275,000 to $500,000. Finally, if the company converts to Windows, employee training costs are estimated to range between $9,000 to $15,000, with the best guess being $10,000.

If the company sticks with Unix, the new server hardware will most likely cost $110,000, but could cost as little as $80,000 or as much as $210,000. Software conversion and upgrade costs are expected to be $300,000 but could be as low as $250,000 and as high as $525,000. Employee training costs should fall between $8,000 to $17,500 with a best guess of $10,000.

In this example, management has developed three estimates for each variable: an optimistic cost, a most likely cost, and a pessimistic cost. Both the beta distribution and the triangular distribution are well suited for modeling variables with these three parameters. However, because the beta distribution is quite complex and not particularly intuitive, we assume that a triangular distribution provides a reasonably good fit for each variable.

It is worth noting that in contrast to other approaches were only the most likely value for each variable is considered, a major benefit of the risk analysis approach is that the full range of possible values is considered. Therefore, the model developed should provide a closer approximation to the actual situation being modeled. Furthermore, the results will likely be more accurate because it is easier to accurately estimate the range of values a variable may assume than trying to predict its exact value. To illustrate, would you have more confidence in your most likely estimate of IBM's stock price one week from now or in a range that was bounded by your estimated lowest stock price to its highest price? More often than not, your range will contain IBM's closing price while your most likely estimate will be off a bit.

Returning to the task at hand, the spreadsheet shown in Figure B.1 was created. The most likely cost estimates were entered in cells B3:C5, while the costs of pursuing each project are calculated in cells B6 and C6 by summing up the hardware, software, and training costs.

	A	B	C
1		**Windows**	**Unix**
2		**Platform**	**Platform**
3	Hardware cost	$125,000	$110,000
4	Software conversion cost	$300,000	$300,000
5	Employee training	$10,000	$10,000
6	Total Project Cost	$435,000	$420,000

Figure B.1 Two web-server options.

Using Crystal Ball to run Monte Carlo simulation requires defining two types of cells in the spreadsheet. The cells that are associated with variables or parameters are defined as **Assumption Cells**. The cells that correspond to outcomes of the simulation model are defined as **Forecast Cells**. Forecast cells typically contain formulas that depend on one or more assumption cells. Simulation models can have multiple assumption and forecast cells, but they must have at least one of each. Referring to Figure B.1, the variables that we will make assumptions about are contained in cells B3:C5. Likewise, the outcomes, or in this case project costs, are calculated in cells B6 and C6.

To illustrate the process of defining an assumption cell, refer to cell B3 corresponding to the hardware costs for the Windows-based platform project. Recall that the most likely cost for hardware if the firm migrates to a Windows-based platform is estimated to be $125,000 with a range of $100,000 to $200,000. Also recall our decision to model all costs with a triangular distribution.

The process of defining an assumption involves the following 6 steps:

1. Click on cell B3 to identify it as the cell the assumption applies to.
2. Select the menu option **Cell** at the top of the screen[1].
3. From the dropdown menu that appears, select **Define Assumption ...**
4. Crystal Ball's Distribution Gallery dialog box is now displayed, as shown in Figure B.2. As you can see, Crystal Ball provides a wide variety of probability distribution to choose from. Double click on the **Triangular** box to select it.
5. Crystal Ball's **Triangular Distribution** dialog box is now displayed as shown in Figure B.3. In the **Assumption Name:** textbox at the top of the dialog box, enter a descriptive name such as *Hardware cost - Windows* to label the assumption. Then enter the optimistic, most likely, and pessimistic costs of $100,000, $125,000, and $200,000 in the **Min**, **Likeliest**, and **Max** textboxes, respectively.
6. Click on the **OK** button.

Repeat steps 1-6 for the other five assumption cells (i.e., cells B4:B5 and cells C3:C5). Note the information entered in step 5 will vary for each assumption cell.

---

[1] If Crystal Ball has been installed on your computer but is not running, select **Tools** and then **Add-Ins...** from Excel's menu. Next, click on the **Crystal Ball** checkbox and select **OK.** If the Crystal Ball Add-In has not been installed on your computer, consult your Excel manual and the CD-ROM that accompanies this book to install it.

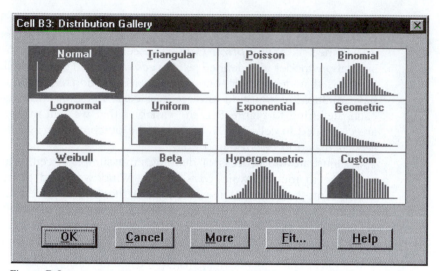

Figure B.2 Crystal Ball distribution gallery.

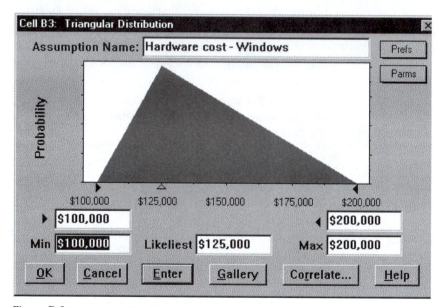

Figure B.3 Triangular distribution dialog box.

Having defined the assumption cells, we now turn our attention to defining the forecast or outcome cells. In our example, we are interested in comparing the costs of the two projects. The process of defining a forecast cell involves the following 5 steps:

1. Click on cell B6 to identify it as containing an outcome we are interested in.

2. Select the menu option **Cell** at the top of the screen.

3. From the dropdown menu that appears, select **Define Forecast ...**

4. Crystal Ball's **Define Forecast** dialog box is now displayed as shown in Figure B.4. In the **Forecast Name:** textbox, enter a descriptive name such as *Total Project Cost - Windows* to label the result. Then enter a descriptive label such as *Dollars* in the **Units:** textbox.

5. Click on **OK**.

Repeat steps 1–5 for cell C6.

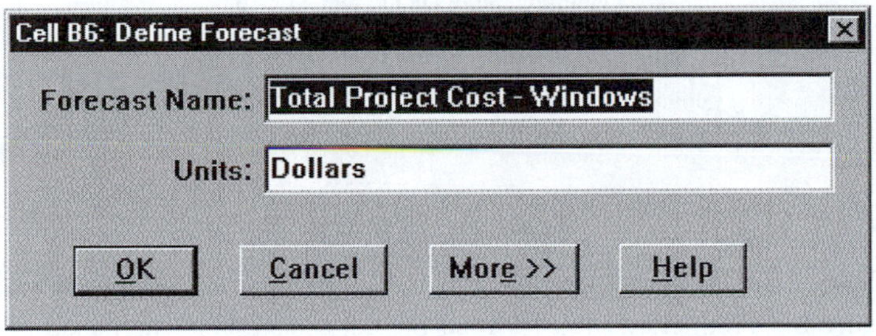

Figure B.4 Define Forecast dialog box.

One iteration of the simulation model involves randomly generating values for each of the assumption cells based on the specified probability distributions and then calculating the total project costs. By repeating this process hundreds or perhaps thousands of times, we can get a sense of the distribution of possible outcomes.

To simulate the completion of these projects 1000 times select the **Run** menu item at the top of the screen. Next, in the dropdown dialog box that appears, select **Run Preferences ...** In the **Run Preferences** dialog box that appears, enter 1000 in the **Maximum Number of Trials:** textbox and then click **OK**. Next, to actually replicate the simulation model 1000 times select the **Run** menu item again and then **Run** from the dropdown menu. Crystal Ball summarizes the results of the simulation models in the form of frequency charts as the model is being executed as shown in Figures B.5 and B.6.

Crystal Ball provides other summary information about the forecast cells in addition to the frequency chart including percentile information, descriptive statistics, the cumulative chart, and a reverse cumulative chart. For example, to see the descriptive statistics for a forecast cell, select the **View** menu option in the **Forecast** window and then select **Statistics** from the dropdown menu that appears. The **Statistics** view for both the Windows-based platform and Unix-based platform projects are shown in Figures B.7 and B.8, respectively.

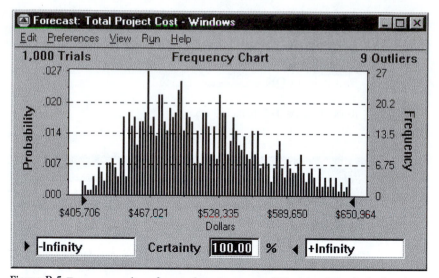

Figure B.5 Frequency chart for total project costs (Windows-based platform).

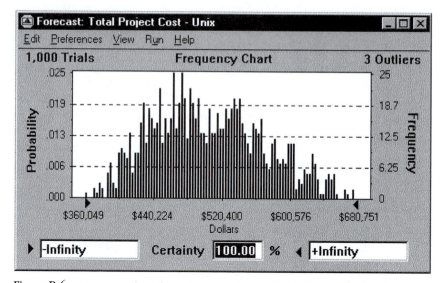

Figure B.6 Frequency chart for total project costs (Unix-based platform).

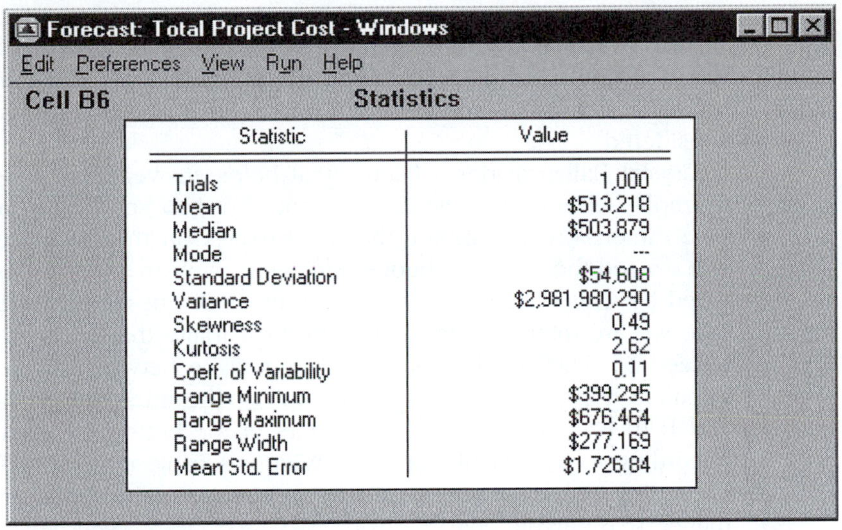

Forecast: Total Project Cost - Windows

Edit Preferences View Run Help

Cell B6   **Statistics**

Statistic	Value
Trials	1,000
Mean	$513,218
Median	$503,879
Mode	---
Standard Deviation	$54,608
Variance	$2,981,980,290
Skewness	0.49
Kurtosis	2.62
Coeff. of Variability	0.11
Range Minimum	$399,295
Range Maximum	$676,464
Range Width	$277,169
Mean Std. Error	$1,726.84

Figure B.7 Descriptive statistics for Windows-based platform project.

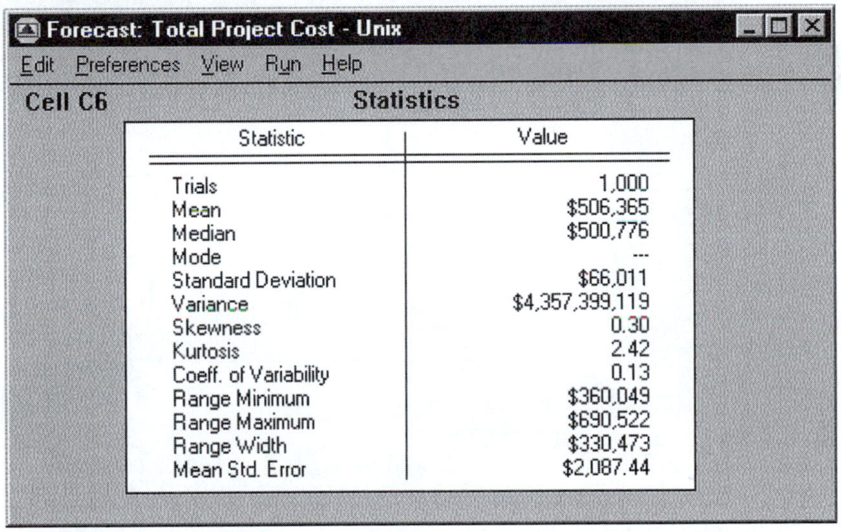

Forecast: Total Project Cost - Unix

Edit Preferences View Run Help

Cell C6   **Statistics**

Statistic	Value
Trials	1,000
Mean	$506,365
Median	$500,776
Mode	---
Standard Deviation	$66,011
Variance	$4,357,399,119
Skewness	0.30
Kurtosis	2.42
Coeff. of Variability	0.13
Range Minimum	$360,049
Range Maximum	$690,522
Range Width	$330,473
Mean Std. Error	$2,087.44

Figure B.8 Descriptive statistics for Unix-based platform project.

Reviewing Figures B.7 and B.8 we observe that the average total cost of the Windows project across the 1000 replications of the simulation model is $513,218 while the average cost of the Unix project is $506,365. On this basis alone, the Unix project appears to be the lower cost project. However, upon examining Figures B.5 and B.6 we can observe that the total cost of the Windows project is expected to range between a little over $400,000 to slightly more than $650,000. In contrast, the Unix project might cost as little as $360,000 or as much as $680,000. The wider range of possible costs associated with the Unix project is an indication of greater uncertainty and therefore greater risks. What should management do in this case? Should it select the Unix project because on average it is expected to cost almost $7,000 less than the Windows project but could potentially end up costing over $680,000? Or should it select the Windows project knowing that it is very unlikely the project costs will exceed $650,000? Clearly, these types of questions only become apparent when the distributions of possible outcomes are considered.

Crystal Ball provides a feature that helps answer these types of questions. For example, assume that the firm cannot afford to spend any more than $575,000. One dimension to compare the two projects on then is the probability that they will exceed the $575,000 budget limitation. We can use the **Forecast** window provided by Crystal Ball to answer these types of questions. More specifically, in this case we are interested in finding the probability that each project's total cost will exceed $575,000 or that its total costs will be between $575,000 and infinity. To calculate this probability for each project, the information shown in Figures B.9 and B.10 was entered in the textboxes at the bottom of each **Forecast** window. According to the calculations, the Windows project has a 14.9 percent chance of exceeding the maximum available funds while the Unix project has a slightly higher 16.6 percent chance.

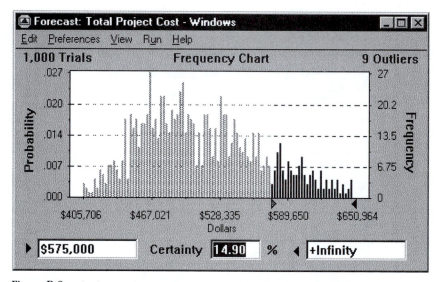

Figure B.9 Calculating the probability that the Windows project's total costs exceed $575,000.

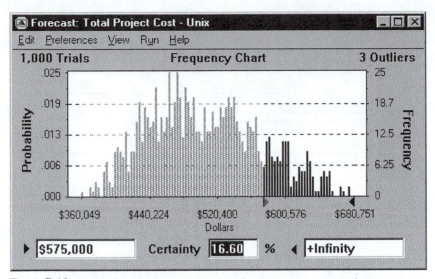

Figure B.10 Calculating the probability that the Unix project's total costs exceed $575,000.

CONSIDERING UNCERTAINTY IN PROJECT BUDGETING

In this section we address the issue of uncertainty in project budgeting. To illustrate, imagine that a consulting company is asked to prepare a budget for a project to develop a relationship management software program to be used by customer service representatives working in a bank's branch locations. Having completed a number of projects of similar scope, the consulting firm accumulated a fair amount of historical data about the time required to complete each of the five major steps typical of these projects. Analysis of this data indicates that the first phase, requirements planning, requires 80 hours of software engineering time on average, with a standard deviation of 15 hours. A summary of the data for all five major phase is provided in Table B.1. Further analysis of the data indicates that the distribution of times to complete each phase is approximately normal.[2] Software engineers are paid an average of $60 per hour including benefits in this particular firm.

---

[2] Note that although we do not demonstrate it here, Crystal Ball (CB) can fit distributions to historical data. This is accomplished by selecting the **F**it button in CB's Distribution Gallery window (see Figure B.2) and then specifying the location of the historical data. In completing this task, CB considers a wide variety of probability distributions and offers the user options regarding the goodness-of-fit test used. The interested reader is referred to Crystal Ball's *User Manual* for additional details.

$\mathcal{T}$ABLE   B.1 • SOFTWARE ENGINEER TIME REQUIRED.

Phase	Average Time (hours)	Standard Deviation
Requirements Planning	80	15
Design	160	25
Prototype Development	320	70
Final Development	640	100
Test	120	20

The spreadsheet shown in Figure B.11 will be used to investigate the implications associated with the uncertainty surrounding the budget for this project. In the spreadsheet, cells B5:B9 were defined as assumption cells with their corresponding assumptions documented in the adjacent cells in column C. Furthermore, the result of interest in this case is the total cost of the project, which is calculated in cell B2. Hence, cell B2 was defined as a forecast cell.

	A	B	C	D	E	F	G	H
1	Wage Rate ($/hour)	60						
2	Total Cost	$79,200	=B1*B10					
3								
4	**Phase**	**Time**						
5	Requirements Planning	80	Normal distribution with mean of 80 and std. dev. of 15.					
6	Design	160	Normal distribution with mean of 160 and std. dev. of 25.					
7	Prototype Development	320	Normal distribution with mean of 320 and std. dev. of 70.					
8	Final Development	640	Normal distribution with mean of 640 and std. dev. of 100.					
9	Test	120	Normal distribution with mean of 120 and std. dev. of 20.					
10	Total Time	1320	SUM(B5:B9)					

Figure B.11 Spreadsheet to investigate project budget.

Because this is our first time dealing with the normal distribution, we illustrate the process of defining an assumption cell based on this distribution for the Requirements Planning phase (cell B5). After clicking on cell **B5**, selecting the **Cell** menu option, and selecting the **Define Assumption** option, the Distribution Gallery is displayed as shown in Figure B.2. In this case we want to define an assumption cell based on the normal distribution. After selecting **Normal** from the Distribution Gallery, the Normal Distribution dialog box is displayed as shown in Figure B.12. Crystal Ball will automatically fill in the Assumption Name Text box with "Requirements Planning" based on the label entered in cell A5. Therefore, the only information that needs to be entered are the two parameters for the normal distribution, namely, the mean and standard deviation.

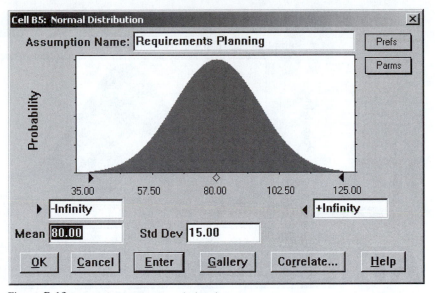

Figure B.12 Normal Distribution dialog box.

Referring to Table B.1, we observe that the Requirements Planning phase is expected to have a mean of 80 hours and a standard deviation of 15. These values were entered in the Mean and Std Dev textboxes, respectively, as shown in Figure B.12. Note that after clicking the **Enter** button, the shape of the distribution changes based on the parameters entered. You can use this feature to visually inspect the distribution and to verify that it provides a reasonable approximation of the variable being modeled.

Referring to Figure B.12, we see that according to the parameters entered, the Requirements Planning phase could take anywhere from 35 to 125 hours, but will most likely require approximately 80 hours. Because the distribution is symmetrical, we are implicitly assuming that it is just as likely for this phase to require more than 80 hours as it is for it to require less than 80 hours. If based on past experience, one or more of these conditions do not seem reasonable, then one or both of the distribution parameters could be altered to try to obtain a better approximation or perhaps a new distribution could be used to model the variable. Also, values can be entered in the textboxes to truncate the upper and lower values returned. For example, if past experience suggests that the Requirements Planning phase never takes less than 55 hours, 55 could be entered for the lower bound as shown in Figure B.13.

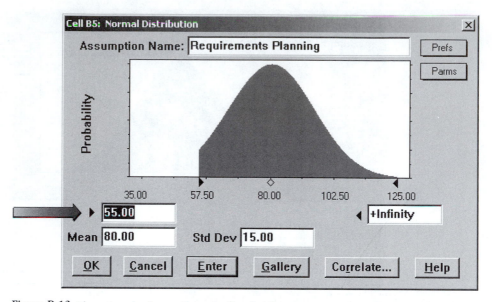

Figure B.13 Changing the lower bound of a distribution.

A summary of the results after replicating the model 1000 times is shown in Figures B.14 and B.15. Analysis of the simulation results indicates that the average or expected cost of completing the project across 1000 trials is $79,180. This is very close to the expected value obtained by simply adding up the average times for each phase and multiplying by the $60 per hour rate, that is (80 + 160 + 320 + 640 + 120)60 = $79,200, which serves to validate our results. Further analysis of the results suggests that on one trial the cost of the project reached $101,748 while on another trial the costs were only $54,025 (see Figure B.15). It is exactly the distribution of likely project costs that determines the risk associated with the project. We would consider a project to have relatively little risk if across all trials of the simulation model the project costs varied little from the average or expected value. As the results from the simulation analysis become more spread out, however, the amount of uncertainty, and therefore, risk increases.

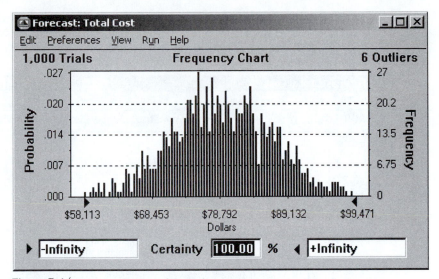

Figure B.14 Frequency chart for total project costs.

Forecast: Total Cost

Edit Preferences View Run Help

Cell B2 — Statistics

Statistic	Value
Trials	1,000
Mean	$79,180
Median	$78,967
Mode	---
Standard Deviation	$7,766
Variance	$60,306,173
Skewness	0.01
Kurtosis	2.82
Coeff. of Variability	0.10
Range Minimum	$54,025
Range Maximum	$101,748
Range Width	$47,723
Mean Std. Error	$245.57

Figure B.15 Summary statistics for total project costs.

One way to quantify the amount of risk associated with a given project is to calculate the standard deviation. For example, across the 1,000 trials of the simulation model, the standard deviation was $7,766. You may recall from an earlier statistics course that 95 percent of the observations fall within plus or minus two standard deviations of the mean for normally distributed data. Based on this, if we are willing to assume that the project completion costs follow a normal distribution, then we can conclude that there is a 95 percent chance that this project will cost between $63,648 and $94,712 (7,7gg) [79,180 ± 2(7,766)]. Observe that the width of this interval increases as the standard deviation increases, again indicating greater uncertainty and more risk.

Another way to help quantify the risk associated with a project is to create a frequency chart of the simulation results as shown in Figure B.14. Using Crystal

Ball, we can use this frequency chart to calculate the probability for any number of scenarios. For example, in Figure B.16 the probability that the total project costs exceed $85,000 was calculated to be 24 percent.

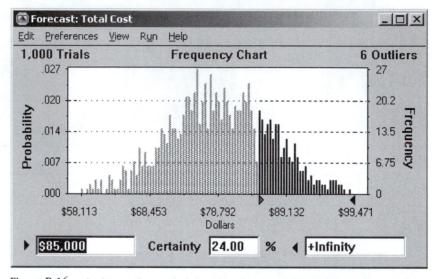

Figure B.16 Calculating the probability that the project's total costs exceed $85,000.

In particular, two characteristics of the frequency chart should be examined. First, the amount of variation (i.e., the spread of the observations) should be noted. As was discussed earlier, higher levels of variation correspond to higher levels of risk. The second characteristic that should be observed is the shape of the frequency chart. A symmetrical distribution such as the normal distribution indicates that the project is just as likely to be completed under budget as it is to be completed over budget. A right-skewed distribution suggests there is a chance that the project will required a much larger than expected budget to complete while a left-skewed distribution suggests that there is a chance that the project will require much less than is expected. The frequency chart in Figure B.14 appears to be symmetrical.

CONCLUDING REMARKS

In this Appendix we utilized two project management examples to illustrate the process of analyzing risk using Crystal Ball. It is not our intention to either provide a comprehensive treatment of Crystal Ball or make you experts in risk analysis. Rather, our purpose is to introduce you to this topic and a user-friendly software program as a way of demonstrating the importance, value, and ease of considering risk. The applicability of risk analysis extends well beyond the applications discussed in this Appendix, as demonstrated by the end-of-chapter problems throughout this text.

References

Crystal Ball 2000 User Manual, Denver: Decisioneering Inc., 2000.

Index